EDUCATING
IMMIGRANT CHILDREN

REFERENCE BOOKS IN INTERNATIONAL EDUCATION
VOLUME 28
GARLAND REFERENCE LIBRARY OF SOCIAL SCIENCE
VOLUME 921

Educating Immigrant Children
Schools and Language Minorities in Twelve Nations

Charles L. Glenn
with Ester J. de Jong

Garland Publishing, Inc.
New York and London
1996

Library of Congress Cataloging-in-Publication Data

Glenn, Charles Leslie, 1938–
    Educating immigrant children: schools and language minorities in twelve
    nations / Charles L. Glenn with Ester J. de Jong.
        p.   cm. — (Reference books in international education ; vol. 28.
    Garland reference library of social science ; vol. 921)
      Includes bibliographical references and index.
      ISBN 0-8153-1469-8 (alk. paper)
      1. Children of immigrants—Education—Cross-cultural studies.   2. Chil-
    dren of minorities—Education—Cross-cultural studies.   I. de Jong, Ester J.
    II. Title.   III. Series: Garland reference library of social science ; v. 921.
    IV. Series: Garland reference library of social science. Reference books in
    international education ; vol. 28.
    LC3745.G54   1996
    371.97—dc20   96-10990
                                                                      CIP

Cover photograph was taken at the Williams School, Chelsea, MA,
by Boston University Photo Services.

Printed on acid-free, 250-year-life paper
Manufactured in the United States of America

Contents

SERIES EDITOR'S FOREWORD

This series of scholarly works in comparative and international education has grown well beyond the initial conception of a collection of reference books. Although retaining its original purpose of providing a resource to scholars, students, and a variety of other professionals who need to understand the role played by education in various societies or world regions, it also strives to provide accurate, relevant, and up-to-date information on a wide variety of selected educational issues, problems, and experiments within an international context.

Contributors to this series are well-known scholars who have devoted their professional lives to the study of their specializations. Without exception these men and women possess an intimate understanding of the subject of their research and writing. Without exception they have studied their subject not only in dusty archives, but have lived and traveled widely in their quest for knowledge. In short, they are "experts" in the best sense of that often overused word.

In our increasingly interdependent world, it is now widely understood that it is a matter of military, economic, and environmental survival that we not only understand better what makes other societies tick, but that we make a serious effort to understand how others, be they Japanese, Hungarian, South African, or Chilean, attempt to solve the same kinds of educational problems that we face in North America. As the late George Z.F. Bereday wrote more than three decades ago: "[E]ducation is a mirror held against the face of a people. Nations may put on blustering shows of strength to conceal public weakness, erect grand façades to conceal shabby backyards, and profess peace while secretly arming for conquest, but how they take care of their children tells unerringly who they are" (*Comparative Methods in Education*, New York: Holt, Rinehart and Winston, 1964, p. 5).

Perhaps equally important, however, is the valuable perspective that studying another education system (or its problems) provides us in understanding our own system (or its problems). When we step beyond our own limited experience and our commonly held assumptions about schools and learning in order to look back at our system in contrast to another, we see it in a very different light. To learn, for example, how China or Belgium handles the education of a multilingual society; how the French provide for the funding of public education; or how the Japanese control access to their universities enables us to better understand that there are reasonable alternatives to our own familiar way of doing things. Not that we can *borrow* directly from other societies. Indeed, educational arrangements are inevitably a reflection of deeply embedded political, economic, and cultural factors that are unique to a particular society. But a conscious recognition that there are other ways of doing things can serve to open our minds and provoke our imaginations in ways that can result in new experiments or approaches that we may not have otherwise considered.

Since this series is intended to be a useful research tool, the editor and contributors welcome suggestions for future volumes, as well as ways in which this series can be improved.

Edward R. Beauchamp
University of Hawaii

Preface

This study is concerned with the ways in which a dozen "knowledge-based societies" of Western Europe and the English-speaking world respond to unprecedented cultural and linguistic diversity resulting from the flow of immigrants and refugees since World War II. It asks how public policy has sought to use schooling to minimize the potentially divisive and inequitable effects of this diversity and to provide opportunities to the children of immigrants. It asks also how the nature of each of these societies affects the meaning of integration into each of them.

For these children, their language and culture of origin—however valuable and worthy of respect—may serve as a forbidding barrier to opportunity and participation. We will examine the solutions that various Organisation for Economic Cooperation and Development (OECD) nations have attempted to the question of whether the schooling of immigrant and language minority children should be organized with the intention of assimilating them into the dominant culture, or, instead, of maintaining their cultural and linguistic distinctiveness. Through what policies and school practices have they sought to pursue one or the other of these goals, or both at once? What do these policies and classroom practices tell us about the assumptions prevalent in different nations about the meaning (indeed, the possibility) of becoming part of the national community? What can this experience, both positive and negative, teach us about effective schooling for language minority children?

The study employs a comparative perspective, showing how similarities and differences among the policies of different countries and among the experiences of different language minority groups illuminate the policy choices. The countries chosen share the characteristics of a highly developed economy, a democratic political system, and continuing controversy over the presence of immigrant minority groups and how they should be treated within the educational system. The main focus is upon Belgium, the Netherlands, Germany, Denmark, Sweden, Switzerland, France, Spain, and the United Kingdom, all within Western Europe, and the United States, Canada, and Australia, with side glances at Italy, Ireland, and New Zealand.

It is based upon very extensive documentation, including both formal studies and periodical literature from each of the countries, as well as upon many discussions and observations by the authors in schools serving language minority children. These school observations have taken place in most but not all of the countries discussed.

We decided not to organize this account with a separate chapter on each of the countries from which information was drawn, since the effect would be highly repetitious and our primary concern has been to describe patterns of response to immigrant children that vary more within each of the countries than among them. In some cases it has seemed useful to devote sections to different countries within the discussion of a particular type of program, but these accounts are intended to be illustrative rather than definitive.

As a result of this approach, the examples drawn from the various countries are in some cases outdated by recent shifts in policy; developments have inevitably continued to occur as the manuscript has gone through its successive revisions, and we have not in every case been able to incorporate these changes. We apologize to our many correspondents that we have not always been able to use their latest information.

The reader will thus not find a systematic, country-by-country comparison of policies and practices, but rather an extended reflection upon certain themes in the schooling of the children of immigrants and in their relationship with societies that seem at times to be simultaneously clasping them too closely and pushing them away. We could say, with Tzvetan Todorov, "I am not comfortable with generalizations or with details; only their encounter satisfies me" (Todorov, 1993, xiii).

The historical, sociological, and policy discussions were the responsibility of Charles Glenn, and the discussion of instructional strategies in relation to linguistic research was that of Ester de Jong. Chapters 1 through 7 and Chapter 9 were written by Glenn, and Chapter 8 by de Jong.

THE POLICY CONTEXT

The first chapter presents the principal controversies that have arisen around the presence of the children of immigrants in schools, and raises many of the issues that will be discussed in the chapters that follow. The second goes on to discuss the current status of immigration to the OECD nations, with some historical background and a brief discussion of policy responses both to immigration and also to the presence of immigrants themselves.

MINORITY GROUPS AND THEIR LANGUAGES

Chapters 3 and 4 focus upon the situation of language minority groups. Chapter 3 discusses "indigenous" language minority groups, those groups that have an historical connection to a territory within the country in which they live but speak a language different from that of the majority in that country. It is suggested that the motivations for seeking to preserve or revive those minority languages, and the strategies employed, provide a context for understanding the prospects of immigrant minority languages as well.

Chapter 4 considers the situation of immigrants and their complex relationship with their host societies, their homelands, and the ethnic minority communities that often develop in the immigration situation. The role of ethnic leadership and of religion in maintaining such communities, and the experience of the second and subsequent generations, will be discussed.

Chapter 5 turns to a discussion of the languages of immigrants: why they are maintained or abandoned, the debates over whether they should be encouraged by public policy, and the types of measures taken to maintain these languages.

PROGRAM MODELS

Chapter 6 provides an overview of the ways in which the children of immigrants have, in some cases, been schooled separately from other children, through discriminatory segregation, separate schools established and maintained by immigrant communities, or separate programs provided with an educational justification.

Chapter 7 reviews the most common models for the schooling of language minority children that are not intended to keep them separate or to stress their distinctiveness, and provides a brief discussion of some of the criticisms raised about each model.

In Chapter 8 de Jong discusses classroom practices that provide language minority children with experiences of integration with nonminority children while stimulating their use of and proficiency in both their home language and also the majority language. She describes a "whole school" approach based upon the best practices employed in many different schools, while acknowledging the difficulties of implementing such an educational strategy.

Finally, Chapter 9 considers the policy implications of the preceding discussion, and ventures a few conclusions about the relative success of the approaches employed in several countries that enroll a significant proportion of language minority children in their schools, as well as what these approaches tell us about how participation in the society is conceptualized. As François Dubet and Didier Lapeyronnie have aptly pointed out,

> The presence of immigrants crystallizes a debate around the definition to give of our society, of the conceptions of solidarity and of the nation, fundamental questions if any are (Dubet & Lapeyronnie, 1992, 80).

EDUCATING
IMMIGRANT CHILDREN

I OVERVIEW

The social and cultural effects of immigration have been in the forefront of policy debate a number of times in American history—and in that of Canada and of Australia—but it is a largely unfamiliar and thus all the more difficult question in Europe. As Willem Fase has noted, "western Europe quickly moves in the direction of immigration countries such as the United States, Canada and Australia" but there is "crossnational variation in social and educational provisions for ethnic minority groups" (Fase, 1994, 7). The concern of this book is with what we can learn from this variation of situation and response.

WHO ARE WE TALKING ABOUT?

The focus of this study is upon the schooling of children of the ethnic minority groups that are developing as a result of recent immigration: Turks, Moroccans, and Algerians; former Yugoslavs of various warring groups and Spanish-speakers of various nationalities; Greeks and Italians; Haitians, Surinamese, and Jamaicans; Indians, Pakistanis, Bangladeshis, and Sri Lankans; Vietnamese and Cambodians; and not primarily upon indigenous language minorities nor upon high-status transnationals. We will be concerned with schoolchildren who are marked both by the linguistic and cultural differences between their homes and schools, and by the low status of their parents and their ethnic identities in the host society. One in six school-age children in the United States (Waggoner, 1988, 81), one in ten in the European Union (ECCE, 1992, 231), comes from a home that uses, much or little, a language different from that of the school.

The first issue is, what shall we call "them"? The child or adolescent who arrives in northwestern Europe with parents who are seeking work or fleeing civil strife might be called a refugee or an immigrant, depending upon a judgment about whether the family is likely to return to their homeland.

The child born of foreign parents may have no sense of another homeland, but is often still considered a "second generation foreigner." Then there is the child of the *following* generation who is still identifiably a member of an ethnic minority group and may arrive at school with little proficiency in its language of instruction, perhaps having been cared for by a grandmother who never learned it. Is that child—who may not automatically possess citizenship in the only country she or he has ever known—still a foreigner?

The terminology used in different countries for children of foreign origin and their parents often implies a political position on the issue of immigration. It may also involve a substantial amount of hypocrisy, as when some German politicians refer to "our dear foreign fellow-citizens" while discouraging them from becoming legally citizens of Germany. Sweden speaks plainly of "immigrants," Canada of "new Canadians." A Turkish writer in Denmark comments,

> They called us "foreign workers," though we were not foreign to working. Anything but. We came precisely to work. Then they called us "guest workers," even though no one ordinarily makes his guests work. And now they call us "new Danes." That sounds a hell of a lot like new potatoes (Andersen & Nielsen, 1987, 22).

And a Danish six-year-old, imitating her elders, may hurl at her Turkish playmate, "You foreign worker!" and be told, "You're one too!" or a little boy may say, of his school, "There are a lot of foreign workers in first grade." These attitudes persist despite the fact that young immigrants in Denmark (or France or Australia), as Mousavizadeh said, "given the chance, would like to think of themselves both as immigrants and Danes."

> (As a Mousavizadeh of Copenhagen, not entirely a Dane and not entirely a Persian, I can understand.) The problem lies in the culture's persistent inability to conceive of the foreign-born as Danes or potential Danes. They are inevitably described as foreigners, or guest-workers, here on borrowed time; their identity as much defined by their otherness as by their place in the work force (Mousavizadeh, 1995, 46).

As we will see, the dynamic is quite different in Australia, Canada, and the United States, where the assumption is that every resident foreigner will become assimilated as quickly as possible, and lingering marks of "otherness" are often considered disloyal indications of resistance.

To add to the confusion, new labels are coined to reflect changing sensibilities or realities, but the older terms continue in use beside them. Thus in Germany the workers recruited in Italy, Turkey, and elsewhere during the 1960s are still sometimes called "guest worker" (*Gastarbeiter*), though the fact that (unlike guests) most show no signs of leaving has led to the substitution of "foreign employees" (*ausländische Arbeitnehmer*), and simply "foreigner" (*Ausländer*) for members of their families into the second and third generations born in Germany. Those concerned about the rise of antiforeigner feeling, however, regard these terms as stigmatizing and often refer to the workers as "migrant employees" (*Wanderarbeitnehmer*). If sympathetic to their desire to remain in Germany, they may use terms like "immigrant" (*Einwanderer*), even though public policy and opinion reject the idea that Germany is a country to which immigrants may come (Just, 1985c, 22–23).

We will sometimes employ the phrase "the children of immigrants," though not thereby intending to exclude children who themselves immigrate, nor yet the grandchildren of the immigrant generation. Other times we will speak of "language minority children," meaning children from homes in which a minority language is spoken, whether or not it is the primary language used.

Although earlier studies and policy documents in Europe tended to focus upon the immigrant generation alone, there is a growing tendency to recognize that the second and even third generations derived from immigration have characteristics that distinguish them—usually to their disadvantage—from the native-origin population (Commissie Allochtone Leerlingen in het Onderwijs, 1992, 6).

Not all groups face such difficulties, of course. Fase has attempted a characterization of the relative success of different immigrant groups in Europe. Each of his "unsuccessful" groups is non-European (North African, Turkish, West Indian, Bangladeshi) and most of his "not unsuccessful" groups are European, with the exception of Indians and Pakistanis in the United Kingdom and "Indo-Europeans" from Indonesia in the Netherlands. A rather different picture would emerge if a classification were made of the relative success of immigrant groups to the United States; for example, West Indians have been notably more successful here than in the United Kingdom, for a variety of reasons (Gibson, 1991a; see Sowell, 1978, 40–49). As Ogbu has noted, much may depend upon the "folk theory" that different minority groups develop to explain their difficulties and the actions needed to deal with them, and this in turn is profoundly affected by the historical circumstances under which the group came into existence as a self-conscious "minority" (Ogbu, 1991b).

5

Ethnic diversity is of course no new phenomenon in the United States, Canada, and Australia, nations built up largely by immigration over the course of the nineteenth and early twentieth centuries, nor have language differences been unproblematic in the nations of Western Europe. Polish workers in the mining districts of Germany and Belgium and Italian workers in France were considered a challenge to social policy in the nineteenth century, and substituting a national language for the local dialects of indigenous regional groups was a major motivation in the development of state-sponsored schooling over the course of the late eighteenth and nineteenth centuries in Europe (Weber, 1976). We should not expect this process to go altogether smothly; after all,

> In the past, major ethnic changes in the pattern of immigration have given rise to social disturbances, followed by periods of adaptation and integration of the immigrants (and adaptation by the U.S. society). The new phase will also likely involve some disturbances and raise new questions about the identity of the "American" (Edmonston & Passel, 1994a, 16).

Two new factors, however, justify the belief that the present phenomenon cannot be considered merely another chapter in the long history of nation-building and migration in the West. One is demographic, the other political and ideological. As we will see, population movement has become a worldwide phenomenon, no longer flowing in a few, well-defined patterns and for transparent reasons as it did in the nineteenth century (Overbeek, 1994, 67). In addition, the *meaning* of ethnic and linguistic diversity has changed.

Ethnicity and its consequences are not only a leading foreign policy challenge of the post–Cold War era (Moynihan, 1993), but also among the most difficult and potentially destabilizing political issues in most of the Western democracies (Overbeek, 1994, 66), as well as in the former Soviet Union and Yugoslavia and the "developing" nations. Within the last several years, political commentators in Germany, in France, and in the United States have ranked immigration as the leading "hot button" topic in political discourse. To take an example at random, a liberal columnist in the *Boston Globe* wrote that President Clinton should "recognize that the dominant issue of the 1996 presidential campaign may be illegal immigration. . . . Look at Western Europe. Immigration is a political time bomb" (Nyhan, 1994).

In Germany, the "foreigners issue" was considered the most important political question by 73 percent of Germans surveyed (Gedmin, 1992, 63), though the far-right *Republikaner* party has been losing support in the wake of shocking incidents of anti-immigrant violence and moves by the ruling Christian Democrats to limit the right of asylum. A government document in 1991 made a fundamental distinction between the *Staatsvolk* of Germans permanently linked to the nation by destiny (the *Schicksalsgemeinschaft*) and the population residing in Germany (*Gebietsbevölkerung*) but not thereby part of the German people (Collet, 1992, 140). Popular support for allowing ethnic Germans to emigrate freely has been declining, as has willingness to accept family reunification and political refugees (*Der Spiegel*, February 5, 1990); even *Übersiedler*, Germans moving to the west from what was East Germany, are increasingly unpopular, and political parties compete to demonstrate their responsiveness to this mood (*Der Spiegel*, February 19, 1990).

Elsewhere political parties making opposition to immigrants a major platform have scored a number of local electoral successes; the *Vlaamse Blok* gained a quarter of the votes in Antwerp in November 1991 and again in October 1994, and the *Deutsche Volksunion* won 10 percent in Bremen, Germany's smallest state, in September 1991. The National Front has consistently gained 10 to 12 percent of the votes in France in recent elections, reaching a high point of 14.4 percent in the presidential election of 1988 (Perrineau, 1992, 84); this inspired the center-right Balladur government to include strong measures against immigrants in its program and made hardline Interior Minister Charles Pasqua a popular figure (*The Economist*, October 15, 1994, 68–70).

The tendency for immigration to become a mainstream political issue was illustrated at the Europewide congress of liberal (probusiness, free-market) parties in 1991, when the head of the Dutch Liberals (VVD) warned of the danger of immigration for European societies and for their cultures (Mahnig, 1992, 119). On the other hand, business groups in the United States and elsewhere commonly argue that continued immigration is economically healthy because of its effects on the supply of labor and thus on wages, while organized labor is often found on the side of proposals for the restriction of immigration and for measures against illegal aliens. Progressive intellectuals tend to be proimmigrant, both from a general sympathy for those in need and also because they welcome cultural diversity as relativizing the hitherto dominant culture.

Thus one of the causes of policy confusion about immigration is that the lines of division on the issue run through rather than between left and right in most OECD countries. This holds true, as well, for the central question of this study, the role of education in promoting assimilation or maintaining distinctiveness: in Europe, "within a decade, the theme of [the importance of protecting] difference has moved from the far Left to the far Right" (Taguieff, 1993–1994, 125).

The situation is further confused by the fact that immigrants themselves tend to be culturally and religiously conservative—thus potential allies of the conservative political movements of the host societies—but to the extent that they manifest a political preference they are strongly favorable toward the social democratic parties, which they perceive as more vigilant about their interests.

Political and social controversies over the presence of immigrants in the OECD countries can be grouped under four headings. One that will not detain us long is the concern that immigrants are a financial burden because of their consumption of social services and because they take jobs from native workers. In effect, they are criticized for not working and also for working too much!

A second cluster of concerns is that an underclass is emerging, consisting of immigrants and their children who are unsuccessful in their participation in the host society and especially its educational system and economy. This concern often focuses upon the academic performance of the children of immigrants in schools.

A third cluster of concerns is that the nature of the society is somehow being changed by the influence of an immigrant minority that is culturally different and, through either its needs or its demands, forces unacceptable changes. Many Americans, for example, resent the use of languages other than English for official purposes (Crawford, 1992a; 1992b). This is often more a vague feeling of unease rather than a specific bill of particulars; it is perhaps best captured by the German word "*Überfremdung*," which might be translated as "an excess of foreignness."

The fourth cluster of concerns is in some tension with the third, since it involves the accusation that immigrants and their descendants are not interacting enough with the host society, that they are an inassimilable minority as a result of cultural differences and excessive devotion to their ethnic community.

A Financial Burden?

California officials estimate that there were more than 2 million illegal immigrants among the 31.5 million residents of the state, and that it costs the state $2.3 billion annually to provide them with legally mandated services.

In July 1993, Governor Wilson proposed legislative changes that would deny automatic citizenship to the children of foreigners in the United States illegally and cut off free health and education services to those families. "Except in emergencies, state assistance would go only to those immigrants who could prove they were in the state legally by presenting a 'tamperproof' identification card" (*The Boston Globe*, July 10, 1993). A referendum question, Proposition 187, adopted in California by a substantial majority in November 1994, requires schools to cooperate with immigration-control efforts by reporting students or parents who may be "reasonably suspected" of being in the country illegally, and denies a variety of public services, including schooling, to illegal immigrants and their children; state education officials estimate that there are 410,000 illegal immigrant students in California schools. The intention, according to the proponents, is to make California less attractive to illegal immigrants, to cut public expenditure, and to challenge the 1982 decision of the U.S. Supreme Court in *Plyler v. Doe* that all children have a constitutional right to public education regardless of their legal status. Proponents denied that the measure was in any way racist, and pointed out that Hispanics (who make up a quarter of the state's population but only 11 percent of its voters) were evenly split on the issue (*Education Week*, October 26, 1994, 18).

The cost figures are subject to more than one interpretation. While public services provide benefits to immigrants, it must be noted that benefits accrue to natives as well, as is pointed out by Michael Fix and Jeffrey Passel:

> The single largest component of immigrant-related public sector costs is the cost of providing public and secondary education, which is approximately $11 billion annually for immigrants. The actual recipients of these expenditures are, for the most part, native-born teachers, school administrators, maintenance staffs, and others employed in school administration, maintenance, and construction (Fix & Passel, 1994, 62).

Opponents of the denial of social and educational services to illegal immigrants argue on the basis both of justice and of the public interest. Noncitizens, they point out, have a higher workforce participation rate than do citizens, and often pay taxes and social insurance contributions over many years. To deny them routine health care will lead to a greater use of emergency medical services and create the possibility of epidemics; to deny their children education will make them less productive as future workers and encourage street crime.

The French government reminded school administrators, in 1984, that schooling was obligatory between the ages of 6 and 16 for all foreigners resident in France, and ordered them not to demand evidence of legal residence when registering children for school. This was a response to occasional decisions, by local authorities, not to admit children to schools if their families were in the country illegally (Henry-Lorcerie, 1989, 49). A French opinion survey conducted in 1989 found 58 percent of respondents in favor of limiting social welfare payments to immigrants (Massenet, 1994, 143).

The same issues have arisen in other countries, particularly in relation to the cost of maintaining asylum-seekers for years while their cases are adjudicated, an especially heavy burden in Germany with its constitutionally guaranteed right of political asylum.

The most common basis for claiming that immigrants represent a financial burden, however, has to do with the jobs that they fill, and their alleged willingness to undercut native workers by accepting less pay and inferior working conditions (*Die Welt*, February 21, 1989). The *Front national* in France, for example, has frequently equated the number of unemployed French men and women with the number of immigrants in France.

Since these debates over the cost of immigration and of immigrants are marginal to our primary themes, we will do no more than note that they provide part of the tumultuous background to concerns over the presence of the children of immigrants in schools.

An Emerging Underclass?

The growing concern about violent crime and disorder in the wealthy nations has been another source of hostility to the presence of immigrants. A disproportionate share of crime is in fact perpetrated by ethnic minority youth, not the immigrant generation themselves but rather their children, young men alienated from the host society without being solidly rooted in a traditional culture. The proportion of foreigners among imprisoned convicts in France increased from 14.4 percent in 1971 to 26.2 percent in 1984 (Voisard & Ducastelle, 1986, 37), and the Interior Ministry now estimates that half of the drug-related crimes are by foreigners (Massenet, 1994, 16). More than half of the prisoners in Dutch jails in 1995 were foreigners (Dunning, 1995, 285). Although it is often argued that minority youth commit crimes because they are young, not in school, and marginalized, not because they are of immigrant backgrounds (Gaspard & Servan-Schreiber, 1985, 124), it is not surprising that the growing preoccupation with crime and violence leads to anti-immigrant sentiment.

In Europe as in the United States, the problem of youth crime is closely associated with youth failure in school (both as an effect and as a cause), and pupils belonging to some immigrant minority groups are more likely than native pupils to experience such failure. This is an area about which it is particularly difficult to generalize, since pupils belonging to other immigrant groups have if anything an advantage in school as a result of high motivation to succeed and isolation from an indigenous youth culture that discourages academic effort (Portes & Zhou, 1994).

Comparisons with Native Pupils

Exceptional groups aside, the educational outcomes of immigrant children are generally inferior to those of native children. One simple measure is the rate at which they are required to repeat a grade. A study in Belgium found that 55 percent of the foreign pupils (and a high 30 percent of the native pupils) were at least a year behind by the end of primary school (Bastenier, cited by Just, 1985c, 141).

Turkish children in Denmark, as in most Western European nations, do, on average, more poorly in school than most other immigrant children (Gimbel, 1988, 117–19). Similarly, in 1980 Turkish pupils who had been born in West Germany were significantly more likely (78.2 percent) to attend the lowest form of secondary education than were other foreign pupils (51.7 percent) who had been in the country less than five years (Nieke, Budde & Henscheid, 1983, 27). Does the stereotyping of these children as *dumme tyrker* (the Danish phrase) or, more benignly, defining them in terms of their special needs contribute to their lagging achievement? A cross-national study of secondary education in the eighties found that

> the enrolment rate of foreign children is always higher than that of nationals in those streams or cycles which either require only minimal qualifications or provide only a short course of instruction. . . . those young foreigners leaving school without these basic qualifications are in a worse situation at the outset of their working lives than were the first generation of immigrants at the moment of their arrival (Centre for Educational Research and Innovation . . . , 1987, 33).

Comparison of the academic achievement and persistence of groups of minority pupils in the United States indicates that those deriving from Latin American immigration have less favorable outcomes than do black Americans, while those deriving from Asian immigration have more favorable outcomes than do white Americans, even though the Asians are as a group the most recently arrived. "By almost any measure," as Beatriz Arias put it, "Hispanics are the most undereducated group of Americans, next to Native Americans" (Arias, 1986, 26). There is some evidence that the low achievement of Hispanic pupils is related to their status in North American society, since their achievement seems to worsen with more time in the United States (Fernandez & Nielson, 1986). This effect may reflect the especially low achievement of Puerto Rican pupils compared with those of other Hispanic groups, since they have typically spent longer in American schools than have Central American immigrant children, but with repeated sojourns on the island that may retard acquisition of academic proficiency in English; "for Puerto Rican students, language difficulties seem to be the beginning of learning problems that are never effectively remedied" (Fligstein & Fernandez, 1985).

Among high school seniors of the lowest 25 percent of socioeconomic status (SES), 12 percent of the Asians later completed college, compared with 7.7 percent of the blacks, 6.9 percent of the non-Hispanic whites, and 4.0 percent of the Hispanics. Of those from the top 25 percent of SES, 40 percent of the Asians, 38.2 percent of the non-Hispanic whites, 25.5 percent of the blacks, and only 18 percent of the Hispanics completed college (National Center for Education Statistics, 1992, 304).

The most recent report on academic achievement on the National Assessment of Educational Progress (NAEP), commonly regarded as the most reliable indicator of the results of schooling in the United States, noted that

> despite progress in reducing the performance differences across the past two decades, . . . the gaps remain large. In 1992, both Black and Hispanic students, on average, demonstrated significantly lower proficiency than White students. This overall difference occurred notwithstanding the fact that students from all three racial/ethnic groups demonstrated performance across a range from high to low achievement (Mullis et al., 1994, 20).

It should be noted that achievement of a largely immigrant group (Hispanics) is roughly comparable to that of an indigenous minority group (blacks) who have an especially low proportion of immigrants; similarly, the average academic achievement of Asians, the most recently immigrated group, is comparable to if not superior to that of the white majority. Indian pupils in the United Kingdom are achieving better academic results than are native British pupils. This is the puzzle that led to Ogbu's distinction between voluntary and involuntary or castelike minorities (Ogbu, 1986;

TABLE 1.1. Foreign Proportion in West Germany by School Type, 1983

	Hauptschule	Gymnasium
Baden-Württemberg	18.3%	3.0%
Bavaria	9.3%	2.6%
Berlin	40.2%	5.2%
Bremen	16.1%	2.6%
Hamburg	22.9%	3.8%
Hesse	12.9%	2.8%
Lower Saxony	5.9%	1.3%
North Rhine/Westphalia	16.5%	2.7%
Rhineland-Palatinate	7.7%	1.2%
Saar	6.8%	1.7%
Schleswig-Holstein	5.7%	1.3%
Total	13.1%	1.3%

Source: Boos-Nünning and Henscheid, 1986.

1991a). Puerto Rican pupils, who legally are not immigrants, have the lowest academic success rate of the Hispanic group; Ogbu considers them, in contrast with immigrants from Asia or Latin America, an "involuntary minority."

TRACKING AND SELECTION BY SCHOOLS

Foreign pupils are significantly less likely to attend an academically demanding *Gymnasium* in West Germany, and more likely to attend a *Hauptschule* with the least capable German pupils (Table 1.1). In 1982 25.6 percent of German pupils but only 3.7 percent of foreign pupils were attending *Gymnasien*. Nearly half of the foreign pupils entering a *Hauptschule*, a study of three states found, did not even obtain the ninth-grade certificate (Nieke, Budde, & Henscheid, 1983, 24, 43).

A Swedish study of ninth-grade pupils nationwide did not find evidence of discrimination against linguistic minority pupils; indeed, "applicants with home languages other than Swedish and with marks below the average for all applicants have been slightly more extensively admitted to upper secondary school than pupils with Swedish as their home language and with equally low marks" (Liljegren & Ullman, 1981, 38).

Similarly, a Dutch study of the transition to the highly-stratified secondary education system found evidence of positive discrimination, since foreign pupils received the same recommendation [as to type of schooling] as native pupils who scored on the average 9 points higher [on the standardized tests]. . . . It appears as though the teachers, who did not know the results of these tests, as it were corrected for the language handicap of the foreign pupils (Jong, 1987, 117).

This finding was confirmed by a nationwide study in 1991: "ethnic minority pupils are generally advised to attend a more advanced form of secondary education than Dutch pupils who performed equally well" (Social and Cultural Planning Office, 1993, 224). In addition, this study found, minority pupils were more likely than Dutch pupils to choose an even higher form of secondary schooling than advised. It has been suggested that this may help to account for the inadequate academic performance of minority youth in secondary schools, including their higher-than-average tendency to repeat the first year or to drop out (Tesser, 1993, 139–41).

Despite a measure of positive discrimination, the gap between Dutch and foreign children, already obvious when they enter school, continues to grow over the course of their schooling, and they fall farther behind not only middle-class but also working-class Dutch pupils (Commissie Allochtone Leerlingen in het Onderwijs, 1992, 23–24). Although lower-level diplomas have recently been introduced for pupils who do not complete secondary education, many immigrant minority youth in the Netherlands leave school without any qualifications at all. "In the past, it was children from labourers' families who were most likely to drop out of school; now this position is held by immigrants, particularly those from Morocco and Turkey." Only 35 percent of Moroccan and no more than half of the Turkish young men who begin secondary education obtain any form of diploma. Those who do not drop out tend to be enrolled in the less academic forms of secondary education in the highly stratified Dutch system. "The lowest position is occupied by Moroccan youngsters, followed by Turkish and Surinamese youngsters and young people from other parts of the Mediterranean. Pupils from an Asian background (mainly Chinese) do better than the average Dutch pupil" (Social and Cultural Planning Office, 1993, 222). A 1989 study found three quarters of the Turkish and Moroccan pupils in Amsterdam in the lowest form of vocational education, compared with less than 40 percent of the (urban) Dutch pupils; 20 percent of the latter go on to academic secondary education—a low proportion by national standards—but only 1 or 2 percent of the Turkish and Moroccan pupils do so (*Samenwijs*, March 1989). These results have been attributed in part to the low level of schooling of most immigrant parents (Tesser, 1993, 159).

A study in France found similarly that, among pupils who reached the final stage of secondary education, two French children out of every five, three foreign children (all nationalities combined) out of five, and four out of every five Turkish, Portuguese, or Algerian children had not taken part in the course of study that leads on to university education (Organisation for Economic Cooperation and Development, 1987, 69). On the other hand, national data indicate that "the preponderant factor in academic success or failure remains the socio-professional status of the parents." Immigrant children from equivalent families have academic results identical to those of their French peers (Boyzon-Fradet & Boulot, 1992, 256). A study in Geneva concluded, similarly, that "social origin being equal, the Swiss have a very slight advantage over the foreigners, but this is quite small against the inequalities revealed by a comparison between different social origins for the same nationality" (Hutmacher, 1987, 246). Such comparisons must be viewed with some caution, however; after all, the status of immigrant families is artificially lowered by their situation in the host society. Immigrants are drawn in most cases from the elite of the working class and lower middle class of their homeland, and have qualities of ambition and optimism that may be missing from the indigenous workers who are equivalent to them in status.

LACK OF PROFICIENCY IN THE LANGUAGE OF THE SCHOOL

Inadequate proficiency in the language of the school is frequently cited as a primary reason for poor academic performance. Only 40 percent of the children of immigrants in German preschool programs, according to one study, were sufficiently proficient in the German language, and 90 percent of those who were not were of Turkish origin. Despite what is now typically several decades of residence in Germany, the social and occupational isolation of many Turkish families has prevented their children from acquiring adequate German (Institut für Zukunftsforschung, 1981, 133). A study of a group of Turkish youth found that 19 percent lived in apartment houses with no German occupants, and 44 percent had no contact with the German neighbors in the same building; only 17 percent had any sort of relationship with their German neighbors; some reported that it caused difficulty with learning German in school that they had no one at home or nearby who could help (Şahin & Heyden, 1982, 116, 119).

Ekstrand argues that the immigration experience is not in itself necessarily traumatic, provided that it is not associated with family breakup, poverty, or other situational problems, and that the frequently evoked concept of "culture shock" may not explain as much as is often assumed (Ekstrand, 1980a, 50). He cites research showing that "immigrant pupils performed about as well as Swedish pupils" *if they had acquired equal proficiency in Swedish* (Ekstrand, 1981a, 208). Lofgren found there was "little difference between students with another home language to that of students with Swedish as their home language. However, the situation differed for those students who did not have a good proficiency in Swedish" (Lofgren, 1984, 6).

An extensive study of all ninth-grade pupils in Sweden using a language other than Swedish at home found

> a relatively large difference between the proportion of pupils with [low] Swedish proficiency . . . admitted to upper secondary school and the proportion admitted with [high] proficiency ratings. . . . The proportion of the total number of pupils with [high] ratings admitted to upper secondary school straight from compulsory [grades 1–9] school comes relatively close to the proportion admitted from among pupils having Swedish as their home language (Liljegren & Ullman, 1981, 47).

Dutch research has found that, social class aside, the language spoken at home affects school performance, but "only those ethnic minority pupils who are in the most favourable circumstances perform as well as Dutch children from similar backgrounds. These are immigrant youngsters who have been in the Netherlands for a relatively long time, have been educated in Dutch from the very beginning and have grown up in a family which is well integrated into Dutch society" (Social and Cultural Planning Office, 1993, 223).

Cultural and Social Class Factors

It is particularly difficult to determine to what extent academic success is harmed by a cultural discontinuity between the home and the school (see Chapter 5). As an alternative to explanations based upon the presumed racism of the host society, some in Europe argue that Turkish and North African children experience a greater cultural gap as they seek to make sense of the schools of the host society. In their enthusiasm for this explanation, they may overlook the fact that many Turkish immigrants come from Ankara or Istanbul rather than the countryside of eastern Anatolia, and that the fathers were often recruited to emigrate because they had been skilled workers in Turkey.

The question is much debated in the Netherlands, where researchers agree that immigrant minority children are underachieving but cannot agree on the reason (Driessen, 1990, 58). The latest major policy document on

the subject concluded that ethnicity should be discounted as a factor leading to educational disadvantage, and additional resources should therefore
be allocated on the basis of social class factors alone (Commissie Allochtone
Leerlingen in het Onderwijs, 1992). On the other hand, a study conducted
for the evaluation of the Dutch compensatory education policy found that

> the deprived position occupied by pupils from ethnic minorities can
> only partly be ascribed to the low socio-economic status of their par-
> ents. Immigrant pupils score lower than Dutch pupils from the same
> social background. The country of origin is particularly significant
> when it comes to language tests, being as important as the parents'
> education and the father's profession (Tesser et al., 1991, cited by
> Social and Cultural Planning Office, 1993, 223).

Encouragingly, it has been noted that about 30 percent of the immigrant
pupils do as well as or better than the national averages (Mol, 1995, 297);
what has been occurring over time is a sorting-out of the immigrant population into those who integrate successfully and those who do not (see
Chapter 4).

While social class factors alone cannot explain the underachievement
of most immigrant minority children, it should be reassuring to those concerned about the future of this group that these factors explain a great deal.
This suggests that with the passage of time the succession of generations will
lead to social mobility. In elementary education in Belgium, 93.6 percent of
Moroccan and 95.8 percent of Turkish mothers have completed no more
than lower intermediate education, compared with 35.1 percent of Belgian
mothers with children in elementary education (Vanhoren, 1991, 53); as the
children of those Moroccan and Turkish mothers, with even a modestly successful education in Belgian schools, become parents themselves, it seems
likely that many of their children will do better than they did as a result of
more effective support in the home.

A French study suggests that the academic difficulties of the children
of immigrants are the result of social class and contextual factors that have
the same effect upon French pupils. "The success rate of foreign students is
comparable to that of French pupils with the same accumulation of unfavorable factors . . . 9 out of 10 have a disadvantaged head of family (compared
with 4 out of 10 of French pupils). The latter has in nine out of ten cases only
a primary education or is illiterate. . . . The results: upon leaving *classes
d'accueil* (welcoming classes) at the lower-secondary level, few pupils enter a
regular course at their age level" (Boulot & Boyzon-Fradet, 1991a, 6).

Whatever the causes of the academic underachievement of some groups of immigrant minority children and youth, its effects are unambiguous: consignment to a low-status and even marginal position in the host society, disappointing the hopes with which their parents undertook their often painful immigration.

The Fear of Überfremdung

It appears to have been in Switzerland that the expression "*Überfremdung*" first came into use in the years before World War I, when a country that had been noted for its emigrants (the Swiss Family Robinson!) began to experience of surplus of immigrants; by 1914, foreigners made up 15.5 percent of the Swiss population (Hoffmann-Nowotny, 1985, 207). The concept was given an official definition in the 1960s, as

> the situation that results when the influence of non-assimilated, or not satisfactorily assimilated, members of other cultures is so strong that the essential and basic values that form the foundation of the native culture are influenced by foreign values and the population's way of living is subsequently no longer based on its own traditions (Hoffmann-Nowotny, 1985, 216).

Concern that the presence of a large number of unassimilated (and perhaps unassimilable) foreigners will somehow alienate a society from itself is thus by no means new; indeed Maurice Barrès raised the alarm in France in the late nineteenth century that "the foreigner, like a parasite, is poisoning us" (quoted by Todorov, 1993, 247). The theme has become increasingly common in recent decades, however. Germany policymakers, fearful of *Überfremdung*, have sought to distinguish between those foreigners who are compatible with their society and should be integrated selectively, and those who are not (Hamburger, 1989, 4). Dutch voters in 1994 told researchers that the issue that concerned them most was not the environment, or joblessness, or the abuse of social services, but the "minority question" (Dunning, 1995, 284). Similarly, a poll conducted at the time of the French elections in 1988 found that 65 percent of the respondents agreed (30 percent) or strongly agreed (35 percent) that "there are too many immigrants in France;" only 19 percent disagreed. This response was associated with another, almost equally strong, agreeing that "one doesn't feel at home like before" (Mayer, 1992, 66).

Not feeling at home because of too many strangers around, with their strange ways, is not the same thing as racism or even xenophobia, the hatred and fear of foreigners; it is a quite understandable discomfort with change in what was familiar and reassuring. At what point the quite tolerable, even interesting, presence of a few foreigners becomes the objectionable presence of too many depends of course upon many factors of circumstance as well as personal psychology, and has been much studied by social scientists who wish to identify a (surely mythical) "tipping point" in housing or in schools. Here it is enough to acknowledge that such a phenomenon does exist and produces a variety of social effects and pressures upon policy makers.

Immigration is a political time bomb in part because of a perceived competition for scarce resources and jobs, but also because of a real or perceived clash of cultures, the sense of discomfort that many citizens of host countries feel about the presence among them of newcomers who differ from them in observable respects.

One might expect the conditions of modernity to make it less urgent to address the question of foreignness. In a traditional society, strangers are always a puzzle and a potential threat; if allowed to remain, they must either be adopted in some way into the status of member of the community, or accorded a special status as a resident alien. An instructive example is provided by the practice of ancient Israel. According to the Law of Moses, "an alien living among you who wants to celebrate the Lord's Passover" (that is, take part in the remembrance of the Exodus as though his ancestors had been among those brought out of Egypt) "must have all the males in his household circumcised; then he may take part like one born in the land" (*Exodus* 12:48 NIV). Those who did not go through this ceremony of incorporation remained distinctly aliens, though accorded protection as a matter of piety and justice: "Do not oppress an alien; you yourselves know how it feels to be aliens, for you were aliens in Egypt" (*Exodus* 23:9 NIV). This requirement itself reflects, however, the vulnerability of the resident alien, comparable to that of widows and orphans. In a climactic event of covenant-making, the whole people is called upon to affirm a series of fundamental assertions of moral order, among them: "Cursed is the man who withholds justice from the alien, the fatherless, or the widow" (*Deuteronomy* 27:19 NIV).

The category of resident alien reflects, not the conditions of a peasant culture, but those of the socially complex cities of the ancient world. In Jerusalem, as in Athens and Rome, there were communities of aliens whose presence was tolerated and regularized without eliminating their distinctiveness through assimilation. Such a system persisted into the twentieth century in the Ottoman Empire, where Christian and Jewish communities were accorded a stable and semi-autonomous if subordinate position as "millets" within a predominantly Muslim society. The persistence of small Jewish and Christian communities for many centuries in India and China reflects a similar acceptance of unassimilated elements as a normal phenomenon of premodern urban society.

In a society where the acids of modernization have dissolved the solidarity of the majority community that had tolerated the presence of alien minorities, where *Gemeinschaft* (community) has given way to *Gesellschaft* (society), the nature of the relationship between majority and minority is likely to change. Members of the minority group are emancipated from their subordinated and marginalized position, but at the same time become subject to intense pressures to give up their distinctiveness. The pressures are not so much deliberately imposed as they are the unintended consequences of individual mobility at the price of conformity to wider societal norms. The classic case is that of Jews in France and Germany during the nineteenth century: civil emancipation brought an incalculable widening of opportunities and of civil rights, but it led also to a widespread secularization and weakening or outright rejection of community ties. The famous offer, "Everything for the Jews as individuals, nothing for the Jews as a people," was both a classic formulation of the universality of human rights and also a challenge to the right to existence of a civil society made up of ethnic communities, voluntary groups, and religious and cultural institutions (Benoist, 1993–1994, 176).

Under the conditions of modernity, "alien-ness" becomes a measure of cultural and social distance rather than of nationality. Physicists and philosophers at the University of Chicago are likely to be in no fundamental respect "alien" from their counterparts at Oxford or Tübingen, or indeed at the University of Lagos, but may inhabit an entirely different social and cultural universe from many fellow-Americans living within ten blocks of the university campus. Those from every nation who participate in the global information society are aware of and may well value the ways in which they are culturally distinctive, but they will not find this distinctiveness a barrier to communication with their counterparts. In this social stratum, "cultural diversity" provides an attractive flavoring to life, but the important transactions of life are based upon a shared international culture.

Those who are opposed to continued immigration to the United States are not agitated over the 45,100 immigrants admitted from India in 1991 or the half-million admitted since 1970, many of them highly educated and none perceived as a social problem. The cultural particularities that these immigrants choose to retain are expressed in the private sphere of life and do not limit their full participation in professional and other activities in the public sphere.

It is the sense that culturally alien attitudes and practices inconsistent with modernity are intruding into and threatening the common public sphere of society that leads to fear of immigrants as a cultural presence. Fear of the growing Muslim population—in France, for example, now estimated at 2.8 million, more than the number of Protestants and Jews combined—is widespread in Western Europe. Among puzzled intellectuals, the "liberal expectancy," described by Milton Gordon, that the distinctiveness of ethnic groups would somehow wear off in the contact with modernity, has been disappointed (De Vos & Romanucci-Ross, 1982a, xiv).

French opinion surveys have found that 74 percent of the respondents are concerned that France is in danger of losing its identity because of the excessive number of immigrants, by which clearly North African rather than Portuguese or Italian resident aliens are meant (Massenet, 1994, 79). Jacques Chirac, the Mayor of Paris, former Prime Minister and now President, described the situation in almost apocalyptic terms in 1990:

> A country can lose a war or experience a serious economic crisis and recover from it. But a country like ours could not recover from losing its identity. . . . in the course of our history, immigration has occurred in little doses that integrated themselves little by little, but we must now confront a real overdose. And that's not all. Formerly, the foreigners who settled in France were of European origin. They had the same culture and the same religion as us. This is no longer the case. That's why the nation feels menaced. I don't understand why some seek to discredit that by talking constantly of racism. Whether the Cassandras like it or not, France is not racist (quoted by Massenet, 1994, 147–48).

The "greatness of France," it is claimed, is that membership in the national political community has nothing to do with *race*, as in Germany and Japan, and takes absolute priority over competing loyalties to ethnic or religious "communities"—which receive little recognition in French law—of the sort that are found in Russia or the United States (Thibaud, 1991, 11). For some commentators, the growing Muslim presence threatens this French approach to diversity. On the one hand, the rejection of North Africans associated with the *Front national* is uncomfortably close to German racialism, while, on the other, the alleged unwillingness of Muslims to assimilate as individuals seems to threaten a future of American-style intergroup conflict.

Nothing has done so much to bring this development to the attention of the French public as the "*Affaire des Foulards,*" which dominated the front pages of French newspapers and journals of opinion for several months in the fall of 1989, as much of the rest of the world was focusing its attention on the collapse of Communism in Eastern Europe. Although involving only three teenage girls, it brought into sharp focus uncertainties about the meaning of participation by ethnic minority groups in French society, as well as raising questions about the continued viability of an ideology of secularity that has been a defining characteristic of French political thinking. The controversy continued to agitate France five years later; a nationwide crackdown in the fall of 1994 led to the expulsion of several dozen students from French schools, after it was reported by the government that 860 of the 150,000 to 200,000 Muslim schoolgirls in the country were insisting upon wearing distinctive dress to school (*The Boston Globe*, October 30, 1994, 5).

This controversy began when three girls (sisters Leila and Fatima, of Moroccan parentage, and Samira, of Tunisian) were excluded from classes in an intermediate school in Creil, on September 18, 1989, because of their insistence upon covering their heads with scarves (the *hijab*, or *foulard* in French), over the strong objection of teachers who saw this as a sign of ethnic particularism and of what they understood to be the subordination of women in Islamic societies. "For many teachers, to conduct a class with veiled pupils represented the very negation of the ideals of emancipation and development of a critical sense that was for them the foundation of secular (*laïque*) education" (Kepel, 1994, 304). The headmaster concluded that the action on the part of the girls was "an attack upon the *laïcité* and the neutrality of a public school"; the three girls were subsequently suspended for a time, and then required to remain in the school library rather than attend classes. Two weeks later, a regional newspaper carried the story, and a national furor developed.

There was something particularly French about this "obsessive fixation of an entire society on the shawl worn on their heads by three adolescents in a run-down *banlieu*" (Kepel, 1994, 239), and it has been paralleled in the francophone provinces of Belgium and Canada. By contrast, it is not uncommon for Muslim girls to wear such scarves to school in Germany, the Netherlands, or the United Kingdom without any fuss made about it by school officials.

The incident was not without background. For several years, about twenty Jewish students at the same school had been refusing to attend classes on Saturday, for religious reasons, and had started school a few days late in

September because of the High Holy Days. The school administration had resolved, the previous June, to begin to treat this as an unexcused absence, and had been reminded of the parallel practice of Muslim girls covering their heads in class. A circular was sent to all teachers informing them that this should no longer be allowed.

While the offense seems a minor one—there was never an allegation that the girls behaved in a disruptive way, or sought to persuade other Muslim girls to cover their hair—the faculty was concerned that one symbol of difference would lead to others, as had occurred at other schools where "once dialogue began with the families involved, other demands quickly appeared: refusal of certain courses, or of [aspects of] their content, demands about co-education, etc.," as one Creil teacher, himself a member of an immigrant minority, wrote, confessing his perplexity about how the school could reconcile respect for diversity with its socializing function (Cardoso, 1990, 7–12). The fact that the school counted 25 nationalities among its 800 pupils made the threat of on-going disruption seem quite substantial. National teacher association leaders promptly paid visits to Creil to express their solidarity with the teachers (Montvalon & Léotard, 1989, 12).

The real issue raised by the *Affaire des Foulards*, however, was its challenge to the *laïcité* of the French public school. *Laïcité*, a word with no precise equivalent in English ("secularity," in the sense not just of neutrality but of a comprehensive ideology—verging on "secular humanism"—based upon a nonreligious understanding of life, would be an approximation), has enormous resonance in French educational policy. From the 1880s until 1914 and indeed beyond, the extension of universal schooling was seen as the surest defense of republicanism and of material and spiritual progress against the forces of reaction as represented (in the thinking of the leading proponents of the public school) by the Catholic Church.

> Having identified the Catholic church as the primary enemy of the Republic, the Radicals paid it the compliment of seeking to emulate the church by creating a state-controlled system of education that was centralized, unified in its doctrines, and concerned above all to transmit values and to shape loyalties (Glenn, 1988b, 243).

The intransigence of the three girls in Creil caused a serious schism within the French Left. On the one hand, there were those (including the wife of President Mitterand) for whom the "right to be different" and respect for the cultural expressions of ethnic minority groups were paramount considerations. Many on the Left had fought for freedom of political expression, rejecting the contention that schools could be neutral, particularly in the generation-shaping confrontations of 1968, and were uneasy about efforts by the authorities to prevent the Muslim girls in Creil from expressing themselves through covering their heads in class. As the Franco-Algerian feminist Leïla Sebbar asked, "Couldn't they, from their position of power, allow young girls, attached to the exterior and interior forms of their religion, to wear a scarf that doesn't veil their faces, as others ornament their hair with ribbons?" (Kepel, 1994, 254). If they were "victims" of Islamic attitudes toward women—as many on the Left believed—they were "not only consenting but also deeply convinced."

In addition, these sympathizers were repelled by what seemed like adults acting repressively toward youth, and toward the hypocrisy of a "brutal *laïc* reaction reaffirming equality and universality in schools that select and divide" their pupils by academic performance (Charlot, 1990, 48). They were appalled to find that *laïcité* was becoming, for many young Muslims, a symbol not of human rights but of intolerance and racism (Kepel, 1993, 33). The "right to be different" was a fundamental demand of S.O.S. Racism, an organization close to the Socialists then in power (Duhamel, 1993, 88). Better that Muslim girls cover their heads in school, many on the Left believed, than that they be excluded by the authorities—or kept from school by their parents (Bonnafous, 1992b, 148).

On the other hand, the French Left was inheritor of the republican tradition of 1793, stressing the indivisibility of the nation; "with the collapse of Marxism, the Jacobin republicanism that [public school teachers] incarnated and propagated is once again becoming one of the most important reference points of the French Left" (Kaplan, 1992, 38). Only five years earlier the Left had engaged in a bitter, costly, and unsuccessful struggle to extend the monopoly role of public education as the primary instrument of national unity, and many of its leaders believed deeply in this agenda (Glenn, 1988b, 1989b). There was thus conflict within the Left between "republicans," committed to the idea of centralized state policies intended to remove social inequalities through treating immigrants and citizens alike, and "democrats," committed to respecting and making room for diversity within French society (Dubet & Lapeyronnie, 1992, 35).

> The "republican fundamentalism" . . . which expresses itself at such length might be nothing but the ideological form of the war of succession [to President Mitterand] taking place within the Socialist Party, opposing symbolically the *laïciste* tradition of the old Socialists to the Third-Worldism and consensualism of the new Socialists (Lorcerie, 1990, 45).

For the French Right, there was an evident conflict between asserting the rights of conscience of Catholic parents, in defense of the autonomy of publicly funded private schools, and opposing expressions of Muslim identity in public schools. The distaste of many conservatives for the growing Muslim presence in France led them into an uneasy alliance with the political descendants of the Jacobins who, two centuries earlier, had tried to suppress any expressions of Christian identity (Casanova, 1989, 20).

Other conservatives, however, pointed out that, had the girls "dressed like little whores like [the rock star] Madonna," no objection would have been raised by school officials; the supposed neutrality of the public school was itself an intolerant cultural particularism that should be resisted in the name of freedom (Alain de Benoist, quoted by Johnstone, 1990, 11). The right to be different and to maintain cultural distinctiveness, to the French New Right, is the essential line of defense against "all totalitarianisms" including that of a dominant universalizing culture identified, by them, with America (Taguieff, 1994–1995, FF, 101). For the newspaper of the xenophobic *Front national*, the controversy was "a slapstick battle of the blind in the closed tunnel of *laïcisme*" which revealed the danger to the national and Christian identity of France not only from the immigrant invasion but also from its real enemy, the secularized elite (Bonnafous, 1992b, 148). France, according to Benoist, "is not threatened with a loss of its identity because there are immigrants. It is, rather, because France has lost its identity that [it] is no longer capable of confronting and resolving the problem of integration" (Benoist, 1993–1994, 174).

As controversy boiled up over the Creil incident, other French schools took action against girls wearing the scarves that, as an English commentator wrote, "to many prominent intellectuals and politicians . . . are more like red flags to a bull." Teachers went on strike in Poissy until a girl removed her scarf; schools in Avignon and Marseilles excluded girls with scarves from classrooms (Follain, 1989). The courts have become involved repeatedly, upholding the right of school administrators to take measures necessary to protect the mission of their schools, but not to single out religious markers that are not otherwise disruptive. For example, the administrative court in Bordeaux ordered reinstatement of a 25–year-old nursing student who had been expelled for wearing a scarf during an internship on the grounds that this prevented her from doing her job, finding that nothing in the record showed her "theoretical or practical inability to pursue her studies" (*Le Monde*, November 6–7, 1994). After all, Catholic nursing sisters traditionally wore head coverings that were at least as constraining.

Islamic organizations threatened a boycott of public schools in response to incautious remarks by Education Minister Bayrou, in September 1994, suggesting that the *hijab* was "too ostentatious" and should be banned (Marshall, 1994). A representative of the *Front national* immediately insisted that yarmulkes were also ostentatious and Jewish students should be forbidden to wear them in public schools (Malherbe, 1994).

Some advocates of the unifying role of the public school saw hidden agendas behind the arguments made, to the Right as well as the Left of them, for accommodation of the wish of the girls to wear their scarves in class. "If the school is successful in achieving integration" of the children of immigrants, "the ideologues of the Right will lose their argument for excluding" immigrants from the country. What is more, "if the school is successful in achieving integration, certain ideologues of the Left, apologists for the right to be different, will find themselves dispossessed of the

TABLE 1.2. Foreigners from Selected Nations in France, 1982, by Age

	Aged 0–14	Total	% 0–14
Spain	44,320	321,440	13.8%
Poland	1,860	64,820	2.9%
Italy	33,480	333,740	10.0%
Portugal	218,620	764,860	28.6%
Algeria	254,920	795,920	32.0%
Turkey	53,420	123,540	43.2%

Source: *Migrants Formation*, December 1986.

TABLE 1.3. Foreigners from Selected Nations in West Germany, 1986, by Age

	Aged 0–15	Total	% 0–15
Greeks	45,686	278,506	16.4%
Italians	73,040	537,067	13.6%
Yugoslavs	95,322	591,116	16.1%
Portuguese	12,709	78,198	16.3%
Spaniards	19,452	150,493	12.9%
Turks	322,727	1,434,256	22.5%
Total	701,325	4,512,679	15.5%

Source: Beauftragten . . . , 1987.

TABLE 1.4. Population of the Netherlands, 1991, by Age

	Percent 0–9	Percent 10–19	Percent 50+
Surinamers	20%	18%	10%
Turks	24%	20%	8%
Moroccans	27%	23%	9%
West Indians	20%	17%	8%
Dutch	12%	13%	28%

Source: Tesser, 1993, 33.

[ethnic minority] population which serves them as a trampoline to attempt to make French society tip toward a model of the Anglo-Saxon type." They asked,

> What do we want? Maintenance of the "French melting pot," or a society organized in communities? What should we do? Talk about [ethnic] customs, honor membership [in ethnic groups], or initiate pupils into the universal, "that part of culture which transcends customs"? (Boulot & Boyzon-Fradet, 1990, 34–35).

To this line of thinking, there is reason to fear that an emphasis upon "problems of 'double reference,' of identity, of specificity, of validation of cultures of origin" will offer to the Right an arsenal of weapons to use in their argument for simply excluding immigrants and even their children born in France from having any part in national life. From this perspective, "it is urgent to renounce struggles for [recognition of] the specificity of children of foreign origin; on the one hand, they are not justified, while on the other, they are the crucible of marginalization and perhaps the instrument of a future eviction" from the country (Boulot & Boyzon-Fradet, 1986, 51–52). Professor Jacques Berque, an expert on Islam who in 1985 had prepared an important report on immigrants in French schools for the Socialist government, warned of the "dark threat of Islam which we thought had passed with the nineteenth-century spirit of positivism" and urged against any accommodation on the issue of wearing the *hijab* (quoted in Spencer, 1989).

Anxiety over the cultural "strangeness" of Muslim immigrants and their children is all the more acute because demographic trends indicate that they will make up an ever larger share of the population. In 1986, 28 percent of the residents of France of French origin were under age twenty, compared with 41 percent of those of Algerian, 43 percent of those of Moroccan, and 51 percent of those of Turkish origin (Voisard & Ducastelle, 1986, 11).

Nor is this true only of France; the Muslim minorities in other nations are also disproportionately young (see Tables 1.4 and 1.4).

The youth of the immigrant minority population is a central factor in the fear of fundamental and (literally) alienating cultural changes, and as a consequence schools are the primary stage upon which the controversy over the extent to which they will be allowed or even encouraged to remain distinctive is played out. This is not to minimize the significance of other settings in which acculturating contacts take place, but it is to recognize that the universal and compulsory nature of schooling makes it the only setting through which public policy in a democracy can work directly, in an explicitly socializing manner. Acculturation can misfire in employment settings, where many workers may get by with a minimal proficiency in the common language and little contact with co-workers from the dominant group, and the voluntary associational life that plays such a large part in modern societies often does not include those who are socially marginal. As Oscar Handlin noted of earlier immigrants to the United States,

> it was expected that those excluded people would alter themselves to earn their portion in Americanism. That process could only come about by increasing the contacts between the older and the newer inhabitants, by sharing jobs, churches, residences. Yet in practice, the man who thought himself an Anglo-Saxon found proximity to the other folk just come to the United States uncomfortable and distasteful and, in his own life, sought to increase rather than to lessen the gap between his position and theirs. . . . It was tempting to resolve the difficulty by arguing that the differences between Americans on the one hand and Italians or Jews or Poles on the other were so deep as to admit of no conciliation (Handlin, 1951, 274).

In the United States, recent anxiety about the effects of the presence of foreigners has focused more on the issue of language than it has in the other countries. Many Americans dislike the visibility of store signs and billboards in Spanish or Asian languages, they are irritated by overhearing conversations in (to them) unintelligible languages, and above all they are opposed to government efforts to accommodate language diversity in public services: schools, hospitals, or voting places. The "Official English" movement is the political expression of these sentiments, and it has shown impressive strength for an effort with no support from the political parties, strongly opposed by the media and "the Establishment," and with a largely symbolic agenda.

> During the first half of 1986, more than a million Californians signed petitions to qualify Proposition 63, an Official English amendment to the state constitution, for placement on the November ballot. . . . Despite much unclarity about its implications, Proposition 63 passed with 73 percent of the vote (Crawford, 1992b, 15–16).

Inassimilable Minorities?

The real issue behind most of the controversy over immigration is the nature of the immigrants themselves, whether they are so different from (implicitly, inferior to) the population of the host country that they will represent a burden rather than a contribution to its economy and society. After all, every society has many different groups that manage (usually) to live together peaceably; for immigrants to be perceived as a social (as distinguished from an economic) problem implies that they are not seen as just another group with more or less interesting distinctive characteristics (Entzinger, 1988, 83). Thus a blue-ribbon commission in France has suggested that the recent immigration flow is different in important ways from that which came earlier, and may prove inassimilable; it is a qualitative rather than strictly a quantitative issue (Massenet, 1994, 56). One sometimes hears, "Don't tell me that immigrants *have* problems; they *are* the problem."

The recent pattern of immigration (and, even more, of refugee flows) is bringing newcomers who differ more from the indigenous population than did their predecessors. Immigration to the United States, Canada, and Australia has shifted dramatically from traditional sources in the British Isles and Western Europe to East and South Asia. Turkish and Moroccan immigrants and Somali and Sri Lankan refugees are perceived by Western Europeans, not incorrectly, as culturally more distant and more difficult to "fit in" than their Italian or Polish predecessors, and there is a widespread fear that millions more of "them" are on their way. After all, "North Africa's population is expected to double over the next 30–35 years. Around 40 percent of Maghrebians are aged under 15. Their income levels are at best a sixth of those in Europe" (*The Economist*, February 15, 1992, 21).

Although many Americans are keenly aware of the gap between their living standards and birthrates and those of Mexico and the other countries of Latin America, the contrast is in fact considerably greater between Europe and the neighboring countries of Africa. After all,

The economic gap between the United States and Latin America is about one-half the gap between the EEC and Africa (measured in purchasing power parities, the ratio is 4:1 between the United States and Latin America and 7:1 between the EEC and Africa). That difference can only grow, because African countries are industrializing much less rapidly than the countries of Latin America. Fertility gaps are striking, too. Latin America has already gone through the major part of demographic transition as the overall fertility index in 1988 is barely over 3.5, having peaked around 6 in 1960. In Africa, by contrast, fertility is at its historic maximum (Chesnais, 1990, 25).

Such shifts in the source and scale of immigration are not unprecedented, of course. There was much handwringing in the United States around the turn of this century when immigration shifted from Western to Southern and Eastern Europe. Polish Jews, Slovaks, or southern Italians were not considered desirable as future citizens compared with Germans and Swedes. Sixty years earlier, of course, the arrival of Germans and Irish immigrants (a distressingly large proportion of whom were Roman Catholic and thus "inassimilable") caused equal consternation. There *is* a greater cultural difference in the most recent shift, however; in addition, the new immigrants are physically identifiable, and they and their children will continue to be so even after they have become proficient in both the language and the social behavior customary in the host society. They are *noticed*, and they will continue to be noticed by those for whom diversity is a source of anxiety. An entire literature has grown up to sound the alarm, books with titles like *The Immigration Time Bomb* (1985) that are rarely noticed by those who shape elite opinion but that are very widely distributed, informing readers that continued immigration is an "invitation to terrorism and subversion" and represents "an alien health threat" as well as a major source of crime and unemployment.

Ethnic distinctiveness is an issue for those who regard it as a threat; it is also advanced, to an increasing extent, as a claim for recognition and social space. It has become a truism—which makes it no less true—that the long ideological confrontation between capitalism and socialism has been replaced, in the wink of an eye, by an older clash of nationalisms and ethnicities. We have become sadly familiar with ethnic hatreds based upon what to outsiders are unimportant distinctions and claims difficult to reconcile with the demands of modernity. The Moroccan Muslim Association in the Netherlands declared, in the early 1980s, that there could be no question of integration given the lack of any common ground between the Islamic and western worldviews (Entzinger, 1984, 145).

Nor is ethnicity significant only in the unhappy case of civil conflict within societies; it has also been a primary incentive not only to the movement of millions across international borders but also to the distinctly uneven reception that these refugees and aspiring immigrants have received. This has nowhere been more evident than in the different treatment accorded by the United States in the fall of 1994 to "boat people" from Haiti and Cuba and, when both were at last consigned on equal terms to incarceration, the willingness of Panama to take in the Cubans after having rejected the Haitians.

Some see the Muslim girls who cover their heads in school as expressing a fundamental refusal to become integrated into French society, which is conceived of as unitary (at least with respect to culture) rather than pluralistic. "The issue of the integration of immigrant minorities reveals the profound uncertainties affecting the conception of the nation. Particularistic demands, [maintenance of ethnic] identity harm a republican model which is secular and universalist" (Dubet & Lapeyronnie, 1992, 14). When the Socialists returned to power (after a brief hiatus) in 1987, they placed increased stress upon integration. While pointing out that, in a free society, individuals had a right to maintain their cultural identities, practice the religions of their choice, and express their opinions, the Minister of National Solidarity and Social Affairs stressed that these rights "must be exercised in the framework of the foundational values which are the heritage of our [French] history and the cement of our society" (Centre for Educational Research and Innovation, 1987, 20). In 1989, a cabinet-rank High Council for Integration was established, and early the following year it adopted most of the recommendations of a report by a top official in the Ministry of Education, calling for a concerted policy of scholastic integration based above all upon the effective teaching of French. Integration, as defined in this report, "is to establish a closer interdependence among the members of a society, which implies that the School of the Republic will transmit to all pupils a common knowledge and values of humanism, equality, liberty, and solidarity, and permit access to rational thought, and will also stress the openness of French society toward the world" (Hussenet, 1991, 46–51).

To an increasing extent, the emphasis upon "the right to be different" was replaced, on the Left, with a concern to revive what was seen as the prewar capability of France to absorb immigrants and make them into Frenchmen (Gaspard, 1992, 18–21). It was not clear whether this would be possible. With the economic difficulties of the 1990s, it became increasingly clear that problems of "insertion" into the job and housing markets were not limited to immigrants and their children; the diagnosis came to be applied to youth in general. The weakening of the socializing power of elementary schools, the army, labor unions, political parties, youth clubs, and the social class structure in its varied associational forms was evident in a growing population of disconnected youth of French ancestry, and left the children of immigrants even more marginal. It may be, indeed, that the new emphasis upon the cultural dimensions of integration are a diversion from the failure to achieve effective "insertion" of the second generation of North Africans; some argue that they are in fact already highly assimilated culturally, but socially and economically marginalized (Dubet & Lapeyronnie, 1992, 141).

The conviction that the primary function of the school was to make citizens and thereby to build the nation was in fact much more significant among those who created the French and American systems of universal schooling than was any idea that schools could be a means of social mobility for individuals (Glenn, 1988b). Catholic schools in France have been willing to allow Muslim pupils to wear the *hijab*, and have insisted that they are under no obligation to comply with the government's instructions to the contrary (*Le Monde*, November 6–7, 1994). The prevailing ideology in public schools would not permit this:

> The republican idea managed to mix Enlightenment Universalism, the Positivist faith in Progress, affirmation of civic virtue, and the construction of a nation that was particularistic in its culture, traditions and spirit, but "universal" in its republican values. The State and public education were the agents of progress; citizenship was required to transcend the regional and social particularisms that, one must remember, were so significant at the beginning of this century (Dubet & Lapeyronnie, 1992, 23).

What is needed, some argue, is a new definition of *laïcité* which takes into account the growing diversity of French society without surrendering to relativism from above or tribalism from below. As the influential academic (and frequent consultant to Socialist ministries of education) Louis Legrand argued, France needed to rediscover a sense of positive secularity, a set of values rooted in a humanistic perspective that could without apology be taught to all students, taking into account "the situation of ethical pluralism in which contemporary France finds itself." "One can ask whether . . . the concept of man in the world that emerges from anthropology would not make it possible to establish a new unifying ethic, acceptable to all." A shared search for truth would replace religion in the unifying role required by education, and "the tolerance thus developed would be the cement of a secular and democratic society" (Legrand, 1981, 62, 78, 118).

Whether Legrand's call for a new unifying ideology of positive *laïcité* was realistic or not, many agreed that it was self-contradictory for "*laïcité* to show itself intolerant; it has set itself up as a State religion" (Khellil, 1991, 149). The "dialectical project" consists of "guaranteeing respect for differences within the framework of a system of attitudes which allows them to be transcended" (Camilleri, 1990, 39–40). Thus a distinction should be made between "intercultural" education, which seeks to facilitate communication and mutual respect between individuals of different backgrounds within the context of an integrated school, and "multicultural" education, which simply emphasizes the differences. Respect for differences would avoid the creation of educational ghettos, because it would not chase all those with religious convictions or cultural distinctiveness out of the public school, leaving it solely the preserve of agnostics and atheists (Duhamel, 1989, 25).

More has come to be at stake, however, in the controversy over the *foulards islamiques*, than school discipline or the accommodation of religious convictions. "It was as if the French had suddenly awakened to the fact that they had a significant poorly integrated, non-European population—twenty years, if not more, after any alert observer could have pointed it out to them" (Kaplan, 1992, 42). For much of the public, influenced by alarmist cover stories in newsweeklies*, the *foulard*, or *hijab*, became a symbol of a purported rejection of French society, indeed of Western culture in general, by the French-born children of immigrants (Charlot, 1990, 49). Although initially many—particularly French youth—told surveys that they couldn't understand why the school wouldn't accept the choice of the girls, over several months public opinion turned sharply against accommodation. A survey published by *Le Monde* found that more than two-thirds of the public had a very negative view of Islam, with 71 percent equating it with fanaticism (Naïr, 1990, 63). There was little support for responding to the concerns of Muslims: only 6 (versus 75) percent of French respondents were willing to accept the *hijab* in public schools, and most (56 versus 36 percent) even opposed offering meals in school cafeterias that respected Muslim alimentary rules. The anti-Muslim backlash (and the controversy over the *hijab*) spilled over to the French-speaking part of Belgium, where 54 percent of the respondents (52 percent in France) told

---

*Cover Stories: *Nouvel Observateur* of October 5, 1989, "Fanaticism: The Religious Menace," with a picture of a girl in traditional Muslim dress (not just a scarf); *L'Express* of October 26, "The Laïc School in Danger: The Strategy of the Fundamentalists," with a picture of a girl in a scarf turning her back; *Le Point* of October 30, "Fundamentalists: The Limits of Tolerance," with picture of a girl in traditional Muslim dress; five years later, two pages in *L'Express* of November 3, 1994 were given over to letters about the issue.

the Eurobarometer survey that there were too many people of other races and nationalities in the country (Dekker & Van Praag, 1990, 45, 55).

The postwar migration to Western Europe of millions of workers from the Mediterranean countries and from former colonies, and the subsequent reunification of their families, has led to the formation of ethnic minority groups in the American sense, heavily concentrated in cities and in the lower levels of employment and educational achievement (Hammar, 1985; Castles, Booth, & Wallace, 1984). Typically with low levels of formal qualifications and concentrated in industries especially vulnerable to economic fluctuations, such as heavy manufacturing and construction, foreign workers have experienced growing levels of unemployment as economies have moved in the direction of high technology and service industries (Kühl, 1987, 35).

In the Netherlands in 1990, 45 percent of those of Mediterranean, Surinamese, and West Indian (Antillian) origin—but only 10 percent of the Dutch—lived in the four largest cities (Tesser, 1993, 39). The same pattern has emerged in Germany: by 1981, the population of Frankfurt included 145,000 foreigners, or 23 percent of the total, that of Stuttgart 106,700 (18.3 percent), and that of Munich 223,500 (17.3 percent) foreigners. Half of the babies born in Brussels and in Geneva have foreign parents. (Brussels illustrates the difficulty of obtaining statistics that are comparable over time and between countries: the number of "foreign births" recorded has been declining since a change in law made those children one of whose parents is Belgian automatically Belgian at birth, rather than limiting automatic citizenship, as previously, to children whose fathers were Belgian.)

One pupil in three is of foreign parentage in many cities in Western Europe; most of these youngsters were born in the host country. The slums and public housing developments where they live, according to an official report in France, "are plunging more and more into a structural crisis where the horizon, if it exists, is lower and lower. Unemployment and its corollaries . . . are no longer experienced as transitory periods between two

TABLE 1.5. Labor Force Participation, Turks in West Germany

	1967	1974	1984
Total	172,400	1,027,800	1,425,800
Workers	131,100	606,800	497,700
% Workers	76.0%	59.0%	34.9%

Source: Sen, 1987.

TABLE 1.6. School Enrollment Trends

	Period	Nationals	Foreigners
Belgium	1974–81	– 9.6%	+ 20.2%
France	1978–82	– 3.1%	+ 13.5%
Netherlands	1978–82	– 5.9%	+ 67.5%
West Germany	1974–81	– 9.4%	+ 95.3%

Source: Centre for Educational Research and Innovation, 1987, 20.

jobs" (quoted by Massenet, 1994, 15).

With the halt to active recruitment of labor migrants, and family re-unification as the foreign workers have settled down in the host societies, the proportion of the foreign population consisting of *workers* has declined, while that of their dependents has increased. This development has been particularly striking in Germany (see Table 1.5).

The decline in birthrate experienced by every Western European nation has underlined the significance of the growing population of children of foreign birth or ancestry. It was projected that, in seven nations, "over the period 1978–2000 the number of children in the 0–14 age group is likely to fall by about six million (half of that figure in Germany, and one-fifth in France) . . . the process of fundamental change in the composition of the school population will continue over the years to come" (Organisation for Economic Cooperation and Development, 1987) (see Table 1.6).

In Sweden, long one of the most ethnically homogeneous nations in the world, the share of elementary school enrollment made up of linguistic minority pupils grew from 1 percent in 1960 to 10 percent in 1980; it is predicted that by the year 2000 the proportion will be one pupil in three (Tingbjorn, 1988b, 86). Other nations have seen comparable changes in school populations.

Thus even as foreign workers have come to have less economic importance, their families have increased as a proportion of the clients of schools and human service agencies. This increase is particularly the case with certain groups: while Italian and Spanish guestworkers came early to northwestern Europe and have in general either returned to their homeland with its increasing prosperity or been substantially assimilated, the Turks in particular show little sign of remigration and are rich in children. Even though they make up only around half of the foreign pupils in German schools, there is a tendency to think of the "foreigner problem" as a "problem of the Turks" (Boos-Nunning & Henscheid, 1986, 65).

The argument for placing strict limits on continuing immigration—legal or illegal—is made not only by those who are hostile to the immigrants who have already arrived. Those persons most concerned about the successful integration of immigrants into the host society, including leaders in the immigrant communities, often fear that such integration is threatened by the continual arrival of newcomers (Massenet, 1994, 54). The natural assimilative effects of the host society, from this concerned perspective, are or would be fatally weakened by new, large-scale immigration.

Concern is also increasing in the United States about the impact of the rapidly growing number of immigrants and illegal aliens, perhaps in part because of their increased visibility and concentration in a few large cities.

> According to the 1990 Census, three-quarters of Miami's population spoke a language other than English in the home, as did 1.6 million of Los Angeles's 3.2 million residents. At the same time, one-half of Miami's and one-third of Los Angeles's residents reported that they were limited English proficient (Fix & Zimmermann, 1994, 257).

Another important factor is the high proportion of immigrants who are recently arrived and thus lack English-language skills. "In 1990, 44 percent of the foreign-born had come in the previous 10 years. In 1970, the share of immigrants who had arrived in the previous decade was only 29 percent." Without a change in immigration policy, it is projected that "about 70 million post-1990 immigrants and their offspring will be added to the U.S. population over the next fifty years, accounting for about two-thirds of net population growth." The proportion of foreign-born to the total population is expected to level off at about 14 percent, "roughly the same level as in the late-nineteenth and early-twentieth century" (Fix & Passel, 1994, 27, 40).

One aspect of this concern is the widespread belief that newly arrived immigrants lower the social and cultural capital of the population, since most come from countries with limited educational systems and a relatively low level of technology. Nearly half of the Moroccan men in the Netherlands and more than half of the women, for example, have had no elementary schooling or at most, a year or two (Tesser, 1993, 119). Mexican immigration to the United States shows the same pattern, though it is balanced in aggregate figures by the higher-than-average education of some other immigrant groups. In fact,

> In 1990, 26 percent of the foreign-born over age 25 had less than nine years of education compared to only 9 percent of the native population. But 20 percent of both natives and immigrants have a college

degree and recent immigrants (24 percent) are more likely than natives to have a college degree. . . . At the high end, 15 percent of Asian immigrants have advanced degrees versus 9 percent for European immigrants, 4 percent for Latin American immigrants, and 7 percent for natives (Fix & Passel, 1994, 33).

Even though average education levels have been rising in the countries from which most immigrants come to the United States, among Mexicans and other Latin Americans "the recent entrants have even lower levels of schooling than the earlier immigrants. . . . at least some immigrants are less skilled than either other immigrant groups or earlier entrants for the same group" (Bean, Chapra, Berg, & Sowards, 1994, 85–86). Such findings should be put in the context of a study of the intelligence of immigrants entering the country in 1913, which "determined that 79 percent of Italians, 80 percent of Hungarians, 83 percent of Jews, and 87 percent of Russians were 'feeble-minded' (that is, below a mental age of 12)" (Crawford, 1992b, 59). Failure to achieve a high level of schooling in a society where schooling is not universally available does not have the same implications that it usually has in the United States and other "knowledge economies" (*The Economist*, May 6, 1995, 15).

Average incomes of immigrants to the United States are lower than those of natives, but "*households* headed by immigrants have virtually the same average income ($37,200) as native-headed households ($37,300), because immigrant-headed households are larger and have more earners." Immigrants (as distinguished from refugees) are significantly (2.0 percent versus 3.7 percent) less likely than working-age natives to receive public welfare support. On the other hand, the proportion of immigrants who live in areas of concentrated poverty, where 40 percent or more of the population is below the poverty line, increased twice as rapidly as that of the native-born during the 1980s (Fix & Passel, 1994, 36, 39, 63).

While ghetto-formation has occurred in northwestern Europe as well, the popular impression that most work migrants who came under the recruitment schemes of the 1960s were drawn from underdeveloped rural areas is wrong. Employers sought skilled workers with experience in industry; a survey in the late 1970s found that only 4 percent of the Turkish workers in West Germany came from the most economically backward areas of Turkey, and many had already participated in internal migration to one of the country's industrial centers (Castles, Booth, & Wallace, 1984, 121). On the other hand, informal and illegal migration, and the more recent refugee streams to the industrialized nations, have brought increasing numbers of foreigners for whom urban life and its demands are unfamiliar. These foreigners may create problems for public services and order.

The perception that "cultural distance" is a fundamental problem of immigrants is based upon a misunderstanding of the elements that contribute to success in the immigrant situation; "in some instances the minorities who are more different in language and culture from the dominant group are the ones who are more successful in school" (Ogbu & Matute-Bianchi, 1986, 78). If the alternative to strong ethnic community isolation is an atomized individualism in urban areas where civil society has largely vanished, it is by no means clear that acculturation is advantageous to the immigrant. The underachievement of Hispanics in the United States and of Turks and Moroccans in northwestern Europe may have less to do with language differences than with status in the society. "Cultural differences" (a notably imprecise term) may work either for or against success. Portes and Zhou contrast Haitians in Miami with Sikhs in California, arguing that the cultural distance and lack of adaptation of the latter help to explain their relative success. Haitian immigrant youth in Miami, by contrast, are overly quick to assimilate to the American models of behavior and attitude most available to them:

> Native-born black youth stereotype the Haitian youngsters as docile and subservient to whites, and make fun of the Haitians' French and Creole as well as their accents [in English]. As a result, second-generation Haitian children find themselves torn between conflicting ideas and values: to remain "Haitian," they must endure ostracism and continuing attacks in school; to become "American" (black American in this case), they must forgo their parents' dreams of making it in America through the preservation of ethnic solidarity and traditional values. . . . As the Haitian example illustrates, adopting the outlook and cultural ways of the native born does not necessarily represent the first step toward social and economic mobility. It may, in fact, lead to exactly the opposite. Meanwhile, immigrant youth who remain firmly ensconced in their ethnic communities may, by virtue of this fact, have a better chance for educational and economic mobility (Portes & Zhou, 1994, 20–21).

Of course, the dysfunctional assimilation experienced by some Haitian youth is as much an indictment of a society that has not prevent-

TABLE 1.7. Unemployment in Five Nations, 1984

	Total Unemployment	Unemployment of Foreigners
West Germany	8.6%	12.7%
France	10.6%	19.0%
Netherlands	14.7%	30.0%
Belgium	15.4%	22.0%
Denmark	8.6%	24.9%

Source: *Beauftragten* . . . , 1987.

ed the development of a demoralized underclass as it is of the choices made by young Haitians to identify with it. The readiness of immigrants to make a success of their new lives is, as Ogbu points out, generally admirable; the relevant question may be, whether the United States and other Western societies have lost their power to assimilate newcomers (Brumlik, 1984, 81), whether they can recover the unspoken conviction and unquestioned habits that allow a civil society to function even as those who make it up change.

PREJUDICE AND HOSTILITY TOWARD IMMIGRANTS

We called workers, and human beings came. They do not gobble up prosperity. To the contrary, they are irreplaceable for prosperity (Frisch, 1967).

The words of Swiss playwright Max Frisch have become the classic statement of a liberal and welcoming attitude toward northwestern Europe's new minority groups. Despite these brave words, social tensions have grown as rising unemployment is blamed upon the presence of foreigners willing to work at low wages. But the truth is that immigrants themselves make up a disproportionate share of the unemployed population.

Even with the recent revival of West European economies, there is an increasing disparity in the impact of unemployment, with 42 percent of Moroccans and 35 percent of Turks in the Netherlands out of work, compared with 7 percent of Dutch workers. In West Berlin, "the number of unemployed foreigners nearly doubled between 1989 and 1993, while the unemployment rate for ethnic Germans rose by less than a third" (*The Economist*, July 30, 1994, 19). Much of this unemployment is long term, and talk is growing of the emergence of an "underclass"—similar to that in the United States—of people who have simply dropped out of the labor market and participation in the civil society.

> Overlapping concentrations of urban decay and immigrant communities . . . provide an easy target for racial and political extremists. . . . Racist political parties have struck a chord in distressed neighbourhoods in France, Belgium, Germany, Holland, Italy and Britain. The technique is simple: blame foreigners (preferably non-white ones) for economic problems, call for them to be kicked out, and collect the vote (*The Economist*, July 30, 1994, 20).

As noted above, there is a tendency for extremist politicians in France (both far-right and far-left) to point out that the number of foreign workers is approximately equal to that of unemployed natives, as though the expulsion of the former would induce the latter to take the low-paid and unpleasant jobs that would then become available. A small but persistent political group in Germany and other countries calls for expulsion of all low-status foreigners, although some demographers insist that more should be admitted to make up for the declining native birthrate (*Der Spiegel*, February 13, 1989; Donselaar, 1982).

> Already the foreign population of the country is comparatively high, at 7.8%. In the past five years, Germany has taken in an average of 830,000 immigrants, as many proportionately as America did during its peak years of immigration in the early part of the century. This makes Germany the nearest thing Europe has to a melting pot—and a place where neo-Nazi groups and violent young people make foreigners the target of their rage (*The Economist*, May 21, 1994).

Between 1978 and 1982 the proportion of West Germans who wanted foreign workers to go home grew from 39 percent to 68 percent; thus when the present West German government took office, Helmut Kohl announced that integration was an important goal which "is only possible if the number of foreigners living among us does not grow further." Those who wanted to return home would be helped to do so, while those remaining in Germany would have to resolve to fit in (quoted in Mahler, 1983, 29, 39). Easier said than done; seven years later, polls showed that the "foreigner problem" was the leading issue for German voters, ahead of unemployment, disarmament, and the environment (*Die Welt*, February 21, 1989).

Nor was this concern limited to the uneducated. The Heidelberg Manifesto of 1981 was a statement by 15 German professors that the German people were being swamped by foreign immigration and the German national character (*Volkstum*) was being undermined. A multicultural society, they wrote, would be an "ethnic catastrophe." Nor was this view limited to cultural and social conservatives; the Social Democratic leader Willy Brandt said around the same time that "we cannot cope with any further immigration" (Castles, Booth, & Wallace, 1984, 205, 209).

A study in 1992 found that 50 percent of youth in the Western *länder* and 62 percent of those in the East agreed that there were too many foreigners in Germany and that no more should be allowed to enter. The contrast between West and East is striking with respect to whether those foreign workers from outside the European Community should be required to go "home"; only 30 percent of those in the West, where Turks and others have been living and working in large numbers for four decades, but 50 percent of those in the East, where there has been little contact with "guestworkers," took this position. Although thousands of Vietnamese guest workers were sent to work in East Germany (the German Democratic Republic), they were kept separated from the German population in residential camps, and most were forcibly repatriated; they were not allowed to bring their families. Perhaps most disturbing, only 29 percent of youth in the West and 17 percent in the East agreed that "there won't be any more problems between Germans and foreigners in the second generation and after" (Heiliger & Kürten, 1992, 113–114).

Youth in East Germany are, as these responses indicate, even more hostile toward low-status minority-group members than are those in the West, perhaps because of the difficult economic adjustments of the former German Democratic Republic. In one recent study, 14 percent of the young women and 25 percent of the young men reported that they had been witnesses to violence against foreigners; 2 percent of the young men in secondary school and 4 percent of the apprentices said that they had taken part in "foreigner hunts" (*Jagd auf Ausländer*). While this was exceptional, the majority of youth were against the presence of foreigners. Reasons given ranged from "because they make the housing situation even more difficult (75 percent of the German youth agreed), and "because they want to live well at the expense of Germany" (58 percent), to "because they have a tendency to violence and crime" (38 percent) (Förster, Friedrich, Müller, & Schubarth, 1992, 105–106).

Hostility is not directed equally at all immigrant groups. A study in 1982 found that 48 percent of German respondents had unsympathetic feelings toward Turks, contrasted with 15 percent who had such feelings toward Spaniards and 16 percent toward Greeks. Positive sympathy was felt toward Spaniards by 26 percent, but only 8 percent had such feelings towards Turks. Most Germans also expressed dubious feelings toward asylum-seekers, with only 7 percent believing them threatened by political persecution in the homelands, and 76 percent attributing to them purely economic motives for coming to Germany (Koch-Arzberger, 1985, 28–29).

Germany is not alone in experiencing such strains. A Eurobarometer study in late 1988 found that a substantial proportion of respondents in six countries of northwestern Europe were concerned about the presence and effects of immigrants. The survey suggests that the Dutch are rather more tolerant of foreigners, and this is confirmed by studies that show rising acceptance of foreign neighbors and co-workers—but, significantly, declining (though still high) acceptance of the integration of classrooms. This contrary result may reflect the growing sense that the schooling of foreign pupils is not going well and that "black schools" are educationally dismal (see Chapter 6).

In the United Kingdom, the early assumption that ethnic minority groups would simply "disappear" into the indigenous majority was "exposed by the rising tide of racial prejudice and hostility" (*Education for All*, 1985, 199). Public opinion was shocked (perhaps excessively so) when a fringe party calling for expulsion of all nonwhites won a local council seat in East London in September 1993; the 1,480 votes gained by the British National Party should in fact have been less alarming than the racist attacks on Asian pupils that followed in the same area (Martinson, 1993, 10).

French observers were reminded of the shock in elite circles when, in 1983, a member of the *Front national* was elected to the municipal council in Dreux, another working-class area, and the polarization that resulted from

---

TABLE 1.8. Opinions in Six Countries on the Presence of Foreigners, 1988

Agree with statement:	Neth	Dnmk	Germ	Belg	Fran	UK
Too many foreigners in country	35%	43%	52%	54%	52%	52%
Foreign pupils hurt school quality	48%	64%	50%	54%	49%	55%
Foreign neighbors cause problems	16%	34%	35%	48%	24%	34%

Source: Dekker and Ester, 1993, 194.

TABLE 1.9. Acceptance of Ethnic Minorities in the Netherlands

No objection at all to . . .	1980	1991
Next-door neighbor of another race	50%	55%
Classmate of child of another race	76%	72%
Colleague at work of another race	76%	82%

Source: Dekker and Ester, 1993, 194.

the deliberate stirring-up of anti-immigrant feelings for political gain (*Le Monde*, September 20, 1993). The Dreux election had made a particular impression because it came less than two years after the victory of the Socialists in the national elections, and seemed to mark their loss of influence over working-class voters (Gaspard & Servan-Schreiber, 1985, 81).

The most extreme form of hostility to foreigners, of course, is the violence directed against them by skinhead groups that often adopt Nazi symbolism along with ideologies of racial purity and superiority (Donselaar, 1982, 1993). While such groups have appeared in every Western nation, they have caused the most consternation in Germany as a result of the country's unhappy past. The incident in the old Hansa port Rostock, in 1992, when more than 500 people attacked a hostel for asylum-seekers, and the fatal attack in Sollingen the next year, shocked many Germans and led to proforeigner counterdemonstrations.

Earlier attacks on Algerians in France, including 32 murders in 1973, led the Algerian government to announce a restriction on further emigration, in the expectation that growing oil revenues would stimulate rapid job growth in Algeria (Entzinger, 1984, 200). Despite such restrictions (more for political effect than enforcement), the North African population in France continued to grow through family reunification and a higher birthrate than that of the French, and anti-immigrant sentiment grew with it. A survey in 1990 found that 42 percent of the majority population admitted antipathy toward North African immigrants and 37 percent did so toward descendants of North Africans born in France. Around 40 percent believed that it would be difficult to integrate them into French society—their "ways of life" were too different—while 70 percent believed that there were too many Muslims in France. Hostility was not nearly so marked toward Black Africans or Asian and Portuguese immigrants (Dubet & Lapeyronnie, 1992, 147–48), though the murder in Marseilles, in February 1995, of young Ibrahim Ali from the Cormoros Islands by members of the *Front national* showed that Africans could be targeted as well.

When a large number of Asian refugees entered the reputedly tolerant Netherlands in 1987, some 300 out of 700 communities refused to participate in their resettlement, and a poll showed that 85 percent of the Dutch wanted a limit on the number admitted. Communities in Sweden and in Denmark have similarly expressed opposition to the settlement of refugees, and in April 1988 Norway's anti-immigrant Progress Party—winner of only 3 percent of the vote in 1985—received over 23 percent in an opinion poll largely as a result of criticizing liberal policies on admitting refugees; its leader remarked, "So long as there are high taxes and Muslims, we've got something to fight for" (*The Economist*, April 30, May 28, 1988). The Norwegian and Swedish governments have found themselves constrained recently to respond to growing anti-immigrant sentiments among youth.

Even Spain, a generally tolerant society, is experiencing outbreaks of hostility toward African workers who came to take the place of the Spanish workers who found better-paying jobs in Northern Europe (Corredera Garcia & Santiago Diez Cano, 1992, 200). Italy has also been the scene of ugly attacks against African and Asian illegal immigrants. The large underground economies in these two nations, in particular, provide ample opportunities for marginal workers (*Le Monde: Dossiers et Documents*, April 1987), but it also leaves them in an essentially marginal position that increases their vulnerability.

The extent of hostility directed against individual immigrants—in contrast with immigrants as an abstraction—may be exaggerated by the tendency of the press to focus upon dramatic incidents rather than upon the day-to-day accommodations that are the rule rather than the exception. Even some of the widely-reported incidents of "racism" turn out to be imaginary, such as the report in 1994 that a handicapped girl in Solingen, in Germany, had a swastika scratched on her cheek by neo-Nazis and the 1990 report that a black girl in Avignon, in France, had her head shaved by white punks; in both cases, it turned out that the girls, like the African American Tawana Brawley in 1987, made up the stories to attract attention (Massenet, 1994, 68–69).

Whatever exaggeration may exist, there can be no question that anti-immigrant sentiments have become increasingly acceptable, at least in some circles. Germany experienced a tenfold increase in reported attacks on foreigners in 1991—more than two thousand incidents were reported—and the country was shocked by the murder of a Turkish woman and two young girls the following year. Attacks also increased in the United Kingdom. Spain experienced its first racially motivated murder in many years (*The Economist*, December 5, 1992, 51).

In the United States, paradoxically, anti-immigrant feeling appears to be strongest among those whose presence in the country derives relatively recently from immigration. The stereotype of middle-class social liberalism toward ethnic diversity was confirmed, at least at the verbal level, by Lambert and Taylor's study in Detroit: "compared to all other ethnic groups in Pontiac, the white middle-class parents have the most favorable attitudes towards all of the other ethnic groups in the community." On the other hand, working-class white parents were "the least enthusiastic of all groups . . . about multiculturalism. . . . working-class whites show no affection for any ethnic or racial group other than their own" (Lambert & Taylor, 1990, 112–116).

Nor is anti-immigrant sentiment in the United States limited to working-class whites. There have been riots in Miami and other cities by blacks expressing their resentment of competition from immigrants; Mayor Dinkins of New York City was accused by some of refusing to intervene effectively when blacks attacked Korean grocery stores. Nor is the belief that immigrants represent competition unfounded; sociologist William Julius Wilson "found that employers generally prefer to hire immigrant Mexicans over blacks, in part because the former are more directly tied into informal job networks that both support individual work effort and reassure employers of the workers' reliability" (Skerry, 1995, 19). Immigrant workers are also less likely than members of native minority groups to "have a chip on their shoulders." Of course, in general they are competitors only for the natives who are at the bottom of the employment ladder, not for the middle class, which can thus afford to be tolerant.

Köbben has pointed out, however, that the more tolerant responses given by the educated in surveys of xenophobia can be doubly misleading:

> First of all, intellectuals are more skilful at giving a socially desirable answer, and second, intellectuals are more tolerant, not because they have more knowledge of the reality, but because they have less! What foreigner does an intellectual associate with? That Surinamese family, three houses away, whose father works as a doctor in the hospital. And, oh yes, the nice young Turk who comes at six-thirty to clean his office and with whom he sometimes has a chat (Köbben, 1985, 57).

Schools as the Focus of Immigrant Policy

It is likely that individual countries—and the European Union—will put in place increasingly restrictive policies on the admission of immigrants and even political refugees, since the latter have a way of turning into permanent residents. Even the United States, with its long and poorly secured land borders, is seeking to gain greater control over who enters the country. In September 1994, Attorney-General Reno announced a "six-point plan to cut down illegal immigration," including a near-doubling of the number of immigration agents (*The Boston Globe*, September 19, 1994, 16); six months later she called for stronger laws and said that the United States intended to triple the number of illegal aliens deported each year to 110,000 (*The Boston Globe*, March 15, 1995). The next chapter will review the patterns of postwar immigration to the OECD nations, and the policies adopted to limit it and to come to terms with its effects.

Such measures will in every case come too late to avoid confronting the theme of this book, that is, the challenge of helping the children of immigrants—and *their* children—to find their way in a society that employs a language and operates on the basis of assumptions that they have not had a chance to learn, as other children do, at home and in their community. Should schools seek to become more powerful instruments of socialization into the language, culture, and worldview of the host society and, if so, should they do so through separate programs for immigrant minority children or through associating them with native pupils, or through some mix of the two? If the children of immigrants are to be schooled together with native pupils, what are the implications for the education of the latter, and how are their parents to be convinced that this is in the best interest of their children?

Or, on the other hand, should schooling be organized on the basis of the assumption that immigrant minority pupils are and will remain different in some fundamental and valuable ways from native pupils, and should be equipped to function effectively within a minority community rather than to integrate into the host society? What would be the implications of such a course of action for equal opportunity in the economy and the political order?

The pursuit of answers to these questions takes us from the glittering generalizations of national policy statements to the observed realities of classroom practice, by way of the arguments of ideologues, ethnic activists, and researchers. It is the schools, above all, which are called upon in every society to come to terms with and to render positive rather than negative the social and linguistic diversity resulting from immigration.

Before we turn to the various approaches taken by schools, and the rationales given for these approaches, we must explore what the literature can tell us about the views and the behavior of immigrant minority children themselves, and their parents, and the ethnic communities to which they are more or less closely associated. What does their behavior, in particular, tell us about the significance and the possibility of assimilation, integration, and separate development?

We should not expect to find clear answers. The evidence is very mixed, for a host of reasons, and perhaps each individual member of an immigrant minority group has conflicting feelings about ethnic distinctiveness and acts in contradictory ways. Indeed, it will be essential to avoid oversimplifying, as many do, the desires and interests of immigrants and their children. The answers may be unclear, but that does not excuse us from paying attention to what evidence there is.

Before we do so, we will consider the situation of language minority groups that are not derived not from immigration but from the manner in which the various countries included in our study took shape. The tensions about and the accommodations of their distinctiveness illuminate the responses, in each society, to immigrant minority groups, and have helped to shape the objective situation of laws and social arrangements that immigrants have encountered as they have entered these societies.

2 IMMIGRATION

Causes and Responses

While it may be true that "past experience shows that it is impossible to predict the scale and direction of future migratory flows" (Organisation for Economic Cooperation and Development, 1994, 13), the questions of policy and practice raised in the last chapter cannot be addressed apart from an understanding of the dynamics of immigration. Why immigrants come, and why they are allowed to come, and with what expectations on the part of the immigrants and (often very different ones) of the host society, are of critical importance for what we are calling the "integration project," and thus for how schools deal with the languages and cultures that children bring with them to the classroom.

It will be the task of this chapter to give some account of the patterns of immigration into the Western industrialized democracies that are members of the Organisation for Economic Cooperation and Development (OECD), with particular emphasis on the period since World War II, and of the public policies which have sometimes encouraged, other times discouraged, and always sought to deal with the consequences of these movements. The emphasis will much more on the receiving countries—the "pull" factors—than on the "push" factors in the sending countries, and there will be no attempt here to describe the impact of immigration upon those who immigrated and their children, which will be the theme of Chapter 4.

THE SCOPE AND NATURE OF IMMIGRATION

Three of the countries included in this study—Australia, Canada, and the United States—are unthinkable in their present form apart from a history of massive immigration to fill their great "empty" spaces; it was not until 1870 that, among white Australians, the native-born came to outnumber immigrants, and a century later immigrants still made up 20 percent of the population (Whitaker et al., 1974, 60). From the 1840s until the First World War, with occasional slowdowns in times of economic recession, tens of millions of immigrants crossed the oceans to these three destinations.

The story of nineteenth-century immigration to the United States is, in its broad outlines, a familiar one. Reliable national statistics go back to 1820. In that decade, 151,000 immigrants arrived; in 1828, the peak year, nearly 18,000 from the United Kingdom and Ireland, 1,851 from Germany, and 4,700 from other countries of northwestern Europe: the Netherlands, Belgium, Switzerland, France. The total increased fourfold to 600,000 in the 1830s. Of 79,340 who came in 1837 (the year Horace Mann became Secretary of the new Massachusetts Board of Education), 28,508 were from Ireland and 23,740 from Germany against 12,218 from the United Kingdom. Germany and Ireland dominated immigration to the United States up to the Civil War. The total nearly tripled in the 1840s to 1,713,000, with 297,024 in 1849; the Irish flow now pulled well ahead, representing 54 percent of the total that year. In the 1850s, 2,314,000 immigrants entered the United States; in 1854, the peak year, Germans represented 50 percent of the total at 215,000, and Irish immigration had dropped to 102,000 (24 percent) in what would be a continuing decline over the next decades (United States Bureau of the Census, 1975, 106).

The 3 million immigrants who entered the United States in the period 1845–1854 were coming to a country that, in 1840, had had a population of only 14,196,000 white and 2,873,000 black inhabitants; thus they added 17.6 percent to the population. In proportion to total population, this influx dwarfs recent immigration: almost 10 million immigrants entered the United States in the 1980s, adding 4.4 percent to a country with 226 million people in 1980. Similarly, in 1907 alone "immigrants added about 3 percent to the U.S. labor force. To have an equivalent labor market impact today, immigration would have to reach at least 9 million per year, 10 times current loads" (Fix & Passel, 1994, 21).

The source of immigration changed toward the end of the nineteenth century. German immigration continued strong, and that from Scandinavia was heavy from 1880 onward. Emigrants from the United Kingdom tended, however, to turn toward western Canada, Australia, and New Zealand as the idea of the Empire took on a certain glamour in the British popular mind. Around 1900 the nature of the immigrant stream to the United States changed decisively, with heavy participation from Southern and Eastern Europe; 1905 was the first year with over 1 million immigrants, primarily from Poland, Russia, and Italy (United States Bureau of the Census, 1975, 105). As M.A. Jones summarizes this change,

Of the 780,000 immigrants who arrived in 1882, 87 per cent came from the countries of northern and western Europe and 13 per cent from the countries of southern and eastern Europe. But in 1907, when 1,285,000 immigrants reached the United States, the proportions were 19.3 and 80.7 per cent, respectively (1960, 179).

Legislation in 1924 imposed a system of quotas by national origin, set at 2 percent of the U.S. residents of that nationality resident in 1890; this replaced a 1921 "emergency quota" that placed a limit of 3 percent of each group as of 1910. The effect of these measures, and especially of the later one, was to reduce sharply the proportion of immigrants from southern and eastern Europe as well as to limit the overall number of immigrants from Europe to 150,000 a year; there was no limit on Western Hemisphere immigration,

TABLE 2.1. Foreign-Born Population of the United States in Thousands, by Country of Birth

Origin	1850	1880	1920	1960	1990
Great Britain	379	918	1,135	765	640
Ireland (incl. Ulster)	962	1,855	1,037	407	170
Germany	584	1,967	1,686	990	712
Poland	—	49	1,140	748	388
Italy	4	44	1,610	1,257	581
Russian Empire	1	36	1,400	754	334
Austro-Hungarian Empire	1	124	576	305	285
Scandinavia		441	1,199	455	131
Other Europe	100	310	2,099	1,553	1,110
Asia	1	108	238	499	4,979
Canada	148	717	1,125	952	745
Mexico	13	68	486	576	4,298
Other Western Hemisphere	7	22	116	333	4,109
All Other	43	21	74	144	468
Total	2,244	6,680	13,921	9,739	19,767

Sources: United States Bureau of the Census, 1975, 117–118; *The American Almanac* 1993, 50.

but Asians were largely excluded. The Immigration and Naturalization Act, followed by the Depression of the 1930s, resulted in a sharp decline in immigration between the wars, and thus in foreign-born population by 1960.

Postwar legislation had the effect of greatly increasing immigration to the United States (Table 2.1); it rose to an historic high of 9 million immigrants during the 1980s, topping the previous record of 8.9 million between 1900 and 1910. Because of overall population growth, however, the share that immigrants represent is substantially lower than in 1910: 4.4 percent as compared with 10.5 percent of the initial population. On the other hand, because of the decline in birthrate among the native-born population, recent immigration accounts for a larger share of the population growth (37 percent) than it did in the earlier period (28 percent) (Edmonston & Passel, 1994a, 15).

The 9 million persons who entered during the 1980s comprised more than 6 million legal immigrants who came under various quotas with the declared intention of remaining permanently, about 900,000 refugees, and more than 2 million individuals who came or remained illegally but whose situation was "regularized" retroactively (see below).

Mexico and the countries of Asia now represent 42.5 percent of the foreign-born population of the United States, up from 5 percent in 1920 and 11 percent in 1960. Large-scale immigration from Mexico began in the 1920s, when railway companies brought in Mexican laborers; during the depression of the 1930s, many of them were deported, only to be welcomed again when World War II brought a demand for industrial and agricultural workers. Most Mexicans who enter the country to work do so for seasonal agricultural labor, but to an increasing extent families have followed or been established. According to some estimates, there are up to 2 million Mexicans living illegally in the United States and 100,000 enter each year (*The Economist*, November 12, 1994, 53).

Although it is often assumed that the large Hispanic population of America's Southwest derives from its possession by Mexico before annexation by the United States during the nineteenth century, in fact immigration is a much more important cause. "If there had been no immigration since 1900, the estimated 1990 Hispanic population would be 3.1 million, or less than one-seventh of the actual 1990 level" (Passel & Edmonston, 1994a, 53).

There is also a growing immigration from the Caribbean, 13 percent of the legal immigration; "the black population is now experiencing the first substantial immigration in the past two centuries, with about 120,000 immigrants arriving from Africa and the Caribbean annually" (Edmonston & Passel, 1994b, 345).

But the most dramatic increase was in Asian immigration to the

TABLE 2.2. Foreign-Born Population of the United States from Asia, 1990

Philippines	913,000
Korea	568,000
Vietnam	543,000
China	530,000
India	450,000
Japan	290,000
Taiwan	244,000
Other Asian countries	1,441,000

Source: *The American Almanac*, 1993, 50.

United States, from 7 percent of the total in 1965 to 46 percent in 1990. Table 2.2 shows the country of origin in 1990 for the major Asian groups.

In contrast to the changeability of U.S. policy, Canada has always welcomed and often promoted immigration. Two-and-a-half million immigrants entered the country between 1896 and 1914, and over 4 million between 1945 and 1974. As in the United States, requirements for admission long discriminated against nonwhite groups—those whose "peculiar cultural traits" had allegedly been "scientifically proven" to make them difficult to assimilate—and recruitment efforts focused on those potential immigrants who were considered most likely to become good Canadians. The government official largely responsible for the efforts around the turn of the century wrote later,

> [I]n Great Britain we confined our efforts very largely to the North of England and Scotland, and for the purpose of sifting the settlers we doubled the bonuses to the agents in the North of England and cut them down as much as possible in the South. The result was that we got a fairly steady stream of people from the North of England and from Scotland and they were the very best settlers in the world. . . . I think a stalwart peasant in a sheepskin coat, born on the soil, whose forefathers have been farmers for ten generations, with a stout wife and a half dozen children, is good quality (quoted by Hawkins, 1989, 5–6).

Immigration to Canada was encouraged in order to fill the nearly empty prairies; for example, between 1897 and 1914 200,000 Ukrainians were recruited for settlement in Manitoba, Saskatchewan, and Alberta, followed by another 70,000 between the wars and 300,000 Ukrainian refugees in 1947–1955 (Samuda, 1986, 104). In 1962 the Conservative government, convinced that Canada must "populate or perish," abandoned the "White Canada" policy and obtained passage of new immigration regulations designed to "eliminate discrimination based on colour, race or creed" (quoted by Hawkins, 1989, 38).

Much of the postwar immigration has been to Canada's cities, attracting especially Chinese, Greek, Portuguese, Italian, and West Indian immigrants. Canada continues to be a preferred destination for residents of Hong Kong anxious about its pending annexation by the People's Republic of China. A striking characteristic of this recent immigration to Canada is that it comes from a much wider range of countries. Of Canadian residents in 1981 who arrived before 1961, more than 80 percent came from just ten countries of birth, with the United Kingdom accounting for 29.8 percent, Italy 12.2 percent, and other European countries among the top ten for 31 percent. By contrast, the top ten countries of origin for those arriving since 1971 accounted for only half of the immigrants (see Table 2.3).

Australia, even longer than Canada, limited immigration largely to those of British and Irish origin, and in the nineteenth century had difficulty competing with North America as a destination; between 1815 and 1850, emigrants to Australia accounted for only 6 percent of those leaving the United Kingdom, contrasted with 51 percent who went to Canada and 43 percent who went to the United States. Small numbers of Indians and Chi-

---

TABLE 2.3. Canada: Ten Leading Countries of Birth of Immigrants Since 1971

Country of Birth	Immigrants 1971–1981	% of All Immigrants
United Kingdom	158,800	13.8%
United States	97,600	8.5%
India	75,000	6.5%
Portugal	66,400	5.8%
Philippines	55,300	4.8%
Vietnam	49,400	4.3%
Hong Kong	42,200	3.7%
Italy	29,100	2.5%
Guyana	27,500	2.4%
All other origins		47.7%

Source: Hawkins, 1989, 261–262.

nese came as laborers from other British colonies, but restrictive legislation was enacted between 1857 and 1901, when a newly self-governing Federation proclaimed what came to be called the White Australia policy: "after 1901, non-whites could only enter Australia on a temporary basis under a permit" (Sherington, 1980, 36, 91).

The restrictions placed on nonwhites was motivated by a mix of concern that Asians would be inassimilable into white Australian society (parallel to the arguments employed at that time in Canada and the United States), together with a sense of strategic vulnerability in relation to China and Japan, whose expatriate communities "were viewed with alarm because they could serve as agents of Asian economic interests, because their [mis]treatment could be used as a pretext for direct intervention or coercive diplomatic interference in Australian affairs" (Freeman, 1993, 91).

In order to develop its underpopulated economy, Australia continued to rely primarily upon immigrants from the United Kingdom, but also admitted some 140,000 from the European continent, or 16 percent of new entries during the decades before World War II, with the largest group coming from Italy (Murphy, 1993, 10, 22, 44, 72).

Australia was shaken out of the complacency of its distance from the troubles of Europe and Asia by World War II, when it appeared for a time that the Japanese would successfully invade its great open spaces. As its first Minister for Immigration pointed out in 1945,

> if Australians have learned one lesson from the Pacific war now moving to a successful conclusion, it is that we cannot continue to hold our island continent for ourselves and our descendants unless we greatly increase our numbers. . . . Our first requirement is additional population. We need it for reasons of defence and for the fullest expansion of our economy (quoted by Hawkins, 1989, 32).

With the slogan "populate or perish," extensive efforts were made after the war to encourage the "right sort" of immigrants from Europe, then overrun with millions of displaced persons. In 1947 the first contingent consisting of 440 Lithuanians, 262 Latvians, and 138 Estonians arrived: they "made a fine appearance and looked bright and intelligent" (quoted by Murphy, 1993, 96). By 1952, 170,000 displaced persons had entered Australia, followed by hundreds of thousands of southern Europeans displaced by poverty rather than by war. The expectation, generally met, was that they would become Australian citizens and assimilate completely into Australian society.

The effectiveness of the "White Australia" policy may be measured by the fact that in 1961 there were more residents born in Latvia than in China or India and more born in Estonia than in Indonesia. Even so, many from Asian countries were Eurasians, White Russians or Dutch [from post-Independence Indonesia] (Jupp, 1966, quoted in Bullivant, 1981, 174).

The White Australia policy became a "dangerous anachronism" and increasingly difficult to retain for foreign policy reasons, and because it led to excluding many who would have been economically desirable immigrants. In 1966 a relaxed policy led to admission of up to ten thousand non-European and part-European immigrants a year, and by 1970 "assisted passage" was being extended to Turks, Arabs, and others. The government was embarrassed that year by criticism from the British Race Relations Board for its decision not to accept the application for financial assistance in immigrating from a well-educated computer engineer, a British citizen, his French-born wife, and their children, because of his Jamaican origin; it was not helped by an official of the State of Victoria, in London on a visit to encourage immigration, who told a reporter that Australia rejected "99 per cent of all people with dark blood, even if only one member of their family has

TABLE 2.4. Origins of Persons Granted Australian Citizenship, 1965–1990

Origin	1965–70	Percent	1989–90	Percent
United Kingdom & colonies	20,531	10%	42,489	32.5%
Italy	43,222	21%	1,801	1.5%
Greece	27,472	13.5%	1,604	1%
Yugoslavia	19,445	9.5%	4,605	3.5%
Netherlands	18,351	9%	624	0.5%
Germany	14,637	7%	900	0.5%
Poland	9,874	5%	2,079	1.5%
Philippines	223	0.1%	7,572	6%
Vietnam	41	0%	9,658	7.5%
All other	49,773	24.5%	59,000	45%
Total	203,569	100%	130,312	100%

Source: Murphy, 1993, 178–79.

dark blood" (Hawkins, 1989, 96–97). Encouraged by the abandonment of restrictions on nonwhite immigration by Canada in 1962 and by the United States in 1965, the new Labour government dropped the White Australia policy in 1973, substituting (as in the other countries) an entry policy based upon skills and potential contributions to the economy and society. Thus in 1971 the Asian immigrants to Australia included 177 medical doctors and 153 teachers (Murphy, 1993, 174).

Whereas in the period 1965–1970 fully 70 percent of those naturalized came from six countries—Italy, the United Kingdom, Greece, Yugoslavia, the Netherlands, and Germany, the 1989–1990 figures show a sharp drop-off in new citizens from the continent of Europe and in general a broader distribution of countries of origin (Table 2.4). The high figure for the United Kingdom "and colonies" in the latter period reflects a strong influx from Hong Kong in anticipation of the reversion of control to China. Australia's population has doubled over the past 40 years and, of the most recent 1 million increase, over half were immigrants, mostly from Asia. "In Australia as a whole, over one quarter of the population were born in households where no one spoke English; less than a third can trace their ancestry directly back to Britain" (*The Economist*, May 30, 1992, 41).

Australia's immigration policy shift seems to have been driven at least as much by considerations of external relations with northeast Asia as by a need for new workers as such; the Asian immigrants represent an important bridge to the part of the world to which Australians are increasingly aware that they belong and in which it cannot rely as confidently as before upon British and then American protection (Freeman, 1993, 92). The White Australia policy had provoked considerable resentment among Australia's Asian neighbors, "whose aptitudes to handle their domestic and international affairs often outstripped Australia's" (Murphy, 1993, 173) and tended to align the country embarrassingly with South Africa on some human rights issues. As Prime Minister Bob Hawke put it in 1988,

> There is no future for an Australia which deludes itself it can be a fortress island with barriers put up around it and says we're not part of this Asian region. If we attempt to do that, we are condemning our children and the generation after that to not just third-rate but sixth-rate status (*The Economist*, August 27, 1988, 28).

Australia "could no longer afford to think of itself as an outpost of British or even European civilization," and the new immigrants would bring language skills and cultural diversity that would enable the country in the future to fit comfortably into an Asian setting. There was a window of opportunity, a report to the government argued in 1990, to recruit highly desirable young immigrants with professional training or business experience from Hong Kong, Taiwan, and Korea; that would be a more immediate solution to Australia's need to learn how to deal economically with northeast Asia than would attempts to develop the language and international business skills of its own people (Freeman, 1993, 84, 96).

Western European countries—with the partial exception of France in periods of low birthrate—have not encouraged immigration and, indeed, at times have encouraged their own surplus population to emigrate. During the nineteenth century, 45 million Europeans crossed the Atlantic to find new homes. The presence now of a large number of persons of foreign origin who are permanently resident and whose children and grandchildren know no other homeland has created a new and challenging situation for these countries. According to the European Union, of the 370 million people living in what has been designated the European Economic Area, 10.4 million or 2.8 percent are from outside the area, while another 5.6 million are from the area but living outside their own countries. Germany has the largest share of non-European residents (41 percent of the total), France 22 percent, and the United Kingdom 11 percent (*The Economist*, October 29, 1994, 6). Nor does this account for all of those who make up the "ethnic minority" population of Europe; the population of most European countries is much more diverse than nativist rhetoric would suggest:

> Today, France has 4.1 million immigrants in the strict sense, that is persons born outside the frontiers, whatever their nationality. Ten million persons were born in the country with an immigrant parent or grandparent (Dubet & Lapeyronnie, 1992, 82).

The figures in Tables 2.5 and 2.6 cannot be strictly compared from country to country. For example, they underestimate the population of for-

TABLE 2.5. Immigrants in Selected Countries

Country	1981	% of Total	1991	% of Total
Australia	3,003,800	20%	3,940,000	23%
Canada	3,848,300	16%	4,342,900	16%
United States	14,079,900	6.2%	19,767,300	7.9%

Source: Organisation for Economic Cooperation and Development, 1994, 187, 214–216; Hawkins 1989, 259.

TABLE 2.6. Foreigners in Selected Countries

Country	1981	% of Total	1991	% of total
Belgium	885,700	9.0%	922,500	9.2%
Denmark	101,900	2.0%	169,500	3.3%
France (1982, 1990)	3,714,200	6.8%	3,596,600	6.3%
Germany*	4,629,800	7.5%	5,882,300	7.3%
Netherlands	537,600	3.8%	732,900	4.8%
Sweden	414,000	5.0%	493,800	5.7%
Switzerland	909,900	14.3%	1,163,200	17.1%
United Kingdom			1,750,000	3.1%

Source: Organisation for Economic Cooperation and Development, 1994, 187, 214–216.
*1991 includes former East Germany; 97 percent of foreigners live in the West.

eign origin in Sweden, with its high rate of naturalization, and do not include ethnic minorities from former colonies, a significant group in the Netherlands and the United Kingdom. Who is a "foreigner" or an "immigrant" is defined differently from country to country, and it would not advance the purposes of this study to linger over questions of legal status except to the extent that, as we will see below, the rate at which citizenship is sought by different groups and granted by different governments may serve as an indicator of long-term intentions on one side or the other.

The use of minority languages in schools—the theme of this study— is in general an issue only with respect to minority groups for whom their own language is one of the markers of distinctiveness and the majority language one of the potential barriers to successful participation in the host society. Under other circumstances there may still be educational reasons why studying a heritage language in school may be educationally appropriate, but the decision is not one that rises to the level of a policy decision.

The largest minority group in the Netherlands is made up of over 300,000 former immigrants from Surinam and the Dutch Antilles and their families, some Creole (of African ancestry) and others Hindu (of East Indian ancestry); "by 1975 more than 30 percent of the whole population of Surinam was residing in the Netherlands" (Eldering, 1989, 109). Members of this group have spoken Dutch as well as several forms of Surinamese patois for generations, and 95 percent are Dutch citizens. Among Surinamese in Utrecht in the early 1980s, only a third of the Hindus spoke exclusively *Sarnami Hindi*, and none of the Creoles spoke exclusively *Sranan Tongo*; the children without exception spoke Dutch among themselves (Fase, 1987, 38). While a recent study found that Surinamese kindergartners scored a full standard deviation below Dutch children on a Dutch language test (Boogaard et al., 1990, cited by Tesser, 1993, 160–61), most Dutch experts believe this reflects social class and parents' schooling level rather than either use or neglect of home languages in the school, and that their situation thus differs from that of the children of immigrants from Turkey or Morocco, or of refugees.

With the passage of time, it has become increasingly difficult to quantify precisely the size of language minority groups in various countries. Children born in the host country may not appear in statistics of the "foreign" population, especially if they acquire citizenship automatically, even though they may arrive in school speaking only the language that their parents brought with them from the homeland. The dimensions of the language challenge faced by schools is not limited to the number of children arriving from other countries, and the relatively high birthrates of immigrant groups together with low birthrates among native populations have the effect that in

TABLE 2.7. Speakers of Languages Other than English and Percent Change (USA)

Language	Speakers 5 and up	Share of Total	Change since 1979
Spanish	14,489,000	58.3%	+ 65.2%
French	1,082,000	4.4%	+ 9.6%
Italian	906,000	3.6%	– 33.1%
German	849,000	3.4%	– 32.7%
Chinese languages	834,000	3.4%	+ 62.3%
Philippine languages	638,000	2.6%	+ 52.2%
Korean	503,000	2.0%	+ 163.1%
Polish	454,000	1.8%	– 37.9%
Vietnamese	398,000	1.6%	+ 153.6%
Portuguese	395,000	1.6%	+ 61.2%
Japanese	370,000	1.5%	+ 39.7%
Asian Indian languages	284,000	1.1%	+ 190.1%
Greek	284,000	1.1%	– 22.3%

Source: McArthur, 1993, 6.

Germany, Belgium, France, England, and Sweden births to foreign residents represent one-tenth or more of all births, while in Luxembourg the proportion is one-third and in Switzerland one-fifth of all births (Organisation for Economic Cooperation and Development, 1994, 30).

The best comprehensive data on this question is from the United States. The 1970 national census had asked about the "mother tongue" or "language spoken in the childhood home" of respondents, but it came to be recognized that this "would lead to overestimates of current non-English language usage" (McArthur, 1993, 3). The Census Bureau included a detailed set of questions about language use in the Current Population Survey (CPS), carried out in 1979 and 1989. The most notable finding is the sharp increase among speakers of Asian languages and the numerically greater though proportionately lesser increase among speakers of Spanish, primarily from Mexico (Table 2.7).

Data available from other countries are less specific, in part because some have traditionally avoided asking questions about race or ethnicity.

> As a result of the migrations from the Indian subcontinent and East Africa, there existed in England as a whole in 1981 a population of well over 1 million people of South Asian origin. Because of the absence of specific "ethnic" and language questions in the census in England . . . it is impossible to give a more precise estimate. . . . the 1981 Census records 378,712 people who were born in India, 179,723 born in Pakistan and 46,868 born in Bangladesh, together with 190,689 people who gave their birthplace as East Africa of whom it is likely that a very high proportion were of South Asian origin (*Linguistic Minorities Project*, 1985, 36).

Just as in the United States, Canada, and Australia, there has been a shift in the makeup of the foreign-born population in Western Europe in recent years. The proportion of resident foreigners from Italy and Spain has declined as workers and their families have returned to their homelands to take advantage of economic progress, and Turkish and North African workers have brought over family members to join them. As a result, the proportion of non-European foreigners has increased sharply. In 1973, about half of the foreigners in the Netherlands from around the Mediterranean were Turks and Moroccans; by 1990, there were 343,000 noncitizen residents of the Netherlands from Turkey and North Africa, contrasted with only 51,000 from southern Europe (Eldering, 1986b, 173). Between 1987 and 1991 the four largest minority groups in the Netherlands (Surinamese, Turks, Moroccans, and West Indians) increased by 131,293; one-third of this increase was from births, two thirds from continuing migration, especially through the formation of new families as resident foreigners of the second generation brought wives and husbands from their ancestral homelands, rather than births (Tesser, 1993, 18, 24).

Of 100,000 immigrants who entered France in 1990, most to join family members already established there, three quarters were North Africans or Turks (Dubet & Lapeyronnie, 1992, 82). While Italians are still the largest group of resident foreigners in Belgium (240,000 in 1991), their numbers are declining, while the population of Moroccans (145,600) and Turks (88,400) is increasing (Organisation for Economic Cooperation and Development, 1994, 191). A similar shift has taken place in the immigrant population of Germany.

The issues created by the presence of a foreign population grow at least in part out of the nature of that population; it is widely perceived in Western Europe that those who come from Islamic and other non-Western homelands experience more profound disorientation and create more difficulties for schools and human service agencies. Such immigrants are by no means evenly distributed; in West Germany, for example, certain states have a substantially higher proportion than others of a foreign population from Islamic countries. The distribution of immigrant minority groups reflects the circumstances under which different groups came to the host country. The Ruhr coal mines recruited mainly in Turkey, so Turks are heavily concentrated in that area, while Italians make up most of the foreign population around Wolfsburg, because Volkswagen recruited in Italy (Castles, Booth, & Wallace, 1984, 118).

In Belgium, Muslim immigrants are disproportionately in Flanders, since the economy of that part of the country was expanding vigorously during the 1960s, while the longer-established Italian immigrants and their

TABLE 2.8. Foreign Population of West Germany, Selected Origins, 1986

	Baden-Württemberg	Berlin	Saarland	Bremen	Total
Europe	475,200	61,900	28,200	11,700	1,955,900
Islamic countries	245,500	106,600	7,900	24,700	1,509,900
% from Islamic countries	34.1%	63.3%	21.9%	67.9%	43.6%

Source: *Beauftragten . . . , 1987.*

TABLE 2.9. Foreign-Born Population by Region of USA, in 1990

Region	Foreign-born Population	Percent of Total
New England	1,043,000	7.9%
Middle Atlantic	4,188,000	11.1%
East North Central	1,783,000	4.2%
West North Central	348,000	2.0%
South Atlantic	2,723,000	6.3%
East South Central	157,000	1.0%
West South Central	1,702,000	6.4%
Mountain	715,000	5.2%
Pacific	7,108,000	18.2%
USA total	19,767,000	7.9%

Source: *The American Almanac, 1993–1994*, 1993, 50.

descendants are disproportionately in Wallonia, drawn there initially by the needs of the mining industry before World War II and in the 1950s.

Similarly, the foreign-born population of the United States is distributed unevenly across the country, with the older European immigration concentrated in the North Central, New England, and Middle Atlantic states, and the more recent immigration from Mexico and Asia more heavily represented in the Southwest and Florida; "the five most highly concentrated ethnic groups are Mexicans, Portuguese, Japanese, Filipinos, and Norwegians. . . . Such stable locations are a far cry from the image of a thoroughly homogenized 'melted' population" (Portes & Rumbaut, 1990, 51).

The different ethnic groups that make up the Spanish-speaking population occupy distinct geographical spaces: 69 percent of the Cubans are in Florida, 66 percent of Puerto Ricans are in the Northeast, and 57 percent of the 11.5 million Mexicans are in the West. Asian-born ethnic groups are also largely concentrated in the West, though Asian Indians and Koreans are distributed more evenly across the United States, the former often in the professions and the latter in retail business.

THE CAUSES OF POSTWAR IMMIGRATION

The scope, direction, and particular forms taken by international migration are the result of complex factors that "push" emigrants out of their homelands and "pull" them to particular host countries. Economic dislocations caused by new forms of agricultural or industrial production, civil war and ethnic conflict, or restlessness arising from increased educational levels without corresponding opportunities, may set individuals, families, whole villages in motion to a new country. The Dutch Prime Minister noted, in 1989, that in Algeria, Tunisia, and Morocco each year 500,000 young people leave school for domestic labor markets that can accommodate only half of them (Lubbers, 1989, 12).

Similarly, the development of new forms of industry may create a need for unskilled labor that can be met by immigrants who will work for less pay than would the skilled workers displaced by the new technology, as was the case in the late nineteenth century in the United States (Jones, 1960, 216). Such labor may continue to be recruited out of a mistaken equation of low wages with low costs even as the economy changes to demand a skilled workforce for capital-intensive industry (Massenet, 1994).

The expanding economies of northwestern Europe after World War II filled their labor needs with workers recruited from Italy and elsewhere in southern Europe, as well as from their fast-disappearing colonial empires. More recently, such former sources of emigration as Greece, Italy, Spain and Portugal have themselves become magnets for immigration, drawing a significant number of labor migrants from farther south: Morocco, Tunisia, Egypt, Pakistan, Iran, and other Asian and African countries (Penninx, 1986, 952).

Recruitment of foreign workers is no recent phenomenon in northwestern Europe. France, with its low birthrate, imported labor throughout the nineteenth century; about 1 million foreigners, mostly Italians and Belgians, came between 1885 and 1895. Another million, from Eastern Europe, came between 1920 and 1925 to work in coal mines, heavy industry, and agricultural labor (Le Bras, 1988). "Between 1914 and the beginning of the Depression the number of foreign workers in France more than doubled, increasing from 1,200,000 (3% of the population) in the former year . . . to 2,700,000 (6.59%) in 1931" (DeLey, 1983, 198). As a result, France is not unfamiliar with the challenge of schooling the children of immigrants: in, 1927 8.4 percent of the pupils in French elementary schools were foreign (Fase, 1994, 15). What is more, French policy explicitly encouraged immigration by families who would remain and add to France's permanent population, perceived as dangerously low by contrast with that of Germany (Weil, 1992, 63).

Immediately after World War II, the French government established the *Office national d'immigration* (O.N.I.) to encourage the orderly recruitment of suitable workers for French industry and agriculture (Massenet, 1994, 133). By 1970, nearly 2 million foreign workers and 690,000 of their dependent family members were in France. Initially, the recruitment centered on northern Italy, but a quarter million Algerians—as of 1947 officially French citizens and thus not required to follow O.N.I. procedures—came seeking jobs, and in the rapid economic expansion of the sixties the official mechanisms were inadequate to keep up with the flow of prospective workers from all around the Mediterranean; by 1968, 82 percent of new labor migrants were coming unofficially and regularizing their situations in the country after finding employment (Just, 1985a, 69).

In 1962, when Algeria became independent, there were 350,000 Muslim Algerians in France (in addition to colonials of European origin) and the peace agreement allowed continued free entry; nearly 500,000 came in the next two years. This number was limited several years later and a quota system imposed in 1968, though family reunification and abuse of tourist visas allowed a substantial continued increase. A Socialist government, concerned to show its good intentions toward immigrants in the face of rising anti-immigrant sentiment, canceled restrictions on immigration from Algeria in 1985; according to President François Mitterand, "the immigrants are at home in France: they will leave only if they want and when they want." The 1990 census counted 614,207 Algerians in France; taking into account children born in France of Algerian parents and others for whom Algerian citizenship was not reported, it appears that there are around 1.3 million persons of Algerian background in France (Massenet, 1994, 10, 98, 206).

In contrast, the Portuguese immigration to France was deliberately encouraged at the time when restrictions were placed on Algerian immigration, out of a belief that the Portuguese would assimilate more readily into French society and that continued growth in the Muslim population would, for the first time in its history, create a racial problem in France. When the Portuguese authorities initially showed some reluctance to issue visas for emigration, France let it be known that immigrants from Portugal would be admitted without them; some 700,000 responded. As the French official then responsible has written recently, "we thus had a way to demonstrate to the Algerians that we no longer needed their labor force" (Massenet, 1994, 50, 131). Over the subsequent decades, the Portuguese workers and their families in France have indeed acquired the reputation of "good immigrants," hard workers, discreet, devout Catholics compared with most of the French, and all the more appreciated by contrast with the feared and disliked Algerians (*Le Monde, dossiers et documents*, April 1987, 1).

The neighboring country of Belgium (or at least French-speaking Wallonia) had similar concerns about underpopulation in the late nineteenth century, and the early industrialization of its mining areas led to recruitment of Italian and Polish workers; by 1890 there were 170,000 foreign workers making up nearly 3 percent of the national population. Active recruitment after World War II increased this number to 570,000 (4.3 percent), mostly still from Italy and Poland, in 1947. With the rapid growth of the Belgian economy in the sixties, recruitment agreements were made with a number of countries, and lax immigration controls allowed many workers to come informally. The number of foreigners in Belgium grew to 9 percent of the total by 1980. Indeed, 95 percent of the increase in Belgian population between 1970 and 1980, and *all* of that in Wallonia, was the result of immigration and births to immigrant parents (Entzinger, 1984, 187).

The earlier labor immigration was largely Italian, and fitted relatively easily into Belgian life [the present Walloon Minister of Education has the Italian name Elio di Rupo]. While the expectation was that these workers would return home with their savings (and many of the Italians and Spaniards have done so), other labor migrants have become immigrants by the passage of time. Their children, born in Belgium, are largely cut off from their lands of origin, though some are only uneasily at home in Limburg, Brussels, or Antwerp. This increase is especially the case with the more recent labor migrants, who come predominantly from Islamic rather than Catholic countries.

The picture in the United Kingdom during the nineteenth century was one in which labor migration was largely from Ireland, then a British possession. Immigration of Eastern European Jews in response to the pogroms at the end of the century led to passage of the restrictive Aliens Act of 1905, and it was not until after World War II that a need was perceived to encourage foreign workers. To a considerable extent they were needed to replace English and Scottish emigrants to Australia and Canada, then vigorously recruiting.

The postwar immigration was largely from former colonies, known collectively as the "New" Commonwealth—the West Indies, the Indian subcontinent, East Africa, Cyprus—as distinguished from "Old" Commonwealth nations like Australia and Canada with predominantly white populations, and was facilitated by what had traditionally been a right for British subjects to live and work in the metropolis. As Britain retreated from Empire, many former subjects were not willing to be left behind, and the influx was essentially uncontrolled until 1962. The event often taken as the start of the New Commonwealth labor migration was the arrival of the arrival of the ship *Empire Windrush* in 1948, filled with Jamaican men eager for work in the "mother country." By 1970, one in six Cypriots was living in the United Kingdom (Taylor, 1988, 4). About 460,000 workers from refugee camps and from Italy were also admitted under a severely restrictive temporary program between 1946 and 1951, and there was recruitment in the 1960s from Spain and Portugal under the "work permit scheme."

As a result of generally permissive policies (but without explicit recruitment as in other countries of northwestern Europe), the number of immigrants from the West Indies and the Indian subcontinent grew from 21,600 in 1959 to 57,700 in 1960, 136,400 in 1961, and 94,900 during the first half of 1962, when the Commonwealth Immigrants Act drastically slowed the influx. This had the paradoxical effect, however (repeated in other countries in the early 1970s), of turning foreign workers into permanent residents, encouraging them to bring their families, and thus to launch a new generation in the host country. Once it was clear that it was not possible to move back and forth between the homeland and the United Kingdom, staying permanently in the host society was the only rational choice and implied bringing one's family or starting one by an arranged marriage with a woman from the homeland. Establishing or uniting families accounted for 96 percent of the movement from Pakistan to the U.K. in 1968, contrasted with 2 percent in 1960 (Crowley, 1992, 84).

Initially, there was bipartisan support for maintenance of the right of citizens of the Commonwealth to reside and work in the U.K.; for progressives in the Labor Party, it signified the humanistic and nonracist character of the postimperial commonwealth, while for traditionalist Conservatives it represented an opportunity to "maintain the integrality of imperial symbols, the 'white man's burden,' and the worldwide role of the United Kingdom" (Crowley, 1992, 77). For both, allowing Commonwealth immigration was a matter more of foreign than of economic policy as it was in Germany or Belgium. In the words of the main opponent of this "colored" immigration, Enoch Powell,

> Largely because of the legal fiction of Commonwealth citizenship and our determination to maintain it, we clung year after year to the assertion that our nearest European neighbours were alien, to be strictly excluded from Britain, but that the myriad inhabitants of independent countries in Asia, Africa and the New World were British, indistinguishable from the native-born inhabitants of these islands, and that no limitation could be placed on their inherent right to enter and leave this country at will (quoted by Crowley, 1992, 81).

With the anti-immigrant rioting in Notting Hill in 1958, the political significance of the immigration question among elements of the British population became clear, and the framework within which the situation of immigrants themselves would be dealt with was established: as a question of race relations more than of economic and social integration.

While most of the "New" Commonwealth residents in Britain in the 1960s had come seeking employment, the most severe test of British responsibility for "subjects" scattered around the world came with political developments in Kenya and Uganda. The Kenyan constitution adopted at the time of independence in 1963 made dual citizenship impossible, and most of the 120,000 Kenyans of Indian descent opted for British passports. The aggressive policy of "Africanization" that began in 1967 caused many of them to seek to emigrate to the United Kingdom. A restrictive Commonwealth Immigrants Act was promptly adopted, distinguishing between those British subjects with ancestral origins in the U.K. and those with no such connections (Crowley, 1992, 91–92).

The second crisis occurred in 1972, when Idi Amin announced that all Asians holding British citizenship—some 50,000—must leave Uganda within 90 days. The United Kingdom felt obliged to admit more than 28,000 of them, and put pressure on Canada and Australia to help; the former admitted more than 7,000, but the latter only a couple hundred of Asians.

The 1981 census attempted to estimate the ethnic minority population of the United Kingdom including those born in the country by counting the number of persons living in a household whose head originated in the New Commonwealth. The total was 2.2 million, of whom 546,000 from the West Indies, 674,000 from India, 295,000 from Pakistan, 65,000 from Bangladesh, 181,000 from East Africa (mostly Indians expelled by the postindependence governments of Kenya and Uganda), 120,000 from the Far East, and 170,000 from the Mediterranean (Cyprus, Malta, Gibraltar) (John Rex, cited by Rogers, 1993, 109).

To continue this survey, Germany, like the United Kingdom but unlike France and Belgium—was a net exporter of population throughout

TABLE 2.10. Foreign-Born Residents in the United Kingdom, in Thousands

Birthplace	1951	1961	1971	1981	% of 1981
"New" Commonwealth	218	541	1,151	1,513	45%
"Old" Commonwealth	99	110	143	153	6%
Ireland	532	709	709	607	18%
Other	724	845	980	1,086	32%
Total	1,573	2,205	2,983	3,360	
% of Population	3.2%	4.3%	5.5%	6.2%	

Source: Castles, Booth, and Wallace, 1984, 43.

much of the nineteenth century. In the "first wave" of 1845 to 1858, 1,361,000 Germans emigrated, as did 1,040,000 in the period 1864–1873 and 1,784,000 in the period 1880–1893. There were only ten years (1895–1905) in the period from 1841 to 1930 when the number of immigrants exceeded that of emigrants (Marschalck, 1984, 179).

To meet the needs of its rapidly growing economy, the newly proclaimed German Empire recruited its Polish-speaking subjects in large numbers from their villages to work as farm laborers and then in mining and industry; to discourage permanent settlement, they were required to return home during the winter months. By 1907 there were more than half-a-million Eastern European workers, 125,000 Italians, and 50,000 Dutch (Fase, 1994, 15). By 1914 there were some 300,000 in the Ruhr area alone (see G. Hansen, 1986). During World War II, Germany recruited Italian and Spanish workers and in 1942 began to deport civilians forcibly from occupied territories to replace mobilized German workers; approximately 5.5 million foreign civilians and 1.5 million prisoners of war were put to work in German industry and agriculture (Just, 1985a, 62).

Immediately after the war there were millions of refugees from German-speaking areas that had become part of Poland and the Soviet Union to absorb into the German economy, followed by further millions who fled East Germany before the construction of the Berlin Wall. With more than 9 million displaced Germans to draw upon, it was not initially necessary to recruit workers from other countries. In 1955, however, with the re-establishment of the Bundeswehr, "Germany had suddenly to replace half a million young Germans who were withdrawn from the labor market, with Italians" (Entzinger, 1984, 177). A recruitment agreement was made with Italy, drawing largely from the south of the country, since France had already absorbed the excess labor of the north, whose economy was in any event picking up. This was followed in the 1960s by arrangements with Spain, Greece, Turkey, Portugal, Tunisia, Morocco, and Yugoslavia (Just, 1985a, 62). Soon, "recruitment of foreign workers was so rapid that West Germany had caught up with the other countries in the use of migrant labour by the end of the decade" (Castles, Booth, & Wallace, 1984, 11). By the time of the oil crisis of 1973, there were 2.6 million foreigners employed in the German economy (Marschalck, 1984, 108).

The most controversial labor migrants were the those from Turkey, who were the least likely to return home and most often perceived as inassimilable. While in 1967 they represented only 9.5 percent of the foreign population, they were 33.4 percent in 1981. Despite the end to formal programs to recruit foreign labor after the oil crisis of the early 1970s, the foreign and especially the Turkish population has continued to grow through family reunification as well as a high birthrate. Anxiety was often expressed about their typically large families: in 1978 the fertility rate of German women was 1.33, that of Turkish women in Germany 3.64 (Marschalck, 1984, 170), though in the 1980s there has been a clear tendency for the foreign birthrate to become more similar to that of Germans (Kühl, 1987, 23). The census taken in 1987 showed a 70 percent increase to 4.1 million in the number of foreigners since the previous census of 1970, but a 1.3 million decrease in the number of Germans (*The Economist* January 7, 1989).

In contrast the Netherlands did not attract labor immigrants as early or as massively as its neighbors. Lack of coal and iron ore meant that its industrial development lagged until after World War II, when technical industries developed that did not need large numbers of unskilled laborers. In addition, the country absorbed some 250,000 repatriated "Indo-Netherlanders" with Dutch citizenship from Indonesia after that country's independence (1946–1949), and accommodated (but did not absorb) 12,500 Moluccans who had served in the Dutch colonial army against the independence movement, and their families. With the highest density of population in Europe, there was a tendency to promote emigration of Dutch natives, especially to Canada and Australia, after the war, encouraged by a "restlessness" that observers noted in the long-placid Dutch society (Sherington, 1980, 145). Some 400,000 Dutch emigrants more than equaled the number of immigrants in this period (Entzinger, 1984, 72).

Recruitment of workers from southern Europe to the Netherlands began in the 1960s, reaching a high of 46,000 in 1966. Although recruitment was stopped with the economic crisis of the early seventies, the Netherlands did not (unlike some of its neighbors) place formal restrictions on immigration of foreign workers, and with family reunification the foreign-born share in the population continued to grow. Between 1975 and 1982, the number of foreigners increased by 71 percent, compared with 12 percent in Germany, 3 percent in Sweden and 2 percent in France over the same period—and with a 15 percent decline in Switzerland (Entzinger, 1984, 22).

In addition, a high proportion of the population of Surinam took advantage of the Dutch citizenship which they possessed until 1975 to emigrate—nearly 40,000 in a panicked rush in the year of independence itself—and, together with a smaller group from the Antilles, make up about 200,000 residents of the Netherlands who are not included in the statistics on foreigners, since 90 percent of them are Dutch citizens (Entzinger, 1984). One third of all Surinamese now live in the Netherlands.

Of the European nations, Switzerland has been especially dependent upon foreign labor, mostly from Italy. By 1973 there were 897,000 foreign workers, representing one third of the total labor force and about half of all factory workers. Despite severe restrictions imposed in the early seventies—and a series of narrowly-defeated referenda calling for expulsion to prevent "*Überfremdung*" or swamping by foreigners—the Swiss economy cannot do without foreign workers to fill the low-pay and low-status jobs (Castles, 1986, 767). Swiss policies, more than those of other nations, are designed to limit admissions to labor migrants from Europe and to prevent the asylum system (see below) from being used by economic refugees from the developing nations (Rogers, 1993, 123).

The rapid growth of the Swedish economy led to recruitment of foreign workers starting in 1950 not only from Italy but also from still-recovering West Germany. In 1964 a policy limiting work permission to immigrants from the Nordic countries was loosened, and about 45,000 labor migrants came each year, many from Yugoslavia, Greece and Turkey. The flow continued until the economic slowdown of the early seventies, despite attempts to limit again non-Nordic immigration after 1967: "the restriction of immigration became a central principle of policy" (Entzinger, 1984, 223). Sweden's generous policy toward refugees, dating to the closing years of World War II (and perhaps to bad conscience over cooperation with Nazi Germany), brought a substantial influx of Hungarians in 1956, of Chileans after the fall of Allende in 1973, and of Kurds and political dissidents from Turkey, of Czechs and Poles. By the end of 1981 there were 631,950 persons born abroad living in Sweden, of whom 246,363 were from Finland, 20,588 from Latin America, 51,688 from Asia (including Turkey), and 10,915 from Africa. Immigration accounted for 31 percent of Sweden's population increase between 1944 and 1975 (*Immigrants and Immigrant Teaching in Sweden*, 1983).

The "guest-worker system" of recruiting labor for temporary employment in more developed European economies came to an end with the oil crisis of the early seventies, and about the same time Britain and the Netherlands moved to close off immigration from their former colonies—even, as in the case of Surinam, by hurriedly granting independence! The primary means of entering these prosperous countries since then have been (1) family reunification, (2) illegal entrance, and (3) claiming refugee status. Currently, "inflows of permanent immigrants to most European OECD countries take place in the context of family reunification. Labour recruitment has not been suspended but, with the notable exception of Switzerland, Austria and Germany, there are relatively few new arrivals" (Organisation for Economic Cooperation and Development, 1994, 19).

The "pull" of the expanding and prosperous economies of northwestern Europe, the United States, Canada, and Australia has been a consistent factor though not always taking the same form from country to country and decade to decade. The "push" of underdevelopment is equally constant, though it should be noted that the most destitute rarely are in a position to emigrate and that the patterns of migration are by no means as simple as that of water flowing from a higher to a lower level. Efforts to slow down the pace of undesired migration through providing development help to the sending countries of the Third World have produced meager results; economic growth pulls people out of rural areas into cities, and for some that is the first step to an attempt to reach the more prosperous cities of Europe or North America. Contrary to popular opinion, most of the Turkish immigrants to Germany, for example, came from cities rather than from the underdeveloped areas of rural Anatolia and were already industrial workers rather than peasants (Institut für Zukunftsforschung, 1981, 69). An exception to this rule is the immigration to Western Europe from Morocco, most of which came out of Berber-speaking mountainous areas with little exposure to schooling or other aspects of modernity (Amersfoort, 1986, 27).

The intended pattern of labor migration of the sort encouraged by intergovernmental agreements in the fifties and sixties was that young men would spend a few years working in the host country and sending money home, after which they would return with newly acquired skills and capital to help to develop the economies of their homelands. This in fact is what Italian, Greek, and Spanish workers largely did, and for a time the remittances of emigré workers were a very significant factor in the economies of a number of countries. In 1973, 18.6 percent of the hard currency earnings of Spain, 33.2 percent of those of Greece, 38.2 percent of those of Portugal, and 47 percent of those of Turkey were derived from the remittances of their workers abroad. That year 10 percent of the Portuguese workforce was employed in France, and their wages represented 9.5 percent of Portugal's gross national product (Hamilton, 1985, 49, 43).

Studies have found, however, that the primary effect of such payments in most cases was to encourage further emigration, not investment in the economies of the homelands (Hamilton, 1985, 40). Labor migrants from countries outside the European Community tended not to return home or, if they did, it was after retirement; they raised their families in the host countries, and their children showed little inclination to make their lives in an ancestral homeland that offered few economic prospects comparable to those available even at the bottom of the social ladder in northwestern Europe.

TABLE 2.11. Spaniards Living Abroad, in Thousands

Place of Residence	1970	1980	1992
France	660	471	327
Germany	246	180	135
Switzerland	102	97	115
other Europe	185	166	192
Latin America	839	764	696
Total	2,233	1,768	1,627

Source: Beck, 1993, 15.

The case of Spain is an instructive exception. Over the past 500 years, Spain has been a net exporter of people, as is evident from the predominant use of the Spanish language in more than twenty other nations. Even after its colonial era ended in 1898, Spain's excess population continued to emigrate, with some 2.3 million crossing the Atlantic to work in food production and industry in Argentina, Uruguay, and other Latin American destinations between 1905 and 1930. Development of petroleum extraction in Mexico and Venezuela stimulated further emigration in the postwar period.

By the sixties, however, the emigration flow turned decisively toward northwestern Europe, with over 100,000 labor migrants in each of the top years (1964, 1969, 1971, and 1972). The primary destinations were France, Germany, and Switzerland (Beck, 1993, 7–9). Starting in the midseventies, however, the number of Spaniards returning home, especially to the industrially prosperous areas of Catalonia, Asturia, and Navarra, came to equal and in some years to exceed the number leaving the country (Table 2.11).

Meanwhile, the number of foreigners moving to Spain was increasing. While the largest number are retirees from northwestern Europe, a growing labor migration from Morocco and other parts of Africa, and even from Latin America, was attracted by Spain's fast-growing economy and have come to fill many low-status jobs in agriculture, construction, and household service (Beck, 1993, 20). "Although for the most part young and unmarried, they hoped through family reunification to bring over family members still remaining in the country of origin. They readily found work in the informal economy. They were highly mobile, both sectorally and geographically" (Organisation for Economic Cooperation and Development, 1994, 92). In short, they greatly resembled the Spaniards who went to more prosperous countries in earlier decades.

A nationwide campaign in Spain to regularize the status of foreign workers without permits, in 1991, led 127,825 to make applications (85 percent were approved); of these, 44 percent were from Morocco and 21 percent from South America (Organisation for Economic Cooperation and Development, 1994, 92). Many of the Africans pay for passage from Morocco in little fishing boats, and not a few drown when they are forced to swim ashore; those who are caught in Spain often cannot be deported because there is no way to prove what country they came from (*The Economist*, September 12, 1992, 56).

Italy, the emigration country *par excellence*, has undergone a similar process. As recently as 1953, a survey suggested that about 1.8 million Italians were eager to emigrate, and about half had relatives who had left Italy since 1945 (Sherington, 1980, 141). Over the next two decades, some 337,000 Italians emigrated to Australia and millions went to northwestern Europe as labor migrants. This pattern has now been reversed; not only have many Italians returned to their newly prosperous country (though not necessarily to the region from which they emigrated), but a growing number of illegal immigrants from developing nations have been entering the country at such a rate that their number was estimated at 1.4 million in 1990; with an additional 380,000 Africans and Asians legally resident, 3.1 percent of the population is from outside Europe. The immigration from Morocco has been especially numerous, as in Spain: only 0.6 percent of the foreign population of Italy in 1985, Moroccans represented 10 percent by 1990 (Rellini, 1992, 180, 193).

Like the Western European nations in their period of postwar economic expansion, the United States was highly dependent upon foreign labor throughout most of the nineteenth century; indeed, the rapid expansion of its agricultural and industrial production would have been impossible without it. "By 1900 the bulk of the employees in each of the leading American industries was of foreign origin, most of them being Italians, Slavs, Russian Jews, Greeks, Portuguese, or French-Canadians" (Jones, 1960, 312).

In the United States, after the restrictions placed on immigration in the 1920s, the need for unskilled labor in northern industry was met in large part by internal migration of both black and white families from the rural south. An additional source of labor was immigrants from the British West Indies, who were able to benefit from the generous quota for British immigrants, subject to meeting literacy qualifications, until the McCarran-Walter Act of 1952 gave them a small separate quota of their own—and turned the West Indian immigration stream decisively toward the United Kingdom (Jones, 1960, 295). This was part of a general outflow of 2 million immigrants from the Caribbean to their "mother countries": to the Netherlands, the United Kingdom, France, and (in the case of Puerto Ricans) the United States (Ferrier, 1985, 65).

Puerto Ricans, as United States citizens, enjoyed an unrestricted right to migrate in search of better economic conditions than were available on an island that "in the middle 1930s, after thirty-five years of American administration, was a scene of almost unrelieved misery" (Glazer & Moynihan, 1963, 86). With the introduction of air service between San Juan and New York City, after World War II, the United States experienced what was surely the world's first mass migration by air, with almost 136,250 Puerto Ricans coming to the United States mainland in 1947. The back-and-forth nature of this migration should be noted, however; 101,115 Puerto Ricans returned to the island in that year, and some years there has been more movement away from than to the mainland. In 1969 a record 2,105,217 came to the mainland, but 2,112,264 left! The peak year of positive net migration was 1953, when 74,603 more Puerto Ricans came to the mainland than left (United States Commission on Civil Rights, 1976, 26–27).

Altogether more than 400,000 Puerto Ricans came to the mainland during the fifties, and by 1957 there were more than 550,000 living in New York City, with another 175,000 elsewhere in northeastern cities. "The economic role of the Puerto Rican immigrant has been to fill in part the vacuum in unskilled and semiskilled labor left by the virtual ending of European immigration" (Jones, 1960, 296). Or, as Clarence Senior wrote, Puerto Rico's "labor force has now become part of the labor force of the whole country" (Senior, 1965, 40).

Like labor migrants to northwestern Europe over the next two decades, Puerto Ricans in New York City sent their remittances home. "In 1940 bank deposits in Puerto Rico were $76 million; in 1961, $674 million" (Sexton, 1965, 16). As in Turkey or North Africa, however, the growing prosperity of their homeland did not tempt most emigrés to return, and their remittances may indeed have encouraged former neighbors to join them in New York.

REFUGEES, ASYLUM-SEEKERS, AND ILLEGALS

There has been no period in this century when the world's attention has not been caught, at least momentarily, by the plight of refugees from war, famine, or persecution. The prosperous nations have provided financial and food assistance in many cases, but in few have they considered opening their own borders as part of the solution. The exceptions to this rule have been when a country (such as Australia and Canada after World War II) has been determined to increase its own population, or when an obligation of kinship is recognized (as with the Germans living in the former Soviet Union), or when a country's own past policies have contributed significantly to the refugee crisis.

Examples of refugee resettlement as a contribution to population would be the admission to Canada of 186,150 European displaced persons between 1945 and 1952, and the admission of 170,000 "D.P.'s" to Australia in the same period.

Examples of reception (and subsequent generous support) of refugees on the basis of a sense of having helped to create their plight would include the admission into the Netherlands of refugees from Indonesia, into France of settlers of European descent from Algeria, into the United States of Cubans after the failure of the Bay of Pigs in April 1961, and into the United States, France, and Australia of Indochinese refugees after the fall of Saigon in April 1975. In addition,

> The flow of boat people from Vietnam to the major countries of first asylum in Southeast Asia increased from 5,833 in July 1978 to 53,133 in June 1979. At the same time, there were major movements of refugees overland. An estimated 160,000 ethnic Chinese from Vietnam fled to China overland in 1978. . . . By the end of June 1979, there were 153,000 Indochinese refugees in camps in Thailand, 74,800 in Malaysia, 42,900 in Indonesia, 64,000 in Hong Kong and 9,800 in other countries of first asylum, making a total of 350,000 refugees in boat and land camps (Hawkins, 1989, 180).

By 1985, many of these refugees had been resettled in those countries where policymakers felt some responsibility for the *débacle* of the Vietnam war (see Table 2.12).

In 1990, about 135,000 persons applied for refugee status in the United States, as did more than 550,000 persons in Europe, 36,000 in

---

TABLE 2.12. Leading Countries of Admission of Vietnamese Refugees, 1975–1985

United States	583,049
China	262,853
Canada	98,424
France	97,827
Australia	96,262

Source: Hawkins, 1989, 182.

TABLE 2.13. Asylum-Seekers per Million Inhabitants, 1984–86

Sweden	4,975
Denmark	4,370
Switzerland	4,000
West Germany	3,350
Austria	2,965
Belgium	1,780
France	1,310
The Netherlands	990
Norway	945
United Kingdom	240

Source: *The Economist*, April 18, 1987.

Canada, and about 10,000 in Australia (Edmonston & Passel, 1994a, 14). These figures represent only a minor proportion of the millions of refugees from war and hunger in Africa and Asia, but even so they include many who do not qualify for admission or residence with refugee status. The United Nations defines a refugee as someone fleeing his country because of persecution or well-founded fear of it on the basis of his "race, religion, nationality, membership of a particular social group or political organization," thus excluding those who are in flight from poverty, famine, or war; the emphasis is upon individuals, not entire groups.

During the eighties the primary source of new immigration has been persons from all over the world claiming the refugee status; since 1986–1987, about 600,000 have sought refuge in Western Europe (*The Economist*, September 19, 1992, 66), including many fugitives from the civil wars in the former Yugoslavia. It would perhaps be more accurate to say that the refugee status has been the primary means of seeking to immigrate in recent years, just as the status of migrant laborer was the primary means in the sixties. It typically takes several years to adjudicate a claim to refugee status, and the claimants are typically either housed and fed at the expense of the host government or allowed to work during the interval. If their claim is disallowed, many vanish into illegal status.

American immigration law makes a distinction between refugees, who apply for admission to the United States from outside the country under a quota system currently set at 120,000 a year, and asylees who "petition to remain in the U.S., usually after having entered illegally. Put differently, the U.S. selects refugees; asylum-seekers select the United States. Asylum applications reached 147,000 in 1993, up from only 56,000 in

1991; only 4,465 petitions were approved in fiscal 1993" (Fix & Passel, 1994, 14).

On the other hand, political circumstances may lead to de facto asylum, as when the American government decided to allow about 30,000 Chinese students and scholars to stay in the United States in the wake of the Tiananmen Square massacre of June 1989.

The dramatic growth in the number of refugees and asylum-seekers is partially a reflection of the troubled state of the world in the wake of the Cold War (such as the massive flight from warring Croatia and Bosnia and the 24,000 Albanians who took ship across the Adriatic to Italy in 1991), but it is also a response to the blocking of other means of immigrating to the wealthy nations, just as the enormous growth of family reunification twenty years ago was a response to restrictions on labor migration. As country after country has placed restrictions on family reunification, the number of "refugees" seeking entry or permission to remain has increased. France had 576 petitions for asylum in 1973 (the year American troops left Vietnam, the Allende government was overthrown in Chile, and the Yom Kippur war occurred in the Near East) but 61,372 in 1989, a far more hopeful year worldwide (Massenet, 1994, 128). Petitions for refugee status are for many the only available means of entering a country with a strong economy or, having entered it illegally, of obtaining legal permission to remain and to be employed. As Patrick Weil explains:

> There are two ways of being irregular: totally or partially. Totally is when one has come as a tourist and remains beyond the permitted time (three months in France) to work illegally without papers. Partially is when one can demand asylum or obtain a student card while working full time. The second approach is now more commonly chosen in France: on the one hand, because illegals have learned to use the loopholes in the system and, on the other, because their employers often encourage them to do so (1992, 69).

Estimates of the number of "illegals" in France range from 300,000 to 1 million; studies in the Paris region found that 42 percent were North Africans and that 70 percent had entered the country as tourists and "forgotten to leave." Despite such abuses, the Foreign Ministry granted 362,000 visas to Algerians in 1993 (Massenet, 1994, 93, 163).

There is every reason to believe that, with the increasing political turmoil in Algeria, the number of visa requests will if anything increase, including many claims of refugee status. Many have legitimate fears of persecution

TABLE 2.14. Asylum-Seekers in Selected Countries of Europe, 1981 and 1991

	1981	1991
Austria	34,600	27,300
Belgium	2,400	15,200
France	19,800	50,000
Germany	49,400	256,100
Italy	—	27,000
Netherlands	800	21,600
Sweden	—	26,500
Switzerland	5,200	41,600
United Kingdom	2,900	57,700
Total	117,081	524,991

Source: Rogers, 1993, 118.

if the Islamic party gains the political control which was denied them by cancellation of elections in 1992, including those who have themselves used brutal means to remain in power. Debate has begun, in France, over whether there is a moral obligation to accept refugees with a well-founded fear of harm if they have deserved it. "The men who have exercised authority in Algeria in a regime based upon the brutal negation of human rights are neither intellectuals nor victims; their quarrel with the Islamic Salvation Front is a dispute among cut-throats. It doesn't concern us" (Massenet, 1994, 180).

The growth in applications for asylum has led governments to adopt more stringent procedures and criteria for recognition of refugee status. Switzerland, which was generous to Hungarian, Czech, and Tibetan refugees fleeing Communist armies, has been less welcoming to the recent wave of Sri Lankan Tamils, Kurds, and Africans; 86 percent of the applications for asylum were approved in 1981, but by 1986 only 10 percent were approved (*The Economist*, March 28, 1987, 54).

The members of the European Community agreed in the Dublin Convention of 1990 to procedures for handling asylum applications, intended to limit abuses of the system but also to ensure each applicant that his or her case will be adjudicated (Rogers, 1993, 122). The asylum seeker will no longer be able to "shop around" from country to country for permission to stay; the petition will be adjudicated in the first country he or she enters. Critics point out that the agreement still allows the members to "compete for the title of most unfriendly toward refugees" (Overbeek, 1994, 79). This was an issue of particular difficulty in West Germany, where the postwar Constitution provided significant guarantees to political refugees:

> the most remarkable phenomenon in all the OECD countries has been the surge in applications in Germany, which increased from 193,000 in 1990 to 256,000 in 1991 and 440,000 in 1992 . . . including almost 123,000 from former Yugoslavia, 104,000 from Romania, over 31,500 from Bulgaria and almost 28,000 from Turkey (Organisation for Economic Cooperation and Development, 1994, 25–26).

In response to this overwhelming flood of foreigners seeking to take advantage of the constitutional protection of refugees, the German Constitution was modified in May 1993 to limit this right; refugee status will be extended only to citizens of countries that have been officially recognized by Germany as violating human rights (Massenet, 1994, 157). As a result, the number of asylum applications has dropped in Germany . . . but increased in neighboring Belgium and the Netherlands (*The Economist*, October 2, 1993, 51).

A further complication for West Germany is that hundreds of thou-

TABLE 2.15. Resident Undocumented Population (USA), October 1992

Origin	Undocumented	Percent
Mexico	1,002,000	31%
El Salvador	298,000	9%
Guatemala	121,000	4%
other Central America/ Caribbean	570,000	18%
Canada	104,000	3%
Poland	102,000	3%
other Europe	215,000	7%
Asia	340,000	11%
South America	205,000	6%
Africa	125,000	4%
Oceania	15,000	—
Total	3,200,000	100%

Source: Fix and Passel, 1994, 24.

sands of individuals of German descent living in Eastern Europe are taking advantage of their legal right to immigrate, most without a working proficiency in German. In 1993, 207,347 came from the former Soviet Union, 5,431 from Poland, and 5,811 from Romania (*Gemeinsam*, August 1994). Fearing that all of the two million Soviet Germans identified in the 1989 census would make use of this right to emigrate to the West, the German government has taken various measures—so far not notably successful—to improve their lives and prospects in place (Brubaker, 1993, 40).

In Europe as in the United States, provisions for asylum are controversial because they conflict with efforts at border control; granting asylum seems to reward the person who has successfully evaded the orderly procedure set up for dealing with refugees. A petition for asylum is a means of avoiding deportation and even receiving authorization to work while what can be extended legal procedures are followed. The United States has a current backlog of some 350,000 applicants for asylum, and few denied applicants are ever actually deported (Fix & Passel, 1994, 15).

In addition to legal immigrants and refugees and asylum-seekers, there are many illegal or "undocumented" foreigners in the United States. A conservative estimate puts the numbers at 200,000 to 300,000 a year; more than a million illegal attempts to cross the border are foiled each year, but there has not in the past been an adequate system for determining how many of these are repeat attempts. Six out of ten illegal immigrants do not cross the border clandestinely, however, but enter legally and overstay their visas (Fix & Passel, 1994, 25).

BECOMING A CITIZEN

The integration of immigrants into the host society, it has been said, consists of three parallel developments: finding a place in the economy, cultural assimilation, and participation in civic life (Dubet & Lapeyronnie, 1992, 81). Of the three, the easiest for an observer to measure is the last, since data are generally available on the rate at which different groups become citizens—or are allowed to become citizens—and participate in elections and other aspects of civic life.

It may seem odd that long-term foreign residents would not seek citizenship of a country that they are unlikely ever to leave, and could even refuse it for their children, but for some it implies abandoning what distinguishes them from a host society whose values they reject. "French citizenship is good for working papers," as a Turkish worker in France put it, "but not for *les moeurs*" (quoted by Kastoryano, 1989, 164). Between 92 and 95 percent of Greek, Italian, and Turkish residents in Germany, in one careful study, did not want German citizenship if that would require rejecting that of their homeland; nearly half would want it if—it were possible, as it presently is not—to have dual citizenship (Koch-Arzberger, 1985, 143).

Controversy has developed in Australia over the fact that about a million immigrants have not yet taken advantage of the opportunity to become citizens, which is seen as indicating a lack of commitment to their new home (*The Economist*, May 6, 1989, 18). The act of becoming a citizen has equal weight in the United States, another "country of immigration" where it connotes "membership in a self-consciously created political community whose cultural identity continuously evolves. Membership is conditional and fluid because it requires continuous adherence to a particular set of political values," rather than descent from ancestors who were part of the same community or *Volk*. Thus "Immigrants become Americans (i.e., naturalize, through publicly pledging allegiance to the creed)—after taking English and civics classes designed to socialize them into the creed" (de la Garza, Falcon, Garcia, & Garcia, 1994, 228).

In contrast with the countries that have historically welcomed and even sought immigrants and thus confer citizenship almost as a matter of right after a period of legal residence (Australia, Canada, the United States), those of Europe treat this as a matter entirely within the discretion of the state to modify in response to the vagaries of political and economic conditions.

Most if not all countries make provision to confer citizenship (naturalization) under some circumstances upon resident foreigners and, more commonly, upon their children, but their requirements and underlying rationale differ considerably depending upon how they conceive of the basis of the citizenship of nonimmigrants. Some stress place of birth on national soil (*jus soli*) as automatically conferring citizenship, while others stress ancestry (*jus sanguinis*). In the first case, children of immigrants born in the host country are automatically citizens or eligible to become citizens, as is the case in France and Spain, provided that one of the parents was also born there. Germany, by contrast, considers the descendants of Germans automatically eligible, even if their families have lived in and been citizens of other countries for generations, while making it difficult for non-Germans born in Germany to become citizens.

The German Constitution guarantees citizenship to descendants of Germans who lived in territory that belonged to Germany before 1938 (thus much of what is now Poland), and this right was extended by a 1953 law to "people whose families left German territory—sometimes centuries ago, often voluntarily—but who keep some German identity" (*The Economist*, August 17, 1991, 43). "The steep rise in the number of naturalisations in Germany since 1989 is due not to any easing of the naturalisation procedures but to citizenship applications from immigrants from Central and

TABLE 2.16. Naturalizations in Selected Countries in 1991

Country	Naturalizations	Rate
Australia	118,510	3.0
Belgium	1,409	0.2
Canada	118,630	2.7
Denmark	5,484	3.4
France	72,213	2.0
Germany	141,630	2.7
Netherlands	29,110	4.2
Sweden	25,907	5.4
Switzerland	8,757	0.8
United Kingdom	58,642	3.4
United States	308,058	1.6

Source: Organisation for Economic Cooperation and Development, 1994, 50.

Eastern Europe who have been able to prove their ethnic German origins" (Organisation for Economic Cooperation and Development, 1994, 50). Long-time residents who are not ethnic Germans face daunting barriers to citizenship, even though two-thirds of the foreign children in the country were born there; fewer than one percent of Turks in Germany were citizens as of 1992 (*The Economist*, February 15, 1992, 22).

The United Kingdom long considered "British subjects" all the peoples of its Empire, succeeded by the British Commonwealth in 1929. The law adopted in 1962 limited entry to those citizens of the Commonwealth who possessed work permits or were students, visitors, or dependents of legal residents. A further distinction was made, in 1973 legislation, between Commonwealth citizens one or more of whose parents or grandparents was born in the U.K. or was a British citizen, and other Commonwealth citizens, whose rights of entry were much more limited. Citizenship was conferred automatically upon children born in the United Kingdom, regardless of the legal status of their parents, until the Nationality Act came into effect in 1983. Such citizenship now requires a naturalization process, subject to evidence of English proficiency and of good conduct (Castles, Booth, & Wallace, 1984, 46).

France is among the countries that encourage permanent residents to become citizens; for example, 5,253 residents from Algeria, Morocco, and Tunisia became citizens in 1978, and 7,212 in 1980 (Sayad, 1987, 124). Sweden has made even more of an effort to encourage naturalization; by 1979 some 300,000 immigrants had become Swedish citizens, to whom may be added an equal number of children of naturalized immigrants (*Immigrants and the Education System*, 1979, 9).

The extent to which taking the citizenship of the host nation is a decisive step depends in part upon whether it is possible to retain that of the homeland. Portuguese workers in France who became French citizens automatically (until 1981) lost Portuguese citizenship, but the North African nations have continued to treat their emigrants and even the France-born children and grandchildren of emigrants as Algerian or Tunisian citizens, whatever their status in France (Khellil, 1991). France, in turn, has seen vigorous political debates in recent years over whether citizenship should continue to be granted automatically to those born on French soil (the *jus soli* last reaffirmed in 1851) or whether there should be a formal requirement of an oath of loyalty to the laws and institutions of France. A distinguished historian insisted, "a *patrie* is something that you choose! . . . Some of these people don't share our values. If they don't feel themselves to be French, we don't want them either! . . . A democracy is fragile, and citizenship must be managed with dignity and care. . . . You don't assimilate in two generations, in a European community, people who belong to a fundamentally different cultural system" (Pierre Chaunu in *L'Express*, October 31, 1986).

Requirements for the acquisition of citizenship vary from country to country, but a common theme in most is demonstration of the ability to speak the prevalent language of the host society. Since 1906 the ability to speak English has been a prerequisite for becoming a citizen of the United States. Although opponents in Congress argued that there were groups who worked hard and contributed a great deal to their communities but lacked the time or opportunity to learn English, proponents held that someone who failed to do so must "be so deficient in mental capacity . . . or so careless of the opportunities afforded to him . . . that he would not make a desirable citizen." As they were "aliens in sentiment," they should remain aliens legally as well (quoted by Crawford, 1992b, 55). This requirement continues to apply in most cases (except for those who have been legal residents of the United States for at least twenty years and are aged fifty or more) but the standard set is not forbidding: "in 1982, an average year, the Immigration and Naturalization Service turned down only twenty-nine out of 201,507 petitions for citizenship because of inability to speak, read, or write the English language" (Crawford, 1992, 196).

The American government is currently simplifying its naturalization procedures in an effort to encourage a larger proportion of "resident aliens" to make a commitment to the responsibilities as well as the rights of American citizenship. Application procedures are being simplified, and there will be a publicity campaign to encourage those eligible to apply. In recent decades, immigrants to the United States from Asia have sought citizenship at a rate three times as great as that of immigrants from the Americas. Of those who arrived in 1970, 48 percent of the Asians had been naturalized a decade later, compared with only 3 percent of those from Mexico and 20 percent of those from Central and South America. Only the Cubans (47 percent) were as prompt as the Asians to become citizens (Portes & Rumbaut, 1990, 121).

Somewhat paradoxically, under some circumstances those who possess citizenship by birth but do not understand English are guaranteed by the Voting Rights Act information and help in their own languages in exercising the vote, though this has become highly controversial. In 1984, for example, 71 percent of California voters approved a referendum question calling for voting materials in English only (Crawford, 1992, 192).

The right to vote remains tied to American citizenship, however, in contrast with several European nations where eligibility to vote in local elections is extended to legally resident foreigners. The practice seems to have started in the Swiss canton of Neufchâtel and in Sweden in 1975, and spread to Denmark in 1982, to Norway and the Netherlands in 1985, and to the German state of Hamburg in 1989 (Leca, 1992, 22).

EVOLUTION OF MIGRANT WORKFORCE INTO ETHNIC MINORITY GROUP

"A willing pair of hands also needs a roof over its head, schools for its kids, and so on" (*The Economist*, February 15, 1992, 22). The result, over time, has been the formation of ethnic minority groups in the American sense in Western Europe, heavily concentrated in cities and in the lower levels of employment and educational achievement (Hammar, 1985b; Castles, Booth, & Wallace, 1984).

In the Netherlands in 1990, 45 percent of those of Mediterranean, Surinamese and West Indian (Antillian) origin—but only 10 percent of the Dutch—lived in the four largest cities (Tesser, 1993, 39). The same pattern has emerged in Germany: by 1981, the population of Frankfurt included 145,000 foreigners, or 23 percent of the total, that of Stuttgart 106,700 (18.3 percent), and that of Munich 223,500 (17.3 percent) foreigners. Half of the babies born in Brussels and in Geneva have foreign parents. (This last case illustrates the difficulty of obtaining statistics that are comparable over time and between countries: the number of "foreign births" recorded declined after a change in law made children one of whose parents is Belgian automatically Belgian at birth, rather than limiting that as previously to children whose fathers were Belgian.)

Within cities, immigrant minority children are concentrated in certain areas, as in the United States. While they made up 10.5 percent of all elementary pupils in France, there were six regions where more than 40 percent of the pupils in "educational priority areas" (see below) were of immigrant origin (Liensol, 1992, 145).

With the halt to active recruitment of labor migrants, and family reunification as the foreign workers have settled down in the host societies, the proportion of the foreign population consisting of *workers* has declined, while that of their dependents has increased. This development has been particularly striking in Germany (Table 2.17).

One pupil in three is of foreign parentage in many cities in Western Europe; most of these children were born in the host country. In Sweden, long one of the most ethnically homogeneous nations in the world, the share

TABLE 2.17. Labor Force Participation, Turks in West Germany

	1967	1974	1984
Total	172,400	1,027,800	1,425,800
Workers	131,100	606,800	497,700
% Workers	76.0%	59.0%	34.9%

Source: Sen, 1987.

TABLE 2.18. School Enrollment Trends

	Period	Nationals	Foreigners
Belgium	1974–81	– 9.6%	+ 20.2%
France	1978–82	– 3.1%	+ 13.5%
Netherlands	1978–82	– 5.9%	+ 67.5%
West Germany	1974–81	– 9.4%	+ 95.3%

Source: Organisation for Economic Cooperation and Development, 1987, 20.

TABLE 2.19. Foreigners from Selected Nations in West Germany, 1986, by Age

	Aged 0–15	Total	% 0–15
Greeks	45,686	278,506	16.4%
Italians	73,040	537,067	13.6%
Yugoslavs	95,322	591,116	16.1%
Portuguese	12,709	78,198	16.3%
Spaniards	19,452	150,493	12.9%
Turks	322,727	1,434,256	22.5%
Total	701,325	4,512,679	15.5%

Source: *Beauftragten* . . . , 1987.

TABLE 2.20. Population of the Netherlands, 1991, by Age

	Percent 0–9 Years	Percent 10–19 Years	Percent 50+ Years
Surinamers	20%	18%	10%
Turks	24%	20%	8%
Moroccans	27%	23%	9%
West Indians	20%	17%	8%
Dutch	12%	13%	28%

Source: Tesser, 1993, 33.

TABLE 2.21. Foreigners from Selected Nations in France, 1982, by Age

	Aged 0–14	Total	% 0–14
Spain	44,320	321,440	13.8%
Poland	1,860	64,820	2.9%
Italy	33,480	333,740	10.0%
Portugal	218,620	764,860	28.6%
Algeria	254,920	795,920	32.0%
Turkey	53,420	123,540	43.2%

Source: *Migrants-Formation*, December 1986.

of elementary school enrollment made up of linguistic minority pupils grew from 1 percent in 1960 to 10 percent in 1980; it is predicted that by the year 2000 the proportion will be one pupil in three (Tingbjorn, 1988a, 86). Other nations have seen comparable changes in school populations (Table 2.18).

The decline in birth rate experienced by every Western European nation has underlined the significance of the growing population of children of foreign birth or ancestry.

Thus even as foreign workers have come to have less economic significance, their families have increased as a proportion of the clients of schools and human service agencies. This is particularly the case with certain groups; while Italian and Spanish guestworkers, as noted above, came early to Northern Europe and have in general either returned to their homeland with its increasing prosperity or have been substantially assimilated, the Turks in particular show little sign of re-migration and are rich in children. Even though they make up only around half of the foreign pupils in German schools, there is a tendency to think of the "foreigner problem" as a "problem of the Turks" (Boos-Nunning & Henscheid, 1986, 65).

The same pattern is evident in the Netherlands (Table 2.20) and France (Table 2.21).

On the other hand, the proportion of foreigners living in Germany who come from nations other than those from which guest-workers were recruited increased from 19 percent to 30 percent between 1983 and 1986 (Beauftragten . . . , 1987). Thus the approaches developed for providing services to relatively homogeneous groups of foreign families—for example, hiring interpreters who speak Turkish or Serbo-Croatian—have been placed under new strains as the diversity of foreigners has increased dramatically.

A similar process of diversification of the immigrant population—previously primarily Algerian and Portuguese—has occurred in France, where between 1980–81 and 1986–87 the number of Moroccan schoolchildren increased by 89 percent, that of Turks by 78 percent, that of Southeast Asians by 70 percent, and that of Tunisians by 56 percent. The enrollment of Algerian pupils remained constant, that of Yugoslav and Portuguese pupils fell somewhat, while that of Spanish and Italian pupils fell substantially. The total number of foreign pupils rose by 13 percent, to 1,085,342 (Liauzu, Henry-Lorcerie, and Liauzu, 1989, 70).

Inevitably, the changing population has had an especially forceful impact upon those schools located in the areas where the immigrants have settled, particularly when this has meant that they are unable to communicate effectively with many of the pupils whom they are charged with edu-

TABLE 2.22. School Enrollments of Foreigners in Selected European Countries

	Year	Primary	Secondary	Total
France	1991–2	407,100	394,400	1,080,800
		10.1%	7.3%	8.5%
Germany	1991–2	539,300	395,200	994,500
		14.0%	8.1%	11.0%
Netherlands	1990–1	106,400	46,100	160,600
		7.4%	3.8%	5.8%
Norway	1991–2	13,700	5,200	18,900
		4.5%	3.3%	4.1%
Sweden	1990–1	103,400	17,200	155,200
		11.7%	6.7%	10.4%
Switzerland	1990–1	71,900	92,400	205,300
		17.8%	16.3%	17.9%

Source: Organisation for Economic Cooperation and Development, 1994, 54. Note: totals include preschool and special education enrollments.

TABLE 2.23. Frequency of Language Use by Persons 5 Years and Over (USA)

Speak Other Language at Home

	Spanish	Other European	Asian	All Other
All the time	17.4%	5.6%	14.7%	6.7%
More often than English	28.4%	13.6%	33.2%	29.2%
About the same	21.0%	14.1%	20.8%	21.6%
Less than	21.7%	31.5%	22.6%	27.3%
Rarely	10.8%	34.2%	8.2%	14.8%

Source: McArthur, 1993, 14.

cating. In the United States, for example, the population 5 years and older speaking a language other than English at home increased by 40 percent between 1979 and 1989; Spanish speakers increased from 3.8 million to 5.2 million (65 percent) and speakers of Asian languages from 321,000 to 727,000 (98 percent) (McArthur, 1993, 12).

In Britain, a language census conducted in London schools in 1987 identified 172 spoken languages, "with 23 per cent of the school population (i.e. 64,987 children) using a language other than or in addition to English at home. . . . at least one-half of all LEAs in England and Wales have a *minimum* of one primary school with over 10 percent of pupils who are bilingual" (Craft, 1989, 136).

The fact that members of an immigrant group are able to speak a language other than that prevalent in the host society does not mean that they (much less their children) necessarily *do* speak it, of course. Here again the data from the United States is the most extensive available. Actual language use appears to vary greatly.

Nor is recent immigration the decisive factor in language use.

Among persons with reported difficulty speaking English, one-quarter were born in the 50 States or the District of Columbia. Among children 5 to 17 years old with difficulty speaking English, about three-fifths were born in the 50 States or the District of Columbia (McArthur, 1993, 17).

The presence of pupils who habitually speak a language at home which differs from that used in the school cannot fail to have an impact upon school practice. Data on the extent of this phenomenon is rather difficult to interpret. For example, a survey conducted in 1990–91 by the International Association for the Evaluation of Educational Achievement (IEA), found the United States among the lowest in proportion of pupils reporting that they sometimes, hardly ever, or never speak the school language at home and, conversely, highest in those reporting doing so always or almost always (see Table 2.24).

The higher proportions in Spain and Switzerland are accounted for by the uneven match between the distribution of territorial language minority populations and administrative areas where one language or another is used in schools (see Chapter 3); that in Italy is presumably a reflection of the continuing importance of regional dialects in that country.

What is at first glance puzzling is the low use of nonschool languages reported for the United States; after all, a very careful study by the Bureau of the Census in 1989 estimated that 2,960,900 schoolchildren aged 8 to 15 spoke a language other than English at home, representing 12.4 percent of the total cohort for whom such data is available. Several factors may have contributed to this discrepancy:

1.   The IEA study may have skipped pupils in separate bilingual programs; language minority pupils in Europe are more likely to be in integrated classrooms than are their counterparts in the United States; and

---

TABLE 2.24. Language Spoken at Home and School Language

9-Year-Olds Reporting Speaking Another Language at Home

United States	3%
Norway	4%
Denmark	5%
France	9%
Sweden	9%
Germany (western)	10%
Belgium (Wallonia)	11%
Netherlands	12%
Spain	13%
Switzerland	21%
Italy	27%

Source: Organisation for Economic Cooperation and Development, 1993, 42.

2.   The use of minority languages in American bilingual programs could have the effect that pupils reported that their home language (e.g., Spanish) was the same as their school language (e.g., Spanish); and

3.   The Bureau of the Census study may have counted all cases in which children used non-school languages at home to any extent at all, while the IEA study asked about the predominant language use. Another finding of the Bureau of the Census study was that 829,700 schoolchildren ages 8 to 15 spoke English with difficulty; this represents 3.5 percent of the total, thus approaching the IEA figure (McArthur, 1993, 24).

Other studies give a much higher proportion of schoolchildren in the United States who require and are not receiving school support through their home language. A study released in 1994, based upon the detailed "long form" filled out by a sample of the population included in the 1990 national census, reports a "language-minority school-age population" of 9.9 million, or 22 percent of the total; the rate rose to nearly 50 percent in California. The definition in this case applies to children who live in households in which one or more people speak a language other than English, even if those persons may speak English most of the time and even if the child speaks only English (Waggoner, 1994).

The discrepancy in data arises from a different set of assumptions about the level of proficiency in English at which a pupil can benefit from instruction provided exclusively through English. Some argue that the ability to speak and understand a second language is a superficial accomplishment and does not represent the basis for academic success, while others argue that it is only through being in situations in which it is necessary to use the second language that sufficient focused effort is made to develop real proficiency. For those who share the first assumption, any child from a home where a language other than English is used to any extent at all should have a school program making use of this language; for those who share the second, a basic proficiency in English is the foundation upon which the whole school program should be based.

THE RECENT POLICY RESPONSE TO IMMIGRATION

Government policy in each of the host countries has responded not only to objective economic and social realities but also to voter perception of those realities, which has more often than not been hostile or at least apprehensive about the presence of foreigners, and particularly of those considered very different culturally. Only in Australia, Canada, and the United States are influential voices raised for continuing immigration, generally on the basis of the presumed economic benefits of an eager and undemanding work force; experts point out that "under the present regime of natural increase and emigration, the U.S. population requires about a million immigrants each year in order to offset a potential population decline in the middle of the next century" (Edmonston & Passel, 1994a, 24). In Europe it is only the exceptionally farsighted who point out that an aging population—particularly in Germany—will need to be supported by more young workers than the native population is currently producing. For example,

> Of the population [of Germany] in 2030, 18% are likely to be over 60. . . . there will be many more dependents than wage-earners. These demographic changes will force big changes in many aspects of German life. . . . Germany might also let in more immigrants. That would boost the labour force. . . . In the past five years, Germany has taken in an average of 830,000 immigrants, as many proportionately as America did during its peak years of immigration in the early part of the century. This makes Germany the nearest thing Europe has to a melting pot—and a place where neo-Nazi groups and violent young people make foreigners the targets of their rage. (*The Economist*, May 21, 1994)

This phase of policy debate ended in the early seventies in northwestern Europe, when economic recession made foreign workers seem superfluous. Most countries took measures to limit immigration at the time of the oil crisis, imposing entry controls (for example, Germany—November 1973, France—July 1974, Belgium—August 1974) but allowing family members to continue to immigrate for some years more (Groenendijk, 1989). The result was to change profoundly the nature and demographic profile of immigrant communities and to increase greatly the impact upon schools. In Bavaria, for example, the number of foreign schoolchildren rose from 27,437 in 1973–74, when labor migration was restricted, to 70,378 in 1982–83, before beginning a gradual decline (Harant, 1987, 243; see also Table 2.18).

Typical of efforts to deal with this phenomenon is the report of a broad-based German commission, in 1983, calling for a three-pronged approach:

1. integration of the foreigners living among us;
2. limitation of new entry of foreigners; and
3. encouragement of return to the homelands.

Since the primary source of new immigration by that point was family reunification, it was proposed that children older than 6 (who were often left in the homeland in care of their extended families) not be allowed to join their parents, and that children of the second immigrant generation not be allowed to bring wives or husbands from the homeland (Just, 1985a, 64–65).

Public policy can thus seek to limit and even reduce the number of foreigners present in a country while at the same time seeking to turn those who will remain into "not-foreigners" through assimilation measures. To the extent to which these measures rely (as they must) upon improving the situation of the immigrant minority group, however, they will tend to make the country more attractive for additional immigrants and reduce the likelihood that any of those already present will return to their homelands or those of their immigrant forebears. This is the fundamental dilemma of public policy with respect to such groups, and no prosperous nation has found a way to seal its borders effectively against illegal immigration; even an island-nation with a highly distinctive culture like Japan is now estimated to have some 300,000 illegal foreign residents (Postel-Vinay, 1992, 269).

Different host countries have responded in rather different ways to the new ethnic diversity created by labor immigration. Sweden and the United Kingdom determined early to limit immigration strictly while assuming that those who came would stay, and thus to press for full integration. Thus while Sweden's policies toward immigrants are unusually generous, the number admitted has been carefully restricted.

Unrestricted immigration to the United Kingdom from its former colonies was limited in 1962, just as other countries of northwest Europe were vigorously recruiting foreign workers. The admission of Commonwealth immigrants of non-British ancestry, it was argued, exceeded the capacity of the British economy and (even more importantly) of British society to absorb them. In 1971 limits were placed on the admission of dependents of those legally resident in the country. More restrictive policies, intentionally discriminatory against nonwhite immigrants from the former colonies, were adopted in the early seventies and again in 1981. For example, residents of Britain whose ancestors were not originally from the country may be deported for criminal offenses. The government did not respond favorably to a proposals advanced during one of the crises over China's intentions toward Hong Kong, that the United Kingdom agree to accept up to 300,000 immigrants from Hong Kong each year, as a way of meeting its moral obligation to the residents of that soon-to-be-former colony.

> Were such a flow to materialize, it would be six times the current net rate of immigration into Britain, but rather less than the rate at which West Germany is now taking in ethnic Germans from Eastern Europe.

It can be done. . . . it would enrich Britain as much as burden it; Hongkongers have a deserved reputation for creating much out of little (*The Economist*, April 22, 1989).

Although citizens of Hong Kong are eligible for British passports, these do not give them the right to settle in the United Kingdom, and most of those seeking a safe refuge have turned instead to Canada or the United States, both of which are eager to welcome immigrants who bring skills, entrepreneurial experience, and substantial amounts of capital with them.

Germany and Switzerland have continued largely to deny that foreign workers would become permanent residents, continuing to insist upon the "rotation principle" according to which foreign workers are expected to go home after a time so their places can be filled by newcomers. Even though more than 77 percent of the resident foreigners had been in the country for more than ten years as of 1984 (Hoffmann-Nowotny, 1987, 59), Switzerland makes it very difficult for them to become citizens. The applicant must have been resident in the country for at least twelve years, and must meet a variety of requirements of language proficiency and character. Switzerland continues to be unusually dependent upon foreign (mostly Italian) workers, but they are discouraged from becoming Swiss.

Germany continues to insist officially that the foreign workers, many of whom have been in Germany for more than two decades, will be going home any day; the Federal Republic is "not an immigration country and will never become one;" that familiar mantra was repeated as recently as late 1991 by the chairman of one of the major political parties (quoted by Shain, 1993, 288). In the 1970s national authorities proclaimed a "dual strategy" of pursuing integration while keeping open the possibility of return to homelands that, for the second and even third generation, seem increasingly remote. A program was established in 1983 to provide financial incentives to re-migrate for foreign workers displaced from their jobs in Germany and for their families, with the proclaimed intention of "resolving the problem" of hastening the integration of those capable of integration (*die Integrationsfähigen*) by ejecting the "foreign elements" that were not (Hamburger, 1989). Some 38,000 adults and children took advantage of this offer over the next year, costing the German government 160 million marks or more than $7,500 for each family which left the country, 90 percent of them for Turkey (Kühl, 1987, 27).

One measure of the reluctance of the German government to regularize the situation of its foreign population is the slow pace at which official permission to stay in the country indefinitely without fear of summary expulsion (an *Aufenhaltsberechtigung*) is extended to residents from outside the European Community. By 1987, only 10 percent of the non-EC residents had received this status, though most had already lived in the country for several decades (Koekebakker, 1990, 47). This is in striking contrast with the rapid regularization of the status of some 3 million illegal residents of the United States around the same time, and it has been suggested that the slowness of Turkish immigrants, in particular, to integrate into German society is a result of the uncertainty of their status (Hamburger, 1989).

Countries that have managed to stabilize the "fluctuation rate," the proportion of all resident foreigners who come and go each year, through regularizing their legal and social status may reap benefits in the form of fewer demands upon their social services as the foreigners become economically productive immigrants. In Belgium, for example, only 8 percent of resident foreigners came or went in 1984, and 10 percent did so in Sweden, contrasted with 20 percent in Germany (Hamburger, 1989, 18).

In response to the rise of anti-immigrant sentiment, most governments have tightened their controls in recent years. In France, for example, "the number of those expelled and escorted to frontiers has been on the increase (estimated at between 7,000 and 9,000 in 1991)" (Organisation for Economic Cooperation and Development, 1993, 75). This hard line was advanced hesitantly by the Socialist governments of Michel Rocard and Édith Cresson, who said in 1991 that "France, while remaining a country that welcomes immigrants (a *terre d'accueil*), cannot open itself to all the misery of the world," and was strongly reinforced by the Center-Right government that followed in 1993 (Massenet, 1994, 32).

Border controls are of only limited effectiveness, and the Schengen agreement to remove them entirely among France, Germany, and seven other countries has made the immigration policies of individual governments in the European Union seem only as effective as the enforcement practices of its neighbors. Police are often hesitant to become involved in "razzias" to check identity papers on the street because of the potential for charges of discrimination (Groenendijk, 1989, 49), and sanctions against employers of illegal workers have not been any more effective in Europe than they have been in the United States.

Australian immigration policy may be entering a new phase in response to a lagging economy and a certain amount of unease about the "multiculturalism" that was promoted so vigorously for a time. Twenty years of heavy immigration from Asia may now be drawing to an end though it will continue at a reduced rate; the government is setting lower admission quotas and some environmentalist groups want new admissions stopped altogether (*The Economist*, May 30, 1992, 41). This development was adumbrated by a government report in 1984 which found that immigration was no longer needed for population growth or in order to supply skilled labor, and should be targeted upon business development (Hawkins, 1989, 250).

Similarly, the Canadian government announced in November 1994 that it will admit fewer legal immigrants each year. The expansion that occurred under Conservative leadership from 84,300 immigrants in 1985 to 245,800 in 1993 and a limit of 250,000 in 1994 will be scaled back to 215,000 in 1995, in part through adopting limits similar to those in the United States on the family members who can be sponsored by immigrants who have obtained legal residency (*The Boston Globe*, November 2, 1994, 2). Even before these new developments, it had become "very difficult if not impossible to be admitted to Canada or Australia . . . *unless* one had relatives (and preferably close relatives) there, or a job offer, or an occupation in very special demand, on unless one was a refugee or could successfully claim refugee status." Of those admitted to Canada in 1983, 65.7 percent came to join relatives, as did 59 percent of those admitted to Australia (Hawkins, 1989, 256–257). The current Canadian government determined to limit family immigrants to 45 percent of the total, in order to give priority to "independent applicants, chosen on a points system that gives high marks to job skills and a knowledge of French or English" (*The Economist*, November 5, 1994, 42).

American immigration policy has gone through many twists and turns. After many decades of essentially unrestricted admission, the United States imposed restrictions in 1882 excluding criminals, prostitutes, and the physically and mentally ill. "Nine years later the category of excluded undesirables was extended to take in as well believers in anarchism and in polygamy. These minimal controls reflected no disposition to check the total volume of immigration" (Handlin, 1951, 287).

An Immigration Restriction League was founded in Boston in 1894, but it was not until organized labor joined the effort that political momentum developed. In the wave of xenophobia accompanying World War I, a requirement of literacy was imposed in 1917. The expectation that this would exclude immigration by the peasants of southern and eastern Europe, while permitting continued immigration from northwestern Europe was disappointed: "peasants, who until then had had no incentive to do so, now set themselves the task of learning to read, and succeeded . . . and the proportion of Mediterranean and Balkan folk among the new arrivals proved no smaller than before" (Handlin, 1951, 291).

The phase of *qualitative* restrictions ended with the National Origins Act of 1924, placing strict *quantitative* restrictions, explicitly designed to limit immigration from the countries of origin that were considered less desirable sources of future citizens.

The Immigration and Naturalization Act Amendments of 1965 repealed the national origin quotas favoring northwestern Europe but set a limit of 20,000 immigrants a year from each nation of the Eastern Hemisphere and placed restrictions for the first time on immigration from the Western Hemisphere; in 1976 this was set at 20,000 from each country. A preference system was set up based upon family reunification and the skills that the prospective immigrant would contribute to the American economy.

The Immigration Reform and Control Act of 1986 provided for legalizing the status of foreigners in the country illegally, while imposing employer sanctions intended to discourage further illegal immigration. This program failed to halt illegal immigration to the United States: despite legalization of the status of nearly 3 million foreigners in the country illegally, representing more than 1 percent of the country's total population, the illegal flow continues. The Census Bureau currently estimates that there are 3.3 million aliens in the country illegally, "roughly the same number that were present at the time of the 1980 Census" despite the reforms of 1986 that were intended to eliminate or greatly reduce their numbers; 200,000 to 300,000 new permanent residents are added illegally to the population each year (Fix & Zimmermann, 1994, 255). Demands are now heard from all sides for better control of the country's borders. Such demands are sometimes softened by associating them with measures to improve the status of those noncitizens who are already within the country's borders, such as allowing them to vote in local elections (Miles, 1994).

The unsuccessful American experience with a strategy of regularizing the situation of illegal residents in the hope of discouraging more from coming has been matched during the 1980s in other countries, including France, Italy, and Spain (Weil, 1992, 64). They too have found that "every a posteriori regularization is accompanied by a new wave of 'clandestines'" (Leca, 1992, 19). The blue-ribbon French commission responsible for integration found that regularization "tends to encourage recourse to clandestine work" (quoted by Massenet, 1994, 136), exactly the opposite of the intention! They might indeed have learned from the long-term consequences of similar efforts in Canada in 1973, the United Kingdom in 1974, and Australia in 1980. Within less than a decade of the widely praised Canadian amnesty program, a government report found that illegal immigration was a major problem and threatened to "reach proportions that will be extremely difficult to control" (Hawkins, 1989, 48, 204–206; Crowley, 1992, 96).

The most recent comprehensive law in the United States, enacted in 1990, increased the legal immigration ceilings by 40 percent, with an emphasis upon admitting those with economically useful skills. "The United States currently admits roughly 700,000 immigrants annually as legal permanent ('green card') residents who after 5 years' continuous residence will be eligible to apply for citizenship. . . . The U.S. admits more such immigrants who are placed on this type of citizenship track than *all other countries combined*" (Fix & Passel, 1994, 11–13; emphasis added). The 1990 law tripled the quota for skilled workers, while reducing entry of family members of legal residents, and reserved 100,000 visas for wealthy immigrants who might invest and create jobs for Americans. In addition, a special provision for Irish immigrants sought to restore them to their earlier favored position among American immigrant groups (Miller, 1992, 253).

America continues to be unusually welcoming to immigrants and refugees who arrive by legal channels, contrasted with other wealthy nations, despite the impression created by the dramatic interdiction at sea of Haitian and Cuban would-be immigrants.

THE POLICY RESPONSE TO POSTWAR IMMIGRANTS

Policies in the Western industrialized democracies countries to integrate those immigrants already present (*immigrant* policy as distinct from *immigration* policy) tend to be longer on rhetoric than on substance. Each host country has taken steps to protect essential civil rights of its foreign residents, and limited political rights have been provided in a few instances (Groth, 1985, 82–111). In some cases, special provisions and even agencies and organizations have been established to address the needs of immigrants, while in other cases there is a reliance upon the existing provisions for poor and marginal native groups.

Despite the political salience of this issue in the United States, it is accurate to say that the country has no coherent immigrant policy. "Indeed, the already limited federal expenditures devoted to immigrant-related programs have been sharply reduced in recent years—even as the number of immigrants have [sic] risen steadily" (Fix & Passel, 1994, 16).

Controversy arose in California over public services to those who are in the country illegally. Proposition 187, supported by 59 percent of the voters in November 1994, denies free nonemergency health care and public education to individuals who are neither American citizens nor legally present in the country, and required every public agency to inform the immigration authorities of any applicants whom it "determines or reasonably suspects . . . [to be] an alien in the United States in violation of federal law."

The preamble to the new law includes a finding that "the People of California . . . have suffered and are suffering economic hardship caused by the presence of illegal aliens in this state" (Baylon, 1994).

American policy is in some ways the mirror image of those of Sweden and other countries with a strong social-democratic political tradition. While the United States is arguably more generous in its *immigration* policy than other countries, it has little in the way of *immigrant* policy—apart from transitional bilingual education (see Chapter 6) in schools—compared with the countries of Western Europe. Americans in general take a sink-or-swim attitude toward immigrants, while generally tolerating the presence even of those in the country illegally. Switzerland is similarly disinclined to pursue specific policies directed at the needs of immigrants:

> Not even among liberal groups that oppose discrimination against foreigners is there much support for special measures in their favor; according to the liberals, special measures would result in positive discrimination, which would conflict with the principles of laissez-faire and might also strengthen the grassroots movement against "foreignization" (Hoffmann-Nowotny, 1985, 224).

Germany has been in a state of denial about the reality that there will be no quick fix of the problems associated with the presence of several million non-Germans within its borders, that policies don't implement themselves, and that only decades of efforts in local schools and communities and indeed the passage of generations will permit the society to master the consequences of the postwar labor migration and the subsequent waves of refugees; integration has taken third place, behind the limitation of further immigration and the ejection of as many as possible of the "un-integratable" (*Integrationsunfähigen*) foreigners and their children. A focus on countering outbreaks of violence against immigrant minority groups, while essential, is no substitute for the sort of concrete measures that have been taken, for example, by the RAA (*Regionale Arbeitsstellen zur Förderung ausländischer Kinder und Jugendlicher*), a publicly funded agency whose branch offices throughout the Ruhr area and beyond work to link schools and community resources to address the needs of immigrant youth (Hofmann et al., 1993).

France and Belgium have pressed for assimilation of immigrants on the assumption that the foreigners and their children would over the course of time lose their foreignness and become citizens. Their approaches differ with respect to the extent of government intervention in social developments.

The Belgian central government is quite weak, and intermediary forces such as Catholic (in Flanders) and Socialist (in Wallonia) groups play a major part in the organization of social life; as a result, policy tends to be something that happens through the interplay of these forces rather than through central decision making as in France (Koekebakker, 1990, 39).

Immigrant policy in the Netherlands operated for several decades on the assumption that foreign workers would go home—"The Netherlands are not an immigration country," the government proclaimed in 1970 and again in 1974 (Entzinger, 1984, 79, 87)—though even the halt to recruitment of workers in the early 1970s did not close the borders successfully; the 84,000 immigrants who arrived in 1991 topped any previous year (Tesser, 1993, 25). Even after their permanence was conceded in the early eighties, public policy hesitated to press for assimilation and talked of the country as a "multicultural society"; the acculturation process should involve mutual accommodation, based upon the assumption that foreign workers had become *de facto* immigrants and would remain. Little has been done to make this a reality, however, and indeed it is difficult to see what public policies would bring about such fundamental social change that minority cultures would have equal standing with that of the majority (Jong, 1987). It is true, on the other hand, that Dutch institutional life is already in many respects pluralistic along religious lines, and Islamic and Hindu parents have been able to obtain public funding for their own schools.

Another characteristic of Dutch policy is its heavy reliance upon social service directed to its foreign population; one comparative study comments that the Netherlands is "without a doubt the country with the highest concentration of social workers, development workers, sociologists, and adult educators" (Koekebakker, 1990, 77). This parallels the Italian government's decision in 1990 to meet the immigrant challenge by adding 200 social workers, a thousand police officers, and a hundred sociologists and psychologists (Rellini, 1992, 186). One imagines that the immigrants might prefer to have jobs for themselves!

The last dozen years have also seen a plethora of government reports and policy statements—"if this is what the immigrants needed, the Netherlands would leave all other countries, including Sweden, behind" (Koekemakker, 1990, 82)—but their impact has been quite limited. Recently the strategy, announced a decade ago, to provide public support to the maintenance of cultural diversity through supporting ethnic organizations, has been criticized as not having done enough to achieve equal outcomes in education and the labor market, and there are calls for more emphasis upon what should be expected of the minority-group members themselves (Rogers, 1993, 130).

Schools are of course an important—perhaps the *most* important—instrument of public policy to achieve the integration of immigrant minority groups into the host society. While specific school programs will be discussed in Chapter 7, it is appropriate to note here the efforts of several countries with large numbers of under-achieving immigrant pupils to create coordinated programs to meet the needs of these students and turn their failure into success. Unfortunately, the programs themselves have by no means been clearly successful.

In the early 1970s the United Kingdom implemented a program for "educational priority areas," which were identified on the basis of a variety of indicators of social distress among which was the presence of children unable to speak English. During the 1980s funding was also made available under the so-called "Section 11" for language support services and antiracism efforts in communities (and especially in schools) with a high proportion of immigrant minority children (Layton-Henry, 1985). In 1991 the emphasis was changed from multiculturalism and teaching of the home languages of immigrant groups to programs to teach English as a second language.

The Dutch variant on this strategy has been the so-called Educational Priority Policy (*Onderwijsvoorrangsbeleid* or OVB) with two primary elements: provision of extra staff to schools with high numbers of disadvantaged pupils, and designation of geographical (mostly inner-city) priority areas where schools and other agencies are encouraged and funded to collaborate. Under the first program, "pupils regarded as deprived are weighted more heavily than average pupils (their value is thus greater than one: the system used is 1.25 for Dutch working class children, 1.4 for the children of barge operators, 1.7 for children living in mobile homes and 1.9 for children from ethnic minorities)" (Social and Cultural Planning Office, 1993, 226).

Two criticisms of this approach have been voiced. The first is that it makes an incorrect assumption that ethnicity may be equated with educational disadvantage. The recent policy document *Ceders in de tuin* (1992) insisted that only social class factors should be considered relevant in allocating extra assistance, while some researchers are equally sure that ethnic minority status has an effect independent of the social class position of parents as measured by their education or employment.

The other criticism is parallel to that of compensatory education funding under Chapter 1 in the United States: that the funds are spread among too many schools to have a serious impact where it is most needed. With almost half of all elementary-level pupils assigned a supplemental funding weight, the additional funds have come to be seen as part of the regular support of schools rather than as a resource with which to enable schools to function altogether differently and more powerfully for poor children.

The program of designated priority areas (there are 70 altogether) has managed to involve some 1,450 schools and over 500 social agencies in collaborative arrangements, though with disappointing results as measured by academic achievement. Pupils'

> performance would appear to be worse than that of comparable pupils outside such areas. However, after correction for social background, this difference largely disappears, although 1.25-category pupils still perform worse in the target-area schools. This may be the result of the negative impact of a high concentration of 1.9-category pupils at these schools (Social and Cultural Planning Office, 1993, 227).

This would seem to be a confirmation of the negative effects of racial/ethnic segregation upon academic achievement.

France has for a number of years implemented a similar program of concentration of resources in designated Educational Priority Zones (*Zones d'éducation prioritaires* or ZEPs). Established by Socialist Minister of Education Alain Savary in 1981, they were put on the back burner during several years of conservative government later in the decade, and revived in 1988 despite results that were no better than modest. At present there are 554 priority zones (including a few abroad in French possessions), representing 12.6 percent of the elementary school pupils, 15.1 percent of those in middle schools, 9.2 percent of those in vocational high schools and 2 percent of those in academic high schools (Liensol, 1992, 10).

Education and other agencies in target areas were encouraged to work together, and additional funding was provided in support of supplemental services, though critics have noted that these did not involve fundamental changes: "a few hours of extra reading help or homework assistance (though the assignments were not changed)" (Zakhartchouk, 1992, 13). The stress upon school teams that would develop and then implement coherent educational strategies too often came to grief on the bureaucratic procedures that reassigned teachers without regard to the necessary stability of the school's program (George, 1992, 14). Pupil:teacher ratios are very slightly better in ZEPs than elsewhere, as is the rate at which 2-year-old children attend preschool programs; pupils in ZEPs on average receive somewhat more instructional time than do others. Beyond such input indicators, there seems little hard evidence that this strategy has produced results for the most at-risk pupils, though national averages conceal the better results in the zones of the Paris region compared with those in the south of France (Liensol, 1992, 63).

The original selection of some 400 ZEPs relied heavily upon data on the distribution of immigrant pupils as an indicator of potential educational difficulties. This approach rested on assumptions about the difficulty of adjustment:

> The early eighties were inclined that way: the advocates who, at the end of the sixties, had drawn attention to the presence of immigrants in the educational system had succeeded too well in ten years: the concern to take into account intercultural realities had been replaced by an excessive polarization of the differences (Bourgarel, 1992, 24).

This emphasis on immigrant pupils as a problem was less marked when the program was relaunched at the end of the decade. Many of those on the Left who had earlier stressed the distinctiveness of immigrants and their cultures became alarmed when the controversy over whether Muslim girls should be allowed to cover their heads in school revealed the essentially religious nature of that distinctiveness; suddenly they wanted "to wrap the children in the tricolor flag and demanded 'schools where no one is a foreigner'" (Bourgarel, 1992, 24).

In general, programs of government intervention in support of improvement of schools in areas where there are many pupils in risk of failure have not been so explicitly targeted to immigrant minority children in the United States as they have been in France and the Netherlands, apart from those programs concerned with language acquisition which will be discussed in subsequent chapters. This is largely the consequence of the fact that the largest of these programs, Title I (now Chapter I) of the Elementary and Secondary Education Act of 1965 was established with other high-need populations in mind: primarily, black pupils in urban and rural areas and white pupils in rural areas. Criteria for selection of schools and communities eligible for these programs were tied directly to income, and eligibility for services was tied to performance on standardized test scores, not to home language or immigrant status. As we have seen, it was that same year that immigration quotas were greatly relaxed, but the effect of this change on schools was not felt for several years. When it was, bilingual education programs were the response at federal and state levels.

An exception at the federal level was the Emergency Immigrant Education Act, which for a time provided about $60 for each immigrant pupil enrolled in certain school districts—1 to 2 percent of typical per-pupil expenditure. The intention was to provide some general support (as distinguished from support tied to particular activities) for school districts experiencing a heavy influx of immigrants; the funding level had been decreasing rather than increasing since 1985, but increased to $50 million in the federal budget for FY 1995 (*Education Week*, October 19, 1994, 18). Unlike the French and Dutch programs, this makes no claim to coordinate a variety of powerful interventions in support of the schooling of immigrant minority children.

Although under American law immigration is under the exclusive control of the federal government, it is largely up to the states to decide what they will do to support immigrants, and especially the schooling of their children. Massachusetts, for example, enacted the Gateway Cities Program in 1986 for areas particularly hard-hit by immigration, and included funding for the schooling of immigrant children. The education funding, administered during its brief career by the author, was provided as general assistance to schools that were forced to add staff because of a sudden influx of children; no claim was made that fundamental changes would occur in the direction or quality of the schooling provided.

Each of the Western democracies has employed a variety of strategies to seek to promote the transition of the children of immigrants into its educational system on an equal basis with native children and, in most cases, other strategies (sometimes in tension with the first) that seek to maintain and build upon the ways they differ from native children. As we will see, these strategies have in almost all cases defined the difficulties faced by immigrant minority children in terms of the languages they do or do not speak, and have in all cases attracted criticism as misguided or ineffective (sometimes as both).

Before turning to the specific programs, however, we must consider the experiences and the hopes of the immigrants, refugees, and migrant workers themselves for their children and for their own relationship with the host society, in Chapter 4. This will be placed in the context of the situation of indigenous language minority groups in these countries, described in Chapter 3.

3 Indigenous Language Minority Groups

The situation of immigrant language minority groups is affected not only by public policies toward immigration and toward immigrants, and by the historical circumstances of their presence in the host country (Chapter 2), but also by pre-existing assumptions about the significance of language and cultural diversity. These assumptions are based in large part upon how the society has dealt with the presence, in its midst, of language minority groups who are *not* immigrants but have a claim to belonging which is equal if not superior to that of the majority. The situation of Moroccan immigrants to Belgium cannot be understood apart from the history of conflict and precarious settlements over the use of French and Dutch, nor can policies toward immigrants to Canada be understood apart from the tensions between English- and French-speaking Canadians.

Such native language minority groups are found in most of the Western democracies—and indeed in other countries as well, with rare exceptions like Iceland. Even though the distribution of speakers of a common language has frequently been the basis for defining the territorial extent of a nation-in-the-making, there are few nations of any size that do not include indigenous language minority groups concentrated (though not always representing the majority of inhabitants) in areas with which their language has traditionally been associated. In some cases they are the remnants of indigenous conquered peoples, like the Welsh, Bretons, and Basques in Western Europe. In other cases, they are groups whose minority status is the result of the untidy process of nation-building and frontier-drawing, like French-speakers in Switzerland, German-speakers in Alsace, and Danish-speakers in Germany. The European Union recognizes 34 "minority languages" that are spoken by about 40 million of its 320 million inhabitants (*Times Educational Supplement*, May 6, 1988).

The maintenance of minority languages may be supported by cross-border contacts, as in the case of the languages of Switzerland. "If French were a language spoken only in one region of Canada, its fate would be sealed, and the same would apply to the language of New York's Puerto Ricans if Spanish were restricted to Puerto Rico" (Siguán & Mackey, 1987, 36).

A special case is represented by those indigenous groups not only linguistically and culturally distinct but also socially marginalized by their relatively brief contact with modernity as well as by the actions and attitudes of the majority, such as Native North Americans (Indians, Eskimos, Hawaiians), Maori in New Zealand, Australian native peoples, Lapps in Scandinavia, and, in a rather different sense, Romany (Gypsy) peoples in much of Europe. The situations of these peoples present complex issues that go well beyond the scope of this study, and will not—apart from a brief overview at the end of this chapter—be considered in any detail.

Speakers of indigenous minority languages are almost invariably able to speak and understand the "national" language, but choose to be bilingual, maintaining the language of their group as well. Continuing to use Frisian in the province of Friesland is essentially a free choice, supported by public recognition and schooling, but virtually everyone can (also) speak Dutch (Jonkman, 1991). Exceptional are those cases—Belgium, Canada, and Switzerland are the most notable examples—in which bilingualism is not necessary and may even be discouraged, since different languages have official status in distinct sections of the country.

In the emergence of nation-states in Central Europe and the Balkans, and more recently in the former Soviet Union, language has frequently served as the basis for defining who is and who is not a member of the nation. Throughout the nineteenth century, the gradual unification of Germany and the struggle for independence by Greeks and Czechs, by Irishmen and Poles, by Hungarians and Finns, from the multinational empires which ruled them were accompanied in every case by a strong emphasis upon a distinctive language. Frequently this entailed transforming a language that had been used primarily by peasants into a vehicle for literature and for political discussion.

> In the last decades of the nineteenth century, the previously limited vocabulary of Estonian expanded to include new political, social, and cultural terms. Yet many abstract concepts were still lacking in the language, and there was not yet agreement on a single system of grammar (Raun, 1987, 77).

It was characteristically the members of the intelligentsia—schoolteachers, clergymen, lawyers and political activists—who undertook these efforts, despite their own success in obtaining education through the dominant language. The purpose of reviving the "national" language was political and symbolic. It was to communicate ideas and to evoke emotions, not primarily to transact the daily business of life. The people would be mobilized to a sense of nationhood and a demand for autonomy if not independence by a stress upon what distinguished them from other subjects of the empire—their language.

> In 1879 the Society for the Spread of Literacy Among Georgians was founded bu Iakob Gogebashvili (1840–1912), a tireless campaigner for education in Georgian and the author of the widely used textbook *deda ena* (Mother Tongue). . . . The dissemination of Georgian national feeling by the patriotic intelligentsia in the last third of the nineteenth century paralleled developments among the Armenians (Suny, 1988, 133).

The massive redrawing of the map of Europe in the early twentieth century, consequent upon the dissolution of the Ottoman, Tsarist, and Austro-Hungarian empires, took language as the primary signifier of group identity and thus of national boundaries. More recently, the discrediting of the Nazi ideology of *race* has led to a "culturalist" emphasis upon language as the marker of distinctiveness, of who is part of the group and who is not (Todorov, 1993, 153).

> When circumstances induce Europeans to shift from the genetic concept of nation [based upon putative common descent], they do not usually take over the American (and, in spite of the differences, also the Soviet) concept of an entity shaped by political faith. They speak rather of a *cultural* heritage, and perhaps the most frequent symbol of a supposed common descent is a common language (Petersen, 1975, 178).

The relationship between nationality and language has taken rather different forms. "Germany" was a way of describing the area in which the German language was spoken long before its hundreds of states became a single political entity, and it was possible for Fichte and others to make an appeal "to the German nation" against French hegemony, though no such nation existed in our present sense (Fichte, 1922). Italy was the area where Italian was spoken long before it was united into a nation-state. Poland continued as an idea even after the nation had been divided among three neighboring empires.

By contrast, the United States was never defined as the area in North America where English was spoken. Of course, it was no historical accident that the original thirteen states shared a language, and made an effort to bring English-speaking Upper Canada into the confederation. The common use of English was a factor in the particular course of events in the founding of this nation, but it was not the defining characteristic: after all, the War of Independence was fought against England.

In many cases, one of the first measures taken by a nation upon attaining independence has been to seek to standardize its "national language" as a sign of separation from that of the previously dominating power. Noah Webster predicted, in 1789, that "a future separation of the American tongue from the English [was] necessary and unavoidable. . . . These causes will produce, in a course of time, a language in North America as different from the future language of England, as the modern Dutch, Danish and Swedish are from the German, or from one another" (Webster, 1992, 35). He insisted that

> a national language is a bond of national union. Every effort should be employed to render the people of this country national; to call their attachments home to their own country; and to inspire them with the pride of national character (quoted by Kohn, 1967, 305).

Similarly, the administrative separation of Norway from Denmark in 1807 was followed by the definition of a distinctive Norwegian language; more recently, Greenlandish has replaced Danish as the official language of Greenland.

This close association of language with nationality creates inevitable tensions around indigenous language minority groups within modern nation-states. After all,

> nationalism is not merely a state of mind, but a political movement highlighting particular aspects of group life. As a movement it creates a new kind of political community, preoccupied with a common cultural heritage, especially in terms of language. It is quite possible for two nationalisms to clash within the boundaries of a single state, and indeed for two nationalisms to overlap, as has recently happened in Canada, where the all-Canadian nationalism asserting the unity of Canada has been rivaled by the separatist nationalism of the French Canadians. . . . even though a nation may be constituted and defined

without reference to the unity of language, nationalism feeds upon the desire and need of people to communicate with each other in their "own" language (Friedrich, 1970, 163–64).

National Minorities in Western Europe

As the nations of Europe took shape in the postmedieval period, they incorporated areas in which both regional dialects and distinct languages were spoken. Use of Latin as the common language of civil as well as ecclesiastical administration made it possible to ignore the variations in common speech, even after the gradual emergence of "high" national languages—generally the dialectical variation of the area of political supremacy. The national center communicated with its peripheries only through the tax collector and the army recruiter, and had no need for linguistic uniformity.

It was the spread of universal elementary schooling as an instrument of state policy that began the destruction of most local languages and dialects; concern about national unity led to the use of schooling to standardize language use.

> Unlike the other forms of state action at the village level, the extension of popular education was an attempt not to take something from the people (their money and their sons) but to *affect* the people, to make them different, to carry out a program of social change. It was at once more benevolent and more deeply intrusive. Guizot expressed this perfectly when he wrote that "the great problem of modern societies is the government of minds" (Glenn, 1988b, 36).

Other nations have set out to revive, for all purposes of civic and economic life, languages that were approaching extinction or were used only for religious purposes and to make them symbols and unifying vehicles of national life. The most successful example of such policies, of course, is the revival of Hebrew in Israel; Ireland's efforts, though persistent, have not been able to achieve widespread use of Irish in the face of a general preference for the use of English. While (as we will see) the language of the Irish-speaking minority in Ireland was given official status and strong government support as the national language, other minority languages in Western societies have depended for their preservation largely upon the enthusiasm of cultural activists or—in some cases—upon the physical or cultural isolation of those who speak them. The Amish in Pennsylvania are an example of a group that preserved a minority language through deliberate isolation, and used that language to reinforce the isolation. Compulsory schooling in the language of the wider sosciety can be a fundamental threat to groups that depend for their continuing existence upon maintaining cultural distance from the majority.

Such groups, generally identified with (often rural) geographical areas and border regions, have been accommodated to a varying degree in tax-funded schools and other aspects of public life (Héraud, 1982). Thus inter-governmental agreements permit the Danish-speaking minority in West Germany and the German-speaking minority in Denmark to operate their own private bilingual schools with government funding (Byram, 1988; Boos-Nünning, 1981). Cross-border consultations between provincial authorities in the northwest of France and the southwest of Belgium turn naturally to increasing efforts to support the home languages of children who are on the "wrong" side of the border (*De Standaard*, September 18/19, 1993).

The European Parliament approved, in October 1987, a resolution to promote the "lesser-used languages" of its member states through allowing their use for education (Gorter, 1991, 57). Some of these are the languages spoken by population groups on the wrong side of a national border, such as the Danes of Germany and the Germans of Denmark, Belgium, France, and Italy, the Flemish/Dutch speakers of northern France, the French-speakers of northwestern Italy, and the speakers of Croatian and Slovenian in northeastern Italy. Their situation is relatively simple, since they can draw upon the publications and the educational resources of a neighboring nation where their language has official status.

Other lesser-used languages have no national basis, but are spoken regionally and in most cases by bilingual speakers of the national language as well; thus their situation can be precarious. Examples include North Frisian in Germany, Occitan in France and Italy, Friulian and Ladin in Italy, and Cornish in England. Bilingualism in these cases is sustained more by sentiment than by practical usefulness, and succeeding generations tend to abandon the use of the regional language.

In some cases, however, there are substantial efforts to revive and maintain these regional languages, often in connection with assertion of a measure of political autonomy. Thus Frisian in the Netherlands and Galician in Spain enjoy support in schools and in public administration. Appel concluded that "Frisian-Dutch bilingual education (with Frisian as an obligatory subject, and with the possibility of using Frisian as the language of instruction throughout primary school) is commonly accepted because the Frisians do not cause sociopolitical problems" (Appel, 1988, 62).

We will begin by reviewing the language diversity of some of the Western European countries where minority languages enjoy a degree of support by native citizens who are otherwise well integrated into the society, before turning to situations of more uneven status in the United States and elsewhere.

Celtic Revivals

The partial revival of Irish is a good example of the symbolic significance of a language with very limited practical usefulness, and its employment as a symbol around which a variety of cultural and political demands were organized.

> The Irish language had been in rapid decline since the late eighteenth century and there was great popular demand for schooling in Ireland both before and after 1831 [when a national system of elementary schooling was initiated] partly because so many Irish speaking parents wished their children to learn English. Only 13 per cent of the cohort born 1861–1871 acquired Irish. Native Irish speakers were preponderantly Catholic but cultivation of the language was not an objective of the Catholic-ethnic Irish nationalism of the early and middle nineteenth centuries (Comerford, 1991, 23).

Although the system of elementary education set up under British rule used only English for instruction, the abandonment of Irish took place at least as much outside of the schoolhouse, where "the Gaels deliberately flung that instrument of beauty and precision from them" (quoted by Edwards, 1988, 207).

With the founding of the Gaelic League in 1893—based in urban middle-class circles, not in the rural areas of the West where Irish was still widely spoken—and the growing political agitation for Home Rule and then for independence, the demand for instruction in Irish in schools grew significantly. This was, it should be noted, Irish for English speakers of Irish descent, not primarily an effort to serve more adequately the Irish speakers of Galway or the Arran Islands. By 1912 more than 2,500 schools (31 percent of the total) were teaching Irish, and that decade more than 60 percent of those taking the secondary-level examinations included Irish among their subjects, up from 5 percent before 1900. In 1913 Irish became a required subject for matriculation in the National University (Comerford, 1991, 25).

This remarkable revival of Irish learned as essentially a luxury good by those educated through English was an important aspect of creating a national identity distinct from that of the United Kingdom, and was thus a prelude to the independence won in 1921. As a recent report by the official body charged with promoting the use of Irish described the process,

> The revitalization came after a long period of cultural assimilation during which expressions of Irishness were aggressively subjugated by the imperial power. The movement had profound and long-term effects. It reversed cultural and psychological demoralisation, and released and refocussed the energies of many Irish people towards the creation of a new, more egalitarian, and self-confident society (An Coiste Comhairleach Pleanála, 1988, xvi).

The new nation of Eire (the name itself is a rejection of the English name for the island) made Irish its official language and a required subject in schools. "Infants' classes, for example, were to be conducted entirely through Irish, even though this would be an unknown language for the over-whelming majority" (John Edwards, 1984, 286). With independence won, however, the enthusiasm for the Irish language began to fade. Although still a required subject of study in all grades of elementary and secondary education, there were widespread signs of resentment.

> A survey of teachers . . . in 1941 reported that a majority of teachers who responded felt that pupils received considerably less benefit from instruction through Irish as compared to instruction through English. . . . [in a 1975 survey] almost 80% of the population felt that many children failed their exams because of Irish and 66% felt that most children resented having to learn Irish. 60% considered that children doing subjects through Irish did not do as well in school as those doing them through English. Widely-held attitudes such as these undoubtedly contributed to the gradual decline in the number of Irish medium schools in English-speaking areas. From a peak of almost 300 in the late 1930s, the number of these schools has fallen to only 18 in the present day (Cummins, 1978, 275).

There does appear to be evidence that the effort to make the entire population bilingual has had negative effects upon academic achievement. A study by Macnamara in 1966 found that

> Native speakers of English in Ireland who have spent 42 percent of their school time learning Irish do not achieve the same standard in written English as British children who have not learned a second lan-

guage. . . . Neither do they achieve the same standard in written Irish as native speakers of Irish. . . . This massive retardation in the development of literacy skills indicates the ineffectiveness of this type of bilingual strategy. For the majority of children and parents in Ireland the teaching of literacy in an L2 was not their positive choice. It was decreed from a remote government (Downing, 1978, 334).

Even more serious for the future of the language, the use of Irish in social and economic life was and is very limited; "only about a quarter if those who once used Irish regularly in their childhood home, now use it to the same extent in their current homes" (Harris, 1991, 88). A language that was spoken by 4 million people in 1800 was spoken by only 300,000 in the year that independence was won (Inglehart and Woodward, 1992, 421n). Its popularity for political reasons did not outlive the independence struggle, however, and

the meanings assigned to the language in the nationalist rhetoric, before and after the establishment of the state, no longer carry the same power to mobilize public action. . . . [There is] a widening gap between the symbolic significance attached to Irish as an official emblem of national identity, and its use as a richly expressive vernacular in everyday life. Many people have learnt to associate Irish with feelings of guilt that they do not speak what national elites told them was their own mother tongue. . . . Irish today, as one hundred years ago, appears to be in serious danger of disappearing as a community language (An Coiste Comhairleach Pleanála, 1988, xvi–xviii).

A survey in 1973 found that in only 3 percent of the homes of respondents was there somebody who used Irish "always" or "often"; 4 percent reported that they used the language often at work, and 10 percent used it sometimes.

There are two aspects to the failure of Irish to become a commonly-used language, despite persistent government efforts to support it, to such an extent that in 1989 the European Community Court of Justice heard a discrimination claim by a Dutch art teacher working in Ireland who was denied a permanent job because she had not learned Irish, even though she did not need to use the language in her teaching (Walshe, 1989). The areas in the West of Ireland where Irish has been dominant are increasingly penetrated by English with the progress of industrialization and attention to the electronic media.

Increased in-migration as a result of greater economic opportunities in Gaeltacht areas clearly constrains the maintenance and transmission of Irish. However, economic change may also affect Irish usage more directly, through the introduction of new contexts, and new power and status relationships, in which Irish is perceived as being less appropriate than English. . . . A product based on local resources, such as fish, could presumably be accommodated into the local language more easily than one that is new and foreign. In a plant producing ophthalmic lenses, it was found that, despite the fact that the workforce was proficient in Irish, numerous English words were being used in describing activity in the factory (An Coiste Comhairleach Pleanála, 1988, 6)

With the winning of independence, the use of Irish no longer has a clear political significance, nor is it a marker for social class, since "no social class has emerged in Ireland which uses primarily Irish rather than English, or where the use of one language as against another is a central element in the processes of class formation and class closure. (In a class context, it is differences in the version of English spoken which seem to be emerging as salient. . . .)" (An Coiste Comhairleach Pleanála, 1988, 37.) While knowledge of Irish continues to be important for government employment, the growth in the labor market over recent decades has been in the private sector and thus "during a period of rapid change in the class structure of Irish society, it has provided no new status advantages to the new middle classes that have emerged" (An Coiste Comhairleach Pleanála, 1988, 37).

What commitment to the use of Irish remains, a 1987 study found, appears largely to be among the well-educated (and thus highly proficient

TABLE 3.1. Commitment to Using Irish

% "committed to using as much Irish as I can"

Socioeconomic Group	State Sector	Private Sector
Professional/Managerial	43	24
Farmers	—	4-7*
Salaried & Self-employed	31	13
Skilled Manual	21	11
Semi-skilled	—	4
Unskilled	—	5

Source: An Coiste Comhairleach Pleanála, n.d., 74.
  *Depending on size of farm

in English), especially those in public employment (see Table 3.1).

Such expressions of commitment must be treated with caution; a 1975 study found that "even in the designated Irish sections of Departments, Irish was rarely, if ever, spoken in the course of the work" (An Coiste Comhairleach Pleanála, 1988, 37).

Although political support continues to exist for requiring the study of Irish throughout the educational system, the lack of broad societal support for its actual use suggests that this is an increasingly futile gesture. Many schools use the language only in music or physical education classes; "one national survey of fifth- and sixth-grade teachers in all types of primary schools showed that an average of 5.6 hours per week was spent on the formal teaching of Irish, about 45 per cent of that on conversational or spoken Irish" (Harris, 1991, 89). Two or three percent of the elementary pupils are in all-Irish schools, but even these

> schools, by themselves, cannot significantly advance a bilingual society, except within the context of a highly visible policy, which adopts a comprehensive approach to language use within society as a whole. It is not practical to continue expecting schools to strive to inculcate high levels of competence in pupils in a language that has little visible presence, functions or advantages in the society in which they live (An Coiste Comhairleach Pleanála, 1988, 37, 34, 71, 99, 104).

Teachers, expected to play the major part in reviving a language that few of their pupils were motivated to speak, grew discouraged, as one of them put it, "flogging a dead horse while the experts debate whether another whip might not revive him" (quoted by Edwards, 1988, 207).

To reverse this pattern of the declining significance of the Irish language would require public policy measures of positive discrimination toward the use of Irish, seen as an essential "ideological resource," in all sectors of society (An Coiste Comhairleach Pleanála, 1986, x). There is no reason to believe that these efforts will be successful. The ever lessening commitment to use of the Irish language in daily life has led one observer to comment that "it is possible that had Ireland remained in the Union [with Great Britain], the Gaelic language would have fared better. At any rate, considerably more people now speak Welsh daily . . . than speak Irish Gaelic" (Wheatcroft, 84).

The partial revival of Welsh (like that of Irish in the period just before independence) is indeed an illustration of the triumph of the symbolic uses of a minority language over the lack of need for it as a means of communication. This revival has occurred in conjunction with a growing demand for a measure of cultural and political autonomy, and has succeeded in bringing Welsh back from the brink of extinction as a living language in most parts of Wales, to become a required supplemental language for pupils who are expected to remain dominant in English. This has represented a dramatic reversal of developments in the last century, when general opinion was that Welsh was a useless anachronism and in no way essential to the maintenance of Welsh national identity; that, indeed, its continued use helped to maintain social stratification because, as an official commission reported in 1847, it isolated "the masses" from the "upper portions of society," keeping them "under hatches" (quoted by Edwards & Redfern, 1992, 7). With growing social mobility, English gained ground and eventually became the predominant language in all but the most isolated areas.

> In-migration to the south Wales coalfield and ports meant that already, by the first language census of 1891, only 54 per cent of the inhabitants of Wales were Welsh speaking. . . . Welsh speaking parents were ceasing to speak Welsh to their children (Okey, 1991, 51–52).

The partial revival of Welsh through schooling has roots in a popular cultural movement with a stress upon music and poetry. A private Welsh-medium elementary school was established in 1939, and after the war Welsh was increasingly introduced into public schools (Dodson & Thomas, 1988, 468). More recently the revival of the Welsh language has been the focus of deliberate official government policy, with the schools playing the major part; the language is being gradually mandated as part of the national curriculum in Wales. Since the new curriculum is already, by most accounts, over-crowded with subjects to be covered, there is an interest in teaching as many subjects as possible through Welsh rather than having to offer it as a separate subject at the secondary level; "the idea is that three subjects can be accommodated in a slot designed for two." Efforts are thus under way to train both veteran and novice teachers to teach physics or French through the medium of Welsh (Croall, 1993b, 34). An assessment in 1990 estimated that only 800 of the 14,600 secondary teachers in Wales were then teaching in Welsh; an additional 1,500 would be needed (Griffiths, 1990a, 1991).

It is reported that the stress level of teachers in Wales is higher than that in other parts of the United Kingdom, in part because of the new language requirements. Even some of the teachers who themselves speak Welsh are concerned that "having undertaken their own education in English, their grasp of Welsh was not sufficiently sophisticated to impart relatively complex pieces of information to a class of pupils" (Griffiths, 1989, 18). There are continuing uncertainties about what a "sufficient command of Welsh" would consist of (Smith, 1987). Others are very concerned with efforts by the Welsh-language teachers' union to persuade authorities to require that all teachers who do not speak the language be required to learn it as a condition of continuing employment (Smith, 1987), and the National Union of Teachers called for peripatetic teachers of Welsh so that others would not have to learn the language (Miller, 1990).

Each local education authority is required to designate some schools as Welsh-medium and others as English-medium with Welsh taught as a required language, and the testing programs mandated under the Education Reform Act of 1988 will include, in Wales, assessment of proficiency in Welsh (Thomas, 1991, 46). Some 450 elementary schools (nearly half the total) now teach primarily through Welsh; by contrast, only one secondary school in six instructs primarily through Welsh, as a result of the more crowded secondary curriculum. Problems arise in small rural communities with only one school, and one teachers' association called for allowing Welsh-medium schools to refuse to admit local pupils who do not speak Welsh, in order to preserve the character of the school (Smith, 1988a).

Among those aged 3 to 15 resident in Wales (many of whom are not of Welsh ancestry), 24 percent reportedly can now speak Welsh, contrasted with 18 percent a decade ago (Croall, 1993a, 2). The goal of the national curriculum is that all pupils in Wales, including the majority from English-speaking homes, will acquire a "substantial degree of fluency" in Welsh by the end of compulsory schooling (Smith, 1988b, 13). Doubt was cast on whether such efforts will actually result in a revival of the language, however, by a recent study finding that, of former pupils in one of the first schools to stress Welsh-language instruction, "60 per cent rarely or never spoke the language once they left the classroom" and only 8 per cent now speak it frequently. On the other hand, 55 per cent said that they would want their own children to learn Welsh (Heath, 1993, 8).

Local education authorities, in setting up programs that use Welsh as a language of instruction, have been influenced by demands from parents, including some who do not themselves speak Welsh, as well as from language advocates; many seem to agree, in the current Welsh slogan, that "a nation without a language is a nation without a heart" (*Cenedl heb iaith, Cenedl heb galon*). One Welsh head-teacher commented that "there are Welsh-medium schools, at both primary and secondary levels, where over 90% of the pupils come from homes where the language is not spoken" (quoted by Baker, 1993a, 22). Thus, the battle in favour [of Welsh-medium schooling] has now shifted to the more anglicised, urban areas. . . . some parents have been campaigning for six years for more such schools. In Swansea, the two Welsh-medium primary schools are overflowing, with some children being taught in the corridor while others are refused a place (Croall, 1993a, 3).

The partial revival of Welsh is attributed, by one expert, to "the general growth of consciousness about the virtues of preserving an indigenous language and culture. Such growth cannot be viewed in simple, functional terms" (Baker, 1993a, 9). The principal of one of the first schools to seek to revive Welsh as a language of instruction insisted that "there is a spiritual importance to the creation of a national identity" (Heath, 1993, 8). Certainly the Welsh language has minimal usefulness for economic purposes (except for those who become teachers of the language or involved in other ways with its promotion), but it serves as a rallying point. It is a way, even for those who have moved to Wales from England, to assert distinctiveness; learning a bit of the language can be an ethnic marker, even for those who are not Welsh by descent. This includes, according to a report from Cardiff, a number of Afro-Caribbean and Indian parents who have enrolled their children in Welsh-medium nursery schools (Smith, 1991).

On the other hand, many English-speaking parents in Wales are not so enthusiastic about their children being taught a language for which they see no utility; others do not object to the Welsh-language lessons, but want all other subjects taught through English. They object to what they describe as "the minority militant section of the community" persuading education authorities to teach every pupil through Welsh in some areas (Griffiths, 1989, 18). There is indeed a certain irony in the fact that the arguments advanced several decades ago against providing the schooling of Welsh-speaking children exclusively through English have apparently been forgotten now that the tables have been turned (Dodson & Thomas, 1988, 468). An organization called Education First is demanding that pupils be provided transportation to an English-medium school if the parents object to an assignment to the local Welsh-medium school. A spokesman argued that

choice does not necessarily negate the aspirations of the language revivalists. Denying choice, however, has alienated people and spawned dissent. Most parents support their children learning Welsh. They do not agree with the method of enforced instruction [in Welsh for the first two years of schooling] for English first-language children (Prestage, 1991).

Parents of one school voted to opt out of the local education authority and become a nationally funded grant-maintained school after a "bitter dispute with Welsh language activists," in order to gain control over language use in instruction (Prestage, 1992, 1993). Others have turned to private schools as an alternative to instruction through Welsh, insisting that language politics should not be allowed to interfere with education. Education officials in Gwynedd, the first county to introduce a fully bilingual policy in its schools, in 1975, point out that their pupils have the best examination results in Wales and insist that

> It is a question of what we call *ewyllys*. If the children have the will they will become bilingual and will suffer no educational disadvantage. Children are no trouble. Very often it is the parents who have this perception of suffering an educational disadvantage. Children cope with Welsh (quoted by Griffiths, 1990b, 26).

On the other hand, a careful study of educational results for pupils instructed in Welsh through a total immersion approach suggests that there are serious costs in concept development for those who speak only English at home and also, to some extent, for those who come to school speaking Welsh, and this holds true for children from all social class backgrounds (Dodson & Thomas, 1988, 484).

There is at present considerable policy discussion about the extent to which schools that do not instruct primarily through Welsh should require the study of the language beyond the elementary grades, when students must cover a great deal of curriculum material in order to perform successfully on the nationwide examinations (*The Times Educational Supplement* August 6, 1993, 7).

Although a general cultural appreciation for things Welsh may be an important factor in the interest of many parents in Welsh-medium instruction for their children, it seems likely that this is also a means of expressing an identity distinct from that of English mass society. Certainly the revival of Welsh in schools must be seen in the context of a general desire for a more independent system of education in Wales. According to a recent report,

> the chairman of the Curriculum Council for Wales . . . believes decision-making will continue to be transferred to Cardiff, not just because of Welsh language and culture but because of "an element of not being content with the decisions made in England." He looks forward to a time when differences are accepted as the norm, as happens in Scotland (Dore, 1993).

It seems likely, by the same token, that the more modest revival of interest in Gaelic is an aspect of the Scottish nationalism that has become so marked in recent years. Few Scots speak or understand Scottish Gaelic— indeed Scottish nationalism first emerged among lowlanders who spoke a northern dialect of English; "those highlanders who used the Gaelic language, living on Islands or in lonely mountain valleys, knew more the loyalty to the clan than to the state" (Kohn, 1967, 637)—but the language has become for some a symbolic element of political as well as cultural movements, sup- porting the contention that "language is far more important to group for- mation that to group maintenance" (Connor, 1985b, 258). An ethnic group is one whose ancestors spoke the same language. Some parents in Scotland are determined that their descendants will speak it as well.

> As in Wales, it is parents who have provided the impetus, setting up Gaelic playgroups, then forcing local education authorities to establish Gaelic- medium units within existing primary schools. Since 1986 the Scottish Office Education Department has provided specific grants to LEAs, to cover 75 per cent of the cost of setting up such units (Croall, 1993c, 2).

There were 833 pupils in Gaelic-medium elementary programs in 1993, far fewer than in Wales, though other programs were planned. The most com- mon model is for the first two years to be immersion in Gaelic, followed by the use of both languages from the third grade. Some argue that this is not enough, given the cultural predominance of English. A parent leader reports that "an increasing number of parents want their children kept in separate streams, so that they can have Gaelic-medium teaching right through," and such segregated programs are now being planned. A head teacher notes that "We're combating the English at home, especially where no Gaelic is being spoken" (quoted by Croall, 1993c, 3). This is increasingly the case, and raises the question whether Gaelic can realistically be restored as a language of daily use, since

> as the older generation of Gaelic speakers die off around 3,000 new speakers are needed every year just to keep the numbers level. If the language is to survive, there will need to be a lot more adult learn- ers, however much Gaelic flourishes in the playgroups and schools (Croall, 1993c, 3).

A more extreme example of the promotion of a disappearing language for symbolic reasons is the current effort to revive the use of Manx and

Cornish, the languages of the Isle of Man and of Cornwall. The last person who spoke only Cornish died in 1777, but "about 120 beginners now join evening classes [to learn Cornish] every year, and a few families are bringing up their children to be bilingual" (Croall, 1993e, 3). The number of speakers of Manx had declined from 12,350 in 1874 to 531 in 1931, and the last native speaker died in the 1970s.

> During the 1930s, several enthusiasts befriended some of the remaining native speakers, learnt the language from them, and later started classes for others. . . . The group who learnt from native speakers has now dwindled to four, and it is *their* students who are now carrying the torch (Croall, 1993d, 3).

A survey in 1990 found that 36 percent of respondents wanted to see Manx taught as an optional subject in the schools, and 1480 pupils registered for such classes (half an hour a week) last year. One local observer noted that this interest reflected developments in Europe, where regional autonomy movements have accompanied the growth of international integration: "Many newcomers are interested in Manx, and want it as a badge of identity" (quoted by Croall, 1993d, 3). A "dead" language with no instrumental utility at all is thus serving as a symbolic expression of group distinctiveness, even for those with no ancestral connection with Manx and no realistic expectation of learning to use it proficiently.

The French government has provided a measure of support to the teaching of Breton, another Celtic language, as an optional second language at the secondary level, but demand is limited; the 1983–84 enrollment in Breton courses was 618, compared with 3,354,617 in English courses (Boulot & Boyzon-Fradet, 1991a, 46–47). It appears, indeed, that the number of Breton-speakers is dropping rapidly as the older generation dies (Fase, 1987, 56).

Spain: Language and Regional Autonomy

If Welsh and Gaelic are being revived to a modest extent as regional languages within the United Kingdom through school programs, the position of Catalan and Basque is substantially stronger in Spain because of their identification with the drive for partial or complete autonomy by those regions. Catalan, in particular, "is spoken by close to 7 million people and is thus the largest stateless language in western Europe" (Artigal, 1991b, 21). In these cases as well, however, it seems likely that the language has become a symbol and vehicle of regional identity and a form of resistance to the centralizing efforts of a national government rather than the primary cause of the sense of the distinctive identity. The languages were sustained, in recent decades, at least in part precisely because of the efforts of the Franco regime to suppress them (Tarrow, 1985, 245; Bassa, 1989). This suggests the unwisdom of official efforts to suppress the use of minority languages; left to themselves, they are likely to fall from use when they no longer serve to rally around.

Spain has sent hundreds of thousands of labor migrants to other European nations, and—like Italy—has actively promoted home language instruction for the children of these workers. It was however only in 1970 that the General Education Law recognized regional languages such as Catalan and Basque as having a role in the schools of Spain itself, and then only as a supplemental subject and not as a vehicle for instruction in the subject areas (Garcia Hoz, 1980, 162–163). The first comprehensive education statute adopted in Spain, in 1857, had provided that instruction in all schools would be through Castilian Spanish and this policy remained in effect under succeeding regimes apart from a few years of Republican government in the 1930s when the teaching of Catalan was encouraged (García Garrido, 1991, 303).

The resistance of outlying regions to the hegemony of Castile and Madrid has deep historical roots, and was not initially concerned with language use. In Catalonia,

> feelings that they were being exploited by the rest of Spain led to revolts in 1640 and again in 1705. . . . Language had very little to do with these basic economic grievances, and in fact, the Catalan language had been on the verge of dying out completely. In 1860 it was spoken only in the most remote and obscure villages, while Castilian was taking hold in cities like Barcelona. The revival of the language was originally the work of a small group of intellectuals and poets (Inglehart & Woodward, 1992, 420).

Catalan language and culture came to be a potent rallying point in the autonomy struggles of the early twentieth century, "taken up and discarded by political leaders of extremely varied interests as it suited their needs. . . . it seems to be an example of ambitious political leaders turning to language as a device to inflame the masses against the central government" (Inglehart & Woodward, 1992, 421).

Despite strong efforts by Franco's Fascist government to impose the uniform use of Castilian Spanish nationwide (Bassa, 1989), and a massive migration of Spanish-speakers into the industrializing Catalan and Basque regions, many parents retained a high degree of loyalty to their regional languages, a loyalty that persists among many of those who have migrated to Madrid, where no language but Spanish (*Castellano*) enjoys institutional support. One study found that, among Catalans living in Madrid, 81 percent reported that they could speak Catalan, 56 percent used it with their children (though *Castellano* was used more frequently), and 50 percent reported that their children could speak it. Of the children with one or more Catalan parents, 69 percent expressed strong motivation to learn Catalan and 94 percent rejected the statement that a Catalan accent (in speaking *Castellano*) was ugly (Truetas, 1978, 133–155).

Instruction in Catalan and in Basque (Euskera) continued in unofficial schools described, by Artigal, as "the fruit of the spontaneous initiative of groups of parents and teachers during the 1960s" and as "a movement of linguistic, cultural and pedagogic renewal" (Artigal, 1993, 33). In 1978, Catalan was reintroduced to the educational system in regions where it was commonly spoken, and parents were given the right to choose instruction through either language (Bassa, 1989, 91). With the establishment of a substantial measure of legal autonomy with respect to education and other cultural matters, in 1979, and subsequent adoption of laws giving Basque and Catalan equal status with *Castellano* in their respective provinces, there has been a concerted effort to maintain and revive the use of these languages through making them media of instruction starting in preschool. The Law of Linguistic Normalization (*Llei de Normalització Lingüística*) for the Catalan-speaking area, approved unanimously in 1983, stated that Catalan was "the symbol of cultural unity, historical tradition and a sign of the faithfulness of the Catalan people to their own specific culture" (Gerth, 1988, 194). The law provided that "children have the right to receive their first instruction in the language that they normally speak, either Catalan or Castilian," and required that "all children, whatever their language at the start of their instruction, must be able to use Castilian and Catalan regularly and correctly at the end of their basic education" or they could not receive an elementary school certificate (Arnau & Boada, 1986, 111). By 1991, nearly 100,000 pupils whose first language was Castilian were participating in Catalan immersion programs (Artigal, 1991b, 22).

It is, of course, one thing to legislate and quite another to change language practices; the 1983 law included a provision that it would apply "taking into account particular sociolinguistic situations" (Bassa, 1989, 108). Only about half of the elementary school teachers were capable of teaching in Catalan, in part because the relatively low status of the profession did not attract Catalan-speakers. It was necessary to bring in uncertified Catalan-speaking teachers in many schools to meet the requirement of at least three periods a week of the language, though gradually the educational system has been training or retraining more teachers capable of using Catalan for instruction. The evolution was rapid, however, from 3 percent of the schools in Catalonia providing instruction partially or totally in Catalan in 1978–79, to 24 percent in 1981–82, to 86 percent doing so in 1985–86 (Bassa, 1989, 113).

Basque was not, under the Franco regime or indeed before, used as a language of instruction in schools—though Catholic priests used it for catechism instruction—but some parents supported the nongovernment schools that, during the period of official suppression of Basque by the Franco regime, were organized to teach the language. These *ikastolas* continue to enroll more preschool children than do the government schools in the area with the highest proportion of Basque-speakers. The Basque provincial government, in turn, has strongly resisted the efforts of the central government in Madrid to bring publicly funded nongovernment schools under uniform requirements (Tarrow, 1985, 258–259).

As in other cases, emphasis upon the Basque language seems more a symptom than a cause of the demand for autonomy. As one language activist wrote,

> Euskera [Basque] will not save the fatherland; patriotism will. Spread patriotism, and with this Euskera will be spread. . . . the difference of language is the great way to preserve us against the contagion of the Spaniards (Sabino Arana, quoted by García Garrido, 1991, 306).

Parents in these provinces were free, until the 1993–94 school year, to choose among modes of instruction, from supplemental lessons in Catalan or Basque to its full-time use in a language immersion program. The immersion approach has proven far more successful in developing real bilingualism in children who speak *Castellano* with their parents. Artigal attributes the gratifying results of the immersion approach in part to its voluntary nature (Artigal, 1993, 49). Because of the dominant position of Spanish in the overall society, he argues, parents and children from *Castellano*-speaking homes do not feel threatened in their cultural and linguistic identity by instruction that is conducted entirely in Catalan (Artigal, 1991a, 7). On the other hand, the effort to encourage real bilingualism in Catalonia has had only a limited success. One elementary teacher noted recently that "In class we will talk Catalan, but in the playground the children will talk and read comics in *Castellano*" (quoted by McGavin, 1993).

In 1982, for instance, 5 years after the establishment of the compulsory minimum number of hours of Catalan throughout basic general education, 40.48% of students were still unable to express themselves in Catalan. . . . [According to another regional government study,] "the mastery of Catalan achieved by Spanish speakers is not even remotely comparable to the command Catalan-speaking students acquire of Spanish (Artigal, 1991a, 68).

As a result, provincial authorities in Catalonia have required that, starting in the 1993–94 school year, all pupils be taught primarily through Catalan, starting at age 3. This has provoked considerable controversy among parents for whom *Castellano* is the primary language and who continue to claim the right to choice of primary language of instruction. The situation in Catalonia is, indeed, unusually complex: "in many ways Spanish is still the strong language, but from certain standpoints Catalan is the prestigious or prime language. The situation may be described as one of dual or 'cross-diglossia'" (Siguán & Mackey, 1987, 33). In contrast with most other minority languages, Catalan occupies a stronger social position than does the majority Castilian; a regional government study in 1981–1982 found that, while Castilian was spoken by 54 percent of the population of Catalonia, it was the primary language of only 39 percent of the pupils completing the baccalaureate, and the proportion of Catalan-speakers in the private schools that serve about half the population was much higher than that in public schools (Arnau & Boada, 1986, 109).

It has been more difficult to restore the position of Euskera or Basque, since its use "for literary and scientific purposes has been cultivated very little in the past and the number of people speaking it as a first language and in the normal course of events is small. Also, unlike Catalan and Galician, which are Romance languages and therefore close to Spanish, Euskarian [sic] is a completely disparate language and is hard to acquire from a basis of Spanish" (Siguán & Mackey, 1987, 57).

France: The Counter Example

In France, more than in any other Western nation, the national language has been the subject of public policy for the past two centuries, and there has been little official support for maintaining regional language and cultural diversity. Even two decades of increasing decentralization of government functions and cultural expression have not been accompanied by significant demand for the revival and use of the regional languages that were widely used only two generations ago. More, perhaps, than any other language is

French itself associated with ideas of nationhood and of a unitary culture, and the insistence of Francophone minorities in Canada, Belgium, and Switzerland upon the official status of their language is not matched by acceptance of minority languages in France itself.

The hegemony of the French language has been especially closely associated with republicanism in France, and indeed the areas where alternate languages and dialects lingered into the nineteenth century—Brittany, the Vendée, the Massif central—were also areas where loyalty to Catholicism and to monarchy lingered as well. One of the primary concerns of the revolutionary government in 1792 was to impose the use of French. "The unity of the Republic demands the unity of speech," they declared, and schools should provide instruction only in French (Weber, 1976, 72). Indeed, parents should be compelled to send their children to "republican schools" in order to make them loyal to the national government and its new order (Glenn, 1988b, 25–29).

Despite this resolve, renewed periodically though never with the desired effectiveness during the succeeding regimes, it is estimated that at least one-fifth of the population spoke no French at all as recently as 1863, and that many others had a very imperfect grasp of the national language. The chief mission of elementary education, made free and compulsory by the Third Republic in the 1880s, was to teach the French language to all future citizens, "a labor of patriotic character" (Weber, 1976, 310–311). It is said that schools in Brittany had signs telling the children, "It is forbidden to spit and to speak Breton" (Gerth, 1988, 198). The efforts to discourage regional languages were so successful that, by the late 1960s, 95 percent of the inhabitants of France, apart from Alsace/Lorraine, identified French as their mother tongue (Bourhis, 1984a, 12).

The success of these efforts on the cultural level should not be exaggerated, however, to the extent of asserting that "the idea of being 'American' does not give people a sense of one large family, the way that being French does for people in France" (Waters, 1990, 153). Ever since the great population shifts that accompanied industrialization during the nineteenth century, "ethnic" groups made up of former peasants from economically-backward provinces of France, from Brittany or Auvergne or Perigord, have clustered in certain *quartiers* of Paris and other cities, dominated particular occupations, and have maintained to some extent their regional dialects or languages.

In France, unlike the United Kingdom, there has been little government support for the maintenance of regional languages and cultures, and very strong official emphasis upon the acquisition of French and of French cultural values. Although schools may offer regional languages as an option, the demand for those of the south of France, across the border from the vigorous revival of Catalan and Basque in Spain, is scarcely greater than that for Breton in the west. In 1983–84, 2,506 French pupils were studying Catalan, and 793 Basque (Boulot and Boyzon-Fradet, 1991a, 46–47). A crucial difference is that, though the area where these languages have historically been spoken extends across the border into France, they do not serve as symbols of a movement for regional autonomy, as they do in Spain. Regional autonomy *is* very much on the political agenda in France, but not in a form which rejects the dominant French culture, as is to some degree the case in Spain.

Denmark and Germany

If the revival and advocacy of minority languages in Spain, Wales, and Ireland are inseparable from demands for regional political autonomy, the situation of indigenous language minority groups in Denmark and Germany reflects the desire of smaller groups with no clearly defined territory to retain their distinctiveness, of which language is the primary marker. For our purposes, the primary interest of this experience is the question it raises about the effect of fostering language maintenance upon the academic success of children.

It is a much-canvassed question, whether it is "good or bad for children to be bilingual?" Kenji Hakuta cites experts who have stated confidently that bilingualism handicaps language growth, and others who are equally sure that it confers intellectual advantages (Hakuta, 1986, 14). The research on this question reflects shifting academic fashion, with the more recent studies concerned with identifying positive effects of deliberately fostered bilingualism upon middle-class children, in contrast with earlier studies which sought to identify handicaps faced by children from immigrant families. The Danish/German experience offers in a sense a third case, of relatively isolated rural populations whose language-maintenance expectations may be of a piece with other efforts to keep the dominant society at a distance.

Allowed, under a bilateral treaty of 1955, to have their own government-funded schools, the leaders of the German minority in Denmark are insistent that these are not bilingual (and thus transitional) schools but explicitly German community schools, established under the Danish law permitting publicly-funded private schools (*friskoler*). Teachers are aware that it is important for the economic future of their pupils that they acquire proficiency in Standard Danish (most, in fact, speak a Danish regional dialect at home), but are under pressure to limit their exposure to the majority language and culture in order to discourage assimilation. "It can therefore be argued that the minority and its policy-makers put the interests of the group above those of its members, especially those of school age" (Byram, 1993, 63).

The corresponding schools of the Danish minority in Germany, according to Søndergaard, are equally unable to teach Standard Danish effectively since it is in fact not the language of the parents. The children speak German at home and Danish is an "institutional language" in which they do not acquire true proficiency.

> One has to recognize that in a situation where the linguistic and cultural influences are not double-sided (from both the home and the educational institutions), even a pedagogical influence over many years will often only give superficial results (Søndergaard, 1993, 76).

The pupils in these schools, he reports, "attained 79% in German and 85% in Danish in relation to monolinguals" in the two languages on vocabulary tests (Søndergaard, 1993, 80). On the positive side, they are functionally bilingual; on the negative side, neither language is as fully developed as is that of typical monolingual students.

The German schools in Denmark, Byram notes, are quite explicitly the schools of a national minority and bearers of a self-consciously minority culture, in contrast with the schools serving the German minority in the officially designated "German language territory" (*deutsches Sprachgebiet*) of eastern Belgium, which are regular Belgian schools that use German as first language of instruction, as other Belgian schools use French or Dutch (Byram, 1988, 393).

Switzerland

Switzerland (like Belgium and Canada) has dealt with its language differences by giving essentially a monopoly position to the prevailing language of each geographic area. While in Belgium and Canada, as we will see, the competition of languages has led to bitter political conflict at points where geographical separation has broken down (the Brussels area, Voeren, the postwar immigration to Quebec), in Switzerland the federal system continues to provide sufficient "space" for each language group, though not without tensions.

There are four "national" languages (German, French, Italian, and Romanche) under the Swiss Constitution; the first three are "official" in the sense that they can be used to petition the federal government, to speak in the federal legislature, and to argue before the federal court; all federal laws and government publications are published in the three official languages (Codding, 1961, 8). In 1980, German was the first language of 73.5 percent of Swiss citizens, French of 20 percent, Italian of 4.5 percent, and Romanche of 0.9 percent; the large number of guest workers from Italy brought the proportion of Italian speakers in the resident population to nearly 10 percent (tables in Fluegel, 1987, 172).

The goal of Swiss language policy has been that all citizens would be able to speak two of the official languages and understand the third, but this is far from being achieved. Switzerland is not a bilingual or multilingual society, but several monolingual societies that share a common federal government. The level of bilingualism is naturally considerably higher than it is in nations with a single predominant language, especially among the many Swiss who work in international finance, tourism, or for international organizations, but education officials are concerned that pupils show the most interest in a language which is not among the four Swiss languages: English. There are movements afoot in Geneva and elsewhere to make English the main second language taught in schools, in lieu of one of the national languages (Plummer, 1988).

Although article 116 of the Swiss Constitution requires the cantons to favor the national languages (that is, not just the locally dominant language), a recent report recognized that to "slow down the English offensive and put a brake on teaching it for the sake of the national languages" would not work. A survey conducted in 1986 asked adult respondents what second language they would choose to study if they went back to school; 58 percent of the German speakers and 65 percent of the French speakers said they would choose English over another of the national languages, and the tendency was even stronger among those under 40 (Fluegel, 1987, 64–65). The perception that this is a problem is not limited to Switzerland; education authorities in Germany urged in 1979 that schools make a special effort to introduce pupils to languages other than English, particularly to those of neighboring countries (Fluegel, 1987, 95).

The implications for educational policy are complex and challenging. Schooling is entirely the responsibility of the cantons—there are 26 independent school systems—and is provided through the language in official use in each canton. Thus schooling in Geneva is provided through French, even for Swiss children from German-speaking homes. German is taught as a mandatory second language, as is French in the German-speaking cantons. In Ticino, the one canton with an Italian-speaking majority, French is the mandatory first foreign language. In Grison, where Romanche is spoken by nearly one-quarter of the population, German is the mandatory second language for those who speak Italian or Romanche, and French for those who speak German. English may not be substituted for the national language

("Recommandations . . . ," 1987, 15–16).

Efforts are under way to ensure that all Swiss have the ability to understand spoken Italian, through including that proficiency among the objectives for French-language instruction, without necessarily seeking to develop the ability to speak or write Italian (Fluegel, 1987, 148).

The situation is further complicated by the fact that the German spoken in Switzerland is highly dialectical. The goal of the cantonal directors of education is that every pupil will be able to understand a second national language; should pupils in Geneva learn to understand standard German, or the spoken Swiss-German? To accomplish the latter would require a emphasis quite different from the usual program of second language instruction. Learning standard German without being able to use it to understand fellow-citizens would defeat the purpose of the language requirement. This implies also that German speakers should learn to speak (as well as read and write) standard German in order to communicate with other Swiss, as well as with German speakers from Germany and Austria (Fluegel, 1987, 62, 114, 147).

Many Swiss teachers are now objecting to demands that the second national language be taught starting in the primary grades, arguing that this places too great a burden upon pupils; parents are mostly in favor (Plummer, 1988).

Sometimes the desire to teach children a group language as a means of maintaining the cohesion and identity of the group may have negative consequences for the opportunities available to those children. Petersen charged that the effect of the policy, in the canton of Grison, of providing instruction to children of the Romanche-speaking minority

> has been to aggravate their cultural isolation and to make it considerably more difficult for peasants' sons to advance themselves. The nationalist spokesmen are inclined to view such upward mobility as disastrous; for them, the survival of the group is a cause to which the welfare of the individuals in it must be sacrificed (Petersen, 1975, 186).

Romanche is in fact a family of five distinct dialects, which together are spoken by around 50,000 Swiss. Even in the canton where Romanche speakers are concentrated they are in the minority, and German is the common language. Efforts to maintain Romanche through schooling have therefore more political and symbolic than instrumental value.

Belgium

The territory now included within Belgium has been divided linguistically along substantially the present lines since the late Roman period, with Walloon dialects of French spoken in the southern provinces (Wallonia) and Flemish dialects of Dutch spoken in the northern provinces (known collectively as Flanders). In both sections, however, French was long the preferred, if not the only, language of the educated elite, and thus the medium of administration and of high culture. This pattern intensified during the two decades (1795–1815) of hegemony by France, when the authorities in Paris sought to assimilate the Belgian people by promoting republican values and French nationalism. The cultural influence that had already given French a privileged position in the Dutch-speaking Flemish provinces was reinforced by official action, including changing of street names, exclusive use of French in legal proceedings, and even a ban on printing anything in Dutch. All secondary education was provided in French. Only in the Catholic Church in Flanders did Dutch remain in public use (Roegiers, 1983, 72–73; Kossmann, 1978, 80).

One of the most important reforms instituted during the brief period of union with the Netherlands (1815–1830) was a substantial expansion of the official use of Dutch, as part of a cultural policy concerned with creating national unity. In Flanders, primary education in Dutch was greatly expanded, and the use of Dutch in secondary schools was gradually extended starting in 1823, while it was offered as an optional subject in schools in Wallonia (Vroede, 1983, 128, 132; Kossmann, 1978, 124).

With the independence of Belgium, the French-speaking elite restored the primacy of French even in Flanders. Educational freedom and the greater diversity of schooling that it brought had the side effect of weakening the position of Dutch in secondary education, since many middle-class Flemish parents preferred schools that would teach their children in the language necessary to worldly success (Vroede, 1983, 141); the French poet Charles Baudelaire noted, in Brussels in 1865, that "everyone pretends not to know Flemish; that's [what is considered] good taste," though he insisted that in fact it was French that they did not [really] know (Baudelaire, 1954, 1296). Until late in the nineteenth century, the French hegemony in education and public life left the more numerous Flemings in a subordinate position, and equal status for the two languages became the highly sensitive political demand that brought down several national governments in recent years. Flemish resentment of the language inequities in national life ran deep: with French alone, it was said, one could become a government minister, but with Dutch alone one could not even become a corporal (Clerck, 1974, 74). "'To be Belgian," complained Flemish intellectuals, "we have to cease being Flemish" (Lorwin, 1966, 160).

Only in 1883 were education laws amended to provide for instruction through the Dutch language in the lower grades of secondary education in

Dutch-speaking regions, and for teacher training in Dutch. Full implementation was slow in coming. Language and religious issues became entangled; Socialists charged in 1910, for example, that Jesuit secondary schools in Flanders were competing unfairly with public schools by continuing to teach in French, thus appealing to "the frenchified bourgeoisie, who have an aristocratic disdain for the language of the people" (Clerck, 1974, 89).

The important education legislation of 1914 instituted the practice of requiring parents, when registering their child for elementary school, to make a declaration of the family's primary language, so it could be used as the language of instruction. Over the next decades, Flemish nationalists continued to seek measures that would prevent a one-way language shift to French, the more prestigious language; in 1932, they called unsuccessfully for an end to classes in French as a second language in elementary schools. Legislation adopted that year provided that second language classes could begin in the fifth grade, and in secondary schools should be provided for at least 4 hours a week. Access to jobs in the national civil service was opened to Dutch-speakers, but a proposal that the entire country be organized on a bilingual basis was rejected by Francophones, and the present system of two language zones and a bilingual capital area was put in place.

Language has continued to play an important part in Belgian political controversy over the past two decades. During the 1960s each of the three major political parties came under the strain of language tension, with the Christian Democrats and the Liberals developing separate Dutch- and French-speaking "wings." The votes won by alternative, language-based political parties increased from 3.5 percent in 1961 to 22.3 percent in 1971, an indication not only of the growing significance of these issues but also of the lessening conflict over religion (Billiet, 1977a, 52; Witte and Meynen, 1982, 228).

While parental choice of the *religious* character of schooling is protected by political compromises enshrined in law, ongoing conflict over language has led to restrictions on the right of parents to choose the language of instruction, even though it would seem clearly in the interest of the nation that Flemish children become fluent in French and Walloon children in Dutch.

Belgian policy does not regard real bilingualism as desirable, however, since it raises the troubling prospect of intergenerational language shift. "In general bilingualism is nowadays viewed as an unfortunate burden by Belgian linguists who certainly do not consider it a blessing which should be pursued beginning at an early age" (Bustamante, Van Overbeke, & Verdoodt, 1978, 20). The census of 1947 showed significant gains in the use of French in the Brussels area, arousing Flemish resentment. In 1846 the capital city's population had been 67 percent Dutch-speaking, but the proportion had declined to 51 percent in 1910 and to 29 percent by 1947; some Flemings described it as a "Frenchifying machine" (Kossmann 1978, 636). Rural migrants from Flanders would adopt French as part of the adaptation to city life, while the gradual spread of French-speaking population into the Dutch-speaking suburbs led to demands that these become officially bilingual; Flemish activists saw these developments as a "robbery of Flemish soil" (Witte & Meynen, 1982, 250).

While French seemed to be taking over Brussels, the language was losing ground nationally with the economic and demographic decline of Wallonia, still dependent upon coal mines and outmoded industry. As an indication of the bitterness of feeling, some Walloon activists blame Hitler for the relative decline of their region, charging that most young Flemish soldiers captured in the defeat of 1940 were released to go home and beget children, while their Walloon counterparts were kept in captivity away from wives and girlfriends. A typical Walloon view is that "the Flemish strategy toward Brussels and Wallonia has been worked out for decades and pursued single-mindedly with continual denials but advanced more vigorously day by day" (Brabant, 1983).

Needless to say, this suspicion and hostility is fully reciprocated in the Dutch-speaking community. A Flemish scholar writing recently apologizes for the title *The Profile of Foreigners in Belgium*: "to publish a book with 'Belgium' in the title is somewhat behind the times. Flanders is our fatherland." Although legally Belgians, he notes, many Dutch-speakers think of themselves primarily as Flemings, and in Brussels they are "undoubtedly an ethnic minority . . . strangers in their own land" (Dumon, 1982, 8, 11).

The major shift that has occurred between the two communities is not so much in relative numbers in the French-speaking and Dutch-speaking areas as in cultural hegemony. Wallonia represented 39.2 percent of the total population of Belgium in 1831 and never rose higher than 42.6 percent in 1866, when the mining and industrial sectors around Liege were booming. The proportion dropped to 38.7 percent of the total in 1920, to 34.5 percent in 1947, and to 32.1 percent at present (André, 1983, 26). This does not include the Brussels region, which represents about 10 percent of the total Belgian population and is, as we have seen, an area in which French is predominant.

While French-speakers have never been in the majority in the Belgian population, they had always seen themselves in the leading role, until a more dynamic economy and a higher birthrate gave a sort of moral advantage to Flanders in recent decades. The persistence of the cultural hegemony of

French in Brussels is all the more resented by Flemings as a result.

In 1962, the language census (which implied continuous renegotiation of the territories within which each language would prevail) was abolished and the boundaries between the French and Dutch regions were frozen in response to Flemish demands. In one of the more unfortunate aspects of the boundary adjustment, the Dutch-speaking province Limburg was given the area of Fourons (French) or Voeren (Dutch), consisting of several communities with French populations and the focal point of recent linguistic conflict that has led to the fall of two national governments. The next year, legislation placed language restrictions on education at all levels except university. No school in Flemish areas could teach primarily in French, nor could schooling be provided in Dutch in the Walloon areas. This situation created some unfortunate results:

> The teaching of the other national language as an individual and separate course is compulsory neither in elementary nor in secondary schools with the exception of Brussels capital, 40 municipalities (mostly very small) near the language borders, and the German-language region. In the rest of the country, the teaching of the other national language(s) is not even allowed before the fifth grade. . . . As a result, parents who move from one linguistic region to another are obliged to send their children to schools with a completely new language of instruction (Bustamante, Van Overbeke, & Verdoodt, 1978, 6).

A child of French-speaking Belgian parents who moved to Ghent or a child of Dutch-speaking Belgian parents who moved to Charleroi could not legally be taught in his or her home language, nor could a Moroccan immigrant child who arrived in Antwerp speaking French as a second language be taught in French. Thus individual rights were sacrificed to the right of the language community to defend its borders. The rationale for these restrictions was stated clearly in 1963 by a Flemish leader:

> In a land like Belgium where three languages are spoken, language peace is possible only when the relationships are stabilized, and when any form of language or cultural imperialism is repudiated. By stabilization of relationships we mean, first of all, that language boundaries and the homogeneity and integrity of the language areas are not only honored but legally guaranteed and protected and defended by the State. For the Brussels area, originally Flemish, where now French- and Dutch-speakers live mixed together, limits must be set

on frenchifying policies, and all measures must be taken that are necessary to prevent language struggle and language imperialism (Van der Elst, quoted by Clerck, 1974, 156–157).

These educational policies were matched by provisions, in the language laws, requiring that jobs in the public service in Brussels be divided evenly between the two groups, though the city was around 80 percent French-speaking, and that top civil service jobs would be open only to those competent in both languages.

In Brussels, as an officially bilingual city, French- and Dutch-language schools may be in close proximity. The 1963 legislation required a careful determination of the primary language of the family, through a special "language inspection" service. Two inspectors, one from each language group, considered each case, with disputes between them referred to a special commission (Baert, 1984, 13). The language of instruction chosen by parents must be that most commonly used by the child. Second-language instruction was required starting in the third grade for three hours a week (Clerck, 1974, 97, 115). This commission adjudicated 133 cases from 1967 to 1971, when the requirements were eased; 55 children were allowed to stay in French-language schools but 41 were required to leave those for Dutch-language schools (Swing, 1982, 279).

The law forbids Dutch and French sections in a single school. Although the second language is taught as a subject, it may not be used as a language of instruction, and English may be substituted for it. Thus, apart from the Brussels area, studying the other national language is not required. Teachers of French in Dutch-language schools are Flemings who have learned French as a second language, not their Walloon compatriots for whom French is native, and Dutch must be taught by native speakers of French in Wallonia. The established view of the two "national languages" is apparent from the new proposed goals for Flemish intermediate schools, which include the section "Modern foreign [sic] languages: French/English." The text points out that the goals for the two languages are the same, and describes those goals in terms of pupils being able to understand television shows, to read instructions with consumer goods, to have simple conversations, and so forth, without the barest acknowledgement that French is the language spoken by nearly half their fellow-citizens (*Voorstel eindtermen . . .* , 1993, 92–110).

As a result of a modification enacted in 1971, parents in the Brussels area may now select the language in which their children will be educated. Since this was a concession to Francophones, the Dutch-speaking community won in exchange a guarantee that their schools would not be closed even if enrollment dropped well below the level at which a French-language school would be closed. This is intended to guarantee that a network of Dutch-language schools will be available despite the enrollment of around 85 percent of the children in the French-language system.

Recently, a trend has appeared (opposite to that expected in 1971) of Francophone parents sending their children to Dutch schools, for several apparent reasons. Although the ostensible reason is that bilingual competency is increasingly necessary for good employment, benefiting the Dutch-speakers who are more likely to know French than vice versa, many observers believe that a more powerful reason is that French-language schools in Brussels tend to have a high proportion of North African and other immigrant students, who may be avoided by selecting a Dutch-language school (Swing, 1982, 285; Smeekens, 1985, 56). In 1985, 16 percent of the children in Dutch-language kindergartens were from homogeneously French-speaking families. In a response characteristic of the Flemish attitude, immigration expert Johan Leman sees this not as a positive sign of the resurgence of Dutch but as a danger, since "a certain 'frenchifying' communication climate will presumably increase in the near future unless drastic action is taken by teachers, administrators, and supervisory personnel" (Leman, 1985a, 25).

Language issues in Belgian education show no sign of going away, nor does wide support exist for a true system of choice under which parents (outside Brussels) could opt for a truly bilingual education. As an illustration of the jealousy that prevents any such development, a local education official for French-language schools in a suburb of Brussels (a city surrounded on all sides by Dutch-speaking areas) recently urged principals not to send children on field trips in Flanders!

The effect of the complicated three-cornered relationship among Flanders, Wallonia, and Brussels is to produce a sense of grievance on all sides—Belgians have been described as one oppressed majority and two oppressed minorities—and an attitude that views language diversity as far more of a problem than an opportunity for enrichment. One study found

> a widespread assumption that bilingualism is at best a necessary evil: a necessity for national unity, at least in bilingual Brussels, but a danger to intellectual development if introduced too early and a one-way road to language loss. Language planning in this bilingual country reflects this assumption, for it fosters the development of linguistic ethnicity through separatism. . . . In the past Flemings were educated

for integration into a Francophone world. Today they are educated for linguistic ethnicity (Swing, 1982, 267).

The result is that "[if] we define bilingual education as the use of two or more languages of instruction in a subject matter other than language instruction per se, we can safely state that only a small minority of students in Belgium receives this type of education" (Bustamante, Van Overbeke, and Verdoodt, 1978, 3). The situation is complicated by the growing number of immigrant children in recent decades, especially in Brussels.

> Dutch-speaking schools in Brussels experience the presence of an increasing group of children who do not speak Dutch as a threat to their Flemish character. Indeed we see that during recess and moments of free play in the kindergarten Dutch is no longer used as the principal language of communication. . . . The school has to make a choice: either nothing is done and very soon the school becomes a melting pot just like home is to many children or the school tries to organise its language situation in a more structured way (Smedt, 1985b, 92).

Such plaints sound familiar; a similar concern about the language used in urban schools is expressed in many countries experiencing immigration. What is perhaps unique in the Belgian situation is that the concern expressed by Flemish educators is not about the use of Greek or of Italian, but of French by Italian and Greek children. Although French is one of the two national languages, and is a required subject in Dutch-language schools in Brussels starting in the third grade, its use at pre-school level by immigrant children is seen as a problem to be overcome through vigorous replacement by Dutch (Smedt, 1985c).

ACCOMMODATING LANGUAGES IN NORTH AMERICA

The language situation is, if anything, even more complex in Canada and the United States, with indigenous (pre-European) language minority groups, regions strongly associated with long-established minority languages, and a complex overlay of immigrant languages.

Canada

In Canada, as in Belgium, the choice of the language of instruction in schools was initially limited by the framework of the "territorial principle"—the official status of a language determined on a geographical basis—with only Quebec being officially bilingual. French speakers in Ontario in effect chose instruction through that language by choosing publicly funded Catholic schools. A study of provincial Quebec the 1930s depicted a compartmentalized society and segmented institutions.

> The great separate institutions are the schools and churches. Around them gather charitable organizations, also separate for the ethnic groups. The churches well illustrate the nature of the institutional division. The Protestant churches are the usual ones of English-speaking countries, from the Anglican to the Salvation Army and the Bible halls. French Protestants are few and soon become English. English Catholics, however, remain English (Hughes, 1963, 85).

In a dramatic reversal, the language of instruction in all parts of Canada *except* Quebec is now based upon parental decisions, while the territorial principle has been imposed with a vengeance in Quebec. There is now a national policy of bilingualism, while bilingualism is regarded as a threat to the dominance of the French language by leaders in Quebec.

The British North America Act, under which the provinces of Upper and Lower Canada were organized as an independent nation,

> affirmed Canada's linguistic duality only in Quebec, where the use of both the French and English languages was required in the Parliament and courts of the province. It was not until 1969 with the passage of the Official Languages Act that both languages were actually accorded official status nationwide . . . at the provincial level, only one province, New Brunswick, recognizes French and English as official languages. The remaining nine provinces are monolingual. . . . In 1971, the federal government adopted an official policy of multiculturalism, whose mandate is ". . . the preservation and sharing of ethnocultural heritages and which facilitate mutual appreciation and understanding among all Canadians" (Genesee, 1987, 5–6).

Canada adopted a Charter of Rights and Freedoms together with a new Constitution in 1982, but Quebec refused to endorse this accord because the Charter "included minority language education rights intended to apply to all Canadian citizens, irrespective of the province in which they reside" (Mallea, 1984, 224). Article 23 of the Charter provides that parents may choose instruction for their children in either French or English wherever the number of children for whom that language is desired is sufficient to warrant a program (Canada's Charter of Rights and Freedoms, 1992,

434); but making language an optional matter is unacceptable to franco-phone activists.

There are those who contend that the policy of nationwide bilingual-ism has been a failure, that "a language policy based on the 'personality' principles for its *citizens* can clash with the right of *public servants* to work in the official language of their choice" (Bourhis, 1984a, 14), and that French is losing ground rapidly under wider North American cultural influences in all parts of Canada except Quebec. The measures taken in Quebec to dis-courage and even penalize the use of English must be understood in the con-text of this trend, which has both demographic and cultural elements.

> Between 1961 and 1971, the percentage of francophones in the Ca-nadian population declined from 30.4 to 28.7. Demographic projec-tions . . . indicated that by the year 2000 the figure would further decrease to 23% and that 95% of Canada's francophones would re-side in Quebec. . . . only 85.4% of the 6,160,120 Canadians of French origin still used French in the home . . . the adoption of English as a mother tongue by francophones outside Quebec was quite substan-tial, ranging from 85% in Newfoundland to 65% in British Colum-bia and to 38% in Ontario. . . . By 1971, the birth rate [in Quebec] had declined from the highest in the country to the lowest of the ten provinces (Anglejan, 1984, 31–33).

This demographic decline has led to the strong concern of authori-ties in Quebec to ensure that the children of immigrants to that province be schooled in French rather than in English. The situation in Quebec is some-what paradoxical, indeed, given the strong national commitment to multicul-turalism and to French/English bilingualism, and to allowing parents to choose schooling in either of the national languages. This issue was not an explicit consideration in the 1867 Act under which Canada was given a con-stitutional foundation: "it was religion and education that aroused people's sentiment then, not language and education" (Wilson and Lazerson, 1982, 9). As the English-speaking population of the province grew and came to occupy leading positions in business life, the situation changed completely. Language came to be the significant "marker" and point of distinction, and religious considerations began to take second place.

A public school system divided four ways on the basis of language and also of denominational distinctions evolved in Quebec, with the Catholic and the Protestant systems each operating French-language and English-lan-guage schools. The earlier association of language and religious denomination continues, however: 92 percent of the students in Protestant schools are taught in English, and 94 percent of those in Catholic schools in French. In a small city in Quebec where numbers did not permit maintenance of a separate system for English-speaking Catholic students, Hughes found in the late 1930s that they attended the Protestant school; language had come to be a more important factor than religious denomination. As Hughes explains,

> The Protestant school is generally called the "English school"; some English-speaking Catholics always so speak of it, with the obvious intent of emphasizing the school's and their own ethnic, rather than religious, affiliation. In fact, it is the school of the English Catholics, of the Jews, of the few families of French Protestants, of a few rather anglicized French Catholics, and of families resulting from marriages of English Protestants with French Catholics. The marginal people choose the legally Protestant, *de facto* English school (Hughes, 1963, 118).

As Mackey observes, "except in private schools or big cities, some French-speaking Protestants and some English-speaking Catholics had to choose between their language and their religion" (Mackey, 1984, 160).

The problem was exacerbated after World War II, when an increasing number of European immigrants (notably Italians and Greeks) chose to identify with the more prosperous English-speaking residents of Montreal: "in 1931, 52% of the Quebecers whose origin was other than British or French had adopted French, while their number had fallen to 29% in 1961" (Laporte, 1984, 59). This group came to be of growing significance with the postwar immigration to Canada. According to the 1971 census, almost 18 percent of the population of Montreal had neither English nor French as their native tongue, as compared to 15 percent of English background and 67 percent of French background.

A law adopted in 1969 (Bill 63), while directing the Ministry of Education to take steps to ensure that all children in Quebec develop proficiency in French, gave parents the choice of language of instruction for their children (Laporte, 1984, 36). Its effects were "detrimental to French" because the great majority used this to choose English; "freedom of choice in the matter of language of education paves the way to assimilation to the dominant language" (Maurais, 1991, 123). About half of the enrollment of Montreal's English Catholic schools, in 1973, was of Italian ancestry (18,000 as against 2,000 in French Catholic schools). Put another way, in 1943 more than half of the Italian children attended French Catholic schools, but only 9 percent did so 30 years later (Anglejan, 1984, 33). "[T]here was one segregated public city school system for English-speaking Protestants and another for French-speaking Catholics. This latter school system maintained English-speaking Catholic schools, in which were found the bulk of European immigrant children, all supported by public funds" (Mackey, 1984, 163).

Other immigrant parents, though themselves Catholic, chose to send their children to Protestant schools in order to provide them with an education in English; in 1972, 89.3 percent of the children of immigrant families in Quebec for whom neither French nor English was the original language (so-called allophones) were attending English-language schools, whether Protestant or Catholic (Anglejan, 1984, 33). Some upwardly mobile families of French background were also choosing English-medium schools, especially at the secondary level, in an attempt to increase future job prospects in a continental—indeed, a world—economy to which English was the key. The comparative attractiveness of the two languages, even in francophone-majority Quebec, is revealed by the fact that, in 1970–71, 8.3 percent of the enrollment in English schools was from French-speaking families, while only 1.9 percent of the enrollment in French schools was from English-speaking homes (Laporte, 1984, 59); 25,000 French-speaking pupils were enrolled in English schools (Maurais, 1991, 123).

As a result, by 1973–74, 35 percent of the "English" school population of Quebec was from homes where French or another language other than English was spoken (Mallea, 1984, 233). The metropolitan Montreal area, in particular, seemed to be in the process of moving toward an English-speaking majority by the end of the century. "Had the trends which prevailed in the sixties and seventies continued unabated, there would have been more children in English than in French elementary schools in Montreal by 1980" (Caldwell, 1984, 209).

For political leaders of the French-speaking community, whose Parti Québécois came to power in provincial elections in 1976, this represented a highly threatening trend, part of an overall assault upon the integrity of the *Québécois* culture and "nationality." "The survival of the French language is of course a primary objective and *raison d'être* of the political culture of Quebec" (Mallea, 1984, 225). The passage of a law (Bill 22), in 1974, limiting access to English-language schools to those children with a sufficient proficiency in English, had been extensively evaded. Bill 22 made French the sole official language of the province (Quebec had, as noted above, been the only officially bilingual province), and restricted access to English-medium schools to pupils who already had "a sufficient knowledge of the language of instruction to receive their instruction in that language" as determined by pretesting (Anglejan, 1984, 39). Schools that needed to enroll additional pupils could find ways to decide that applicants from immigrant families were ready to learn through English.

In 1977 the new government, invoking its campaign slogan "*Maître chez nous*," adopted a Charter of the French Language (Bill 101) to regulate further the use of language in all aspects of public life in Quebec, viewed by some as "a denial of the reality of Quebec's cultural and linguistic diversity" (Anglejan, 1984, 45). The people of Quebec were "in the majority French-speaking," the preamble stated, and French "is the language by which that people has articulated its identity"; the government was determined to make it not only the official language but also "the normal and everyday language of work, instruction, communication, commerce and business" (Crawford, 1992a, 436). Efforts to promote bilingualism—gathering force at the national level in an effort to respond to the concerns of French-speakers—were dismissed. According to Quebec's Minister for Cultural Affairs,

> the Quebec we build will be essentially French. The fact that the majority of its population is French will be clearly visible—at work, in communications and in the countryside. It will also be a country in which the traditional balance of power will be altered, especially in regard to the economy; the use of French will not merely be universalized to hide the predominance of *foreign* powers from the French-speaking population; this will accompany, symbolize and support a reconquest by the French-speaking majority in Quebec of that control over the economy which it ought to have. To sum up, the Quebec whose features are sketched in the Charter is a French-language society (quoted in Williams, 1984, 210; emphasis added).

Accordingly, French would be the language of instruction in all schools in Quebec except for specifically permitted exceptions, and the requirement of Bill 22 that English be taught as a second language to pupils in French schools was dropped (Anglejan, 1984, 42). The Charter (text in Bourhis, 1984b, 262–284) restricted admission to English-language schools to children whose parents had themselves attended English-language elementary schools in Quebec, while permitting those already enrolled and their siblings to complete their education in English (Council of Ministers of Education, 1983, 134); the criteria were broadened somewhat by a Supreme Court ruling in 1984 (Maurais, 1991, 123). The development of French-language "Protestant" (really, religiously neutral) schools was promoted, so that new immigrants would not have the excuse of avoiding a French-language school because of its Catholic character. Jewish children had traditionally attended English Protestant schools, but now many attend French Protestant schools.

Thus as children of immigrant parents entered the educational system, the French sector would grow in relation to the English (*Ministère de l'Education* [Montreal], 1984). The effect of these measures was immediate. In 1976–77, only 17.8 percent of foreign students attended French-language schools, but the number increased to 40.4 percent by 1983–84 (*L'Ecole québécoise*, 1985, 22). A partial relaxation of the requirement of French-medium schooling was made for English-speaking families who could demonstrate that they would be in Quebec for a limited period of time and not as permanent residents, in response to business concerns about the recruitment of skilled employees from other parts of Canada and from other English-speaking countries (Laporte, 1984, 69).

The language policies in Quebec have clearly not been directed toward establishing bilingualism as the norm for the entire population; it has rather been to protect French from competition from English. French language activists refer to the "bilingual requirement often artificially imposed on francophones by English-speaking employers," while insisting that anglophone employers must use French (Laporte, 1984, 64). The new requirements for language use have the effect of making life more difficult for English-speaking residents of the province. Laporte reports with approval a survey that found that

> among francophones the percentage of respondents reporting that they experienced difficulties obtaining services in French decreased from 13% in 1971 to 8.8% in 1979. Among anglophones, however, the percentage of respondents who reported they experienced difficulties in obtaining services in English increased to 34% in 1979 from 26% in 1971. At least on the basis of such survey results we have evidence that francization is gaining ground (Laporte, 1984, 62).

A Greek-Canadian member of the Quebec National Assembly asked, somewhat plaintively, in 1982 "Does Quebec belong to all its citizens and, therefore, must respond to the needs of the population as a whole, or does it belong to the French majority first, and only owe tolerance to its minorities?" (Christos Sirros, quoted by Anglejan, 1984, 47). Meanwhile, many English-speaking Canadians no longer felt welcome in Quebec and left the province; there was "a decline of 11.8% in Quebec's English-speaking population between 1976 and 1981" (Anglejan, 1984, 44).

On the other hand, other English speakers have made significant efforts to help their children to become bilingual. A 1977 survey of university students found that the francophones "felt very strongly about the importance of speaking French in Quebec and about sending their children to French unilingual schools," while anglophones "felt it was important to speak *both* French and English and favored sending their children to bilingual schools rather than to either French or English unilingual schools" (Bourhis, 1984b, 181).

A development that originated in Quebec and has received international attention grows out of this parental interest in bilingualism. *English*-speaking parents have the option for their children to be instructed in French by total or partial immersion (Lambert and Tucker, 1972; Swain and Barik, 1978). In 1979–80 a half-dozen English-language school boards converted some 20 schools to the use of French as the language of instruction for at least some of their students. More than 10 percent of the students in English-language schools were taking part in such programs in 1981–82, and similar programs have been developed across Canada, though, ironically, English-immersion programs for French-speaking students are not legally permitted in Quebec.

It should be noted that these French immersion programs are *not* integrated, bringing together French-dominant and English-dominant students to learn together and from each other, as in the "two-way bilingual education" model promoted in Massachusetts, New York, and elsewhere in the United States. Such a model would entail providing instruction partly through English for francophone pupils, which would violate Bill 101's requirement of sheltering pupils from English. These segregated programs do little to promote the sort of active use of the second language with native speakers that leads to a high level of proficiency.

Quebec educational policy, indeed, does not promote active bilingualism for the French-speaking majority. In 1983, for example, 61 schools had separate French and English programs, but there were no truly bilingual schools in which some subjects were taught in each language to a mixed group of students (Council of Ministers of Education, 1983, 137). Anglophone parents who want their children to develop a high level of proficiency in French must enroll them in French schools where they will receive no support in their home language; one observer suggests that "the entire English élite sends its children of elementary age to French schools" (Caldwell, 1984, 210).

The situation in Quebec contrasts sharply with that in the rest of Canada. "Quebec moved from a personality [that is, individual choice] to a territorial approach . . . while in contrast the Canadian Federal Government since 1969 has been moving towards a personality approach" (Bourhis, 1984a, 15). This has resulted from a conscious policy decision, by political leadership which has sought complete national independence for Quebec, to use language as a marker of distinctiveness that increases the distance between Quebec and the rest of Canada. An official of the office charged with enforcing the program of "francization" noted that "language legislation in Quebec, as it is in many 'new nations' of Africa and Asia, is now a nation-building mechanism" (Laporte, quoted by Anglejan, 1984, 43). There is no room for a valuing of societal bilingualism in this program; it is, its opponents have charged, "a denial of the reality of Quebec's cultural and linguistic diversity" (Anglejan, 1984, 45).

By contrast, federal policy has been to seek to reduce the threat of separation by stressing national bilingualism, even as provincial bilingualism is abandoned in Quebec. Since educational policy is set at the provincial level, the following specific examples will give a sense of the diversity of arrangements.

Since the late 1960s, New Brunswick has guaranteed to children from French-speaking and English-speaking homes the right to instruction in their own languages, and in 1969 the province became officially bilingual, the only Canadian province which has taken this step. The language of instruction of each school is that of the majority of the students, with other children (if there is no alternative for them) given supplemental instruction in their home language. Separate but parallel systems exist, with separate school boards based on the dominant language in each area. Under legislation adopted in 1981, the minister of education is obligated to establish a minority language school board in areas dominated by the other language, if 30 parents request it. In 1981–82, 48,614 students were enrolled in the French-language sector, with 15 school boards, and 100,803 in the English-language sector, with 26 school boards.

Prince Edward Island requires that school boards provide instruction through French on the request of parents representing at least 25 students enrolled in three consecutive grades. Two schools provide instruction primarily in French. Of five local school districts, one is French (operating a single k–12 school) and the others English. In Nova Scotia, instruction of French speakers through their native language is not required, but school boards are free to provide it. Twenty-three out of 374 elementary schools offered (in 1981) instruction to some students in French and to others in English, as did 10 out of 107 secondary schools. Out of 40 local school boards, 2 are French.

In Ontario the Catholic flavoring of French-language public schools traditionally made it possible for parents to choose Catholic schooling by choosing French-language schooling. Since the recent policy change permitting public funding of the upper secondary grades of Catholic schools, this indirect approach is no longer necessary.

Ontario requires that school boards provide instruction in French if a sufficient number of parents request it. Languages other than French and English may not be used as media of instruction in public schools, except on a transitional basis, but instruction in "heritage languages" may be provided for up to 2 hours a week outside of regular school hours. In 1981–82, nearly 82,000 students enrolled in such classes in more than 50 languages (Cummins, 1984b, 8).

In Manitoba local school boards must establish French-language classes wherever parents of at least 23 elementary or 23 secondary students can be assembled. The Manitoba minister of education stressed, in 1977, that parents had the responsibility to choose the language of instruction for their children, though local school boards could decide, for the sake of efficiency, in which schools each language would be offered (Council of Ministers of Education, 1983, 73–76). The French-speaking minority—about 6 percent of the total population—thus has had a choice, in recent years, of schools in which French is the primary language of instruction.

The change which made possible the creation of such schools was the [designation] by the federal government of official minorities, French and English, on a national basis, and the recognition by the Manitoba government, after a century of struggle by their French-speaking minority for language rights in matters of education. Not all members of the French-speaking minority, however, reacted in the same way to these changes in the political environment. Although many were willing to adopt an educational formula that would give the optimal guarantees for the survival of the language, some were unwilling to compromise the future of their children in an English-speaking world, and still others were willing to split the risks (Mackey, 1984, 170)

As a result of this ambivalence on the part of parents, "four types of schools had to be recognized to permit a range [of choice] from almost unilingual irredentism [in French] to unilingual assimilation [in English]" (Mackey, 1984, 170).

In British Columbia the language of instruction was not regulated by law until 1978, when policies were adopted to promote French programs for the French-speaking population. School boards were required to provide French-language core curriculum (*Programme-cadre de français*), with all instruction in French except for a period of English as a second language each day, when the parents of ten French-speaking children requested it. English-dominant students who had been enrolled in a French immersion program and transferred to a school without one could be admitted to a *Programme-cadre de français*, if available, but otherwise no provision has been made for integrated bilingual education in British Columbia.

Thus, language policy in Canada is moving in contrasting directions, with Quebec seeking to limit the use of English while other provinces, and the national government, seek to expand the use of French in education and in government. The Quebec policy of unilingualism seems rather more successful than the national policy of bilingualism:

> Quebec has rejected bilingualism, allowing only the use of French in every sphere of public life, at the same time that the Federal government has imposed French/English bilingualism on the rest of the country from coast to coast, even though French-speakers constitute less than 5 percent of the population outside the provinces of Quebec, Ontario, and the Maritime Provinces. . . . In the 1981 census 15 percent of the respondents identified themselves as able to carry on a conversation in the two official languages—a proportion that has not changed in over twenty years. One reason may be that as the number of English-speaking people learning French has increased, the number of French-speaking citizens in Quebec who have a command of English has decreased, since there is no incentive for bilingualism in that province (Porter, 1990, 174).

Multilingual societies with a clear territorial base for language use such as Belgium, Switzerland, and—in contrast with the rest of Canada—Quebec may find it difficult to accommodate immigrant minority languages that disturb a precarious set of arrangements designed to protect the rights of indigenous language groups. In Belgium, for example, although many Moroccans speak French, it would be unthinkable for their children to be taught primarily in that language in Flanders or in Dutch-language schools in Brussels: that would run directly counter to the language settlement reached at the highest levels of Belgian politics.

Similarly, the emphasis on Canada as a "multi-cultural" nation was not welcomed by those francophone leaders for whom it suggested a downgrading of French, and Quebec declined to endorse the Charter of Rights and Freedoms because of its implications for the province's treatment of its own language minority groups, including those speaking English (Mallea, 1984, 224). The multicultural position was also criticized by some French-Canadians as threatening to reduce the status of French from one of the two (equal) founding languages of Canada to simply one ethnic minority language among others and thus reinforcing the dominance of English-speaking Canadians of British origin. "Without doubt, the most consistent and virulent opponents of the multicultural ideology are those who consider that the most appropriate model for Canada is the bilingual (anglophone/francophone) one" (Bullivant, 1981, 66).

The official recognition, in Canada, of language differences along the axis of two dominant languages has had the effect of politicizing the question of language in a way that may make it more difficult to accommodate other languages and those who speak them.

The United States

The very moderate success of efforts to achieve societal bilingualism in Canada casts doubt upon the realism of those advocates of minority languages—and especially of Spanish—who urge that similar governmental efforts be undertaken in the United States (N. Epstein, 1992, 338). What has emerged in Canada, as in Belgium, is a dual monolingualism with highly polarizing political consequences. There is no indication so far that the elements for such a linguistic polarization exist in the United States, where the situation of indigenous language minority groups is in fact very different from that in Canada.

Territorial language minority groups in the United States fall into two categories: those Americans of Spanish descent whose ancestors were in the present United States before annexation by the expanding nation, and "native peoples." The situation of the latter is so different from that of Catalans and Frisians, Welsh and Québecois, that it seems more appropriate to discuss them in a final, separate section, together with such similarly situated peoples as Maori in New Zealand and Lapps in Scandinavia.

MEXICAN AMERICANS

Of the Spanish-speaking inhabitants of areas that were added to the United States following the Mexican War, much the largest group—an estimated 80 percent—lived in what is now New Mexico. The Treaty of Guadalupe

Hidalgo (1848) granted citizenship to the approximately 75,000 Mexican nationals who remained in what would become Arizona, California, Colorado, New Mexico, and Texas, and extended to them a measure of cultural, religious, and language rights. The chief of the American peace delegation negotiating that treaty had reported, on the part of the Mexican negotiators, "a perfect devotion to their distinct nationality, and a most vehement aversion to its becoming merged in or blended with ours" (quoted by Crawford, 1992b, 63).

New Mexico has retained a rather distinctive character in comparison with the rest of the American Southwest, as a result of the long-established population of Spanish descent and also the presence of a significant and well-organized Native American (Indian) population. The New Mexico state constitution, adopted in 1911, provided that teachers should learn Spanish as well as English but also insisted that "children of Spanish descent . . . shall never be classed in separate schools" (U.S. Commission on Civil Rights, 1992, 61). During the national controversy over whether English should be given official status as the exclusive language of public life, the New Mexico legislature adopted a resolution reaffirming "its advocacy of the teaching of other languages in the United States and its belief that the position of English is not threatened" (New Mexico Legislature, 1992, 154). On the other hand, a high proportion of New Mexicans of Spanish descent use English as their first language and the situation is in no respect parallel to that of Quebec.

Apart from New Mexico, the vast majority of Americans of Mexican descent came to the country as immigrants in this century and might be expected to be subject to all of the assimilating pressures upon immigrants that will be discussed in Chapters 4 and 5. Skerry presents the following data for 1848:

> [A]t the close of hostilities between Mexico and the United States in 1848, Mexicans comprised at most 4 percent of the population of the Southwest—or about 80,000 people. Since this was only about 1 percent of Mexico's population at the time, very few Mexican Americans today can trace their lineage back to that conquest (Skerry, 1993, 23).

The Mexican-born population of the United States was 100,00 in 1900, 200,000 in 1910, and (with federally-funded irrigation projects in the Southwest and the economic boom fueled by World War I), 427,000 in 1920. The numbers did not begin to grow significantly again until around 1960 (Brussell, 1968, 11).

It is difficult to generalize about Mexican Americans, who consist of recent arrivals as well as families who lived in the United States well before the arrival of Europeans. Predominantly a rural and agricultural people through the early 1900s, Mexican origin persons now are more urbanized than the general U.S. population. This rapid transformation, over a period of four to five decades, has changed the nature of this group (National Commission on Secondary Education for Hispanics, 1984, II, 35).

Even as the second and third—and tenth—generations of earlier immigrants from Mexico are moving out of agricultural labor into industrial and professional positions in the urban economies of the Southwest and Midwest, millions of new immigrants have arrived to complicate the picture.

Although California, Texas, and other southwestern states have a very large population of Mexican Americans who are beginning to move into political prominence, it would be misleading to think of them as a territorial minority group, nor is there anything like a serious claim of regional autonomy of the sort that gives significance to a minority language like Basque or Catalan. Veltman points out that only 2 percent of the French speakers in Quebec have become primarily English-speakers, contrasted with 60 percent of the Spanish speakers in the American Southwest (cited by Leibowicz, 1992, 104). The situation is very different in the case of another Hispanic group in the United States.

Puerto Ricans

Puerto Ricans living in Puerto Rico are the one group in the United States who correspond generally to the situation of Catalans; indeed, Puerto Rico's situation has until the recent developments in Spain been considerably more autonomous than that of Catalonia. Its people have been citizens of the United States since 1917, without an English language requirement for citizenship. More than one-third of all Puerto Ricans live in the continental United States, and will be discussed in connection with immigrants, though technically they are internal labor migrants; our primary concern here is with those who live on the island.

Spanish and English were both made official languages of government in 1902, soon after the American occupation in 1898. The prevailing language used in schools for the first decades after the establishment of a system of popular education, however, was English, and virtually every Puerto Rican has studied the language for years in school. Only a quarter of the population, however, is estimated to be truly bilingual, and "perhaps half of the island's population has no usable English" (*The Economist*, March 23, 1991).

The attitude of the North Americans who set up and ran the Puerto Rican system of schooling was expressed by an early education commissioner who warned that "the Spanish language is precious to these people. All their history, and their traditions, and their civilization are bound to it" (quoted by Steiner, 1975, 379). It would be necessary to teach them English in order to change them into real Americans. By 1912, 98 percent of the schoolchildren in Puerto Rico were being instructed through English, despite intense political controversy over the language question. A subsequent commissioner insisted in 1919 that "as citizens of the United States the children of Porto [*sic*] Rico possess an inalienable right to learn the English language," and as late as 1937 President Franklin Roosevelt expressed his regret that Puerto Ricans were resisting becoming bilingual (Crawford, 1992b, 242) and called for renewed efforts to develop active bilingualism as an aspect of "the blessing of American citizenship," which could only be achieved,

> if the teaching of English throughout the insular educational system is entered into at once with vigor, purposefulness, and devotion, and with the understanding that English is the official language [*sic*] of our country (quoted by the Language Policy Task Force, 1992, 66).

It should be noted that it was political progressives like Roosevelt and his Secretary of the Interior Harold Ickes who felt most strongly about promoting active bilingualism in Puerto Rico, as a means of extending the benefits of democracy and shaking the Puerto Ricans free from the sleepy effects of four centuries of Spanish colonial rule. Ickes expressed his confidence, in 1943, that "practical bilingualism is desirable and can be achieved, consistent with the president's promise that 'there is no desire or purpose to diminish the enjoyment or the usefulness of the rich Spanish cultural legacy of the people of Puerto Rico'" (Ickes, 1970, 27).

Efforts to provide universal schooling in Puerto Rico led to widespread educational failure. As an official study pointed out in 1925, children did not remain long enough in school to become proficient in English, and the other subjects were learned inadequately because they were studied in an unfamiliar language (G.K. Lewis, 1968, 383). Advocates for the use of Spanish as the language of instruction, with English taught as a second language, had no doubt that an excessive emphasis upon English in the early grades were responsible.

The extreme policy of using the English medium in all the grades was tried during the twelve years after 1904. Its failure was officially admitted . . . in 1916, and English as the medium of instruction was limited to the grades above the fourth until 1934 (Cebollero, 1970, 169).

The use of English as the medium of instruction was further limited to high school in 1934, and with the adoption of the Constitution of the Commonwealth of Puerto Rico, in 1948, Spanish was declared the official language of instruction in public schools. This did not put to rest the issue of language use and the relative claims of the two languages, given the ambiguous political status of Puerto Rico and its love/hate relationship with the United States and with North American culture. Indeed,

> few countries have had so much anguish over how to maintain the identity of their national culture. . . . That a sizeable number of Puerto Ricans desire statehood and are willing to divide their loyalties between their own island and the United States suggests that Puerto Rico's identity is ambivalent. . . . Puerto Ricans might still feel they have something in common with the *jíbaro* (Puerto Rican folk-hero) of fifty years ago, but they are becoming increasingly less secure in their attachment to traditional ways and symbols (Epstein 1970a, vii).

There is a widely-held belief that Puerto Ricans must choose between loyalty to their traditional culture and language and their desire to take advantage of the opportunities available to them through automatic American citizenship.

> To the extent that Puerto Ricans wish to maintain their unity and uniqueness, they must support and defend the most distinctive aspects of their culture. Often this means to retard acculturation. . . . English . . . is symbolic of change. . . . it is believed generally that excessive change would rob Puerto Rico of its cultural vitality (E.H. Epstein, 1970b, 11).

Those who hold this view tend to reject the idea that Puerto Rico is or ever should be a bilingual or bicultural society. "We are, simply, a people with a cultural superstructure which is equal to those of other nations of the world, the product of the ingredients which have melted together in the course of history within our geographic situation" (Iglesias, 1970, 180). There is no room in this concept, apparently, for a further admixture of ingredients from North America, least of all the English language. Advocates of independence (who have the support of less than 10 percent of the voters on the island, and somewhat higher support on the mainland) use the language question, and grievances about the alleged cultural domination of the United States and its corrupting influence, as means of mobilizing support for their cause. It has become almost a truism to assert that Puerto Rico has suffered culturally compared with other nations of Latin America and that its dialect of Spanish is hopelessly debased by *yanqui* elements. The linguist Rubén Del Rosario, himself a supporter of independence, denied this charge, insisting that English words have entered Puerto Rican speech by a natural process, parallel to that by which loan-words enter any language that is culturally alive; he insisted that the culture of Puerto Rico was intact and not sliding into the cultural orbit of the United States.

> What has happened here is not, as some believe, a linguistic mutilation, but a process of synthesis, of accommodation of European Spanish to the material and spiritual needs of the Puerto Rican people. . . . As long as political and cultural relations continue with the Anglo-American world, as long as it is they who invent new things and we who receive them, as long as Hispanic peoples prefer rhetoric to scientific creation, we will have anglicisms. Progressively more anglicisms (Rosario, 1977, 16, 22).

On the other hand, according to Rosario, the effect of statehood would be the inevitable dissolution of Puerto Rican culture and language; "I believe that the only way to save our identity and our Spanish language is independence" (quoted by Rodriguez, 1970, 188).

Others argue that many of the strongest supporters of limiting the influence of English and of North American culture are highly acculturated and fluent in English and should not seek to deny to others what they have benefitted from themselves. A leader of the Statehood Party, supporting development of full bilingualism in Puerto Rican society, criticized an opponent for a "tirade because of the use of English . . . delivered by a man who is perfectly bilingual and who masters English so well that is has been his most efficacious tool . . ."(Toro, 1970, 35).

Swing comments on the irony of "the establishment in this outlying area of the United States of monolingual linguistic policies similar to those found in Belgium and Quebec . . . Indeed, the only way that Anglophones living on the island can now obtain an English language education for their children is to enrol them in private schools" (Swing, 1985, 312). There is indeed a growing number of private schools in which English is the language of instruction, with as many as one pupil in four—including many from Spanish-speaking homes—attending these schools (Language Policy Task Force, 1992, 69). By 1962, 58 of the 132 accredited private schools on the island were teaching through English, including 38 of the 71 Catholic schools. Commissioner of Education Oliveras attacked these schools in 1962, threatening to withdraw their accreditation if they continued this practice, insisting that it was not the policy of the government to allow parents to choose the language of instruction for their children. "The schools of Puerto Rico are for Puerto Ricans," he told a press conference, "and they are to serve the good people of Puerto Rico with all their cultural values." In particular, they must not be used to further the Americanization of the island and its people (Oliveras, 1970, 106–110). He explicitly rejected the idea of providing an effective bilingual education:

> I don't believe in the idea that if we teach both English and Spanish well in the first four grades, afterwards we'll be free to choose any sort of instruction. I believe that the Puerto Rican tends to pray in Spanish and tends to communicate his most intimate feelings in Spanish and tends to use Spanish as a part of his way of being and I believe that Spanish must be the medium of teaching in Puerto Rican schools (Oliveras, 1970, 113).

Statehood advocate (and later governor) Luis Ferré immediately attacked this attempt to dictate the language of instruction of private schools, calling it a "dangerous attitude" of the government, seeking "to use the educational system as a means of indoctrinating our youth for its political purposes [and] denying the natural right of parents to educate their children." He adds,

> As the American citizens that we are, in order to enjoy the equality of opportunities which is basic to our democracy, we must know the English language adequately. Otherwise we Puerto Ricans will continue to be second-class citizens within our nation (Ferré, 1970, 119–20).

For many upwardly mobile Puerto Rican parents, the language question is less symbolic than instrumental; their children already know Spanish, and they would like the school to teach them English. The opportunity for their children to obtain English-language skills that would be important for future employment has justified what was for many a considerable sacrifice to pay tuition to private schools which, until 1993, received no public subsidies. (Under an educational reform program, more than 2,000 pupils benefitted from public scholarships to attend private schools in 1994–95, but the Commonwealth Supreme Court ruled in November 1994 that Law 71 was in violation of the Puerto Rican Constitution.) It does not appear that the choice of private schools was for most parents a decision to sacrifice Spanish language and culture for the sake of English.

Research carried out for the Puerto Rican Department of Public Instruction in 1960 found that "public school children had no Spanish-language superiority over children taught in English private schools. Further, they revealed little perceived connection, among either student population, between language and cultural identity." Indeed, paradoxically, "twice as many public school [taught through Spanish] as private-school pupils felt it was necessary for Puerto Ricans to become more Americanized. . . . Students said their contact with English had not jeopardized or changed their feelings of national identity. The English language was perceived as a valuable political, intellectual, and economic resource" (Language Policy Task Force, 1992, 70). Epstein noted two decades earlier that research findings "do not suggest that proportionately more Catholic school pupils than public school pupils wish to become more American and less Latin or that more of them regard English as a vehicle of americanization" (Epstein, 1970c, 151).

There is no inherent reason why proficiency in English should lead to the abandonment of Spanish, or to the rejection of Puerto Rican culture; to the extent that it leads to greater economic success, it may indeed permit their cultivation. Unlike Mexican Americans or Puerto Ricans in the continental United States, the people of Puerto Rico have sufficient physical isolation from North America, and sufficient economic and cultural ties with Latin America, that there seems to be no sociological reason why they would abandon the use of Spanish (Epstein, 1970d, 239). What a more widespread proficiency in English *would* be likely to do, however, is to increase the already strong support for Puerto Rico becoming a state and thus permanently part of the United States. Advocates of independence, though especially strong among Puerto Ricans on the mainland, express concern that returning migrants "will carry the 'contagion of English back to the island'" (Swing, 1985, 312).

In 1966, a Commission on the Status of Puerto Rico concluded that "statehood would necessarily involve a cultural and language accommodation to the rest of the federated states of the Union. The commission does not see this as an insurmountable barrier, nor does this require the surrender of the Spanish language nor the abandonment of a rich cultural heritage" ("Statehood as a Status Alternative," 1970, 231). Two of its members, U.S. Senators Jackson and Javits, spelled out the implications for language more explicitly.

> The people of Puerto Rico represent an old and rich culture. We welcome diversity; therefore, the distinctive culture of Puerto Rico presents no bar as such to statehood. The unity of our federal-state structure, however, requires a common tongue. We do not have to look far to see what has happened in certain countries that have failed to adhere to this fundamental practice. Surely, at a time when we are trying to eliminate ghettos of all kinds, we should not establish within our federal-state system a "language ghetto." A condition precedent to statehood must be the recognition and acceptance of English as the official language (Jackson and Javits, 1970, 45).

Ultimately, the language question is as much a political as a social issue in Puerto Rico. What is the "nation" of Puerto Ricans? That is the question that lies behind and provides so much emotional intensity to the language question. Those who are for incorporation into the United States as the fifty-first state stress the need for a greatly increased level of proficiency in English in order to make this union work—and to overcome the hesitations of the American Congress about granting statehood. While millions of new Americans over the years have come with alien languages and cultures, they have always been accepted as *individuals*; American political culture recognizes individual rights but not group rights. Puerto Rican statehood would for the first time give *institutional* form to a system based upon a language other than English, and would do so at a time of popular anxiety about whether pluralism has gone too far and of legislation, in a number of states, establishing English as official language.

In this context, the adoption of a law in Puerto Rico, in 1991, making Spanish the only official language and ending the bilingual provision in effect since 1902 was interpreted by some as a measure by Commonwealth advocates and Governor Rafael Hernandez Colón seeking to reduce the chance that the American Congress would admit Puerto Rico as a state. In 1993, newly elected Governor Pedro Rossello of the pro-statehood New Progressive Party signed a law again giving English equal status with Spanish in Puerto Rican government, though Spanish will continue to be the primary language of instruction in public schools (*Education Week*, February 10, 1993).

In the months leading up to the referendum on the status of Puerto Rico in November 1993, the issue of the extent to which English should play an important part in the island's life and education system was hotly debated. Statehood advocates repeated the earlier argument that an enhanced use of English was perfectly consistent with Puerto Rico "conserving its personality, its culture (certainly older and more solid than that of North America) and its vernacular language as the expression and vehicle of that culture" (Morales, 1970, 30). Those who believed that complete independence would be more conducive to the integrity of the Puerto Rican people sought to reduce the role of English to that of a foreign language like any other.

> The [present] commonwealth arrangement places English in a state of limbo; it is suspect to those who stress the distinctiveness of Puerto Rican culture and view independence as the only just condition, and it is extolled by those who advocate assimilation with the United States. An uncertain political status places Puerto Rican educators in a difficult position. Supporting increased English instruction leaves them open to nationalist accusations that they follow a policy of assimilative colonialism. Limiting English further in the schools draws charges that Puerto Rican education does not go far enough to promote americanism. . . . It is notable that no language policy has been safe from bitter criticism (Epstein, 1970c).

Language is a central factor in the political debates that continue over the status of Puerto Rico.

> Psychically, commonwealth status implies a certain distance from the United States—a commitment to the preservation of the Spanish language and of Puerto Rican culture . . . Puerto Rico's idea of itself is as an island of earthy, unpretentious, good-hearted people who treat each other with *dulce cariño*, "sweet caring." It's easy to see how American culture could be perceived as a threat to this ethos, and thus something that should be kept at arm's length. . . . Advocates of statehood—a mixture of business interests and the rising lower and middle classes, like Margaret Thatcher's coalition in Britain—acknowledge that [the economic situation] would be worse in the short term, and stress the overriding historical importance of the island's becoming fully American (Lemann, 1991, 108, 110).

The closeness of the vote on the status of Puerto Rico in 1993, and the high proportion of its population which comes and goes between the island and the mainland, have not only prevented the wholehearted implementation of strategies to promote active bilingualism—though the island is bilingual by default—but have also apparently prevented many Puerto Rican migrants to the mainland from making the commitment to a new society which have led to the economic and educational success of most immigrant groups.

Puerto Ricans on the mainland fall somewhere between the categories of "immigrant" (which they are not, since they are United States citizens by birthright) and "indigenous minority" (which they are not, since no more than two or three generations, in most cases, have lived on the mainland). Ogbu includes them in his category of "involuntary minorities," and this status of imposed marginalization (as contrasted with the self-imposed marginal situation of voluntary immigrants) may help to explain why Puerto Ricans have the most unfavorable social and economic indicators of all the Hispanic groups in the United States (National Commission on Secondary Education for Hispanics, 1984, II, 32–33).

"Native Peoples"

We have not so far considered "indigenous minority" groups speaking languages that lack a written tradition: the aboriginal languages of Australia and New Zealand, Inuit languages of the Arctic regions, and the languages of the native peoples of the United States, Canada, and Scandinavia. Speakers of these languages have even more difficulty than those mentioned above in preserving valued elements of their ancestral languages and cultures, or in doing so without a high cost in blocked opportunities. The "native peoples" of the United States and Canada, for example, are reported to have spoken more than 600 different languages at the time of European settlement; "only 300 still survive, and of these, over one-half are spoken by a handful of elderly people" (Bunge, 1992, 377). The 1990 United States Census identified 136 different groups of Indian languages.

> Of these, 47 were spoken in the home by fewer than 100 persons; an additional 22 were spoken by fewer than 200. And this is probably a conservative estimate of linguistic erosion, because the Census has no way of knowing how well or how often these people actually use the language (Crawford, 1995, 19).

Others count 155 indigenous languages in the United States, 135 of which are moribund; "all of California's 31 Indian languages are moribund; of these, 22 are spoken only by small groups of elders" (Crawford, 1995, 18).

Before and during the period of government-sponsored assimilation efforts at the high tide of Western colonialism in the second half of the nineteenth century, the educational programs of Christian churches among native peoples were considerably more respectful of their languages, if not always of their cultures. Effective evangelization had always been associated, since the first Pentecost, with the preaching of the Gospel in whatever language would communicate effectively with the target group (*Acts of the Apostles* 2:1–12). In many cases, as with the Goths and Slavs in early medieval Europe, the first written form of the language was developed in order to provide portions of the Bible and religious instruction materials. This practice continued among the Micmac of Canada (Battiste, 1986) and the Maori of New Zealand, where

> over a thousand items were printed in Maori between 1815 and 1900; in 1872, Bishop Colenso wrote a text book for teaching Maoris to read English remarking in the preface (which was written in Maori) that seeing they could already read their own language so well, they should have no difficulty in learning to read a second one (Spolsky & Holm, 1991, 64).

In the early years of European settlement in New Zealand, "mission schools were established and proved enormously popular. Instruction was provided in the Maori language, and . . . a cautious estimate would be that by the early 1840s a little over half the adult population of 90,000 could read or write a little in their own language" (Barrington, 1991, 310).

Government policymakers were less sympathetic than were church leaders toward native languages, and often came into conflict with efforts by missionary groups. Maori was banned from New Zealand schools in 1870, and the same year President Grant criticized the use of Indian languages in American mission schools, then publicly funded. An official report in 1881 stated that

> so long as the American people now demand that Indians shall become white men within one generation . . . [they] must be compelled to adopt the English language, must be so placed that attendance at school shall be regular . . . and must breathe the atmosphere is a civilized instead of a . . . barbarous community (quoted by Leibowitz, 1971, 3).

In the same spirit, the top government official charged with Indian affairs wrote, in 1887, that the language "which is good enough for a white man or a black man ought to be good enough for a red man," and suggested that "teaching an Indian youth in his own barbarous dialect is a positive detriment to him" (Atkins, quoted by Szasz, 1974, 71). Similarly, the *Toronto Globe* insisted, in 1872, upon making the Indian peoples into assimilated Canadians:

> Englishman and Frenchman, Scot, Irishman, German and Swede, are content to yield up their boasted nationalities, and mingle in the common Canadian stock. They are not exterminated by becoming Canadians; and neither need the civilized Indian be exterminated, though he share in the same lot, and merge in the common stock of our Canadian people (Wilson, 1986, 82).

By contrast, a nineteenth-century Anglican missionary in Ontario who worked energetically to create schools for Indian children concluded at last by condemning efforts to "un-Indianize the Indian, and make him in every sense a white man. . . . Why should we expect that Indians alone should be ready quietly to give up all old customs and traditions and language, and adopt those of the aggressor upon their soil?" (quoted by Wilson, 1986, 82).

The native (pre-European) peoples of the United States were initially treated as a feature of the external environment of the nation; formal treaties were made with them, and an ever-retreating space was provided within which they could to some extent control their own destinies. In 1871, however, "Congress ended all treaty-making with tribes. This action marked a shift in government plans for the Indian, from relocation to the unsettled West to assimilation into the general population" (Reyhner, 1992, 42). One of the primary goals of government policy was to ensure that all Indian children learn the English language. The goal had a substantial element of cultural imperialism about it, but it was also motivated by a concern to ensure that Indian children would be able to participate fully in the opportunities offered by American life. "In the difference of language today lies two-thirds of our trouble," wrote a government-appointed "Peace Commission" in 1868. "Schools should be established which children should be required to attend; their barbarous dialects would be blotted out and the English language substituted" (quoted by Leibowitz, 1971, 2).

Both in the United States and in Canada (Gresko, 1986, 97) government pressure was placed on mission schools that insisted upon continuing to use the native language together with English. The American government even challenged the right of tribes to use their own funds to assist these schools, but "Indians were vehement defenders of sectarian schools threatened by closure" (Szasz, 1974, 12). More recently, criticism of these schools has become a standard trope in the rhetoric of Indian activists, with an emphasis upon forced assimilation, denigration of native culture, and suppression of Indian languages. The critics "condemn the deleterious effects of White man's education of Indian people over a century and a half," a Canadian scholar points out, "but make no effort to document the true nature of that education. However dismal the record of church-run Indian schools in the nineteenth and twentieth centuries, it remains a fact that most of today's Indian-rights leaders are products of those very schools" (Wilson, 1986, 64), which "educated young Indians about one another and politicized them about their place in the larger society" (Gresko, 1986, 102). Denominational schools also played an important role in New Zealand, where

> a high proportion of Maori leaders, at both local and national levels, graduated from these schools and the schools' pupils have had a significantly better record of passes in national examinations for Maoris than [have those of] state schools. A major reason for the success of these schools has been the emphasis they place on Maori language and culture and on their being "Maori" institutions (Barrington, 1991, 322).

After the American government's own schools for Indians—many of them boarding schools where pupils from a number of tribes were brought together for instruction provided exclusively through English—had gained an unfortunate reputation, a policy of integrating Indian pupils into nearby public schools sought to place them in the mainstream of American life. Between 1930 and 1970 the proportion of Indian children attending local public schools—with the costs of this schooling subsidized by the federal government—increased from 53 to 65 percent (Szasz, 1974, 89), with the intention that the proportion would continue to increase as integration took hold and the isolation of reservation life was broken down. The same strategy of placing Indian pupils in local schools was officially adopted in Canada in 1951 (Persson, 1986, 157) and in New Zealand in 1955 (Barrington, 1991, 317). In effect, in all three countries, native peoples were given the same status as that of immigrant minority groups (Kramer, 1991, 293).

This change of strategy created the unintended consequence of an increased vulnerability to the ineptitude or ill-will of local officials. "Without the protective federal involvement to maintain their unique status as sovereign domestic nations . . . American Indians were relegated to the same status as other American ethnic groups" (Kramer, 1991, 293). They were to be helped in a variety of ways by government programs, but always with the expectation that they would become "normal" Americans in time. As the (white) chief of Indian education wrote in 1946,

> without sacrificing racial pride or identification with their Indian past, Indian parents and pupils are determined to gain from education a mastery of the English language and of the manual and intellectual skills of their white brethren. . . . [seeking] mastery of the material culture of the dominant race (Beatty, quoted by Szasz, 1974, 119).

Abandoning group solutions for integration on an individual basis was proposed in 1967, in a study arguing "the necessity of integrating Indians into Canadian society" (Battiste, 1986, 36), and was adopted by the Canadian government in 1969, after the election of Pierre Trudeau's Liberals. Parliament was told that the separate legal status of Indians "and the policies which have flowed from it have kept the Indian people apart from and behind other Canadians" (Persson, 1986, 165). The new approach was

> premised on the achievement of individual Indian equality at the expense of cultural survival. All legislative and constitutional bases of discrimination [positive as well as negative] were to be removed; Indians would receive the same services, including education, available to members of the dominant society. The Department of Indian Affairs would be abolished and the reserve [reservation] system dismantled. Indians as individuals would become equal participants in the "just society" (Barman, Hébert, & McCaskill, 1986, 15).

Reaction by Indian leadership to the change of government policy was overwhelmingly negative; it was a "thinly disguised program of extermination through assimilation" (Cardinal, quoted by Barman, Hébert, & McCaskill, 1986, 15). Of course, there would be no need for Indian leadership once integration was achieved.

Eventually there was a swing back to Indian control of schooling in Canada, and by 1983–84 20 percent of Indian children were attending schools operated by the different tribes, particularly in Western Canada (Barman, Hébert, and McCaskill, 1986, 16). This was in effect a belated validation of the position maintained by the missionary education efforts of the churches, that Indian youth could best be educated in schools exclusively dedicated to them (Persson, 1986, 150).

The failure of integration of Indian children into local school systems in the United States was asserted powerfully in 1969 by a Special Subcommittee on Indian Education of Congress which

> concluded that the "dominant policy of the Federal Government towards the American Indian had been one of coercive assimilation," and that this policy "has had disastrous effects on the education of Indian children. . . . Schools attended by Indian children have become a "kind of battleground where the Indian child attempts to protect his integrity and identity as an individual by defeating the purposes of the school"; these schools have failed to "understand or adapt to, and in fact often denigrate, cultural differences"; the schools have blamed "their own failures on the Indian student," which reinforces his "defensiveness"; the schools have failed "to recognize the importance and vitality of the Indian community"; and the community and child have retaliated "by treating the school as an alien institution" (Szasz, 1974, 150).

The committee called for less coercive approaches to meeting the goal of assimilation, but it did not call that goal into questions. Others, among the Indian leadership, were doing so, insisting that Indians were not simply another ethnic minority group but were sovereign nations under treaties made by the United States government during the period of westward expansion. Thus, in the words of a white supporter of Indian self-sufficiency, "American Indians only stand to lose by integration into the larger society" (Kramer, 1991, 302).

It is certainly possible to see the sense in which this is true, but it does not answer the question of how a sufficient number of opportunities can be provided for Indian youth within a separate Indian sector of the economy so that they will not have to acquire the language and other skills and habits necessary for employment in the wider economy. There is a nice ring to asserting that "the most viable political and economic position for Indian tribes has been coexistence with American society, not entry into it" (Kramer, 1991, 302), but that holds true only for those tribes, like the Ute, who are supported by royalties from oil and mineral rights without compromising their splendid independence.

As it became clear in the United States that public school systems were not meeting the needs of their Indian pupils, "federal policy again shifted, this time toward self-determination, encouraging Indian tribes to become responsible for their children's schooling" (Kramer, 1991, 294).

Indian leadership in the United States also became more assertive in the 1960s, in part under the influence of the Civil Rights Movement. Great attention was focused on a few "community controlled" schools such as Rough Rock Community School (Begay et al., 1995) and Rock Point on the Navajo Reservation, where initial literacy instruction was through Navajo and the language continued to be used for instruction (though to a diminishing extent) through intermediate and high school (Holm & Holm, 1990, 1995).

Efforts to use native languages as a vehicle for at least initial education and transition to English had gained temporary government support in the thirties, when bilingual readers were produced in Navajo, Hopi, and Sioux, and Spanish-English materials were produced for Pueblo and Papago children (Bauer, 1971, 30). Even among the more isolated peoples, however, there has generally a strong orientation toward acquiring proficiency in English, not as a rejection of the native culture but because of the instrumental importance of the majority language. Kluckhohn and Leighton found among Navajo parents before the Second World War a strong concern that their children be able to speak and write English, and after the war the returning veterans and defense workers were much more familiar with the advantages of proficiency in a wider means of communication.

> A public demand grew for more and better education and for education in English. Thus, in the context of a nation-wide distrust of differences as being un-American, and a governmental policy of transition to state public schools, was fatal to the relatively modest Navajo language programs (Kluckhohn and Leighton, 1946).

Although Navajo continues to be spoken extensively—the Navajo reservation has over 140,000 residents and an extensive administrative structure that uses the language to some extent—English is used for written communication "despite what is probably the largest absolute number, and largest relative percentage, of native-language monolinguals of any tribe in the United States, the written business of the tribe goes on in English" (Spolsky & Holm, 1971, 60). Among Navajo aged 5 to 17 living on the reservation, the proportion who spoke only English rose from 11.8 percent in 1980 to 28.4 percent in 1990 (Crawford, 1995, 21).

On the other hand, the native languages continue in some cases to retain considerable symbolic importance, even for those who experience their cultures largely through English. The Navajo Community College, founded in 1968, established a program to teach the Navajo language to those "who have apparently lost their ability to speak Navajo" (Werner, 1969, quoted by Coombs, 1971, 15), as an aspect of an overall rejection of the hegemony of American culture; non-Indian faculty members were also denied a voice in the decision-making process of the college, and served only until Navajo replacements could be found (Szasz, 1974, 177–178).

For at least one tribe, the use of their language by the school was initially unwelcome, since it seemed to presage a breach in the wall which the language provided between their own life and that of the wider—and generally hostile—society. "Parents feared that written Ute language materials might give any literate person, including non-Utes, access to esoteric dimensions of Ute culture." For this tribe, like many others, "political success meant maintaining its own institutions, not integrating into the county, state and national systems" (Kramer, 1991, 298–299), much less becoming part of a "multicultural mosaic."

One result of such efforts was the Indian Education Act of 1972, which provided support not only for programs on and near reservations, but also for efforts to reach and serve Indian children living in cities and in the East. Federal support had already been expanded with the enactment of a program to support various forms of bilingual instruction, in 1968. Though the primary focus was upon the needs of Spanish-speaking children, a variety of pilot programs were implemented in Cherokee and Navajo (1969), Chocktaw, Ute, Yuk, Crow, Cree, and Northern Cheyenne (1970), and Zuñi, Lakota, and Passamaquoddy (1971) (Tennant, 1971, 35–36). Other languages have been added over the years, in some cases only after written forms were developed for the first time.

These programs, it should be noted, have mostly been concentrated at the lower grades of schooling, and have been designed more for transition to English than for maintenance of the native language as the primary means of communication; though "culturally related topics and special heritage classes" (Predaris, 1984, 27) are common, they have done little to slow the abandonment of Indian languages in cases where they do not receive strong support outside the school. The situation is especially complicated by the fact that "many reservation schools serve students from multiple Indian nations thus creating the problem of deciding what languages and what cultural traditions should be taught" (Pitman, 1995, 2).

According to a report of discussion at a conference in 1968 to develop preschool programs in Navajo,

> the importance of beginning the child's education in his own language and in his own cultural background, building a sense of security and pride in his own culture, and the need for strengthening this sense of pride were stressed again and again during the conference. Indeed,

the conference felt that to be truly effective bilingual education should be extended into the elementary school, though it was realized that attempts to use Navajo at higher levels might increase the already existing problems in the use of Navajo as a medium of instruction, the teaching of Navajo to those who are monolingual in English both in purely Navajo and mixed schools, and the preparation of materials and teachers for instruction in and through the medium of the Navajo language (Ohannessian, 1971, 68).

Even this group of enthusiasts for early instruction through Navajo conceded that "there was a great variety of attitudes among Indian parents and leaders towards the teaching of Navajo language and culture in the schools, and that many felt these were better taught by parents at home . . . others felt that there was insufficient information on what Indian parents really thought on the subject" (Ohannessian, 1971, 69). On the other hand, there were compelling reasons of self-interest for promoting and—once established—for defending an educational program employing, with federal government funds, a language which few outsiders were qualified to teach in. As Bernard Spolsky observed,

> The decision to establish bilingual education, even a transitional variety for the first three grades, implied the need for a thousand Navajo-speaking teachers. Whatever other educational or linguistic rationales might have been presented, it is clear that bilingual education in this situation offered the possibility of jobs within the community for a sizable number of people. . . . [This] would immediately establish within the community a well-paid middle class whose potential influence on the political development of the Navajo Nation is obvious (Spolsky, 1978a, 278).

More broadly, Spolsky concludes, "in the United States, one of the rationales for bilingual education has been to give previously underrepresented groups control over the resources of the educational systems that affect their children; it serves then as part of the general affirmative action movement" (Spolsky, 1978a, 279).

There has been a growing interest in New Zealand, as well, in the use of Maori as a language for instruction as well as for enrichment and cultural maintenance; by 1989 there were "eleven official bilingual schools and over 100 primary schools with bilingual classes" (Barrington, 1991, 321).

A policy adopted by the American Congress (without funding or enforcement provisions) in 1990 stated that "the United States has the responsibility to act together with Native Americans to ensure the survival of these unique cultures and languages;" in 1994 $1 million was granted for language conservation and renewal projects. The policy went on to assert that

> the traditional languages of Native Americans are an integral part of their cultures and identities and form the basic medium for the transmission, and thus survival, of Native American cultures, literatures, histories, religions, political institutions, and values" (Native American Language Act, 1992, 155).

This seemed to imply that those Americans of Indian descent who did not speak their ancestral languages—the great majority—had no share in the cultures and identities of their ancestors. There are Indian language activists who assert precisely that: that "one cannot be Mohawk without speaking the language, and that the culture dies with the language" (Freeman et al., 1995, 53), but this would be vehemently denied by hundreds of thousands of Native Americans who continue to identify strongly with their ancestral traditions even though they speak at most a few words or phrases of Micmac or Cheyenne. The Indian peoples for whom the ancestral language has been adapted to the demands of contemporary life, and is spoken on a daily basis, are in general those whose numbers and geographical remoteness shelter them to some degree from external influences, like the Navajo. Research in the late 1960s found that "the farther children live away from Reservation population centers and/or paved or all-weather roads, the more likely they are to speak Navajo at home" (Spolsky & Holm, 1971, 63).

The situation of the Lapps (or Sámi) of Scandinavia is analogous to that of the Navajo, including an economy based upon herding in a forbidding environment. There were estimated to be about 70,000 Lapps in the 1980s, 40,000 of them in Norway, 20,000 in Sweden, and the balance in Finland and Russia (Aikio, 1991, 95).

> They were a nomadic people of hunters and fishermen, who step by step were forced back from the more desirable lands, until they were left with territory that proved to be suitable only for reindeer herding. . . . By now many have drifted off into urban areas and have slowly been climbing the ladder of Swedish life, a few succeeding to the extent of going to a university. The jobs most of them have found, however, have been positions as kitchen maids, shop assistants, of-

fice clerks, nurses, or teachers, railway workers, unskilled laborers, miners, or builders' workmen (Haugen, 1992, 403–404).

Those who have abandoned reindeer herding are heavily exposed to the influence of Swedish, Norwegian, or Finnish culture. The Swedish government, according to Deirdre Jordan, long categorized the Sámi as an occupational group engaged in herding reindeer, not as an ethnic group. As a result, no recognition or support was given to maintenance of their language or culture. With the development, after World War II, of a heightened consciousness among the Lapps, a Scandinavian Lapp Council was formed and included, among its demands upon the Norwegian, Swedish, and Finnish governments, that children should be taught to read and write first in Sámi before learning the official language of the country (Jordan, 1988, 195). There was some increase in instruction through Sámi, but as of 1991 "no Sámi-speaker has majored in the Sámi language at a university in Finland although Sámi has been a university subject for more than ten years. Their proficiency in Sámi—as defined by outsiders—has not been sufficient" (Aikio, 1991, 98).

The Lapps themselves are by no means united in support of the demand to maintain their ancestral language; indeed "some parents speak Swedish on purpose to their children."

> Some of them value their Lappish mother tongue highly, others would care little or nothing if it should disappear—and there are many attitudes in between. . . . Some Lapps are firmly convinced of the superiority of Swedish in comparison with Lappish (and Finnish) as a means of communication, as a cultural instrument and as a logical symbol (Hansegård, quoted by Haugen, 1992, 404).

Research in Finland found that there was a fundamental shift in the 1940s; "people spoke with youth using both languages while they spoke almost exclusively Finnish with children. From the 1950s on, no one used Sámi with children. This was caused primarily by the established school environment: the language was Finnish and it was more or less overtly recommended for exclusive use when speaking to children" (Aikio, 1991, 96). Similarly, Norwegian schools banished the use of Sámi from 1870 until the aftermath of the Second World War, when it was introduced as a teaching language and a subject. "In 1967 the first experiment with teaching reading, writing and arithmetic through the mother-tongue only was started. The Norwegian language was used only half an hour every day, and only for elementary oral exercises" (Boon, quoted by Coombs, 1971, 18).

In recent decades, the Swedish Government has extended a measure of support to the maintenance of Lapp culture, adopting a law in 1962 that provided:

> As far as the schooling of the Lapps is concerned, they have the right to an instruction which is in all respects equal, but does not therefore have to be identical with that which the majority receives. By virtue of being a minority group, they have certain peculiar instructional needs which society cannot overlook. They have the right to get in their schools an orientation concerning the development of their own culture and its status in the present, an orientation which does not merely aim to communicate knowledge, but also to awaken respect for and piety towards the heritage from earlier generations, as well as a feeling of solidarity with their own people (quoted by Haugen, 1992, 409).

This modestly phrased statement, with its emphasis upon respect for a culture which is acknowledged to be evolving rather than upon its maintenance intact, seems far sounder as a statement of national policy than that implied by the action of the American Congress in 1992. Despite these efforts, Sámi has been characterized as a dying language, "sliding towards extinction," though without this meaning that group identity is becoming meaningless (Aikio, 1991).

Denmark adopted a local option provision which permitted communities in Greenland to provide instruction through native languages, and more recently Greenlandic has become the official language (though Danish continues to be widely used). This choice of a traditional language with no international currency parallels the decision in Ireland, two generations ago, to designate Irish as official national language in its sentimentality.

The question remains, whether the culture (and its associated language) of a people making a rapid transition to modernity can itself evolve rapidly enough to manifest a new vitality as the culture and language through which they orient themselves to a radically transformed situation. There are unfortunately many examples of "native peoples" who have apparently become stuck halfway through the transition, having abandoned the coherent culture and way of life that once sustained them without successfully mastering those of the dominant society. It may be (though it is "politically incorrect" to suggest it) that the effort to bridge the gap is doomed to fail, and that those who make the transition successfully must accomplish the feat by an intensely painful act of renunciation of the old ways and a mastery of the dominant culture and its associated language. It is not a question of whether they have the *right* to maintain their ancestral traditions (and there are few governments, today, that would deny them that right), but rather of whether those traditions can be more than a marginal aspect of successful participation in the wider society.

In the case of the United States, the fact that tens of thousands of people are "rediscovering" (or, in many cases, inventing) Indian ancestry out of a romantic identification with what has been presented in schools and the media as a less corrupted culture or out of a desire to benefit from schooling and employment preferences available to members of minority groups—or, indeed, because of the new prosperity of those tribes that are operating gambling casinos—is further weakening the case for treating native languages as an essential element of the Indian identity. Whereas less than 800,000 persons identified themselves as American Indians in the 1970 census (and only a little over half a million a decade earlier), the number is projected to be 2.3 million in the 2000 census; it seems highly unlikely that much of this dramatic growth consists of persons who speak Indian languages. The situation is thus sharply different from that of the other fast-growing groups, persons of Mexican and of Asian ancestry, among whom immigrants are constantly replacing those who make the transition to primary use of English.

CONCLUSIONS

This review of the situation of indigenous language minority groups cannot tell us conclusively whether the language and culture of immigrant groups will be maintained by their own efforts or by government policies. The evidence that such a review can provide is at best negative. Successful maintenance or revival of Welsh or Catalan, by a group with a local majority and a substantial measure of political autonomy, would not prove that an immigrant group scattered among a majority speaking another language and with little political influence could maintain its own language over several generations on more than a token basis. On the other hand, official bilingualism might create a climate of opinion and of public policy that would allow additional languages to find acceptance and support. Immigrant groups might thus stand a better chance of maintaining their languages in societies where there are strongly established indigenous language minority groups.

Experience does not provide support for this optimistic scenario. In nations with more than one official language, such as Belgium, Canada, and

Switzerland, there is indeed a heightened sensitivity about the use of languages, but it takes the form of a jealous prescription of which official language will be used in what place and under what circumstances. Legislation and public policy designed to protect the official language considered to be in a weaker position (in these three cases, French) leave little room for unofficial languages to receive public recognition and support. As we have seen, in Canada the federal government support for "heritage languages" has been perceived by some Francophones as part of a plot to reduce the status of French to the same level. Under such circumstances, it is more appropriate to speak of societal *diglossia*, "an enduring societal arrangement, extending at least beyond a three generation period, such that two 'languages' each have their secure, phenomenologically legitimate and widely implemented functions" (Fishman, 1980, 3), rather than of individual *bilingualism*. Only the sort of vigorous efforts undertaken in Catalonia has much prospect of turning a situation of diglossia into one in which most people are in fact bilingual, and Belgium and Switzerland show that it is quite possible to live as a monolingual person in a diglossic society.

The experience of territorial language minority groups in modern societies suggests that such groups are able to maintain full use of their language as more than a means of domestic communication only (a) when it is, like French or Spanish, a language of strong international viability, or (b) when it is, like Catalan or Welsh, associated with strongly articulated claims to political autonomy. In the latter case, anyone who participates in the modern economy must also have full mastery of the predominant national language; the declining significance of Irish after the winning of independence suggests that the second set of circumstances may be only a temporary shelter for a minority language which has only symbolic significance. This is not to say that all use of the language will be lost with its political role, but that it is likely to be relegated to dialect status, as an aspect of ethnic identity with more sentimental than practical significance, an interest of devotees rather than an essential means of communication.

A third set of circumstances under which a minority language is preserved has not been discussed in the examples cited in this chapter. Certain groups maintain an intense inwardly focused communal life which does not depend upon and indeed precludes extensive communication with and integration into the wider society; under such circumstances, a minority language may be not only preserved but essential to the preservation of the group's distinctiveness.

The examples that come to mind—an archaic form of German among the Amish, Yiddish among Hasidic Jews—are associated with religious conviction and practice. As we will see in Chapters 4 and 5, there is reason to believe that maintenance of the languages and cultures of immigrant groups is indeed more likely to be furthered by religious than by political agendas, to the chagrin of "ethnic activists," but over time most religious institutions and loyalties seem quite capable of adapting to new languages without abandoning anything essential. Many "ethnic churches" in the United States have offered two Sunday services, one in the immigrant language and the other in English for the younger generation, only to cancel the former eventually when the younger became the older generation.

The example of "territorial language minority groups" in highly integrated modern industrial societies, then, suggests that immigrant groups, lacking a physical space within which to construct a distinct cultural and linguistic space, are unlikely to be able to maintain their ancestral languages over the course of several generations. It also suggests that efforts to teach those languages to the second and third generations, while ultimately incapable in most cases of achieving proficient bilingualism (Chapter 5), do not represent any sort of threat to social unity, absent territorially-based political conflicts. As one linguist has pointed out, "successful transitional programs will encourage more rapid acquisition of English and consequent loss of use of the native language by groups which have no strong internal desire for language maintenance" (Spolsky, 1978a, 281).

The wisest public policy toward a minority language might therefore be a benevolent one of its encouragement *as a second language*, to avoid the possibility of alienation based upon language grievances. A good rule of thumb might be that the more government seeks to suppress a minority language (as in Catalonia under Franco's rule), the more importance it comes to have and the more resolutely and defiantly it will be retained. Minority-group maintenance of a language, especially with some public support, is unlikely to lead to political polarization. It is essential, however, that the minority language not be maintained at the expense of full proficiency in the language of the majority and thus of opportunity and participation in society, political decision making, and the general economy.

Thousands of works of fiction, autobiography, and scholarship have attempted to describe the immigrant experience. The academic field of sociology in the United States largely grew out of attempts to understand the relationship among immigrants, between assimilation to the host society and maintenance of elements of cultural distinctiveness and ethnic organization, and this American experience with immigration and the ways in which it was analyzed by Mayo Smith, Thomas, Park, and others has tended to shape thinking about interethnic relations in other countries where very different circumstances exist (Bastenier & Dassetto, 1993). This can lead to the misleading assumption that "since Germans, Poles, and the like have become 'Americans,' Walloons and Flemings can be expected to become 'Belgians' and Hausa-Fulani to become 'Nigerians'" (Connor, 1985a, 9).

It is not so much the distance between cultures (however measured) that determines how an ethnic minority will relate to the majority as it is the attitude that members of each group have toward members of the other, and the prevailing assumptions about what it means to be a member of the host society.

> It is one thing, for example, for a member of the Korean minority in Japan to contemplate Nipponization and quite another for a Korean-American to contemplate Americanization. The latter can be undertaken with one's emotional memory bank intact, because the new identity is ethnically neutral. Americanization does not require one to deny or hide his or her ancestry (Connor, 1985a, 9).

Our theme—the accommodations made or not made by schools to the home languages of some of their pupils—must be seen against the background of the continuing significance of these languages to those who immigrate and to their children and grandchildren, and the significance of a language cannot be understood apart from the communities within which it is used or for which, unused, it has symbolic importance. As we saw in Chapter 3, minority languages like Welsh that have little "bankable" usefulness may yet serve to express and maintain community solidarity or support a symbolic identity.

In this chapter the varying social situations of individual immigrants and of immigrant groups will be discussed; in Chapter 5, the focus will be upon their varying cultural situations, including the languages that they or their parents spoke before immigration. This discussion will then lead in Chapters 6 through 8 to the arrangements for schooling (and for language use in schooling) which host societies, and immigrant groups themselves, have made for children growing up in the ambiguous situation resulting from the immigration of their parents.

The factors that influence the extent to which immigrants maintain or give up their distinctiveness can usefully be grouped as (1) characteristics of the host society, and (2) characteristics of the immigrant group and of the individual's relationship with it. After discussing each of these, we will consider the roles of religion and of ethnic leadership in maintaining communities or fostering the participation of individuals in the wider society, and then discuss the uneasy balance that immigrants and their children must strike between accommodation and the maintenance of distinctive identity.

CHARACTERISTICS OF HOST SOCIETIES

One of the factors that influence the experience of immigrants is whether the conditions of the host society are such that foreign workers are sought to meet the labor needs of the economy, as in Germany and France in the 1960s, or that whole families of foreign origin are sought to enlarge the population, as in Australia and Canada through most of their history, or that immigrants come as a back-wave of an earlier phase of imperialism on the part of the host country, as in the United Kingdom and the Netherlands during the 1950s, or that (in times of economic difficulty) the doors are closed and those immigrants who are already present are perceived as a burden and a threat to renewed prosperity, and political refugees, if admitted at all, are accorded scant welcome (Chapter 2).

In the first situation, there is likely to be little effort to adapt schooling to the needs of the children accompanying guestworkers, since the presumption is that they will return to their homelands once the labor of their parents is no longer needed. Perhaps the most that will be done (as in several West European countries in the 1960s) is to make an arrangement with the education authorities of the homeland to send teachers and textbooks so that children can continue schooling in their native language with a view to reintegration into the homeland upon the return of their families. Those who come as "guest workers" with every intention of returning with accumulated earnings may believe it unnecessary to adapt to the host society beyond the minimum necessary to get along. With the passage of time, however, many of the first generation and most of the second are likely (absent heroic efforts to the contrary) to find themselves entering more and more into the life of the host society and gradually making it their own—if they are allowed to do so. Parents may observe with anxiety the tendency of their children to adopt the language and mores of the host society, fearing correctly that this may undermine their ability and even willingness to return to the homeland.

In the second situation, by contrast, there are likely to be deliberate programs to help the children of immigrants to adapt rapidly to the host society and its educational system, like the "steamer classes" provided in the early twentieth century in many American cities, and the strongly assimilationist policies followed by the Australian government in the postwar years, when "neither the underlying philosophy nor the procedures to produce 'good Australians' was open for debate" (Murphy, 1993, 143). If some use is made of the home languages of immigrant children under these circumstances, it is purely instrumental, to enable them and their parents to understand what is expected of them and how to go about becoming assimilated.

The third situation creates a rather different dynamic, since the admission of the former colonials is justified on political or humanitarian grounds without a perceived benefit—either of labor force or of population—to the host society and continues an ambivalent colonial relationship of "civilizing" and exploitation on the one side and failed or resisted assimilation on the other that gives a complex resonance to the presence of the formerly colonized in the "mother country." Former colonials may have already acquired patterns of relationship with representatives of the colonizing power that carry over into the new situation in the form of a certain cultural and psychological distance. They may also be prone to continue to re-enact aspects of their liberation struggle in this new context, as has been especially evident in the United Kingdom.

This complexity extends to the use of their languages in schooling, since (unlike typical labor migrants) they tend already to be somewhat familiar with the language of the host society but may share a history in which the assertion of their own language was an important element of the decolonization struggle, to which their struggle for rights in the host country is often analogized. Former colonials may thus, paradoxically, be both more proficient in the majority language than other immigrants, and more politically insistent upon official recognition for their minority languages.

Former colonials and labor migrants overlap in some countries, of course, and help to explain the complexity characterizing the attitude toward and experience of immigrants. Formerly colonized Surinamese in The Netherlands, Finns in Sweden, Puerto Ricans and Filipinos in the United States, and Algerians in France share the immigrant situation with other populations, Turks and Serbs, Koreans and Portuguese, who have come for strictly economic reasons and without a prior love-hate relationship with the language and culture of the host society. The fact that almost all immigrants to the United Kingdom—the Irish in large numbers for the past two centuries, West Indians, Cypriots, Pakistanis, Bangladeshis, and Indians since World War II—are from former colonies may help to account for the special intensity of rejection and segregation in that country, and the early politicization of the immigration question there.

The countries that we are considering are mostly now in the fourth situation, when it has come to be perceived (accurately or not) that immigrants and their children represent a social problem that will not conveniently go away, when the immigrants themselves have experienced economic and social marginalization, and when the educational strategies employed initially—whether involving separate development or rapid assimilation—have proved unsuccessful. Stopping formal immigration ironically has the effect of increasing the demands made by the immigrant population on the host society; no longer able to come and go freely, guestworkers settle down and send for their families. Under these conditions, the question of whether to use minority languages in school can take on a significance which is no longer simply instrumental but deeply symbolic, both for many of the immigrants themselves and also for the host society.

Within any one of these situations there are factors that account for significant differences in the experience of immigrant groups. For example, the presence of a large low-status black population in the United States at the time of the European immigration of the nineteenth century may have enabled the new immigrants to avoid sinking to the lowest position in the society, one which was already occupied; it has been suggested that ethnic identity among American whites owes its continuing significance largely to the way it implicitly locates them on the advantaged side of the color line (Alba, 1990, 317). Part of the explanation for the significance of race in American life may be the way it has allowed white people of many different backgrounds and religions to experience a sense of "fictitious related-ness" sustaining an egalitarian democracy—for whites only (Todd, 1994, 52). The same presence of a native black lower class may explain the relatively greater success of black West Indian immigrants in the United States, where they were able to form the upper levels of the black population, than in England, where they tended to move into the lowest positions in the society (Sowell, 1978, 42; Ogbu, 1991a, 13).

The arrival of particular immigrant groups may have political significance which that of other groups, at the same time and place, does not possess. The warm welcome extended to Hungarian and Cuban refugees in the United States during the 1950s and 1960s had much to do with their symbolic significance as opponents of communist régimes, while the hostility toward Algerian immigrant workers in France during the same period reflects the bitterness of the decolonization process (Lapeyronnie, 1993, 102). There was much greater controversy over the arrival of immigrants in the United Kingdom than in France (apart from Algerians) in the postwar period because in the latter case it was a purely economic matter, centrally managed, while in the former it was associated with the loss of Empire and was largely dealt with, in the decentralized British system, as a local political matter (Freeman, 1979).

Hostility of the majority population to the presence of immigrants may also be based upon the extent to which that presence disrupts existing patterns of life, especially in crowded urban neighborhoods (Haest, 1989). We should not overlook "the distress that immigration creates for people who are already there. No people likes to have its way of life upset, and large-scale migration always upsets it. . . . It is wise not to confuse this with prejudice and discrimination" (Fitzpatrick, 1967, 278–279).

Prejudice is of course also a factor, especially in relation to immigrants whose physical appearance or manner distinguishes them readily from the majority. Sometimes an immigrant group may be considered "inassimilable," as was the case with the Chinese in California in the nineteenth century. During the debate over ratification of the Fourteenth Amendment, in 1866, Congressman Higby of California informed his colleagues that

> the Chinese are nothing but a pagan race. They are an enigma to me, though I have lived among them for fifteen years. You cannot make good citizens of them; they do not learn the language of the country; and you can communicate with them only with the greatest difficulty. . . . virtue is an exception to the general rule. They buy and sell their women like cattle, and the trade is mostly for the purpose of

prostitution. That is their character. You cannot make citizens of them (Schwartz, 1970, 197).

A similar judgment has sometimes been expressed about Turks in Germany and Algerians in France (Lapeyronnie, 1993, 71). This is even given a benign cast by Alain Benoist and other spokesmen of the French "New Right," who stress commitment to pluralism and solicitude to protect immigrants from "universalistic" assaults on their cultural distinctiveness. "Dialogue," he told an interviewer, "is only possible if heterogeneity is respected" (Benoist, 1993–1994, 181), and immigration is to be condemned because it harms the immigrant culturally as much as it does the host society (Taguieff, 1992b, 50). Pierre-André Taguieff, the leading French authority on racism, charges that it has taken a new "culturalist" form under the guise of a form of multiculturalism for which the "right to be different" (formerly a slogan of the Left) has become a justification for maintaining a strict separation between Europeans and immigrants from other areas, lest they contaminate each other culturally. "What I call *differentialist racism* . . . is imbued with the categorical imperative of preserving the identity of the group." Thus, the "'right to difference' changed from being a means of defending oppressed minorities and their 'cultural rights' into an instrument for legitimating the most extreme appeals for the self-defense of a 'threatened' national (and/or European) identity" (Taguieff, 1993–1994, 122–125).

It was on the basis of assumptions about fundamental cultural incompatibility that quotas based on the national origin of prospective immigrants were long in effect in the United States, Canada, and Australia (see Chapter 2). This was then reinforced by the results of early intelligence testing, which "found" that 83 percent of the Jewish, 87 percent of the Russian, 80 percent of the Hungarian, and 79 percent of the Italian immigrants to the United States were "mentally defective" (Bastenier & Dassetto, 1993, 71). The assumption that culture is immutably associated with race or ancestry is now thoroughly discredited—except, curiously, among some advocates of multiculturalism in the school and university curriculum.

Social, political, and economic conditions do not exhaust the ways in which the nature of the host society influences the experience of immigrants. Values that are central to the self-understanding of different societies are certain to influence how they perceive the strangers in their midst; for example, the conviction on the part of French elites that France is, in Michelet's phrase, the "universal Fatherland" and that the greatest favor it can bestow upon foreigners is to make them over into Frenchmen could not fail to shape policies toward immigrants (Todorov, 1993, 259). Deeply rooted assumptions on the part of the rank-and-file native population about the significance of human differences may also have an effect upon how immigrants are treated and what social positions are open to them. Emmanuel Todd traces these assumptions and behaviors to fundamentally different traditional family patterns in host societies which, on the surface, are characterized by a common modernity, as well as in the societies from which immigrants have come. Thus the population of the dominant Paris region of France, he argues, share assumptions about differences that are based upon symmetrical inheritance patterns (all of the males inheriting equally) characteristic of that area for many centuries (in contrast with the traditional German practice of the eldest son inheriting, or with the Anglo-Saxon pattern in which parents have considerable discretion in designating their heirs); these have led to a universalistic mentality that attributes little fundamental significance to human differences. It is primarily for this reason, Todd argues, that France has been less willing than have Germany or the United Kingdom to make provision for the maintenance of ethnic minority groups or to accommodate their distinctiveness, and more determined to promote full participation by members of those groups *as individuals* (Todd, 1994, 12). To become assimilated to French culture, in this view, is at the same time to acquire the universal culture of Enlightenment, and resistance to such a program could only be based upon a refusal of modernity, not upon loyalty to any valid alternative (Lapeyronnie, 1993, 69).

Todd sees the United States as the principal exporter of an ideology of multiculturalism based upon tolerance, while itself practicing a brutal form of separation based upon race, as measured by an especially low rate of interracial marriage. In California in 1980, for example, the rate of exogamous (outside of group) marriage was 36 percent for Japanese-, 22 percent for Mexican-, 14 percent for Chinese-, but only 3 percent for African-American women (Todd, 1994, 81). This is only an apparent paradox, he argues; it is the "designation of a [particular] minority as the bearer of the idea of difference that makes it possible to obliterate all other differences, to redefine the other minorities as equivalent to the dominant group and [thus] assimilable" (Todd, 1994, 14). The insistence by blacks in the 1960s upon equal treatment led, not coincidentally, to discovery of the wonders of ethnic distinctiveness and thus to a new rationale for separateness, accepted too readily by some black leaders. "There is something terrifying," writes Todd, "in seeing black intellectuals championing the old association between a biological substratum and psychic organization which was the very heart of European racial doctrines from 1880 to 1945" (Todd, 1994, 99). Self-segregation of blacks (as in many American universities) makes it possible for the majority to assert its commitment to equality without bearing the costs of a reduced social distance between blacks and whites.

As applied, in turn, to the Mexican and other Latin immigration of recent decades, the ideology of multiculturalism is "profoundly dysfunctional for American society" because it threatens to prevent Latinos from integrating over the course of several generations, as other immigrant groups did before them.

> Toward the beginning of the sixties, Mexicans could be described like other immigrants in the process of assimilation. By the second half of the sixties, they and other hispanics were reached by the differentialist wave that touched all of American society. . . . American culture in the seventies wanted differences (Todd, 1994, 103–104).

As a result, he argues, and despite the almost universal adoption of English as primary language, the academic performance of the third generation did not equal that of the second, there was a falling rate of naturalization, and the rate of marriage outside the group fell. This is all the more striking in that Mexican culture has traditionally been highly universalistic and open to differences; "Mexico is one of the few nations in the world to have completely dissolved a population of African origin by intermarriage" (Todd, 1994, 105–106; see also Rout, 1976).

This is an example, then, of a process occurring in the intellectual and social climate of the host society—an unanticipated consequence of real achievements in implementing civil rights—that has had a profound impact upon the situation of recent immigrant groups to the extent that they think of themselves and are thought of by others (in part because of the fashion of ethnic assertion) by analogy with the American experience of blacks rather than with that of earlier immigrant groups. Peter Skerry notes that

> in the past, when Mexican Americans were more likely to be treated like a racial minority, they sought protection by denying any racial distinctiveness; while today, when they experience dramatically fewer such racial barriers, their leaders are intent on defining them as a minority (Skerry, 1993, 18).

Dazzled by the legal and political successes of African Americans in recent decades, Mexican-American leaders may overlook the fact that African-American social and economic progress on average has been much less than that of immigrant groups that have followed another path to success.

Germans, according to Todd, have a long tradition (rooted in family patterns) of hostility to assimilation, as manifested in the continuing distinctiveness of the Germans who migrated to eastern Europe and the Volga region between the Middle Ages and the eighteenth century (Todd, 1994, 18). The federal structure of German government, and the preservation of regional dialects, are expressions of resistance to universalism (and centralism) in the French style. So is the lack of full acceptance of the Turks who are now in their second and even third generation in Germany, though there is some evidence that the resistance to assimilation is mutual and based upon patterns of exclusiveness as deeply rooted among Turks as among Germans. Bernard Lewis, in his history of modern Turkey, noted that

> the Ottoman Empire was tolerant of other religions. . . . But they were strictly separated from the Muslims, in their own separate communities. . . . even today, 500 years after the conquest of Constantinople, neither the Greeks nor the Jews in the city have yet mastered the Turkish language. . . . after thirty-five years of the secular Turkish republic, a non-Muslim in Turkey may be called a Turkish citizen, but never a Turk (quoted by Gellner, 1987, 7),

just as a third-generation resident of Germany of Turkish ancestry will never be considered a German!

The German policy of granting citizenship primarily on the basis of ancestry, wherever one is born or however many generations one's family has lived in another country, reflects the assumption that it is almost exclusively socialization provided by the family that is decisive for the ability to participate as a member of the society. This implies that the child growing up in an immigrant family, even though born, raised, and schooled in Germany, will not have acquired the habits and attitudes characteristic of Germans. By contrast, the French grant of citizenship to all those born in France (lately somewhat modified) reflects assumptions about the power of French culture, as mediated above all through the school, to make Frenchmen out of anyone (Todd, 1994, 164). This would help to explain also the far greater symbolical significance attached to the public school in France—and the United States, another country that seeks to assimilate immigrants—than is the case in most countries (Glenn, 1988b), and the ongoing furor over allowing symbols of minority religious identity in schools.

French universalism also explains, according to Todd, the characteristic pattern of French colonialism, which sought to conform the colonized to French administrative and social patterns (or, as it would have been stated at the time, to confer the benefits of French civilization upon the natives). The British pattern, by contrast, was to rule indirectly through using the existing structures of authority within West African or Indian society, and the British found it easier than did the French to abandon their empire because it had always been clear to them that Arabs, Africans, and Indians could never become British (Todd, 1994, 298). This contrast has become a truism of accounts of nineteenth-century colonialism; in Todd's framework, it helps to explain why the British accepted and even encouraged ethnic organizations among immigrants to the United Kingdom, tolerating a high degree of segregation, while the French have placed much more emphasis upon assimilation of individuals to French norms with the assumption that they would become full participants in the society. The exception to the otherwise prevalent French pattern of colonial assimilation was in Algeria, where (for reasons too complicated to explain here) the French accepted a high degree of segregation between themselves and the Arab and Berber peoples (Todd, 1994, 292–297). A continuing consequence of the fundamental conflict between competing universalisms (French and Arab), he argues, is the greater hostility of the French people toward the Algerians among them, physically of the Mediterranean type, than toward the far more different black Africans who live in France.

It is not true that host societies experience tensions toward minority groups primarily because of the cultural distance between them; in fact, as the obvious differences between members of an excluded minority group and the majority decrease, or as the rate of social mobility increases, the level of tension may rise; members of the majority may feel a need to keep the minority in their place (Gellner, 1987, 94). Thus the number of violent xenophobic attacks in Germany increased from 270 in 1990 to 2,010 in 1992, after the procedures for them to become German citizens were relaxed in January 1991 (Todd, 1994, 190).

Whether or not we accept Todd's thesis in all its rich particularity, there can be no question that immigrants to different Western countries are affected by a social climate that goes beyond economic opportunities and the formal legal and political structure which they encounter. Immigrants to North America or to Australia, societies that have traditionally welcomed—indeed, depended upon—immigrants have less difficulty than do those to Europe in making the adjustments that enable them to fit in, and are thus less likely to remain relatively unchanged by the experience.

Caribbean immigrants to Britain, for example, express considerably less satisfaction with their own situations and the prospects of their children than do Caribbean immigrants to the United States and to Canada. This does not reflect merely subjective perceptions of acceptance. A study by Bagley and Verma found that Jamaican children who immigrated from rural areas to London and to Toronto improved their "perceptual disembedding skills" (their ability to perceive figures in a complex background) in both cases, but that this change was significantly more rapid in Canada. Change in this skill was also more rapid, though in a negative direction, for Japanese children in Canada than for those in Britain; they became *less* capable of perceiving embedded figures.

> Although we had no direct measure, we assumed that the more rapid absorption of Jamaican children into Canadian society would reflect the degree to which the migrant children were motivated to absorb the general folkways, tenets, norms, values and styles of interaction which the major culture represents. Canada, being a more open society and more receptive to immigrants than Britain, promotes such absorption at a faster rate (just as it promoted Japanese children's acculturation at a seemingly faster rate) (Bagley, 1989, 104–105).

Similarly, Goldscheider and Goldstein found in 1967 that the distinctive family patterns of Jewish immigrants to the United States, patterns that had survived for centuries of isolation in the hostile environment of Eastern Europe, were abandoned by the third generation in the United States. "Jewish parents distinguished themselves from their Protestant or Catholic counterparts only by an even greater insistence upon the ideal of the autonomy of children, a normal American value. That difference suggested a hyperconformist assimilation rather than a perpetuation of an old anthropological system" (cited by Todd, 1994, 64–65; see Gordon, 1964, 190).

CHARACTERISTICS OF IMMIGRANTS

The examples given so far of factors affecting the experience of immigrants and their children have focused upon the host societies; there are of course many ways in which immigrants make their own situations or in which their previous lives create a trajectory which continues to determine their careers in a new society. Consider, for example, how different are likely to be the lives of four Dominican immigrant men in New York City: one a university graduate with professional training, another an illiterate peasant, the third an urban worker, and the fourth a small businessman. While it is possible that none would end up doing the same sort of work and living the same sort of life that he had lived in the Dominican Republic, their adaptations to the new situation would most likely vary widely. The same immigrants, if chance led them all to a small town in Sweden instead, would continue to differ in their adaptations, but in rather different ways as they interacted with that environment and with Swedish public policies. If, other things being equal, the four were Turks, or Somalis, or Sri Lankans, or Portuguese, or Russian Jews, the situations would turn out rather differently in each case. And, of course, we cannot discount the influence of individual factors resulting from early socialization, birth order, genetic endowment, and simple happenstance, as well as the choices—free in some sense, however constrained by all of these considerations—which each of our immigrants would make, and which others would make about him.

In brief, the factors that contribute to the situation of a particular immigrant are bewildering in their complexity, and should warn us against attempting to generalize about "the immigrant experience." We are on solider ground comparing Dutch and Belgian policies toward the schooling of the children of Moroccan immigrants than we would be in attempting to contrast the situation of Moroccan immigrants in the two countries; in the second case, we would be aware, in describing typical examples, that every statement could be qualified by contrary examples. "Ideal types" are always confounded by stubborn particularities, without thereby losing their usefulness (Weber, 1964, 92, 110).

Anthropological studies of Mexican Americans suggest that they cannot be understood as located somewhere on a continuum stretching from Mexican to North American cultural characteristics, but in a number of ways represent a distinctive culture that in some ways may differ more from either Mexican or North American than either does from the other. Thus

> second- or third-generation Mexican Americans may be knowledgeable of and adequately versed in the American culture and yet not strongly identify with "Anglo-ness." They may also be relatively uneducated in and removed from the Mexican tradition; that is, they may speak limited Spanish, thus reflecting a low commitment there also. At the same time, they may primarily identify [with] and interact with other persons of a similar background (Bayard, 1978, 111).

Despite these cautions, it is possible to bring some analytical order into the variety of responses to the immigration situation, and thus to the conflicting claims of two (or more) languages. We will consider variations in the relationship of immigrants and their children to (1) the homeland, (2) the immigrant or ethnic community, (3) religious practice, and (4) ethnic leadership.

Many do not initially think of themselves as immigrants; they come to earn money that they intend to spend at home, and a significant proportion of them do just that, especially in the early stages of labor migration. This was nearly as much the case with Europeans who came to the United States at the turn of century as with southern Europeans who came to northwestern Europe in the 1950s. Of immigrants to the United States in 1906–1910, 83.4 percent were men; there were 3.9 million who left the country between 1908 and 1914, for 7.9 million who arrived (Bastenier & Dassetto, 1993, 19).

Labor migrants with the intention of returning home often send home remittances to support their families and as investments—a piece of land, a small business—in their future. For example, in 1991 Portuguese living abroad sent home $4,503 million, up 5.7 per cent on the previous year (Organisation for Economic Cooperation and Development, 1994, 90). Typically, however, such remittances decline over time, as families come to join their working members in the host society and as the intentions of those workers change. Turkey and Morocco earned as much from the export of workers (through remittances sent home) as from the export of goods in 1974, but the connection is weakening; remittances from Turkish workers abroad, once a mainstay of the Turkish economy, have declined in recent years, falling to $2,829 million in 1991, though official reports are believed to underestimate greatly the actual amount (Schumacher, 1981, 34; Organisation for Economic Cooperation and Development, 1994, 100).

Fugitives from political conditions may expect their stay in the host society to be temporary, and center their lives on the exile community. Paris and London, New York and Zurich have always hosted such groups, like the Algerian intellectuals who fled to Paris from Islamic terrorism in 1994: "To leave is to die a little," one told *L'Express* sardonically; "to remain is to die a lot!" (Dupont, 1994, 122). Like earlier exiles, they may find themselves forced to make new lives in new homelands. Bertold Brecht, when in exile from Nazi Germany, expressed the resulting ambivalence in his "Thoughts about the Length of Exile":

> Hammer no nail in the wall
> Throw your coat on the chair.
> Why make arrangements for four days?
> You will go home tomorrow.
> Leave the little tree without water.
> Why plant another tree?
> Before it's as high as a step
> You will go joyfully away from here. . . .

Look at the nail in the wall that you hammered in:
When, do you think, will you return?
Do you want to know what you really believe, deep down?
Day after day
You work for Liberation
Sitting in the room you write.
Do you want to know what you think of your work?
Look at the little chestnut tree in the corner of the courtyard
To which you carry the pot full of water!
(Brecht, 1959, 292–293; translation mine)

Intentions change over time. The Algerian Constitution optimistically states as "one of the primary objectives of the socialist revolution" the return of Algerian guestworkers from France, and those who returned (bringing with them, in theory, both capital and skills acquired abroad) were to be given preferential treatment in the allocation of housing, schooling, and other support for their reintegration into Algerian society. The extended family treats return to the village as a social duty, and young men were often pressured into marrying before going abroad to seek work, leaving their wives behind in the care of their families (Khellil, 1991, 23). French authorities provide financial support for Algerians to return to their homeland, and the racially motivated attacks that some have experienced are a further inducement to remigration. As a result of all these factors, many Algerians in France intend and expect to return once they have acquired sufficient savings to buy a house or start a small business . . . but most will never do so. A survey in 1986 found that 45 percent of the immigrants interviewed believed that racism was becoming more severe in France, but 66 percent reported they were satisfied with their life in France and 52 percent hoped to remain there (Khellil, 1991, 30). Another in 1991 found a majority of Muslims in France nervous about their future in the country but 70 percent saying it was where they preferred to live, and only 20 percent preferring their homelands or that of their parents (Kepel, 1994, 283).

A survey of guestworkers in Germany in the late 1970s found that "70 percent of those interviewed had originally intended to stay . . . for less than five years. . . . [However,] only 17 percent had not changed their original plans" (Castles, Booth, & Wallace, 1984, 123). Turkish guestworkers, in particular, have tended to stay in Western Europe because of their poor economic prospects in Turkey, and because the low status of their occupations in Germany has often not permitted them to develop sufficient savings to realize their original intention of starting a small business at home; their hopes have changed in the contact with reality. This is especially true of migrants from the less developed areas of Turkey, who have less to return to (Wilpert, 1987, 209). A Dutch survey in 1991 found, similarly, that only 23 percent of the Turks and 27 percent of the Moroccans wished to return to their homeland, and of those expressing that desire, less than 40 percent in each case saw any possibility of doing so (Tesser, 1993, 32). For most, "Europe doesn't seem to be as short and sure a way to a future in their homelands as they had expected" (Vermeulen, 1984, 132).

One group that lies outside the scope of this study tends to be correctly confident that they will return when they have satisfied the needs that brought them to immigrate: those who occupied a privileged position in their homelands, for whom a relatively short-term stay in the host country is an opportunity to complete professional training or to gain business experience. Higher education or the exercise of a high-status occupation ordinarily requires proficiency in the language of the host society, but well educated professionals tend to have no difficulty in also maintaining their native language and, if they intend to return to their homeland, in ensuring that their children become proficient in it as well. The parents may become well-acculturated, fitting easily into comparable social circles in the host society, without surrendering any valued aspects of their original culture, including the use of its language at a sophisticated level.

Working-class immigrants may also return to their homelands when they have reached the age (or have accumulated sufficient resources) to retire to an ancestral village where life will be cheaper and less stressful. They may find to their sorrow that their children are unwilling to follow them into what for them is an unrewardingly backward environment—or, if they do, find it extremely difficult to make the adjustment and are commonly regarded as foreigners in their "homeland" (Byram, 1990a, 93). A study of a Mexican village from which most of the active-age population migrates to California in search of work stressed the poignancy of the return visits to visit grandparents:

> The children of migrants in the U.S. do not want to leave their friends and schools; they have become accustomed to the amenities of life in California. In the summer one sees these reluctant visitors. . . . The teenagers have little in common with their Napízaro peers—boys like Virgilio who spend their days with the animals. . . . The relatives from California are critical of the dirt roads, lack of plumbing, the tortilla-and-beans diet. In turn, some villagers criticize the Californians' manners, how the teenage girls walk freely around the streets, their clothes, their poor Spanish (Fletcher & Taylor, 1990, 15).

While the triumphant return of a short-term immigrant who "made it" to his home village is not uncommon—indeed, if it had never occurred, there would have been less immigration to the United States in the nineteenth century or to Western Europe in the postwar decades—there have always been some who returned defeated as well. On the other hand, many Spanish and Italian labor migrants to northwestern Europe, as we saw in Chapter 2, have returned to their homelands with the growing economic prosperity of those countries.

If the children of immigrants gradually distance themselves from their parents' intention of going "home," it may be in part because the parents themselves come to hold that intention less and less strongly. Among Portuguese immigrants in France, "even those who had built a house [in Portugal] became aware of how difficult the return would be." Perhaps they see themselves retiring in their homeland (indeed, thousands have done so), but not as re-entering the workforce or as persuading their children to return to Portugal with them to live (Cunha, 1989, 119). Portugal is where you go for vacation, perhaps several times a year, as of course do many northern Europeans not of Portuguese descent. The village remains an important reference-point for the second generation, but they are no longer "from there" (Villanova, 1986, 135). The first generation migrants from Napízaro continue to return for the annual festival of the Virgin of Guadalupe, and have contributed the money for the villagers to build a new church, but few will even retire in Mexico, far from their American children.

The homeland seems to be even less attractive for West Africans living in France. If they have half-serious thoughts of returning to Africa, it is often to a city rather than to the village from which they emigrated and where, as they are keenly aware, no real opportunities exist for them. "Living in France, the African families have acquired the habit of using a certain number of services that they would find more easily, in Africa, in cities than in the countryside. That changes their perspectives on returning" (Barou, 1989, 15). As an immigrant from Mali put it, "Return home? One could, but it's so expensive. And when you're there, it's hard to be considered a foreigner. The people imagine that everyone coming back from France are rich. . . . They can't understand that it's very difficult to live in France; they believe that we live like the French" (Massenet, 1994, 22).

Some homeland governments make efforts to maintain the loyalty of their citizens living in diaspora, through support for full-time or supplemental schools and through promoting associational life, as among North Africans in France (Verbunt, 1985, 159). By organizing and supporting an extensive system of immigrant organizations (*amicales*), the Algerian, Tunisian, and

Moroccan governments have sought to maintain a sense of connectedness to the homeland, though under present economic conditions the hope is more for remittances than for returning workers. More recently, the Islamic movement that is seeking to overthrow the Algerian government has been building a network of support organizations among Algerians in France and there is a certain re-islamization of the second generation (see below).

Turkish governments and opposition political parties actively work to gain support among Turkish migrants in Western Europe, and their conflicts are often played out on a foreign stage. In 1979, for example, the Association of Turkish teachers of North Rhine–Westphalia accused the Islamic cultural centers of being agents of the reactionary Turkish parties (Elsas, 1983, 92). Such orientation toward homeland politics can have a negative effect on the adaptation of immigrant groups to their host societies; "It is not only the German state through its guest-worker system which has marginalized Turks, but the Turkish state is also vitally concerned that these Turks in Germany maintain their ties with Turkey" (Wilpert, 1988, 90).

The Yugoslav, Italian, Greek, and Spanish governments, homelands of millions of labor migrants to Western Europe during the 1950s and 1960s, were reluctant to see their citizens living in West Germany and elsewhere as permanent emigrants. They opposed any form of school segregation imposed by the host society, but took an active role in promoting educational self-segregation by their expatriate citizens in the interest of transmitting a sense of national identity to the second and even third generation. The Greek government was particularly active in helping to organize Greek schools in Germany, and found support in the concern of many Greek parents not to allow their children to become "germanized" (Institut für Zukunftsforschung, 1981, 399). Elements of the immigrant communities themselves—or those who claimed to be ethnic leaders—took the position of Italians in Nuremberg who demanded, in 1982,

> Let *us* decide about our children. The Federal Republic allows itself the luxury of being convinced that it treats foreigners as human beings, and speaks of "our foreign fellow-citizens," of equal rights, but it submits foreign children to German compulsory schooling and does not allow national schools (quoted in Mahler, 1983, 83).

That year 688 foreign pupils in Munich were advised to make the switch to regular German classes because of their proficiency in German; only 158 (97 Turks, 53 Yugoslavs, and 8 Italians) did so (Mahler, 1983, 84). The proportions are suggestive; Italians (and Spaniards) are in fact much more likely to re-emigrate than are Turks and others whose homelands have not undergone an economic boom in recent decades. A decision, by an Italian family, to choose a predominantly Italian schooling in Germany may be thoroughly rational, while a parallel decision by a Turkish family would limit the future opportunities of its children.

Under some circumstances, however, a quite different—though no more realistic—picture may emerge. There are reports that the cultural identity of some young Turks and Yugoslavs is strongly tied with the country of origin of their parents, and that many would like to return there to live (Morokvasic, 1986, 100), though few seem to act upon this desire. It is impossible to judge whether this is simply a reaction against experiences of discrimination in the host society, or is based upon a unrealistic assessment of the prospects of "re-insertion" into an unfamiliar homeland which has in any event profoundly changed since the parents emigrated. This may be the case with the young people of West Indian ancestry in the Netherlands, who are more eager than their elders to return to the Antilles, where employment opportunities and the social safety net are poor (Tesser, 1993, 32). Unlike the immigrant generation, who "leave their land for a better tomorrow" and, as one researcher put it,

> often paused and made comparative evaluations between the "here" and "there," subsequent generations, if unsuccessful, can make no such comparisons (indeed, the never-seen "homeland" may be bathed in a rosy glow of imagination), and are left with "a perception of a basic continuity in the pattern of exploitation and crushed efforts" (Suarez-Orozco, 1991, 47).

There is undoubtedly an element of *nostalgie pour l'inconnu* in this attraction to a homeland that was in most cases left for a good reason and not without sacrifice.

> "Here" is the domain of the concrete, the directly perceivable, of complexity. . . . "There" is the domain of the abstract, mediated by memory, by the storytelling by elders, even by the imagination. (M. de Certeau, quoted by Boulot & Boyzon-Fradet, 1986, 38).

More characteristic, however, is an almost complete lack of interest in the "homeland" on the part of those who have known it only through half-understood stories by parents and grandparents whose own status and educational level was in most cases not such that they had access to those aspects of its life that might be of interest to a generation growing up in a more developed society. The culture that the children of immigrants acquire from their everyday experience is not that of the country of origin of their parents, but rather a variation on that of the host society (Luchtenberg, 1984, 420). Even the *Re-Türkisierung* of some younger Turks in Germany "is not a genuine cultural import" but something made up out of fragments of a shattered tradition; teenaged girls who adopted "traditional Turkish" clothing as a means of showing pride in their identity "would have rejected such clothing in Ankara or Istanbul as a symbol of repression" (Elwert, 1984, 68–71).

A *nationality* that functions within a wider nation, like the Welsh in the United Kingdom or the Catalans and Basques in Spain (see Chapter 3), is of course quite different from an ethnic community, unless the individuals who identify with that community can be persuaded to see their fundamental interests as being distinct from and even in some respects in opposition to those of national unity.

This is not how ethnic groups have functioned in the United States: at moments of crisis, they have reacted with dramatic manifestations of loyalty, even when this required explicit opposition to their former "homeland." Thus the largest immigrant group during the nineteenth century, the Germans, dismantled many of their organizations when Germany became the national enemy in 1917–1918, and Americans of Japanese, Italian, and German background showed conspicuous loyalty during World War II. Nor has this pattern changed, as some latter-day nativists fear: "Mexican-Americans seem to have no great interest in homeland issues, and they seem to have no great interest—no more than that of other Americans—in Latin American issues" (Glazer, 1985, 212). This is confirmed by the fact that, "when offered the opportunity in the 1980 census to designate themselves as 'Mexican, Mexican-American, [or] Chicano,' nearly 1.25 million people living within the five states that are commonly considered to constitute the homeland (Arizona, California, Colorado, New Mexico, and Texas) opted instead for a category ('Spanish/Hispanic') which denied any hint of Mexican ancestry" (Connor, 1985a, 18).

Mexican Americans are not alone in reorienting themselves strongly toward their new home; the efforts of the Korean government to make political use of Korean Americans have produced more resentment than positive results (Portes & Rumbaut, 1990, 110). Immigrants to the United States, Canada, and Australia seem to have little inclination to look back with a great deal of interest to their homelands, though they may send remittances or go on vacation visits, nor have the governments of those countries had much success in seeking to enlist them in their interests. The most notable domestic lobby for a foreign nation, in fact, is that supporting Israel, made up largely of Jews who have never lived there.

The efforts of the governments of the countries of origin of immigrants to Western Europe to maintain their loyalty have produced almost as meager results. During the Gulf War, for example, there was little restiveness among the millions of immigrant Muslims about the Western mobilization against an Islamic state. What is emerging as the children and grandchildren of the postwar immigrants become a permanent part of the societies of Western Europe is at most new ethnic communities, not new national groupings. Many choose simply to identify with the majority society and cut all ties with their national background.

It is important to remember, finally, that "the home country is not one thing to all migrants;" some wish to retain close ties with their country of origin, while others—for example, Kurds and Assyrians from Turkey—want as little as possible to do with their former "homeland."

Relation to the Immigrant Community

A desire to remain in the host society does not necessarily translate into the intention of becoming a full part of that society. In 1978 there were 130,000 Turkish citizens in West Germany who met the qualifications for German citizenship, but only 312 actually were naturalized (Mahler, 1983, 27). In part, this reflects the difficulty of the naturalization process in Germany (see Chapter 2); it also reflects, however, the formation of an ethnic community made up in large part of individuals who, whatever their legal status, are no longer members of Turkish society and may never have visited Turkey but are not yet (if they will ever be) fully members of German society. For such persons, *ethnicity* rather than *nationality* becomes salient as the primary source of identity and of relationship with others both inside and outside of the ethnic group, and as a way of coming to terms with rejection by the latter.

In contrast with organizations promoted by homeland governments or political parties are those that immigrants themselves create. In Australia, with the sponsored immigration after World War II,

> when most of them were poor, badly housed, unsettled, lonely and incompetent in English, these Eastern European immigrants founded embryonic groups in a search for companionship and for relief from the dreariness and frustration of their daily round. Before long these needs became absorbed into the more self-conscious aim of preserv-

ing ethnic cultural traditions and identity. Most minorities soon set about establishing choirs, folk-dancing groups, theatres, Saturday schools, and Scout groups" (Jean Martin, 1972, quoted by Sherington, 1980, 136).

Research on turn-of-the-century immigration to the United States has found that even before the immigrants came many of them were familiar with self-organization. The social disruptions associated with industrialization in Europe, which created the mobile populations available to emigrate, also led to the vigorous creation of "voluntary associations . . . [for] collective response to their new vulnerability. There emerged an enormous variety of associations after 1870 to insure for illness and death, to supervise education, to form agricultural and artisan organizations, to pursue political aims" (Barton, 1978, 154). Such organizations had not been required by traditional village life, but they proved readily adaptable to the immigrant situation in the cities of North America. In turn, the immigrant situation stimulated such groups as a way to respond to issues of identity that were not problematical before migration. The first step toward assimilation, the sociologists of the Chicago School believed, was paradoxically to recreate some aspects of the environment of the homeland through a vigorous ethnic community life (Beaud & Noiriel, 1992, 268)

> Czech newcomers in Chicago . . . formed forty-nine mutual benefit societies between 1870 and 1890, thirty-six of which began as branches of societies in homeland villages. . . . Italians in Cleveland organized thirty-five mutual benefit societies between 1903 and 1910, twenty-five of which were branches of societies in Southern Italian villages. In the Slovak community of Cleveland the formation of some twenty-five societies between 1885 and 1900 served to create a stable community. . . . In these new urban settlements, voluntary associations became the characteristic social unit. (Barton, 1978, 159–160).

Similarly, Polish migrant workers in the coalfields of the Ruhr maintained 182 Polish libraries in 1912 and had a much more elaborate organizational life than in the areas of Prussia with predominantly Polish population (G. Hansen, 1986, 50).

Despite such efforts to maintain valued elements of cultural distinctiveness, each immigrant group, with rare exceptions, becomes something new in its contact with the host society. Thus, for example, "the affirmation of a specific Italian culture is developed in the relationship maintained with the host society," and "Australian-Italians are sometimes much more Australian than they think" (Lapeyronnie, 1993, 30). Rather than being, as the stereotype has it, "torn between two cultures," immigrants participate in the development of a new culture of adaptation to new circumstances on the basis of the cultural goods they bring with them. Connections with the homeland become attenuated, traditional customs become detached from their original functions, and the immigrant who does not assimilate into the new society does not remain what she was in the old country. "After several decades in the industrial environment [of the United States], the displaced peasants of Southern Europe were neither wandering adrift, embracing traditional American middle-class values, nor living European life-styles. They were creating a new milieu that was a blend of their cultural heritage and emerging working-class status" (Hoerder, 1988, 11).

Or, as a study by Donna Gabaccia of immigrant women puts it, "the new identities they created for themselves and their communities were neither foreign, nor American, but a complex blend of the two. . . . Often, in fact, the customs that seemed most exotically foreign to native-born Americans were new accommodations to life in the United States." Gabaccia continues,

> Acculturation was partly a process of interpretation, as immigrants collectively assigned meaning to their experiences in the United States. . . . in reality many Italians had never glorified close ties to distant kin, nor had they even used the term *la famiglia* in their home-lands. *La famiglia* represented an adaptation to the migration process and to life in mobile migrant communities (Gabaccia, 1988, 17).

This new, transitional culture and social existence is lived out, for most, in an ethnic community that enables immigrants and their children to share with others the challenges of adaptation, and to limit their relations with the majority population to limited spheres in which potential conflict is minimized and distinctive aspects of the values and private lives of the immigrants are not subject to constant challenge. As Louis Wirth wrote seventy years ago,

> the relation between the two groups in such instances are usually re-lations of externality. Problems are settled by rules and laws, not by personal contact and intimate discussion. It is because the contact between the larger and the smaller, between the dominant and the subordinate groups, are confined to mere externals that they are able to live so close to each other at all. . . . among human beings con-

sciousness and feelings will arise, and two groups can occupy a given area without losing their separate identity because each side is permitted live its own inner life. . . . This relationship has been properly described as accommodation, to distinguish it from the assimilation which takes place when two people succeed in getting under each other's skins, so to speak, and come to share each other's inner life and thus become one (Wirth, 1956, 282–283).

While groups of immigrants from the same village or province often cluster together, it is also common for the host society to lump together immigrants who would have had very little in common before immigration. Tunisians and Moroccans, from very different societies a thousand miles apart, find themselves regarded as "North Africans" (*Magrébins*) in France; they may form alliances, or not, despite the tendency of the wider society to lump them together. Nor is a common language necessarily the basis for recognition, by those who speak it, of a shared ethnicity; an Arab-speaking Egyptian Muslim in Sweden has little affinity with the Arab-speaking Christian Syrians with whom he may be lumped together by the school (Paulston, 1982, 34). "Ethnic identity is potentially fluid and adjustable, not necessarily tied to deep-seated, old country values which are automatically elicited in segregated, disadvantaged life experiences, or in intergroup contacts that highlight ethnic contrasts" (Lambert & Taylor, 1988, 32).

"Ethnic resilience," it has been claimed, "is a uniquely American product because it has seldom reflected linear continuity with the immigrants' culture, but rather has emerged in reaction to the situation, views, and discrimination they faced on arrival" (Portes and Rumbaut, 1990, 96). In fact, of course, immigrant groups in *every* host society become something different as they adjust to new circumstances, though (as Bagley and Verma's research suggests) the culture of North America may in some respects, because more welcoming or more in flux, have a more powerfully transformative effect than do those of Western Europe (Bagley, 1989).

Mention of "ethnicity" requires a brief discussion of the meaning of this term, which has been used in countless poorly defined ways. It seems to have been first employed as a label for those groups on the periphery of national states, with a common language and elements of identity but without formal political structure, at least from the perspective of the West. This reflects the ancient Greek use of *ethnoi* to refer to those peoples not organized into city-states and, in the Greek version of the Hebrew Scriptures, to translate *goyim* or "gentiles." The word "ethnic," correctly used, always has a connotation of being somehow marginal to the mainstream.

More recently, the term has been used too broadly to describe any category of a population with an identifiable common national origin. In this sense, for example, the English ancestry of many Americans is sometimes seen as the basis for the existence of an English "ethnic group." There is no such thing, in any meaningful sense; the millions of Americans of English ancestry do not see themselves as a community with shared interests and customs. Anglophiles (whatever their ancestry) may of course associate together on a voluntary basis for a variety of reasons, but that is a very different matter. Indeed, "for some ancestries—for example, Dutch and Scots—even ethnically interested persons would have difficulty locating the cultural materials needed to give substance to their inner orientations." Even for Italian Americans, deriving from a more recent immigration and perceived enviously by other Americans of European descent as retaining a larger measure of ethnic flavor, the rate of participation in ethnically based organizations is low and the distinctive cultural expressions are largely limited to "practices that lend some ethnic flourishes to major holidays" (Alba, 1990, 117, 123).

In his now classic study of the assimilation of immigrants, Milton Gordon identified three primary functions served by ethnic groups. They provide "a source of group self-identification" which can offer a sense of security under the stressful conditions of adjustment to a new society, and they provide "a patterned network of groups and institutions which allows an individual to confine his primary group relationships to his own ethnic group throughout all the stages of the life cycle." An ethnic group also "refracts the national cultural patterns of behavior and values through the prism of its own cultural heritage" (Gordon, 1964, 38). Assumptions shared by the group that deviate from those of the majority encourage its members to have different priorities and different ways of understanding the world than those taken for granted in the society around them. To return to the example of the *foulards islamiques* in France, the meaning attached to wearing these scarves on the part of many Muslim girls, according to those who have been interviewed by the press, was entirely different from that assigned to them by French feminists. Not one of the girls agreed that it had anything at all to do with being subordinate to men; according to several it was a way of insisting that they were not sexual objects offered for the enjoyment of strangers.

While it is often true that ethnicity has a strong component of cultural distinctiveness, it should not be identified with a static cultural "package," but is rather a form of identity within a social and historical context, changing constantly in response to circumstances (Vermeulen, 1984, 13,

195). Gordon himself notes that "in extrinsic culture traits, native-born [American] Jews at various class levels are very similar to native-born non-Jews of the same social class (Gordon, 1964, 190). Jews from Yemen or Ethiopia, on the other hand, share a common ethnic identity with Jews from New York City, but culturally they could scarcely be more different. Their culture, in each case, was almost completely shaped by their relationship with non-Jewish peoples around them, but this (largely) shared culture did not erase the significance of ethnic differences. On the other hand, a sense of ethnicity, or of the importance of ethnic identity, can be and often is lost, when it is sustained neither by a religious dimension nor by stigmatization by the surrounding society. Nathan Glazer has captured the essentially transitional nature of most ethnic communities, asking

> What after all is the history of American ethnic groups but a history of group and individual adaptation to difficult circumstances? All the histories move in the same pattern. The immigrants arrive . . . ignorant of our language and customs, exploited and abused. They huddle together in the ghettos of the cities, beginning slowly to attend to their most immediate needs—organization for companionship, patterns of self-aid in crisis, churches for worship, schools to maintain the old culture. American society and government is indifferent to their needs and desires; they are allowed to do what they wish, but neither hindered nor aided. In this amorphous setting where no limits are set to group organization, they gradually form a community. Their children move through the public schools and perhaps advance themselves—if not, it may be the grandchildren who do. . . . They move into the spheres of American life in which many or all groups meet—the larger economy, politics, social life, education. Eventually many of the institutions created by the immigrants become a hindrance rather than a necessity; some are abandoned, some are changed (Glazer, 1967, 145–146).

A hundred years ago, Germans in the United States could have been accurately described as an ethnic group, but they are so no longer. It was they, in fact, who first developed the concept of a pluralistic society—in contrast with the prevailing Anglo-Saxon individualism—based upon a collective identity *within* but distinguishable from the larger society, reinforced by group institutions and intended to preserve the distinctiveness of the "Teutonic race" in the New World (Bastenier & Dassetto, 1993, 123). In a sense, then, "ethnicity" in the American sense was created by leaders of the German immigrant group, but even with their strong sense of a superior culture (reinforced by the contemporary triumphs of Bismarck's Germany) they were not able to protect their group against the assimilating pressures of American society. These pressures, it should be noted, had little to do with explicit "Americanization" policies directed at Germans, apart from the brief episode connected with World War I. It was less public campaigns than private decisions that led to the general abandonment of the German language and other cultural distinctions. "The Germans in America . . . were so diverse socially, economically, culturally, and politically that there was no common interest strong enough to bind them together. They were as heterogeneous as the nation itself" (Luebkc, 1978, 67).

Similarly, among those who came to Australia after World War II, "not all refugee groups continued to maintain . . . close cultural contacts. By the early 1960s, some had withdrawn to more private lives, attached and committed to their own family rather than any ethnic association" (Sherington, 1980, 137). The West African men working in France lived initially in immigrant rooming houses (*foyers*) "which may be even more conservative culturally than villages 'back home,' because they are constantly under assault by Western influences," but as their wives have followed and new households have formed, "the community becomes less closely linked and relates largely around religious and secular festivals; it becomes a cultural rather than a physical community" (Barou, 1986).

In fact, most "ethnic Americans" today have only the faintest connection with anything that could accurately be described as an "ethnic group," even though they will readily (though not necessarily consistently) identify their ancestry. Mary Waters has described the "symbolic ethnicity that fulfills this particularly American need to be 'from somewhere'" (Waters, 1990, 150) and makes none of the demands of group membership or specific cultural—much less linguistic—practices. Among Americans of European descent, "interethnic marriage appears prevalent and endogamy infrequent;" Alba's study in the Albany, New York area found that "close to 85 percent of respondents of Italian background have spouses with no Italian ancestry at all" (Alba, 1990, 177, 185); nationwide, the 1990 census found that 56 percent of white Americans "have spouses whose ethnic backgrounds do not overlap with their own at all" and "only one-fifth have spouses with identical ethnic backgrounds" (Alba, 1995, 13). This is consistent with Parsons's description of the "desocialization of ethnic groupings," the attenuation of ethnicity over time from a social to a cultural/symbolic reality (Parsons, 1975).

Max Weber (1864–1920) made an important distinction in his discussion of the characteristics of a community within a modern society:

It is by no means true that the existence of common qualities, a common situation, or common modes of behaviour imply the existence of a communal social relationship. Thus, for instance, the possession of a common biological inheritance by virtue of which persons are classified as belonging to the same "race," naturally implies no sort of communal social relationship between them. By restrictions on social intercourse and on marriage persons may find themselves in a similar situation, a situation of isolation from the environment which imposes these distinctions. But even if they all react to this situation in the same way, this does not constitute a communal relationship. The latter does not even exist if they have a common "feeling" about this situation and its consequences. It is only when this feeling leads to a mutual orientation of their behaviour to each other that a social relationship arises between them, a social relationship to each other and not only to persons in the environment. Furthermore, it is only so far as this relationship involves feelings of belonging together than it is a "communal" relationship (Weber, 1964, 138).

The term "ethnic group," then, should be reserved to describe groups with a common cultural and (at least in theory) ancestral basis who define themselves as such in contrast with the majority, and who organize their lives in significant ways on the basis of this self-definition. By these criteria, most Americans of European ancestry can no longer be considered members of ethnic groups. Nor are all recent immigrants automatically members of ethnically defined communities. The fact that the majority in the United States may think of all "Hispanics"—or, even more bizarrely, all "Asians"— as members of the same social category does not make them an ethnic community.

If former immigrants continue to see themselves and to behave as though they have something important in common that distinguishes them from others of similar circumstances, then they can be considered an ethnic minority group, defined at least as much by how the wider society perceives them as by a shared heritage (Bastenier & Dassetto, 1993, 151). Immigrants from disparate backgrounds, and even from different homelands, may come to function as an ethnic group simply because the host society insists upon treating them as one. The category "Hispanic" does not serve as a basis for group formation among Hondurans and Guatemalans in Honduras, but it may do so when they come to the United States (Portes & Rumbaut, 1990, 137). Alternatively, perhaps it may not.

Mexican Americans are no more "similar" to Puerto Ricans [in their own view] than are black or white Americans. Furthermore, a very sharp contrast is drawn on the issue of "American": Puerto Ricans see themselves as being as American as are black and white Americans whereas Mexican Americans are [in the view of Puerto Ricans] decidedly *not* American. . . . the reciprocal view of Mexican American parents was substantially different: they saw both their own group and the Puerto Rican as being *not* American" (Lambert & Taylor, 1988, 93).

Sociologist Robert Park (1864–1944), writing in the 1920s, described the process through which immigrants go as including *accommodation*, the social arrangements (including concentration in certain neighborhoods, churches, associations and forms of employment) through which their needs are met while conflict with the host society is minimized, and *assimilation*, the inner process through which new attitudes are formed which allow the immigrant to become part of a common culture (Bastenier & Dassetto, 1993, 89–97).

An ethnic group, we may say, is a form of relatively temporary accommodation to the immigrant minority situation on the transgenerational path toward assimilation; it could of course be perpetuated for many generations in a society that continues to deny real integration to members of that group, but then it would be better to use the term "caste," which implies a permanent status. African Americans are more accurately described as a caste, permanently relegated to separate status as evidenced by the very low rate of intermarriage with other groups, than as an ethnic group.

Immigrants who come to a country with the intention of maintaining their cultural distinctiveness may find themselves and especially their children abandoning it. Others who intend to fit in by abandoning their distinctiveness may find that intention rejected by the host society and they, or their children, may seek to reclaim elements of it. Different groups respond in different ways which can best be explained by the anthropologist. Traditional family patterns are more intact and ethnic community participation more intense among Pakistanis and Bangladeshis in the United Kingdom, for example, than among Indians in the United Kingdom or North Africans in France, whose young women, in particular, move into the majority society with relative ease. In France, there is "a confrontation, and the destruction of the minority [anthropological] system by that of the majority," in contrast with the continuing ethnic enclaves in the United Kingdom and Germany; "the openness of the host society brings on a process of disintegration" of ethnic community (Todd, 1994, 314–317).

Efforts at forced assimilation of immigrants sometimes have the effect of increasing their determination to retain their distinctiveness. In some cases, this takes the form of continued use of the minority language and culture:

> The Russification program for Finland, the Germanization program for Poles, the Magyarization program for Slovaks led to massive counter-activities. The experience of Czech migrant workers in Vienna and Polish miners in the Ruhr (migration within a political unit) were ambivalent. The economic situation indeed meant an objective pressure to fit in for the sake of better employment positions and salaries, and this pressure was experienced subjectively by the migrants as a temptation. Working to slow this down was the political exclusion of migrant workers who were prepared to acculturate. . . . To protect themselves against political attacks and repression the migrant workers had to band together on an ethnic basis (Hoerder, 1988, 9).

Such ethnic separatism comes at a cost, however. As Fase points out, "It is Utopia where ethnicity advances the cultural mix or melting pot only, while it remains neutral in matters of hierarchy, stratification, and inequality" (Fase, 1994, 36). The pluses and minuses are not easily netted out: ethnic separation may retard the adaptation of the second generation even as it reduces the psychological cost of such an adaptation (Hoffmann-Nowotny, 1987, 57). A (usually) less conflictual and segregating way of continuing to maintain a distinctive identity and community life over several generations is through religion, which provides a thread of essential continuity even as language, customs, and family patterns change.

There is much to suggest, then, that ethnicity is a transitional and often helpful expression of group identity and mutual support for immigrant groups that are moving toward successful participation in the host society, but that the process is by no means a simple or inevitable one. Marx's view of ethnicity as an archaic form of social organization rapidly being replaced by class is confounded by the fact that class is becoming less significant than ethnicity in social and political conflicts.

This is not to proclaim the triumph of a Weberian emphasis upon culture as the determinative factor, since it appears that ethnicity—or caste, suggesting a more permanent category with institutional rather than cultural boundaries—can continue to structure profound social divisions even when there are insignificant cultural differences between the groups thus separated within the same society.

The situation of African Americans is the classic instance of this castelike separation with minimal reinforcement by cultural differences (admittedly an unfashionable view). We can see something of the same pattern emerging in European countries as well as in North America, where the second generation of an immigrant minority group is assimilated culturally to the host society but at the same time many of its members are separated from it structurally, forming an "underclass" that cannot be attributed simply to the functioning of the economy but emerges from the failure of a process of social integration. It is for this reason that schools are heavily implicated both in the search for causes of and in the effort to find solutions to the problem of social marginalization.

It is important to keep in mind that a minority group can be marginalized—ghettoized—without thereby forming a coherent ethnic community with the positive effects that such communities may have (Elwert, 1984, 53). Thus the marginalization of some immigrant minority youth is not a function of their being part of a functioning ethnic community—quite the contrary.

Religion as a Source of Solidarity and of Alienation
Sociologist Peter Berger has noted that, under the pressures of modernity, "private life is experienced as the single most important area for the discovery and actualization of meaning and identity." Thus

> as long as private life is not anomic, the alienations of the megastructures are at least tolerable. The situation becomes intolerable if "home," that refuge of stability and value in an alien world, ceases to be such a refuge—when, say, my wife leaves me, my children take on life styles that are strange and unacceptable to me, my church becomes incomprehensible, my neighborhood becomes a place of danger, and so on . . . the best defenses against the threat are those institutions, however weakened, which still give a measure of stability to private life. These are, precisely, the mediating institutions, notably those of family, church, voluntary association, neighborhood, and subculture (Berger, 1977, 134).

For Dutch, German, and Scandinavian Protestant immigrants who organized local churches and associations on a national basis, for the members of autocephalic (national) Orthodox churches which became American denominations, and for Roman Catholics who organized "national parishes" in many cities, religious life was the primary expression of community and anchor of identity on a national as well as a religious basis. In 1886, for example, a priest in Milwaukee memorialized the Vatican to ensure "that German parishes shall be entirely independent of Irish parishes." The idea was abroad, he wrote, that "the ecclesiastical status of the Germans is . . . a transitory one" and, once German immigrants had acquired English, they could be simply incorporated into Irish-dominated parishes. No, the differences in approach to the Catholic faith went much deeper than the language in which it was expressed.

> With the lapse of time, by a certain natural formative process one will become more assimilated to the other. But, God forbid that anyone should dare, and most of all, that bishops and priests should endeavor to accelerate this assimilation by suppressing the language and customs of the Germans. The German temperament and a most sad experience demonstrate that their effort is not conducive to edification, but for the destruction and ruin of souls (Gaustad, 1983, 44–45).

The organization of religious life around national origin rather than the specifics of belief is more than questionable theologically, at least for Christians, but it makes very good sense sociologically, as recent studies of "mission strategy" have acknowledged. The relatively low level of community organization and political mobilization among recent immigrants of Catholic background may derive in part from the abandonment of this much criticized practice. Thus, in New York City, "there has been no attempt to set up national parishes but rather to integrate Puerto Ricans into the already existing parish structure" in which leadership roles are already filled by other groups (Poblete, 165). This may also help to explain the very rapid growth of evangelical and pentecostal denominations among Hispanic, Haitian, and Brazilian immigrants to the United States; "the sect represents a search for a way out of [the socially-disorganized] condition and is therefore an attempt to redevelop the community in the new urban situation." For the deracinated immigrant, "the group solidarity" of a storefront church "appears to the converted not as a loss of individuality but rather as a chance to develop his own personality—to experience a worthwhile fulfillment" (Poblete, 1986, 171, 175).

The liberalized Roman Catholic church, by contrast, seems less able to carry out this sociological function. Michael Novak notes that, for earlier immigrants,

> more than any other institution . . . the [Catholic] church gave the immigrants cultural reinforcement and a sense of dignity; a feeling of belonging; support in the hours of being born, and dying; and com-

fort in the anxieties and disasters in between. . . . The church taught the immigrants to work hard, to obey the law, to respect their leaders, and to concentrate on private, familial relationships.

Recently, however, Novak continues, "the church in America . . . has become Protestant, individualistic, and pietist in character" (Novak, 1973, 11), and no longer is able to structure the lives of Catholics—including those newly arrived—in the same manner.

The Catholic and Protestant churches of Western Europe have generally been in the forefront of extending a welcome and social services to immigrants, and in the decades after World War II many labor migrants from Italy, Spain, or Portugal were linked into their host societies through Catholic parishes with priests from their homelands. More recent immigration has in few cases brought co-religionists, however, and the churches have grown fastidious about seeming to seek conversions. Refusing to see the immigrant as a potential convert precludes in a sense taking him completely seriously as a potential member of the same community. There is thus a rather patronizing and arms-length quality to many of the well-meaning intercultural activities sponsored by the churches.

The most notable example, at the present time, of religion serving as a primary organizing principle and expression of minority life is that of Islam. There are 2 to 3 million Muslims in the United States, and some 10 million in Europe. In common with the Christian immigrants to North America in the nineteenth century, the Muslim immigrants to Western Europe have tended to organize their community life around religious institutions which, though invoking a universalistic faith, have at least initially borne a national character as well. Significantly, it was Dutch converts to Islam who attempted to create, in the 1970s, an organization uniting Muslims in the Netherlands from every national origin and, just as significantly, they failed (Waardenburg, 1988, 16).

Adapting to subordinate minority status was a challenge for Roman Catholics in the United States in the nineteenth century, and it is a challenge to Muslims in Western Europe (and, less dramatically, in the other countries included in our study) in the twentieth. Gilles Kepel suggests that the dress rehearsal was in India after 1857, when the Muslim minority lost political control to the British and had to find another basis for survival as a group among the Hindu majority. Kepel describes the two primary forms of this adaptation as an "internal *hejira*" toward strict observance or toward Sufi mysticism, on the one hand, and political mobilization on a communitarian basis on the other, the latter leading eventually to the partition of India on a religious basis and the creation of Pakistan in 1947. This mobilization was based upon defining Islam as the basis of a minority identity that transcended the village or even the province, "promoted by political leaders who wished to attain power by presenting themselves as the exclusive representatives of a 'community' with only a single will by uniting diverse populations on the basis of a sociological definition of their Muslimness" (Kepel, 1994, 132).

The pattern thus established has been carried over into the migration of Muslims into Western Europe, starting with the United Kingdom, where the idea took root that British society was multicultural, "conceived as the juxtaposition of 'minorities' and of 'communities' which are the depositories of the political identity of their members and the entitled intermediaries of their participation in relations with the State" (Kepel, 1994, 135). Just as Scots and Welshmen are members of distinct nations who possess British citizenship, so the various "black" groups (not only West Indians and Africans but Indians, Pakistanis, Bangladeshis, and even Greek and Turkish Cypriots) in the United Kingdom could be fully citizens without assimilation or even acculturation to a common British nationality. The distinction between citizenship and nationality, unfamiliar to Americans for whom the two are assumed to go together, is the source of continuing strain in British society, inheritor of the traditions of a multinational Empire with a common citizenship (Crowley, 1992).

Assertion of a community identity based upon religion (though, as elsewhere, with a lingering component of national origin) thus took place earlier in the United Kingdom than it did on the Continent; the first mosques serving immigrants were established in the 1950s, twenty years before those in France (though both countries already had mosques serving their high-status colonial and diplomatic visitors). British government policy toward the immigrants was, as earlier in the British colonies, to prefer to deal with group leadership rather than with individuals, and legal status and funding were provided to minority organizations; carrying over the patterns of India, both the leaders and their organizations were often religiously identifiable.

As the Muslim population in the United Kingdom continued to grow in the 1960s, its leaders expressed increasing concern about the effects that the "open society" and especially schools would have upon children whose families lived by entirely different assumptions, as a result of the "inner *hejira*" by which earlier generations had responded to minority status in India. A leading Labour politician reassured them, in 1966, that a pluralistic society had no desire to assimilate minorities, and funds were allocated for multicultural activities in communities and in schools—and, in turn, to employ many of the more articulate members of ethnic communities; the same year, the Muslim Educational Trust was established by immigrants, with one of its goals to protect a distinct Muslim identity among children exposed to a permissive society and schools where they would encounter "the materialistic Western culture, broken families, sexual promiscuity, alcoholism, and the relaxation of morality" (Kepel, 1994, 153–154). A recent study of young women from immigrant families found, indeed, that

> over half of the young people interviewed faced problems connected with religion (food, dress, school curriculum, facilities for prayer) whilst many Muslim parents continued to express distress at the permissive attitudes of young people in British society which gave rise to concern about the moral socialisation of their children at school (Wade and Souter, 1992, 17).

Schooling became—until the Rushdie affair and now again as that has quieted somewhat—the central defining issue for the community politics of Muslims in the United Kingdom. The Swann Commission found that "for many ethnic minority communities, especially those from the various faiths within the Asian community [sic], respect and recognition for their religious beliefs is seen as one of the, and, in some cases, *the* central factor in maintaining their community's strength and cohesiveness" (*Education for All*, 1985, 466). In the cities, well-mobilized Muslim communities have been able to obtain significant concessions from local education authorities, including in some cases the designation of rooms for prayers, exemption of girls over 10 from coeducational activities, the right for them to wear traditional dress (including the headscarves that were forbidden in France) in the colors of the school uniform, and *halal* food in school cafeterias (Kepel, 1994, 162). Despite these victories, British authorities have been reluctant to provide funding for separate Islamic schools, as in the Netherlands, and the twenty or so that operate are privately financed (see Chapter 6), despite the existence of hundreds of publicly supported Christian and a few Jewish schools.

The organization of immigrants into mobilized communities based upon religious identity (rather than, as in the contemporary United States, a separation of religious institutions from most aspects of public life based upon the privatization of religious expression) has led to political strains reflecting an incompatibility of values. In Birmingham, for example, despite the efforts of the Labour Party to court immigrant voters, the party

> is criticized for its permissiveness, the issue of support for homosexuals being often quoted. . . . the feeling is that the Council should give

money not merely for language (mother-tongue) classes, but for moral and religious education. Combining both points, several mosque leaders have expressed the opinion that the Labour[-controlled] Council gives money to support homosexuals and other deviants and yet refuses to support a kind of education which promotes law and order (Rex, 1988, 214).

As the British example shows, religion can simultaneously serve as the basis for group solidarity and mutual support and for a degree of alienation from the wider society; indeed, solidarity and alienation may well reinforce each other. The fact that Muslims have been especially inclined to such religiously based estrangement from their host societies may derive as much from the international political situation, of which the confrontation between Islam and the West has been a major theme for a quarter-century, as it does from the claims which Islam makes to regulate all aspects of the lives of the faithful. This latter consideration should not be exaggerated, since in fact it is a characteristic of all vital religious faiths to attempt to do so, and the examples of Hasidic Jews in the United States, and of German Anabaptist Protestants (Amish, Mennonites) in both Russia and North America demonstrate that Islam has no monopoly on polarization from "the World."

Religious affiliation has proved an effective vehicle for the mobilization of immigrant minority group in the Netherlands, as well, but for a different reason. Dutch society and public life have been structured, since the midnineteenth century, along religious lines; despite considerable secularization since World War II, many Dutch institutions including schools are identified as Catholic or Protestant or Humanist, and political decisions are often made through a process of negotiation among the *zuilen* ("pillars") that make up Dutch society, sometimes termed "the politics of accommodation" (Lijphart, 1968). Muslim and Hindu groups have been able to fit into this context and to obtain significant concessions for their religious and other needs (Rath, Groenendijk, and Penninx, 1992). They have received support from a government policy, articulated in 1983, that called for "the realization of a social life in which the members of minority groups who remain in the Netherlands can have an equal and unlimited opportunity to develop individually and as groups" (*Regeringsnota*, 1983, 10). However secularized the intentions of those who articulated the goal of "the Netherlands as a multi-cultural society" may have been, the reality is that immigrants there have organized themselves primarily as Muslims and Hindus, though with lingering distinctions based upon national background, as among the early generations of Protestant, Catholic, and Orthodox immigrants to the United

States. So powerful is this religious identity that "it is not easy for Moroccans and Turks even in the Netherlands to withdraw from being Muslims" (Tennekes, 1991, 11). This Muslim identity has become more important, for many, than it ever was in their homelands; in the words of one young Turk,

> since I came to the Netherlands I feel more drawn to Islam than ever before. We're discriminated against by the Dutch as Turkish Muslim . . . they look on us as inferior. But we have the strength of our religion. We're not at all afraid, not of anyone, only of Allah. We have the greatest religion. One Turk can, with his religion, take on 50,000 Dutchmen. . . . I think that we migrants will bring the true Islam back to Turkey through our experiences here" (quoted by Sunier, 1994, 19).

The structuring of public life on a religious basis by Muslim immigrants is a reversal of the secularization and privatization of religion that have characterized Western European societies, and immigrants to them, for the past hundred years. Like pentecostal and evangelical Christianity in the United States, Islam has come to be extremely important for many immigrants in Western Europe, including some whose religious practice in the homeland may have been perfunctory; it is

> the religion of marginalized immigrants whose inclusion has been a failure. . . . Religion works to construct a community and an identity which make it possible to endure the failure of inclusion and to give a positive meaning to marginality and to a dependence upon social services (Dubet & Lapeyronnie, 1992, 95).

In particular, it is a means by which immigrants and their children can reject a dominant culture which appears (if only by neglect) to be rejecting them, and assert continuities when much in their lives is changing. More than "ethnic" values and traditions, and far more than minority languages, religion is seen as the essential element of connectedness with the family and the community. Thus sub-Saharan African ethnic groups in France are countering what they perceive as the inevitable loss of their languages by a strong emphasis upon Islam as a cultural marker and a basis for identity. Within a growing number of families from Senegal, for example,

> Learning the "language of origin" is more or less abandoned and communication is carried on in the language of the child: French. In fact,

the Muslim identity is given more positive emphasis [*valorisée*] than is the ethnic identity, often perceived as negative (Timera, 1989, 22).

"The process of socialization through taking part in [Muslim] associations, both comforts the immigrant, who sees in it his 'salvation' and that of his children, and also re-Islamicizes him, sometimes with various difficulties" in relation to the host society (Nebioglu, 1989, 181). As a result, "many Turks who came to Germany as atheists have become practicing Muslims in Germany as a result of the conflicts over identity which they experience there" (Elsas, 1983, 41).

French government policy, which insists upon dealing with immigrants as individuals and has no tradition of recognizing community representatives, has found it particularly difficult to come to terms with this new political salience of religiously based issues.

> The French republican tradition with respect to immigration is assimilation. . . . France in the 1990s does not intend to become a federation of ethnic, religious and cultural communities. She refuses the logic of juxtaposition that leads directly to ghettos. . . . France does not want to be a mosaic (Duhamel, 1993, 86–88).

The French understanding of an appropriate political order is rooted in the Jacobin tradition of 1792 and in French sociological thinking which, since Durkheim, has stressed socialization by national institutions rather than by "communities," as in the American sociological tradition (Kastoryano, 1992, 169). This understanding of political socialization overlooks the role of labor unions in providing structure and a means of political participation to earlier generations of French migrants from rural to industrial areas (Bastenier & Dassetto, 1993, 253; Lapeyronnie, 1993, 40), as unions did for an earlier generation of Eastern European immigrants to the United States, a role that, in their weakened state, they are no longer able to play so effectively for contemporary immigrants.

The prevailing French viewpoint, historically correct or not, accepts no "mediating structures" between the state and the individual (Berger & Neuhaus, 1977), and indeed the social history of France in the nineteenth century—culminating in a law enacted in 1905—was dominated by the struggle of republican "radicals" to marginalize the Catholic church and to confine the role of religion to the private sphere (Glenn, 1988b). Gérard Israël, president of the umbrella group of the Jewish community in France insisted, in 1992, that the question is: does the, can the indivisible French republic recognize the existence of a community . . . ? As paradoxical as it may seem, one must respond in the negative. The French institutional order does not recognize communities. The French are free and equal, that's all. Of course, they are free to associate together, to meet, but their community does not constitute an institution. France does not recognize the phenomenon of minorities. There have never been national minorities among the French people (Massenet, 1994, 153–154).

Similarly, in ratifying the International Covenant on Civil and Political Rights, in 1980, the French government insisted that article 27, protecting the rights of "ethnic, religious or linguistic minorities," did not apply to France since, constitutionally, it was "an indivisible Republic" (Storimans, 1993, 47).

It is for this reason that the *affaire des foulards* which began in 1989 and shows no sign of resolving itself (see Chapter 1) has been such a shock for France. For much of the previous decade, under the benevolent eye of the ruling Socialists, members of the second generation of North Africans living in France had proclaimed their intention of being fully integrated, and large demonstrations had brought together young people of all groups to say "No to Racism!" The presence of a few young women among them in traditional Islamic garb had attracted attention against the background of the largely assimilated and secularized crowds, most of whom would have agreed that "Islam, that was something for my parents" (Leveau, 1988, 117).

Surveys suggest that, in fact, Muslims in France are about as religious, on average, as are other groups; that is, not very. A 1988 found that 32 percent of young women but only 17 percent of young men among the *beurs* (born in France, of North-African origin) declared themselves as "without religion," reflecting the greater integration of the former; among French youth and among Catholic immigrants (the other response groups), women were slightly more religious than men. Muslim young men were the most religious, and Muslim young women the least religious, of the six categories, though it should be noted that Muslim women were more likely than men to actually live by the obligations of the Koran (Duraffour & Guittonneau, 1992, 194–195). According to a poll conducted for *Le Monde* in November 1989, only 38 percent of "Muslims" in France described themselves as believers. The World Islamic Alliance estimated that only 10 to 12 percent were actively practicing Islam, a level of practice close to that of "Christians" in France. This suggested that there might be fewer practicing Muslims than there are practicing Jehovah's Witnesses in France (Cordeiro,

1990, 56–57). It could be predicted with confidence that "contrary to a widely-held view, the inclusion of Muslims in a nation with a strong assimilationist pressure, like France, modifies 'our' cultural norms less profoundly than the norms of 'their' religious membership" (Roux, 1990, 94).

Although there is no reason to believe that Islamic militancy is sweeping through the Muslim population resident in France, the controversy over the girls who refused to remove their headscarves represented a challenge to fundamental assumptions about the place of religion in French society, and has been especially baffling to those on the Left who have often demonstrated in support of the rights of immigrants, but associate the wearing of the "veil" (which actually covers the hair but not the face) with the subordination of women in traditional Islamic societies. It was deeply puzzling for them when "liberated" women of the second generation, fully acculturated to French life and norms, defended the right of the girls to cover their heads in school. In several schools where girls were allowed to cover their hair, leftwing teachers went on strike against this accommodation of "the right to be different" which they had themselves proclaimed under other circumstances. They had perhaps forgotten that

> in the Algerian struggle against the French colonial power, as in the Iranian revolution against the Shah, the veil became a leading symbol of the religious but above all of the nationalistic or national-religious self-awareness and self-affirmation. For a short time, it was not an institution and symbol of oppression, but the flag of a common struggle against foreign domination and exploitation (Enderwitz, 1983, 171).

The rising militancy of Islamic groups in Europe has invested the headscarf (*chador* or *hijab*), together with the full beard for men, with another symbolic meaning, as a rejection of secularized governments that are seen as being too infected with Western values. Among Turks in Berlin, traditional dress is considered a political statement of opposition to the "Turkish secularism, or laicism, [which] may be considered in some sense as an ideology which competes with religious belief for the loyalty and core identity of the citizens of the Turkish nation state." As a result, "religious dress became a red flag aggravating ideologized Turkish secularists" and associated, by them, with political extremism (Wilpert, 1988, 88–89).

The Tunisian government of Ben Ali, after taking control in 1987, successfully forbade the headscarves in schools as part of its crackdown on Islamic militancy. Significantly, this was accompanied by an extensive effort to use schools to create "democratic citizens." Hundreds of new teachers of history and philosophy were appointed, and two hours of civic education each week replaced two hours of religious instruction; pupils are required to study the *Universal Declaration of Human Rights* each year (Sitbon, 1994, 32–34).

The internal contradiction of such an effort is evident: human rights include the right to religious expression. As a young Muslim woman in France pointed out in a dialogue with Taslima Nasreen, the Bangladeshi feminist,

> It's very serious after all that you want to make us happy despite ourselves! To want to impose your ideas on others, to make a law forbidding the headscarf, that's [the real] fundamentalism! According to you, I'm the obscurantist, but you are demonstrating an immense intolerance. . . . You are superficial. It's not because a woman gives the appearance of being liberated that she really is deep inside. . . . Why don't you want to show your body, and wear a dress? From modesty. Well, it's from modesty that we don't want to uncover our hair!" (Schemla, 1994, 94).

The charge could be made, as it was against nineteenth-century Catholic spokesmen in the United States, that such arguments are opportunistic and insincere; after all, Muslims who insist upon freedom of expression in France are not prepared to grant it in Algeria. How free societies should treat those who do not share the commitment to freedom is of course a recurring issue; most have concluded that they must be tolerated in their opinions and expressions, so long as they do not offend against the common law, but the countries of Western Europe have been less inclined than is the United States to posit an absolute freedom of expression. Many of the Nazi materials that are distributed clandestinely in Germany are printed in the United States, since German law forbids them. Similarly, France long forbade, under a law adopted in 1939, associations of foreigners on its territory (Costa-Lascoux, 1989b, 61); more than half the members of any legal organization had to be French citizens.

The law was changed in 1981, giving foreigners full freedom of association for lawful purposes (Henry-Lorcerie, 1989, 43), and the number of Islamic associations in France doubled in a decade to more than two thousand; Muslims in France began increasingly to relate to the host society through a form of "communitarian integration" (Kastoryano, 1992, 173). Despite fears of militant Islamic fundamentalism, the degree to which those identified as Muslim orient their lives by Islam varies greatly, with many almost completely indifferent to religious practices but at least a strong minority deeply committed. Among the latter group are many—influenced by the (Turkish) Islamic Center of Cologne in Germany and by the newly militant Islamic Salvation Front of Algeria—who explicitly reject what they have seen of Western values, and are concerned to build an Islamic community-in-exile that will be capable of "recapturing" the second and third generation that have been drifting away from any meaningful connection with Islam (Raufer, 1993, 31). This is a quite new phenomenon in France in contrast with Germany, taking root especially in the depressed industrial areas around Lyons, and calling for the form of "separate development" that commentators tend to consider uniquely "Anglo-Saxon" and inimical to the French tradition of assimilation (Kepel, 1993, 33). The media focus attention on this intransigent element among Muslims in France, abetted by the leaders of these groups, in whose interest it is to appear as the true representatives of their coreligionists, even those who are successfully integrating (Stora, 1992, 221).

Inevitably, schools experience in an acute form the controversies over religious expression and its meaning for the minority and the majority; it was no accident that the *affaire des foulards* took place in a school. For Islamic militants, French schools are intended to brainwash Muslim pupils; "you have to learn it all by heart so you can get good grades, but remember that it's false" (Kepel, 1994, 289). The claim to neutrality is perceived as profoundly deceptive, since secularity itself takes a position against faith and undermines its very foundation, its epistemological validity (Kepel, 1994, 289). This is, of course, identical to the charge brought by many Christians against American public schools (see Glenn, 1987b).

> [D]ifficulties arise because minority groups (ethnic, religious, linguistic) may perceive the education system as providing and transmitting the cultural values of the majority group which they fear or reject as subversive of their own culture. This is undoubtedly a position taken by some of the Asian, especially Muslim Asian, community [sic] in the U.K., and is a view shared by an increasing number of Pentecostal Christians (Watson, 1988, 536).

Although most immigrants place a high value upon the schooling of their children—often unrealistically so—there are thus some groups that regard it *in the form available to their children* as a threat to their cultural and religious identities (Gibson & Bhachu, 1991, 88). What accommodations to make for religious convictions—a fundamental human right—in schools is a question that has troubled nations other than the United States. Schools may remove or grant excusals from practices that the devout find offensive (as Muslims do coeducational physical education classes) and may modify the curriculum to give more recognition to the significance of religious belief, for example by teaching about world religions. These accommodations within a "common school" are often unsatisfactory to all involved (Glenn & Glenn, 1991). Muslims, for example, have expressed opposition to allowing non-Muslims to explain their faith to Muslim pupils (Zaki, 1982).

Islamic religious instruction (as contrasted with teaching about Islam) has been fitted relatively easily within the legal framework of educational systems which already provide for voluntary religious instruction for other groups. In Belgian public education, for example, such classes are taught by teachers approved by the religious leaders of the Islamic community.

> For the school year 1984/85, more than 300 Turkish and Arabic speaking teachers of religion were appointed in Belgian schools. Some 20,000 pupils in primary school and some 9000 pupils in secondary school attended such courses (that is about 50 per cent of all those potentially concerned). . . . The system of appointing religious teachers permits foreign governments to select personnel, according to their own criteria, who are to function within the Belgian framework. By relinquishing to other states part of its own prerogatives in such a sensitive area as education, did not the Belgian government somewhat hastily give away the possibility of evaluating correctly the actual role played by the teachers in the process of cultural and social integration? (Bastenier, 1988, 140).

The recent development of more radical tendencies, rejecting much of Western culture, among Muslims has led to second thoughts about allowing into the schools instructors whose message (because in Arabic or Turkish) cannot be monitored by education authorities: the government now requires that teachers of Islam in schools possess Belgian citizenship and have lived in the country for at least 5 years (Ephimenco, 1986).

One reason to provide Islamic instruction within schools is to seek to reduce the influence of the supplemental "Koran schools" supported by many immigrant parents. Many observers perceive these schools as overtaxing students and alienating them from life in Western Europe by dismissing all of its manifestations as evil (Alfatli & Alfatli, 1980, 177; Karaman, 1980, 260).

Such independent Koran schools were outlawed in Turkey, where religious instruction at the elementary level could be provided only in the government's own schools, and their popularity in Western Europe is deplored by many as a threatening sign of Islamic fundamentalism. A fairer assessment might be that (however deplorable some may be pedagogically) the Koran schools represent an effort of immigrant parents, faced by mandatory school attendance laws, to retain control over at least one aspect of their children's socialization. Koran schools are in some ways comparable to the parochial schools supported by Irish and German immigrants to the United States in the nineteenth century, and equally deplored then by educational and political leaders (Glenn, 1988b, Ch. 8). In this perspective they reflect a way of resisting "modernity and its discontents" (Berger, Berger, & Kellner, 1974).

Islamic religious instruction (like Protestant and Catholic instruction) is provided in many German schools on a voluntary basis, and education authorities have put considerable effort into working with Muslim authorities in Turkey to develop suitable curriculum, as an alternative to Koran schools. In response to criticism by the Association of Turkish Teachers of North Rhine/Westphalia, the Islamic Cultural Center in Cologne replied that "the establishment of Koran courses is a consequence of the fact that no Islamic religious instruction is provided in German schools [and parents want] cultural and national identity to be maintained" (Elsas, 1983, 92)

Many Turkish children in Berlin whose parents have by no means been extreme nationalists are sent to Koran schools operated by groups very hostile to Western society because the public schools which they attend teach them very little of Turkish history or culture and provide them with no Muslim religious instruction (Elsas, 1983, 66). Education authorities have responded to this criticism by organizing Islamic instruction in public schools. This is intended to replace an

> imported Islam, taught by teachers who have little knowledge of daily life of Turkish children in Berlin, [which] will have an alien and probably nostalgic character for the children. . . . An example is the programme for grade two . . . "My fatherland is Turkey. I love Turkey more than my life. I love the beautiful banner with the crescent and the star. I love Mustafa Kemal Atatürk, our saviour, our founder of the Republic and our great hero. I love all our great Turkish personages."
> In other Federal States there exist curricula which avoid the confinement to only one Islamic direction, as the German school authorities take over the supervision of the Islamic religious instruction and discuss its content with the Islamic groupings. In Hamburg, Turkish teachers are employed by the German school districts to provide Islamic re-

ligious instruction. . . . This form of institutionalization of the Islamic religious education in the German schools will also help determine whether Islam in Germany becomes an integral part of the cultural, social and religious life of the country or whether it will remain a foreign element related to life abroad (Thomä-Venske, 1988, 86).

Religious instruction in public schools has been strongly resisted in France, where indeed it is contrary to a long-established law. Most members of the French public would oppose it, at least with respect to Islam,

> religious instruction entrusted to representatives [of the different religious confessions], as the religious authorities demand with more and more insistence under the false pretext that this will contribute to understanding our own culture better, is unacceptable. . . . Conflict is unavoidable between a religion which wants to impose itself as law and the *laïcité* in which we live (Pierrot, 1990, 31).

Resistance on the part of public authorities has if anything strengthened the desire of many immigrant parents and their children to be allowed to give public expression to their faith, as a central element of identity, since "religion . . . is often the only culture that parents have to transmit to their children" (Khellil, 1991, 155)

The role of religion in the continuing experience of immigrant groups does not have to be based upon a group life that is a refuge from unsuccessful participation in the host society, as is assumed by many observers for whom religious faith is a sign of failure to adapt to modernity and who suggest that "it is as a result of the failure of their integration as a result of rejection by the host society that many of them have returned to an Islam about which most of them had not known much" (Khellil, 1991, 79). The continuing vitality of denominations in the United States that derive from earlier immigrations demonstrates how well religious organizations can adapt to new circumstances, changing as their members acculturate to the host society.

In general, religious institutions have stood the test of acculturation far better than have organizations with a primary focus upon ethnic language or culture, usually adopting the language of the host society for teaching and then for liturgical purposes in order to retain the second generation. In the United States, "for the [German] churches, ethnicity had been primarily a means to achieve religious ends; when it tended to hinder rather than to ease the attainment of their goals, they readily abandoned programs of language and culture maintenance" (Luebke, 1978, 68).

Koreans in the United States, for example, have founded hundreds of Protestant congregations, many of which hold services in Korean for the older generation and also in English for students and young professionals. Though only 20 percent of the population of Korea is Christian, it is estimated that 70 percent of the Korean immigrants in the United States attend Christian churches, which have served as the primary focal point of community life. These churches provide an occasion for an unusually high level of personal involvement (Kim, 1988, 265): "It is the one place that has always allowed us to be Korean," one Korean-American banker told a reporter. By adapting to the language shift of the second generation, the Korean churches make it possible for them to continue to identify with their ethnic community while doing so in an "American" fashion (Dezell, 1995, 32). Chinese-American churches have often adopted the same practice of separate services in English and Cantonese or Mandarin to accommodate the intergenerational language shift (Wong, 1988, 317).

Although recently confrontation has marked the relationship between Islam in particular and the host societies of Western Europe, there are some signs of evolution within Muslim religious institutions. In France, for example, there are efforts to shake off the long-standing dominance by the religious authorities of Algeria—originally negotiated by the French government—in a determination to develop what might be called an assimilated Islam, expressing itself in French and taking its place alongside the other religious communities on equal terms (Girardon, Huguex, & Stein, 1993, 27). Some predict "religious currents which will use much more widely the local languages, beginning with French; since Arabic is spoken and read less and less frequently among immigrants, despite efforts to re-appropriate it" (Roux, 1990, 95). This in turn is likely to lead to a liberalized understanding of the requirements of Islamic practice. Similarly, among Turks in Germany, there has been a growing interest in "what it means in our modern industrial society to live as a Muslim and to draw motivation and strength from faith in order to give humane and democratic form to current and future opportunities in life" (Elsas, 1983, 134).

Religious affiliation can, we have seen, function in several different ways for immigrants and their children. It can serve to reinforce and justify the sense of alienation that may arise from experiences of marginalization, as when the Moroccan Muslim organization in the Netherlands declared that "integration and assimilation can only have a place when there is a common basis and starting point" which do not exist between Islam and the West (Entzinger, 1984, 145). Or it can, as for Koreans in the United States, serve as a framework within which acculturation is experienced as a smooth transition.

"Professional Ethnics"

Students of the history of ethnic organizations in the United States have noted that a new type of leadership emerged in the 1920s, less concerned with maintaining traditions and more with mobilizing members to exert political pressure "to maximize material and social gains in the larger society" (Barton, 1978, 170). Ethnic activists may endorse cultural pluralism out of a belief that "permanent minority status might be advantageous," at least for themselves (Higham, 1975, 211). It has been noted, for example, that many educated Surinamese in the Netherlands changed their occupations in the late 1970s, from the "Dutch" jobs for which they were trained to more rewarding jobs concerned with discrimination and the problems experienced by their compatriots; from being a disadvantage, their minority identity became a distinct advantage to their careers (Vermeulen, 1984, 52).

The role of ethnic communities and religious organizations in shaping the relationship of immigrants to their host societies is profoundly affected by the nature of the leadership which they receive, and how public authorities choose to relate to that leadership. Those who become identified as ethnic leaders may promote vigorously the participation of their rank and file in the host society, or they may seek to keep them apart and monopolize significant contacts (Amersfoort, 1986, 39). They may, for example, select among the preoccupations of their community those that lend themselves to solidifying their own position, as with the priority some see as given by Latino leadership in the United States to affirmative action rather than to crime, which is of more direct concern to the rank and file. It may indeed, because of sensitivity to political allies, lead to their taking positions—such as on abortion—which conflict with those of rank and file (Skerry, 1993, 277–279).

> Because so many Mexican Americans do not, or cannot, participate [in voting], the means of ascertaining and representing the group's interests are necessarily limited. Yet at the same time, the wider society places enormous demands on Mexican-American leaders to represent those interests. With only weak ties to their nominal constituents, who remain in a state of political passivity, it is hardly surprising that these leaders should rely on the resources of non-Mexican-American allies and sponsors. Inevitably, these allies and sponsors

play a role, however indirect, in setting the Mexican-American political agenda (Skerry, 1993, 311).

The role of ethnic leaders as a primary channel of information may in turn shape the ways in which the demands and opportunities of the host society are communicated across a language barrier to members of their ethnic community.

Ethnic leadership is often drawn from among those elements of an immigrant population who are successful, not by acculturating to and participating in the host society, but precisely by stressing their ethnic distinctiveness. In some cases they are "enclave entrepreneurs" who serve the immigrant community, with products or services that are not otherwise available, like the Al Halal Supermarket in Birmingham, England, justified by its founder as a way for Muslims to invest without violating Islamic law against usury, as a place for Muslim women to wear traditional garb while employed, and as a source of ritually clean food (Kepel, 1994, 150). Every Latino neighborhood in the United States has its *tiendas* that sell *productos tropicales* and Spanish-language videos and newspapers and arrange international transfers of funds.

In other cases, ethnic businesspeople operate restaurants and businesses, often of an ethnic character, that serve the majority population: Koreans control the retail grocery business in many urban areas, and Greeks, Italians, and Chinese have run thousands of small restaurants in North America, Western Europe, and Australia.

For such self-employed men and women the language and culture of their homeland are an essential economic resource; indeed

> the children of enclave entrepreneurs are likely to become fluent bilinguals because of access to quality English language education financed by their parents' resources combined with strong ethnic support for continuing use of the mother tongue. Fluent bilingualism in these contexts is associated with superior opportunities (Portes & Rumbaut, 1990, 217).

They are successful precisely because they can live in two cultural worlds, and negotiate the relationship between the two. The fact that continuing use of the language of their homeland or that of their parents is part of their repertory in business or profession leads naturally to a strong belief in bilingualism and biculturalism as an alternative to assimilation. Also inclining them to this position is the fact (perhaps not consciously recognized) that their livelihood or at least their status would be threatened by the disappearance of the distinct ethnic community as a consequence of their fellow-immigrants achieving full participation in the host society.

The cessation in the early 1920s of large-scale immigration from Italy to the United States (more arrived in 1921 alone than from 1925 through 1957), and the successful economic and social integration of the descendants of the immigrant generations, have had the consequence that speaking Italian is no particular advantage in obtaining employment as a teacher, social worker, or government employee, nor is the language spoken much any more in Italian restaurants, pizza shops, or barber shops. As the economic function of the Italian language has declined in American life, it is not surprising that few Italian Americans (apart from the elderly) speak the language. By contrast, the more recent Italian immigration to the United Kingdom, and the attractiveness of an Italian ambience in some services, has produced an occupational bilingualism. "Restauranteurs, waiters, hairdressers, etc., clearly have to learn English in order to function and communicate effectively, yet economically the Italian position is maintained by emphasizing and trading on their ethnicity. Ethnicity is encouraged at the same time as linguistic acculturation" (Taylor, 1988, 233). It seems unlikely, however, that this effect will continue into the generation born in the United Kingdom (Tosi, 1984).

Other ethnic leaders are even more explicitly concerned with maintenance of a distinct ethnic community, and of the characteristics (especially language) that keep it distinct. Those working in the ethnic media, or in cultural and mutual-support organization, or in religious institutions, have a direct stake in the continuing existence of an unassimilated minority community. Becoming virtuosi in "the manipulation of the symbolic, the instrumental, and the affective," they achieve a high level of participation in the host society while doing so on the basis of the continued existence of a group of followers who are precisely not integrated (Kastoryano, 1992, 174).

American experience suggests that, like ethnic groups themselves, such ethnic leadership is a transitional phenomenon. "When German immigration dropped off sharply at the end of the 19th century, ethnic leaders sought to inhibit the inevitable disintegration of the group by espousing a new cultural chauvinism," but after the anti-German sentiment of World War I, "few were ready to respond to a leader who promised to solve the problems of the Germans as an ethnic minority group. The majority were not interested in the promotion of ethnic consciousness or in the political defense of *das Deutschtum*" (Luebke, 1978, 65–66). By the 1920s, "the Germans constituted a disintegrating constituency—a melting iceberg, in the words of one observer" (Luebke, 1978, 78), and the various nationality-based Lutheran denominations gradually merged.

A third group whose interests depend upon the continuing distinctiveness of an ethnic community are those who work for public and other institutions of the host society as representatives of and communicators with the minority, or as providers of public services to its members.

> Gordon (1975) has identified two major forms of cultural pluralism: liberal and corporate. In the first form, difference is tolerated but not officially recognized, for example, by the allocation of supportive resources. In the second form, there is explicit recognition of ethnic groups as a basis for the allocation of social and political power and access to economic rewards and resources. Bullivant (1984) has recently extended this proposition, arguing that ethnic minorities need to establish separate structures and institutions in order to survive (Lynch, 1989, 123–24)

Several European countries provide public financial support to various kinds of recognized voluntary associations, among which are ethnic groups; in Sweden, in the late 1980s, there were thirty-six nationwide federations of ethnic organizations, from the *Assyriska Riksförbundet* for Assyrian refugees from Turkey to the *Ungerska Riksförbundet* for refugees from the suppressed Hungarian rising in 1956. The Yugoslavian association represented 125 groups and 19,000 members, and that of the Finns included 166 organizations and 42,000 members (Koekebakker, 1990, 59). Support is provided to the groups themselves, to the newspapers that they publish, and to their various cultural and youth activities (Hammar, 1985a, 39). The Dutch government has provided subsidies to private organizations serving immigrant groups (though often dominated by Dutch self-appointed spokespersons for the interests of those they serve) since 1964 (Schumacher, 1981, 35); not surprisingly, ethnic associations have sprung up rapidly and in great numbers (Buiks, 1986, 215). In other cases, homeland governments support organizations of their emigrated citizens, with the goal of maintaining a measure of political influence and of ensuring continuing remittances (Just, 1985c).

Such a vigorous organizational life provides ample scope for individuals to make it their primary occupation to be "ethnic" and to seek to maintain the distinctiveness of the group and the incommensurability of its needs and interests with those of others in the society. It also gives rise to questions about the extent to which advocacy groups are representative of the ethnic rank-and-file (Entzinger, 1984, 110). It promotes the provision of *categorical* services directed to particular groups, while weakening the possibility of coordinated interventions to address social problems; this is particularly the case with the Southern European immigrant groups (Yugoslav, Italian, Spanish, Portuguese), though less so with the Turks and Moroccans (Buiks, 1986, 221).

Teachers in programs designed for minority children, social workers and community organizers, ethnic elected and appointed officials, professors and researchers specializing in minority cultures and languages, and leaders in advocacy groups all contribute to "development of community awareness and identity through various forms of consciousness raising," though themselves are entirely capable of functioning in the host society. To the extent that, as in some British cities, public authorities choose to provide services to immigrants through mosques and other ethnic organizations,

> the emergence of certain types of leaders is encouraged, who have an interest in perpetuating the bounded ethnic community for which they are the necessary intermediaries between public institutions and populations whose distinctiveness is prized by official multiculturalism (Kepel, 1994, 158).

It is not necessarily the marginalized or the not yet acculturated immigrants "who experience ethnic identity most clearly and who champion ethnic mobilization movements" (Lambert & Taylor, 1988, 33). Individuals who are highly qualified academically to occupy positions in the host society may come to feel that "permanent minority status might be advantageous" (Higham, 1975, 211) as might insistence upon maintenance of the minority language. In some cases, their sense of calling can take on literally apocalyptic dimensions, as when Finnish language activist Tove Skutnabb-Kangas writes that

> monolingualism . . . is an illness, a disease which should be eradicated as soon as possible, because it is dangerous for world peace. . . . In a world at five to twelve (= on the verge of self-destruction) what is needed is *not* monolingual technical idiots (white, middle-class, male) who can make the missile and push the button. They are people who have never been forced to and who are probably not able to see matters from the inside from somebody else's point of view. You can obviously not discuss with a missile, but a real bilingual/bicultural might be able to mediate before the button is released, provided she has the instruments for analysis, and the solidarity (Skutnabb-Kangas, 1988a, 13, 38).

The effort to maintain a minority language through community initiatives or through lobbying for government support and inclusion as a prominent part of formal schooling may be based upon sound pedagogical principles (see Chapter 8); it may also, however, "become a means of assuring social control and social ascendancy for those ethnically related interests that are already in power, just as it becomes a desideratum for those ethnically related interests that seek to increase their power or at least to gain sufficient control over their own lives to assure their intergenerational ethnocultural continuity" (Fishman, 1989, 266).

The essence of such political agendas is their oppositional nature; they are premised upon a necessary conflict between the interests of ethnic minority groups and those of the host society, and a consequent refusal of the token accommodations of diversity which public policies sometimes offer. As Foster and Stockley comment,

> The options seem to be either to reduce multiculturalism to simply another term or to promote a politicization of ethnicity operating outside the mainstream political parties and aiming for genuine *institutional* change in the mainstream institutions of Australia. Politicization would involve a proliferation of pressure groups. A conscious strategy of avoiding the process of co-option which governments have previously used and an acceptance that *structural* pluralism is inevitable unless the mainstream culture does, in fact, undergo a radical (and unlikely) transformation. Such a re-direction of energies seems to us to be the only way of saving multiculturalism from becoming just another issue of the 1970s and 1980s (Foster & Stockley, 1988, 247).

A "re-direction of energies" of this sort requires—or would require, if it came to pass—a Maoist "heightening of the contradictions" and a refusal of compromise or reforms within existing structural arrangements. This was identified as a danger in a Dutch draft policy document, which warned that "group formation can direct itself against the society and promote isolation through calling strongly upon values and/or interests that are in conflict with those of Dutch society" (*Ontwerp-Minderhedennota*, 1981, 23). In these situations, "leaders . . . play down potential cleavages and conflicts among their own members and exaggerate the salience of conflicts with outsiders. . . . Because associations help to fragment the concerns of citizens, interests that many citizens might share . . . may be slighted" (Dahl, 1982, 44).

Separate educational provisions for minority children (such as, for example, bilingual classes in schools) are supported by some ethnic leadership in part as a basis for development of alternative institutions that can serve as a power base in relation to the host society. The idea that such programs are intended to be provisional and to transition the child as quickly as possible into the educational and societal mainstream—the expectation of most immigrant parents—may be strongly resisted by those who place the interests of the group above those of the individual child (Entzinger, 1984, 131).

This was dramatically illustrated in Massachusetts in the spring of 1995, in the response to a legislative bill filed by the governor to reinforce the transitional nature of the state's bilingual education law by reaffirming the three-year limit on enrollment in a separate program and encouraging long-term enrollment in integrated ("two-way") programs. Although bilingual educators would admit privately that the existing law, the oldest in the nation, could profitably be amended to correct problems revealed by more than twenty years of experience, they orchestrated a show of opposition by bringing hundreds of children (during school hours) to demonstrate at the legislative hearing. Fliers went home to parents, in Spanish, saying that the governor's amendments would "abolish bilingual education," a patent untruth. The hearing was completely one-sided; apparently the only witness in support of the changes was bilingual education critic Christine Rossell. Not surprisingly, the amendment was tabled by the legislature.

Reinforcing minority language use by children through bilingual programs could in theory help to maintain into the next generation the boundaries and thus the potential for political mobilization of the ethnic community; this accounts for the fact that use of Spanish for instruction in American schools "is a program initiated and shepherded by mostly middle-class Chicano activists—not barrio masses" (Skerry, 1993, 288). Actually, as we will see in Chapter 5, there is little prospect that bilingual programs will have the effect of maintaining active use of minority languages.

There are some indications, nevertheless, that Latino spokespersons in the United States are concerned to retard the pace of assimilation, convinced that strategies of confrontation and defining of group interests that have served black leadership (though not black rank and file) can serve them as well. Linda Chavez has warned that this "would mean that for the first time a major ethnic immigrant group, guided by its leaders, had eschewed the path of assimilation." In pursuit of this strategy, rather than boasting of their hard work and contributions to American society, as other ethnic leaders had done, "Hispanic leaders developed a vested interest in showing that Hispanics were, as the head of one Hispanic organization described it, 'the poorest of the poor. . . .' To succeed at the affirmative action game, Hispanics had to establish their failure in other areas" (Chavez, 1991, 2, 5).

Ethnic politics, new style, is no longer concerned to gain a share of the municipal jobs or the paving contracts, but a separate societal space guaranteed, not by the self-organization of an ethnic community but by government sponsorship (Edwards, 1984). Anything less is "the denial of a people's development and use of its native tongue . . . a denial of its participation in society and of its very peoplehood" (Hernández-Chávez, 1988, 45). The assumption in such statements, of course, is that individuals of Mexican ancestry in the United States form a separate "people" rather than part of the American people, as though all Americans of Polish or German ancestry were also distinct "peoples."

The same author made a similar appeal for a form of separate development in a collection published (oddly enough) by the California Department of Education. Academic achievement on the part of minority children, however important, was not enough, he wrote,

> for the full and equal participation of language minorities in American society requires not that these groups try to become indistinguishable from the white majority, but rather that they strengthen themselves from within—culturally, socially, politically, and economically. . . . Academically prepared individuals who are alienated from their community and who are culturally adrift cannot be assets either to themselves or to society (Hernández-Chávez, 1984, 170–171).

This breathtaking judgment—who, after all, is not to some extent "culturally adrift" under conditions of modernity?—leads to a policy argument for making the minority language the primary vehicle for schooling of language minority children, precisely in order to retard rather than to promote their assimilation into the mainstream. "Neither the educational or linguistic theories nor the sociocultural or sociolinguistic realities of minorities in the United States require the immediate acculturation and acquisition of English fluency" (Hernández-Chávez, 1984, 171).

As in the communitarian politics employed by Muslims in the United Kingdom, "in order for this political strategy to work, Hispanics must stay in the barrio. It is a political victory that can be won only at the expense of the ultimate social and economic integration of Hispanics in this society" (Chavez, 1991, 40). There is little evidence, however, that immigrant groups have abandoned their characteristic strategy of progressive integration over the course of several generations in response to this political counsel. No political parties in any of the countries included in this study have been successful on an ethnic basis; the attempt to organize a Mexican-American party,

"*La Raza Unida*, was never able, despite great effort, to acquire even one-third of the necessary 66,000 registrants to qualify as a legally recognized political party in California" (Connor, 1985a, 27).

Many question the wisdom of strategies to advance the interests of immigrant minority groups that are based upon how they differ from the majority. Germany explicitly forbids political activity by foreigners, and in Belgium associations are required by law to have a certain number of members who are Belgian citizens (Koekebakker, 1990, 90). Emphasis upon the distinctive needs of a minority creates the danger that the majority will come to believe that they have no interests in common. When immigrants and their children are defined as a problem in terms of the ways in which they are different from the norm, and social and educational services are designed and provided in the name of responding to and eliminating these differences, this can serve as a substitute for opening access to real participation in the society, with the effect of keeping members of ethnic minority groups in a subordinate and dependent position (Rath, 1991; see criticisms by Strijbosch, 1992).

Separate development is sometimes promoted, not to serve the political interests of the immigrant groups, but rather those of the country of origin, as when the Tunisian ambassador to France claimed, much evidence to the contrary, that most of his fellow countrymen really wanted to live apart, remain Tunisians, and not be integrated into French society (Gaspard & Servan-Schreiber, 1985, 147).

The cultural politics of some ethnic spokespersons shade over into demands for radical changes that would affect not just the ethnic minority group but the entire society. After all, if "schools are ideological state apparatuses . . . education also operates as part of the *repressive* state apparatus" (Skutnab-Kangas, 1988b, 259), then the state itself and the social and economic order which it defends must be challenged. From this perspective, many of the efforts made in the supposed interest of minority children are mere palliatives that may do more harm than good, by reducing the pressure for fundamental change.

> Whilst the multicultural approach sees discrimination and isolation of minority pupils in schools as an error of history, the anti-racist approach sees this situation as an outcome of imbalances in power relationships within society: racism and discrimination operate through structural mechanisms and processes in social institutions such as the school (Fernández Bragado, 1992, 131).

Although the immigrant minority groups tend to vote (when given the opportunity) for Socialist and other parties that support welfare-state policies, not all ethnic mobilization is on the Left. Cubans in the United States have been wooed successfully by the Republicans, and Moroccans in Western Europe are divided on the basis of opposition to or support for the authoritarian regime of Morocco (Schumacher, 1981, 175). Bitter struggles can take place within immigrant communities, often around issues that have little to do with their situation in the host society (Just, 1985c, 172).

> The Turkish far right is . . . able to mobilize large numbers of Turkish workers in West Germany around racist ideas of ethnic superiority and Pan-Turkish expansionism. . . . the consequence is a policy of cultural separatism which plays into the hands of the German right in their rejection of settlement [by immigrants] and their call for repatriation [to Turkey] (Castles, Booth, & Wallace, 1984, 222).

Race and ethnicity are proposed by some as the focus for struggle leading to the revolutionary transformation of society, with the postwar anticolonial struggles proposed as a model in place of the class struggles that have proved such a disappointing basis for recent political mobilization in the advanced economies.

> Proto-elites whose change-over aspirations may have been stymied recognize and capitalize upon the potentialities for power as leaders of the bearers of a distinguished paternity and patrimony such as is "really" theirs. When the class struggle and political action along class-related lines have proved themselves incapable of rectifying the inequities . . . then ethnicity becomes an even more logical basis of instrumental organization (Fishman, 1989, 42–43)

Of course, such efforts at ethnic mobilization are undercut by the fact that much of the potential leadership is continually being absorbed into the opportunity structure of the host societies. There is little evidence, indeed, that members of immigrant minority groups are eager to be mobilized in opposition to society; for most, it is undoubtedly the fondest desire to "join the oppressors" by becoming a fully participating member of the society. The personal freedom that is an essential component of modernity continually undermines identity-based organization, the attempt to create a "culturally-autonomous space for each cultural minority that wishes one" (Kugelmann & Löw-Beer, 1984, 48–49). The exception is when ethnicity has hardened into caste, and then we may appropriately call it segregation into an inferior status. Ghettoes may be gilded, but they remain what they have always been.

Ironically enough, progressive intellectuals who insist upon the right of linguistic minority parents to control the schooling of their children in the name of linguistic pluralism and political empowerment tend to have little sympathy for the more common demand of such parents for religiously based schooling, which runs counter to the aversion to traditional religion which progressive counter-elites share with liberal elites. In Germany, immigrant blue-collar workers and their families are more likely to be associated with religious organizations (Muslim, Catholic, or Orthodox) than with the intellectual-dominated ethnic groups that call themselves "workers' associations" (Schoeneberg, 1985, 427).

There are other ethnic intellectuals who argue for the preservation of their minority languages and cultures (even if they are themselves thoroughly acculturated to the host society) out of what Gunnar Myrdal called "an abstract craving for historical identity," charging that "they have not clarified . . . what cultural traits are implied, who wants this identity, who should want it, and why, and how it should and could come about. I am afraid, therefore, one must characterize this movement as an upper-class intellectual romanticism" (quoted by Steinberg, 1982, 50).

In the last analysis, ethnic elites seem usually to have little effect upon the actual process by which immigrants and their children negotiate their evolving relationship with the host society. Most immigrants in Germany, according to a careful study, had never once participated in an ethnic association (Schoeneberg, 1985, 421). With a rank and file that is constantly slipping away, the role of ethnic leadership seems destined to grow less and less significant, *unless they can somehow* persuade the dominant groups in the host society to accord them a continuing importance—for example, in professorships of "ethnic studies." From such positions they may affect the public policies of the host society in ways that run counter to the actual process under way among those they claim to speak for. To that uncertain process we must now turn.

THE SECOND GENERATION

"Second generation" is sometimes used to include those who came as young children with their immigrant parents; these are now sometimes called the one-and-a-half generation. With the relative decline of new immigration, at least to Western Europe, the second generation more commonly refers to those born in the host society of immigrant parents. If those parents came as young children, and thus were themselves schooled entirely in the same educational system that their children attend, the latter may be referred to as the two-and-a-half generation. In short, the sequence of generations, like other aspects of the situation of immigrant minority groups, is too varied for simple categorization.

The situation of the children of immigrants rather than that of immigrants who come as adults is the major preoccupation of public policy in this area. This priority is imposed by the numbers themselves—almost three-quarters of the 2 million young people in France derived from immigration were born in France (Abou-Sada & Milet, 1986, 14)—and also by the fact that it is characteristically in the second generation that the immigration project is a success or a failure.

The trajectories followed by the immigrant generation are relatively predictable, but those of the second generation show more variation than those of any other sociological group, based upon individual decisions and happenstance as well as social pressures and opportunities. Some retain highly traditional values and relationships with their families, while others adapt eagerly to the host society, leading to sharp divisions within the second generation itself (Sung, 1971). When asked, the children of immigrants will often say that they are "simply themselves: a little bit of this, a little of that" (Tappeiner, 1990, 41). It is possible to identify useful patterns in this confusing picture, however, provided that such patterns are not applied rigidly or deterministically.

> Three distinct situations of dominant socialization—the family, the school and the street—can lead to three different destinies: the predominance of the family favors retaining certain traditional economical or anthropological behaviors; the victory of the school implies the complete assimilation of dominant French values and upward social mobility; the choice of the street leads into a hazy world which includes the possibilities of unemployment and of delinquency (Todd, 1994, 315).

Alejandro Portes makes the same three-way distinction among ways of adapting to the immigrant situation: remaining closely tied to the immigrant community, becoming part of the working or middle class through acculturation to mainstream values and behaviors, or "becoming impoverished and assimilating into an underclass" (Schmidt, 1993, 14). As a school administrator in California put it, there is "just as great a chasm not only between the immigrant youngster and the larger society, but within a minority community itself—a chasm of language, culture, and the drive to be assimilated" (Olsen, 1988, 36).

The Choice for the Family and Ethnic Community

Among the marginalized who continue to cling together as an immigrant community, the frustration of their project of success in the adopted society may lead to a revival of awareness of distinctiveness. Characteristics which may at first have seemed primarily impediments to successful adjustment to the new situation may come to have a powerful symbolic importance. "Many immigrants who have experienced a strong cultural assimilation discover their ethnicity in the face of difficulties of economic inclusion and of racism and discrimination. Ethnicity functions in such a case as the rationalization of a disappointed love" (Dubet & Lapeyronnie, 1992, 93).

Accepting a self-definition as members of a group who will inevitably be discriminated against and can do little to improve their prospects is one way of handling the "affective dissonance" that accompanies failure in the process of achieving success in the host society. Another way is to retreat into the ethnic group at the cost of accepting limited prospects. For many rank-and-file immigrants, especially those in low-status employment, the language and culture of their homeland can come to enjoy increased significance even as the homeland itself recedes in time, enabling them to retain a sense of personal worth; these may indeed become central to an *"oppositional cultural system or cultural frame of reference* that contains mechanisms for maintaining and protecting the group's social identity" (Ogbu & Matute-Bianchi, 1986, 94). Use of the majority language, acceptance of the majority culture, may under these circumstances come to be seen as a betrayal of the ethnic minority group, and

> schools are perceived as agents of assimilation or linear acculturation into the Anglo cultural system. And, since linear or one-way acculturation is considered detrimental to the integrity of Mexican-American identity, culture, language, school policies, and practices are viewed as things to be resisted, challenged, and changed. Some students go as far as asserting that doing school work is doing "the white people's thing." . . . They may complain that the schools are teaching only Anglo language or English and not their own language: Spanish. There is, thus, an element of opposition that is not always conscious or overt. Often, it takes the form of mental withdrawal (Ogbu & Matute-Bianchi, 1986, 129).

Precisely because the society in which they must live and work offers them few satisfactions beyond (scanty) material goods, the parents of these pupils may have little inclination to adopt its values with enthusiasm. It is particularly excruciating when the society seems to invade the sphere of private satisfactions, the home and family, through alienating children from the values of their parents. While the media and peer influences have much to do with this acute generation gap, parents can to some extent, if they choose, keep those at bay in the private sphere of life. It is through compulsory schooling that the values—or lack of values—of the society are most powerfully inculcated in the children of immigrants, and thus the demand for alternative forms of schooling can take on great significance to them.

On the other hand, the host society itself may tend to reinforce the ethnic distinctiveness of the immigrant family. One result of the unreceptiveness of German society to outsiders is that there is a much higher rate of endogamy (intergroup marriage) among Turks in Germany than there is among North Africans in France, where young women of this group are perceived as being highly motivated to assimilate and are encouraged by social acceptance to do so. By contrast, "Turkish women in Germany, like black women in the United States, are defined [by the majority] as tabu" (Todd, 1994, 179). In such cases, ethnic distinctiveness is not the result of insufficient time or opportunity to acculturate, or even of a prior disinclination on the part of the minority to do so (though, as we have seen, that may be the case with Turks), but of intergroup tensions and the political assertion of ethnicity as a group marker and claim for consideration. Todd comments that "German society seems to be engaged in the manufacture of a stably marginal group, marked by a distinctiveness which is simultaneously ethnic and religious" (Todd, 1994, 184).

Close family cohesion, although it may in some cases promote school success and consequent societal participation, may also have the effect of limiting opportunities to acquire the language of the host society. That is,

> Working-class immigrants who cluster in certain areas give rise to homogeneous ethnic neighborhoods that help preserve mother-tongue monolingualism among adults. Their children are likely to be limited bilinguals because they are insufficiently exposed either to English—as is the case with recent arrivals—or to full use of the mother tongue—as is the case with the U.S. born (Portes & Rumbaut, 1990, 217).

A study of Asian girls in the United Kingdom found that "an important factor in academic achievement amongst the sample is the pre-school learning of English" and that "the provision of specialist English lessons did not appear to have redressed the balance for those who had not had the opportunity of early contact with the language" (Wade & Souter, 1992, 62, 53). Children who, though born in the host country, grow up in families that are resisting acculturation by continuing to use the language of their countries of origin may experience particular difficulty in school, even compared with children who immigrate after some schooling in that language (see Chapter 5).

Rejection by the host society can lead in either of two directions: toward a hyperconformism, a compulsive assimilation, that seeks to remove all traces of the behavior that is presumed offensive or that serves as a ready label of "otherness," or (particularly when physical characteristics make the first impossible) toward a defiant rejection of that society through an affirmation of distinctiveness. The "Black is beautiful" movement in the United States is such a compensatory self-affirmation.

Perhaps the most striking instance is that of the Turks who came as guestworkers to Germany. Most were already well on the way to modernity before emigration; despite the common stereotype in Germany, most Turkish immigrants had lived in urban areas and held industrial jobs before they left Turkey (Institut für Zukunftsforschung, 1981, 69). Rural patterns, such as the extended family, had already been abandoned by most of them while in Turkey (Wilpert, 1987, 201). In response to widespread rejection by German society, however, many who had been highly secularized embraced Islam and asserted the superiority of Muslim ways. "Coming from one of the few Muslim countries which has a real secular tradition, the Turkish minority in Germany have become a stronghold of Islamic fundamentalism." An objective measure of this reaction is provided by the rising birthrate of Turkish women in Germany, which by 1990 was higher than that in the west of Anatolia, from which most of them came (Todd, 1994, 159, 174).

> Typically it is groups who have remained on the economic margin who have been insulated from assimilating forces, and thus relatively successful at preserving their ethnic distinctiveness. Groups that have experienced widespread mobility, in contrast, are producing such high rates of intermarriage that their futures are very much in doubt. Without these class inequalities, therefore, one can imagine only an accelerated rate of ethnic defection as the forces of assimilation are freed from the restraints of class (Steinberg, 1982, 261).

Success in the schools of the host society is, for most children of immigrants, both the means to and an expression of a substantial degree of assimilation. This word is now often avoided in policy discussions, since it has taken on a connotation of cultural imperialism leading to the suppression of all ethnic distinctiveness by a hegemonic culture. As used by Robert Park, assimilation had a less politically charged meaning:

> In the United States an immigrant is ordinarily considered assimilated as soon as he has acquired the language and the social ritual of the native community and can participate, without encountering prejudice, in the common life, economic and political. . . . This implies among other things that in all the ordinary affairs of life he is able to find a place in the community on the basis of his individual merits without invidious or qualifying references to his racial origin or to his cultural inheritance (quoted by Gordon, 1964, 63).

A high proportion of those immigrants who come to the United States, to Canada, or to Australia come with the intention of becoming a part of those societies. While they may have every intention of retaining a variety of aspects of their previous lives, this intention is in most cases secondary to the project of fitting in, and practices that conflict with fitting in are quickly abandoned so as not to appear a "greenhorn." After all, "people have not migrated to maintain the conditions of village-agricultural society in Australia. . . . They have migrated to leave situations which they might have found socially/culturally unsatisfactory or limiting, for a new culture" (Kalantzis, Cope, & Slade, 1989, 20). Similarly,

> ethnic groups [in the United States] were not just passive victims of cultural repression, but played an active role in their own demise— not out of any collective self-hatred, but because circumstances forced them to make choices that undermined the basis for cultural survival. To be sure, their choices were difficult ones, and they were accompanied by a painful sense of cultural loss (Steinberg, 1982, 257).

The same process may be observed in France, where

> the grandsons and especially the granddaughters of the immigrants have a French culture, learn English rather than Arabic, neglect their original religion, have a fertility rate that is rapidly conforming itself

to that of the French, and demonstrate strong desire to adopt the local customs and ways of life (Duhamel, 1993, 100).

A study of *beurs*—born in France, of North-African origin—found that 88 percent of them wanted to be fully integrated into French society (Duraffour & Guittonneau, 1992, 211). As a result of this desire for full participation in the host society, "among immigrant families in France, an "[i]ncreasing disliking on the part of pupils towards courses 'for immigrants' has been observed. The demands of the parents themselves tend now towards . . . 'Let French schools do what they know how to do!'" (Costa-Lascoux, 1989a, 77). Research in the Netherlands has found that the children of immigrants have a very positive attitude toward Dutch schooling, more so than do Dutch children! (Batenburg & De Jong, 1985, 106).

The focus upon what it takes to make a success of life in the host society is likely to have an effect on the desire to maintain, into the second and third generation, the use of the language of the homeland. Analysis of the foreign language courses selected by Portuguese-speaking pupils and their parents in France shows that the great majority select English rather than Portuguese. "For families concerned about the social mobility of their children, the mother-tongue becomes secondary at this stage in their education" (Villanova, 1986, 172). Parents who have pushed their children to be successful in the educational system may suddenly become aware, to their intense distress, that an entire cultural heritage that they themselves took for granted is closed to those children (Dubreuil, 1989, 125).

The same pattern emerged during an earlier period of heavy migration to the United States. Advocates for the use of minority languages in American schools have frequently pointed out that the public schools in some cities provided instruction through German and other languages of large immigrant groups during the late nineteenth century; they do not always mention that the discontinuance of this practice owed as much to lack of interest on the part of parents as it did to nativist reaction.

[T]he demand for such schools dissipated in the face of increasing parental desire for their children to have the same opportunities as did those graduating from English-language schools. More recently, parental concern has resulted in a sharp decrease in the demand for French-language parochial schools among Americans of French-Canadian background (Connor, 1985b, 283).

The evidence—admittedly unsystematic—suggests that language minority parents vary greatly in their desire for programs in public schools to maintain and develop the proficiency of their children in the language of the home, or of the country from which the parents, or *their* parents, emigrated.

> If the people themselves cannot perceive their institutions, and in particular their [ethnic] educational institutions, as offering positive opportunities and reinforcing identity, then, where command of language and physical characteristics permit people to "pass" into the dominant society, voluntary "migration" into the dominant group will be the most compelling option open (Jordan, 1988, 214).

This is in fact the "most compelling option" for many children from immigrant families who are fortunate enough to experience early and continued school success. Although the effect may be to increase the distance between themselves and their parents, as poignantly described by Richard Rodriguez in his autobiographical essay (Rodriguez, 1983), it corresponds in most cases, as in his, with the intentions of the parents. For many, the immigration project is undertaken precisely so that their children may enter without reservation into the host society, cost what it may.

> Parents who firmly decided to succeed in the host country and plan and provide for their children a definitive residence and career in that country, will act in such a way that their children succeed much better than those of families that see the migration as a temporary phase and that continue to cling to the relations that stayed behind and to their region of origin. A family group of the former type will more easily overcome all the hindrances of the migration, including the linguistic and cultural difficulties (Roosens, 1989, 99).

The relative lack of academic and economic success of Puerto Ricans in the continental United States, despite their advantage of citizenship, may have much to do with ambivalence about facing the usual consequences of immigration. Automatic citizenship has encouraged them to behave as migrants rather than as immigrants, coming to New York or other cities for some temporary benefit without the intention of making a definitive move. The constant flow in both directions between Puerto Rico and the mainland—"by 1977, homebound Puerto Ricans outnumbered emigrants by nearly 47,000"—has caused serious problems at both ends. "Some 57,000 young returnees [from the continental United States] in the public schools of Puerto Rico in 1977 were limited Spanish-proficient and were suffering severe adaptation problems—cultural as well as linguistic" (Castellanos & Leggio, 1983, 159). On the other hand, schools in mainland cities found it difficult to educate children who come and go several times during the school year.

Immigrants, it must be stressed again, do not generally come with previous experience of being members of a minority group; they have usually been part of the *majority* in their homeland. Rather than acquiring the attitudes and habits that would sustain group existence as a minority, many simply integrate as families or as individuals into the host society, particularly if that society is reasonably open to persons who look like them.

The well-meaning efforts of school staff to promote the self-esteem of the children of immigrants by stressing their cultural and linguistic distinctiveness may thus run counter to the desires of their parents. "Many immigrants," as John Rex notes of the English situation,

> do not expect, and sometimes do not want, their children to be educated in their own minority cultures. Having made the decision to migrate they want to ensure above all that their children get on in the society of settlement. Arguably, too much stress on their cultural difference might act as an obstacle to this process of "getting on" (Rex, 1989, 13).

Maureen Stone has described the resentment of many West Indian parents in the United Kingdom at multicultural programs that she characterizes as "a misguided liberal strategy to compensate black children for not being white," and as "aimed at 'watering down' the curriculum and 'cooling out' black city children while at the same time creating for teachers, both radical and liberal, the illusion that they are doing something special for a particularly disadvantaged group." Ironically, the emphasis of such programs upon feelings and relationships undercuts the stress of the West Indian community upon "hard work, high aspirations, willingness to sacrifice and belief in one's ability to succeed" (Stone, 1981, 100, 149).

Rather than seeking to promote minority cultures, Stone argues, schools should concentrate on providing minority children with access to successful participation in the mainstream of society. She insists that "the community, parents and children are sufficient guardians of the black cultural inheritance. Schools have to be about something else." After all, "if you really want to reduce educational and racial inequality, the best way is by providing your pupils with the skills and knowledge they need to make their own way in the society in which they live" (Stone, 1981, 6).

In the same spirit, one can applaud the generosity expressed in a California study subtitled "Crossing the Schoolhouse Border" without being sure what, if anything, it means:

> We can either say to the newcomers in our midst, we accept you provisionally to the extent you can re-create yourselves into a standard American mold—or we can say we welcome you as full members of our state and accept that we as a people have a new richness and diversity which requires new forms of public institutions to celebrate and support that diversity while uniting us as a state (Olsen, 1988, 9).

"New forms of public institutions" designed for immigrant populations run the great risk of giving an institutional fixedness to their separation from the majority, which would otherwise be constantly lessened by almost imperceptible adaptations to the new situation in which they find themselves. The fact is that the children of Filipino and Vietnamese and Armenian and Mexican immigrants to California (to the extent the last have not been segregated in large urban *barrios*) are precisely re-creating themselves as Americans, though not in any standard mold, for there is not and has never been such a standard model American. To the extent that they are making a success of their schooling and their participation in the host society, they are becoming something different from what their parents are. Like the successful among the second generation of Algerians in France,

> the young develop individual strategies of integration: military service, marriage, economic success, etc. To wish to assign to them a specific culture, a particular religion, would come back to marginalizing them and thus to slowing down their integration (Khellil, 1991, 168).

For at least some of the second generation, the "choice for the school" proves successful: young people of Turkish and Moroccan origin born in the Netherlands have a clear advantage over their contemporaries who arrived as immigrants (Table 4.1). Among Moroccans, whose academic achievement on average is lowest among the ethnic groups in the Netherlands, there is a clearly emerging minority whose inter-generational progress is notable.

TABLE 4.1. Completed Education of Persons Aged 15–35, The Netherlands, 1988

Highest Level of Education Completed	Elementary Only	Higher Education
Turks born in Turkey	67%	1%
Turks born in the Netherlands	53%	2%
Moroccans born in Morocco	86%	1%
Moroccans born in the Netherlands	50%	6%
Native Dutch persons	13%	20%

Source: Roelandt and Veenman, 1991, 33.

Among a sample of Turkish youth in Germany, 30 percent of those who attended elementary school in Germany but none of those who arrived as adolescents obtained positions as skilled workers in their first jobs (Mehrländer, 1986, 14). This is no doubt related to the greater proficiency in German of those who came as young children; another study found that 77 percent of the foreigners who had arrived before the age of 11 were fluent in reading, writing, and speaking German, but that the proportion dropped to 19 percent among those arriving ages 11 to 25 and 9 percent to those arriving age 26 and older. Of those arriving age 41 and above, an astonishing 46 percent knew almost no German at all (Koch-Arzberger, 1985, 169). Such findings should warn us against a too pessimistic view of the effects of schooling and other acculturative processes on immigrants who are exposed to them young enough.

It remains to be seen whether, in Europe as lately in the United States, the progress of minority students in higher education will reach a plateau at a level significantly lower than that of the majority.

The Choice for the Street

Immigration is of course not an inevitable success story, and its significance for public policy lies less in those who move smoothly into the societal mainstream than in those who fail to find a secure place, perhaps into the second or third generation. "Those who fail are marginalized in an absolute manner. The larger the opening the more their incapacity to assimilate seems irreparable and their own responsibility. It is their culture which seems incompatible, not so much with French culture but, more deeply, with democratic modernity and the market. Rejected, they barricade themselves in their identity, a fortress all the more closed because they oppose it to a modern culture which is too open" (Dubet & Lapeyronnie, 1992, 108–109).

Among pupils of Mexican descent in a California city, those born in Mexico or identifying with Mexico may have had academic difficulties (though in general they were more successful in school), "because they do not have satisfactory English-language skills and/or because they lack competence in academic skills in Spanish and English and because they are perceived to come from a rural peasant Mexican background which has not prepared them to meet the demands of schooling in the United States." By contrast, those pupils with no real connection with the immigrant experience were "perceived to be unsuccessful because they lack the 'motivation, interest and respect for schooling.' They are perceived to fail in school because they reject what the school has to offer" (Matute-Bianchi, 1991, 227).

The first major American study in fifty years, of second-generation immigrant children, conducted in South Florida and San Diego, has found that "assimilation can have a negative effect on academic achievement if the children of immigrants are becoming part of a marginalized, low-income subculture" (Schmidt, 1993, 14). The children of Haitian immigrants, living in urban ghettoes,

> find themselves torn between conflicting ideas and values: to remain "Haitian," they must endure ostracism and continuing attacks in school; to become "American," (black American in this case), they must forgo their parents' dreams of making it in America. . . . the assimilation is not to mainstream culture, but to the values and norms of the inner city (Portes & Zhou, 1994, 21).

To the extent that the children of immigrants to the United States choose or are led by circumstances to identify with underclass elements of the native population, they are likely to come to share many of the self-defeating attitudes of what Ogbu has dubbed "involuntary minorities." Although a 1973 study found that even "more Mexican-American students than Anglo students (67.5 to 64.7 percent) agree that 'the United States of America is the best country in the world,'" and overall there were only small attitudinal differences between the two groups of students, this fundamental confidence may not survive contact with the culture of victimization. The same study found that "black students show increasingly negative affective orientations toward the political system with age" (Horowitz, 1985, 85). The increasing ghettoization of Mexican American and Puerto Rican youth in Los Angeles and other cities seems to be inducing a growing proportion of them to understand their situation in American society by analogy with that of African Americans, as though they too were an "involuntary minority" rather than an ethnic group present on a voluntary basis, seeking (and finding) opportunities in the host society.

Immigrant parents may also fear the emulation, by their children, of majority children in the host society, perceiving the latter as spoiled and lacking the discipline required to make a success of the challenges of the immigration situation. Sikh parents in the United States, for example, may warn their children, "if we just follow the whites and do as they do, then we are going to be lost." "When our children get together with the white children," the parents lament, "they start doing things that affect our family honor" (Gibson & Blachu, 1991, 76–77).

The process of dysfunctional adaptation appears to be at work in the United Kingdom as well, as in the case of the Turkish- and Greek-speaking Cypriot children who have been "attracted by the 'street credibility' of Creole forms of English and have not uncommonly been found to employ 'London Jamaican' speech" (Hewitt, 1982, cited by Taylor, 1988, 69). Muslim youth,

> whatever the difficulties of their social insertion, of their access to the job market, know this society from the inside and have mastered at least part of its cultural code; for them, the criticism of British society in the name of Islam can no longer speak the language of externality and of the protection of community that characterize the first generation of immigrants. That doesn't mean that this criticism is necessarily less radical (Kepel, 1994, 174).

Some Hindu and Muslim youth in the Netherlands are emulating the "hustling" [*hosselen*] lifestyle of black youth from Surinam (Gelder, 1990), who in turn are acculturating to the most marginal elements of Dutch society.

> The cultural capital that poorly-educated black individuals need to rise in society is not acquired through hanging around with poorly-educated white youth. . . . Not every form of acculturation leads to an improved position. . . . Growing up in the Netherlands . . . and being at home in white discotheques don't prevent long-term unemployment and are no guarantee of living comfortably. . . . What's

important is not the frequency of contacts with whites, but the quality of those contacts and with which whites one associates (Sansone, 1992, 239).

The French look with concern upon the "economic, social, above all cultural instability of a population [of immigrant youth] using an abbreviated jargon, who would be almost more alienated in the villages of their grandparents than in the housing projects of their parents, who gladly reject all authority, ready to complain of injustice in response to the most ordinary constraints, and don't feel at home anywhere" (Pautard, 1986, 15). Among the second generation of immigrant families in France is appearing "an ethnicity which has nothing about it of the traditional. . . . Young immigrants are not defined by a strongly different community and by a large cultural distance from groups in the host society. On the contrary, they are extremely close to them and the major problem of most of them is based on the lived contradiction between a strong cultural assimilation and a weak social integration" (Dubet & Lapeyronnie, 1993, 28–29). For these marginalized youth, North African and French alike, "street life [*la galère*] is not the expression of a popular tradition and of sub-culture. The adults do not recognize in their children their own youth. . . . Moreover, it is not these [working-class] traditions and their particulars which lead toward street life, but rather their absence; research on this population indicates that young delinquents are clearly more identified with the norms and values of society than are other [working-class youth]" (Dubet and Lapeyronnie, 1993, 128).

The valuation of ethnicity by marginalized members of immigrant minority groups is of a very different quality and resonance from that characteristic of successfully assimilated descendants of immigrants for whom a little ethnic flavor in life is attractive but not central. Neither group, however, is generally able to preserve anything approximating their heritage culture in its original form. If for the latter the distinctive culture tends to reduce itself to a few ethnic dishes and traditional customs at holiday times, for the former it often came to little more. As a classic study of ethnicity in New York City noted, "if Puerto Ricans were not illiterate in both languages, it is certainly true that on the whole they learned English poorly, and at the same time the Spanish cultural heritage was transmitted inadequately" (Glazer & Moynihan, 1963, 87). Or, as a Belgian study found, "the children of an immigrant family are confronted not by a coherent culture but with cultural fragments, and . . . they psychologically internalize this fragmentation" (Roosens, 1989, 89).

In some respects, the marginalization and sense of not having any place may become greater on the part of those who have not themselves shared the immigration experience. The immigrant has a recognizable identity, after all: he or she is the stranger who works hard in a menial occupation, sacrificing for the sake of the following generations. There is little cultural ambiguity about this role. It is the native-born child of immigrants, knowing no other home, who may feel most homeless.

THE UNEASY BALANCE

It would be too simple to understand the choices faced by immigrants and their children as lying along a single continuum running between maintenance of the original identity, language, and mores intact, and their complete abandonment for those of the host society. Didier Lapeyronnie has suggested a more nuanced and useful classification of responses to the immigrant situation along the two dimensions of *participation* and *integration*. The first describes the degree to which an immigrant takes advantage of the economic and (less significantly) political opportunities of the host society, while the second describes the degree to which he or she adopts the worldview and mores of that society (Lapeyronnie, 1993, 104).

An immigrant can have a high level of participation, in this sense, while maintaining a strongly distinctive ethnic group life; indeed, the latter is for some groups an essential condition for their economic success, as in the case of some immigrant groups in the United States who have found economic niches which did not require a high degree of social or cultural integration. For Koreans in the grocery business, or, earlier, Eastern European Jews in the New York garment industry, the closeness of the ethnic group contributed to a high level of economic participation based upon mutual support, but also to a lower level of integration into the society (Kotkin, 1992, 105). As subsequent generations of Jews have acculturated themselves to American life, they have largely abandoned the garment industry to newer immigrants and moved into occupations in which ethnic group membership provides no advantage.

Economic success requires coming to terms with modernization, but not necessarily with *modernity* in the sense of the individualized state of consciousness called for by integration into contemporary Western societies. Such integration almost necessitates abandonment of the ethnic group, even on the part of those who serve as representatives of such groups before the wider society; some choose it, others do not, for conscious or unconscious reasons. The assimilated immigrant or child of immigrants is high on participation and on integration, even though he or she may continue in largely symbolic ways to assert an ethnic identity.

At the other pole from the successful ethnic businessman is the second-generation immigrant youth who has "chosen the street" by internalizing a version of the culture of the host society without acquiring the skills or the drive that leads to successful participation. There are of course also, at the opposite pole from assimilated immigrants, others who "choose the family" and the maintenance of an ethnic culture and language at the expense of successful participation in the host society.

Any such schematic representation of a complex reality must make room for exceptions, such as those hapless immigrants who find it difficult *both* to make the adjustment to the new society *and also* to retain important aspects of the culture and even the language of their homeland.

Is there such a thing as being "bicultural"? The following is often held out as an ideal, because flexible, form of adaptation:

> [I]t might be more accurate to speak of the children of immigrants as being bicultural rather than between two cultures . . . adopting by choice, within identifiable constraints, the most appropriate norm or practice, depending on the circumstances they face (R. Miles, 1978, quoted by Wade & Souter, 1992, 14)

Many in the second generation, we are told, experience no particular tension but move quite easily between their "plural life-worlds."

> Biculturalism results from the interaction of two healthy cultural systems within a single individual or group, with neither system dominating the other. It also represents a nonextreme and unfinished solution, one that must be worked out, bit by bit, over time (Fishman, 1967, 179).

It seems likely, however, that true biculturalism is a rare and difficult accomplishment. We may question how frequently and to what extent members of the second generation actually achieve such a balancing act. After all,

> the persistence of ethnic identity and affiliation may be satisfying, but in continuing this affiliation members may lack the social knowledge required for mobility into positions controlled by the dominant group. . . . The time and effort required to learn and maintain ethnic languages and customs could inhibit the acquisition of skills and

knowledge which, while in absolute terms are no better than ethnically valued ones, are nevertheless more useful in securing jobs, promotion, influence and the like (Birrell, 1978, quoted by Bullivant, 1981, 238).

Even the most positive aspect of ethnic identification, the psychological and sometimes practical support that comes from membership in a distinctive sociocultural group, has its drawbacks for individuals who are concerned above all to become successful in the new society. After all, "ethnic-network assistance comes at the cost of ethnic pressures for conformity . . . " (Portes and Rumbaut, 1990, 88), and this source of comfort may hinder the adaptations necessary to have full access to opportunities. It is not uncommon for the more ambitious members of an immigrant group to make a clean break from ethnic institutions and social networks, even from family members who continue to behave in "ethnic" ways.

There are some, however, for whom their heritage language and culture continue to have deep significance, despite their successful acquisition of those of the host society. Faced with the anonymity of mass society, "ethnicity [may] become more salient because it can combine an interest with an affective tie. Ethnicity provides a tangible set of common identifications— in language, food, music, names—when other social roles become more abstract and impersonal" (Bell, 1975, 169). This may lead some members of the third and subsequent generations to an interest in recovering ethnic "roots," significantly mostly on the part of those for whom integration and participation are no longer in question. Elements of the heritage language may continue to have some significance as a luxury, a residual cultural good, valued precisely because such generations do not have to make use of it. Language and other cultural elements may, for those several generations removed from the actual immigrant experience, serve as a token of what Steinberg has called "reconstructed ethnicity . . . pieced together out of fragments of the abandoned culture that do not conflict with middle-class American cultural patterns" (Steinberg, 1982, 60–61).

The "ethnic revival" of the 1960s in the United States may have been in large part a reaction among Americans of European ancestry to the enhanced sense of group pride and solidarity on the part of Americans of African and Hispanic descent; it has turned out to be for most a relatively superficial aspect of group identity with few practical consequences. Most Americans of European ancestry have given up such cultural "markers" as their ancestral language that distinguish them from the majority society and do not participate actively in an ethnic community, but may continue to have a sense of ethnic identity that serves valued functions in their lives. "[T]he cultural *content* of each ethnic group in the United States seems to have become similar to that of others, but the emotional significance of attachment to the ethnic group seems to persist (Glazer & Moynihan, 1975, 8).

Sociologist Herbert Gans has pointed out that "symbolic Judaism," for example, is a highly tenuous culture, pieced together out of fragments of the abandoned culture that do not conflict with middle-class American cultural patterns (cited by Steinberg, 1982, 61). Gans perceives the trend towards assimilation as still powerful and dominant; only those aspects of ethnicity which can be transformed into symbols and which can be easily practiced will persist (Lambert & Taylor, 1988, 27).

One source of confusion in discussing immigrant minorities is the difficulty of judging whether their observable behaviors are a step in the integration process or a manifestation of resistance to integration (Lapeyronnie, 1993, 22). A correct answer would probably be that the same act can be a little of both. Organizing an ethnically-based retirement facility or supermarket is a way for immigrants to participate in the institutional life of the host society while to some extent doing so on their own terms. On the other hand, taking part in an ethnically-based criminal gang may also be an adversarial way of participating in the opportunity structure of the host society.

This is not to say that the process of integration, though taking different routes, is an inevitable one. The ethnic group community may be a way station on the road to assimilation, but it may also remain frozen on the margins of the host society until it becomes a permanently subordinated caste.

> The generally accepted assimilationist model posits that it takes approximately three generations for immigrants to become "Americans." . . . This approach assumes that neither long-term obstacles to incorporation nor recurring socializing experiences that result in alienation, i.e., anti-incorporative attitudes, exist. . . . An alternative model—the "emergent ethnicity model"—suggests that ethnic identities emerge in response to shared experiences such as group-based discrimination (De la Garza et al., 1994, 231).

A study of Turkish adolescents in twenty-two German cities in 1980 found that only 6 percent wanted to become German citizens; they had been confirmed in a marginal status by their reception in Germany. Those who lived in predominantly Turkish neighborhoods were less motivated to return to Turkey than those in neighborhoods with primarily German population, "probably because these young Turks . . . are to a greater degree confronted with the German population's prejudices and discrimination" (Mehrlander, 1986, 21–22).

Contrary to what might be expected, cultural distance between the host society and an immigrant group does not necessarily result in problems of adaptation for the latter. West Indians have experienced more difficulty and less success in the United Kingdom than have Asian Indians, even though they have far more in common culturally with the British. It appears that their cultural similarity to the majority population makes it all the more difficult to deal with the rejection that they experience; the only alternative cultural expression available to West Indian youth is Rastafarianism, which marginalizes without empowering them. Sikhs in the United Kingdom, by contrast, have a long tradition of belonging to a cultural minority. Their reaction to the racial hostility of the sixties was to take psychological refuge in growing their beards and resuming the wearing of turbans, expressions of a disciplined way of life consistent with work, family stability, and relative success in British society (Todd, 1994, 125).

Such cases appear to be the exception, however; it will not do to exaggerate the extent of alienation among immigrants and their children. "The striking thing is that generally 'young muslims' do not find the fact of existing 'between two cultures' and of being a 'halfway generation' intrinsically problematic" (Kitwood, 1983, quoted by Verkuyten, 1985, 89). Acculturation over the course of a few generations is the usual outcome of immigration; the children or grandchildren of immigrants come to identify with the attitudes and assumptions of the host society, and no longer feel "between two cultures" (Verkuyten, 1985, 89). This process does not preclude maintenance, by various groups within the society, of sentiments, associations, and customs which relate to their distinctive ancestry, but these are likely to become marginal, except perhaps when there are marked physical differences such as skin color which may preserve a degree of separation; and even in such cases the remaining cultural differences may be insignificant.

Of course, the process of adaptation to a new society carries with it a definite—and frequently a poignant—cost.

We imagine that the immigrant will somehow be able to maintain his way of life and culture unchanged and at the same time enter fully into Danish society. That is unrealistic. There is a cultural cost of moving from one country to another, and immigrants must accept a certain cultural and social adaptation. In some spheres the immigrant must give up his cultural characteristics and live according to the norms that prevail in the Danish system. In other spheres the immigrant will be able to maintain his own traditions, and Danes must accept that (Hemmingsen, 1988, 61).

The painful situation of the first generation of immigrants in Western European societies is reflected in an interview with an Italian couple in Brussels, still seeing themselves as Italian, knowing they will never be accepted as Belgian, yet also knowing that their children will not identify strongly with the homeland and that they themselves, if they went "home," would be regarded as foreigners there, as well. "We are foreigners [both] here and there, we don't really have any place" (quoted by Byram, 1990a, 79).

Public policy can do little to alleviate this sense of loss, so well captured by Richard Rodriguez in his description of the silence that fell over the family dinner table as he and his siblings made the transition from Spanish to English. The challenge is rather to foster a culture of participation in place of the culture of opposition that has been created by the discrimination of the majority, the self-interest of some ethnic activists, and the excesses of an ideology of multiculturalism among those who believe they speak for the interests of ethnic minority groups. After all, "the tendency to align oneself with the majority behaviors of the host society . . . is irresistible, when the latter does not demand of immigrants that they incarnate an ideal of difference" (Todd, 1994, 320).

Social segregation and the consequent marginalization of immigrant minority groups may be promoted by host societies in two ways that contrast sharply in underlying intentions but which ironically converge in their results. Rejection of human differences, even to the extent of physical violence, is the classic reason for the formation of ghettoes and the development of an intense group life that resists assimilation to the surrounding social environment. Enthusiastic and well-meaning acceptance of human differences by the majority, if it goes to the extent of encouraging and even rewarding members of the minority group to remain different, may have much the same result. Policies that define ethnic minority groups as "problems"—confusing ethnic identity with social class—may, by the same token, reinforce the separation of those groups from the rest of the society and make it all the more difficult for their members to negotiate their own way into the mainstream (Beaud & Noiriel, 1992, 281).

The social location of the two reactions to minority groups is typically very different, with the first found among the indigenous working class and the second among the "new class" of educators, social workers, therapists, and journalists. This helps to explain the very different tone in which they are typically expressed, but xenophobia and ideological multiculturalism have in common that they deny the possibility or desirability of immigrants becoming "like us."

There are those who charge that the form of multiculturalism that insists upon the uniqueness and incommensurability of the experiences, "perspectives," and values of different racial and cultural groups is itself a form of "soft racism," with ultimate results not unlike those of outright rejection, and thus that "multiculturalism remains fundamentally incompatible with the liberal state" (Piccone, 1993/1994, 15). Racist ideology, according to Taguieff, has replaced the thesis of biological inequality with an absolutization of cultural differences, thus throwing those who oppose racism into a profound intellectual confusion. By an ominous transposition, any appeal to universal values is now condemned as "Eurocentric" and thus by definition racist (Taguieff, 1992b, 15, 35).

There has been a loss of nerve among elites, in recent decades, about the possibility that immigrants or their children can—or should—become fully assimilated members of the host society. This has been more the result of currents of intellectual fashion than of any actual loss, on the part of Western countries, of their capacity to absorb and transform new populations. The *process* of assimilation has been continuing, by and large, even as the concept has been challenged.

This loss of nerve has even affected the French, with their strong commitment to universalism; among the "natural and imprescribable" human rights of which since 1789 they have thought of themselves as the special guardians has recently appeared that of being "different." *Le droit à la différence* was proclaimed initially by antiracist groups closely allied with the Socialists, but it has proven a useful slogan for anti-immigrant conservatives as well. Former President Valéry Giscard d'Estaing wrote in 1991 that the question of integration should not arise in relation to legally resident foreigners, who "must be allowed to preserve their culture and their own values" (quoted by Todd, 1994, 375).

> The "right to be different" has retarded the recognition, by immigrant parents and their children, of the anthropological and social rules of the host society. It has softened the first shock experienced by the parents. But it has aggravated a delayed shock: that which can crush the old age of the retired North African worker if he must, in the evening of life, become aware simultaneously of the abandon by his children of his own culture and their inadaptation to French culture, if he must see them wander without landmarks in a sort of

anthropological no man's land. The ideology of the right to be different has not made possible the preservation of any immigrant culture, but it has contributed substantially to the psychological and social disorientation of the second generation deriving from the North African immigration. In slowing down adherence to the values of French society by adolescents who are cut off from the values of their backgrounds, it has been a factor [in creating] *anomie* (Todd, 1994, 382).

It was for this reason that the majority of a UNESCO commission studying racism and prejudice rejected the proposal of some of its members, that the "right to be different" be included among its recommendations, fearing that this would be used as a justification for *apartheid* (Hofmann et al., 1993, 47).

To express concern about the excesses of pluralism is not to insist upon an absolute uniformity, but to recognize the importance of a

hard core of social practices which demand to be respected . . . the daily consensus which crosses the lines of social class to shape the attitudes that affect, if not the great institutions, at least the daily life of the common people . . . [such as] the discipline of work and the apprenticeship of a regulated use of work time, certain conventions of public sociability such as the use of the local language, standards of moderation and self-control in use of the voice and body, relations between the sexes and with authority, etc." (Bastenier & Dassetto, 1993, 291).

Beyond this "*noyau dur*" of social practices, complex modern societies leave ample room for living lives that are culturally quite diverse (Goetze, 1987, 71). Wise social policy does nothing to discourage the private expression of cultural distinctiveness, within limits of public safety and the protection of children, but it avoids extending its patronage to any of its forms.

The constitutional protection of the free exercise of religion—in some respects, the essence of culture—in the United States is wisely paired with a prohibition against government sponsorship of any particular form of religion. This "disestablishment" has been as healthy for religion as it has been for public policy. As government takes on more and more of the functions that once were the domain of the civil society, however, there has latterly been an unhealthy tendency to discriminate against religious expression by comparison with other forms of expression; free speech is protected, in some cases, so long as it is not religious in character, in obvious conflict with the intention of the Constitution's First Amendment. The parallel with the *affaire des foulards* in France is obvious.

When we talk of the "private" exercise of the right to cultural distinctiveness (including religious expression) we do not—or should not—mean that it must be somehow covert, out of the public sphere of life (Neuhaus, 1984). We are, rather, using the word in the sense in which we speak of "private enterprise," that is, activities that are neither controlled nor supported by government. Cultural distinctiveness based upon ethnic identity has every right to be expressed in the public sphere, including in schools, provided that it is not disruptive of order, but it has no legitimate claim to the sponsorship of public authorities through the curriculum or organization of the school.

To what extent do immigrant groups actively seek to maintain their languages? The question is hotly debated; evidence is mixed on how important immigrants *themselves* believe it is to their identity and psychological well-being, their valued relationships and hope of posterity, to maintain their original language and culture and to see them perpetuated in their children and grandchildren. Surveys often find that immigrant parents place considerable importance on their children continuing to speak the languages of their homelands, but do little to ensure such a result; many, like the parents of Richard Rodriguez, are primarily concerned to ensure, cost what it may, that their children not experience the difficulties that attended their own adjustment to life in the host society (Rodriguez, 1983).

THE PROSPECTS FOR IMMIGRANT LANGUAGES

It was very important to "preserve the Spanish language for their children," agreed 85 percent of Hispanic respondents in a California survey in 1983, and a 1987 national study found that 75 percent of Mexican American parents "said it was important that their children speak Spanish well" (Skerry, 1993, 286). On the other hand, the actual practices of these parents, as we will see, do not promote that result, nor do the children of immigrants in most cases make extensive use of the language of their parents. "The simple rule seems to be that people will not indefinitely maintain two languages where one will serve all their needs" (Edwards, 1988, 203).

Subsequent generations may feel a fair amount of guilt associated with the failure to become proficient in a language that they perceive emotionally as an important aspect of identity, even as they largely neglect its use. Portuguese youth in France, while reporting that they no longer used their home language much, expressed regret that they did not know it better (Munoz, 1987). All but two of the elementary children from Senegal interviewed in another French study reported that they spoke only French—never Wolof—with their parents; the two had been in the country for less than two years. One of the others reported that he could understand some Wolof from hearing his parents speak it with friends, but had virtually no ability to speak it (Platiel, 1989, 43). Another French study of Lao children found that Laotian was used only to talk with older family members, and that the children had difficulty mastering the complexities of polite address, thus "disorganizing the perception of relations between the generations." Most did not know the Laotian alphabet (Choron-Baix, 1989, 83).

In a study of Australian secondary school pupils, those whose parents spoke a language other than English reported their parents as mildly supportive of bilingual instruction in schools (Lewis, Rado, & Foster, 1982). Immigrants from Germany were more likely than those from Macedonia (68 percent to 41 percent) to use English at home (Kalantzis, Cope, & Slade, 1989, 169). Attitudes and practices vary among groups: 3 percent of Greek and 6 percent of Italian, contrasted with 44 percent of Dutch, first-generation Australians reported that they no longer used their original language at all (Smolicz, 1983, 333).

In the Netherlands, interviews with the children of Spanish immigrants found that all reported using mostly Dutch among themselves. A study of Turkish immigrant children found that, "in 12 out of 20 families, the children spoke mainly Dutch to each other, according to the parents; in four families alternately Dutch and Turkish, and in four other families primarily or only Turkish." Yugoslav children, according to another Dutch study, "lack motivation to use their mother tongue in communicating with Yugoslavian peers" (Appel, 1988, 68–69). An unusually careful study of the language proficiency of young Moroccans found that Dutch was their dominant language, and they had a good grasp of its grammatical structure though not always a sufficient vocabulary to say what they intended to say; their ability to communicate in their "home" language (Berber or Moroccan Arabic) was "limited or poorly developed." It was inaccurate, the author suggested, to describe Dutch as their "second language;" it was rather their "language 1/2" that produced "a stagnation in the use and acquisition of their first language" (Ruiter, 1990, 16).

Most available data report the extent to which the children of immigrants have acquired proficiency in the language of the school and the host society, though of course this does not tell us whether they are fluent bilinguals or have become essentially monolingual in the majority language. German education officials estimated, in 1989, that about half of the children of immigrants could no longer be distinguished from German children with respect to language use; another 30 to 40 percent could use German reasonably well, though with some limitations ("Mit der Nadel . . . ," 1989, 74). Much the same pattern exists in Sweden, where in 1982, 41 percent of the foreign pupils in grades 1–9 had "the same command of Swedish as an average Swedish pupil" while 8 percent had a very low proficiency in Swedish. This second category, pupils with a low level of proficiency in Swedish, rose as high as 25 percent among Turkish-speaking, 39 percent among Chinese-speaking, and 23 percent among speakers of Assyrian and related languages, while these groups included only 16 percent, 7 percent, and 7 percent, respectively, of fully-proficient users of Swedish (*Immigrants and Immigrant Teaching* . . . , 1983, 38).

Such evidence as exists does not support the long-term prospects of fluent bilingualism, except under special circumstances. Postwar Polish immigrants in the United States for ten years or more and their children were found to have "native-like skills in English, but have not kept up Polish" (Lambert & Taylor, 1988, 169).

> Asian immigrants appear consistently more inclined to shed their native tongue than [do] those from Latin America . . . [but] Spanish monolingualism does not outlast the first generation. The shift toward English is massive, with up to 96 percent of U.S.-born adults adopting it as their main or only language. . . . A minority of about 20 percent of U.S.-born Mexicans, Puerto Ricans, and Cubans continues to report use of Spanish as their preferred, though not exclusive language" (Portes & Rumbaut, 1990, 204).

Similarly, "Cypriot children born in the UK tended to be bilingual but often had little Greek. By 1968 Hylson-Smith claimed that many of the Greek Cypriots attending youth clubs . . . spoke almost no Greek. From a socio-anthropological study in the mid-1970s Constantinides (1977) also claimed that the second generation, in spite of parents' efforts, often spoke very little Greek" (Taylor, 1988, 55). "Visiting Ukrainian community centres and clubs, Khan (1976) noted that few adolescents of Ukrainian origin spoke really fluent Ukrainian and that dance classes, for example, were conducted in a mixture of English and Ukrainian, with English predominating" (Taylor, 1988, 319). Many second-generation youth do not even take advantage of chances provided in school to maintain their home language; less than 5 percent of the Turkish secondary students in Berlin, according to Fase, were taking Turkish rather than English as a foreign language (Fase, 1986b, 113).

The most common pattern is for an "inter-language" to develop based upon the specific circumstances of the family, evolving toward an exclusive use of the language of the host society as more and more of the experiences of family members have taken place within that society. "Bilingualism is often a transitional state" (Ruiz, 1995, 77). This evolution can be illustrated from the responses of South Asian youth in Bradford, in England: 6 percent reported speaking English with their grandparents, 11 percent with their mothers, 16 percent with their fathers, 54 percent with their sisters, 60 percent with their brothers, and 84 percent with their friends at school recess (Reid, 1988, 185).

In Australia, "some new immigrants move between domestic interchange in their first language and the use of the host country's dominant language to explain new institutions, technologies and social relations, rather than take on the forms of their language of origin which express and manipulate life in advanced industrial quarters in their place of origin" (Kalantzis, Cope, & Slade, 1989, 26). This is reminiscent of the use of English in connection with manufacturing processes in Irish-speaking parts of Ireland (see Chapter 3).

The best data on retention or loss of the languages of immigrants is from the United States, where several large-scale studies have been carried out in recent years. Research on ethnicity within American society has stressed repeatedly the almost complete loss, by second-generation Americans, of the languages spoken by their immigrant ancestors. Interviews by Waters with sixty American Catholics from various white ethnic groups found that only four claimed to speak their ancestral languages; one had studied it in school, while three had used it with their parents but had become "rusty" since the parents' death and had not taught the language to their own children (Waters, 1990, 116).

> [T]he American experience is remarkable for its near mass extinction of non-English languages: In no other country . . . did the rate of mother tongue shift toward (English) monolingualism approach the rapidity of that found in the United States. Within the United States, some relatively isolated groups (such as the Old Spanish, the Navaho and [some] other American Indians, and the Louisiana French) have changed at a much slower rate; but language minority immigrants shifted to English at a rate far in excess of that obtained in all other countries. . . . Bilingualism, American style, has been unstable and transitional—at least until recently (Portes & Rumbaut, 1990, 183).

Two academic supporters of bilingual education concede that "the United States is, at the societal level, staunchly monolingual. Legislating monolingualism as a requirement for citizenship could hardly have been more successful in creating a monolingual society than have been the unofficial economic and social forces at work." Among immigrant minority groups, "only the old folks, the very young, and the recent arrivals, in general, speak these other languages; the school children and young adults have often switched to 'dominance' in English" (Snow & Hakuta, 1992, 385). Of the 270,000 Chinese Americans born in the United States, most speak English as their primary language; in 1970, less than 30,000 of those whose parents were also native-born spoke Chinese, indicating a massive shift to English (Wong, 1988, 210, 212). Filipino immigrants, already familiar with English in their homeland, make a rapid shift to exclusive use of the language on the mainland, though they may retain some use of Ilocano or Tagalog if they settle in Hawaii (Galang, 1988). This pattern of language shift among Asian immigrants in the United States is presumably related to the fact that their languages are less likely than is Spanish to have currency outside the home. On the other hand, Mexican-American youth are more likely than are Asian youth to use English with their families (Baratz-Snowden et al., 1988a, 38, 87). In other words, bilingual Asian youth appear to segregate the use of their two languages more sharply than do Mexican-American youth.

The possible exception to the pattern of language shift is that of Spanish in the United States which, like Finnish in Sweden, is a "next door" language constantly reinforced by family and business connections with the homeland and by labor migration. Spanish is unique among immigrant languages in the United States in that "it is continually invigorated by these linguistically high-contact situations. Consequently, Spanish persists in the Hispanic population longer than other languages have remained with immigrant groups" (Arias, 1986, 42).

Some critics of immigration or of bilingual education have expressed concern that the number of Spanish-speakers may become so great that language shift—and thus assimilation—will become stalled with grave social and political consequences. They cite the example of Miami, where, as then-Mayor Ferré boasted in 1983, "You can be born here in a Cuban hospital, be baptized by a Cuban priest, buy all your food from a Cuban grocer, take your insurance from a Cuban bank. You can get all the news in Spanish. . . . You can go through life without having to speak English at all" (quoted by Crawford, 1992b, 91).

Often cited against this "another Quebec" hypothesis is the study by Calvin Veltman, who concluded that "approximately 70 percent of the youngest immigrants and 40 percent of those aged 10–14 at time of arrival will make English their usual, personal language. As a result, they will give birth to children of English, not Spanish, mother tongue" (Veltman, 1988, 45). Even in Miami, a 1985 survey of Cuban-American students at Miami-Dade Community College found that 86 percent preferred to use English with their friends (Crawford, 1992b, 119). A study in Miami schools found that "only 17 percent of students who have Spanish as their native language elect to take [the course in] Spanish for Spanish-speakers" (Benderson, 1986, 10). Under the influence of electronic media and of a more open job market for Hispanics,

> the rate of language shift to English has been accelerating over the past half-century. Less than 30 percent of the oldest age group made English their usual personal language when they were young, and only 60 percent spoke it on a regular basis. Nearly all native-born teenagers now speak English on a regular basis, and five in eight already have made a language transfer to the English language group" (Veltman, 1988, 49).

On the other hand, Veltman suggested, something like the fluent bilingualism that is generally a transitional phenomenon for immigrant populations could develop in parts of the United States. "There is no reason to believe that the rates of English monolingualism will increase over time. . . . In fact, it is possible that English monolingualism is undergoing some slight decline" as the use of Spanish receives a measure of support in school and society (Veltman, 1988, 49). This is a regional phenomenon in areas where a large number of recent immigrants continue to make Spanish a valuable asset, even for those who have come to use English as their primary language. As a result of the economic opportunities offered by such Spanish-medium markets, "many second- and third-generation Hispanics who haven't learned any Spanish at home, whose parents and siblings may have stopped speaking it themselves, learn it from life in the immigrant-impacted neighborhoods" (Fishman, 1992, 168). In parts of Los Angeles and Miami, "monolingual monopoly seems unlikely to return. Bilingualism is becoming institutionalized, a new way of living and doing business" (Crawford, 1992b, 119).

What Veltman calls the "rate of anglicization may be undergoing a slow, long-term decline in California, presumably because the large influx of immigrants makes it easier for people to retain Spanish as their principal language of use" (Veltman, 1988, 56). This continuing use of Spanish in California, however, has not slowed the rate of shift to English as the primary language for individuals of Hispanic descent; while "in most areas of the United States approximately 70 percent of the native born currently are adopting English as their usual language," the rate is 85 percent in California (Veltman, 1988, 66). In brief, the continuing role of Spanish in American life seems likely to be as a second language for occasional use by those native-born Hispanics for whom it serves as a useful bridge to recent immigrants.

A study of Mexican-origin Americans based on data drawn from the Latino National Political Survey (1989–1990) found that this pattern prevails in the homes of those born in the United States, and increases with subsequent generations (see Table 5.1)

TABLE 5.1. Home Language of Mexicans in the United States, 1989–1990

Language Reportedly Spoken at Home (%)

	Only English	Mostly English	Mostly Spanish	Only Spanish
Foreign-born	2.9	6.1	26.2	52.3
Two foreign-born parents	12.3	28.9	17.1	7.0
One foreign-born parent	21.9	41.1	13.4	1.8
Two native-born parents	42.2	29.8	1.2	1.6
At least one native-born grandparent	36.3	34.0	5.6	1.5

Source: Garza et al., 1994, 237; respondents who reported "both" were left out.

It is notable that this study indicates a slight up-tick in reported use of Spanish in the third generation, as would be predicted by those studies suggesting that in many immigrant groups some members of the third generation take an interest in the cultural heritage that their parents neglected in their urgency to make a success of their participation in the host society. The third generation, to paraphrase Marcus Lee Hansen (1938), wishes to remember what the second generation wishes to forget!

Aside from a nostalgic interest in linguistic as well as genealogical roots—seldom extending to the hard work of actually mastering the ancestral language—the overall trend is clear: an ever-increasing reliance upon the language of the host society as the primary means of communication even within the home, that last refuge of potential cultural distinctiveness. Even among Puerto Ricans in the continental United States, with their frequent returns to the island, "communication in English is the norm for school age sisters and brothers" (Zentella, 1988, 151); Cuban Americans "use English widely among themselves and even in their Spanish-speaking homes" (García & Otheguy, 1988, 186). Analysis of data from the national *High School and Beyond* study on Mexican-American pupils who had been in bilingual programs documented a shift to primary use of English by the second year of high school (Olson, 1990).

After reviewing some of the forces that tend toward the abandonment of immigrant languages, however, we will consider those that make such languages a continuing policy challenge and an important reality for at least some immigrants and their descendants.

Factors in the Abandonment of Immigrant Languages

The continuing significance of ethnicity into the third generation, and beyond for some (Chapter 4), does not ordinarily translate into maintenance of the language associated with ethnic identity. The competition with the language of the host society is extremely uneven. "The two languages often represent different social networks and associated value systems, and the choice of language can come to symbolize an individual's identification with either system" (Hakuta 1986, 233); since ethnic communities are usually a transitional phenomenon, it is not surprising that, over time, most of the second and third generations identify with the host society rather than with the subgroup, and thus come to use the language of the majority.

Despite occasional charges that immigrants are compelled to abandon their ancestral languages, there is ample evidence that most are eager to become sufficiently proficient in that of the host society that they can function in it fully; "most groups are assimilationist in their attitudes," Edwards observes, adding that "pragmatism and the desire to make the painful act of immigration worthwhile have led inexorably to language shift" (J. Edwards, 1984, 292–293).

Consistent use in the home is of course the most important means of sustaining a language that is not used commonly in the wider society. Families can do much to maintain a minority language through making a point of using it without exception to communicate with their children. Evidence suggests that relatively few parents make this effort, unless they are themselves highly sensitive to language issues, even though they may articulate the intention of doing so. In one study, 99 percent of Korean American parents said that they wanted their children to speak only Korean at home, but more than half of the Los Angeles sample also responded that they wanted their children to use only English at home (Kim, 1988, 268)! As this suggests, ambivalence is common and consistent practice more the exception than the rule, even in a situation as charged with feeling about language as that in Canada. In a survey of French-speakers in Ontario, "less than 50 per cent responded that they mostly, or always, used French with their children. In spite of attending Francophone schools, some students of this background were not able to master standard French by grade 12" (Kalantzis, Cope, & Slade, 1989, 38). That this shift occurred "in spite of parallel [i.e. French-using] institutions of church, school, recreation, etc." (Paulston, 1992b, 58) illustrates how powerfully the general societal ambience influences language shift.

Research by Cummins and others in western Canada found that "francophone students who speak French at home and whose school program is 80 percent French (kindergarten through the sixth grade) still preferred to use English with friends outside the classroom . . . and rated themselves as being somewhat more comfortable in English than in French (Lapkin & Cummins, 1984, 74). Anxiety about the gradual loss of French in Canada despite the language-maintenance efforts of school programs, because of the omnipresence of media and other influences encouraging use of English, is thus not unjustified, especially outside of Quebec.

Groups like the Finnish minority community in Sweden and the French-Canadians of Ontario may develop ethnic ambivalence, experienced by those who

> often feel hostile towards the majority culture because they know that members of the majority group regard them and their culture as inferior. For their children, this translates into an ambiguous message about the importance of the majority language and culture. Along with this, families in these groups tend not to encourage their children to maintain the home language nor to identify with the minority community's culture (Teunissen, 1992, 102).

A 1973 study in Los Angeles found that, among third-generation Mexican-American women, 4 percent spoke only Spanish at home, and 84 percent only English. The transition to English among men was even more rapid (Portes & Rumbaut, 1990, 205). According to another study of language use in the Los Angeles area, the persistence of use of Spanish was largely a function of continuing replenishment of the Spanish-speaking population through legal and illegal immigration. Lopez concluded that "were it not for new arrivals from Mexico, Spanish would disappear from Los Angeles nearly as rapidly as most European immigrant languages vanished from cities in the East" (quoted by Connor, 1985a, 21).

A 1979 national study of "cohorts of U.S.-born South-Central-East European ethnics" found a "plummeting level of childhood exposure to ethnic mother tongues. About three-quarters of the two older cohorts had such exposure in their childhood homes, compared to just 10 percent among persons born after 1960." A more recent study in the Albany, New York area found that, of white ethnics born in the United States, nearly half had no knowledge at all of their ancestral language, "even in the restricted sense of occasional words and phrases in conversation" (Alba, 1990, 11). Alba found that

> about 17 percent of native-born whites reported that a non-English language was spoken in their childhood home. . . . But only 11 percent claim to speak a mother tongue now. Of those exposed to a mother tongue during childhood, just half can currently speak the language (Alba, 1990, 93–95).

Of the total group interviewed in the Albany study, "only 5 percent said that they use a mother tongue in their daily lives." Half of this use was with their parents, and only one-quarter of the small group who use the ancestral language at all reported that they used it with their own children (Alba, 1990, 98). The data on home use of Spanish (Table 5.1) point in the same direction. *Children are unlikely to become fluent speakers of a language which their parents use rarely in the home.*

This is not to say that such families do not retain and transmit *other* elements of their heritage to their children, only that a minority language is unlikely to be maintained through school or supplemental programs unless it is sustained in the home and the community. After all, "the serious maintenance of traditional culture does not need bilingual programmes in schools but the material/structural basis for its reproduction" (Kalantzis, Cope, & Slade, 1989, 55), and it is difficult to sustain the relevance of a minority language. Joshua Fishman observes that "the combination of relative linguistic inflexibility and relative ethnocultural flexibility finally results in the triumph of overall ethnocultural continuity experiences over ethnolinguistic discontinuity experiences" (Fishman, 1985, 340). In plainer terms, people maintain valued elements of culture from generation to generation even as they give up the use of a language that separates them more sharply than (essentially private) cultural traditions do from the mainstream of the host society. Nor is language change incompatible with an emphasis upon ethnic distinctiveness, as in the United Kingdom where

> restauranteurs, waiters, hairdressers, etc., clearly have to learn English in order to function and communicate effectively, yet economically the Italian position is maintained by emphasizing and trading on their ethnicity. Ethnicity is encouraged at the same time as linguistic acculturation (Taylor, 1988, 233).

It is interesting to compare the generalized survey response to the idea of language maintenance with the actual language practices of American ethnic groups. Fishman notes that the maintenance of ethnic language and culture "are both far greater at an attitudinal level than at an overt behavioral one" (Fishman, 1985, 340). Members of ethnic groups, in other words, claim to be more "ethnic" than their actions demonstrate. Lambert and Taylor's Polish-American respondents were supportive (5.77 on the 1 to 7 scale) of using Polish "for most or all speaking within the family," but in fact few did so. Puerto Ricans were the most emphatic of the ethnic groups studied "in their endorsement of various steps that should be taken to maintain heritage *cultures* in America. They feel that their styles of foods, dress, songs and dances, as well as their own cultural values should be maintained." Curiously, though, they did not show support for the idea that such cultural elements could be maintained by community efforts; instead, they wanted the schools to do it. Puerto Rican history, they agreed, should be given equal emphasis with that of the United States (Lambert & Taylor, 1990, 91). The paradox is that it is Puerto Ricans, of all recently arrived language minority groups, whose culture has been most deeply influenced by that of the United States, in both its white majority and black minority forms.

Puerto Ricans on the mainland also had a contradictory response to the question of language maintenance. While on the one hand they responded that Spanish should be used in the home, and that it was the responsibility of the public school and not of the Puerto Rican community to ensure that children could speak Spanish, their responses on a question about what it would mean for their children to be bilingual or to speak only English indicated that the two options seemed equally preferable to the parents (Lambert & Taylor, 1990, 91–92).

The primary reason for the loss of an immigrant minority language is that, over time, it loses any function as all of the members of a family come to speak the language of the host society and, particularly, as the younger generation comes to prefer to use the majority language because of its association with attractive features of the life around them. Catherine Snow and Kenji Hakuta suggest that this process is not particularly mysterious: "Why do the children in such a family gravitate to English monolingualism? English, because it is the language of prestige and the majority culture; monolingualism, because for the child, as much as for the adult, maintaining two languages is harder than learning, maintaining, and using just one" (Snow & Hakuta, 1992, 388). A Moroccan family in the Netherlands will use three languages: (1) their Berber or Moroccan Arabic dialect for conversation between the parents and with their friends, to do errands in ethnic stores, and in ethnic community associations if they take part in any; (2) Dutch between the children and in school, at work, and for business with government agencies and in Dutch stores; and (3) Standard Arabic in the mosque and Koran school (Muysken & Vries, 1982, 108; Ruiter, 1990). There is no particular reason, given this distribution of language use, that the children would choose to use the dialect of their parents for other than simple household matters nor would they, in time, use it with their own children.

Inevitably, the majority language will come to be associated with the glamour of modernity and the wide world outside the home, and the home language—though possessing lingering intimations of family warmth—will be associated with the disappointments and humiliations experienced by immigrant parents. A Catalan specialist on language recalls that, when he was a child,

> all movies were shown in Spanish (never in Catalan), and this created a social model so powerful that it was "impossible" to use any language but Spanish. We knew of course, even at that age, that "¡manos arriba!" ("stick 'em up!") could be rendered in Catalan as "mans enlaire!" But this knowledge was of no use. The Catalan expression had no "punch" in the situation created by the game. . . . my friends and I were able, from a very early age, to "play" Cowboys and Indians in Spanish without knowing any Spanish. In other words, thanks to movies about the Wild West, we were able to use a language that we did not yet know (Artigal, 1991a, 23).

Cypriot children in England "refuse to speak their mother tongue except when essential, demonstrating not only the dominance of their fluency in English, but also the value which they accord to English and by implication the values inherent in the language itself" (Taylor, 1988, 163).

Opportunities to maintain the language of the homeland may be limited, especially for the low-status immigrant with few opportunities to visit or to obtain books and periodicals from the homeland. Television and radio are likely to provide few opportunities to hear the language used in relation to a broad range of issues, and so it may come to function only in relation to domestic and religious matters and not to the other concerns of life in the new situation. Under such circumstances, "the role models of their home languages can change as parents incorporate words, structures and meanings from the mainstream language into their own" (Kalantzis, Cope, & Slade, 1989, 31).

For those who are higher status and for whom the high culture of their homeland is important, language use may be maintained through deliberate efforts though seldom at a nativelike level (Ekstrand, 1979, 48), but such individuals also have more opportunity to participate actively in the host society if they adopt its language as their own. German ethnic leadership in the United States complained, in the 1930s, that the political refugees arriving from Germany "were interested in a rapid acculturation and hence tended to regard the use of the German language as a necessary evil during the transition period" (Luebke, 1978, 82). Though some 9 million residents of the United States had spoken German two decades earlier, the language was rapidly being lost as a result of lack of renewal through immigration; by the 1960s, there were at most 50 thousand persons under 18 who used the language natively (Molesky, 1988, 42–43).

In general, the religious institutions and practices of ethnic communities have more staying power than their languages (see Chapter 4). Jewish immigrants to the United States, for example, quickly abandoned use of Yiddish without thereby assimilating fully into the host society;

> secular Yiddish schools, theaters, and newspapers have all but disappeared, while, by contrast, religiously and ethnically distinct Jewish institutions, from synagogues and yeshivas to summer camps and English-language publications, continue to thrive. It turns out that of the various components of a cultural legacy, language may well be the least durable (Friedberg, 1988, 63).

An important factor in the abandonment of immigrant languages is the growing importance of educational qualifications for desirable employment in postindustrial economies. Well-paid assembly line jobs of the sort that immigrants have typically aspired to are less and less available. In Australia, it was reported in 1994, "migrants with an English-speaking background have lower unemployment rates than other migrants (9.9 and 14.2 per cent respectively)" (Organisation for Economic Cooperation and Development, 1994, 65). The same process is at work in the United States, where "during the 1980s, the penalty for speaking English poorly or not at all increased for all immigrants" (Sorensen & Enchautegui, 1994, 155).

Continuing to use an immigrant language may also indicate rejection of the host society (and implicitly of its advanced economy), while conversely rapid language shift may be a sign of eagerness to do whatever is necessary to get ahead. The 19–year-old son of Moroccan immigrants to the Netherlands who had won a prize for a field study of changes in the village in which his parents had been born told a Dutch magazine that

> from the start I was determined on integration, on doing things with the others; I had lots of Dutch friends, belonged to a football team and so forth. That way I had learned Dutch within 6 months. . . . I did have one year of Arabic [in a school language-maintenance program] on Wednesday afternoons, but that wasn't my own language. At home we speak Berber (*Samenwijs* 13, 2 (October) 1992, 60).

Ambition may be a powerful factor in language shift. "When a distinction is made between those language minority students in Sweden who prefer to use their home language ('active') and those who prefer to use Swedish ('passive home language'), the second group shows higher results on tests in their mandatory English course than does the first group, and also higher results than monolingual Swedish students!" (Balke-Aurell & Lindblad, 1983, 86). The varying rate of acquisition of—and use of—the language of the host society by various groups in turn contributes to different social and economic outcomes, as does their acquisition of English as a third language. The children of Chinese immigrants in the Netherlands, for example, are more interested in learning English than they are in learning Chinese (Vermeulen, 1984, 112), and the same phenomenon has been noted in France, where less than 14 thousand pupils choose to study Arabic, and a similar number Portuguese, in secondary education, contrasted with 4.7 million who choose English (Henry-Lorcerie, 1989, 79).

This is not to suggest that a simple choice exists between maintenance of full proficiency in the ancestral language and acquisition of full proficiency in that of the host society. Children of immigrant parents may have few opportunities to hear their parents use extended forms of the home language, since it does not serve as a vehicle for communication with the world outside the home, or to acquire the language of the host society as native children do, through using it in natural contexts (Salameh, 1988, 45–46); this is sometimes called "semilingualism," the condition of an inadequate proficiency in both languages spoken, with consequent limitation of higher-order intellectual skills. It should be noted that whether such a condition results from confusion between the two languages, or simply from the non-standard language use characteristic of lower class persons in general, including those who are monolingual, is much debated (Ekstrand, 1978, 64, 75, 84; Paulston, 1982, 42), and will be discussed below.

There is reason to doubt that even a segregated school program that uses primarily the home language (see Chapter 6) can in fact develop full nativelike proficiency in a language that is not otherwise reinforced in the surrounding society and its media. A pupil in such a program could end up with a "school knowledge" only of the first language, and insufficient proficiency in the second. While the concept of "semilingualism, with its heavy emphasis on the necessity of developing mother-tongue skills, has often been a major factor in educational and political arguments for mother-tongue classes" (Hyltenstam & Arnberg, 1988, 497), such classes may in fact result in the very condition they are intended to prevent.

Most researchers doubt that the maintenance of proficient bilingualism is achievable, even when the home language enjoys high status and is the primary means of instruction (Lofgren, 1986, 12; Ekstrand, 1978, 18). "For the conservation of minority languages," Johan Leman has written, "it is assumed that the social context outside the school, i.e. language homogeneity or heterogeneity, and social status of the minority language, will be largely determinative over the long run" (Leman, 1991, 132). Simply providing school instruction in the language, or even *through* the language, is unlikely to lead to its long-term maintenance absent social supports for its use.

A widely held view among French specialists on the immigrant experience is that the educational system has no solution to offer to the historically inevitable process of language transition. Recent efforts to revive French regional languages have had little impact, and there is no reason to believe that Arabic or Portuguese will continue to be spoken by the children and grandchildren of the immigrant generation. Like many other second-generation groups, young Portuguese in France prefer to use French in talking with their brothers and sisters, though 34 percent of them use Portuguese with their parents; Portugal is a place where they go for the summers, but only 24 percent would want to live there (Boumaza & Neves, 1994, 22). During the political conflicts that arose out of the *affaire des foulards*, the Muslim associations in Avignon resisted the demand of the most radical group, in the name of "cultural purity," that Arabic be used in lieu of French in their strategy discussions (Lapeyronnie, 1993, 332).

The likelihood is that, absent forced segregation and a brutal marginalization of an immigrant group, its original language will not be maintained effectively into the third generation, and its culture will evolve rapidly in the immigration situation, just as that culture, under the impact of modernization, is undoubtedly evolving in the homeland. Vestiges of language, and somewhat larger vestiges of cultural habit and observances, will be preserved by some but not all of the descendants of the immigrating generation. This is true even when an immigrant language becomes a "minority language" whose preservation has political resonance, unless—as with Catalan, Basque, and perhaps Welsh—the language is associated with and fortified by a territorial redoubt. Fishman concludes that "reliance on Spanish is weakening ideologically, attitudinally, and overtly at only a somewhat slower rate than have mother tongues among other ethnolinguistic minorities in the United States" (Fishman, 1985, 341).

Factors in the Maintenance of Immigrant Languages

Language as a means of communication and of acquiring information may have a simply functional significance, as when we listen to tapes or take a course at Berlitz in preparation for a trip to another country. The "national" language alone would be needed and maintained if this were the only purpose of language use. But language can also have an evocative, an emotional, and even a powerfully symbolic meaning in many situations. This reality is acknowledged in the terms used by different educational systems for the languages which the children of immigrants may speak when they come to school: *Muttersprache* ("mother language") in Germany, *eigen taal* ("own language") in the Netherlands, *hemspråk* ("home speech") in Sweden, or *langue d'origine* ("language of origin") in France.

Fishman points out that

> By its very nature language is the quintessential symbol. . . . All language stands in this very relation to the rest of reality: it refers to, it expresses, it evokes "something" in addition to itself. . . . Language is the recorder of paternity, the expresser of patrimony and the carrier of phenomenology. Any vehicle carrying such precious freight must come to be viewed as equally precious, as part of the freight, indeed, as precious in and of itself. The link between language and ethnicity is thus one of sanctity-by-association. . . . Anything can become symbolic of ethnicity (whether food, dress, shelter, land tenure, artifacts, work, patterns of worship), but since language is the prime symbol system to begin with and since it is commonly relied upon so

heavily (even if not exclusively) to enact, celebrate and "call forth" all ethnic activity, the likelihood that it will be recognized and singled out as symbolic of ethnicity is great indeed. This likelihood is both increased and exploited when ethnicity is manipulated into ethnic consciousness since language is crucial for relaying the good word, the message, the call, and, as such—even without any linguistic features that make it unintelligible to others—it easily becomes "more than" a means of communication, even more than symbolic of the ethnic message; indeed, it becomes a prime ethnic value in and of itself (Fishman, 1989, 32).

As a result of these associations, language has far more than merely communicative significance; it may have a symbolic function which leads parents to wish it to be taught to their children by others precisely *because* they themselves are incapable of developing it adequately in those children themselves. The clearest example of this is the language revival movements in provinces of several nations where an ancestral language has come to serve as a symbol of independence *vis à vis* the larger society and its centralizing and homogenizing tendencies, such as Catalonia and Wales. In such cases, a minority language can become a symbol of the resistance of the periphery to the center, a symbol all the more precious because it has few practical consequences or economic advantages (Chapter 3).

Under circumstances of sufficient residential concentration and business enterprise, an immigrant community can also create a world in which many of its members do not find it necessary to use the majority language for their daily activities. In postwar London it was noted that the use of Greek and Turkish were perpetuated "because of the close knit Cypriot community which makes it unnecessary to use English in daily life since it is now possible to shop in Cypriot stores. . . . even in the mid-1970s Constantinides (1977) noted that second-generation Greek Cypriot adults often spoke to each other in a mixture of colloquial English and Cypriot Greek liberally sprinkled with Hellenized terms invented by first-generation Cypriots to describe aspects of the dressmaking and restaurant trades" (Taylor, 1988, 68). "Little Havana" in Miami is a similar case, where shoppers and professionals have continued to use Spanish as their primary means of communication for several decades. Six years after arrival in 1973, 45 percent of Cubans surveyed still had no knowledge of English and only 9 percent were fluent, but they had made substantial economic progress: one fifth owned businesses and two-fifths owned their own homes. "Living and working in Spanish, many Cubans felt little urgency about learning English—much like the Germans, Norwegians, Greeks,

and other groups before them, who for a time had succeeded in building in-
sular communities" (Crawford, 1992b, 95).

Development, by the immigrant generation itself, of proficiency in the
language of the host society may depend in large part upon whether they
work outside the home, and whether the work performed requires the use
of language and provides constant opportunity for practice; thus a waiter
in an Italian or a Chinese restaurant is likely to become more proficient in
the societal language than is the cook. The concentration of immigrant workers in Germany in the heavy manufacturing and construction industries has
undoubtedly retarded their linguistic integration, and thus indirectly their
eligibility for German citizenship. The failure of many of the first generation to become proficient in the host language may have less to do with unwillingness than it does with the nature of the work opportunities available
to them. Paulston points out that Mexican Indians did not learn Spanish until
jobs became available for which the language was necessary; "without access to rewards, Spanish was not and is not salient" (Paulston, 1992a, 20).
Spokesmen for language-minority groups argue that "populations acquire
new languages if and when they are admitted to new social roles requiring
these languages rather than vice versa" (Fishman, 1989, 441). Of course, it
can be difficult to be "admitted to new social roles" if those roles require
proficiency in a language which one does not speak.

An immigrant minority language can also be maintained to some extent by the deliberate efforts of an ethnic community that values its continued use. In New York City in the 1960s,

> people active in politics and the leaders of the Puerto Rican commu-
> nity expect that Spanish will be the major language in use in the com-
> munity for as long ahead as anyone can see. As against the situation
> in some earlier immigrant groups, where dominant opinion in the city
> and in the group insisted on the need to learn English and relegate
> the immigrant tongue to a minority position, in the Puerto Rican
> group many leaders . . . expect and hope that Spanish will maintain
> a strong position in the group. . . . Spanish already has a much stron-
> ger official position in New York than either Italian or Yiddish ever
> had (Glazer & Moynihan, 1963, 101).

This was attributed by some observers, not only to the back-and-forth movement between Puerto Rico and the mainland, but to a determination to continue the use of Spanish. "[T]he newer immigrants (their leaders, at least) are
pressing for bilingualism clearly not for pragmatic reasons . . . but for reasons

of the values they hold" (Glazer, 1983, 152). Similarly, in the western states, "as middle-income Mexicans reach even higher income levels they begin to look for, create, and support part-time or full-time schools to develop and retain Spanish among their children. . . . The favored income position [in California and New Mexico] was for bilinguals having English as the dominant and Spanish the subordinate language" (Macias, 1985, 302). Consistent with American studies suggesting that a strong interest in ethnic language may be more a characteristic of those who have been successful in "making it" in the host society than of those who are still struggling for a foothold (Alba, 1990, 73), French research found that highly-educated young Portuguese women placed a high value on maintaining the Portuguese language as a token of their identity, though in fact they usually spoke French, even with their Portuguese contemporaries at the university (Villanova, 1986).

> Acculturation signifies the ability to master the dominant cultural codes and is not necessarily synonymous with the dissolution of the heritage culture or with the loss of the specificities of the immigrant *milieu*. . . . To the contrary, success and acculturation, in facilitating mastery of the social environment, permit immigrants to maintain a living connection with their origins (Dubet & Lapeyronnie, 1992, 91–92).

On the other hand, research in Quebec found that francophone university students "who were least fluent in English were those who felt their cultural identity to be most threatened" (Lambert & Taylor, 1990, 19).

Progressive intellectuals are of course not unique in having material and ideal interests in the separate schooling of linguistic minority pupils. For many rank-and-file immigrants, especially those who experience discrimination and low-status employment, the language and culture of their homeland can come to enjoy increased significance as a means of retaining a sense of personal worth, even as the homeland itself recedes in time. The Spanish language is an important marker of identity for many Hispanic immigrants and their children, continuing to be significant even after connection with or even interest in their homeland has been lost. A study in the mid-1960s found that, "when asked to choose from a list of attributes those aspects of the Mexican heritage they would like to preserve in their children, only 5 percent of the respondents in Los Angeles and only 3 percent in San Antonio selected 'identity as Mexican' . . . [but] 51 percent in Los Angeles and 32 percent in San Antonio selected 'Spanish language'" (cited by Connor, 1985, 19).

It seems likely that the relatively strong maintenance of Spanish in the United States has a political as well as the sociological basis of continued new immigration and heavy concentration in certain areas. For Mexican Americans or Puerto Ricans who (encouraged by government and advocacy groups) have come to see themselves as members of an "Hispanic" minority group with claims upon the wider society based upon a history of victimization parallel to that of African Americans, the Spanish language is the primary basis for group identity. After all, culturally and even racially there are significant differences among Americans of Latin American origin; what they have in common is a language, whether they actually speak it or not. But this common language functions as a symbol of group membership only to the extent that it is possible to believe that Puerto Ricans and Mexican Americans and Dominicans have also somehow been victimized in the same way by North American society as a function of their *hispanidad*. As Max Weber pointed out, even

> Community of language . . . taken by itself is not sufficient to constitute a communal relationship. It is only with the emergence of a consciousness of difference from third persons who speak a different language that the fact that two persons speak the same language, and in that respect share a common situation, can lead them to a feeling of community and to modes of social organization consciously based on the sharing of the common language (Weber, 1964, 138–139).

In a typical expression of such a political agenda for language maintenance, a left-of-center Greek Cypriot newspaper in London wrote, in 1959, that "the struggle for the Greek education of our community is one of a national nature, a struggle for the protection of our children against the danger of their anglicization that the conqueror of our suffering island so much desires" (Taylor, 1988, 79). Similarly, the leaders of the Polish workers in the Ruhr (where they made up about a third of the labor force) around the turn of the century urged them to keep themselves apart in order to maintain the solidarity of the group, insisting that—though legally citizens of the German Reich—"no true Pole allows his children to become German" (G. Hansen, 1986, 47).

Of course, as in the case of those Polish children, identification with a minority tradition can be promoted in a way that prevents some who have not made that choice for themselves from participating freely in the broader society. In fact regulations were issued in 1899 by German authorities, making proficiency in German a prerequisite for all senior jobs (Esser & Korte,

1985, 167). Despite the impact upon such opportunities, ethnic leaders may go so far as to advise members of language minority groups not to learn the majority language, lest group bilingualism lead over time to loss of the minority language (Gaarder, cited by Paulston, 1992d, 89), and the heavy-handed attempt to suppress the minority language may lead, as it did among the Poles in the Ruhr, to an increased sense of ethnic solidarity (Koekebakker, 1990, 45).

Lack of successful participation in the host society can, in turn, lead to a social position that does not encourage using the language required by such participation, in a vicious circle of marginalization and self-limitation. Under such circumstances, "the real and perceived barriers to socioeconomic attainment operate to discourage socioeconomic achievement, to reinforce the distinctiveness of the ethnic group, and to reaffirm and revitalize ethnic patterns and customs" (Bean et al., 1994, 77). This is one possible explanation for the lagging achievement in education and income of third-generation Mexican Americans in the United States, but it does not seem to be supported by the data on home language use (Table 5.1). Another possible explanation is that many native-born Mexican Americans have come to think of themselves as what Ogbu calls "involuntary minorities," on the analogy of African Americans, rather than as immigrants. Skerry suggests that "contemporary political institutions encourage many Mexican Americans to 'assimilate' precisely by defining themselves as an oppressed racial minority" (Skerry, 1993, 265). This sets up a very different psychological dynamic than that characteristic of immigrants.

> Involuntary minorities do not, unlike the immigrants, interpret the language and cultural differences they encounter in school and society as barriers they have to overcome. Rather, they interpret these differences as *symbols of identity to be maintained.* . . . The oppositional identity combines with the oppositional cultural frame of reference to make crossing cultural boundaries and engaging in cross-cultural learning more problematic for involuntary minorities than for the immigrants, since utilizing the cultural frame of reference of the dominant group is threatening to the minority identity and security as well as to their solidarity (Ogbu, 1991a, 15–16).

Bastenier, reversing Robert Merton's concept of "anticipatory socialization," describes a "preventative non-socialization" on the part of immigrants placed in an inferior social position and seeking "to preserve their initial socio-cultural capital (their original identity) that they intend eventually to use again" (Bastenier, 1986, 85).

Representations of the claims of Mexican Americans (and Puerto Ricans) in the political arena has been primarily on the basis of "a presumed moral trump: the group's claim as a victimized racial minority," and by professional advocates funded largely by foundation grants. The result may be a certain passivity on the part of members of the group (Skerry, 1993, 376). The logic of a rights-based strategy for social advancement is that neither personal effort nor grass-roots political mobilization is necessary; the claims are advanced instead by lawyers and publicists.

It is entirely consistent with such an attitude that the overwhelming majority of spokesmen for Mexican Americans and Puerto Ricans in the United States are strong supporters of bilingual education as a means of maintaining the use of Spanish, described as a fundamental right, and yet few native-born members of those groups use the language consistently in their homes, which is the only way that any minority language is in fact maintained. To the extent that Spanish continues in active use, it tends to be in dialectical forms such as *caló*, "the jargon of young male Chicanos, which changes rapidly and consists of lexical innovations (some of which reflect English influences) in the preexistent Spanish linguistic mold." It is reported that children who attempt to speak the standard Spanish they are taught in school may be mocked by their peers, thus limiting their motivation to acquire real proficiency (McLaughlin, 1985, 187).

Consistent use of a minority language helps to maintain group boundaries, and therefore can be one of the means by which a group may assert and maintain its distinctiveness in relation to other groups. In extreme cases, it may serve to identify the enemy; the Gileadites at the fords of the Jordan river knew whom to kill by the Ephraimite inability to pronounce *shibboleth* (Judges 12:6).

> National languages are protected by national boundaries. Where minority cultures are strong enough to protect their cultural boundaries (and, of course, interested in doing so), they produce the same defenses for their ethnocultural mother tongues. They separate populations into insiders and outsiders and they define the cultural desiderata— including language—which are required for inside membership. Under such circumstances, even small minorities can attain intergenerational mother tongue continuity (viz. Old Order Amish); lacking them, even large ones cannot (viz. Spanish-Americans, German-Americans, Polish-Americans, Franco-Americans, etc. (Fishman, 1985, 225).

This judgment of history has not prevented some ethnic activists from seeking to draw a boundary around their group and maintain its cohesion by promoting the use of its distinctive language. The imposing challenge that such efforts face is to persuade individuals that participation in the group is more valuable than access to the opportunities offered by the wider society.

Under such circumstances, *individual bilingualism* can come to seem the enemy of group maintenance, since it is correctly perceived as a transitional phase leading over time to primary use of the language of the wider society and, in the following generation, to complete loss of the minority language. "Group bilingualism is frequently accompanied by language shift to the official language when there are ample, material rewards in so doing" (Paulston, 1992b, 58). The same shift can occur even when the culturally-subordinate language is "official," simply because the dominant language may seem more useful or attractive; this is why francophone language activists in Quebec are *not*, as one might expect, supporters of bilingualism, nor do the Dutch-speaking and French-speaking communities of Belgium encourage real bilingualism in the two primary languages of the nation (see Chapter 3).

> If circumstances are such that the majority language could dominate, and ultimately lead to language shift, then it is through the individual bilingualism of members of the minority that this threat will materialize. In circumstances where such a shift could happen, it is likely that it is in the *personal* interests of the individual to be bilingual, and this is where a tension begins to appear between group and individual. The group's need is to maintain a monolingual ethnic identity. . . . From the minority group viewpoint, however, the majority language threatens to take over functions additional to the economic ones and gradually eradicate the minority language (Byram, 1991, 15–16).

The offer of public schools to give the children of immigrants the key to a wider society may seem to some parents and, perhaps even more, to ethnic activists as a poisoned apple. Nor has this function of popular schooling been less than explicit over the two hundred years of its active promotion by governments, as when John Dewey, in *Democracy and Education*, described "the office of the school environment" as the obligation "to see to it that each individual gets an opportunity to escape from the limitations of the social group in which he was born, and to come into living contact with a broader environment" (see Glenn, 1988b, for an historical account of this mission of popular schooling and resistance to it in France, the Netherlands, and the United States).

It would not be accurate to portray this as a conflict between group interests and individual interests, of course, since it is usually in the interest of individuals to belong to groups that function well, and it is certainly in the interest of groups that the individuals who belong to them prosper. There is, however, an unavoidable tension of interests around the question of the extent to which schooling will seek to present universal values and thus relativize and diminish those of particular groups, as there is around that of developing proficiency in the language of the wider society at the possible cost of losing use of the full range of an ethnic minority language. Sometimes the good intentions of those who seek to support ethnic distinctiveness may have effects which are as negative for members of minority groups as those achieved by the bad intentions of their oppressors.

Under normal circumstances, language is too diffuse a characteristic to make for group solidarity. When such solidarity exists for other reasons, the majority language may be used to express the identity and values of a minority ethnic group which has largely or entirely abandoned the use of its distinctive language. After all,

> no matter how all-embracing language is experienced to be as the vehicle or as the symbol of the total ethnocultural package . . . , it is really only a part, and a detachable part at that, rather than the whole of that package. This is all the more so when, as in the case of the American ethnic revival, language ideologies and language movements *per se* are almost entirely lacking (Fishman, 1989, 674).

Group maintenance (if that is desired) is thus by no means dependent upon continued use of the heritage language. Genesee cites Canadian research by Adiv that found that "native French-speaking Jewish Canadian children saw themselves as more similar to other Canadians who were Jewish but English-speaking than to French-speaking [non-Jewish] Canadians (Genesee, 1987, 102). Lambert and Taylor found that Puerto Ricans and Mexican Americans, though sharing the use of Spanish, felt no closer to each other than did either to other groups of Americans (Lambert & Taylor, 1988).

Similarly, "being an Italian-American has little to do with the Italian language or with most features of Italian culture. Rather, it has to do with a sense of continuity with the past, of group loyalty, and of a similarity of emotional experience within the home which makes the individual look for self-assertion in the form of ethnic group belonging" (De Vos, 1982, 32). After all, "identity can proceed without language, as in ethnic music or customs, also in political and social organizations" (Brock and Tulasiewicz, 1985, 8). Connor suggests, indeed, that "language is far more important to group formation that to group maintenance": an ethnic group is one whose ancestors spoke the same language (Connor, 1985b, 258).

A sustainable generalization, then, is that "language is . . . not inevitably associated or linked with culture nor relevant in every situation. Certain minorities may perceive their language to be a crucial characteristic of their culture and identity, and essential to knowledge and belief of their religion. In others it is not an essential attribute of ethnic or religious identity or group membership" (Saifullah Khan, 1980, 84). Or, as Paulston puts it drily in a study commissioned by the Swedish government, "contrary to popular belief, even among Swedish researchers, ethnicity is rarely sufficient for language maintenance, nor is language maintenance necessary for culture or ethnicity maintenance" (Paulston, 1982, 36).

Privileged Spheres of Minority Language Use

It is not the length of time that groups are in contact that determines whether the minority will adopt the language of the majority as the ordinary means of communication within the group, so much as the intentions of the minority and whether they possess established institutions through which they sustain their existence as a distinct group and which employ the minority language in a consistent way. Even under such conditions "communicative language shift may occur while leaving behind a symbolic value of importance" (Edwards, 1988, 205).

A group may maintain its distinctive culture and language while living in contact with those of a host society, but only through the most heroic measures of renunciation of many of the benefits that the majority society offers. "In the absence of a rather rigid and fargoing compartmentalization which is difficult to maintain (and, therefore, rare) in modern interactive life . . . such as is available, e.g. to Amish, Hasidic, or traditional Islamic families (or other communities sheltered by distance, rurality or major philosophical-religious-ideological ramparts), what begins as the language of social and economic mobility ends, within three generations or so, as the language of the crib as well, even in democratic and pluralism-permitting contexts" (Fishman, 1989, 206).

Mart-Jan de Jong points out the futility of language and cultural maintenance programs which do not enjoy such support:

Learning the official national language of the country of origin will not do much to contribute to the maintenance of the old values and norms. Neither can a knowledge of the geography of the country of origin or fragments of its history be expected to preserve its culture. When groups seek to preserve their own culture there is only one way available: to maintain an intensive group life and minimize contact with natives and with other foreigners. . . . An important factor is a strongly orthodox religious life (Jong, 1987, 42).

After all, "stable societal bilingualism (diglossia) depends on institutionally protected functional sociolinguistic compartmentalization, so no ethnocultural collectivity can maintain two cultures on a stable basis past three generations if they are implemented in the same social functions (family, friendship, work, education, religion, etc.) . . . (Fishman, 1989, 193). In other words, most people maintain active use of a language only to the extent that they are essentially *monolingual* in that language in at least one essential dimension of their lives.

There are many examples, in the nations under review, of immigrant groups that maintain the use of their original language for various 'private' functions such as family life and religious practice, but none in which use the minority language is used as the primary vehicle of effective political participation, as in Catalonia or (to some degree) in Wales. Paulston recalls how she began research on the use of Catalan in Spain as a study in ethnic boundary maintenance, only to come to realize that it was an issue of Catalan nationalism with a territorial base and clear political claims, not one of ethnicity (Paulston, 1992e, 133).

As Fishman has advised those concerned with the preservation of "endangered languages," "they must be intimately tied to a thousand intimate or small-scale network processes, processes too gratifying and rewarding to surrender even if they do not quite amount to the pursuit of the higher reaches of power and modernity" (Fishman, 1989, 399).

The Policy Debates over Minority Languages
Arguments Based on Minority Language Rights

At the end of Chapter 4, we considered briefly the principle expressed in the American Constitution, that distinctive understandings of the world should be allowed free exercise in the public sphere, but not established by government sponsorship. Attempts have sometimes been made to assert a body of "language rights" parallel to the rights to free speech and free exercise of religion. It has been argued, for example, that separate religions can be self-sustaining and self-fulfilling if government does not favor one over another. For whatever reason, the [American] government presently favors one language, English, over all others and provides that language with massive support through public education and other means. Without even limited support for other languages, language rights cannot be protected. . . . Language rights, unlike religious rights, cannot be effectively protected by being left alone in an underdeveloped and culturally backward state while only one language is promoted vigorously (Landry, 1983, 374–375).

Such arguments are historically and sociologically naive; the American government uses English because that is the language that the great majority of the American people have spoken at all stages of the nation's history. Publicly funded schools mostly use English for the same reason. Despite occasional flurries of linguistic xenophobia, public policy toward languages is far more pragmatic than it is ideological.

From the days of the Pilgrim fathers American leaders have ideologized morality, opportunity, progress, and freedom. Ethnicity has been considered irrelevant. . . . The English language does not figure prominently in the scheme of values, loyalties, and traditions by which Americans define themselves as "American." . . . More linguistic and cultural treasures were buried and eroded due to mutual permissiveness and apathy than would ever have been the case had repression and opposition been attempted (Fishman, 1970, 85).

There *is* an ideological case to be made for support for minority languages, but it has more to do with the idea of group rights—an idea which has little support in American constitutional law—than it does with individual freedoms. The closest analogy would be, not accommodation (*never* support) of religious organizations, but affirmative action for the benefit of those considered to have some group-based claim upon preferential treatment. Race, physical handicap and sex are (in most cases) immutable characteristics, of course, while most people are capable of changing the language that they use, so it has been necessary to add the premise that minority language is indissolubly linked (even for those capable of speaking the majority language) with an irreplaceable identity and worth.

The emphasis upon language as the primary marker of group identity is closely associated with the rise of the ideology of nationalism in the late eighteenth and early nineteenth centuries. Until the rise of nationalism as a mobilizing idea, indeed, "language was very rarely stressed as a fact upon which the prestige and power of a group depended." Thus, for example, "the Breton estates, which were very jealous of their independence [within France], nevertheless spoke French, and in the Act of Union for the Defense of the Liberties of Brittany of 1719 the Breton spokesmen did not mention language grievances" (Kohn, 1967, 7).

The idea that language is a distinctive and irreplaceable element of group identity was given definitive form by Johann Herder, who asserted in a school address published in 1764 that "every language has its definite national character, and therefore nature obliges us to learn only our native tongue, which is the most appropriate to our character, and which is most commensurate with our way of thought." The spirit and character of a people was, according to Herder, indissolubly linked with its own language, with obvious implications for the contemporary practice of providing schooling to German-speaking youth in Latin and in French.

> If language is the organ of our soul-forces, the medium of our innermost education, then we cannot be educated otherwise than in the language of our people and our country; a so-called French education in Germany must by necessity deform and misguide German minds (quoted by Kohn, 1967, 433).

A further implication was that the idea then prevalent, in educated circles, that a universal culture could gradually, through popular enlightenment and universal schooling, be spread to wider and wider circles of the population, was fundamentally misguided. Schooling would have to be distinctively national, for "no individual, no country, no people, no history of a people, no state is like any other. Therefore the true, the beautiful, and the good are not the same for them" (quoted by Kohn, 1967, 433). This led Herder to oppose the efforts, by Habsburg ruler Joseph II, to unify the administration of his multinational empire through the universal use of German for all educational and official purposes, "at a time when the Bohemians, Rumanians [sic], Croatians, and others had hardly any consciousness themselves of their nationality" (Kohn, 1967, 432). Herder asked, in 1783,

> Has a nationality anything dearer than the speech of its fathers? In its speech resides its whole thought domain, its tradition, history, religion and basis of life, all its heart and soul. To deprive a people of its speech is to deprive it of its one eternal good. . . . With language is created the heart of a people (quoted by Fishman, 1989, 105).

Though usually expressed in less exalted language, this belief in an almost mystical identification between a nation and its language has persisted. One of the most influential French thinkers of the mid-nineteenth century, Ernest Renan, insisted that language, much more than "blood" (or, as we would say, genetic inheritance), created the great divisions of humanity; "the spirit of each people and its language are very closely connected: the spirit creates the language and the language in turn serves as formula and limit for the spirit." Or, as he said on another occasion, "a Musulman who knows French will never be a dangerous Musulman" since "fanaticism is impossible in French" (quoted by Todorov, 1993, 143, 146). Here we see an early expression of the French insistence (discussed in Chapter 4) upon the necessity—and the possibility—of transforming culturally-alien persons through assimilation by French culture and language.

If language is inseparable from culture, to this way of thinking, so cultures are so fundamentally different as to be incommensurable. We can see one of the roots of the ideology of multiculturalism in the conviction expressed a hundred years ago by Gustave Le Bon, that "different races cannot feel, think, or act in the same manner, and . . . in consequence, they cannot comprehend one another" (quoted by Todorov, 1993, 55). For many present-day advocates of measures to preserve the use of minority languages, "the assumption is that language is the necessary support for a specific cultural identity" (Byram, 1990b, 127), and that ethnic identity is an essential treasure to be handed on to successive generations through continued use of the heritage language. Its loss—even if the loss is voluntary on the part of individuals who do not choose to use the language of their parents—is a tragedy and evidence of oppression:

> To me monolingualism, both individual and societal, is not so much a linguistic phenomenon (even if it has to do with language). It is rather a question of a psychological state, backed up by political power. Monolingualism is a psychological island. It is an ideological cramp. It is an illness, a disease which should be eradicated as soon as possible, because it is dangerous for world peace. It is a reflection of *linguicism* (Skutnabb-Kangas, 1988a, 13).

But, of course, a belief in the necessary connection between a language and membership in a national community can lead to intolerance of other languages within the national sphere. To the extent that a common language functions as an expression of a common nationality, the status of minority languages is always liable to be called into question. Conflict over language policy (such as over the "Official English" movement in the United States) does not reflect xenophobia so much as it does conflicting ideas about what it means to be a full member of the society. Is societal membership appropriately mediated through associations and communities to which a primary loyalty may be felt and which may communicate among themselves in a language incomprehensible to the wider society, or are such mediating structures inimical to national unity and the rights of individuals?

Ethnic groups and their institutions, some argue, are an important aspect of the civil society; they are mediating structures that may reduce the *anomie* attendant upon modernization and a mass society and perform an important function in the relation between individuals and the nation as a whole. To the extent that such groups depend upon the maintenance across generations of a distinctive language, compulsory schooling can be either a fundamental threat or a valuable support to their continuing existence, depending upon the policy that the school adopts toward the use of that language.

> Prolonged participation in the British education system is thought by parents to cause a loss of "Greek identity" as individual children conform to the values and behaviors of their school peers. Participation in the Greek-language schools is quite specifically designed to counteract some of the effects of State schooling (Constantinides 1977, quoted by Taylor, 1988, 145).

There is a fundamental human right, by this logic, to preserve a language and cultural heritage; "the smallest and most insignificant language groups or individuals, like the largest and most powerful, have a right to exist and prosper regardless of any calculation of profit and loss" (Lewis, 1978, 680). But of course such statements, by equating groups with individuals, avoid the question of whether the former, like the latter, enjoy fundamental human rights. Although such rights have been recognized repeatedly in international law, it is not so easy to specify what this recognition entails; for example, the *International Covenant on Civil and Political Rights*, adopted by the United Nations in December 1966, provides in Article 27 that

> In those States in which ethnic, religious or linguistic minorities exist, persons belonging to such minorities shall not be denied the right, in community with the other members of their group, to enjoy their own culture, to profess and practice their own religion, or to use their own language (Storimans, 1993, 31).

The influence of modern compulsory schooling is so profound, some argue, that this right can only be guaranteed through alternative forms of schooling for ethnic and language minority groups, comparable to the alternative religiously-based schools which most nations allow and even support. The *Convention Against Discrimination in Education* adopted by UNESCO in December 1960, asserts such a right but hedges it about severely in Article 5:

> It is essential to recognize the right of members of national minorities [note that this does not include *immigrant* minorities] to carry on their own educational activities, including the maintenance of schools and, depending on the educational policy of each State, the use or the teaching of their own language, provided however:
>
> (i) That this right is not exercised in a manner which prevents the members of these minorities from understanding the culture and language of the community as a whole and from participating in its activities, or which prejudices national sovereignty;
>
> (ii) That the standard of education is not lower than the general standard laid down or approved by the competent authorities; and
>
> (iii) That attendance at such schools is optional. (OIDEL, nd, 28)

It should be noted that the logic of this statement is quite distinct from that of an earlier (1953) UNESCO position, growing out of a conference held in 1951, which stated that "we take it as axiomatic . . . that the best medium for teaching is the mother tongue of the child" (quoted in Baral, 1983a, 6). The 1953 statement was focused upon what the assembled experts believed was in the best interests of the early schooling of children, especially those in developing nations still ruled by colonial powers, whereas the 1960 statement is concerned to assert the group rights of national minorities.

The *Final Helsinki Accord*, adopted in June 1990 by all the European nations except Albania and by the United States and Canada, stated a right to ethnic schools but without suggesting any obligation on the part of government to fund such schools or even to recognize them as equivalent to its own schools.

> To belong to a national minority is a matter of a person's individual choice and no disadvantage may arise from the exercise of such choice. Persons belonging to national minorities have the right freely to express, preserve and develop their ethnic, cultural, linguistic or

religious identity and to maintain and develop their culture in all its aspects, free of any attempts at assimilation against their will. In particular, they have the right . . . to establish and maintain their own educational, cultural and religious institutions (Storimans, 1993, 37).

Several international agreements have taken another tack, asserting a right to a measure of minority language maintenance within the context of regular schooling. The Council of Europe adopted a resolution in 1969 that urged countries hosting labor migrants to keep open the possibility of return through "mother tongue teaching corresponding with the curricular requirements of the countries of origin" (Wittek, 1992, 3). Even as the prospect of return to the homeland has faded, a series of resolutions and pilot programs of the European Community have called for "intercultural education" with an emphasis on optional mother tongue instruction. Similarly, the chapter on migrant workers of the *Final Helsinki Accord* committed the states signing it "to ensure that the children of migrant workers established in the host country have access to the education usually given there, under the same conditions as the children of the country and, furthermore, to permit them to receive supplementary education in their own language, national culture, history and geography" (Storimans, 1993, 40). Similarly, the *European Charter for Regional or Minority Languages* (Strasbourg, November 1992) provides, in Article 8, Section 1:

> With regard to education, the Parties undertake, within the territory in which such languages are used, according to the situation of each of these languages, *and without prejudice to the teaching of the official language(s) of the State*: . . .
>
> (i) to make available primary education in the relevant regional or minority languages; or
>
> (ii) to make available a substantial part of primary education in the relevant regional or minority languages; or
>
> (iii) to provide, within primary education, for the teaching of the relevant regional or minority languages as an integral part of the curriculum; or
>
> (iv) to apply one of the measures provided for under i to iii above at least to those pupils whose families so request and whose number is considered sufficient . . (Storimans, 1993, 39, emphasis added).

This argument has been applied to linguistic minority children in Denmark in these terms:

the child must have the possibility of using his or her resources actively in interaction with children from the same culture, with adults from the same culture, and in surroundings that, in their symbolism and imagery, mirror their culture (C. Horst, 1988, 22).

According to this interpretation of "minority rights," ethnic groups "have the same democratic right to cultural reproduction as do the majority population" (Clausen & Horst, 1987, 102).

As we have seen, immigrant languages are not usually sustained (other than in marginal ways) into the second and third generations by immigrant communities themselves. This has led to demands by language advocates that public education systems take on the task, through supplemental programs, of teaching these languages to children who have not learned them from their parents, and those of most nations under review have made some efforts in that direction.

Lambert and Taylor have studied the attitude of several ethnic groups in the American Mid-West toward the role of public schools in maintaining the heritage language of their children. One of the questions they asked was whether that language should be used "for part of the teaching and learning in public schools." Another question was whether children should "learn to read and write our own language not through school, but through church-run or community-run classes." On a scale from 1 ("definitely disagree") to 7 ("definitely agree"), the two least assimilated groups, Arab Americans and Albanian Americans, were strongly supportive of both forms of language maintenance. Mexican Americans and Polish Americans were also positive about programs to maintain their languages, but rather less so. Perhaps the most interesting finding was that Puerto Ricans were among the most insistent on language maintenance efforts in schools, but much the least supportive of community-based efforts to maintain their language outside of school (Table 5.2).

TABLE 5.2. Support for Maintenance of Ancestral Language
(1="definitely disagree"; 7="definitely agree")

Ethnic Group	Support Language Maintenance Outside School	Support Language Maintenance in School
Mexican American	5.43	5.55
Puerto Rican	3.05	6.63
Polish American	5.23	4.52
Arab American	6.69	6.74
Albanian American	6.72	6.21

Source: from Lambert & Taylor, 1990, 77, 100

In answer to the argument that every group is free to continue to use any language they wish privately, without involving the government or publicly supported education, Swedish advocates for home language classes insist that the prospects of developing and maintaining full competence in a minority language are unfavorable. There are few opportunities to receive stimulation or positive support for use of the home language. In Tingbjorn's analysis:

> Sweden is far from being a bilingual country—it is a mono-lingual country with many small minority languages. The limited opportunity for active or passive language stimulation applies even to the minority that is in a class by itself, the Finns. The few hours of broadcast time for Finns in Finnish on radio and TV, Finnish sections in some large daily newspapers and instruction in Finnish in home language classes (for a certain part of school attendance for pupils in densely Finnish areas) are naturally not comparable to the circumstances of Finns in Finland. Moreover the use of Finnish in Sweden is limited . . . to the private sphere such as relations with family and friends. Much more limited are the opportunities for other language groups, especially those which are very small, to use their languages. This places a heavy burden upon the schools to compensate as far as is possible for the limits imposed by the milieu on language learning through comprehensive and well-planned instruction *in* and *through* the pupil's first language (Tingbjorn, 1988b, 87).

Whether schools make such efforts or not, only individuals, in the final analysis, can continue to use a language or not do so, as they choose. A government official pointed out to the author a nuance in the wording of the Swedish national curriculum adopted in 1980, which stated that

> the purpose of instruction in home languages is for the pupils to develop their language so that it will provide them with a means of growing into individuals with a strong sense of identity and a clear opinion of themselves, their group identity and their living situation. Home language instruction must help the pupils to retain contact with their family and their language group. This will enhance the prospects of their linguistic development. Instruction must lay the foundations of the pupils' development of active bilingualism (National Swedish Board of Education, 1980).

This curriculum, and thus the Swedish educational system, did not claim to *develop* an active bilingualism but simply to lay the foundations for one which the individual might or might not choose to build upon (interview with Swedish government education official Bertil Jacobsson, February 6, 1989). For Finnish educational activist Tove Skutnabb-Kangas, on the other hand, "it should be the task of the school to give the migrant children as good a command of the mother tongue as they would get in a school in their native land" (Skutnabb-Kangas, 1979, 5).

"Proclamations concerning bilingual education," according to Richard Rodriguez, "are weighted at bottom with Hispanic political grievances and, too, with middle-class romanticism" (Rodriguez, 1992, 352). Even though it is the ethnic group whose interests are most closely associated with maintenance of a minority language, there may be individual interests to do so as well, quite distinct from any calculation of profit. Dismissal of romantic yearnings for an ancestral language fails to do justice to the purpose that can be served by ethnic identity, however vestigial, in defining oneself in contrast with a majority culture that seems stifling or insufficiently respectful. No harm is done, surely, when individuals choose to emphasize some aspect of their ancestral heritage for reasons that seem good to them.

Whether public funding should support private decisions to maintain an ancestral language (or, indeed, to learn another language of choice) is a question more of curriculum planning than of fundamental educational policy. Publicly supported schools commonly offer optional enrichment activities, especially at the secondary level, and it may be that classes to maintain ancestral languages should be thought of in this context. The supplemental home language classes provided on a voluntary basis to the children of immigrants by most of the countries included in this study (see Chapter 7) might be considered an appropriate enrichment apart from considerations of success in the academic mainstream.

As an American critic of bilingual education has pointed out, "there are several reasons . . . for teaching children in their home language instead of the language of the majority community, such as promoting language loyalty, community closeness, political hegemony, and control by ethnic leaders. However, such reasons exist quite apart from reasons of equal educational opportunity or effective second-language learning or social integration" (Porter, 1990, 63).

The case for public support for the maintenance of minority languages is commonly made, however, in the name, not of individual rights, but of the rights of groups, and by analogy with the much-litigated rights of African Americans to be accorded some remedies by American society because of the disabilities under which they, because of their involuntary group membership, previously suffered. For African Americans, it was the color of their skin and not any individual merits or demerits that determined their treatment under the laws of a number of American states. Whether even in this instance there is such a thing as a "group right" is much debated, notably in the legal cases and political controversies over affirmative action.

It is true that the federal courts, since the *Soria v. Oxnard* (488 F2d 579) and *Keyes* (413 U.S. 189, 203) cases in 1973, have extended to Hispanics the standard of strict scrutiny for group-based discrimination and eligibility for certain kinds of group-based remedies. The ruling in *Soria* found that Hispanics and blacks "suffer identical discrimination in treatment compared with the treatment afforded Anglo students." In no case, however, has the right to a remedy of past discrimination been extended to a right to public support in maintaining the group's identity or language. Indeed Shirley Hufstedler, the federal judge who was on the winning side of the *Lau* decision of the Supreme Court, when later serving as Secretary of Education, insisted that "the Lau regulations [issued by her agency] are *not* designed to maintain any language or subculture in the United States" (quoted by Ruíz, 1988, 9).

National minorities in several European countries—Frisians in the Netherlands, Germans in Belgium, as well as those groups discussed in Chapter 3—are often entitled to support in their distinctiveness, though more commonly through political than legal decisions, and on a territorial basis. The latter, for example, have a right to instruction of their children through German so long as they live in the small section of Belgium where that right is established, but no such right if they move to Charleroi (where French would be the language of instruction) or Antwerp (where it would be Dutch).

English-speakers in Quebec and French-speakers in Ontario have rights anchored in the Act of Union of 1840 and the British North America Act of 1867, by which Canada was established, and the Charter of Rights and Freedoms of 1972 extended the right to instruction through these two languages to all parts of Canada—but it has not been ratified by Quebec, which continues to assert a territorial basis for language use which does not acknowledge an individual right of language choice.

The only language minority groups in the United States with the right to be treated as members of a group rather than as individuals are members of Indian peoples that made treaties with the national government in the course of the westward expansion of its control; this is the basis for the greater organizational autonomy and distinctiveness that is at least possible for Indian education under tribal jurisdiction compared with the education provided to the children of immigrants.

In general, however, and despite the international covenants and statements of principle, only individual and not group rights are recognized by the Western democracies, and the assertion of a right to public support in the maintenance of a non-territorial group—particularly one constituted on an ethnic basis—is an invitation to political debate. As described in Chapter 4, some countries (the United Kingdom, the Netherlands) are inclined to look favorably upon such demands because of their traditions of institutional pluralism; others (France in particular) find them repugnant. American policy-makers, with characteristic equivocation, provide separate schooling through minority languages on a massive scale, but do so in the name of "transition" to the educational mainstream and not of any recognition of group rights.

There is little reason to believe, indeed, that the supplemental lessons provided in several countries, or even the full-time but transitional bilingual classes in the United States, have the effect of maintaining the active use of minority languages, and thus the policy argument is often made for separate programs or schools that will give primary emphasis to ensuring that the children of immigrants will develop proficient bilingualism, or even dominance in the minority language (see Chapter 6). Tove Skutnabb-Kangas has insisted that "a couple of hours a week of mother tongue instruction for a minority child is more therapeutic cosmetics than language teaching" (Skutnabb-Kangas, 1988a, 29).

One conclusion of Paulston's review of Swedish research was that "Mother tongue classes [that is, separate home language classes] are partly an excuse, a mechanism for segregation, which happens to coincide with Finnish national demands, and therefore meets with Finnish support" (Paulston, 1982, 54). Such a motivation has been advanced without apology by Finnish language theorist Skutnabb-Kangas, who sees the choice of the language of instruction as an instrument of oppression or of liberation; the decision to provide schooling through the majority language is a deliberate strategy by a capitalist system to keep immigrants in a subordinate, economically exploitable position. Thus she argued in 1979 that "the large scale educational, psychological, and social problems of minority children are *not* a failure inherent in the ethnic group status of the children, but are more or less caused by the policy of forced assimilation" (Skutnabb-Kangas, 1979, 1). The reader may recognize the influence of French sociologists Bourdieu and Passeron (1964), according to whose theory the low academic achievement of working class children is the result, not of ineffective schools, but of schools that are highly effective in their intended task, in a capitalist society, of legitimating inherited social inequality and producing an unskilled class available for exploitation.

Skutnabb-Kangas and other language activists played a major role in a so-called "school strike" in Rinkeby, a working-class suburb of Stockholm, demanding "first of all, to stop the so-called integration model. We wanted all the new concepts in subject matter teaching to be introduced through the medium of Finnish, during the first six years. . . . We wanted Swedish to be taught as a second language (not a mother tongue), and we wanted it taught by bilingual teachers" (Honkala, et al., 1988, 244). The "we" included Finnish school directors and bilingual teachers (described as "some of the most active participants") who objected to the integration of Finnish with Swedish pupils starting in the fourth grade; Tove Skutnabb-Kangas was, by her own account, deeply involved in the organization process (Skutnabb-Kangas 1988b, 265, 274). These specialists and teachers were obviously not disinterested participants in the demand for their services.

The case that government support for language maintenance is a fundamental right has been advanced most successfully in Sweden and the United States, two nations with a strong and self-aware linguistic minority group anchored in a neighboring nation with which a semi-colonial relationship long existed. Under such conditions the possibility arises of political mobilization through (as the jargon has it) "the conversion of quiescent ethnic phenomenology collectivities into dynamic ethnic ideology collectivities." Like the Hispanic population of the United States, the Finnish population of Sweden is caught between societal pressures toward assimilation and the desire of many—perhaps especially among the educated elite—to maintain a separate identity, language and culture. Ekstrand traces this to nineteenth century controversies when

> part of the Swedish upper class in Finland launched a nationalistic movement, one aim of which was to establish Finnish as the sole language in the so far bilingual Finland . . . Other parts of the establishment opposed, and a bitter feud followed, to a large extent carried on in Swedish. . . . Although the feud is said to have ended during the 1930s, attitudes from it still survive. The strong claims for unilingual Finnish schooling in Sweden, primary as well as secondary, are by many believed to be an extension of the language feud. (Ekstrand, 1981b, 31f).

A slogan in these controversies was "without Finnish we are not Finns" (quoted in Fishman, 1988, 277). There is thus considerable demand on the part of Finnish organizations for all-Finnish home language classes.

> The Finnish associations have strongly urged that a parallel Finnish school system should be set up in Sweden. The Finnish speaking pupils would therefore, according to this point of view, have the opportunity of completing their schooling entirely in Finnish (Norbelie, 1983, 44).

If the minority group language fails to be used as the primary vehicle for social, affective, and cognitive development, it is argued, these aspects of the child's growth will be damaged, bringing great harm to the child's educational potential. Nor is this an accidental result, since

> the educational system in industrial Western countries helps to ensure the continuation of the class system and the conservation of the social structure of society. Since the system operates on majority terms and the majority will need assembly line workers even in the future, the educational system reproduces the migrant's existing professional and social structure, even if its official aim is to give migrant children the same opportunities in the host country. In this respect the function of the semilingualism of migrant children as a factor transferring and increasing inequality is understandable (Skutnabb-Kangas, 1979, 18).

Skutnabb-Kangas returned to this conspiracy theory in 1984, insisting that even for those "programmes which are said to be bilingual or to lead to bilingualism (or not) there are not only linguistic, psychological, pedagogical or sociolinguistic reasons and goals, but always very substantial economic-political rationales and goals, regardless of whether those who choose the programmes admit it or not" (Skutnabb-Kangas, 1984a, 18).

Separate classes that stress maintenance of the home language have thus arisen, in some cases, not because this is a more effective way of easing the transition into the language and culture of the host society—the major claim for bilingual education in the United States—but "as a protest against suppression of minorities, and often their existence shows that the minority community has started a dynamic struggle to get their share of the goods and services of the majority society" (Skutnabb-Kangas, 1984a, 38). In such classes, she and Cummins wrote in the conclusion of a collection of essays, the mother tongue can be emphasized partly in its own right, as a *self-evident human right*, and partly in order to be able to give a *better instrument* for coping with both the learning of the second language and the learning of other skills, and to include *analysis, understanding, evaluation and action in relation to societal questions of economic and political power.* An emphasis on minority mother tongues can thus be for *exclusion*, for *pacification* or for *empowerment.* It is the last of these approaches, advocating language for empowerment, that [we advocate] (Skutnabb-Kangas & Cummins, 1988, 394; emphasis in original).

For language activists,

> the maintenance of language and culture by the school . . . is not a frill. It is a matter of academic and social survival and must be considered a civil right. For these reasons, bilingual education must be supported, if at all, as a maintenance effort. . . . the history of language rights legislation demonstrates that its function—even that of modern permissive laws and regulations—is to restrain the access of linguistic minorities to American institutions at the same time that it demands the acquisition and use of English for full participation in society (Hernández-Chávez, 1988, 54).

The demand for "language rights" has been a major focus of political action on the part of minority language activists, who ask for "a concerned political struggle that encompasses all segments of the Chicano people and other linguistic minorities and that is based on a solid ideological foundation" (Hernández-Chávez, 1988, 55), which would be an unprecedented (and deplorable) phenomenon in American political life. Schooling through the minority language is valid, he argued earlier, even for minority children who are dominant in English when they enter school, since "the minority language in these circumstances remains an extremely important determinant of sociocultural identity" (Hernández-Chávez, 1984, 175).

> A sound educational approach for minority children . . . must have as one of its highest priorities the first establishment of a deep sense of social and cultural identity that is grounded in the ethnic community. A central component of this goal is the development of a keen awareness of the social, economic, and political processes that condition the subordinate role of many minority groups in society in the

United States (Freire, 1970). Students who do not understand these processes or who do not have the critical-analytical skills necessary to acquire an understanding of them will not be likely to develop a sense of loyalty and responsibility toward their communities (Hernández-Chávez, 1984, 171).

Because of the salience of these considerations of strengthening identification with the ethnic group as a means of political mobilization in opposition to the existing social and economic system, Hernández-Chávez is not entirely satisfied even with San Diego programs which use only Spanish in the initial instruction of pupils, and which have "a long-term commitment to the native language as the principal medium of instruction." Despite this gratifying emphasis on Spanish, "there is no emphasis on the development of sociocultural identity." As a result, such programs do not satisfy the central criterion of promising "to revitalize ethnolinguistic communities in the United States . . . and, ultimately, to build the capacity of these communities for self-sufficiency" (Hernández-Chávez, 1984, 177–179), whatever that could possibly mean in a highly integrated economy.

Such assertions by language activists seem rather detached from the realities of social and political development. After all, language is not usually a surrogate for class interests in political mobilization, except in the cases noted in Chapter 3 in which it is a symbol of national minority territorial claims. While school use of the minority language in an area where it is home language of most of the population—as in Catalonia—may be a crucial political goal, an occasion for mobilization (Mallea, 1984), there is no reason to believe that such instructional use itself leads to further effective mobilization. Thus the political arguments for separate education based upon the home language are understandably vague in their scenarios for how language maintenance will translate into social justice and political power. It is more common to find the charge that adoption of the language of the host society is itself somehow disempowering, establishing a relationship of subordination and of internal colonization, without a very clear description of how an alternative of separate development might work under conditions of minority status.

In the United States as elsewhere calls for minority language maintenance support have come largely from the relatively new middle class of advocates and educators who are themselves proficient in the majority language needed for advancement in education and the economy. Many of these activists, though they have left their old communities, find it difficult to accept the eagerness of new arrivals who want to learn English and become "American" (Heath, 1985, 277).

In debates over bilingual education the political arguments—however important in motivating the choice of this approach—are generally given less emphasis than those based upon learning theory and psychological consid- erations. In part this is no doubt for tactical reasons, but in addition the political benefits argued for schooling based on the minority language turn out to be remarkably vague. Not that examples are lacking of language serv- ing as the rallying-point for ethnic group political mobilization over against the dominant society, cases in which (as discussed in chapter 3) ethnic elites are able to "heighten awarenesses that are only latent, so that not only will masses come to feel that they constitute a nationality but that they will also be willing to act upon the basis of that feeling" (Fishman, 1989, 121).

The partial revival of Welsh is attributed by Baker to "the general growth of consciousness about the virtues of preserving an indigenous lan- guage and culture. Such growth cannot be viewed in simple, functional terms" (Baker, 1993a, 9). Certainly the Welsh language has minimal useful- ness for economic purposes (except for those who become teachers of the language or involved in other ways with its promotion), but it serves as a rallying-point. It is a way, even for those who have moved to Wales from England, to assert distinctiveness and identification with a romantic tradi- tion of bards and castles. Learning a bit of the language can be an ethnic marker, even for those who are not Welsh by descent.

Arguments Based on Academic Underachievement

More powerful as a policy argument for publicly-funded efforts to maintain minority languages than the possibility of political mobilization is the con- tention that the weak academic performance of some groups of immigrant children and their descendants is caused by a failure of the society and es- pecially of its schools to provide positive messages about the minority lan- guage and culture, and thus about the children themselves. There is a widely shared belief among those who devise programs to serve language minority children, that "[t]he impact of the monocultural orientation of the educa- tional system on the self-respect and identity of ethnic minority children and adolescents is shattering" (Verma, 1989, 238). The Dutch Ministry of Edu- cation and Science changed the focus of its policy for teaching home lan- guages of language minority children in 1980, acknowledging that the ear- lier purpose, to facilitate reintegration into the society of origin when the families returned to Turkey or Morocco, was no longer valid as guest work- ers settled down as immigrants. The new rationale was stated in "*psycho- logical rather than in linguistic terms*: fostering the well-being and the eth- nic awareness of children" (Eldering, 1989, 120).

Programs that maintain or teach in the home language are supposed to have a positive effect upon the emotional development of linguistic minority pupils, contribute to a positive self-image, and thus make it more likely that they will do well in school and in life. This position "maintains that bilingual children's emotional conflicts result from tensions between linguistic settings. Their emotional maladjustment is not so much generated by the complexity of thinking and speaking in two languages, as by cultural conflict" (Tosi, 1984, 162). As a congressional committee was told at the time the Bilingual Education Act was under consideration, it was essential to cultivate in the minority child

> ancestral pride; to reinforce—not destroy—the language he natively speaks; to capitalize on the bicultural situation; . . . to make use of a curriculum to reflect Spanish—and Puerto Rican—as well as American tradition, and to retain as teachers those trained and identified with both cultures. Only through such education can the Spanish speaking child be given the sense of personal identification so essential to his educational maturation (Francesco Cordasco, quoted by Spolsky, 1978a, 275).

Separate minority-oriented programs, including bilingual classes, according to this argument, educate the children of immigrants in a setting that gives strongly positive messages about their ethnic and cultural identity, and to some extent shelters them from the negative evaluation which the surrounding society may place upon that identity. An identity crisis with negative effects upon personal and academic development is allegedly prevented by such measures. Indeed the benefits claimed are so global that, in the acerbic description of a Swedish expert, "the idea of the home language as the basis for second language learning, identity and personality development, as well as cognitive and emotional development, appears to have grown into something akin to a religious revival" (Ekstrand, 1981a, 188). Thus the reports about one project in the Netherlands

> were lavishly strewn with such concepts as healthy personality development, experiencing of identity, basic security and positive self-concept. It was never specified what precise meaning these concepts had, what factors promote a healthy personality development, and under what conditions education in native language and culture can contribute to that. Theory-formation about bicultural specialization and the identity development of migrant children is still at a primitive stage and the research results are not in accord (Eldering, 1986a, 195).

Bertil Malmberg of Sweden helped to popularize this idea in 1964 with his assertion that "only the mother-tongue with its link to the child's own environment and experiences can introduce the child to the world of abstract experiences and higher culture" (quoted in Kerr, 1984, 180). This would seem to imply that a child whose mother-tongue is not a language of "higher culture" cannot hope to have access to it in another language, no matter how early nor how proficiently this might be learned. Malmberg drew upon Toukomaa's research on the Finnish minority in Sweden to argue that

> any introduction of another language into the child's world, before the native language is safely anchored as an emotional and cognitive means of expression, has a retarding effect on the intellectual development in general and the linguistic in particular. . . . this becomes a disturbing component which hinders the harmonic emotional and cognitive development and hurts the solid development of the native tongue, without which a continued linguistic development may not come about (quoted in Ekstrand, 1979, 15–16).

A UNESCO gathering, in 1969, advanced an argument for use of the home language as first language for instruction that differed from the language rights position discussed above, asserting that "psychological and linguistic studies are of comparatively recent origins and it was not formerly recognised how closely related are the development of thought and speech, and how closely bound up with speech is the growth of the personality in its individual and social aspects. (quoted by Johannesson, 1975, 349). Separate home language classes (see Chapters 6 and 7) are now commonly advocated on the basis of theories of language learning supported by UNESCO-funded research conducted during the seventies among Finnish pupils in Sweden, in several cities and in the Torne River region along the Finnish border.

For many years only Swedish was used in schools in the Tornedal area, but since the 1970s Finnish has been used as an optional language of instruction as a result of broader Swedish policies concerned primarily with immigrant pupils, though

> the measures in favour of Finnish, which are as a matter of fact part of the reason for the ethnic revival, have come too late. Swedish has got such a strong position in the region that there is hardly need for Finnish any more just for making oneself understood linguistically in communication with peers. There are few if any monolingual Finn-

ish-speaking people among the original population of Tornedal Finns . . . the number of monolingual Finnish-speaking beginners in the elementary school: in 1945 about 72% of the beginners were monolingual Finnish, in 1957 38%, in 1965 (1967) 16% and in 1976 *one* per cent (Wande, 1984, 236–237).

The heart of the argument for mother-tongue schooling was the reportedly superior performance of Finnish-speaking pupils who came to Sweden after some years of instruction in a Finnish school, in contrast with those who had been born in Sweden and schooled in Swedish from the start. Pertti Toukomaa found that children with good skills in Finnish tended to have good skills in Swedish, and argued that their proficiency in Finnish (rather than intelligence, social class, or aptitude for language) caused their proficiency in Swedish. The poor achievement of the pupils from Finnish-speaking homes in Sweden who had been schooled in Swedish was, he argued, the result of inadequate development of their home language in school. The results of this research, widely cited in literature supporting bilingual education, were interpreted by some to argue that linguistic minority children who are taught in the official language rather than in their home language will be cognitively and educationally handicapped. Finnish researchers Toukomaa and Tove Skutnabb-Kangas claimed, in a profoundly influential publication in 1977, that

> if in an early stage of development a minority child finds itself in a foreign-language learning environment without contemporaneously receiving the requisite support in its mother tongue, the development of its skill in the mother tongue will slow down or even cease, leaving the child without a basis for learning the second language well enough to attain the threshold level in it [that will permit continuing development] (Toukomaa & Skutnabb-Kangas, 1977, 28)

This condition is often referred to as "semilingualism," described by the Swedish researcher N.E. Hansegard in 1968 as "functioning in two languages without being really proficient in either." On one level, of course, this is an unexceptional concept; there are millions of individuals who use only English but are less "proficient" than a baseball announcer or William F. Buckley, Jr. The concept becomes more controversial when it is asserted that using two languages at an early age makes it more likely that neither will develop to the point of real proficiency by some standard. If such "premature bilingualism" is a real danger, immigrant and other linguistic minority children should—to prevent semilingualism—be taught in and through their home language primarily, with supplemental instruction in the host language, until the age of 12 or 13. Such "sheltered" instruction would, the researchers claimed, lead to development of full proficiency in both the home language and the second language after a number of years.

Concentrating on the home language until it was well established would prevent the insufficient development of cognitive and social skills as a result of premature bilingualism. Toukomaa asserted that his research demonstrated that acquisition of a second language (in this case, Swedish) was entirely contingent upon an adequate development of the home language (Finnish) (cited by Ekstrand, 1979, 13). Skutnabb-Kangas argued that "there is good reason to believe that children who cannot fully develop their mother tongue have great difficulties in learning [a second language] properly" (Skutnabb-Kangas, 1979, 15).

The conclusions drawn from this research have been criticized extensively in Sweden, though in general only the Toukomaa/Skutnabb-Kangas conclusions and not the criticisms have been reported in references to Swedish research in arguments for bilingual education in other countries. An early criticism, by Loman, found no empirical support for the concept of semilingualism: "when social factors were controlled for, no differences in Swedish skills were found between residents of the Torne Valley and those in other areas of Sweden" (cited by Hyltenstam & Arnberg, 1988, 496). This suggests that the poor test scores for Finnish pupils in Toukomaa's research were the result of social class and not of their having been "prematurely" educated in Swedish. Hansegard, on the other hand, contended that Loman had not taken into account the (less easily measurable) intellectual and emotional functions, and the concept of semilingualism had thus not been disproved.

Other researchers working with linguistic minority pupils in Sweden have rejected the concept of semilingualism and stressed that early bilingualism has positive effects if children's use of language is appropriately stimulated. Ekstrand pointed out that Toukomaa "disregards the positive effects of [second language] learning on [first language] development, and the effects of the general cognitive development" on acquisition of any language (Ekstrand, 1979, 13; see also Kerr, 1984, 179). His own research indicated "that native language does not play a major part in [second language] learning," while "data indicating that an almost unilingual native-language approach will be the most efficient form of bilingual-bicultural education are still missing." A number of studies had led "their authors to the conclusion that the hypothesis of semilingualism in [the frontier region where Toukomaa did his research] is not supported by their findings" (Ekstrand, 1978, 64, 75, 84).

In a study of Swedish research commissioned by national authorities, Christina Bratt Paulston of the University of Pittsburgh observed that "the notion of semilingualism" is based more in struggles over language policy than in research:

> The fact of the matter is that there is *no* empirical evidence to support the existence of such a language development hiatus as Hansegard claims. Linguist after linguist in Sweden . . . have criticized the notion. . . . The widespread mythology of semilingualism when there are no data is astounding to the outsider. Such mythology has obviously served a purpose: people believe what they want to. It has served as rationale for the Finnish groups in their demands for monolingual Finnish schooling in Sweden. It has also served as a rationale for the Swedish parents in Sodertalje who do not want the Assyrian children in the same classes as their own children. . . . I expect the press may deserve part of the blame (Paulston, 1982, 42).

Semilingualism as an explanation for low achievement of linguistic minority pupils has thus been called into question among Swedish researchers. Similar criticism has been directed to the contention that early instruction through the home language contributes more to later proficiency in the second language than does early instruction in the second language. A nationwide study of all linguistic minority pupils in Sweden who were in the ninth grade in 1978–79 found that those who had immigrated early were substantially more proficient in Swedish than those who came at a later age, even though the latter had benefitted from more extensive home language instruction and supportive Swedish instruction (Liljegren & Ullman, 1982, 3). This study also found that those early immigrants who had received home language support in Swedish schools were not necessarily doing better than those who had not, contrary to what Toukomaa's research would predict.

Some of the pupils who immigrated in 1971 or earlier (i.e., by grade 2 at junior level) received home language instruction . . . at all levels of compulsory school. The Swedish proficiency of these pupils in grade 9 (1978–79) is judged somewhat inferior to that of other pupils who immigrated in 1971 or earlier (Liljegren & Ullman, 1982, 27). Thus the contention that late immigrants who had already been well-grounded in their home language before leaving their homelands would do better in Swedish was not supported by this broad-scale study, nor was the contention that home language instruction in Swedish schools would lead to superior performance in Swedish.

Despite such criticism from researchers, the continuing impact of this small-scale study is comparable to that of the Clarks in the United States with the response of Negro children to white and Negro dolls. Just as the conclusions which the Clarks drew continue to resonate and shape discussions of American race relations, via the celebrated footnote 11 of the 1954 *Brown* decision, even though later studies have tended to disprove its central contention of a damaged self-concept among minority children, so Toukomaa's conclusions about the importance of developing the first language before a second is introduced are cited in virtually every serious discussion of the need for bilingual education. To take a few examples, Toukomaa's research is cited as decisive evidence by Saifullah Khan in Britain (1980, 79), by Appel in the Netherlands (1980, 77), and by advocates of home language instruction in France, West Germany, Australia, India, and Canada, as well as those in the United States. It is above all the writing of Jim Cummins of Toronto which has given the ideas advanced by Toukomaa and Skutnabb-Kangas tremendous resonance in policy discussions around the world. For example, Cummins wrote in a publication prepared for the California Department of Education in 1982,

> Finnish children in Swedish-only programs were found to perform worse in Finnish than 90 percent of equivalent socio-economic status Finnish children in Finland and worse in Swedish that about 90 percent of Swedish children (Skutnabb-Kangas and Toukomaa, 1976). The Sodertalje program, however, used Finnish as the major initial language of instruction and continued its use throughout elementary school. Swedish became the major language of instruction from third grade. By sixth grade, children's performances in this program in both Finnish and Swedish were almost at the same level as that of Swedish-speaking children in Finland. (Cummins, 1982, 27)

It was on the basis of this and a few other studies that Cummins elaborated his "threshold hypothesis," that the home language should be solidly developed, since "maintenance of L1 skills can lead to cognitive benefits for minority language children" (Cummins, 1979, 232). Cummins explicitly rejected the common justification for the use of home languages in school, that (as put by the United States Commission on Civil Rights in 1975), that "lack of English proficiency is the major reason for language minority students' academic failure. Bilingual education is intended to ensure that students do not fall behind in subject matter content while they are learning English." The idea that the "linguistic mis-match" between home and school was the central problem was rejected by Cummins as no longer supported by research. He boldly asserted that

> there is no evidence for the belief that a switch between the language of the home and that of the school, i.e., "linguistic mis-match", is in itself a cause of school failure . . . [Thus] instruction through [the home language] is regarded as much more than an interim carrier of subject matter content; it is rather the means through which the conceptual and communicative proficiency which underlies *both* [the home language] and English literacy is developed (Cummins, 1981, 31, 39, 43).

Cummins—and through him Skutnabb-Kangas and Toukomaa—are the most frequently cited authorities for the development of separate programs based upon the home language. This model represents the norm for bilingual programs in the United States, with classes made up exclusively of pupils of a single language group, who are instructed in that language and in English for a number of years before they are physically and instructionally integrated with majority pupils. Many advocates now suggest that five to seven years would be the optimal period for participation in a bilingual before placement in a "mainstream" class (see Chapter 6).

While this set of ideas clearly has the intellectual initiative—and indeed is often presented as though endorsed by all experts—the official Swann Report in Great Britain concluded, on the basis of a review of the research evidence, that

> it would not seem possible for the case for any form of mother tongue provision to rest upon the research evidence alone . . . in many instances the most that can be claimed from particular projects is that the child's learning of English is not impaired and *may* in some respects be enhanced (*Education for All*, 1985, 404, 406).

Similarly, a German specialist on intercultural education points out that the hope based on Cummins' theories, that foreign children would be academically successful if they came to Germany at the age of ten or later—ideal from the "threshold hypothesis," since their acquisition of the home language would be essentially complete—and then were instructed in that language in German schools for as long as possible, had been disproved by experience (Pommerin, 1988a, 20).

While for cautious researchers like Kenji Hakuta this remains "a question to which the answer must await future research" (Hakuta, 1986, 100), for many advocates of bilingual education it is an article of faith that research has proved Toukomaa's theory. On the other hand, the concept of "semi-lingualism" itself has been brought into disrepute even among academics who support the Toukomaa/Skutnabb-Kangas theory which ultimately depends upon its accuracy, since use of arguments based on this concept may have "negative consequences . . . for immigrant children both in terms of low self-esteem and decreased expectations from the wider environment." In addition, "by focusing on the linguistic issues, it has diverted attention from the cluster of factors that contribute to immigrant children's poor school achievement which, in addition to linguistic factors, also involves social, cultural, cognitive, and emotional factors" (Hyltenstam & Arnberg, 1988, 496)

Cummins himself continued to argue for the reality of semilingualism, while urging that the term itself be avoided as conveying "a deficit view of minority children" and "deflecting attention from social and educational variables;" explaining that "despite the fact that the construct is, in principle, defensible and follows logically from the acknowledgement that there are individual differences among bilinguals in [first and second language], its use is extremely ill-advised" (Cummins, 1984, 128–129).

Separate development in home language-based programs might itself contribute to linguistic deficiencies, others argue, resulting in unequal access to educational opportunity. After a review of the debate over semilingualism and sheltered home language programs, one scholar suggested that a more useful formulation of the issue might be that

> working-class im/migrant children in programmes with predominant teaching in the mother tongue, little instruction in the majority language and little access to standard-speaking models in the communities, might develop a non-Standard variety of the majority language, so resulting in one more difficulty when they are introduced to [second language] classes (cited by Tosi, 1984, 27–28).

There is reason to doubt that even a sheltered home language program can in fact develop full native-like proficiency in a language that is not otherwise reinforced in the surrounding society and its media. Ironically, a pupil in such a program could end up with a "school knowledge" only of the first language, and insufficient proficiency in the second. While the concept of *semilingualism*, with its heavy emphasis on the necessity of developing mother-tongue skills, has often been a major factor in educational and political arguments for mother-tongue classes" (Hyltenstam & Arnberg, 1988, 497), such classes may in fact result in the very condition they are intended to prevent.

A more cautious formulation of the argument that first language development is important for general school success does not tie it directly to a case that cognitive development can occur only in the mother-tongue, but simply stresses that schools should avoid the loss of precious learning time for children who have not yet developed sufficient proficiency in the language of instruction.

> If the mother tongue is not continuously practiced during the time when [the second language] has not yet reached a satisfactory level, there would be a period in which pupils would lack any adequate medium for knowledge attainment. (Linde & Lofgren, 1988, 134)

If, on the other hand, the child's first language is already well-developed and is used actively in the home, "there is no reason not to start [second language] training when the child begins school." In such a case there is no reason to seek to shelter the child from the language used in the society—a hopeless enterprise in any case. Nor is there a need, some would argue, to make special efforts to develop the first language at that point, since it will develop naturally if it is used. "If the home, so to speak, can guarantee the development of the mother tongue through daily usage, then the school is able to concentrate, as best as it can, on the development of the dominant language (Linde & Lofgren, 1988, 143). The target group for home language development, according to this position, should be those linguistic minority children whose families do not use their language actively. Unfortunately, the opposite generally happens:

> Pupils speaking both Swedish and another language at home need more home language instruction than others in order to remain actively bilingual. But most of the pupils speaking two languages at home have not attended home language instruction in compulsory school (Liljegren & Ullman, 1982, 2).

A rather different argument for a stress upon maintenance, in schools, of the home language of immigrant children is based upon what is presented as their need for ethnic identification as one source of the stability and self-respect which much in a modern society undermines, especially for those at the economic margins. "Under conditions of rapid social change and certain tendencies to anomic social disorganization and alienation, intensification of 'groupism' and the high emotional loading of the status of group membership and identity is one major type of reaction" (Parsons, 1975, 68). This is undoubtedly one of the reasons why, in the United States, "[m]any surveys show that only 10–15 percent of whites . . . fail to answer questions about ethnic background" (Alba, 1990, 16). Lack of attachment to and continued use of the heritage language may be no indication of abandonment of ethnicity, particularly when language has not been "manipulated into ethnic consciousness" to serve a political or separatist agenda. Under such conditions, the majority language may, as Fishman points out, be used to express the identity and values of a minority ethnic group which has largely or entirely abandoned the use of its distinctive language. "This is all the more so when, as in the case of the American ethnic revival, language ideologies and language movements *per se* are almost entirely lacking" (Fishman, 1989, 674).

But this is not to conclude that ethnicity is of overwhelming importance for most Americans. "Insofar as ethnicity has a role [in American society], then, it is increasingly voluntary, dependent on deliberate actions of individuals to maintain activities and relationships that have an ethnic character" (Alba, 1990, 20). Or, as Waters puts it, "ethnicity is not something that influences their lives unless they *want* it to. . . . Ethnicity has become a subjective identity, invoked at will by the individual" (Waters, 1990, 7).

The theory of self-concept in contemporary social psychology is "the notion that the social world is composed of social categories and membership groups, in terms of which the individual must define him- or herself and be defined by others. . . . Commitment is the degree of investment in relationships to others that is premised on a specific identity, and thus the social cost of renouncing it, and salience is the 'probability, for a given person, of a given identity being invoked in a variety of situations'" (Stryker, 1968, quoted by Alba, 1990, 22–23). Some argue that the process of teaching a second and socially dominant language, or a standard dialect of that language, to children who learned to speak in a different manner has the result that they "are made somehow to feel inferior and are thereby turned off from the learning process" (quoted by Crawford, 1992b, 257).

Others question whether self-concept and ethnic identity are really problems for linguistic minority pupils—any more than such concerns trouble every adolescent. It is in fact astonishing how resilient the idea of poor self-concept on the part of minority children is, given that it has been refuted again and again by research. As long ago as 1968, Carter found that Mexican American youth actually rated themselves somewhat higher than did Anglo youth (cited by Brussell, 1968, 32), and similar results have turned up in many subsequent studies. On the basis of research among immigrant pupils—especially Turks, Moroccans, and Surinamers—in the Netherlands, Verkuyten concluded that ethnic identity was only a relatively secondary factor (compared, for example, with physique) in their self-concept: "youth from ethnic minorities are not more burdened than others with tensions related to their self-concept." School achievement was in fact a more significant factor to minority youth than to their Dutch schoolmates, and thus the constant approach to foreign youth on the basis of their ethnic background does an injustice to the richness of the life experience and personal functioning of the youth and can perhaps lead to a rank growth of this identity. In school and in class, foreign youth are first of all pupils who achieve well or poorly (Verkuyten, 1988, 235, 238, 242). Teachers who place emphasis on developing the ethnic identity of linguistic minority pupils, Verkuyten suggested, would be likely to do so at the expense of helping these pupils to develop the academic skills essential to authentic self-respect (Verkuyten, 1988, 248). His conclusions thus parallel those of Maureen Stone, discussed in Chapter 4, and those of Madan Sarup, who argues that "'Black Studies' and the therapeutic teaching approach may have actually increased educational inequity" in the United Kingdom (Sarup, 1986, 101).

Lars Ekstrand, in Sweden, reviewed the literature on psychological problems of immigrants and concluded that they were greatly exaggerated in popular and policy discussions and frequently confused with problems that had more to do with poverty or rural background—or emotional difficulties ante-dating immigration—than with immigration as such (Ekstrand, 1978). More stress should be placed upon finding solutions to issues of employment, housing, and language-learning than to psychologically oriented interventions. This is consistent with the findings of a study of immigrant pupils in Australia, which made it "clear that esteem and identity came with succeeding at what school required and with the possibility of getting a job. Students were less concerned with language as an artefact or symbol of identity" (Kalantzis, Cope, & Slade, 1989, 57).

Bilingual education programs in the United States are increasingly justified not so much for linguistic reasons as on the psychopolitical basis that some years (five to seven are commonly suggested) of instruction primarily through the ancestral language is essential to the self-esteem and subsequent educational success of language minority children. Perhaps the most cited authority on bilingual education is Jim Cummins, who concedes that well-structured programs based exclusively upon the second language of children may be quite effective linguistically, but do not deal with the other causes of the underachievement of minority pupils, including their alleged ambivalence about both languages and need to have their "cultural identity" reinforced (Cummins, 1984a, 156–157). Cummins has been known to urge that instruction primarily through Spanish be provided even to those Hispanic pupils who come to school speaking only English, since "the language spoken by the child in the home is, in itself, essentially irrelevant" (Cummins, 1981); bilingual education is merely part of the changes that are needed through schooling to "counteract the power relations that exist within the broader society" (quoted by Crawford, 1989, 108). A shift of emphasis in the argument for using the ancestral language for school instruction can be traced in the question Cummins raised in a later essay:

> data from both Sweden and the United States suggest that minority students who immigrate relatively late (about ten years of age) often appear to have better academic prospects than students of similar socioeconomic status born in the host country (Cummins, 1984; Skutnabb-Kangas, 1984). *Is this because their L1 cognitive/academic skills on arrival provide a better foundation for L2 cognitive/academic skills acquisition* [the only explanation given earlier], *or alternatively, because they have not experienced devaluation of their identity in the societal institutions, namely schools of the host country?* (Cummins, 1986, 23; emphasis added)

Sometimes this argument is put in an even more extreme form, as when an American education official told a congressional committee that

> When you come to the Indian child, given what seems to be the fact that he cherishes his Indian status to a remarkable extent, and given the fact that his cultural patterns are markedly different from those of the dominant American group, he is not simply cheated out of a language that does not matter internationally any more, he is not just damaged in school: he is almost destroyed. As a matter of fact, historically, that is what we tried to do with them: destroy them" [testimony of Bruce Gaarder at House bilingual education act hearing June 1967, quoted by Coombs, 1971, 10].

According to this line of argument, providing instruction through the home language, without more fundamental changes designed to give a message of empowerment, does not go far enough, since it is not sufficient to merely use the students' home language in bilingual programs, nor is it sufficient to employ members of the minority group in the school only as teachers and support personnel. What is called for is the use of the students' home language and the employment of minority language group members in ways that upgrade their status and power relative to that of English and English-speaking people. This might mean "over-using" the minority language or "over-representing" the minority group in the administrative hierarchy of the school, relative to their predominance in the community at large, in order to offset the inferior social status otherwise associated with the group (Genesee, 1987, 168).

"Relative linguistic and social status" are central to this justification for a primary emphasis upon the home or ancestral language in schooling minority children. "In situations where the home language is denigrated by the community at large, where many teachers . . . are insensitive to their values and traditions, where there does not exist a pressure within the home to encourage literacy and language maintenance," the school should precisely make that language the basis for instruction (Tucker, 1977, 39).

Perhaps the most influential exponent of this view in the formulation of educational policy in the United States was José Cardenas, who testified in several landmark cases that a child's ethnic characteristics should not be considered "handicaps" that lie outside the school's responsibility; a school's unwillingness to adapt to these characteristics by providing a bilingual and "bicultural" program that would overcome the incompatibilities between minority children and the school of the majority should be deemed "discrimination." The judge in the *Otero* case commented drily that "although enlightened educational theory may well demand as much, the Constitution does not" (Rebell & Block, 1982, 167). Legislation enacted in Colorado in 1975, also inspired by the Cardenas theory of incompatibilities, provided that "students from 'culturally different environments,' *whatever the present extent of their English language proficiency*, are entitled to special programming" (Rebell & Block, 1982, 179, emphasis added).

Research support for this policy prescription is notably weak. In the first place, as we have seen, there is no solid evidence that members of linguistic minority groups have low self-esteem, as Arias points out in reviewing the research on Mexican Americans (Arias, 1982, 39–40). And, in the second place, there is no reason to believe that an emphasis upon the heritage language and culture is a sovereign remedy to whatever problems of self-esteem may exist. For example, a study of 270 Puerto Rican children, grades 4–6, in Chicago found that "bilingual students who read only English adequately had significantly more positive self-esteem scores than those who read only Spanish adequately. . . . Students who had participated in a bilingual program reported significantly less positive self-esteem scores than those who had never had this type of experience. . . . The language of the dominant culture appears to be a key factor in the self-concept development of these students" (Peters, 1979). A study of Mexican-American students in California found that those in bilingual programs had lower self-concept (and reading scores) than those in the regular program (Lopez, 1980). Another found that limited-English speaking children matched English-speaking children in self-concept, and concluded that "[w]hile instruction through the native language may provide linguistic and conceptual advantages, these findings called into question one of the most frequently-cited rationales for bilingual education, its positive effects on self-concept" (Seligson, 1979). Similarly, a three-year study in Dade County (Miami) compared two groups of limited-English proficient (LEP) children who were matched for age and social class and randomly assigned to schools using Spanish and schools using English (in a curriculum designed for LEP pupils) as the primary language for instruction.

> The teachers, all of whom are bilingual, rated student attitudes toward learning and toward school in general to be comparable for the two groups. In other words, the children who were being taught in English from the first day of school were apparently not suffering emotional distress or anomie, and those who were taught in Spanish did not have a noticeably higher level of self-pride (Porter, 1990, 72–73).

If linguistic minority pupils do not experience themselves as "between two cultures" (Verkuyten, 1985), the psychological argument for special programs to promote their ancestral language and culture is greatly weakened. Batenburg and De Jong found that foreign pupils in fact were more contented in secondary schools than were their Dutch classmates. The problems that the foreign pupils identified had to do primarily with academic achievement, particularly proficiency in Dutch, not with their "motivation, self-image, or the development of their own (ethnic) identity" (Batenburg & De Jong, 1985, 108).

Glazer has pointed out the lack of evidence of a connection between the improvement of a minority pupil's self-image through an emphasis upon his culture and his academic achievement; Jewish, Armenian, Chinese, and Japanese pupils have done very well in American schools despite the lack of programs emphasizing their cultural heritage (Glazer, 1977, 18–21). Verma and Bagley (1982) have claimed that research has failed to show any differences in level of self-esteem between white, West Indian, Asian, and Cypriot children (cited by Taylor, 1988, 182). More recent "research in different countries finds small or non-existent correlations between different operationalisations of self-concept and educational results" (Verkuyten, 1988, 94; Koot, Tjon-a-Ten, & Uniken Venema, 1985, 102). Such research results seem to have very little discouraging effect upon those who place self-esteem at the center of the objectives of schooling, and argue on that basis for a stress upon ancestral languages. In the United Kingdom,

> Other aims of the [Italian] language classes . . . include strengthening the relationships between the generations and the development of the child's self-confidence. But there appear to be divided views on this. On the one hand, teachers involved in the Mother Tongue and Culture Project (MTCP) claimed that this was an unnecessary aim, for many of the Italian children exhibited natural confidence and had communicative personalities, and one teacher commented that since many of these children of primary school age regarded themselves as English the aim of building up their self-image by teaching them the Italian language was inappropriate. Moreover, Weston (1979) observed that one effect of the attendance of Italian children at voluntary language classes was to make them more aware of the gap between the dialect which they spoke at home with their parents and the Standard Italian of the language classes, evoking feelings of shame rather than enhancing self-confidence (Taylor, 1988, 304).

As Maureen Stone observes mildly, "Programs designed to bolster a minority's self-esteem may well be misjudged when confidence is no longer the basic problem" (Stone, 1985, 126).

Others argue that use of the home language in an elementary school (whatever its merits for other reasons) does not have an identity-affirming value, since identity is not a question that children are dealing with at that age; for elementary pupils, "isn't studying the language and culture of his parents' origins considered, by the child under 11, as one among others of the things that have to be learned [*éléments de connaissance*] about the outside world, without impact upon his own identity?" In adolescence, by contrast, questions of ethnic identity and what that means for a wide range of aspects of personal beliefs, loyalties, and behaviors will arise inevitably for language minority youth. This does not necessarily mean that they will choose to identify with the culture of their parents, or welcome being told, by the school, that it is "their" culture.

It is only the adolescent who can grasp the language of origin, the religious, eating, or dressing practices of his family to affirm an identity as "other", if he feels in conflict with French society, or to adopt, instead, as a challenge to family values, the French practices which are most shocking for his parents if integration [into French society] seems to him most able to form his personality. But isn't it characteristic of the adolescent to adopt values that will allow him to believe himself "different"? (Boulot & Boyzon-Fradet, 1986, 41)

The idea that the problem of language minority youth is that they are, as it is often put in Europe, "sitting between two chairs" was rejected by a young French-Algerian woman in an interview with *Le Monde*. "That business of chairs is a hoax of French sociologists. . . . We live with the only culture which is really ours: that of our neighborhoods. . . . We don't have our ass between two chairs. It's big enough to sit on both of them!" (quoted by Boulot & Boyzon-Fradet 1986, 41).

There is some possibility, indeed, that stress upon maintaining a language minority identity may have a negative effect upon school achievement, at least for some groups. A study in a California high school found that "[a]mong Mexican-descent students [compared with Japanese-American students] . . . there are multiple identities in which symbols, stereotypes, and styles assume great significance. . . . They must choose between doing well in school or being a Chicano. From this perspective, it is not possible or legitimate to participate in both the culture of the dominant group, that is, the school culture, and in the Chicano culture. To cross these cultural boundaries means denying one's identity as a Chicano and is viewed as incompatible with maintaining the integrity of a Chicano identity" (Matute-Bianchi, 1986, 255).

Finally, some would argue that the competition between the cultures represented by the home language and the language of the host society is so unequal that it is wishful thinking to believe that language minority children can be persuaded that their equal dignity and value rests upon ability to speak the language of their grandparents. After all, "can equivalence of cultures exist in a society in which the respective ethnic-cultural groups hold different socio-economic positions?" (Eldering, 1989, 121). There may be many reasons why the child of immigrants might want to know the language of his ancestors—though it seems not to be a high priority with most—but there are easier ways to maintain a sense of identity (Schuricht, 1982, 78–80).

Arguments against Maintaining Minority Languages

Those who oppose efforts, by schools and other public institutions, to maintain the active use of minority languages generally employ two arguments; which is the more urgent may vary. The first has to do with the needs of the host society; the second, with life-opportunities for minority children.

Language can, as we have seen, have a strongly symbolic meaning for an immigrant group seeking to create an ethnic community or a territorial language minority seeking a measure of political autonomy, whether or not it is actually used in an active way (De Vos, 1982, 15). It can also have a strongly symbolic meaning for the majority. In many—perhaps most—cases, a central element in the definition of each of the European nations has been the sense of being a language community; the term "nation" was applied to groups who shared a common language long before it came to mean a territorial entity with a single government. The exceptions, like Belgium and Switzerland (and Canada), prove the point by continuing tensions between subnations defined by language.

The European Union, while awakening in many a sense of European citizenship and decreasing to some extent the significance of the *political* nations of Western Europe, has heightened sensitivity about the rights of its *language* communities to continue a distinct identity. This is further exacerbated by fear that continuing immigration, in the form of asylum-seekers and illegal entrants, will undermine these language communities from within.

Much the same generalized anxiety about a changing population seems to lie behind "English Only" campaigns in the United States (Draper & Jiménez, 1992). The only precedent for the recent wave of "official English" laws in a number of states is the reaction to the heavy immigration that preceded World War I; Nebraska made English its official state language in 1920, and Illinois in 1923 (Crawford, 1992b, 122). The Nebraska law, as the state Supreme Court (which was subsequently reversed by the United States Supreme Court) noted in *Meyer v. Nebraska*, a case involving instruction in German in a Lutheran school, was intended to prevent

> the baneful effects of permitting foreigners, who had taken residence in this country, to rear and educate their children in the language of their native land. The result of that condition was found [by the Legislature] to be inimical to our own safety. To allow the children of foreigners, who had emigrated here, to be taught from early childhood the language of the country of their parents was . . . to educate them

so that they must always think in that language, and, as a consequence, naturally inculcate in them the ideas and sentiments foreign to the best interests of this country (quoted by Crawford, 1992b, 183).

Demand for recognition and promotion of a single national language is related to the perceived role of language in "making citizens." As a Texas teacher put it a generation ago,

> when they [Mexican Americans] get rid of these superstitions, they will be good Americans. The schools help more than anything else. In time, the Latins will think and act like Americans. A lot depends on whether or not we can get them to switch from Spanish to English. When they speak Spanish, they think Mexican. When the day comes that they speak English at home like the rest of us, they will be part of the American way of life. I just don't understand why they are so insistent about using Spanish. They should realize that it's not the American tongue (quoted by Madsen, 1964, 106).

Somewhat ironically, advocates of English-only strategies for the children of immigrants, by positing a direct link between making a transition to primary use of the language of a society and a primary loyalty to that society and its values are in agreement in their fundamental premises with ethnic activists who urge that minority languages be maintained at any cost. Just as language activists assert that "language is a key symbol of human identity and . . . it is a right of all people to *recover*, maintain and develop their languages" (Seminario Internacional, 1986, emphasis added), so advocates of teaching in the majority language stress that

> the process of acquiring a language is never innocent. To learn French is to learn much more than the French language, it is to make one's own [*intégrer*] a strongly-marked relationship with the world, a way of structuring, of constructing reality, it is to use the tools, the methods handed down by a culture, it is also to participate, in a way, even if only by using the language which expresses it, in the future of that culture (Blot, 1978a, 88).

The French government ordered, as long ago as 1851, that "only French shall be used in schools," thus forbidding the practice of using the local *patois*, particularly in Catholic schools (Boyzon-Fradet with Boulot, 1992, 241); this was consistent with the belief that "the Republic has made the school, the school will make the Republic" (see Glenn, 1988b).

Apart from considerations of linguistic nationalism, there are arguments based upon what is understood to be the best interest of the children of immigrants. The desire to teach children a minority language as a means of maintaining the cohesion and identity of the group, it is said, may have negative consequences for the opportunities available to those children. "With the perhaps praise-worthy intention of respecting everyone's identity, a system has been put in place which turns out to be a factor of discrimination more than of integration: foreign-origin children are isolated to receive instruction which others do not and which will not even be taken into account in measuring their academic success" (Voisard & Ducastelle, 1986, 75).

A study of Spanish-speaking first-graders, in 1985, found that "those in bilingual programs receive 25 percent less instruction in the basic skills than do those in all-English classes . . . in order to make time for Spanish courses, these children spent 24 percent less time on oral development in English, 96 percent less on reading in English, and 14 percent less on mathematics" (Benderson, 1986, 11). Data collected by the federal Office for Civil Rights found that prior enrollment in bilingual classes had, for Hispanic pupils, a strong negative relationship with subsequent assignment to classes for gifted pupils (Meier and Stewart, 1991, 170).

Nor is the problem limited to competition for instructional time. Petersen suggests that the policy, in the Swiss canton of Grisons, of providing instruction to children of the Romansh-speaking minority

> has been to aggravate their cultural isolation and to make it considerably more difficult for peasants' sons to advance themselves. The nationalist spokesmen are inclined to view such upward mobility as disastrous; for them, the survival of the group is a cause to which the welfare of the individuals in it must be sacrificed" (Petersen, 1975, 186).

The Dutch Labor Party has expressed some impatience with supplemental school programs to maintain the language and culture of immigrants, which it long supported. The party now believes that more emphasis must be put on teaching Dutch: "Don't overburden the pupil with yet another language, like Standard Arabic, when Berber is spoken in his home. Try to emphasize Dutch as much as possible" (Vliet, 1991, 90). A similar urgency is sometimes heard from advocates for minority children in the United States; it is pointed out that "the effectiveness of bilingual-bicultural programs in improving overall academic achievement of Chicanos is much in dispute. By comparison, there is hardly any question that schools can effectively teach Chinese or Mexican-

American children how to speak English" (Rebell & Block, 1982, 153). [There *is* a question whether, having learned to speak English, these children will go on to achieve as well academically as they would have if they had been taught by an effective bilingual method; see Chapter 8.]

It is difficult to see how minority groups can maintain a distinctive language as their primary means of communication over several generations without paying a high price in isolation from the societal mainstream and the opportunities that it offers. A distinctive culture, adapted as necessary to the language and mores of the host society, is less demanding than is a minority language to keep in good working order within the family and ethnic religious and other organizations, whatever adjustments must be made to the culture of the wider society in the public domain.

> The persistence of ethnic identity and affiliation may be satisfying, but in continuing this affiliation members may lack the social knowledge required for mobility into positions controlled by the dominant group. . . . The time and effort required to learn and maintain ethnic languages and customs could inhibit the acquisition of skills and knowledge which, while in absolute terms no better than ethnically valued ones, are nevertheless more useful in securing jobs, promotion, influence and the like (Birrell, 1978, quoted by Bullivant, 1981, 238).

Or, as Steinberg puts it bluntly, "the literature of the ethnic pluralists devotes remarkably little space to the problem of inequality" (Steinberg, 1982, 255).

Lisa Delpit is one of the black educators who argue that to give minority children an effective command of the language and style of the dominant majority is not to disrespect their own forms of speech, but is precisely to respect *them* and their potential to be successful in the mainstream. Maureen Stone is another; she argues that "it is the job of the school to enable children to function with ease in the standard language. By the same token it is the job of the home, family and community to keep the dialect alive" (M. Stone, 1981, 111). The well-intentioned introduction, into public schools serving poor black children, of "dialect readers" was seen by many black educators as "dooming black children to a permanent outsider caste (Delpit, 1995, 29). They agree with Italian Marxist Antonio Gramsci, that

> without the mastery of the common standard version of a national language, one is inevitably destined to function only at the periphery of national life, and, especially, outside its national and political mainstream (quoted in Tosi, 1984, 167).

Under some circumstances, it appears that the maintenance of an ethnic group language, when that is promoted by social conditions or by public policy, tends to support the continued separateness—even the segregation—of the group that speaks it, in a way that is harmful to the general interest, as well as to that of individuals in the ethnic group. It is undoubtedly for this reason that "despite much propaganda, we do *not* have unequivocal evidence of widespread support for active policies of bilingual education (in its maintenance form) and cultural pluralism. Nor do we have such evidence from ethnic groups themselves" (Edwards, 1981, 37). This is true even in the United States, where bilingual education has been for several decades the touchstone issue for Hispanic activists.

> Elected Hispanic officials surveyed in 1983 supported bilingual programs in general but with some questions about the programs' effectiveness. . . . Half said that all regular school classes should be taught in English with Spanish used only for "supplementary courses". . . . Ninety-seven percent of the leaders were opposed to teaching all courses in Spanish, and few saw language as the basic cause of either dropouts or youth unemployment. The leaders tended to favor some kind of an effort to retain Spanish in other ways but not as an educational panacea or a substitute for learning English (Orfield, 1986, 11).

Immigrant parents are especially likely to question language-maintenance efforts in schools if they believe there is any chance this will limit the acquisition, by their children, of the majority language that they, themselves, may be keenly aware they cannot teach them well. "Significantly, much of the pressure for learning English comes from Hispanic parents" (Benderson, 1986, 9). Mexican-American parents surveyed by the Educational Testing Service in 1987 supported bilingual education and said it was important that their children speak Spanish well, but rejected instruction in Spanish nearly four to one if it would take away from learning English. Cuban Americans were even more adamantly opposed to cutting into the time available for teaching English (Baratz-Snowden et al., 1988b). Paulston reported that all nine of the Turkish language teachers in a school she visited while conducting her study of language-maintenance efforts in Sweden had chosen to put their own children in regular Swedish classes (Paulston, 1982, 54). Spolsky mentions an Indian pueblo where bilingual education was opposed "because it might bring the school into areas best left to the home and the community," and other cases in which language minority groups see it as threatening the access of their children to the economic rewards associated with proficiency in the majority language (Spolsky, 1978a, 277).

Maintenance of their home language is thus not always a primary concern in the demands made by immigrant parents upon official education systems, despite the painful language gap that may exist between the immigrant generations. Proposals to teach the Indonesian language (*bahasa Indonesia*) to Moluccan refugee children in the Netherlands, when there seemed a good prospect that they would be returning home, was strongly resisted by parents who wanted to ensure that their children could take full advantage of Dutch education (Schumacher, 1981, 95). In the United States, Asian parents are much more likely than Hispanic parents to favor teaching their children "only in English," and to believe that instruction through the home language would interfere with learning English (Skerry, 1993, 289). Parents recognize that their children need to acquire proficiency in the language of the society, and when instruction through the home language becomes the primary focus, that is usually because of the involvement of progressive intellectuals and educators in formulating the agenda of the parents. Some critics of bilingual education ask, "Are we paying more heed to the demands of the group than to the rights of individuals in the matter of ethnic identification and enforced group loyalty, both elements of intergenerational tensions in immigrant families?" (Porter, 1990, 159).

The irony of this debate is that even multiyear separate bilingual education programs of the sort common in the United States do not in most cases preserve the active use of the minority language, unless that use is strongly reinforced by the social environment in which the pupil and her family live. Fishman charges that the federal Bilingual Education Act of 1967 "was primarily an act for the Anglification of non-English speakers and not an act for *Bilingualism*" (Fishman, 1989, 405). The danger associated with bilingual programs of inadequate quality is not that they will reinforce pupils in a minority language which they are almost invariably in the process of abandoning, but that they will prepare them inadequately to function with a high degree of proficiency in the majority language. In other words, the danger is that the pupils will come out badly educated, not that they will be well-educated in a minority language; would that they were!

Louis Porcher noted, several decades ago, that the ideological commitments of the French Left to "Third-Worldism" had led to efforts to address the needs of the children of immigrants as though they had nothing in common with French children from poor families, efforts that stressed institutional and structural remedies, linguistic over conceptual considerations, at the expense of attention to pedagogical strategies in the classroom. He continues,

All of a sudden, with the generous intention of preserving the cultural identity of the foreign child, he is thrown involuntarily into a world different from that of his French peer: thus objectively, though without anyone noticing it, he is cut off from the world in which he lives here and now (Porcher, 1978a, 13–14).

It should be noted that proficiency in a language other than that of the school is by no means *of itself* a barrier to success in school, and may indeed be associated (whether as cause or effect) with academic achievement, *provided that* the pupil is also proficient in the school language. A study conducted by the Educational Testing Service in conjunction with the National Assessment of Educational Progress concluded that "whether or not one comes from a home where a second language [that is, other than English] is frequently spoken is not the critical issue, but rather the central question is whether or not one is competent in English" (Baratz-Snowden et al., 1988a, iii). Among Indochinese refugee youth, "English proficiency was the key sociocultural variable which was predictive of psycho-social adjustment" (Bureau for Refugee Programs, 1987, 3).

Such findings have nothing surprising about them, of course; speaking the language of the host society well is fundamental to success and positive adjustment. The hesitation that many immigrant parents feel about school policies that promote retention of their home languages has to do, not with a rejection of those languages, but with concern about diversion of energy and time from the majority language and from academic subject-matter, and with isolation of their children in a separate instructional track.

MEASURES TO MAINTAIN MINORITY LANGUAGES

Language maintenance efforts can be sponsored by homeland governments, organized and supported by the ethnic communities themselves, or provided by the regular educational systems. Some homeland governments seek to maintain their influence over their citizens working in other countries—even children born in those countries and unlikely ever to return—by sending teachers and sponsoring cultural programs. Ethnic groups themselves have frequently chosen to maintain aspects of their language and culture through their own efforts, whether part-time programs or full-time alternative schools. In this way, they seek to reconcile what could otherwise be competing goals: for language-minority groups, "state schools provide avenues for desired economic assimilation while supplementary schools are agents for preserving cultural identity" (McLean, 1985, 329). In other cases, education authorities decide to bring minority language teaching under their direct control by sponsoring it themselves.

Homeland-Sponsored Language Programs

The Chinese immigrants to America in the late nineteenth century were assisted by the Imperial Government, otherwise so unable to relieve their misery and exploitation, to operate part-time language schools for their children (Ogbu & Matute-Bianchi, 1986, 107); in general, however, such efforts in the United States have been organized by the immigrants themselves, through their churches and mutual-aid associations. The pattern has been very different in Europe, where migrant workers and their families tended to be considered citizens abroad rather than permanent emigrants.

When a large number of Polish mineworkers were imported to Belgium, in the 1920s, Polish schools were established with teachers from Poland. The buildings were provided by the mine companies, but the teachers were paid by the Polish government and followed the Polish elementary school curriculum. "The idea of going back was always alive for our parents," one of the former pupils said decades later, "they were always sitting on their suitcases" (Wulf & Janssen, 1992, 442).

The Polish schools fell victim to the perennial Belgian conflict over language policy. The language law of 1932 provided that instruction could be provided only through the official language of the area in which the school was located, whatever was the language of the parents. Although aimed primarily at French-language schools in Dutch-speaking areas, the effect was to outlaw Polish-medium schools as well. Polish lessons could still be provided for a couple of hours a week, but Polish could not be the language of instruction (Wulf & Janssen, 1992, 442). Soon the children of Polish immigrants were becoming Belgians.

During the heavy labor migration to Western Europe of the 1950s and 1960s, the homelands in some cases sent teachers or otherwise sponsored programs to provide supplemental instruction in their languages to the children of citizens who were expected to return with their savings of hard currency in two or three years. In 1970 the Council of Europe adopted a resolution calling upon authorities in countries with guestworkers to take full responsibility for the education of the children of migrant workers. This was followed in July 1977 by a Directive with theoretically binding authority. Article 3 requires that

> Member States shall, in accordance with their national circumstances
> and legal systems [this qualifying language was added to provide a

loophole!], and in cooperation with States of origin, take appropriate measures to promote, in coordination with normal education, teaching of the mother tongue and culture of the country of origin (in Boos-Nunning & Henscheid, 1986, 11).

The loophole was added at the insistence of several members, including Great Britain, which insisted that local control of education made it impossible to impose a single model upon all schools; in the 1976 draft, home language provision had been mandatory.

In 1974, Turkish authorities selected some 250 teachers to send to West Germany to teach supplemental courses to 11,600 immigrant pupils (Abadan-Unat, 1975, 315). There were 351 Turkish and 172 Moroccan teachers in the Netherlands by 1982 (Eldering, 1986a, 183). France also entered into a series of agreements with other countries to provide teachers for supplemental classes at the secondary level; there were an estimated 1,390 such teachers in 1989, serving about 115,660 pupils (Lapeyronnie, 1993, 167; see Chapter 7).

The presence of foreign teachers, offering lessons in the native language and culture of immigrant students, was intended to maintain contact with the unknown homeland as well as communication between the immigrant generations. In itself, however, it raised serious pedagogical questions. Should these teachers, for example, stress the "official culture" of the homeland, or the customs of the (often rural) milieu from which the parents came, or should they deal with the new cultural forms coming into existence in the immigrant situation? Instruction could end up presenting a culture that no longer really existed, as modernization brought change in Anatolia and the Moroccan Riff, in Calabria and Thrace. On the other hand, those outmoded customs and values were to some extent what parents clung to in their exile, and desired to see taught to their children.

And did maintaining contact with the homeland mean serving the agenda of its government? Some critics felt that it might suit the foreign government that paid the teachers to stress an essentially irrelevant version of the native culture, to foster conservative values and a sense of alienation from the situation in Western Europe. In Belgium as in West Germany, the liberal or radical educated Turks working in social agencies and public schools tended to be hostile toward not only the religiously conservative Koran schools but also toward the after-school programs sponsored by their own government. They charged that programs in Turkish language and culture "involved a barely-concealed form of propaganda and political control, based on a semi-fascist ideology," while the function of the Koran schools was "to furnish to capitalism an ignorant, isolated and inoffensive labor force, by diverting its potential energy from the struggle between exploiters and the exploited" (Karaman, 1980, 262).

Teachers recruited by the Turkish or the Italian government who looked upon their work abroad as a temporary interlude in a career at home might have difficulty relating to the special circumstances of pupils growing up in an immigrant situation, even if in theory those children would eventually return to a "home" they scarcely knew; they were not well-served by programs which assumed that they had the same needs or the same capabilities as schoolchildren in the homeland. "Turkish children in the Netherlands are growing up in a migrant culture. . . . Sometimes teachers try to teach them about . . . things that were alive in Turkey fifty years ago but don't exist any more. Culture is not static" (Buvelot, 1986, viii).

There has also been controversy over whether accepting the assistance of Moroccan authorities in recruiting home language teachers would result in their being agents of an authoritarian government and in conflict with the political view of many Moroccans abroad (Schumacher 1981, 62, 112). Even though the local Dutch authorities made the final selection, the nature of Moroccan society is such, according to the Dutch education attaché in Rabat, that teachers found it difficult to conceive of themselves as simply individuals taking a job rather than as agents of their government (*Samenwijs*, 6, 7, March 1986).

The role of foreign governments in controlling part of the socialization of children who are living and may always live in another country is often questioned in West Germany, as well. Some claim that "the idea was not only to reduce the cultural "alienation" of foreign youths; the government also wanted to strengthen their willingness to return home (Esser & Korte, 1985, 183), while others believe that, as a Turkish teacher told me, "our government wants us to continue to be Turks . . . in Germany!" The remittances of labor migrants have been a mainstay of several economies around the Mediterranean, and those economies would have no way to reabsorb those migrants; thus their continuing loyalty—and absence—were both important.

A common complaint is that

> the instructional work in home language classes that are supported and organized by the consulates can be in contradiction with the German educational system, indeed to the political basis of the German Constitution, without the German authorities being aware of or having any control over it. There must be assurances that home language and regular education will not conflict (quoted in Rixius & Thurmann, 1987, 52).

Schoolbooks available in Turkish and other languages may be largely irrelevant to the experience of foreign children living in the immigration situation, and too difficult as well for pupils whose proficiency in their home language is not developed to their age equivalency. For many pupils, in fact, the official language of the country of origin—in which the home language instruction is given—may not be spoken in their home. Kurds and Assyrians from Turkey, in particular, may have emigrated in part because their groups and their languages were under pressure from the national government (Meyer-Ingwersen, 1988).

The political and social views expressed in such materials may also conflict with those taught in the schools of the host society. There have been frequent calls for the development of materials in the home languages that are directly relevant to the host society where the children live and have a future. The Turkish government, took the position that it should develop and print all books that deal with Turkish language and culture and provide them at cost to German authorities (Dericioglu & Orfali, 1982, 44).

The Italian government has, since 1971, employed teachers "to provide children [of] Italian origin all over the world with the opportunity to maintain the Italian language and culture," with help, in Northern Europe, from the social fund of the European Community, in an effort to preserve the connection of the families of labor migrants with their homeland. Classes have to an increasing extent been organized in cooperation with the regular schools (Kroon, 1990, 61). The instruction seems to have been at least partially successful in limiting loss of the first language as well as in teaching the standard language of the homeland with which many children of immigrants have not previously been familiar. In Taylor's words,

> The very existence of such schools with the backing of government and church support appears to have reinforced through community pressure any personal inclination Italian adults may have had to ensure that their children developed skills in Standard Italian in addition to oral skills in the parents' dialect (Taylor, 1988, 244).

There are concerns that this may lead to undesirable consequences, at least with respect to those immigrants who are settling down as ethnic minority groups. Sometimes, indeed, the homeland governments discourage efforts organized by the immigrant communities themselves, since these are less readily controlled (McLean, 1985, 332).

It may be that supplemental programs, like those maintained for many years by the Chinese, Jewish, and Greek communities in the United States, are the only satisfactory alternatives for language minority parents who wish to send their children to integrated schools instructing through the majority language but also to expose them in a systematic way to their linguistic and cultural heritage. Home language instruction outside of the setting of a public school is often associated with the transmission of religious beliefs and traditions. In Britain,

> classes in, for example, mosques and gurdwaras, the earlier established Polish Saturday schools, and Welsh language Sunday schools, often associated language teaching with religious instruction . . . the growth of mother tongue teaching was related in part to parents' wishes to keep open the verbal channels of communication between the generations, partly to their wish to combat some of the Western European secular values promoted by [public] schools (Linguistic Minorities Project, 1985, 287).

As we will see below, the efforts of official educational systems to include among their goals the maintenance of minority languages and cultures have been plagued with controversy and with practical difficulties. Some of these difficulties are avoided when the function is carried out by community-based supplemental schools, which children attend by the choice of their parents, providing instruction that

> cannot be taken over easily by state schools when the degree of demand for culture maintenance varies so considerably within each ethnic group, and when different members of the same cultural group expect different kinds of mother culture maintenance. This can be seen in the variations in character and aims between supplementary schools of the same cultural group (McLean, 1985, 333).

Glazer makes the same point:

> In any group there will be division: there will be assimilationists, those who demand linguistic competence, those who want only maintenance of cultural attachment, those who insist on full education in language and culture. It is hard to see how school districts operating under government regulations will satisfy such a variety

of interests. Purely voluntary educational activities, conducted in private schools under only limited public authority, might respond to this variety of needs. In the case of Jewish education, for example, we have seen schools that are religious and secular, Orthodox (of several varieties), Conservative, and Reform, all-day, afternoon, and Sunday, variously emphasizing Hebrew, Yiddish, or English, reflecting a history of political tendencies including Zionism, diaspora nationalism, territorialism, anarchism, socialism, and communism. One wonders, after this history, what kind of bilingual-bicultural education established under public auspices and common central rules can possibly satisfy or be relevant to—to take one example—the children of Hebrew-speaking Israeli immigrants who are now coming to this country in substantial numbers. Or, to take another recent immigrant group, those from India and Pakistan; they speak a dozen languages, are in religion divided among Moslems, Hindus, Sikhs, Jains, and others, and reflect a variety of cultures. Will it now be up to school districts in which their numbers are substantial to provide a program? And even though their parents probably insist their education be in English, fully and completely? (Glazer, 1983, 140–141)

Lambert and Taylor found that white American parents not strongly identified with an ethnic minority group were supportive of the use, by more recent immigrants, of their original languages for community celebrations, for religious services, and in their families. They approved of the maintenance of these languages through community-run classes, but they did not support the use of minority languages in public schools.

It suggests to us that a compromise is expected from ethnic newcomers: keep your culture alive, but do so within ethnic boundaries; our system has many ethnic heritages to consider and public institutions, like the school system, are "common grounds" where a common language and a common way of life become preeminent (Lambert & Taylor, 1990, 111).

The most common form of home-language support has long been that provided by community based organizations, especially those for which minority-language maintenance is in some way associated with participation in the religious community, both socially and ritually. Jewish and Greek immigrants to the United States in the early twentieth century did not expect the public schools to teach their children the necessary amount of Hebrew or Greek to take part in worship and study of their religious heritage, but entrusted that (in most cases) to after-school or weekend programs; those who wanted a more intensive exposure to their language, culture and religion paid for their children to attend full-time ethnic nonpublic schools, in some cases extending through higher education. For example, in the early 1960s there were some 6,500 pupils in weekend Ukrainian programs in the United States, and about 8,500 pupils in Ukrainian parochial schools—where the language was no longer a required subject (Frost, 1970, 236). Similarly, many Indian immigrants to the United Kingdom brought with them an experience in East Africa of language maintenance through community-run schools "alongside the mainstream English-medium schooling which many of them experienced in those countries" and continued that tradition in their new home (Linguistic Minorities Project, 1985, 48).

Although the idea that the common public school should uphold universalistic values on behalf of national unity has a special resonance in France, there have been concerns expressed in other countries as well about whether it is consistent with this mission for public schooling to seek to accommodate the diversity of cultural and linguistic expression that language minority pupils bring with them to school. Some believe that supplemental schools sponsored by ethnic minority communities should be encouraged by public policy, rather than perceived as a threat, because they can more appropriately respond to the diversity of parental goals for education than could the public common school. After all, "state schools could not accommodate easily the desire of parents in many ethnic groups to choose between the different kinds of mother culture teaching that are at present available [in supplemental schools that do not pretend to cater to all interests]" (McLean, 1985, 343).

Canada, like the United States, has always faced the challenge of integrating immigrants into the national life, and thus of determining how to respond to their linguistic and cultural diversity. Historically, Canadian educational policy has been as assimilationist toward immigrants as that in the United States, but in recent years an effort has been made to find a place for the immigrant cultures and languages in the Canadian "mosaic." Public funds are made available for the maintenance of heritage languages—those spoken by immigrant as well as by indigenous language minority groups—either within public school programs or through programs sponsored by community organizations. This stance toward minority languages contrasts with the United States, where bilingual education is justified in policy debates almost exclusively as an effective way to promote the transition to successful academic work in English.

Community-based home-language programs may be operated in co-operation with schools and even, as in Canada, supported with public funding. The Multiculturalism Act of 1988 directed all federal government institutions to make use of the language skills of all of the peoples of Canada, and $200 million was committed over five years for heritage language teaching and related activities (Edwards & Redfern, 1992, 12). Despite such support, these programs may remain primarily an "alternative space" for ethnic minority children and youth, a place to socialize with others of the same ethnicity, or—for parents—as a setting within which alternative and preferred values prevail. Chinese community language schools in the United States may offer classes in calligraphy, brush painting, Chinese crafts, folk dancing, and martial arts; "in the face of massive shift to English, parents would be willing to give up insistence on functional proficiency in the Chinese language in order to preserve the children's interest and pride in being Chinese" (S. Wong, 1988, 216).

Even without being as oppositional as some of the part-time Koran schools in Western Europe, community-based programs occupy a distinctive role and one that may be central to the group-preservation strategies of an immigrant community. Whether to ask for home-language classes within the regular school program or in a community setting has divided immigrant parents in some cases; the former implies an official recognition which some find desirable, while the latter provides a setting for the community activity which others seek—and ensures that no time will be lost from regular lessons in school (Fase, 1987, 19).

Concerns have frequently been expressed, in Western Europe, about the presumed ill effects, both on language learning and on social adjustment, of full-time and part-time schools operated by ethnic minority communities. The most intense concern has been expressed about afterschool Koran schools where Muslim children are allegedly subjected to severe punishments and mindnumbing memorization of scripture verses in a Classical Arabic of which they understand little. Teachers complain that children in their classes come to school exhausted and without home assignments completed because of these programs, and sometimes urge parents not to send their children; home language teachers in regular schools are sometimes especially hostile toward these community-based rivals (Triesscheijn, 1985, 94). This inadvertently reinforces the common perception, among parents and ethnic leaders, that teachers wish Muslim children to apostatize from Islam.

Authorities have responded in two ways to the perception that community-based programs to maintain ethnic languages and cultures are in some respect academically harmful or socially alienating for the children of immigrants. Often they have sought to offer such programs, either at public expenses or at that of the governments of the homelands of immigrants, under the auspices and thus the control of schools. (School-sponsored language and culture programs will be discussed in the next section.) In other cases, authorities have worked with ethnic community organizations to raise the quality of their educational programs. For example, authorities in the London Borough of Haringey set up a center for bilingualism with fifteen teachers, "to serve both voluntary and mainstream sectors for in-service training and resources" (Taylor, 1988, 45). As early as 1960, it was reported that

> the Greek Orthodox Church classes in nine areas of London were attended by about 600 pupils, and that a further 300 pupils throughout London studied in classes run by the Greek Parents' Association. . . . In 1980 . . . 2,866 pupils attended 23 Greek mother-tongue schools and 1,306 pupils attended 11 Turkish mother-tongue schools. . . . These represented in 1981 just over two-thirds of all the Greek-speaking pupils and just under a third of all Turkish-speaking pupils in ILEA schools (Taylor, 1988, 86).

Ensuring that these "mother-tongue" part-time schools were usefully supplemental to and not in tension with the work of regular schools seemed an important objective, especially in light of the strong disinclination in the United Kingdom to separate language minority children within the school program, even for part-time instruction in their home language and culture. Thus,

> Georgiou (1983) whilst suggesting that the provision of Greek in the school curriculum might assist the integration of Greek Cypriot pupils, nevertheless was of the opinion that children attending such classes might feel singled out and might miss some other curricular subject. She suggested that Greek Cypriot parents might still prefer to send their children to an extra-curricular Greek school in order that they should receive tuition not only in language, but also have the opportunity to learn to appreciate Greek and Cypriot culture (Taylor, 1988, 104).

Although community-sponsored language programs are very common—indeed, almost a universal phenomenon among immigrant groups—

they are seldom successful in maintaining a language for long. Afterschool programs sponsored by the Vietnamese refugee associations in California, for example, have been unable to maintain student interest or to stimulate their active use of the language (Chung, 1988). Efforts by American Indian activists to promote the use of their tribal languages—though seldom as utopian as the proposal to revive the Miluk language of Oregon through tape recordings made in the 1930s of the last living speakers (Crawford, 1995, 29)—seem unlikely to succeed beyond the mastery of a few phrases. An especially widespread effort has been that of the hundreds of Portuguese associations in France, but even in that case it appears that less than one immigrant family in three has participated, and it is French language and cultural elements that are most attractive to the younger generation (Cordeiro, 1989). Almost invariably, over time the emphasis of community programs shifts from language teaching to social and recreational activities that seek to overcome the reluctance of children and youth to participate.

Minority Language Programs in Mainstream Schools

Several countries have chosen to provide supplemental instruction in the languages of immigrant minority groups as part of their regular school programs. For example, Swedish schools were providing supplemental home-language instruction in 52 languages to more than 47,000 pupils in 1979, with teachers recruited, paid, and supervised by local education authorities (Kerr, 1984, 184). Bringing such instruction under the sponsorship and thus the control of education authorities has been perceived as a way of avoiding dangers associated with "wildcat" community-based programs that may overburden children and contribute to segregation, and to programs sponsored by other countries that may promote undesirably conservative political agendas. In some cases, indeed, the home language teachers employed by regular schools use the opportunity to promote their own, more liberal, political agendas, earning the mistrust of minority parents (Triesscheijn, 1987a, 169).

To take examples from opposite sides of the globe, the Norwegian government stated as its policy, in 1979–80, to provide to immigrant pupils "opportunities to maintain their own language, religion, culture, etc., while at the same time providing them with opportunities for instruction in Norwegian and Norwegian social conditions" (quoted in Hemmingsen, 1988, 65), while that of New South Wales, in Australia, stressed that

the use of English is essential for full participation in the life of the nation. All children must therefore be assisted to become fluent in all aspects of English. . . . Nevertheless, for many people in Australia, the language and culture of their ethnic background play a significant role in their communal life. . . . Therefore, the teaching of community languages and cultures both for native and non-native speakers will be supported and encouraged in our schools (New South Wales Department of Education, 1983, 1–2).

Programs of supplemental home language instruction were established initially, in most cases, to keep open the possibility that guestworkers and their families could return to their homelands and fit in without difficulty to its society and educational system. While this has been abandoned as a policy goal in the Netherlands—and was never a goal in Sweden—it continued to be an important consideration in West Germany as recently as the report of a government commission in 1983 (Mahler, 1983, 199). Home language instruction in schools is now most often justified in terms of the supposed cultural pluralism of society.

In the United States, by contrast, minority language maintenance has never been advanced as an official goal of bilingual programs. As a federal official put it in 1974, "the cultural pluralism of American society is one of its greatest assets, but such pluralism is a private matter of local choice, and not a proper responsibility of the federal government." Thus the goal of bilingual programs was to help children "to gain competency in English so that they may enjoy equal educational opportunity—and not to require cultural pluralism" (Crawford, 1989, 38).

What evidence is there about whether language minority parents *themselves* want their home languages to be maintained by the formal educational system? There is no simple answer to this question; not only do individuals within ethnic groups differ, but the groups themselves in each host society may differ both in their expressed desires and in their actual practices. For example, a majority of the parents of a particular group may tell researchers that they want their heritage language maintained and taught, and yet fail to use it themselves with their children in a consistent way, as we have seen. Or considerations may prevail which have little to do with language maintenance as such:

the Swann Committee reported that . . . Cypriot youngsters . . . were very much against mainstream provision. . . . It has also been suggested that Greek-speaking pupils tend to see community-run schools as places where they socialize as much as places for learning Greek (Taylor, 1988, 105).

Home-language programs within regular schools have an ambiguous resonance, and inevitably raise policy questions. It is one thing for an ethnic community to seek to segregate itself to preserve valued elements of distinctiveness, but quite another for school authorities to promote distinctions among their pupils based upon ethnicity. Should the function of home-language programs be primarily the development of academic competence in a useful language, or should it be primarily cultural, even psychological, as in claims about the need to develop self-esteem?

There are some cases, though not so many as one might anticipate, in which offering supplemental or enrichment language programs in a language spoken by a minority population is a means of attracting pupils under conditions of competition for enrollment. The declining birthrate in Western Europe and the United States in recent decades, together with the provisions in most democracies for some form of parental choice of schools (Glenn, 1989b), has led some schools to seek to improve their competitive position through offering the opportunity to maintain a minority language.

In Brussels, for example, some Dutch-language schools have sought to bolster their enrollment through competing with French-language schools for the children of the city's large immigrant population. The natural inclination of Italian or Moroccan parents is to enroll their children in schools that employ French as the language of instruction; some Dutch schools provide half-time instruction through Italian, Arabic, or other languages to attract these children (Leman, 1990, 13).

Dutch-speaking schools in Brussels experience the presence of an increasing group of children who do not speak Dutch as a threat to their Flemish character. Indeed we see that during recess and moments of free play in the kindergarten Dutch is no longer used as the principal language of communication. . . . The school has to make a choice: either nothing is done and very soon the school becomes a melting pot just like home is to many children or the school tries to organise its language situation in a more structured way (Smedt, 1985b, 92). What is unique in Brussels—and in Montreal—is that the concern expressed by policymakers is not about the continuing use of the languages of immigrants, but about the possibility that they will adopt the *other* official language of the host society: not that they will fail to be assimilated, but that they will assimilate to the wrong camp. Although French is a required subject in Dutch-language schools in Brussels starting in the third grade, its use at preschool level by immigrant children is seen as a problem to be overcome through vigorous replacement by Dutch (Smedt, 1985c). The situation is parallel to that of immigrant children in Quebec who were enrolling—until forbidden by law in 1974—in

English-language rather than French-language schools, and thus threatening to throw their weight on the wrong side of a delicate political and linguistic balance (see Chapter 3).

The Foyer is a private social agency in Brussels that seeks to meet the adjustment needs of migrant workers and their families. One of its programs (started in 1981) involves working with kindergarten and primary school classes in Dutch-language schools to provide native-language support that is integral to the instructional program rather than a supplemental enrichment. In two of the project schools, the majority of students (56 and 69 percent) were from immigrant families and a substantial proportion (18 and 14 percent) from French-speaking Belgian families, so that children from Dutch-speaking families were in a distinct minority (Smeekens, 1985, 56). The hope was that foreign children (many of whom speak French with their parents) could be weaned away from a threatened identification with the French-speaking community by a stress, in the context of Dutch schooling, on their native language (Coppens 1985); of course, the Foyer believed also that using the native language would be educationally beneficial. The "Frenchifying" of Brussels might be to some extent retarded by preventing at least some immigrants from joining the Walloon camp through offering them an attractive incentive; better that immigrants be reinforced in their ethnic identity as a minority within the Dutch-speaking community than that they be assimilated within the French-speaking community. After all,

> language is one of the boundary markers for these parents . . . in some cases, parents are aware that their own knowledge of Italian (standard or dialect) is not adequate for them to be able to mark the boundary themselves, or pass on that ability to their children. The school is seen as a source of that ability, as a means of ensuring that their children can symbolize their Italian identity in language (Byram 1990a, 85).

The Foyer project has reached out vigorously to recruit students who in some cases were attending French-language schools, to the resentment of the latter. A number of Turkish families who already patronized French schools were persuaded to enroll their children in the Foyer program: "The fact that the project runs in a Flemish school plays an ambiguous part. As an alternative to the French schools and to avoid a preponderance of Moroccan children Turkish parents see a Flemish school as a positive change. But they do not attach, initially at least, too much importance to the Dutch language" (Smedt, 1985d). It was primarily the possibility of instruction in

Turkish language and culture (and home visits by the Foyer's Turkish teacher) that persuaded most of them to entrust their children to this project, even when the older siblings were attending French-language schools.

In contrast with most bilingual programs in the United States, the Foyer model and other European programs for Moroccan and other immigrant children are concerned with what immigrant parents *want* rather than with what linguistic theorists believe is good for their children. Moroccan children of Berber ancestry are not taught through the language of their home (either Berber or Moroccan Arabic), but through Standard Arabic, the language which their parents want them to learn for religious and cultural purposes. This has created its own problems, since it would take years to develop the children's proficiency in Standard Arabic to a sufficient degree that it could be used as the medium for instruction; thus it is taught as an enrichment language, while instruction goes forward in Dutch. Similarly, Berber-speaking children in the Netherlands are a challenge to theories that using the "home language" is cognitively advantageous, since it is simply impractical (as well as contrary to the wishes of parents) to find a sufficient number of trained teachers of the various Berber dialects to match with pupils who speak those dialects at home (Eldering, 1983b, 20).

By contrast, advocates for bilingual programs in the United States tend to insist upon using the language of the home as the first medium for reading, whether or not it is a language in which a substantial literature exists and without regard for whether it is likely to be useful in later life. In Massachusetts, for example, Cape Verdean Kriolu is used for instruction in bilingual programs, even though it is never used in schools in Cape Verde and

> there is no written Kriolu, no alphabet, and so there are no Kriolu books. With no written language, sending notes home to parents . . . becomes problematic. Additionally, there are many Kriolu dialects, and teachers often must translate from one to the other for certain children in their class. . . . Massachusetts is thought to be the only place in the world to have Kriolu classrooms from kindergarten through high school.

In Boston alone, there are 750 pupils and 40 teachers in the Cape Verdean program, including classes at two of the city's high schools. The Cape Verdean government has asked for Massachusetts assistance in developing a standard written form of the language. On the other hand, a Cape Verdean parent in Boston was quoted as complaining that the school "sent me a note apparently to tell me something. I never understood what it was trying to say. I called to say that if the intent of the letter is to communicate, it would be better in Portuguese" (Jong, Cheryl de, 1995, A94).

Parents from the Indian subcontinent in the United Kingdom tend to speak local rural vernaculars, but to want their children to be taught a standard form of Urdu or Panjabi in school (Kroon, 1990, 11). Similarly, Italian immigrants tend to talk regional dialects, though they may understand standard Italian as a result of schooling in Italy, but "many second generation persons who speak a dialect fluently say that their knowledge of standard Italian is so insufficient that they cannot even understand it" (Mizrahi, 1970, 139). Their parents may wish their children to be taught standard Italian in school, just as they would be in Italy, despite the inclination of educators who have absorbed current thinking about bilingual education to seek to use dialect because it is the "mother tongue" of the children.

> It looks as if there is a fundamental difference between 'white liberals' who support the inclusion of the actual languages or varieties used by families as part of the content of mother tongue teaching, and, on the other hand, parents, teachers and official representatives of the countries of origin, who tend to favour a narrower focus on the standard languages (Reich & Reid, 1992, 152–153).

Troubling questions arise when the minority language is used in the schooling of children because parents or others value its symbolic significance as a token of relationship to the ancestral homeland, and not because it is spoken (even embryonically) by the children themselves. It is one thing, presumably, to use a familiar minority language that will enable children who are potentially at risk of failure to make the transition to school more successfully, and quite another to impose an additional burden upon them as they struggle to become proficient in the language of the host society. "Would it be advantageous to Italian children, for example, to be able to speak and write Italian in Brussels?" asks the founder of the Foyer. And if the answer is positive, "does it also apply to non-European children, particularly now that they can, in the second generation, or will, in the third, be Belgians? Is it sufficient for the parents to consider it important?" (Leman, 1993, 89). The same question has been raised in an American context: "what social and practical value can there be for childhood literacy in a language such as Hmong or Cape Verdean Creole for which there is no corresponding community [adult] literacy" (Dolson, 1985a, 21).

We have considered two sets of arguments for efforts to maintain the languages of immigrants into the second and following generations. The first line of argument is based upon the asserted right of ethnic groups to maintain an identity inseparably linked to the ancestral language. In one form of the argument, this identity is associated with an irreplaceable and untranslatable cultural heritage that would be lost forever without continued use of the language; in another, the identity based upon a shared language is conceived of as a basis for unity in political action; in yet another, it is seen as the basis for community solidarity and mutual support.

Each of these variations upon the argument for a group right to language maintenance could—and indeed does—legitimately serve as the basis for efforts by ethnic groups themselves to encourage their young members to continue to use the language of their parents and in other ways to identify with the group. These efforts are likely to be successful with a few, but not with most. That fact does not, however, justify ethnic group leaders and language activists in calling upon the assistance of government to maintain the minority language through making it an aspect of the required school program for children who "should" speak the language of their ancestors. To do so is politically inappropriate and sociologically futile. Inappropriate because it seeks to use the authority and resources of government in support of group interests that are likely to conflict with individual interests in a sphere—ethnic identity—which should, in a free society, be reserved to personal choice. Futile because, even when taught by the school that they should value and maintain a language and an identity that separates them from the majority in the society, most ethnic minority children and youth are more eager to find a place within the wider society than to stay within the narrow world of their immigrant parents.

> There is no evidence to suggest that any meaningful aspects of ethnicity can be held in place by outside intervention, much less ones which are visible markers (like communicative language). There is, also, no evidence that this policy—misguided though it is—is supported in any active sense of large segments of the population, minority or majority (J. Edwards, 1984, 301–302).

In brief, the first line of argument for minority language maintenance points, at the most, to group efforts but does not make a strong case for public support. Such efforts—in some cases *with* public support—will be discussed in Chapter 6.

The second line of argument for language maintenance through schooling is based upon what is alleged to be its importance for the psychological well-being of ethnic minority pupils, for their "self-concept" or "self-esteem," whether or not they speak the ancestral language when they come to school. This argument makes a potentially stronger case for public support, since it invokes the public interest in the academic success of individuals, rather than any asserted group rights.

The weakness of the psychological argument for the use of minority languages in schools lies in the lack of convincing evidence that (1) self-concept is a problem for minority youth, and (2) that teaching a minority language has a positive effect on how minority pupils think of themselves. Both anecdotal and research evidence suggest that many pupils experience separate programs for minority pupils as an assault upon rather than a boost to their sense of well-being and self-respect, and are not deceived into accepting the success they may experience in such programs as any substitute for demonstrated ability to achieve in the mainstream.

In assessing the arguments made for programs that seek to maintain the ancestral languages of the children of immigrants, it is important to ask who is making the argument. Paulston notes that "many if not most proponents for mother tongue teaching have a vested interest in the maintained lack of assimilation of migrant children . . . their lack of objectivity is marked, and their advice vis à vis educational language policy needs to be considered *cum grano salis*" (Paulston, 1982, 54). Is it legitimate for progressive academics or well-assimilated ethnic elites to argue and for politicians and government officials of the host society to decide, on behalf of language minority children, that they are better off if schooled separately from the majority, in order to preserve their home language and ethnic identity? No, the only ones who can legitimately—and effectively—decide whether language minority children and youth will maintain and develop the language and the culture of their ancestors are those children and youth and parents acting on their behalf, and they will have to do so in their daily lives. School programs that will support that resolution are a generous and possibly a wise accommodation, so long as participation is truly voluntary and not based upon an automatic assignment of minority children in ways which make their schooling differ from that of their majority peers.

We have also considered two lines of argument *against* the use of minority languages in schooling. The first is concerned with national unity, and is based upon fears that immigrant groups will not fit within society and that social order will be threatened if immigrants and their children are not required to use the majority language. From this perspective, any support or even tolerance, by government, of minority language use is considered highly unwise.

These fears, and the insistence that schooling serve above all to "knit the nation together," have a long pedigree (Glenn, 1988b), but they are sociologically naive. As we have seen in Chapter 3, minority languages are politically polarizing only when there are underlying agendas—notably the demand for territorial autonomy—for which they serve as a convenient symbol and rallying-point. There is no instance, in any of the countries included in this study, of the formation of successful political organizations based upon an immigrant minority language, nor are there immigrant groups which for political (as distinguished from religious) reasons have successfully maintained the primary use of their minority language into the second and following generations. National and social unity are *not* threatened by immigrant languages, and conflict is likely to arise only in cases when the majority seek to suppress the use of a minority language by a group for whom it serves an important function.

This is not to dismiss the possibility that members of the second and third generations of an immigrant group may come to form a marginalized group that is characterized by failure in schooling and in the economy, and by a high level of social disorganization. The presence, in Paris and Birmingham, Rotterdam and Chicago, of youth whose parents came as hopeful immigrants but who themselves face dismal prospects is evidence that the immigration project can fail, and that this failure can pose a serious challenge to public order. Their problem, however, is not one of lack of acculturation— few continue to speak the language or to observe the cultural practices of their parents—but rather lack of successful participation in the host society (Chapter 4).

This leads to the second line of argument against an emphasis, in schooling, upon minority languages and cultures, that it may divert attention and time away from giving the children of immigrants the skills and habits, the attitudes and expectations that they will need to participate successfully in the host society, in its political system, and in its economy. As Han Entzinger has put it, by an over-emphasis upon the *background* of the pupils, it may give insufficient attention to their *future* (Triesscheijn, 1987b, 192).

This argument cannot be regarded as conclusive—or refuted—apart from the particulars of the programs provided by schools that seek to make use of the languages spoken by ethnic minority families; these will be considered in Chapter 7.

The evidence and arguments considered to this point neither make a case for public policy support of the maintenance of minority languages, through their instructional use in schools, not do they suggest that language maintenance is to be discouraged as a threat to society. Chapter 8 will consider a third, potentially the strongest, argument for the use of minority languages in schooling, based upon how language is learned rather than upon ethnic group interests or dubious psychological theories.

Conflicts of culture and of intention between immigrant minority groups and the societies to which they are strangers have led in some cases to the segregation of their children from the children of the majority. Sometimes this is the result of discriminatory policies or practices by government, or of decisions by host society parents; in other cases, the result of self-segregation by the minority group. There are even cases in which segregation results from (or is at least justified by) educational considerations; well-meaning decisions by education authorities, often encouraged by ethnic activists, to educate minority children separately "for their own good."

DISCRIMINATORY SEGREGATION AND REMEDIES

The United States

School segregation by deliberately discriminatory policy is often thought of as affecting black children until theoretically ended by the 1954 Supreme Court ruling in *Brown v. Board of Education* (347 U.S. 483), but it has affected other groups in the United States—notably Hispanics and Asians—as well.

Children of Chinese immigrants were segregated by law in a number of states in the 19th century. The California Legislature enacted a requirement during its 1859–1860 session that "Negroes, Mongolians, and Indians, shall not be admitted into the public schools," while allowing local school boards to establish separate schools for such children; this was reaffirmed in the school code adopted ten years later. The state issued a regulation in 1885 that gave local school officials "the power to exclude children of filthy or vicious habits, or children suffering from contagious or infectious diseases, and also to establish separate schools for children of Mongolian or Chinese descent" and exclude those children from other schools ("The Evolution . . . ," 1974, 1761–1763). This association of Chinese children with contamination was reflected in a report of the school board in San

Francisco, in the 1880s, on the "722 children of Chinese parentage in Chinatown," most—if not all of them—born in California:

> Speaking no language but the Chinese, born and nurtured in filth and degradation, it is scarcely probable that any serious attempt could be made to mingle them with the other children of our public schools without kindling a blaze of revolution in our midst . . . the laws of morality, and the law of self-protection, must compel our own people to sternly prohibit them from mingling with our children in the public schools, or as companions and playmates . . . what we shall do with the Chinese children is a question that may well rest in abeyance. Meanwhile, guard well the doors of our public schools, that they do not enter ("The Evolution . . . ," 1974, 1769–1770).

Twenty years later (1905), the same board took the stern view that "co-mingling" the children of Japanese immigrants "with Caucasian children is harmful and demoralizing in the extreme, the ideas entertained and practiced by people of Mongolian or Japanese affiliation being widely divergent from those of Americans;" thus "our children should not be placed in any position where their youthful impressions may be affected by association with pupils of the Mongolian race" ("The Evolution . . . ," 1974, 2971).

Nor was such discrimination confined to California. The United States Supreme Court ruled in 1927, in *Gong Lum v. Rice* (275 U.S. 78) that school officials in Mississippi could exclude a Chinese-American child from the local "white" school. Martha Lum had "the right to attend and enjoy the privileges of a common school education in a colored school" or her father could send her to a private school at his own expense.

Although persons of Mexican descent (the only Hispanic group in the United States in significant numbers until recent decades) were considered "white" under state laws requiring school segregation of blacks, they were often segregated by local practices. These included drawing of school attendance lines to correspond with residential segregation and—within schools— "ability grouping" assigning all Mexican-American children automatically to the lowest instructional track (Salinas, 1971). A Los Angeles education official conceded in 1933 that "our educational theory does not make any racial distinction between Mexican and native white population. However, pressure from white residents of certain sections forced a modification of this principle to the extent that certain neighborhood schools have been placed to absorb the majority of the Mexican pupils" (quoted by Wollenberg, 1974, 320). As a result of such practices, "in 1931, 85 per cent of California schools surveyed by the state government reported segregating Mexican students either in separate classrooms or in separate schools. . . . By 1930, 90 per cent of the schools in Texas were racially segregated" (Donato, Menchaca, & Valencia, 1991, 35).

Such official segregation has been outlawed in the United States, even when caused not by laws but by manipulation of attendance districts and other administrative measures, as in many northern cities; the *Mendez v. Westminster* decision of 1946 "outlawed the assigning of California Mexican-American students to segregated schools or classrooms on the basis of surname or heritage" (Cortés, 1986, 11). Great efforts and some progress have been made, in recent decades, in reducing the segregation of black pupils, but unofficial or *de facto* segregation resulting from demographic shifts continues to be common. That of Hispanic pupils has actually increased as a growing population is concentrated in cities that the majority population is continuing to abandon.

> In 1968, 23 per cent of Latinos attended 90 to 100 per cent minority schools. By 1984, nearly 1 in 3 (31 per cent) of Latinos attended such ethnically segregated schools. . . . "Hispanic students tend to be concentrated in schools where the tone and the level of instruction are set by large proportions of poorly prepared students" (Orfield 1988, quoted by Valencia, 1991, 7).

As a result, "as time goes by, Hispanic students are more and more likely to find themselves in schools with large numbers of urban poor, of non-English speaking, and of other racial minorities" (Arias, 1986, 51).

> Hispanic children are now the most segregated group in our schools. In 1984, 70.6% of Hispanic students attended "predominantly minority" public schools . . . 31% attended "intensely segregated" schools where more than 90% of the student body were minorities. These percentages have risen consistently since these data first became nationally available in 1968. . . . Regrettably, Hispanic students of the mid-1980s had much less interaction with English-speaking whites during their schooling than did those attending school 16 years earlier (Medina, 1988, 340)

By 1993, according to a study by Orfield, about half of the Hispanic students in the northeast of the United States attended "intensely segregated" schools (Schmidt, 1994, 5).

This is a problem that extends beyond social marginalization to educational marginalization and unequal opportunity to learn; minority children in these segregated schools are in general educated under less stimulating circumstances where low academic expectations are the norm.

California Hispanic students, even in the earliest grades, are highly concentrated in segregated schools where the average achievement level is seriously lower than in schools attended by Anglo students. This same pattern holds through all the grade levels. . . . a student of above-average potential in a Hispanic neighborhood would be very likely to attend a school with less challenging classmates and lower than average expectations than a similar Anglo student. . . . This may well point to one of the key mechanisms by which educational inequality is perpetuated and by which talented students are denied the opportunity for equal preparation for college (Espinosa & Ochoa, 1986, 95).

American government and courts have been notably ineffective in addressing the segregation of Hispanic pupils, in part because of a fundamental contradiction between policy prescriptions. On the one hand, the federal courts have held that this segregation has the same unconstitutional significance and requires the same remedies as does the segregation of black pupils; on the other, courts and policymakers have frequently ordered distinctive measures for the schooling of Hispanic (and other language minority) pupils that have the effect of segregating them, as described later in this chapter.

Although Mexican Americans are, in the great majority, within two or three generations of the experience of immigration, there has been a clear tendency to equate them (and other Hispanics) with African Americans. When a federal judge ruled in *United States v. Texas* (1971) that the court could "see no reason to believe that ethnic segregation is any less detrimental than racial segregation" and ordered the creation of a unitary school system "with no Mexican schools and no White schools but just schools" (Castellanos, 1983, 90–91), he was extending the logic of the 1954 *Brown* decision, which had forbidden separate schooling on the basis of race alone, citing the "equal protection" clause of the Fourteenth Amendment, adopted to protect the rights of those who had previously been slaves. The subordinate and vulnerable position of African Americans was the result of three centuries of unjust behavior toward them by the white majority.

Judge Justice reached conclusions about Mexican Americans, however, that would seem equally applicable to other immigrant groups that are not treated by law or policy or public opinion as requiring special consideration by government; he pointed out that they "exhibit numerous characteristics which have a causal connection with their general inability to benefit from an educational program primarily designed to meet the needs of so-called Anglo Americans. These characteristics include 'cultural incompatibilities' and English language deficiencies . . . it is largely these ethnically-linked traits . . . which account for the identifiability of Mexican American students as a group" (quoted by Ruíz, 1988, 7). Most immigrants to the United States or to other countries, of course, experience "cultural incompatibilities" and need to learn or improve their proficiency in the societal language, but it has not generally been assumed that these challenges of the immigration situation constitute a legitimate claim of victim status in relation to the government of the host society.

Similarly, in the *Cisneros* case, in June 1970, another judge ruled that "on the basis of their physical characteristics, their Spanish language, their Catholic religion, their distinct culture, and their Spanish surnames, Mexican Americans were an identifiable ethnic minority group for desegregation purposes" and therefore that the series of rulings since *Brown* in 1954 applied to them (San Miguel, 1987b, 178). The logic seems weak; after all, many ethnic groups in the United States have distinct languages, cultures, surnames, and religious connections, but are not thereby treated analogously with African Americans, whose history of victimization by both government and society would seem to be of altogether a different order than that— unquestionably deplorable as it was—experienced by Mexican Americans. It seems especially odd that a newly arrived immigrant from Mexico is, as a consequence of such rulings, considered *prima facie* a victim of past discrimination comparable to that of African Americans with generations of ancestors held as slaves in the United States, and a century of officially enforced second-class status, behind them. Although illogical, the prevailing view is consistent with the sociological reality that Mexican Americans are "thought of as indigenous rather than as immigrants" (Mead, 1982, 179). The fact that earlier generations of Mexican Americans experienced various forms of discrimination and that "the new Mexican immigrants were fitted into the existing colonial structure" (Barrera, 1979, 63) has encouraged the courts, the host society and, most fatally, many Mexican-American leaders in the belief that only compensatory measures based upon ethnicity can ensure their successful participation in the society.

This assumption is directly contrary to that held by most European policymakers, who resist any measures that single out individuals on the basis of ethnic origin, while supporting measures that target those of low socio-economic status or education, of any background.

The decision to treat Hispanics as a discriminated-against group entitled to special treatment was also based on the realization that, otherwise, school systems in the Southwest would try to meet their obligation to desegregate black children by putting them with Hispanic children and so avoid arousing the wrath of the more influential white parents. In the *Keyes* ruling, in Denver in 1973, "the Court had to define Mexican Americans as part of the white population and pair them with black students, or define [them] as an identifiable minority and pair them with Anglo students. To assign them the status of identifiable minority, the . . . judges would have to conclude that Mexican Americans had been subjected to a system of pervasive official discrimination" (San Miguel, 1987b, 181). In order to make desegregation sociologically meaningful, in other words, the school system could not be allowed to assign poor black children to schools with poor Mexican-American children.

While it is therefore legally obligatory upon public school systems to avoid actions that would have the effect of segregating Hispanic pupils and, in fashioning remedies of past segregation, to seek affirmatively to integrate them, there is another legal and policy mandate that runs in the opposite direction. School systems have been obligated, since the Supreme Court decision in *Lau v. Nichols* in 1974, to provide a program for "students who do not understand English" that will provide them with access to "meaningful education." The Court left to the discretion of school districts—in the *Lau* case, San Francisco—how to meet their obligation. "Teaching English to the students of Chinese ancestry who do not speak the [English] language is one choice. Giving instructions to this group in Chinese is another. There may be others" (quoted by Baker & de Kanter, 1983, 205). In the mood of the 1970s, the obvious solution was to provide a separate program tailored to these pupils, and then to assign pupils of a single language group to the program in such a way that, unavoidably, they received a segregated education.

One of the judges who heard the appeal in the *Lau* case, Shirley Hufstedler (later the United States Commissioner of Education), made an explicit analogy between the segregation of black pupils by assignment to separate buildings and "the language barrier, which the state helps to maintain, [which] insulates the [Chinese] children from their classmates as effectively as any physical bulwarks" (quoted by Castellanos, 1983, 116). The Court's ruling took care to point out that it would not be appropriate to separate minority children more than was required by their educational needs, quoting from an earlier federal government regulation specifying that "any ability grouping or tracking system employed by the school system to deal with the special language skill needs of national origin-minority children must be designed to meet such language skill needs as soon as possible and must not operate as an educational deadend or permanent track" (quoted by Baker & de Kanter, 1983, 207). In retrospect, however, it seems almost inevitable that such a targeted program would develop a momentum of its own and that those educators who made it their specialty would discover an ever-increasing need for what only they could provide, and ever-new reasons not to integrate language minority children into the mainstream.

As a result, the inherent tension between desegregating these children and providing them with specialized services was almost always resolved in favor of the latter (see chapter 8 for exceptions); when it was not, advocacy groups and government officials complained that school systems were neglecting their responsibilities toward minority children, or worse. As Orfield put it in the late 1970s, "when Congress and HEW [the federal Department of Health, Education and Welfare] finally recognized the discrimination against Hispanics, they chose to act on the linguistic and cultural issues and ignore the issue of segregation" (Orfield, 1978, 206). As desegregation plans have evolved over the past several decades, there has been a perverse incentive to keep language minority children in programs designed to meet the needs of pupils with very limited proficiency in English, long after that was no longer necessary.

The author conducted a study of Boston on behalf of the Federal District Court, in the mid-1980s, which found that hundreds of pupils were remaining in "transitional" bilingual programs for 6, 8, even 10 or more years, in many cases long after they could have been successful in regular classes.

> Two distinct patterns were identified: (1) a substantial number of Hispanic students remain in the [bilingual] program for six or more years without—according to the data available—achieving the working knowledge of English which would permit them to take advantage of the educational and career opportunities available in the Boston area, and (2) a substantial number of Italian-speaking (and, to a lesser extent, of Greek-speaking) students remain in the program for six or more years despite having achieved full fluency in English (Glenn, 1985b, 57–58).

There were 485 pupils in the middle school grades 6 through 8 who had been in a separate bilingual program since kindergarten or first grade (the first year of mandatory schooling); this included 46 percent of the Spanish-speaking middle school pupils. Even more shocking, 37 percent of the middle school students who had been in a separate bilingual program since the start of their schooling were still classified as "speaking a language other than English exclusively." On the other hand, Greek pupils were graduating from the bilingual program at the end of twelfth grade—having been shielded from racially integrated classes throughout their schooling in a desegregated system—and going directly into college programs conducted entirely in English, with no academic difficulties. While this was a desegregation compliance issue, the graver issue was the failure of the school system to meet the needs of many Hispanic pupils. As I advised the court, if "students are taught English ineffectively or, having mastered English, are not 'mainstreamed,' then the system has created an 'educational deadend or permanent track.' In either of these cases student rights would be violated, desegregation would be frustrated, and the requirements of Massachusetts law would be evaded" (Glenn, 1985b, 58).

On the other hand, language minority pupils deemed not to require a separate program were typically provided with no support at all related to language development; they were simply placed in the mainstream and given desegregative assignments unrelated to their home language use.

The practice of segregating minority pupils in order to provide specialized educational benefits will be discussed later in this chapter.

The United Kingdom

None of the other countries included in this study has a history of segregation and subordination of a minority group as shameful as that of the United States toward African Americans; none has government programs to promote school desegregation with anything like the energy and resources that have been devoted to that goal in most American cities. In general, European cities are less residentially segregated than many of those in the United States. On the other hand, there is significant ethnic segregation in European schools, through "white flight" (the American term is often used untranslated) and through the concentration of immigrants in areas of inexpensive housing. One unintended consequence of the implementation of full parent choice of schools in the United Kingdom in the mid-1980s was that some schools became 100 percent minority (Hofmann et al., 1993, 41).

When, consistent with the central assumptions of the assimilation strategy, immigrant pupils are put directly into regular classes, these classes turn out in many cases to be made up exclusively of other foreigners, and thus offer little opportunity for real integration.

European school segregation emerged earliest in certain cities in England, with the postwar Caribbean immigration resulting in part from the

1952 closing of American borders to immigrants from the British West Indies. In 1963 the Minister of Education told the House of Commons that an enrollment of more than 30 percent of immigrant pupils was undesirable on educational grounds and should be avoided by taking steps to promote desegregation, and a year later the Commonwealth Immigrants Advisory Council expressed concern over

> a tendency towards the creation of predominantly immigrant schools, partly because of the increase in the number of immigrant children in certain neighborhoods, but also partly because some parents tend to take native-born children away from schools when the proportion of immigrant pupils exceeds a level which suggests to them that the school is becoming an immigrant school. If this trend continues, both the social and the educational consequences might be very grave (quoted in *Education for All*, 1985, 193).

A bulletin from the Ministry of Education and Science in 1965 suggested "dispersal" of immigrant pupils so that in no school would they represent more than 30 percent of the enrollment; this was considered "the maximum that is normally acceptable in a school if social strains are to be avoided and educational standards maintained" (quoted in Linguistic Minorities Project, 1985, 282). No effective measures have been taken to prevent segregation, however, in part as a result of rulings that assignments or admissions on the basis of race would violate the Race Relations Act. More recently, the policy of the British government to expand parent choice threatens to increase racial segregation. The Under Secretary of State for Education, Baroness Hooper, insisted in 1987 that "If we are allowing freedom of choice to parents we must allow that choice to operate. If it ends up with a segregated system, then so be it" (*Times Educational Supplement*, December 4, 1987).

This could happen in two ways. Asian and other minority parents could take advantage of provisions in the 1988 education legislation to organize separate schools (see below), or English parents could insist upon their right to choose a school other than the integrated school to which their children are assigned by local authorities. The second possibility became real in an incident which attracted tremendous attention in 1987–88. The parents of 26 children in Dewsbury, West Yorkshire, objected when their primary-level children were assigned to Headfield Junior School rather than to Overthorpe School, which they had requested even though it was farther from their homes. While both are publicly funded Church of England schools, the enrollment of the first was 85 percent Asian and that of the second was only 10 percent minority. The particular assignment to which objection was made was not an attempt at desegregation; it was simply based on administrative convenience.

> Stories have been spread about Headfield school (for example, that it does not celebrate Christmas, and children make *chapattis* on Shrove Tuesday instead of pancakes) which have brought counter accusations of racism. These have been denied by the school, the [local education authority], and the local diocesan board, who say multicultural education, including the teaching of Christianity, is provided in the same way as [in] most state schools. The allegations that their motives are racist are denied by the parents, who say their objections to Headfield are cultural, not racial (*Times Educational Supplement*, September 11, 1987).

At least one Asian parent had been able to obtain a transfer of her child from Headfield to another school because she did not want her in an all-Asian class, out of concern that the child would not learn English well. The English parents complained that this was a case of reverse discrimination. Meanwhile, a leader in the local Asian community said, "We send our children to Headfield because it is the local community school, and white parents should do the same. Segregated schools are wrong" (*Times Educational Supplement*, September 18, 1987). The English parents refused to accept the assignment, and operated a classroom in the room over a pub, with volunteer retired teachers, for nine months while their lawsuit against the local education authority made its way to the High Court. The suit received strong support from elements of the Tory Right, which saw it as a test case for parent rights as well as for their objections to multicultural education (*Times Educational Supplement,* July 8, 1988; Naylor, 1989). The authority's case collapsed over the issue of whether appropriate procedures for setting enrollment limits had been followed, and the parents were allowed to enroll their children in Overthorpe school. They continued to insist, through their attorney, that race was not the issue but that they "have a natural desire that their children should be educated in a traditional English and Christian environment" (*Times Educational Supplement,* July 15, 1988).

Even as this resolution was announced, a paper was published by a Conservative research group, urging a policy of desegregation through persuading minority parents that their children would receive a better education if they used the parent-choice policy to seek an integrated school.

German families often move out of areas with a growing foreign population, and avoid the lower level of secondary education (*Hauptschule*) where foreign pupils are increasingly concentrated (Boos-Nünning & Henscheid, 1986, 65). In Frankfurt, in 1989, foreign pupils made up 15 percent of the *Gymnasium* pupils but 59 percent of those in *Hauptschule*, and 88 percent in one of them ("Mit der Nadel . . . ," 1989, 71). In order to reassure German parents, and to promote the social integration of foreign pupils, the West German authorities recommended in 1976 that the proportion of the latter in each class be limited to 20 percent. If the numbers in a school made this impossible, they suggested, separate classes could be created made up *exclusively* of foreign pupils. Clearly reassuring German parents was considered more important than integration!

A poll in 1980 found that 41 percent of German parents supported the separate education of foreign pupils in their own classes. Even many parents whose political views are on the Left, and who strongly support the integration of Turkish pupils, find ways to send their own children to schools with few of them; Catholic schools are used by many non-Catholics for the same reason. These parents were convinced that education would inevitably be inferior in classes with many Turkish pupils, and teachers sometimes supported this view ("Mit der Nadel . . . ," 1989, 71). In response to such concerns, the Berlin legislators insisted in 1982 that "the common schooling of foreign and German pupils must not lead to the German children feeling like strangers in their own school and education system; German pupils should not experience being a minority in their classes." Thus no class serving German pupils should have more than 50 percent foreigners, even if these were perfectly proficient in German. On the other hand, classes made up exclusively of foreign pupils were acceptable (Mahler, 1983, 204, 220). The result has been that by 1989 55 percent of immigrant minority pupils in *Hauptschule* were in such "foreign classes"; Turkish teachers referred to this as "a West-European version of *apartheid*" ("Mit der Nadel . . . ," 1989, 82).

This growing tendency toward officially promoted segregation of the children of immigrants had a negative effect upon their opportunities to learn the language of the school as a second language (Nieke, Budde, & Henscheid, 1983, 39, 86), reducing the motivation of foreign pupils and their parents to take seriously schooling in which no native pupils participate (Boos-Nünning, 1981a, 45).

One German community that made a determined and comprehensive effort to promote ethnic integration is Krefeld in North Rhine/Westphalia. While the "Krefeld Model" is most notable for its stress upon pedagogical integration, it also includes an element of deliberate assignment of pupils to create the pre-conditions for successful integration. Of the three schools in the original model, the one concentrating on integrating Greek and German pupils was able to draw almost its entire enrollment from the assignment district already established for the school, with a few additional Greek pupils from elsewhere in the city. One of those integrating Turkish and German pupils drew the latter from the vicinity of the school and the former from a single housing area with a substantial Turkish population; the other drew Turkish pupils from a number of areas to a facility in a predominantly German area (Dickopp, 1982, 68).

The Netherlands

During the first postwar immigration from Indonesia, the government made deliberate efforts to ensure that the newcomers would not be overly concentrated in identifiable areas; all municipalities were required to reserve 5 percent of their new subsidized housing for these refugees, and it seems likely that this policy deserves part of the credit for the good integration that this group has achieved (Jong, Mart Jan de, 1987, 6). On the other hand, the Moluccans who came at the same time (soldiers for the Dutch colonial administration, and their families) were settled in physically segregated clusters, and they have remained to a large extent apart from the majority. When immigrants came from Surinam, an attempt was made to disperse them as with the Dutch Indonesians, but with less success:

> Surinamers were less motivated to integrate (the return option continued to exist) and work was less readily available to them, partly because they did not possess the proper qualifications. What had proved workable in the 1950s was no longer effective in the 1970s (Entzinger, 1985, 75–76).

The policy employed with Dutch Indonesians was not continued with the labor migrants who began to arrive in the 1960s, and they ended up concentrated disproportionately in the four major cities. As Dutch society becomes more multicultural, some schools in "concentration districts" (*concentratiewijken*) paradoxically become less diverse; Dutch parents took their children out of them (Bolhuis, 1994), reportedly fearing that they would be held back because of the language and academic difficulties of minority children (Schumacher, 1981, 105). The phenomenon is not limited to Dutch parents, however, since many immigrant parents also seek to enroll their children in schools outside of the areas where they live in hopes of better schooling (Anderiesen & Reijndorp, 1991, 59). This phenomenon was first noted in the early seventies, when a Socialist newspaper asked whether *apartheid* was being created in a suburb of Amsterdam with a high proportion of Surinamese families (*Het Parool*, March 24, 1971). The same paper, in 1987, carried a series of in-depth articles by Maria Sitniakowsky and others on this phenomenon and its consequences for education of ethnic minority and Dutch children alike.

In 1987, there were 147 schools in the Netherlands with an enrollment more than 70 percent of foreign pupils, and 511 more than 50 percent foreign; 18 percent of the schools in the four largest cities enrolled more than 70 percent, and 32 percent more than 50 percent of foreign pupils (Wit, 1990, 12). In many cases, especially in the smaller cities, these concentrations were caused in part by official actions: with the "family reunification" of immigrants in the 1970s, reception programs were established at certain schools and over time these came to be perceived as "black schools" by ethnic minority and Dutch parents alike. A study of the immigrant community in Utrecht describes how initially a few schools specialized in serving immigrant children and soon were avoided by Dutch parents, while other schools found pretexts to refuse admission to immigrants. In 1978, the local Council of Churches formed a working group to ensure that all Catholic and Protestant schools were welcoming to minority children. With the declining enrollments of the 1970s (resulting from a fall in the birth rate and increasing suburbanization), there came to be an actual competition for immigrant children as schools were threatened with closing. Attempts to specify, for educational reasons, that Turkish children would be enrolled in one school, Moroccan children in another, and Surinamese children in a third broke down under this competitive pressure (Bovenkerk et al., 1985, 288–293).

The phenomenon of "white flight" has been much discussed in the Netherlands; many principals attribute their declining numbers of Dutch pupils to avoidance, by parents, of schools with substantial minority enrollment. Dutch parents may use the right of choice—established to respect religious differences—as a way to desert schools which they perceive as being "black" and in consequence providing a low standard of instruction (Dors et al., 1991, 47, 105). Research has not produced clear evidence to explain this phenomenon (Fase, 1990, 23), though there is some evidence that in fact both Dutch and foreign children have lower achievement levels in classes with a large number of the latter (Tesser & Mulder, 1990). While there is considerable movement in and out of inner-city areas for school attendance, it involves minority as well as Dutch pupils and is based on a variety of factors of which ethnicity is not especially salient. Interviews with parents in

Amsterdam found very complex motivations for school choice.

> The parents who chose a white school outside the neighborhood did
> so after a careful weighing of the cultural climate at the school, the
> pupils and their parents, the teachers and the curriculum. They wanted
> to join with parents of a similar social position and formed intellec-
> tual and artistic networks with them. They distanced themselves
> thereby from parents of a lower social class. On the other hand, con-
> tacts with ethnic minority [parents] were considered important, but
> it must be with those whose life-styles fitted with their own (De Lange
> & Van Veghel, 1986, cited by Wit, 1990, 15–16).

Dutch education policy has particular difficulty in dealing with the problem of ethnic segregation, in that the Constitution protects the free choice
of a school (Glenn, 1989b). It is very difficult to find ways to assign pupils
on the basis of their ethnicity, or even to keep Dutch pupils in schools in
residential areas with a growing number of foreign families.

Mohammed Rabbae, the Moroccan director of the Netherlands Center for Foreigners, called for a local and national debate on this issue
(*Samenwijs*, November 1987). The presence of foreign pupils in more
schools, he insisted, would have an enriching effect for Dutch pupils as well.
For the foreign pupils it might make all the difference in their learning Dutch
adequately, and thus being able to keep their heads above water (*Het Parool*,
October 17, 1987).

The most successful effort to achieve school desegregation in the
Netherlands seems to be that in Gouda, where both public and nonpublic
schools agreed to a policy designed to enroll minority pupils in many schools
rather than to have them concentrated in a few. The policy implemented in
Gouda is based upon an agreement that every public school will have up to
25 percent linguistic minority pupils, and every nonpublic school (mostly
Protestant and Catholic) up to 20 percent, with transportation provided as
necessary—children 10 and older are expected to use their bicycles! Only a
few ultra-Protestant schools, which admit only the children of those who
share their beliefs, find it impossible to meet this goal.

Linguistic minority children who enter the system at age 4 do not go
automatically to their nearest school, but are enrolled in a reception program for one or in a few cases two years, after which they are assigned to a
school on a basis which promotes desegregation. A difficulty has been that
some schools in outlying areas to which linguistic minority pupils are trans-
ported do little to respond to their educational needs (Miedema, 1988, 291).

Others, including a Protestant school that I visited, make significant adjustments to show respect for diversity without giving up their distinctive identity. It has unfortunately not been possible, however, to attract Dutch children to the Anne Frank School, perceived as the "black school" since it provided the original program for Moroccan and other immigrant children (*Het Parool*, October 10, 1987).

There has been continuing discussion of measures to reduce the concentration of ethnic minority pupils in other communities. At one point, authorities in Rotterdam sought to address this problem through residential distribution of immigrant families, but this came to grief over legal and political problems (Fase, 1990, 23). Such measures can only be successful, in the Dutch context, through collaboration between the various types of schools. In the thickly populated Netherlands, nearly all pupils live within walking distance of several schools (Boef, Bronneman, & Konings, 1983), and parents can make use of their constitutionally protected right of choice to avoid schools that they perceive as enrolling too many minority children, if nearby schools enroll few.

Under an agreement among the governing boards of Protestant, Catholic, and public schools in Leiden, language minority children will be enrolled from age 3 in a multiyear program with a strong emphasis upon developing their proficiency in Dutch. As soon as they progress to the point of mastery of the first-grade curriculum, they will be distributed among the various schools for second grade. Every school will receive assistance in providing appropriate support to these pupils (*Samenwijs*, 12, 7 (March) 1992, 306).

Municipal authorities in Amsterdam, where in 1985 41 schools were over 70 percent minority, have been wrestling with this problem. Since the authorities seek to make the education in all schools exactly alike with respect to resources, but not to influence where anyone sends their children, it is natural that middle-class parents make sophisticated choices on the basis of the social class of the pupils already in the school. This has led to a sort of double standard, with such parents holding government accountable for improving the quality and equality of education for minority (and other poor) children while themselves making choices which promote class and ethnic divisions precisely in education (Dors et al., 1991, 74).

The Amsterdam authorities are considering several options to prevent the development of "black schools." Three possibilities were identified:

1.   Limiting of free choice of schools or the development of an admissions policy under which ethnicity does not lead to separation between groups of pupils.

2. Influencing the choice process of parents in such a way that without limiting their free choice of schools a change is created in [the school's] intake. Essentially this would be a matter of improving the quality of the education, the teachers, the buildings, and other material provisions.

3. Combining option 1 and option 2 (Afdeling Onderwijs, 1988, 34).

Any such policy must be developed and implemented in consultation with nonpublic school authorities, since only some 30 percent of elementary school pupils in the Netherlands attend schools operated by local government. Nonpublic schools—mostly Catholic and Protestant—might be tempted to become "white havens" during a period when declining enrollments are putting pressure on some to close. Nationwide, in 1981, 50 percent of all foreign pupils were in public and 50 percent in nonpublic schools; the disproportion in part reflects the greater concentration of denominationally based schools in more rural areas with few immigrants. Public schools must admit every pupil who wishes admission, subject only to capacity and age limitations, and the advocates of such schooling make this a major point in their argument that government policy should be less generous toward nonpublic schools (Vereniging voor Openbaar Onderwijs, 1983; Schoten & Wansink, 1984). Nonpublic schools, though fully funded by the government, are permitted to select students as a means of protecting their identity. Thus a Catholic school could not choose among Catholic pupils, but it could choose not to admit a Protestant or a Moslem. In fact, however, most nonpublic schools in areas with substantial immigrant populations have been eager to admit such pupils. Among Protestant schools, for example, there are some which identify themselves clearly as teaching a particular tradition, others which see themselves as standing within such a tradition but stressing encounter with other traditions, and yet others which consider themselves open to all forms of belief with perhaps a residual tincture of Christianity (Stuurgroep, no date, 14).

Catholic and Protestant schools in some cases have enrollments up to 80 or 90 percent ethnic minority, and make significant adjustments in their programs to operate in an "inter-cultural" style (Glenn, 1985). The associations of Protestant and of Catholic schools in the Netherlands have produced materials and held conferences and teacher training institutes to support such adjustments (see, for example, *Handbook voor de ontmoeting*, 1987; *GAMMA: bronnenboek intercultureel onderwijs*, 1987; *Ontmoetingsonderwijs*, 1985). In general it is only the relatively small number of stricter "Reformational" Protestant schools and similar Catholic schools which fear that such adjustments would undermine their fundamental mission.

Any successful strategy to reduce the *de facto* segregation of ethnic minority children in the Netherlands will have to respect the freedom of both schools and parents. An important element will be improved efforts to provide information to parents on the basis of which they may gain the confidence to select a school with an ethnically diverse enrollment (Dors et al., 1991, 48). The SENECA Project in Amsterdam is seeking to develop such a system, with special attention to the issues that concern immigrant families. There is considerable opportunity for cooperative policies to ensure that both public and nonpublic schools in an area reflect the overall ethnic makeup of the area (Glenn, 1990).

Belgium

A study in three areas of Flemish Belgium with a high proportion of immigrants found that more than a third of the elementary schools enrolled over 50 percent ethnic minority pupils (Vanhoren, 1991, 53). There was evidence that some nongovernment schools (most pupils in Flanders attend publicly-funded Catholic schools) found ways—despite laws and formal commitments to the contrary—to refuse admission to such pupils, or to accept only the most promising. Immigrant parents complained about the quality of education in the schools where their children were concentrated: the children spoke Turkish among themselves, they said, and the teachers spoke a sort of "Tarzan Dutch" so they can be understood. Without good language models, the children failed to develop fluency in Dutch and felt marginalized by their lack of contact with Flemish children (Laquière, 1993, 31). Concern has been heightened by the strong showing made by the anti-immigrant *Vlaams Blok* in municipal elections in Antwerp, attributed by the mayor to the visibility of Moroccans (Peeters, 1992, 301–302).

The Flemish government has recently sought to reduce the concentration of minority pupils in certain schools by requiring that schools seeking supplemental funds to serve immigrant pupils collaborate with other schools to this end (Laquière, 1992, 78–80; Laquière, 1993, 29–31, 47). The strategy has two well-coordinated elements. In selected cities with a large number of children of immigrant origin, the government used the threat of withholding funding to require consultation among the various networks of schooling and school principals, working with the agencies and organizations that serve immigrant families, to encourage a voluntary distribution of minority children among the schools; this parallels the desegregation strategy in Gouda in the Netherlands. Minority parents are counseled to consider alternative assignments, and each school is expected to accept at least a minimum proportion of minority pupils (for example, 12 percent in

Mechelen), so that there will no longer be "white schools." Although maximum proportions (22 percent in Mechelen) were also set under these local agreements, Education Minister Luc Van den Bossche has said that these could not be used to deny admission to a pupil whose parents selected the school (Laquière, 1994, 18).

To encourage efforts to promote voluntary integration, the extra funding provided for the schooling of these children varies depending upon the makeup of the school that they attend. It was decided in 1990 that a "weight" of 2.0 (that is, twice the regular per-pupil funding) would be provided for minority pupils in schools with 30 to 50 percent minority enrollment, while a weight of 1.5 would be provided in schools with 50 to 80 percent minorities, 1.7 in schools with under 30 percent, and no extra funding in schools with over 80 percent minority enrollment (Fase, 1994, 95). In effect, the Flemish policy creates a "weighted voucher" of the sort that has been proposed in the United States by Coons and Sugarman and by the author, to ensure that public funding of nongovernment schools would promote social class and racial integration (interviews with Johan Leman, Marc Verlot, & Lief Vandevoort, December 14–15, 1994).

The funding is not provided automatically; schools must develop plans showing how they will use the additional resources for minority pupils and by what standard they will judge their results (Jansen & Terkessidis, 1992, 61). In one project, in Ghent, a "black" school (with a high proportion of minority pupils) has entered into a voluntary pairing with a "white" school to implement a curriculum involving cooperative learning projects for the pupils from both, with as one of the goals that the black school will become an American-style magnet school attracting majority pupils on a voluntary basis (Wulf, 1993, 206–207).

Overview and Summary

Much school segregation is the result of patterns of housing segregation, and efforts to achieve integrated housing are often blocked by anti- discrimination requirements, as in the Danish community Ishøj (*Berlingske*, 2/24–3/2/ 89). Half of the pupils in 15 Danish schools are immigrants, as are 80 percent of those in two others (Andersen, 1992, 28). Governments have adopted but then abandoned policies to require the physical dispersion of foreigners, like the futile West German requirement that none be allowed to settle in areas that were already more than 12 percent foreign (Mahler, 1983, 23).

In other cases, avoidance by majority parents of schools with large numbers of immigrant children may have much the same effect as residential segregation, leaving some schools significantly less heterogeneous in enrollment than are the areas which theoretically they serve. Educational reasons are often cited, as when some Swedish parents demanded "that their children attend only classes where all pupils have Swedish as their mother tongue; in support of this position they cite the requests made by Finnish parents that their children be placed in classes where everyone's mother tongue is Finnish" (Hammar, 1985b, 269).

In effect, the historic mission of schooling as the integrator of those on the periphery of a society has been largely abandoned in such cases. Nowhere is this mission more explicitly enunciated than in France, where it continues to have deep political resonance. It was with a sense of shock that French commentators greeted the decision of the Communist mayor of Clichy to draw school attendance zones in such a way that one school would have only 6 percent immigrant minority pupils, and another 95 percent (Navarre, 1990, 33). For much of the public, however, such measures were only a necessary response to what they perceived as the refusal of Muslim immigrants, in particular, to integrate voluntarily into French society.

If the goal of integration policies is to absorb foreign pupils fully into the host society, it is difficult to see how this can be accomplished by measures that keep them physically separate and provide few chances for spontaneous and natural interaction with native children. Such separation is, however, often the reality in the schools and programs to which these pupils are assigned. The effort of acculturation, under such circumstances, becomes a matter of teaching a language and smatterings of a culture much as they might be taught to children living in another country. Just as foreign language instruction in schools is not, in most cases, successful in making pupils fully competent in the language, much less in the culture of the target society, so these segregated programs for immigrant children tend to be ineffective.

Separate Schooling by Community Initiative

There is something paradoxical about the fact that some ethnic minority groups create separate educational provisions for their children even as policymakers seek to find ways to reduce the isolation in which many of those children are schooled, as a result of residential patterns, "white flight," and discriminatory assignment practices. For example, there are those who argue that programs to support home language and culture will always be a poor relation in mainstream schools and would flourish if made the responsibility of community-based organizations. Public funding is sometimes provided—notably has this been the case in Australia and Canada—for part-time supplemental programs under the auspices of ethnic organizations.

Gilles Verbunt suggests that such external programs may be preferable:

> Allow me to dream a little. If public education did not have a mo-
> nopoly on the time available for school schedules, nor of staff, nor
> of financial means, nor of the power of recognition and sanction, but
> had at its side institutions with an ethnic, regional, or "ideological"
> (in the highest meaning of that word) character, would it not be easier
> to square the circle of promoting diversity within an institution whose
> mission is to equalize? . . . The dream implies that a share of the re-
> sources, staff, power and available time would be transferred to other
> institutions which are closer to the collective identities other than the
> national one. . . . we are thinking in terms of complementarity, the
> first condition for achieving an inter-cultural society (Verbunt, 1986).

Community-based home-language instruction of the sort described in Chapter 5 is sometimes supported by government, which thereby surrenders to a
large extent its control over the content of not only the language instruction but also the cultural and religious message associated with it. This is,
of course, as it should be in a free society.

Home language instruction outside of the setting of a public school
is more commonly associated with the transmission of religious beliefs and
traditions, and typically has no connection with government, either of the
homeland or of the host society. Sung reported in 1971 that "about a fourth
of the children in the vicinity of New York's Chinatown attend Chinese
school following American school from 5 to 7 P.M. daily." Most of these
Chinese after-school programs nationwide were sponsored by Chinese
churches, and often included Saturday-morning classes as well (Sung,
1971, 179, 228). Although these programs were initially designed to ensure that the children of immigrants would continue to be able to speak
with members of the older generation, and to read and write Chinese
characters, the emphasis has reportedly shifted in recent years to "softer"
aspects of Chinese culture (interview with Anping Shen, November 1994).
In Britain,

> classes in, for example, mosques and *gurdwaras*, the earlier estab-
> lished Polish Saturday schools, and Welsh language Sunday schools,
> often associated language teaching with religious instruction. . . . the
> growth of mother tongue teaching was related in part to parents'
> wishes to keep open the verbal channels of communication between
> the generations, partly to their wish to combat some of the Western

European secular values promoted by [public] schools . . . (Linguistic Minorities Project, 1985, 287).

Many programs motivated primarily by religious considerations conduct such instruction in the language of the immigrant parents until that no longer proves an effective medium for reaching the rising generation. This is a largely invisible phenomenon; there were 4,893 part-time "ethnic schools" identified in an American survey in the late 1970s, "maintained, by and large, by ethnic communities that are competently English-speaking" but for whom "language maintenance is viewed as a moral necessity." Fishman points out that the primary focus of these schools was not upon foreign-born children who did not speak English, but upon children born in the United States whose first language was English but whose parents—themselves well-acculturated—wished to maintain their ethnic connections. Paradoxically, "the entry of Chicano, Puerto Rican and Native American children into such schools is a sign of their 'Americanization'" (Fishman 1989, 454, 458).

American experience shows that immigrant groups can preserve their ethnic churches and associations, and through them express and pass on at least the most valued elements of their traditions, for several generations after abandoning the use of their original language. Turkish, Moroccan, Pakistani parents in Western Europe who stress the teaching of Islam over that of their mother tongue exhibit a sound grasp of which elements of identity have power to resist acculturation. Establishing and maintaining a supplemental Koran school—so often deplored by progressive ethnic elites and mainstream educators—may be perceived by a Muslim community as the most important element of maintaining religious practice:

> For parents seeking legitimacy in relation to their children, it is invested with a role which they have not—or which they believe they have not—been able to play; it is up to the mosque to transmit the heritage which they believe is lost or in danger, at best, of disappearing, . . . to revive the values that are believed to be on deposit, to apply them literally in the first instance and then to bequeath them. Under this perspective, the need for a Koran school is the first need; it precedes and serves as the basis for the demand for places of prayer (El Yazami, 1988, 74).

Inevitably, however, such part-time provision does not satisfy those who wish to ensure that the children of immigrants be so solidly rooted in their ethnic identity that they resist the seduction of the culture and language of the host society, or so solidly anchored in the religious faith and practice of their parents that they will persist in them loyally despite an unfriendly environment. Such confirmation of distinctiveness is sought not in marginal after-school time, but at the very heart of the educational enterprise: full-time schooling was the strategy followed by Catholic immigrants to American cities a century ago, building their parochial schools before their churches. Similarly today, when supplemental instruction does not seem adequate to counter the effects of mandatory state schooling on children's values and loyalties, immigrant parents may begin to demand separate full-time schools that place their own goals for education above or alongside those of the host society.

The United States

The situation has evolved rather differently in recent decades in the United States: there has been a vigorous development of deliberately separate schools through African-American initiatives, but relatively few by immigrant minority groups. This is a reversal of the pattern of the late 19th century, when most nonpublic schools were founded by Catholic and Lutheran immigrants, some of whom wanted instruction to be at least partly in their home languages. In Massachusetts, for example, there were 90 nonpublic schools in 1914 where instruction—in contrast with that in public schools—was bilingual, half a day in English and half in Polish, Italian, Portuguese, French, or Greek. A state report that year pointed out:

> that the knowledge of a second language has cultural advantages is beyond dispute, and should be encouraged, for in the history, traditions, literature and art of the various nations there is much that would enrich American life. But it is not in the pursuit of culture that the overwhelming majority of these children are to spend their lives. The far more practical and far more difficult problem of bread-winning is the one to which—day in and day out—they will be forced to devote their unremitting attention.

Nonpublic schools should therefore be encouraged to stress the study of English without abandoning the study of the native languages, since "to speak English and to understand it is the vital need of the immigrant" (Commission on Immigration, 1914, 150); a few years later, Massachusetts briefly required that instruction even in nonpublic schools be in English (Castellanos, 1983, 39).

The state report criticized the quality of instruction provided in many of these schools, while conceding the "exalted character, disinterested service and untiring zeal of the teachers." They had not been trained in American teaching methods, nor were some of them familiar "with American civic or social ideals." An even greater problem, the commission concluded, was that the parish priests upon whom these schools primarily depended were often what we would now call highly ethnocentric and concerned to maintain the distinctiveness of the group of immigrants entrusted to them. "While some of these pastors are thoroughly imbued with American ideals, the majority are of foreign birth, education and training, so intensely devoted to their native land that their patriotism permits no divided allegiance" such as a stress, in the parochial school, "upon American traditions and ideals" (Commission on Immigration, 1914, 149).

It is interesting to note the official concern about the "ideals"—what we would now less elegantly call the "values"—taught in schools dependent upon the ethnic community rather than upon public authorities, as well as about the quality of instruction and of second-language learning in such schools. These are, of course, the schools whose effects, in our own times, upon the academic success and the character of poor and vulnerable children have been celebrated by researchers James Coleman and Anthony Bryk. Today it is more likely to be public schools that are called into question on the basis of the "values" that they are believed to represent and teach, and immigrant groups which do the questioning.

Discussion in the United States has, until recently, largely overlooked the quiet "second growth" of alternatives to public schooling through initiatives in minority communities. While there was national debate over the decision by Detroit school authorities to create three public schools designated for black pupils, the simultaneous creation of three "interfaith" schools serving the same population received little attention (*Education Week*, September 4, 1991). A study in 1991 identified 284 "independent neighborhood schools" in the United States, most of which enrolled predominantly or exclusively black pupils; altogether this represented more than 50,000 pupils compared with some 6.7 million black pupils attending public schools. The largest number of black pupils outside the public system—some 220,000—are in Catholic schools, including schools in the South founded long ago to serve the children of freed slaves, and schools in northern urban neighborhoods abandoned by white ethnic Catholics. Upwardly mobile black families living in these areas frequently choose a Catholic school as "a functional alternative . . . for quality suburban schools;" 53% of the black pupils in heavily minority Catholic schools, one study found, were not Catholics (Cibulka, O'Brien, & Zewe, 1982, 47). Considerable interest has been shown recently in indications that these schools may be particularly effective in educating pupils who would otherwise be at risk of academic and social failure (Benson & others, 1986; Coleman & Hoffer, 1987).

A number of Protestant schools have been started by black churches, in Los Angeles, Kansas City, Detroit, Milwaukee, Boston, and other cities. In these schools, the emphasis is much less upon "Afro-Centric" elements and much more upon the failure of public schools to provide the moral and religious instruction that the parents who choose these schools want for their children. It is not the "Euro-Centric" nature of public schools so much as their pervasive secularism and moral incoherence that gives impetus to these schools.

Muslim education in the United States has developed completely outside of the publicly supported sector, making perhaps its first appearance in the unorthodox form of the "Black Muslim" schools started by Elijah Muhammad's movement in Detroit and Chicago in the early 1930s, with the intention of the "moral transformation of the [black] population" (quoted by Paulston, 1992, 49). Since the mid-1970s, 38 of the schools associated with this movement have become orthodox Muslim schools known as Sister Clara Muhammad Schools, with much less stress upon rejection of the majority society (and race), and much more upon Islamic teaching (Rashid & Muhammad, 1992, 178–185).

The Council of Independent Black Institutions represents about 30 schools across the United States which subscribe to various aspects of an "Afro-Centric" curriculum, including the *Nguzo Saba* or "Seven Principles of Blackness" formulated by Karenga in the 1960s. The purpose of this approach has been described by one principal as "to improve the self-esteem, self-worth and self-confidence of the [black] child so he will have the coping skills necessary to merge into the broader pluralistic society and to deal with racism and some of the things he will confront as a Black man" (Kenneth Holt, quoted by Lomotey, 1992, 461).

It should be noted that the emphasis of these schools is not generally upon educating children to live apart from American society, much less to function proficiently in a minority language (as is the goal of Hasidic or Amish schooling), but to equip them to contend successfully with the pressures of life in the society as a person of color. Parents of children in black independent schools interviewed in one survey "indicated that they utilized the schools to 'buy time' for their children in settings that allowed them to develop as free as possible from the limitations imposed by racism" (Shujaa, 1992, 154).

Although "Afrocentric transformation"—defined as struggling "to define social reality with Africa at the center" of consciousness—may be the goal of some of the founders of black independent schools, it appears that the motivation of parents in paying tuition and sending their children has more to do with concerns about the deficiencies of public schooling. A survey of black parents with children in 36 independent schools in the Washington, D.C. area found that "lack of Afrocentric curriculum" ranked 21 out of 24 factors in their rejection of public schools; "lack of discipline" and "poor standards" ranked first and second (Jones-Wilson, Arnez, & Asbury, 1992, 131). Most black independent schools focus more upon academic achievement and a supportive environment than upon recovering an African heritage, though it is the latter agenda that has caused the most policy debate and has inspired efforts to create racially separate public schools.

There are some indications that pupils in black independent schools *do* achieve above national norms (Ratteray, 1992, 143–46), though John Witte's ongoing evaluation of the voucher program under which poor children in Milwaukee may attend nonreligious independent schools has found no consistent advantage.

An exception to the rule that recent immigrants to the United States have generally not established separate full-time schools is the existence of a number of nonpublic schools in the Miami area for young Cuban Americans, serving an estimated 20 percent of that population. "These ethnic schools provide middle and working class Cuban American children with a context where Spanish is to some degree the language of power and prestige" (García & Otheguy, 1988, 177).

A special case is represented by the Indian-controlled schools on some reservations, in some of which tribal languages are used for instruction (Crawford, 1995, 29). In most cases, these are bilingual programs, but there are scattered instances of attempts to revive a nearly disappeared language through immersion programs in which Mohawk or Odawa is used exclusively for at least pre-school. It does not seem likely that these schools will manage to persuade Indian youth to make tribal languages their primary means of communication and, as we have seen in Chapter 5, anything less is unlikely to result in real bilingualism in a society which is far from diglossic. As even advocates of language revival concede, "we have sometimes seen community-controlled schools be a force toward Western values, roles, knowledge and language despite deepest intentions" (Freeman & others, 1995, 44–45).

The prospects for continuing use of tribal languages are best in situations in which through large numbers and relative isolation have preserved the active use of an alternative to English, most notably on the Navajo reservation, and it is there that the most successful Indian bilingual schools have operated since the 1970s. At Fort Defiance, Arizona parents whose children had at least some passive knowledge of Navajo volunteered them for a kindergarten immersion program in that language, and this was gradually extended into a bilingual program through the elementary grades. Similar bilingual schools have been developed in other reservation communities, though they are by no means the norm, and a survey by one of their main promoters, in 1993, found that less than 1 percent of 3,300 Navajo pupils surveyed knew no English, and only 31 percent were fluent speakers of Navajo (Holm & Holm, 1995).

> Until recently, the language of the home and the community was mainly Navajo; children entered school as dominant speakers of their ancestral language, and the district promoted and taught English. In recent years, however, the situation has changed dramatically. The language of the home and community is no longer Navajo but English. Fewer and fewer children some to school speaking Navajo. . . . growing numbers of parents, teachers, administrators and school board members have realized the resultant threat of Navajo language loss . . . and asked, "Can't the schools teach English *and* Navajo? Won't instruction in Navajo help the children better understand themselves, and also help stabilize the Navajo language?" (McLaughlin, 1995, 170).

Even the strongest advocates of such efforts concede that their purpose is "not for cognitive" or instrumental reasons, to increase the ability of the children to think or to function effectively in the society in which they will live as adults, but "for cultural identity purposes." It depends upon enlisting the support of families, since most have themselves chosen to use English for communication in the home, and ultimately "demands nothing less than acute understandings of local religion, history, politics, sociology, and anthropology so that the right social engineering decisions might be made in the right ways" (McLaughlin, 1995, 176–177). Of course, this raises the fundamental question: What authorizes educators to engage in social engineering?

Canada

Postwar immigrants from the Netherlands brought to Canada with them a tradition of denominational schooling that led to the founding of the first "Christian Reformed" school in 1945. By 1985–86 there were more than 19,000 students attending schools in the Reformed tradition (there are also many such Dutch-founded schools in the Midwest of the United States). Mennonites have also been concerned to educate their children in their own schools. The first Mennonite settlers, German speakers from Russia, were recruited to the Canadian plains of Manitoba a century ago by promises of land and of religious freedom, including that of educating their own children.

Because of their residential grouping, the Mennonites found the local rural public schools possible to influence and thus generally acceptable until in recent decades the consolidation of smaller schools (where alternative values had flourished apart from the mainstream) and the increased secularization of the curriculum led to their increasing alienation (Bergen, 1978c). In 1977 members of the Church of God in Christ, Mennonite, known as the Holdemans, took their children out of local public schools in Alberta and placed them in a school they had built and staffed themselves. Since this alternative had not been approved by provincial authorities, they were prosecuted. One of the leaders of this group wrote to the Premier of Alberta that

> We definitely feel that we have a culture and a way of life to preserve for our children and that the trends in our greater society are not conducive for this. We plan to give our children a curriculum that will foster self-discipline rather than permissiveness; respect for authority rather than disrespect; interdependence rather than independence; consideration for the rights of others rather than "I'll do my own thing"; and respect for God, his creation, and his institutions (quoted in Bergen, 1978b, 14).

The judge hearing the case found, in a 1978 ruling (*Regina vs. Wiebe*), that the guarantees of freedom of religion under the Alberta Bill of Rights "rendered inoperative" the attendance requirements of the school legislation. He concluded that the instruction in public schools was incompatible with the religious faith and practices of the Holdeman Mennonites (Bergen, 1978b, 8; Bergen, 1978a; Thiessen, 1986).

Another immigrant group with a strong commitment to schooling informed by their religious views are the Hutterites, an extremely conservative Anabaptist church related to the Mennonites. Because they live in homogeneous farming colonies in the prairie provinces, the Hutterites have been able to make use of their local public schools, supplemented by language and religion instruction before or after school. Local authorities have been willing to accommodate the Hutterite practice of recognizing 15-year-olds as members of the adult community; they are excused from school on the basis of receiving training as apprentices through their responsibilities in the Hutterite community (Bergen, 1982, 326).

In many cases, it appears that the primary motivation of those creating and patronizing alternative ethnic schools is not so much an insistence upon a distinctive identity as it is profound dissatisfaction with the schooling—and the values upon which that schooling rests—of the host society. Concerns about government-operated schooling have been acute among Asian parents in the United Kingdom (Parekh 1986, 21), and "Turkish Cypriot parents . . . were horrified by what they perceived as the permissiveness of English schools" (Taylor, 1988, 146); "some Italian parents are distrustful of the apparently more liberal atmosphere of their children's schools and wonder whether their children can grow up to be serious, industrious and hard-working in such an environment. Some Italian parents would like schools and teachers to be more disciplined and authoritarian" (Taylor, 1988, 293). One Asian girl told an interviewer that her parents were more restrictive than they would otherwise be because of their revulsion at what they saw around them in the host society; she reported "that the situation is different in Pakistan, that the girls there are allowed to go outside their homes, whereas in Britain parents are afraid that daughters will 'adopt a white way of life'" (Wade & Souter, 1992, 40).

There is at present considerable controversy in the United Kingdom over separate schools organized on an ethnic or religious basis. Demand for such schools may come from parents and ethnic leaders of very different political perspectives. Sometimes a blatantly segregationist argument is advanced. A few minority ideologues, like the author of *Black England*, argue "for a more racially divided society if the ethnic minorities are to maintain their cultural identities, preferring this to any form of anglicisation or mutual influence" (Narayan, quoted by Saunders, 1980, 37). Bernard Coard, before his ill-fated return to Grenada, insisted that "We need to open Black nursery schools and supplementary schools throughout the areas we live in, in Britain. . . . Our children need to have a sense of identity, pride and belonging" (quoted in Homan, 1986, 168). The Swan Committee found that

> certain leading West Indian educationalists have continued to believe that the only way in which West Indian children can hope to succeed in educational terms is through attending separate "Black" schools since they regard existing schools as irremediably racist and dismiss any moves towards developing multicultural education as merely cosmetic and as in no way tackling the fundamental inequalities and injustices inherent in the system. Advocates of "Black" schools thus see

them as the only hope of West Indian children escaping from the "culture of failure" (*Education for All*, 1985, 515).

Nor are race and discrimination the only considerations. A Greek church in London declared its intention that "the young Cypriot children of our community will be educated and strengthened with nourishment from the national and religious ideals of the Orthodox Church and the Greek Motherland and not with the lure of dehellenization and assimilation" (Taylor, 1988, 79).

But nationalistic and ethnic considerations appear to be less prominent than those having to do with the values taught—or neglected—in British schools. A survey in 1977 found that among Cypriot parents "a very small percentage were positively satisfied with the discipline in their child's school," and another study in 1981 found that Cypriot parents "criticized schools for failure to instil moral codes" (Taylor, 1988, 152–3). Similarly, "some Italian parents are distrustful of the apparently more liberal atmosphere of their children's schools and wonder whether their children can grow up to be serious, industrious and hard-working in such an environment" (Taylor, 1988, 293).

There is mounting evidence to suggest that minority parents expect a good deal from the education system, far more, in many cases, than do majority parents. Parents of West Indian origin, in particular, are now more vocal in expressing their dissatisfactions with schools. A government commission found that a wide gulf in trust and understanding appeared to be growing between school and home: "parents appear to be losing confidence in what schools are teaching their children, and schools seem to be having limited success in explaining their aims and practices" (Tomlinson, 1984, 146).

The demand for separate minority schools in England has grown partly out of the highly organized nature of the Islamic community there, and has been stimulated recently by the heightened militancy which found expression in efforts to organize an Islamic vote in the 1987 elections and in the "Rushdie Affair" (which began with imams in Britain and not with Khomeini). The "Charter of Muslim Demands" included various measures to permit a partially separate existence for British Muslims, of which schools were merely one expression (Kepel, 1991, 62). This was possible within the context of British laws and policies that encouraged "the institutionalization of minority identities, providing important legal and financial means to representatives of 'minorities,' favoring those leaders who reified these minority identities" (Kepel, 1994, 140). The Muslim Educational Trust, founded in 1966, has sought "to safeguard and defend the distinct Muslim identity among Muslim children," protecting them from contact with "the materialistic Western culture, broken families, sexual promiscuity, alcoholism and the abandonment of morality," and the Trust has eight or ten rivals to represent the fragmented Muslim community. Islamic education has thus become a rallying point for ethnic political demands (Kepel, 1994, 153).

Minority separatism has also responded to incidents in which English parents withdraw their children from integrated schools, as in the Dewsbury incident described above. A curious aspect of this affair, in which some parents charged that the multicultural education in their local school neglected traditional Christianity, was the support they received from the separatist Muslim Parents' Association, which pointed out that "our children are at the same disadvantage because the state system makes no provision for Islamic teaching or our moral way of life, our culture or heritage" (*Times Educational Supplement*, September 11, 1987; see also Naylor, 1989). As an editorial in the *Times Educational Supplement* commented, the Dewsbury incident

> will encourage those among the Muslim community who already want to start their own schools, and discourage those—probably a majority till now—who have resisted segregation because they want to participate fully in the English educational tradition (September 11, 1987).

Some Asian community leaders in the United Kingdom have indeed been arguing for the right to receive government support for separate schools based upon Islam, parallel to the support given to Catholic and Protestant schools (Rex, 1988, 213). The leader of the group sponsoring the Islamia School pointed out that it was "mixed racially and has 23 nationalities;" the goal was not ethnic nor linguistic but religious:

> Christians and Jews are allowed to have [government-]aided schools but all sorts of reasons are given for stopping Muslims from having them. The "suppression" of equal opportunities for girls, for example, has been cited more than once and yet Muslim girls' schools have been established precisely because such equality is missing in the state system where untold pressures are brought to bear on devout youngsters, harming their education progress (Hewitt, 1988).

All of the teachers at Islamia, he pointed out, "even the religious education teacher, are state-trained and have taught in mainstream schools" (Klein, 1993).

The basis for such efforts is a growing conviction that no accommodation to Muslim beliefs and values was "feasible or indeed desirable within the existing system and in order to provide a true Islamic education for their children, it is necessary to provide Muslim [publicly funded] schools." Reportedly, many British teachers see a part of their mission as being "to liberate [Muslim] girls from their families. . . . In no other community do you find parents thought of as prison warders and villains" (Noshaba Hussain quoted by Klein, 1992b). As a government commission was told,

> a major worry for Muslim parents is the fact that their children soon begin to adopt English standards and ideas. . . . Islam is not something which can be learnt and adhered to overnight. It must be lived, breathed and fostered until it cannot be separated from life itself. Most Muslims acknowledge that Britain is a fair place to live, and in many ways they have come to depend upon it for their livelihood, but it is hard to judge how possible it is to live as a Muslim within the society as a whole (*Education for All*, 1985, 504).

The commission suggested that accommodation of the concerns of Muslim parents could be made within the educational system, reducing the demand for separate schools,

> if schools were seen by parents to be offering a more broadly-based curriculum, which reflected the multi-racial, multi-lingual and multi-faith nature of Britain today we feel this would counter many of the anxieties which have been expressed (*Education for All*, 1985, 509).

This seems contrary, however, to the same group's observation that

> much of the evidence which we have received in favour of Muslim schools stresses the need to create an Islamic ethos permeating every aspect of school life. The major aspiration of such a school is seen as educating children to be first and foremost "good Muslims" and all the other aspects of education being seen of secondary concern (*Education for All*, 1985, 504).

The Swann Commission saw pluralism as a means of achieving integration, but failed to understand the distinction between a *relativizing* pluralism and a *structural* pluralism (as in the Netherlands) that would permit distinct groups within a society to maintain their distinctiveness. "The ulti-

mate objective of Muslim education," according to an ad hoc group responding to the Swann report, "is the realization of a total submission to God on
the part of the individual, the community and humanity in general" (retrans-
lated from Kepel, 1994, 166). Parents seeking such an education for their
children would not easily be satisfied with a curriculum relativizing all forms
of religious expression. As one leader told a reporter, "parents need to feel
secure that what goes on in schools doesn't alienate their children from Islam" (Nargis Rashid, quoted by Klein, 1992b). There is some opposition
within the Muslim community in Britain even to inclusion of teaching about
Islam within the mandatory religious education instruction, unless taught
by a Muslim (Zaki, 1982, 33–38).

Demands for adaptation of English schooling to minority concerns
are generally opposed and often condemned as "racist, segregationist, and
socially divisive" by policymakers and progressive academics alike, without
acknowledgment that parents may have a legitimate interest in seeking to
pass on their own values to their children. As one Muslim leader put it, "State
schools lack an educational and moral philosophy. In all spheres of human
experience, we need answers to what's right and wrong. It shouldn't be left
to children to discover this for themselves" (Muhammed Naseem, quoted
by Klein, 1992b, 2).

Not all Muslim parents in Britain, by any means, are in favor of separate schools for their children; a study among Bangladeshi parents in Tower
Hamlets "found that parents wanted their children to attend the local state
school, providing some concessions are made such as offering *halal* meat
[corresponding to Islamic dietary requirements], a prayer room and a school
uniform that includes trousers for girls. . . . While they wanted the children
to learn their home or cultural language, they stressed that learning English
should take precedence" (Pyke, 1991, 11). Asians in Bradford were also divided over whether to demand separate schools (Dean, 1990). There are
some indications, indeed, that support for Islamic schooling is stronger
among Asian parents who are themselves fairly well acculturated and fear
that their children will become too much so, rather than among the more
marginal Bangladeshis.

Controversy flared up in 1990 when the Commission for Racial
Equality issued a report suggesting that "a multiracial society might be better off without [any] religious schools," and assuming that the primary motivations on the part of minority parents for seeking such schools were "ethnocentric bias, low teacher expectations leading to under-achievement,
racism or co-education." A Christian critic pointed out that even a growing number of Christian parents were alienated from state education and that

"the idea seldom seems to occur to the Commission that religious parents ask for religious schools for religious reasons;" the Commission reflected a secularist attitude that sees "religious phenomena as harmless cultural odds and ends instead of expressive of a whole religious world view" (Richard Wilkins, quoted by Lodge & Sanders, 1990). A Muslim leader joined in the criticism, charging that "instead of being a source of moral strength, state schools in this country bias children towards a neutral, uncommitted frame of mind" (Syed Ali Ashraf, quoted in *Times Educational Supplement*, September 21, 1990).

Muslims are not alone in seeking alternatives to the public schools. West Indian parents in England have created many "Saturday schools" which "are not intended primarily to transmit a black culture—though this has some part in the schools—but to cover the state school curriculum so that the pupils' performance in external examinations and thus economic opportunities are improved" (McLean, 1985, 329–330). The original impetus was the overidentification of Afro-Caribbean pupils in British schools as "educationally sub-normal." From their beginnings in the mid-1960s, such part-time schools have "become a part of black British life," and there is growing interest in developing private schools under the recent legislation (Klein, 1992a, 26). As noted in Chapter 4, sociologist Maureen Stone, herself West Indian, concluded that English "schools have concentrated on 'relationships' and on the 'soft-option' approach. Without exception, people working in West Indian community groups stress the importance of hard work, high aspirations, willingness to sacrifice and belief in one's ability to succeed as the only possible way forward" (Stone, 1981, 149). In this instance, then, the problem identified by the minority community as calling for the creation of parallel learning opportunities for their children was not the insensitivity of public schools to their *culture*, but insufficient respect for their *aspirations*.

By 1992, there were 26 private Islamic schools in the United Kingdom, most of them serving only girls or only boys; by 1994, some had closed, others opened, and the number stood at 27, enrolling about 1 percent of the half-million Muslim children. They vary considerably in the strictness with which they express Islam in every aspect of school life and in their efforts to teach the national curriculum; one British observer noted

a polarity between two models: a school for Muslims or a Muslim school. . . . Within the former, the institution offers a quasi-British education with aspects of Islam and Islamic studies grafted on where appropriate and subject to funding. The latter model, however, aims to provide a totally Islamic ethos within an Islamic framework, incorporating the Islamisation of knowledge, and staffed solely by Muslim teachers able actively to impart the faith (Parker-Jenkins, 1994, 13).

As of the start of the 1994–95 school year, no Islamic schools had been granted public funds, but it was widely anticipated that that situation would change in the near future, given the commitment of the Conservative government to support parental choice of schools. The government's policy document *Choice and Diversity: A New Framework for Schools* (July 1992) signaled this direction by including a provision to allow schools to "opt in" to the publicly funded system; this is expected to result eventually in public funding for Muslim as well as ultra-Orthodox Jewish and Evangelical Christian schools, which have not been able to benefit from the arrangements under which more mainstream religious schools have long been supported by the government (Beckett, 1993; Dean, 1993; Hackett, 1992). Controversy broke out again in February 1995, however, with the rejection of an application for "voluntary aided status" (that was enjoyed by hundreds of Anglican and Roman Catholic and some Jewish schools) from an Islamic girls' school in Bradford; the government insisted that it had nothing against Islamic schools as such but that this school had management and structural deficiencies; Muslim leaders complained of a continuing pattern of unfair treatment (Pyke, 1995, 11).

There have been stirrings of a demand for publicly-supported Islamic schools in Scotland as well (Henderson, 1994, 12).

The Netherlands

As it became clear to most labor migrants that they and their families would not be going home, that they were becoming *de facto* immigrants, it became increasingly pressing for many of them to learn how they could maintain the most important elements of their culture and religion (Strijp, 1990, 26). Nowhere has this been supported by public policy so generously as in the Netherlands.

The Dutch education system is based upon a constitutional guarantee of the freedom to establish and obtain public funding for any school that is able to attract a sufficient number of pupils and meets other government requirements, but authorities for some years did not encourage the use of this freedom for the operation of schools by ethnic and linguistic minority groups (Entzinger, 1984, 116). While recognizing that each group had a right "to live and give shape to their own identity," the government insisted that "in general there is no difference between minorities and the rest of the population" (*Regeringsnota over het minderhedenbeleid*, 1983). An earlier draft of the government policy had stressed that

> if minorities mostly or exclusively call on values and/or interests that differ from those of the host society and set themselves apart from this society, that will lead to isolation. Members of the group can then be held back from actually orienting themselves to the surrounding society, at the cost of their chances within the society (*Ontwerp-Minderhedennota*, 1981).

Although there was no question of the *right* of Hindu and Muslim groups to set up schools and—if enough parents selected these schools— to receive full public funding, local authorities were not eager to give their approval. A Hindu group in The Hague experienced many delays in obtaining approval, while the education officials of Eindhoven and Rotterdam expressed their regret over the necessity of allowing Islamic schools (*Samenwijs*, May 1988, January 1989). A protest petition from 14 elementary schools in Rotterdam, in 1990, warned that approval of an additional Islamic school would increase ethnic segregation, though it has been pointed out that the enrollment of most of those schools was already heavily minority. Though many of the protesting schools were themselves Catholic or Protestant, the petition curiously did not acknowledge any positive side to creation of a school corresponding to the religious beliefs of parents (Shadid & Van Koningsveld, 1990, 22).

The resistance reflected in large part the opposition of many Labor Party leaders—in control of the government of most cities where immigrants are concentrated—to non-public schooling in general, and to the teaching of religion within the framework of formal schooling. Muslims complain that their long-standing requests for Islamic instruction within public schools have been ignored, or trivialized with a comparative religion approach that stresses festivals but not beliefs. As the chairman of the Hindu Education Foundation pointed out,

> You don't bring a Hindu child up as a Hindu by organizing a Hindu festival or an exotic day. Our philosophy of life does not find a place in the public school. . . . We don't want the superficial alone, and that's why we want a Hindu school.

Another frequent objection was that such schools would lead to isolation.

Advocates insist that this is hypocrisy. After all, a Muslim leader argued that "there's no difference between the [public] inner-city schools and our school. In those schools the foreign children are separate." Similarly, a Hindu leader noted that

> in The Hague there is a Catholic school with 70 to 80 percent Hindu children. All the Hindu festivals are celebrated. When we say, take the Catholic label off and make it Hindu, we're accused of trying to segregate and polarize (Balinge, 1988, 324–326).

Despite the resistance of authorities, a publicly funded Islamic school was able to get off the ground with a hundred pupils in late 1988. The leaders insisted that it was "a Dutch elementary school on an Islamic basis," and noted that all five teachers were Dutch, supplemented by a Moroccan and a Turkish teacher to provide language and culture lessons. The lesson plan was that of other Dutch schools, except that the periods of religious (or humanistic) instruction provided in other Dutch schools were devoted to Islam. Dutch was the language of instruction except for the periods of religion and of supplemental language and culture. The Moroccan chairman of the school's trustees pointed out that non-Muslim pupils were welcome and would be treated with the same respect that Muslim pupils have experienced in Catholic and Protestant schools; apparently no irony was intended.

In this connection it is interesting that it was the local Protestant School Association that provided the necessary guarantees so that this Islamic school could get started, and that there was no contact with the embassies of Morocco or of Turkey. The Muslim community is making use of the existing structures for denominational organization within Dutch society, rather than operating as an outpost of the homeland.

The Tarieq-ibn-Ziyad School (mostly Moroccan) was founded in Eindhoven and the Al-Ghazali School (mostly Turkish) in Rotterdam in 1988–89. The founders were from traditional Muslim circles. In 1988, however, the Islamitic Foundation for Education in the Netherlands (ISNO) was founded, in part as a less highly traditional alternative, influenced by the "establishment" Islam of Turkey. In 1989 it opened elementary schools in Amsterdam, The Hague, and Rotterdam. Members of the board are mostly middle-class Turks, "enlightened" Sunni Muslims. The chairman said "our children will become more Dutch all the time, but they need to know where they stand, they need to have their own *zuil* [sector of society] and not be counted in with the Catholics or Protestants." Another board member said, "it is precisely our policy to make sure that our children can make good progress in the society right away. We are trying to convey Islam in a Dutch form." According to a Dutch observer, "An important reason to start their own schools now is that many parents are growing ever more concerned over the rapid pace at which their children become 'Westerners'" (Teunissen, 1990, 46). Enough signatures of parents willing to commit their school-aged children were gathered in the large cities to justify six to eight new schools. The initiators are thinking about secondary schools and even about a Muslim university in ten years or so. The ISNO schools are very much like Dutch elementary schools, "under Turkish-Muslim governance."

The same year (1988–89), the Shri-Visnoe School was started in The Hague, and the next year other Hindu schools were founded in Amsterdam and Rotterdam; by May 1993 the three schools enrolled over 400 pupils (Bloemberg & Nijhuis, 1993, 35, 37). The first Hindu school admitted children from all varieties of Hinduism, and teaches customs and practices which many parents are no longer able to pass on to their children (Teunissen, 1990, 50). The Dutch school inspector found in 1992 no clear definition of what the Hindu character of this school consisted of, and concluded that it was basically pluralistic and tolerant; the posters and drawings by children were not distinctively Hindu (Bloemburg & Nijhuis, 1993, 38). These schools do not instruct pupils primarily in their home language, nor seek to shelter them from the language of the host society. Several hours a week of instruction in Hindi is provided as part of religious instruction in the three Hindu schools; otherwise Dutch is the language of instruction in all subjects. The children speak Dutch and some Sarnami (a creole of Hindi spoken in Surinam); the material used for Hindi instruction is imported from India and does not relate well to the actual experience of the children. Both Hindu and Christian feastdays are observed, to ensure that the children are not out of touch with either their tradition or their environment (Bloemburg & Nijhuis, 1993).

The concern of the Islamic and Hindu schools is less with language than with providing the children with an alternative to the *values* of Dutch society and thus of Dutch schools; they seek to provide an alternative schooling that is more consistent with the beliefs of immigrant parents, while equipping pupils to participate fully in the Dutch economy. A study of Turkish immigrants found that they had concerns not only with the norms and values presented in Dutch schools, but even more with the fact that teachers took no responsibility for overseeing the relationships between boys and girls; they deplored what they perceived as a lack of discipline and respect for adults. "It is thus not so much the content of education as the manner in which it is provided that determines the image [held by immigrants] of Dutch education" (Willems & Cottaar, 1990, 19). Similarly, a study of Surinamese parents found many concerned that their children were imitating the behavior of Dutch children (Koot, Tjon-a-Ten, & Uniken Venema, 1985, 61).

Groups in the Muslim and Hindu communities are seeking to reinforce their ability to socialize their children in values with which they are comfortable, in order to protect and isolate them in some respects from the acids of modernity. The fact that different models of Hindu schooling (Schwencke, 1994) as of Islamic schooling have now emerged reflects the fact that within each community there are those who choose to stay at arm's length from the host society, while others seek to occupy a middle position between two cultures. The call for Hindu and Islamic schools is in either case not related to ethnic nationalism or to a "myth of return," but to the universal desire of parents to have a major say in the raising of their children. The optimistic scenario for these schools is that

> this institutional segregation must lead later to societal integration. Through separate establishment schools can strengthen the cultural distinctiveness and self-worth of pupils. The schools make pupils conscious of their culture and their position in The Netherlands. . . . As their identity is strengthened, they will be better able—as individuals and as a group—to protect themselves from domination and discrimination. More [Islamic] schools should therefore be established. Self-organization can contribute to a considerable extent to the maintenance of culture and to better school achievement (Teunissen, 1990, 54).

It should be noted that the new schools (now numbering several dozen) serving the Muslim immigrant community in the Netherlands are *Islamic* rather than Turkish or Moroccan, and one proposed school in Utrecht was turned down because it would be explicitly Turkish. Even though all the pupils could turn out to be of one ethnic origin, this was the case with only one of six Islamic schools studied in 1990. That in the Hague, for example, enrolled 20 Turkish, 99 Moroccan, 7 Tunisian, and 6 Pakistani pupils; 4 of the 9 teachers were Dutch, and another 4 (somewhat curiously) Surinamese, while of the 9 only 2 were Muslim. Indeed, in none of this sample of six Islamic schools was a majority of the faculty Muslim, though all teachers and pupils were expected to abide by Islamic behavioral standards, including modest dress and some form of head covering for women; non-Muslim pupils, if any, would not be required to take part in religious observances (Shadid & Van Koningsveld, 1990, 19–20).

As noted above, these minority schools teach in Dutch, with two hours a week of "home language and culture" instruction comparable to that provided to ethnic minority children in other Dutch schools (see Chapter 7). The religious instruction—one or two hours a week, as in other schools—is sometimes given in home languages as well, with the result that one school must provide this instruction in Turkish, Moroccan Arabic, and Urdu (Shadid & Van Koningsveld, 1990, 20). Under Dutch educational law and policy, a school could not be established on the basis of language or ethnicity, but religion is a privileged basis for school selection, enjoying protection as a right of conscience (Rath, Groenendijk, & Penninx, 1992, 32).

Advice and in-service training for the new Islamic schools was provided initially by the (Protestant) Christian Pedagogical Study Center, but with its help a similar Islamic organization was established in 1991 (Triesscheijn & Geelen, 1991, 160–161).

A government inspection of existing Islamic schools in early 1990 concluded that they differed very little from other schools in the Netherlands (Shadid & Van Koningsveld, 1990, 23). It was notable, indeed, that at a time when the Rushdie affair in the United Kingdom and the controversy over Muslim girls covering their hair in France and Belgium suggested an irreconcilable opposition between Islam and Western societies, the structurally pluralistic Dutch society was able to accommodate the desire of some—by no means all—Muslim parents for schools reflecting their beliefs. It seems likely that this helps to explain the relative unimportance of Islamic fundamentalism in the Netherlands (Güler & Van der Heijden, 1990, 71–72).

Germany

The promotion of separate schooling by ethnic community groups has owed as much to a rejection of the schools of the host society as it has to a desire to promote an alternative culture or religious tradition. Parents from what was then Yugoslavia were reported to have considered German schools inferior to those of their homeland, with respect to academic level and discipline. Tension exists between the home language-and-culture instruction provided by arrangement with school authorities in most Western European nations and the competing after-school Koran instruction. One of the responses of Turkish families to their experiences in West Germany as elsewhere in Western Europe has been an increase in the fervor of Islamic observances, including the support of highly traditional religious instruction, and avoidance of the recreational activities available (Institut für Zukunftsforschung, 1981, 247, 30).

In the Greek press the situation of Greek children in German schools is commonly described in very negative terms, echoed by the Greek authorities, and immigrant parents in one German community kept their children out of school for a time in order to support their demand for a separate school (Giotitsas, 1988, 93). The Greek government has urged German authorities to provide two alternatives for Greek parents. One group, it said, would like its children in German schools, in regular classes, with supplemental home language and culture instruction provided by the community with assistance from their consulates. This option should continue to be provided. But there is another group, "and it doesn't appear to be smaller than the first, which does not agree to having its children integrated." Their concerns had not been met by German proposals for all-Greek bilingual classes located in regular German schools and under the authority of German administrators, since these classes were planned as transitional with a declining proportion of the instruction in Greek over the course of several years. This was not satisfactory for parents who intended to return to Greece with their children, and doubly unsatisfactory because the German schools offered no guarantees that their children would be able to keep up with their German schoolmates and thus enjoy equal opportunity. There were suspicions, on the Greek side, that the eagerness of German educators to integrate their children had more to do with the declining German birthrate and a desire to protect jobs than it did with real concern for the future of the children. What was needed were separate schools designed to meet the needs of Greek children in Germany (Karayannidis, 1982).

Such schools have in fact existed since 1965, when a private Greek elementary school was founded in Munich, serving 400 pupils the first year. Subsequently an intermediate and a secondary school were established there, and by 1980 the system enrolled some 3,500 Greek pupils full time. The pupils are prepared for both Greek and German school certificates; the Greek university system reserves about 5 percent of its places for Greek students living in other countries. In other parts of Germany, as well, the strong Greek interest in education has led to a demand for separate schools (Kanavakis, 1982).

A study of ethnic organizations in the Frankfurt-am-Main area found that the Greek community was more deeply divided over the question of whether its children should attend German schools or separate Greek schools than over any other issue. After a long struggle both within the Greek community and with German school authorities, the proponents of separate schools had their way and a separate school was established, particularly due to the efforts of two of the parents' associations, one of the "Greek communities," and the Greek Orthodox Church. Thus the primary polarization within the Greek community is over this assimilation issue and only secondarily based on political conflict between Left and Right (Schoeneberg, 1985, 423–424)

There are other cases in which separate schooling has been developed in order to resist the encroachments of a majority culture perceived as being so attractive to the younger generation that they are at risk of losing their connection with their cultural heritage and ethnic community. This has notably been true of most of the indigenous language minority groups discussed in Chapter 3; thus ethnic activists among the Navajo in the United States and Saami (Lapps) in Scandinavia have sought to use schooling to mobilize adults as well as children "into a politicized ethnic-interest group" (Paulston, 1992, 55).

As a securely French Islam evolves, with its own institutions independent of foreign powers and expressing themselves in French, it is inevitable that the demand will grow for approval of and public funding for Islamic schools, parallel with the Catholic and other schools that already function under the provisions of the *Loi Debré*, adopted at the start of the Fifth Republic in 1959, extended by the *Loi Guermeur* of 1977. The *Loi Debré* created a number of alternatives for nonpublic schools: (1) to continue completely independent of government intervention, subject to employing qualified teachers; (2) to be absorbed into the national public education system; (3) to accept government requirements as to curriculum and testing in exchange for staff salaries (*contrat simple*); or (4) to accept, in addition, some government control over pedagogy and the selection of teachers, in exchange for operating expenses as well as salaries (*contrat d'association*) (Georgel & Thorel, 1995).

If the idea that the common public school should uphold universalistic values on behalf of national unity led to nationwide political conflict in France in 1984, when the alternative was Catholic schooling (Savary, 1985; Leclerc, 1985), it can be anticipated that demands for approval and public funding for Islamic schools will be even more controversial (Malaurie, 1990, 11). A survey carried out for *Le Monde* in 1989 found 57 percent of Muslim respondents in favor of Islamic schools (36 percent were opposed), while French respondents opposed the idea by 63 to 27 percent.

Creation of Islamic schools is not always controversial, in other political contexts. "A number of new Muslim day schools have been established in Melbourne [Australia] with the assistance of funds from the Federal government" (Foster & Stockley, 1988, 109). Even in Ireland, with its relatively very low rate of immigration, separate schools have been established for the children of immigrants. President Mary Robinson of Ireland attended the opening of a new Islamic school facility; like recently founded Islamic schools in Australia and the Netherlands, it receives public funding (*Times Educa-*

tional Supplement, May 7, 1993). As in those cases, the primary motivation is religion, not the maintenance of a minority language.

Summary

There are thus many schools that have been organized outside of the regular public education system to serve the children of minority communities. To some, these are important opportunities for the exercise of community initiative in order to maintain shared values and to pass them along to the rising generation. Other ethnic minority leaders reject such "dwarf schools," in which the home language is used as a medium of instruction and a ghetto effect is created, as contrary to the long-term interests of their communities (Abadan-Unat, 1975, 314).

Those who argue that separate schooling will lead to community mobilization and thus to eventual political power are probably deluding themselves. Maintaining a language and other cultural symbols *can* serve as a rallying point for political mobilization over against a dominant majority, when ethnic elites manage to "heighten awarenesses that are only latent, so that not only will masses come to feel that they constitute a nationality but that they will also be willing to act upon the basis of that feeling" (Fishman, 1989, 121), but, as we have seen in Chapter 5, the conditions under which this is at all likely to occur are quite rare. Short-term arrangements, like the "freedom schools" organized in many parts of the American South and in northern cities like Boston during the civil rights struggle are the exception that proves the rule: they were established to make a point about the schooling (and, more broadly, consciousness-raising) of minority youth, and were disbanded once the point was made sufficiently clearly that those youth returned to their regular schools. Freedom schools for Chinese-American pupils flourished briefly in San Francisco in the early 1970s, in protest against a desegregation plan that Chinese community leaders did not feel took the needs of these pupils sufficiently into account. The three community-operated schools enrolled 1,465 pupils, 85 percent of whom were new immigrants. A study of the Chinese freedom schools concluded that "culture and language were not the main reason for the establishment of the competing system . . . the Freedom Schools . . . concentrated on basic curriculum, not on Chinese Studies" (Lum, 1978, 70). And when the political crisis was over, they closed.

SEPARATE SCHOOLING BY GOVERNMENT INITIATIVE

American educational policy has promoted short-term segregation of language minority pupils through bilingual and other programs developed to respond to what is understood, by the planners, to be their distinctive educational needs. Other countries tend to be more alert to the possibility that separate programs may turn into long-term segregated tracks; the British Commission for Racial Equality found, in 1986, that the way that language minority pupils were being grouped for English-language instruction in one community had the effect of segregating them in violation of the 1976 Race Relations Act (Tomlinson, 1989a, 31). French policy, in particular, is strongly resistant to separate provision for the schooling of minority children.

Most such programs are intended to be transitional and thus short term, as are the reception programs (some bilingual, others not) for immigrant pupils that have been developed in the other countries under consideration (Chapter 7). There are also instances of what may turn out to be permanently separate tracks developed for language minority children in public schools and justified by the special characteristics of their learning styles or goals. The primary examples are in the United States, Germany, and Sweden.

THE UNITED STATES

The assignment of ethnic minority children to segregated schools has often been justified on grounds of educational needs. There is a long American tradition of separate schooling for American Indian (Native American) children, reaching back to colonial times, and based upon the conviction that only an unusually powerful treatment could be sufficiently influential for pupils so fundamentally different from white children. Thus a government report in 1867 concluded that

> all experience has demonstrated the impossibility of educating Indian children while they are permitted to consort and associate with their ignorant, barbarous, and superstitious parents. . . . The only Indian schools which have attained to any degree of success are those where the means have been supplied to feed, clothe, and lodge the children separate from their parents and members of their tribes (Doolittle, 1974, 1736).

Schooling of African-American children was also generally in segregated schools in the North and, after Emancipation, in the South as well.

In general, no separate schooling was established for the children of immigrants, however, apart from short-term reception classes in which they could learn the rudiments of English. To the contrary, much of the impetus behind the formation of the "common school" system was concern for the rapid assimilation of these children, as when Calvin Stowe urged, in 1836, that

> it is altogether essential to our national strength and peace, if not even to our national existence, that the foreigners who settle on our soil should cease to be Europeans and become Americans. . . . The most effectual, and indeed the only effectual way, to produce this individuality and harmony of national feeling and character, is to bring our children into the same schools and have them educated together. The children of immigrants must be taught English and prepared for the common English schools. (Stowe, 1974, 994).

The great exception consisted of the children of German immigrants, for whom public authorities maintained a considerable number of bilingual programs and even schools for a time during the nineteenth century, largely as a means of persuading German parents to enroll their children in "common schools" rather than in Lutheran or Catholic parochial schools. This exception reflected the fact that German immigrants had a rather higher cultural and educational level than that of many of the midwestern Americans in whose midst they settled; the German-English public school in St. Louis was established in 1837, a year before that city had an all-English public school (Genesee, 1987, 2).

The schooling of Mexican-American children, however, was not generally treated like that of immigrants; there was a presumption that separate treatment was educationally appropriate for them. To what extent this reflected the desire of the dominant white population to keep its children separate from them is difficult to judge. Segregation of Mexican Americans, unlike that of blacks, Indians, and in some cases Chinese, was accomplished without a legal mandate. Thus a Texas court ruled in *Del Rio Independent School District v. Salvatierra* (1930) that Mexicans were white and should not be subject to the legally mandated segregation of black pupils. "The judgment, however, was overturned by the appellate court on the basis that the school board had the right to segregate Mexican students because of their 'language problems'" (Donato, Menchaca, & Valencia, 37). Assigning Mexican-American pupils in grades one through three to a different school than their Anglo counterparts, the higher court found, was a legitimate exercise of pedagogical judgment. "Correction of language deficiency as determined by the educational experience of the Del Rio administrators was deemed adequate justification for separation," but the district was required to use a test administered to all pupils as a basis for this judgment (Allsup, 1977, 31).

The bulk of professional opinion during the 1920's was on the side of segregation for educational reasons. . . . Mexican children needed a special curriculum to suit their special abilities. . . . American values, sanitation practices, and work habits were stressed. And educators argued that the process could best be accomplished by separate schools and classrooms. . . . Segregation of Mexican and Mexican-American students, then, was a product of community pressure, sanctioned by professional educators and supported by the studies of educational psychologists (Wollenberg, 1974, 320–321).

A California superintendent wrote that "pupils should not be put into Mexican classes because they are Mexican, they should be put there because they can profit most by instruction offered in such classes" (quoted by Wollenberg, 1974, 321).

Even when Mexican children were not assigned to segregated schools, they were often segregated within schools on the basis of what was assumed to be their educational needs. A study by George Sánchez of ten Texas school districts in the 1940s found widespread assignment to separate classes, varying considerably from district to district in which grades were affected and how extensive was the segregation of extracurricular activities, in which, presumably, language proficiency was of less significance but social considerations very important. Seven of the ten, for example, did not allow Mexican-American pupils to participate with Anglo pupils in sports (San Miguel, 1987b, 121). In another related Texas study, school superintendents gave the following reasons to justify separate schooling for Mexican Americans:

- Local prejudice and inability to speak English.
- Latin-Americans favor the plan; children are much more at ease and they will naturally segregate anyway. They are not at the disadvantage of being graded in English on same standards.
- Public opinion.
- Children with language difficulty can be given special treatment and special methods in teaching may be employed.
- So many in the first grade, and need cleaning up to be taught. Lack of English language knowledge.
- School board is antagonistic toward housing [them] in the same building. These children need five or six years of Americanization before being placed with American children. Their standard of living is too low—they are dirty, lousy, and need special teaching in health and cleanliness. They also need special teaching in the English language (quoted by Kibbe, 1946, 96–97).

"So many in the first grade . . .," reflects the fact that, in the early 1940s, Texas had 37,000 Hispanic pupils enrolled in first grade, and only 19,000 persisting to second grade; by eighth grade there were fewer than 6,000 (Kibbe, 1946, 87).

The mixture of educational and social reasons given for the practice of separate schooling for language minority pupils has persisted into present discussions. The educational arguments could not be dismissed then, and they cannot be dismissed now, as simply a rationalization of prejudice on the one hand and of ethnic separatism on the other, but neither can they be entirely detached from such motivations.

In *Delgado v. Bastrop Independent School District* (1948), in Texas, the court ruled that placing Mexican students in separate schools was discriminatory and illegal (Schlossman, 1983, 895). The court did allow school boards to segregate Mexican students in separate classes within a school "solely for instructional purposes" on the basis of their limited English proficiency as measured by "scientific and standardized" tests (Allsup, 1977, 34). "Thus, this initiated a new form of school segregation within desegregated school settings based on a language rationale" (Donato, Menchaca, & Valencia, 38).

George Sánchez, one of the most distinguished experts on the schooling of Mexican-American children in the postwar period, "considered it dangerous for a minority group often stigmatized and segregated for language handicap to endorse pedagogical reforms that might rationalize the beliefs and actions of its enemies" (Schlossman, 1983, 900). Insisting upon the use of Spanish for the instruction of Mexican-American pupils might reinforce the common perception that they were incapable of being successful in the mainstream of an English-speaking society. "While vernacular instruction may have demonstrated its pedagogical value in other countries, it was inappropriate in America because it required a degree of segregation 'not only objectionable but intolerable under our philosophy of the "unitary" school and our denial of "separate but equal" doctrine'" (Schlossman, 1983, 901).

Although evidence for the superior effectiveness of separate programs is distinctly mixed, various government initiatives in recent years have provided such schooling in the name of improving the academic and social achievement of minority pupils. The most extensive form of government-sponsored ethnic segregation—though it is seldom understood in this way—has been through separate bilingual education programs of the sort that Sánchez warned against.

While officially intended as a transitional means to enable pupils to acquire the majority language quickly while continuing studies in their home language, bilingual programs have sometimes acquired a momentum of their own, in which maintenance of the minority language and culture have become the dominant concern and there is no urgency felt about placing children in mainstream classes. An important study of federally funded bilingual education programs in the United States, in the late 1970s, found that "less than a third of the students in these classrooms were there because of their limited English-speaking ability. Project directors were openly proud of their maintenance programs, and only 5 percent of them said that Spanish-dominant students were transferred to an English-only classroom once they had learned enough English to function in school" (Hakuta, 1986, 215).

State laws requiring or permitting bilingual instruction for pupils unable to perform classwork in English invariably stress the transitional and voluntary nature of these programs, but those who advocate bilingual education are often uncomfortable with the idea that parents whose children are eligible might be allowed to opt for assignment to a class in which only English is used. Lawyers for the plaintiffs in New York City's *Aspira* (1974) case argued—unsuccessfully—that assignment to a bilingual class should be mandatory for all eligible children (Glazer, 1983, 155). The judge ruled, however, that his order that bilingual programs be made available "imposed no *duties* upon the members of the class to 'enjoy' those rights" (quoted by Weinberg, 1983, 30).

After the 1974 *Lau* decision, school administrators had every reason to believe that they were not only permitted but required to educate language minority pupils separately, at least for whatever period of time was required to bring them up to speed in English. The argument, by some linguists and minority language advocates, that the best way to learn English was through a number of years (5 to 7 years is the figure most commonly used) of a bilingual program provided a strong rationale for extending this period of separation. When the argument was further broadened, as we have seen in Chapter 5, to include the alleged need to include pupils in separate bilingual programs to affirm their ethnic identity, whether or not they made predominant use of a minority language, such programs came to work directly against school desegregation efforts. "Bilingual programs, when they are established as one-way maintenance programs for Hispanics only, are equivalent to the establishment of a dual educational system," which is the very definition of racial segregation (Eyler, Cook & Ward, 1983, 139). Rather than being a short-term measure (like reception classes in many European countries) to enable the newcomer to acquire some proficiency in the language of the school, "English-speaking Hispanics are heavily represented in bilingual transitional programs [because] transfer out is rare in many of these programs, which creates Hispanic tracks within the school" (Eyler, Cook, & Ward, 1983, 139–140).

This is partly the result of administrative practices that (presumably unintentionally) work against the integration of language-minority pupils. For example, "although . . . guidelines allow a percentage of non-LEP students to participate in bilingual programs paid for by federal and state funds, reimbursement is usually tied to the number of LEP students served in each classroom. There is, therefore, a disincentive to include non-LEP students, white or black, in these programs, since extra local monies would be needed" (Fernández & Guskin, 1981, 121). It is not surprising that a study by the leading Mexican-American organization, "the National Task Force de la Raza, reporting on the fifth year of federal bilingual programs in 1974, found that the enrolment in programs for Chicano children was 88 percent Spanish-speaking and only 12 percent English-speaking students" (Orfield, 1978, 218).

There was also an element of intentionality in these separate assignments on the part of the majority society as represented by local school boards and administrators; it has been correctly pointed out that "white society seems most supportive of bilingual efforts when bilingual education is translated into 'separate' education for Hispanics" (Noboa, 1980, 21). This willingness to make provisions for language minority pupils that do not require integrating them with the children of the majority is abetted by the desire of many ethnic leaders to preserve the distinctiveness of their group into the next generation (see Chapter 4). It is not surprising that in hearings in 1973 before a Senate committee, "the Puerto Rican Association for National Affairs denounced proposals that at least 30 percent of English speakers be included in bilingual programs as an unnecessary waste of scarce funds" (Orfield, 1978, 219), or that the plaintiffs in the *Aspira* case in New York City asked the court (unsuccessfully) to order the school system to provide a "maintenance bilingual education program" for Puerto Rican children whose parents requested it, even if they were proficient in English and thus able to function adequately in regular integrated classes (Santiago, 1986, 158).

The tendency of ethnic group leaders to call for separate programs is compounded by the fact that separate programs, in education as in other human services, provide a major source of professional employment for educated and fully bilingual members of the group (Hakuta, 1986, 227). A study by Lois Steinberg in the 1970s noted the creation in New York City of "an informal network of Puerto Rican educators whose careers have been promoted through federal initiatives." Indeed, their "upward mobility was confined to federally-funded bilingual positions" (Weinberg, 1983, 24). Similarly, Bernard Spolsky pointed out that

> in the Navajo situation, the most important outcome of bilingual education is probably related to changes in the economic and political situation. At the moment, the 53,000 Navajo students in school, 90% of whom speak Navajo, are taught by 2600 teachers, only 100 of whom speak Navajo. A decision to establish bilingual education, even a transitional variety for the first three grades, sets up a need for a thousand Navajo speaking teachers. Whatever effects this may have on the educational or linguistic situation, it is clear that it immediately provides jobs within the community for a sizeable group of people (quoted by Paulston, 1992, 90).

Of course, as we have seen, 90 percent is far too high an estimate of the number of Navajo children speaking their tribal language; less than one third are actually fluent in Navajo, but this does not prevent language activists from arguing that schooling should seek to restore active use of language not only by using it for instruction but also by creating many jobs for which it is a prerequisite, to overcome the main cause of loss of any minority language, its lack of utility.

Separate education is also consistent with the priority given, by the organizers of many of these programs (and contrary to the stated intention of the authorizing legislation), to minority language maintenance. "Almost nine-tenths of the programs were aimed at permanent maintenance of Spanish competence rather than at a more effective transition to English" (Orfield, 1978, 218).

Two Arizona legislators who were instrumental in passage of a law, in 1984, that gave local districts more discretion about what types of services to be provided to LEP pupils were critical of bilingual education advocates as more interested in "preserving their own culture" than in improving the academic performance of Hispanic pupils. "Both interpreted earlier efforts to increase bilingual services as supporting an ideological agenda of isolating Hispanic children in bilingual programs" (Medina & Sacken, 1988, 293).

This is too bluntly stated. In fact, most advocates for separate programs are convinced that they offer the only hope to improve academic performance by pupils who belong to "subordinated groups," by improving both their individual self-esteem and also their positive identification with their ethnic group. As noted in Chapter 5, this agenda has come, for many, to outweigh the earlier arguments for the use of the home language, which was based upon theories of how language and cognitive function develop.

Amado Padilla enumerates the elements of the political/cultural agenda for separate minority education:

> first, there is the explicit philosophy that education should be in the hands of culturally similar teachers (i.e., members of the same ethnic group). Second, there is the belief that the curriculum should be as highly relevant to the culture of the student as possible. To ensure this, the medium of instruction should be weighted heavily on the side of the home language, rather than English. Finally, there is the belief that the students must be instilled with and/or reinforced for having pride in their cultural membership. This orientation is more than just cultural maintenance. It is . . . the antithesis of assimilation. Separatists would prefer to exclude "American" cultural values and traditions from the curriculum to the extent possible (Padilla, 1982, 58).

Here a personal note may be permitted. The author was the Massachusetts state official responsible for urban education and civil rights for more than twenty years. Approximately one-third of the Hispanic pupils in the Commonwealth were, at any one time, enrolled in bilingual education programs. Almost all of the advocacy by Hispanic organizations, however, was in support of these programs; very rarely were issues raised about the larger group of pupils who were dominant in English but faring poorly, by and large, in the mainstream.

In effect, then, there has been a tacit agreement between many educational administrators and many ethnic leaders: the former will support a separate program within which ethnic-group maintenance is encouraged and employment is provided on the basis of ethnicity, in exchange for which the latter will not insist upon integration. The idea that bilingual programs should be a temporary, transitional measure, parallel to the reception classes for newly arrived immigrant pupils in many countries, is rejected by many advocates, who argue that transitional

> bilingual education programs, even when committed to language maintenance, can reproduce a symbolic universe that subordinates and obscures ethnic culture, identity, and values. . . . Insistence that bilingual education be temporary and transitional, moving children from "special" classrooms to "regular" classrooms, reinforces the identification of equality with access to a given social order; suggests that assimilation, conformity, and sameness are prerequisites to equal participation (Olneck, 1990, 239).

Language-based segregation has persisted in American schools with large numbers of language-minority pupils despite the Federal Appeals Court ruling, in *Keyes v. School District No. 1* (Denver), that maintaining a segregated school—even for purposes of bilingual instruction—violated the Constitution. In the *Keyes* case, Hispanic groups called for bilingual/bicultural programs "as the best approach to counterbalance the educational inequality caused by Anglo-oriented curricula." They asked "that schools in which the programs were located not be desegregated during the period the programs were being developed." The Tenth Circuit ruled, however, that "bilingual education is not a substitute for desegregation . . . such instruction must be subordinate to a plan of school desegregation" (quoted by San Miguel, 1987b, 183–184).

At the level of explicit American policy, bilingual education has been advocated as a method of making a transition to proficiency in English rather than as a means of maintaining the minority language or an identity based upon cultural and political distinctiveness. However, for the reasons given, "Federal programs in bilingual education and in civil rights enforcement, though nominally affirming integration, have actually strengthened segregation" (Orfield, 1978, 220).

Administrators of bilingual programs have sometimes sought to make it difficult for parents to remove their children from a class taught in their home language. In Massachusetts, for example, the requirement was imposed that a parent write a letter making this request, and school officials were warned not to prompt with wording; this can be a significant barrier for immigrant parents, often illiterate or at least intimidated by composing an "official" letter to a government agency. Language minority parents are sometimes told, by school officials, that their children will be ineligible for *any* supplemental support, including English as a second language, if they are not enrolled in the bilingual program. No choice is then offered between the extremes of language and academic support in a segregated program and being placed in a regular class with no attention to needs arising in the course of second-language acquisition. Children in the second situation (including those in schools where no bilingual program is offered) not infrequently are subsequently diagnosed as having learning disabilities or other needs and end up segregated in a special education program.

The segregated educational settings experienced by many language minority pupils in the United States appear to have negative educational effects. Analysis of nationwide data collected by the Office for Civil Rights showed that "large bilingual class loadings are associated with a lack of future educational attainment [defined as not dropping out of school and graduating from high school] for Hispanics. Such a finding is consistent with the use of bilingual classes as an Hispanic track rather than a program that builds skills needed to succeed in school" (Meier & Stewart, 1991, 143). As a form of academic tracking, "bilingual education . . . emphasizes grouping students in homogeneous units and teaching different students with different curricula. Such a program fits the pattern of academic grouping but uses language rather than IQ as the grouping criterion" (Meier & Stewart, 1991, 78). As a result,

> schools with little Hispanic-Anglo contact in bilingual classes had fewer Hispanics in gifted classes and fewer Hispanic students graduating from high school. . . . Regardless of how much Hispanic students are helped by these transitional bilingual classes, they are hurt greatly by the separation from Anglo students. When they rejoin their Anglo classmates, they are less likely to gain access to the best educational opportunities within the school district (e.g., gifted classes) and less likely to graduate (Meier & Stewart, 1991, 204–205).

It appears, indeed, that segregation based on language is at least as harmful as segregation based on race or ethnicity (Donato, Menchaca, & Valencia, 1991, 44). This was not at all the intention of the 1970 government guidelines on the basis of which bilingual programs were set up to benefit language minority pupils, and which were given authoritative status by the 1974 Supreme Court ruling in *Lau v. Nichols*; the guidelines insisted that

> any ability grouping or tracking system employed by the school system to deal with the special language skill needs of national origin-minority group children must be designed to meet such language skill needs as soon as possible and must not operate as an educational deadend or permanent track (quoted by Baker & de Kanter, 1983, 207).

Despite this unequivocal warning against allowing bilingual programs to become a separate educational track, it has become the prevalent view among advocates that pupils require five-to-seven years in such programs before they are ready to be "mainstreamed." "The lack of clear entry and exit criteria was extending the children's participation in bilingual programs long after they were able to function in the standard classroom and curriculum—giving these programs the unnecessary and undesirable stigma of permanent tracks" (Castellanos, 1983, 145). The inevitable result is a high degree of segregation within schools, even when the schools themselves have been painfully desegregated. Indeed,

Hispanic groups have often accepted bilingual education in lieu of desegregation; in fact, some Hispanic educators oppose desegregation because it would limit the use of bilingual education. . . . [The data show that] bilingual education not only increases in more segregated schools, it reduces the level of intergroup contact. Overall, the results show modest support for the idea that second-generation discrimination is a substitute for segregation (Meier and Stewart, 1991, 185).

As a result of the way in which bilingual education is organized in many American school districts, the linguistic separation of limited English proficient] students in desegregated schools is becoming a form of resegregation. Efforts to provide bilingual education on an integrated basis, as in the "two-way" programs developed by a few schools (Glenn & LaLyre, 1991), have not spread widely, less because of any unwillingness on the part of nonlinguistic minority parents to enroll their children than on a lack of commitment by school authorities—and sometimes lack of support by bilingual education advocates (Castellanos, 1983, 87).

This was by no means the intention of the pioneers in the field of bilingual education, one of whom stated that, "given only two polar choices—ethnic segregation with instruction in Spanish or desegregation without it—I would choose the latter as the most beneficial to the child and society" (Thomas Carter quoted by Castellanos, 1983, 144). Separate bilingual education programs have become such a powerful symbol and such an important source of employment for the articulate middle class of language minority groups that even "a discriminatory school system might . . . have seen bilingual education as an easy way to create an Hispanic track and still retain support from the Hispanic community" (Meier and Stewart, 1991, 170).

Given the projection that over the next thirty years the Chicano/Latino youth population will account for *nearly all* of the increase in the country's youth sector . . ., it is sad to predict that the next generation of Chicano students will experience school segregation far more severely than the current generation (Donato, Menchaca & Valencia, 1991, 57).

Germany

The growing ethnic segregation in Western Europe is not a matter only of housing patterns or of majority-group parents choosing to avoid schools enrolling many minority pupils; it results also from educational policies that seek to serve the immigrant children through separate provisions. While these may be justified on educational grounds, there is reason to believe that a more powerful motivation may be the concern to keep majority parents content.

> In 1971 Berlin was already permitting model types of secondary school that segregated migrants. . . . Bavaria justified its "open model" which is actually equivalent to a totally segregated school system for the whole duration of the compulsory school attendance period, even if the transfer to regular classes is formally possible, by pointing out . . . that the importance of the native language for the children's mental and spiritual development had been underestimated until then. . . . The regulations for school organization in the 1970s were based on the aim of achieving migrant pupils' adjustment to the German school system. This aim was not achieved . . . except at the cost of separating the migrant pupils, and thereby reducing their possibilities of switching to the German system (and hence curtailing their professional and social chances in the Federal Republic of Germany). . . . migrant pupils were separated: in separate classes; in support groups, which rarely supported the migrant pupils, but merely served to relieve the problems of regular classes; in special schools; in measures established to prepare migrants for professions [that is, vocational education] (Boos-Nünning & Hohmann, 1989, 42, 52–53).

Local school officials may support separate classes because of an interest in the frictionless functioning of their systems; thus

> schools and native parents in areas with a concentration of immigrants thus become in an astonishing fashion allies of foreign parents who are interested in maintaining their language into the next generation. . . . However we have noted that the majority of foreign parents consider the academic success of their children in the host country more important than language maintenance; the exceptions are only politically self-conscious, nationalistic groups (Reich, 1982, 8).

It is the most conservative of the German states, Bavaria, which has been most willing to support separate instruction for linguistic minority pupils in their home language, taking encouragement from a decision of the coordinating group of state education ministers, in 1976, not to press for integrated classes in the first years of elementary school or eventual transition to regular classes (Fase, 1994, 107). Under the so-called "open model," parents are allowed to choose whether their children will receive an integrated education or remain in separate classes (Mahler, 1983, 64). As elsewhere in Germany, this is partially a stop-gap means of avoiding "overloading" classes with too many foreign pupils (*Überfremdung*).

> The Education ministers justify the existence of national classes by claiming that they are respecting the wishes of foreign parents. In reality they are respecting the wishes of German parents, who are unwilling to have their children schooled together with foreign children (Reich 1982, 20).

Pilot home language classes were implemented in Nürnberg in 1972–73, with "at least half of the instruction provided in the thinking language of the children, which as a rule is their mother tongue." The goal of their schooling, it was decided, should no longer be integration into German society, but rather

> an education which, in view of the uncertainty about which country the child will live in in the future, makes possible the optimal schooling for the child and thereby assures him of the same educational opportunities as for German children (Mahler, 1983, 63).

Thus, the child should be prepared for further study in either of two educational systems, that of Germany and that of Italy or Greece or another homeland. Four principles undergirded the approach chosen:

1.   Foreign children who have already lived for a long time in the Federal Republic of German and will remain there with their parents in the future should be placed in regular German classes, provided that they are proficient in the language and that their parents want it.

2.   Children whose parents see their stay in the Federal Republic as limited and who intend to restore their connection to the school system of their homeland must be enabled to continue their education at home.

3.   The foreign child cannot master two languages at once and must choose for a first language. He must be taught first in this language. The first language for children who immigrate to the Federal Republic is their mother tongue.

4.   As soon as the child has mastered German as a second language the parents may decide whether he will transfer to classes using German as the language of instruction or will continue his schooling in classes with the mother tongue as the language of instruction. A supplementary offer of mother tongue instruction will also be provided to those in German-language classes (Mahler, 1983, 64).

Eight arguments were advanced by Bavarian authorities for separate classes: (a) bilingual classes promote the development and integration of foreign children better than do other measures; (b) bilingual classes keep open the possibility of return to the homeland; (c) the first language should be developed first as a basis for thinking; (d) the Bavarian model takes the wishes of parents into account; (e) bilingual education prevents estrangement between pupils and their parents; (f) bilingual classes help to preserve cultural identity; (g) bilingual classes prevent the germanization of foreign children; and (h) the Bavarian model offers different options for the varied interests of children and parents (Boos-Nünning, 1981a).

While separate "foreigner classes" in Berlin and elsewhere are instructed in German and follow the local curriculum, those in Bavaria use the home language as the basis for a significant part of the instruction. Another difference is that preparatory and remedial classes in other *Länder* are generally made up of pupils from a number of different immigrant groups, in contrast with the "national classes" in Bavaria. The former are designed either to concentrate appropriate short-term services upon foreign children or (more cynically) to keep them out of the classrooms of German children, as they acculturate to German norms. The Bavarian model, by contrast, is intended to maintain the cultural and linguistic distinctiveness of the foreign children, while providing them with the skills required by German schooling as well. See Table 6.1.

Separate home language classes on the Bavarian model have enjoyed strong support from many immigrant parents, particularly those from Greece. The decision whether their children were to remain in separate classes or be integrated with German pupils after acquiring sufficient proficiency in German was left entirely up to the parents in Bavaria. Critics

TABLE 6.1. Foreign Pupils in Bavarian Schools, by Year and Program Type

Year	Regular German Classes	Home Language Classes	Number of Home Language Classes	Percent in Home Language Classes
1973–74	26,279	2,590	82	9.0%
1976–77	26,985	10,457	318	27.9%
1980–81	33,628	30,328	897	47.4%
Change	28%	1,071%	994%	

Source: Nieke, Budde, and Henscheid, 1983, 37.

TABLE 6.2. Foreign Pupils in Bavarian Schools by Nationality, 1982–83

Nationality	Total	Separate Classes	Separate Private Schools	Percent Separate
Greek	8,033	1,518	5,037	0.82
Italian	7,122	2,088		0.29
Yugoslavian	10,099	2,862		0.28
Portuguese	570			0.00
Spanish	1,121	164		0.15
Turkish	43,433	21,043		0.48

Source: Based on Mahler, 1983, 235.

argued that many of these parents had an unrealistic expectation that they and their children will go "home," even after many years in West Germany, and that placing their children in a home language class was a way of nurturing that hope at the expense of their children's future in the German society and economy. Children attending such classes, according to this viewpoint, were essentially in a ghetto with very little contact with German contemporaries.

Supporters of the program respond that such contact between non-German and German pupils was insignificant in any case, and that the increased self-confidence of foreign children attending mother tongue classes creates a sound basis for meaningful integration in those aspects of school life that are shared (Mahler, 1983, 66). Most German specialists on the education of foreign pupils, however, would probably agree that

> the essential disadvantage of bilingual classes [on the Bavarian model] lies in their structurally-based effect of isolating by nationality. In this way the social and cultural segregation characteristic of the guest worker ghettoes of large cities is carried over into the German school. The opportunity to assimilate oneself to the society of residence is thereby reduced to a substantial extent, without thereby increasing the possibility of educational opportunities in the event of re-immigration (Harant, 1987, 257)

The number of pilot classes based upon the home language was expanded to 82 in 1973–74 and to 215 in 1974–75. The enrollment of such classes grew rapidly through the seventies, and it became possible for a pupil to receive his or her entire schooling without being integrated with German pupils. See Table 6.2. The number of parents choosing such separate instruction began to drop during the 1980s, however, and reportedly was 26 percent in 1989 ("Mit der Nadel." 1989, 82).

The education provided by these Bavarian classes has been criticized on the ground that they are not truly "bilingual," since German does not become a language of instruction on equal terms until the fifth year. The fact that the curriculum used does not correspond to that used in the mainstream makes it difficult for the participating linguistic minority pupils ever to make the transition. The bilingual classes are more likely than preparatory classes to become an educational pretext for never integrating the children of immigrants (Boos-Nünning, 1981a, 39–43).

> Many of the bilingual teachers, recruited from the homelands of the immigrants, must immediately, without knowledge of German, without information about German society and the German school system, without knowledge of the situation of foreign children and of immigrant families, without sufficient up-to-date textbooks, without training in the special guidelines which apply to the situation of foreign pupils, teach in the bilingual classes. (Boos-Nünning, 1981a, 49)

A careful review of the evidence found no support for claims that separate bilingual instruction on the Bavarian model produces better outcomes than other methods of schooling linguistic minority pupils. Generally, pupils in separate bilingual classes did no better and no worse than do those in other parts of West Germany, and relatively few made a successful transition to regular classes.

> Eight hours of German instruction a week without communicative use of the language outside of that instruction cannot, in a time frame of four to six years, create the preconditions for participation in the instruction in a German class. Most children lack, after this time, factual knowledge and language competence. The chances for a transition decrease with the length of time that is passed in the bilingual class. In addition there is a loss of realism by pupils and teachers about the achievement level of the classes. There is no pressure to bring the classes to the level of regular classes. [Thus] a transition into the German education system occurs only in exceptional cases; such a transition is not facilitated, but made more difficult. There are, for example, no measures provided to support the change (Boos-Nünning, 1981a, 53).

Although Bavaria placed unusual emphasis upon separate instruction in order to maintain the home language and thus to facilitate re-migration of the second or third generation to their (perhaps unknown) "homeland," the organization of instruction for minority children in other *Länder* often had much the same effect. Several, including North Rhine/Westphalia, have experimented with deliberately separate programs providing instruction primarily through the home language. At a school in Duisburg, for example, Turkish pupils not proficient in German

> are placed in exclusively Turkish classes, which nonetheless follow the normal German curriculum . . . with twice as much tuition in German as in Turkish. . . . The [legally required] common teaching intended to enable immigrant and German pupils to cement collective bonds is provided in this school, owing to the large number of foreign children, only during the first two years of compulsory schooling and only in art subjects and physical education (Hohmann, 1983, 15).

This was officially permitted by the national policy-coordinating group, the Conference of Education Ministers, in 1976, modifying their earlier position under which it was allowed only on a pilot basis (Boos-Nunning, 1981a, 29). There were second thoughts about the extent of instruction provided in the home language, however, as many foreign families showed no signs of returning to their homelands. Thus in Baden-Württemberg, which established separate home language classes in 1975–76, the proportion of time devoted to the home language and to German for Turkish and Italian pupils was reversed in 1982–83, from 2:1 to 1:2 (Mahler, 1983, 220). As North Rhine/Westphalia Prime Minister Kuhn pointed out in 1979, it had become clear that the children of immigrants would not be returning to their parents' homelands, and therefore the emphasis should be upon drawing them into the German education system and removing any impediments to their full participation (Frederking, 1985, 20). This conclusion led to the abandonment, in 1982, of experiments with "bilingual preparatory classes in extended form" which had kept ethnically homogeneous groups together for a number of years of schooling. Education authorities in other German states often do not support separate home language classes; according to the Minister of Education of Hesse

> if we put the foreigners in national classes today, in which they cannot obtain German school certificates, we will have to cope

with the social effects in a few years' time, in the form of unemployment, ghetto-formation and criminality (quoted in Castle, 1984, 160)

Hesse does, however, permit "national classes" (made up of pupils of a single foreign origin) which follow the regular German curriculum, enriched by additional hours within the weekly schedule for study of and through a language other than German (Giotitsas, 1988, 93).

Tove Skutnabb-Kangas and other progressive language activists seek to distinguish their advocacy of separate schooling to maintain ethnicity and minority languages from the identical prescription when it is advanced by conservatives like those in Bavaria. The latter, they argue, call for separate schooling as a way to keep linguistic minority children in a subordinate position, while they themselves see it as a way to liberate and empower them. Home language classes in Germany are deliberately intended to prevent development of "native competence in the majority language" in order to keep immigrants in a subordinate position in which they can be exploited as a labor reserve for the benefit of rapacious capitalism. It is also essential to this capitalist agenda that immigrant children be unfitted to return to their homelands by a deficient schooling in their home language.

> These programmes produce bad results because the bad results serve certain social, economic and political functions. . . . In West Germany enemy number one for the [guest worker] in the educational context is *forced segregation*. . . . [From the progressive perspective] for the time being, putting the children into German classes is the only way to ensure (especially for Turkish children) that they: (a) learn at least some German; (b) get instruction which is not directly, at least, undemocratic and strongly authoritarian; . . . In Scandinavia, especially Sweden, the worst enemy is not segregation, but *forced assimilation* (Skutnabb-Kangas, 1984, 43).

What appears formally to be the same form of treatment, then, may have a very different significance and effect (according to this argument) depending upon the overall political context and intentions upon which it is based. For Skutnabb-Kangas it might be a matter of some embarrassment that the policy demand for separate instruction, of which she has a leading advocate in Sweden, is very similar to the policy implemented by the conservative government of Bavaria in association with reactionary foreign governments. Nothing of the sort; progressive educators and advocates should, in her view, employ very different arguments and seek different goals, depending upon the political situation. What is needed under unfavorable conditions, as in West Germany, according to Skutnabb-Kangas,

> is necessarily a defensive strategy, a defensive line of argumentation, that must be used, as long a societal conditions do not allow the type of offensive strategies we use in Scandinavia, and as long as the results of using an offensive strategy might be misused so as to strengthen the segregation. . . . The defensive strategy, necessary in openly linguicist [a new coinage, parallel to "racist"] countries like West Germany, thus involves using arguments to legitimize the minority mother tongue in schools, which emphasize its instrumental value in learning the majority language. The offensive strategy used in Scandinavia emphasizes the human rights argument for legitimizing the minority mother tongues. The defensive line of argumentation may later on function as a negative boomerang, because the argument itself is linguicist. But choice of argument to be used is determined by the stage at which the society in question finds itself in the historical development of minority education (Skutnabb-Kangas, 1988a, 31).

Sweden

Bilingual education has been developed most extensively in the United States, but the example of Sweden is frequently cited in American policy debates as evidence of the superiority of an emphasis upon the home language in schooling. The discussion of Sweden is often misleading: contrary to the impression that might be gained from references in the literature advocating bilingual education, separate home language classes are not the norm for foreign pupils in Sweden, but several hundred are in operation, primarily for Finnish-speaking pupils. These separate classes served 7 percent of the 88,284 linguistic minority pupils in Swedish schools in 1987–1988; nine times as many participate in supplemental home language instruction (*hemspråksundervisning*) as do in full-time separate home language classes (*hemspråksklasser*). Even among Finnish-speaking pupils, nearly four times as many take part in supplemental home language instruction while enrolled in integrated Swedish-medium classes as are enrolled in separate home language classes. See Table 6.3.

In a home language class (as distinct from supplemental home language instruction) an ethnically-homogeneous group of pupils is taught primarily in their home language. In some cases Swedish instruction is not

TABLE 6.3. Separate Home Language Classes in Sweden, 1987–88

Language	Classes	Pupils
Arabic	7	65
English	7	76
Estonian	6	37
Finnish	454	4,959
Greek	27	302
Macedonian	6	65
Persian	11	32
Portuguese	3	37
Serbo-Croatian	13	176
Spanish	19	211
Tigrin	4	12
Turkish	34	424
Total	591	6,396

Source: *Hemspråk* . . . , 1988.

started until the fourth grade, though this has become less common because of difficulties experienced by such pupils later. In principle, the pupils are mainstreamed after the sixth grade, but there is an increasing trend toward extending the home language class through the ninth grade, the last year of compulsory schooling in Sweden.

Concerns have been expressed about whether effective acculturation is retarded by these language maintenance efforts, since "the interest for immigrant classes with much training in the native language and teaching conducted with [native language] as a means of instruction, and only a few hours per week assigned to the new language, may be based upon a desire to use education as a means for minority groups to maintain their autonomy rather than upon a genuine wish to help children to grow into the new culture" (Ekstrand, 1978, 73).

Since there is intense controversy over the value of such classes it seems fair to include two descriptions, the first by a supporter, the other by an opponent.

These classes run for at least the first three years, but preferably at least through the first six grades, with an increasing number of lessons in Swedish, and later also through the medium of Swedish. This is the model which the immigrant organizations want and most researchers recommend . . . because it seems to produce the best results with respect to bilingualism, school achievement and the happiness of children. . . . Even if most of the existing classes are Finnish (468), many other languages are also represented, and the immigrant organizations are unanimous in demanding them. In 1981 there were 5 Arabic-medium classes, 2 Assyrian, 6 Chinese, 1 English, 2 German, 29 Greek, 1 Polish, 23 Spanish, 26 Turkish, 34 Yugoslav language (mostly Serbocroatian-medium) and three for other languages. . . . Mother-tongue classes physically segregate the immigrant children in the beginning, but *not* in relation to content or ideology (as the German national classes do) (Skutnabb-Kangas, 1984, 30–31).

According to Ekstrand, however, most research does not support such classes, nor do most immigrant groups in Sweden, other than the Finns, desire them for their children. Although the classes were based upon an attractive theory of language learning, experience has been disappointing; "poor results in Swedish have become more and more common lately," with the proportion of immigrant pupils requiring extra help in the language growing from 41 percent in 1975 to 69 percent in 1988. Ekstrand suggests that this may in part be attributable to inadequate education and teacher training of home language teachers, which "may in fact create a restricted environment for the immigrant children" (Ekstrand, 1979, 31), and to devoting inadequate time to instruction through Swedish in home language classes.

There is no Swedish until grade 3. In grade 3 there are two periods of Swedish weekly (a period is forty minutes). . . . In grade 4, Swedish is used as a medium of instruction to some extent. . . . According to an evaluation report by the National Board of Education in Sweden (1982), only 20% of the time is devoted to using Swedish for teaching by grade 6. The percentage of teaching in the home language is 41% and in both languages 39%. Furthermore, Swedish is used mostly as the medium of instruction in subjects such as drawing, athletics, handicraft and music, while the home language is used for mathematics, natural and social sciences and English. . . . Of course, it is not possible for these students to follow teaching in grades 7–9 in Swedish. Instead [home language] classes throughout this stage have become more and more common (Ekstrand, 1988, 2–3).

As evidence for the poor results of separate home language classes compared with integrated classes, Ekstrand cites a number of studies of

Finnish pupils in Sweden, including three by Sylvia Linde of UCLA. Linde found

> a high positive correlation between Swedish medium instruction and achievement in Mathematics, English and Swedish. . . . The more Finnish is used in school, the poorer is the student's knowledge of Swedish, but Swedish is an important causal factor for mathematics. Finnish medium instruction has a positive effect on Finnish achievement if Finnish is not spoken in the home, otherwise not (Ekstrand, 1988, 15–16; see Linde & Lofgren, 1988).

Elsewhere

A different sort of linguistic minority school has existed for several decades in the border area of Schleswig (see Chapter 3). The German minority in Denmark and the Danish minority in Germany receive government subsidies paying most of the costs of operating their own schools. The schools are first and above all German schools (in North Schleswig) and Danish schools (in South Schleswig). Their primary purpose is to introduce their pupils to the language and culture of their national allegiance, to further the pupils' consciousness of their belonging to the minority and to the nation beyond the border (Byram, 1981, 178). The Danish minority, in particular, is threatened by the cultural hegemony of German, and its schools work hard to reinforce the linguistic basis of non-German identity. "It is indeed clear in the daily life of the school that German dominates the thinking of many pupils, that even in Danish lessons there is a strong tendency to fall back on German where problems of comprehension appear" (Byram, 1981, 180).

Such schools occupy a difficult position, with "two purposes—to induct pupils into one culture and to prepare them for living in another—which pull in opposing linguistic directions." This creates particular difficulties for

> those pupils who have only the legal minimum of schooling and must then find their place in the majority society. For these pupils the purpose which the minority schools place second—to prepare their pupils to live in the majority society—looms larger than the first purpose—to introduce them to the minority culture (Byram, 1981, 181).

Similar problems were experienced by the children of Polish farmhands in Denmark, later interviewed as adults:

Those who had gone to Polish schools had certainly preserved more of their background language and culture. On the other hand, they had suffered more discrimination [subsequently]. Many were highly critical of having been put into Polish schools, as they felt this had made their social careers more difficult (Ekstrand, 1981a, 207).

The Swedish-speaking minority in Finland—14 percent of the population a century ago but only 6.2 percent today—is also entitled to its own separate school system, teacher training, textbooks, and in-service training. There are no bilingual schools in which both languages are used for instruction (S-E Hansen, 1987, 79). This accommodation has fueled the political demands by language activists of the Finnish minority, in Sweden, for separate schooling in their language. It should be noted, however, that the significance of Swedish in Finland is very different from that of Finnish in Sweden. Swedish-speakers in Finland are the former ruling class, and speak the *lingua franca* of Scandinavia (Paulston, 1992b, 39), while Finnish-speakers in Sweden are mostly working-class labor migrants or peasants of the Tornedalen region annexed into Sweden by an arbitrary border. Researchers have found that Tornedalen is "characterized by very rapid language shift with numerous reports on families shifting to Swedish after the first child or two" (Paulston, 1992a, 28); Finnish is a "marker" of inferior status and exclusion in Sweden, while Swedish is a marker of positive distinction in Finland; thus, according to Paulston, "the Finns totally agreed with the Swedes on the collective goals for the former—rapid and total assimilation" (Paulston, 1992a, 25).

DISCUSSION

Although the demand by some ethnic leaders and language activists for separate schooling is often opposed by policymakers as inimical to the socializing and acculturating mission of the "common school," there are some instances in which it is translated into official policy; this has particularly been the case in Bavaria. Local school officials in other parts of Germany and in other countries may also support separate classes because of an interest in the frictionless functioning of their systems or because they are not sure how best to educate the children of immigrants and are willing to entrust the task to specialists rather than to make changes that might affect native children.

While it appears that most immigrant minority parents wish their children to participate fully in the educational opportunities provided to the children of the native majority, there is considerable demand for separate programs (whether during school time or supplemental to it) that seek to maintain elements of ethnic distinctiveness. Such programs and their relation to the general curriculum are discussed in Chapter 7.

Less common is a desire, on the part of immigrant parents, for fully separate schooling based upon the language of their homeland. Our survey suggests that a much stronger motivation for separate schooling than language maintenance is a concern to transmit a religious heritage with its associated behavioral norms, especially when the latter are threatened by a host society that seems anomic and corrupting. It seems, indeed, that the demand for schooling based on religious dimensions of the immigrant heritage is growing even as (and perhaps because) the linguistic minority community becomes better-established and more comfortable with the language of the host society. After all, as children become proficient in the language of the host society, it becomes more difficult for parents to protect them from its corrupting influences—especially those which the parents themselves do not understand. In some cases, indeed, religious institutions like schools serve as an important focal point for ethnic community organization (Rath, Groenedijk, & Penninx, 1992, 29). Again, religion and not language appears to be the primary motivating factor in the creation of separate ethnic schools.

This is illustrated by the Netherlands, where a wise public policy supports Islamic and Hindu schools provided that the instruction is primarily through the Dutch language and the curricular goals of the Dutch educational system are met, and there is little social conflict around religious or language differences. The situation of ethnic minority groups in the Netherlands is eased by the fact that there has not been the sort of institutional abandonment of areas with high minority concentration that has occurred in the United States, nor is there an ethnically identifiable underclass in the American sense (Anderiesen & Reijndorp, 1991, 60). Obviously, ethnic schools are much less problematical in a situation in which heavy government regulation associated with full public funding, and a moderate degree of ghetto-formation, make ethnic separatism less ominous than it seems in the United States. Questions remain, however, about whether minority children can be effectively prepared to participate in the host society without the opportunity for regular interaction with majority children (see Chapter 8).

The demand for schooling based upon beliefs and values which parents hold dear may be less of a threat to the successful adaptation of immigrant minority children to their host societies than are the well-meaning efforts of educators to adapt their systems to the supposed needs of these children by providing separate programs. As a French authority pointed out a quarter-century ago,

We must have the courage to recognize that most of the "specialists" who have up to now concerned themselves with [the schooling of the children of immigrants] have fallen into this trap: considering that this population demands pedagogical responses which are *absolutely specific*, they have shut them, whether they wished to or not, whether they were aware of it or not, in the educational ghetto which in most cases they assert should be avoided (Porcher 1978a, 11).

After all,

Ghettoes are *always* dangerous. To socialize individuals separately is to run the risk of making them permanently unable to be anything but separate. The school ghetto has the essential characteristic of perpetuating itself and of producing other ghettoes (or, if one prefers, of perpetuating the social ghettoes which already exist. . . . it's hard to understand how marginalization can help to fight against marginality (Porcher, 1978b, 122–123).

French policy-makers and informed opinion remain firmly opposed to separate schooling for language minority pupils, and continue to raise questions even about the value of short-term reception classes; "nothing, in our educational system, must differentiate the schooling of pupils, whether they be French or foreign" (Boulot & Boyzon-Fradet, 1991b, 16). While a certain separation from the majority, as in ethnic neighborhoods and associations, may play an important part in the initial psychosocial adjustment of immigrants, it is dangerous if they become a form of permanent retreat in "distinctive cultural memberships" (*appartenances culturelles singulières*), and certainly it is not the role of the school to encourage such a development (Bastenier & Dassetto, 1993, 251).

American law and policy recognize a crucial distinction between self-segregation, which is the right of any group, and segregation of ethnic groups through government decision, which gives a fatal message of exclusion and unworthiness. The former may often, as the history of immigration to America illustrates, be a stage on the way to effective participation in the host society. The latter, as our history also illustrates, leads too easily to the creation of a caste system with profoundly inequitable results. As the Supreme Court found in *Brown v. Board of Education*,

[t]he impact [of segregation] is greater when it has the sanction of law; for the policy of separating the races is usually interpreted as denot-

ing the inferiority of the Negro group. A sense of inferiority affects the motivation of a child to learn. Segregation with the sanction of law, then, has a tendency to retard the educational and mental development of Negro children and to deprive them of some of the benefits they would receive in a racially integrated school system (347 U.S. 483, at 494).

Support for the languages and cultures of the children of immigrants within public education is entirely appropriate; segregating them by public policy for any significant portion of their schooling, even with the best of intentions, is not consistent with American law or policy. Too often, in American schools and in the schools of the other countries included in this study, an emphasis upon home languages translates into separate schooling and unequal access to educational opportunities.

Chapter 7 will review in a schematic way the most common arrangements for the schooling of the children of immigrants, and the meager evidence—mostly anecdotal—that exists for the effectiveness of each. This will be followed, in Chapter 8, by a description of the elements of an effective schooling for these children as illustrated by schools that promote integration of language minority and majority pupils while stimulating the use of both languages.

School Programs for Language Minority Children

Long-term separate schooling is often provided to the children of immigrants and other language-minority pupils; in most cases, however, the *intention*, at least, of public policy is that these pupils be integrated with the children of the majority, both as a goal and as a means to reach that goal. This chapter reviews the most commonly employed models of schooling for integration into the mainstream.

The development of school programs to serve the children of immigrants has often been hesitant and sometimes self-contradictory. It is complicated by the great variation in the situation and capabilities of the children themselves. A publication by the Victoria (Australia) Ministry of Education identifies six distinct groups of pupils who might need English as a Second Language services:

A.   Children beginning school in Australia at the normal . . . age (4.5–6 years) who have had minimal or no exposure to English.

B.   Students who are beginning school in Australia after normal . . . age and who have had no previous formal schooling in any country.

C.   Students beginning school after normal . . . age, with severely disrupted schooling.

D.   Students who arrive from overseas with about the equivalent amount of schooling as their peers have had in English.

E.   Students who have had the major part of their schooling in Australia but who have difficulty with the English demands made upon them in mainstream classes. Included in this group are students who were born in Australia.

F.   NESB [non-English-speaking background] students who have specific learning difficulties (Curriculum Branch, 1987).

This typology, which could be applied to the situation in any of the countries in this study, illustrates the extreme complexity of providing appropriate educational services within the normally rather rigid framework of an educational system.

Some children of immigrants and refugees—especially those who arrive after the age of compulsory schooling in their homelands—do not go to school at all in the host country. Girls from Muslim families may be kept at home after they reach puberty, because of the coeducational classes in most European schools. In 1973 the Turkish consulates in West Germany estimated that only 54 percent of Turkish children of school age were attending German schools (Abadan-Unat, 1975, 313), though the participation rate has since increased dramatically. Others take part in educational and adjustment programs operated by community and social agencies. For example, there is a program in The Hague for young women aged 12 to 17 from orthodox Muslim families that keep them out of Dutch schools after puberty because of government insistence on coeducation. They study Dutch, consumer math, sewing, gymnastics, social studies, and Arabic or Turkish (Groenendijk, P., 1992, 33); a similar program exists in Rotterdam (Dongen, 1993, 196–198). Specialists on the schooling of ethnic minority children confess themselves uncertain about the advantages and disadvantages of such arrangements (Triesscheijn, 1994, 203).

More commonly, however, and to an extent that has come to represent a major challenge for teachers and administrators, the children of immigrants are accommodated in schools. A 1987 survey identified 172 spoken languages in London schools, with 23 percent of the school population (64,987 children) using a language other than or in addition to English at home. At least one-half of the school systems in England and Wales "have a *minimum* of one primary school with over 10 per cent of pupils who are bilingual" (Craft, 1989, 136).

From the perspective of education officials, these children speaking other languages have appeared in large numbers virtually overnight as a result of unanticipated population movements. Improvisation has frequently marked the response at the school level, and confusion on the part of policymakers. In extreme cases, the response of policymakers has been to deny that a problem existed, as when the Australian government for some years refused to collect information on the number of immigrant pupils in schools; the Director of Education for New South Wales explained in 1963 that "we deliberately refrain from collecting any statistics in regard to pupils from overseas. Once they are enrolled in school they are, from our point of view, Australian children" (quoted in Bullivant, 1982, 132)

In many instances, programs or policies developed in response to one set of circumstances have been continued even when no longer serving a useful purpose under new conditions. A notable example is the common practice in Europe thirty years ago of providing the curriculum of schools in the homeland for the (relatively rare) children of labor migrants, on the assumption that they would return to live in that homeland after their parents had accumulated sufficient savings. This was indeed the pattern followed by many Italian, Spanish, and Greek families. This policy was recognized (though by some governments more slowly than by others) as inadequate when it became evident that most families would *not* re-migrate (Entzinger, 1984).

The curriculum appropriate to a Turkish school was not appropriate for children brought up in Berlin or Rotterdam, and knowing no other home; they needed to learn the same lessons as their German or Dutch peers. On the other hand, an adolescent arriving from Anatolia as a result of family reunification would not benefit from simply being assigned to an age-appropriate class conducted in an unfamiliar language, but required an opportunity to develop "survival skills." How these should be taught varied greatly depending upon the level and quality of schooling which the young immigrants had already received; acquiring basic skills in a new language is a relatively simple matter compared with mastering literacy and the culture and expectations of schooling as a teenager. Schools all too often provided services that were entirely appropriate to some other pupils, but not to the actual language minority children arriving on their doorsteps.

Official policy in West Germany toward the education of immigrant pupils went through several stages. The first (nonbinding) national guidelines, in 1964, spoke of providing appropriate support including supplemental instruction in German to foreign pupils, together with instruction in the official languages of their homelands (not necessarily the languages spoken in their homes). Guidelines issued in 1971—when it had become clear that many migrants would not return to their homelands—placed increased stress on the integration of foreign children into regular classes, and mentioned home language instruction only as an optional extra. Immigrant children who reached school age while resident in Germany should be placed directly in a German first grade, while older children with language difficulties should be placed in reception classes located in German schools, normally for a single year before mainstreaming. The reception classes should follow so far as possible the ordinary curriculum, and immigrant pupils should be integrated with their German peers for as many activities as possible (Röhr-Sendimeier, 1986, 54).

After the economic reverses brought on by the oil crisis of the early seventies, the guidelines issued in 1976 returned to the theme of keeping open the possibility of re-migration. Bilateral collaboration had been worked out with education authorities in several of the homelands from which the immigrants had come, and the guidelines made provision for assigning foreign pupils to "national classes" made up exclusively of a single language group and without a limit of time of participation—a practice already implemented in Bavaria (Boos-Nünning & Henscheid, 1986; see texts in Mahler, 1983). This recommendation was couched in the rhetoric of enabling the children to live in "two worlds," but only three years later the commissioner for immigrant issues called for a consistent policy of full integration, charging that the ambiguous nature of the schooling of immigrants was to blame for disastrous results (Esser & Korte, 1985, 194). New guidelines in 1982 discouraged separate schooling (either in reception classes of mixed nationalities or in "national classes") for more than two years, and made integration with German peers the priority, while seeking to strengthen supplemental classes in home language and culture (Röhr-Sendimeier, 1986, 62).

Before there were policies, of course, there were practices; schools could not wait for policies to be formulated and debated when pupils were sitting in their classrooms who could not follow the language of instruction. Diego Castellanos categorizes the responses of American schools in the 1950s to the presence of language minority pupils as (1) "Sink or Swim" assignment to an ordinary class with no support or preparation of the teacher, (2) "Downgrading" to a class several years below that indicated by the age of the pupil, (3) "Slow Learner," or placement in a group of low-intelligence or learning-disabled language majority children, and (4) "Vocabulary-building" strategies that assumed that language-learning was primarily a matter of acquiring necessary vocabulary in English (Castellanos, 1983, 54–56). In Germany, as a result of the growing awareness that special measures were needed, at least the following alternatives were officially available as of the mid-1980s: (1) assignment to a regular German class, with the possibility of supplemental "home language" instruction, (2) assignment to a separate bilingual class with other pupils of the same nationality, or (3) assignment to a reception class for intensive instruction in German (Harant, 1987, 253–255).

Assignment to a Regular Class
"Sink or Swim"

Simply placing immigrant children in regular classes and hoping that they will pick up the language and catch up in academic content is the almost universal practice in situations when the first such pupils appear in a community. It would be extremely difficult to give a systematic account of its results. Anecdotal evidence, on the other hand, is abundant, both in auto-biographical and fictional accounts of the immigrant experience and in policy debates over special provisions for language minority pupils. The debates are often enlivened by anecdotes on the order of "We made it without special help, why can't they?" from former immigrants. There can be no question, indeed, that some and perhaps many immigrant children pick up a new language in school and on the streets with relative ease.

Advocates for special programs counter with accounts of children sitting in stunned incomprehension for years before dropping out of school, or of others punished for using their home language at recess. A Puerto Rican parent told a hearing of the United States Commission on Civil Rights, in 1972, that children

> are practically wasting their time because they are not learning anything. First of all, they don't understand the language. What good does it do to sit there in front of the teacher and just look at her face? It is wasting their time. They don't learn anything because they don't understand what she is saying (quoted in United States Commission on Civil Rights, 1976, 99).

In practice, the language situation of the children of immigrants arriving on the doorstep of a school is often complex. They may speak the language of the school to a certain—and perhaps deceptive—extent. This is especially the case with pupils who arrived in the host society a year or more before starting school, or indeed were born there. It may also be the case in schools where English (or, to a lesser extent, French) is the language of instruction, due to the international currency of those languages. The foreign pupil who arrives at school speaking the language of instruction with fair fluency is often presumed to require no support related to language acquisition (Portmann, 1988, 80). In such cases there is seldom any adaptation of the curriculum to respond to the child's needs and strengths.

Much depends upon the age of the pupil upon entering the schools of the host society. All of the children in a primary classroom are learning many basic language skills, though of course native speakers of the language of the school have a great advantage. Starting in the fourth or fifth grade, the subject matter grows progressively more complex, as does the language proficiency required to handle it successfully. The pupil who, as the Germans put it, "climbs in sideways" (a *Seiteneinsteiger*; Dutch *zij-instromer* or *neveninstromer*) to the educational system may find it impossible ever to catch up (Şahin & Heyden, 1982, 119). The school faces a dilemma: Should a 14–year-old who has only had three years of formal schooling in his homeland be put in a class with 9–year-old native pupils who are learning what he needs to learn, or in a class with native pupils his own age, with no capability of keeping up, language proficiency aside (Esch, 1982, 131)? During the period of family reunification in the late 1970s and early 1980s, this was the situation of many: a study in the Netherlands in 1977–1978 of 564 foreign pupils at the secondary level found that 44 percent of them had come directly from their homelands (Janssen-van Dieten, 1982, 42).

Linguistic minority pupils may not receive the language development support that they require because of a faulty assessment based upon superficial fluency in the language of the school.

> [Their] utterances in English are of a highly imitative nature . . . they manifest local pronunciation and intonation: fluency in the local accent is often interpreted by teachers as a sign that the immigrant pupil has acquired a native command of English. . . . Yet beyond the initial stages of the curriculum, when more conceptual and less practical linguistic functions are demanded by the teacher, difficulty in elaborating abstractions and in using sophisticated vocabulary may arise. The Head teacher, teachers and educational psychologists (all mono-lingual in English) could assess these as cognitive problems not linguistic ones (Tosi, 1984, 111).

Even the pupil whose proficiency in the language of instruction is minimal may be left to "sink or swim." This is often the case when refugees are settled in nonurban communities with no established group using their language, where school staff are without previous experience with language minorities (Haeffele, 1988, 29). A school in a suburban German community that the author visited in 1989 enrolled some pupils whose only language was Polish or Russian, allowed to immigrate on the basis of their German ancestry, and others speaking Tamil or Iranian, admitted as political refugees. Such pupils may be fortunate enough to know a little English, or to find a teacher or fellow-pupil with some knowledge of their home language, but otherwise would have to pick up German through ad hoc arrangements.

Chinese families in the United Kingdom, the Netherlands, and other countries are unusually scattered because of the parents' tendency to work in restaurants, with the result that the children are "found in ones and twos in individual schools, often in isolated, rural areas which otherwise have no experience of providing for the educational needs of ethnic minorities"

(*Education for All*, 1985, 654). Similarly, only 51 percent of Asian pupils, contrasted with 76 percent of Hispanic pupils, were enrolled in schools in the larger cities of Massachusetts in 1986 (Glenn, 1987, 100–101). This has had the result that they are less likely—whether for good or ill—to be assigned to special program than are pupils who are more concentrated residentially.

Often the development of programs to receive and support foreign pupils lags years behind their presence in significant numbers in a community. This was the case nationwide in France; while most newly arrived pupils at primary level were served in reception programs by 1980–81, it was not until five years later that similar provision was available for newly-arrived pupils aged between 12 and 15 (Boulot & Boyzon-Fradet, 1988, 13).

Other pupils are "submerged" in mainstream classes without support because their parents refuse to allow them to be enrolled in special programs for immigrants, in the expectation that this will hasten their adaptation. This is common even in Sweden, the nation with the most extensive program to teach home languages. Swedish policy is that a pupil is not required to study in his home language, but *is* required to take part in Swedish-as-a-second-language instruction if in the judgment of the principal this is necessary. But of course such support is not available in every school, even in Sweden, and most European communities do not bring language minority pupils together at a single site for support programs.

A distinction is made in some educational systems between language minority children who begin their schooling or preschooling in the host society—usually having been born there, though in homes where a minority language is spoken—and those who enter later. In France it is assumed that the first group should be treated like and integrated with French children of the same age, should learn numbers and colors and reading in French, and should receive supplemental help only as individually needed, just as a child from a French-speaking home would. Only for the second group, who start French schools at ages when their classmates would already be well-advanced in their studies, are special reception programs regarded as an essential transitional measure (Boulot & Boyzon-Fradet, 1991, 6).

The [government] circular of March 13th 1986 on the teaching of French for foreign children newly arrived in France calls attention to the situation of foreign pupils born or arriving very young in France (who are much more numerous): the difficulties which they encounter, whether it involves an insufficient mastery of the written language or of an insufficiency in other fundamental subjects must be treated in the same framework as the analogous difficulties of French pupils (Boulot & Boyzon-Fradet, 1991, 7).

British policy has also leaned strongly toward treating native-born language minority children as though they were children of English ancestry of comparable social class. Fase and other observers have attributed this to the peculiarly intense concern with class stratification in England compared with other OECD nations (Triesscheijn, 1994, 202). It has become clear that in fact lack of in-depth proficiency in English, even for pupils whose families have been in Britain for decades, contributes to the pattern of low achievement. A survey in 1985 indicated that as many as half of the Greek-speaking and two-thirds of the Turkish-speaking pupils needed additional help with English proficiency (Taylor, 1988, 119).

Despite the growing proportion of foreign students who were born in the host countries, many enter school without a readiness for success in the regular program. A study in Frankfurt in 1981, for example, found that 45 percent of the Turkish children beginning school were not prepared to perform ordinary schoolwork in German, and that another 30 percent could do so only with intensive supplementary support.

> In Berlin 36 children were enrolled for first grade. All had been born in Berlin; 14 did not speak a word of German. We find the same situation in all the large cities. What is decisive for the readiness to participate in a purely German class is not whether the child was born here, but how and where he spent his first six years of life (Mahler, 1983, 88).

The problem is exacerbated by the fact that immigrant children, especially those of the most marginalized and low-status groups, are less likely to attend kindergarten in most host nations. Thus in Germany in 1980, 80 percent of the German, 76 percent of the Portuguese, 68 percent of the Yugoslavian, 56 percent of the Spanish, 46 percent of the Italian, 43 percent of the Greek, and only 39 percent of the Turkish children aged three through six attended kindergarten (Mahler, 1983, 72).

Many foreign children come to school unprepared to meet the expectations of the regular schooling process in the host country. If the school is also unprepared for them and unresponsive to the needs and the strengths associated with their family and community background, it is unsurprising that academic under-achievement and social isolation are the results.

Assigning newly arrived foreign pupils to a regular class does not necessarily imply a "sink or swim" attitude toward them; many educators are convinced that an integrated approach can provide adequate support while extending also the benefits of interaction with native pupils and a stimulating language-development program. This requires extra staff support as well as training for classroom teachers to diagnose the progress of the language minority pupil as well as to prescribe appropriate remedies on an on-going and flexible basis (Knijpstra, 1993a, 331–332).

In many cases, language minority pupils assigned to regular classes are also given supplemental support by specialized teachers. As we have seen, children of immigrants who are born in France are as a matter of policy assigned to regular classes from the start but may receive supplemental instruction in learning French, since it may not be the language of their homes. In Denmark there is a strong policy preference for treating language minority pupils experiencing difficulty with schoolwork through the regular compensatory education provisions for native pupils in academic difficulty (Hetmar & Jørgensen, 1991).

In Germany, foreign students are typically provided two to four periods a week of supplemental language development activities (Mahler, 1983, 212). Extra staff were used, in a model program visited by the author in Gelsenkirchen, to provide additional support within the framework of regular instruction. Each of three fifth grades (the first year of *Hauptschule*, the lowest form of secondary school) was assigned two teachers in order to provide more individual and small-group attention, with flexible grouping for instruction in history, earth sciences, and German. A *Gymnasium* (selective secondary school) in Oberhausen made a special effort, in another experimental project, to enroll pupils newly arrived from Turkey but with strong academic preparation; they were selected carefully and enrolled in regular classes for all academic subjects, with supplemental help. For the first two years they were given progress reports rather than graded like their German classmates; after that time, they were expected to achieve to the same standards (Hofmann et al., 1993, 90–93).

In the Netherlands, additional staff time is provided to schools where there are a sufficient number of pupils who have been in the country less than four years, to provide them with supplemental assistance "to learn the academic skills that are necessary to take part in the Dutch educational process;" a study in the late 1970s found this amounted to an average of an hour and a half a week (Coenen, 1982, 35).

In the decentralized English educational system, local authorities have employed a wide variety of approaches to providing extra language support, though with a preference for part-time withdrawal from regular classes rather than for separate programs or language centers, which are believed to segregate inappropriately and even unlawfully (*Education for All*, 1985, 387). The 1966 Local Government Act provided funding ("Section 11") to benefit the immigrant communities, and initially the positions were used primarily to teach English; local education authorities were reimbursed 50 percent (later 75 percent) of the cost of extra teachers and other staff appointed to provide assistance to ethnic minority children (Watson, 1988, 541). Over time these funds were often diverted to trendy "anti-racism" activities (for a critical view, see Flew, 1986a & b; Palmer, 1986a & b). More recently, guidelines adopted by the Conservative government have required that the use of these funds be limited to language teaching and reaching out to minority parents (Edwards & Redfern, 19, 22). Efforts targeted to immigrant minority children have been threatened recently by a sharp reduction in Section 11 funding (Passmore, 1994).

In Sweden, when the first guidelines for Swedish as a second language were published, the government assumed that six weeks of intensive instruction would be sufficient to enable them to be integrated into regular classes (Willke, 1975, 365). It soon became clear that it was necessary to provide follow up lessons in Swedish after pupils were mainstreamed, sometimes for a number of years. The Swedish 1980 national curriculum for grades 1 through 9 (the "compulsory school") described the goals of Swedish as a Foreign Language in ambitious terms; it should give

> the pupils the necessary linguistic knowledge which pupils having Swedish as their home language have already acquired before reaching school age and which pupils of the same age have acquired in their Swedish lessons. The pupils are also to learn words and concepts which they need in order to participate meaningfully in instruction in various subjects. . . . The pupils should become acquainted with everyday life and working life in Sweden, with the local community and with Swedish social conditions. They should be enabled to participate in Swedish culture as represented by music, literature etc., and in this way augment their opportunities of experiencing a sense of community with people in Sweden and of identifying both with their original culture and with Swedish culture. Schools should help their pupils to establish contact with other pupils, associations, etc. . . . The teaching of Swedish as a foreign language should help the pupils to

acquire a knowledge and understanding of the different living conditions and living patterns of different people (National Swedish Board of Education, 1980).

There was a fourfold increase in the number of teacher periods devoted to supportive Swedish instruction between 1970 and 1980 (Liljegren & Ullman, 1982), as the educational system came to terms with the presence of a large number of foreign pupils, and a decade later it was estimated that "89% of the pupils in the compulsory schools who report a home language other than Swedish attend regular classes," and that two-thirds of these receive supplemental instruction in Swedish as a second language (Boyd, 1993, 278); school principals have authority to require participation.

The American Supreme Court's 1974 decision in the landmark *Lau v. Nichols* case (see Chapter 6), noted that

> there are 2,856 students of Chinese ancestry in the [San Francisco] school system who do not speak English. Of those who have that language deficiency, about 1,000 are given supplemental courses in the English language. About 1,800 however do not receive that instruction (*Lau v. Nichols*, 1983, 205).

The implication was that no violation of the Civil Rights Act of 1964 would have been found if all of the pupils in question had participated in supplemental English instruction ("ESL"), though ironically the "*Lau* remedies" issued subsequently by the government, influenced by bilingual education advocates, leaned heavily toward requiring use of the home language for instruction in a separate program. School districts "were directed to identify the student's primary language, not by his proficiency in English but by determining which language was most often spoken in the student's home . . . thus a student would be eligible for a bilingual program even if he were entirely fluent in English." The national administration (not accidentally) "overlooked the fact that the failure of the San Francisco schools to provide ESL to all Chinese children in the system was the basis of the *Lau* decision" (Ravitch, 1983, 274–275).

Home Language Enrichment

While most school programs focus upon adjusting language minority pupils to the requirements of the school by reducing the salience of their differences from native pupils, home-language programs precisely stress these differences and seek to build upon them. It is not uncommon for these contrary efforts to be combined in the actual experience of an individual foreign pupil. Pupils assigned to mainstream classes have the opportunity, in most of the countries under review, of taking part in supplemental "language and culture" classes made up exclusively of classmates of the same ethnic background, though in some cases the grouping is based upon the homeland of pupils or their parents and may not take into account language differences. Kurdish-speaking children may thus be assigned to a supplemental class based upon Turkish, a language they would have learned in school in Turkey but do not learn from their parents in the immigrant diaspora— and which may represent a hated reminder of oppression to their parents. Children who have learned to speak one of the (mutually unintelligible) Berber languages may be assigned to a class in which Moroccan Arabic is used and taught. In these cases, it would be more accurate to describe the programs as "homeland official language" instruction, and that should be understood in the discussion that follows.

This situation reflects the fact that the original impetus for such programs was more political than it was educational, a way of sustaining the myth that the guestworkers and their families would be returning to their homelands. The belief was important to both the host government and that of the country of origin, and in a number of cases bilateral agreements were made with the explicit purpose of facilitating the re-entry of the children of immigrants into the educational and social systems of the homeland of their parents (Boos-Nünning, et al., 1986, 200).

Home language enrichment classes are in part also a response to the European Community directive of July 1977 that called for "appropriate measures to promote the teaching of the mother tongue and the culture of [the children of guestworkers] with a view principally to facilitating their possible reintegration" into their homelands (see Chapter 5). While a further resolution, in July 1985, carefully qualifies this mandate by stating that "this does not result in an automatic right to such teaching," most member states make some arrangements to provide it. Though the directive applied to children coming from other member states (for example, Italian children in Germany), it was accompanied by an expression of the hope that minority language programs would be provided also for children coming from outside the European Community (European Communities, 1985, 13).

Reich offers a helpful typology of the responses to this directive and to the pressure, by some homeland governments and ethnic communities, for supplemental home language instruction. There is one group of educational systems (France, Belgium, the German *Länder* of Baden-Württemberg, Bremen, and Hamburg) in which such instruction is provided through bilateral agreements with the homeland governments, which recruits, pays, and supervises the teachers. In a second group of systems (Sweden, Denmark, the Netherlands, and the *Länder* Hesse and North Rhine-Westphalia) minority language instruction is provided and supervised by the host government, which thereby exercises substantially more control over its content and objectives. The third approach is that of some school systems in the United States and the United Kingdom, where supplemental instruction in minority languages may be offered by arrangement with the local ethnic community (Reich, 1991, 168). A variation on this last is represented by Canada and Australia, where national government funding has been provided for community-based as well as school-based language programs; this was also the case briefly in the United States, under the Ethnic Heritage Act (see Chapter 5 for examples of these alternative approaches to minority language teaching).

Australia

A group of Greek organizations in Melbourne, in 1973, called for "inclusion of migrant languages such as Greek, Italian, Turkish, in the school curricular [sic]. Retraining of teachers, both new and existing, to teach ethnic languages—a reservoir of such teachers is already available" (quoted by Foster & Stockley, 1988, 71). A nationwide support effort called the Ethnic Schools Program ["ESP"] was established in 1981 "to supplement community efforts to teach the languages spoken within the Australian community." Funding is provided both to after-school classes supporting language maintenance (serving about one third of the 196,000 pupils participating in 1991) and also to "insertion classes" within the regular school schedule. The latter commonly involve nonprofessional teachers providing 30 to 60 minutes a week of instruction in both language and culture. In these insertion classes, about 80 percent of the pupils are Australian-born and speak English as their first language.

> In 1986 a ceiling was imposed on new enrollments and new ethnic schools, in order to curb the exponential growth previously experienced in the insertion classes. This ceiling tended to exclude the most recently arrived immigrant groups because, since 1986, new ethnic schools have generally not been eligible to receive ESP funds. In 1990, 69% of ESP funding supported Italian, 10% Greek, 5% Chinese, 4% Arabic, 2% Vietnamese, and 1% Turkish. The remaining 43 languages funded under the program together received less than 9% of the funding (Department of Employment, Education and Training, 1991b, 64–65).

Several reports criticized the organization of this program, especially with respect to the quality of instruction and the relevance of materials used in the after-school programs. While recognizing that "the efforts of the ethnic communities to promote language teaching through the ESP, particularly for primary school children, have made a significant contribution to language teaching and cultural awareness in Australia," a 1991 government report called for measures to strengthen the program (Department of Employment, Education and Training 1991b, 80). The decision was made to align the program with regular language programs in schools, including shifting funding for after-school programs from community organizations to school systems; the pill was sweetened by a 30 percent increase in funding (Department of Employment, Education and Training 1991a, 18).

Home languages are also supported through regular school language classes and through "Saturday Schools of Languages" funded by the state education authorities that operate the public schools in Australia. The first community language program in public schools in South Australia was Italian, beginning in 1958 and offered for school credit after 1967. Dutch followed in 1969, Hebrew in 1973, Ukrainian and Lithuanian in 1975, Modern Greek in 1976, Latvian and Polish in 1977, Hungarian in 1978, and more recently Vietnamese and other languages (Smolicz, 1984, 25). The National Language Policy recognizes the following categories of languages for school-based instruction: "the languages of ethnic groups within the Australian community, languages of significant economic and political importance to Australia, major world languages, and some Aboriginal languages." The first category would include Dutch and Ukrainian, languages of significant immigrant groups; the second would include Indonesian, since Australia has important economic ties to that neighboring nation; the third would include French and Japanese—the latter seems to be receiving particular emphasis.

The states (which, as in the United States and West Germany, are responsible for education) have issued their own guidelines for language programs. More than thirty languages are taught in the public and nonpublic schools of Victoria, and that state's Ministry of Education recommends starting at the primary level. In 1985 there were 130 supplemental teachers of languages other than English in public primary schools, teaching sixteen languages, while Catholic primary schools offered twelve languages with Italian by far the most popular (36,355 out of 49,103 pupils). Fifty-three independent (non-Catholic) primary schools offered sixteen languages, including three Aboriginal (Curriculum Branch, 1988, 95).

An interesting pattern emerges in comparing the programs offered in state (public), Catholic, and independent primary schools in Victoria. The independent schools tend to offer the more prestigious international languages, along with Hebrew in Jewish schools and the classics, while Catholic schools stress Italian and Spanish for their immigrant clientele. Greek and Turkish immigrants, it appears, tend to be in the state schools.

Belgium

Coordination of supplemental home language with regular instruction is a problem in every nation, in part because of scheduling and in part because of teacher attitudes. It becomes much more of a problem when, as in Belgium, the instruction is funded and supervised by the consulates of other countries on the basis of what may be very different goals and assumptions than those of the host educational system.

Belgian French-language authorities suspended their cooperation with Moroccan home language instruction for a time, and then reached a recent agreement with the Moroccan embassy for a home language and culture program beginning in November 1987 in six elementary schools. The Moroccan Ambassador agreed to nominate more teachers than required, all of them appropriately trained and certified and completely proficient in French; teachers were selected in consultation with Belgian authorities though paid by Morocco.

Schools participate voluntarily, and Moroccan parents have the choice whether their children will participate in the Arabic classes. The Moroccan teachers are under the supervision of the school principal and

> will work in coordination with the classroom teachers in an intercultural spirit and mutual understanding, will respect the educational mission of the school [this would include the Catholic identity of two of the schools], and will adhere to the rules governing the relations of teachers and students.

The Moroccan teachers under this agreement limit their teaching to Moroccan culture and are not to seek to interpret Islam, since students are taught religion in another course. This provision reflects the concern over foreign governments using religious teaching as a means of maintaining their influence over their expatriated citizens. They are expected to take part in the instruction of Belgian students, as well, in the interest of intercultural education. Their instruction in Arabic includes only the spoken language, since Belgian authorities are concerned lest teaching written Arabic before intermediate school lead to difficulties with French.

Perhaps most important, the agreement stresses that the precise manner in which teaching of Moroccan language and culture is to be integrated with other subjects will be worked out by negotiation in each school, thus making clear that the Moroccan teacher is a part of the school team and not someone who comes to do a few hours of supplemental instruction each week.

The primary purpose of this program is stated clearly as being to improve the integration of Moroccan children who will decide to stay in Belgium, and especially to improve their rate of success in Belgian education. Improved involvement of Moroccan parents in the life of the school is also an objective. The official memorandum explaining the agreement concludes

> Statistics force us to consider extremely unlikely what is incorrectly called the 'return' to the country of origin (most Moroccan students were born in Belgium); it follows that study of the Arabic language must have more a psychological and cultural function than one that is truly functional (Duquesne, 1987).

Canada

Supplemental classes in home languages are seldom provided with public funding in the United States, but both Canada and Australia have chosen to do so. The Canadian government adopted a policy of "multiculturalism within a bilingual framework" in 1971 (see Chapter 5), and ethnic groups were encouraged "to enrich Canadian society by continuing to develop their unique cultures" (McLaughlin, 1985, 75). The Heritage Language Program provides almost full funding to school boards that implement supplemental classes in native languages at the request of community groups, and by the mid-1980s there were over 100,000 pupils taking part in Ukrainian language and culture programs, and programs in many other languages. This is seen as an "enrichment" opportunity rather than as an intervention designed to reinforce students' conceptual foundation (Cummins, 1988, 141), and there has been little discussion of the possible relevance of bilingual education programs to promoting the academic achievement of minority students who are at risk of academic difficulties, which is the primary rationale employed in the United States. Many of the pupils participating do not speak the minority language upon entering school, and they are therefore studying a language to which their connection could be called sentimental.

> The Heritage Language Program was established in 1977 in Ontario as a way of accommodating ethnic-group demands without creating a backlash from those who opposed official sponsorship of language maintenance. Under the HLP, the Ministry provides virtually 100%

of the operating costs, based on a per-pupil formula for 2 1/2 hours of instruction per week, to school boards that agree to implement a programme at the request of community groups. Thus, the initiative must come from the community and school boards are under no obligation to accede to community requests. . . . There are three basic options for when classes may be held: (1) on weekends; (2) after the regular 5-hour school day; and (3) integrated into a school day extended by half-an-hour. This last option is the predominant one. (Cummins, 1984, 99).

By 1982–83 there were almost 80,000 pupils participating under this program, which included cultural festivals, music and dance classes and other activities as well as language instruction.

In addition, the national government's "Cultural Enrichment Program" awarded (in 1984–1985) nearly $3.5 million (Canadian) to heritage language and culture programs operating outside of the public education system; some 120,000 students participated in classes teaching 59 different languages. Chinese, Greek, German, Italian and Ukrainian were the languages most in demand (*Federal Government Initiatives*, 1987). Although the target groups are mostly identified by language, by some accounts these programs "have tended to stress folk culture often more than ethnic language maintenance, thus incurring the dissatisfaction of ethnic minority spokesmen who want more attention to language" (Bullivant, 1981, 74).

There are also home language programs offered in many public and nonpublic schools, though policies vary widely among the provinces. These in-school programs respond to the concern expressed by many that real societal multiculturalism could not become a reality unless the authority of the schools was seen to support it. After-school programs organized by ethnic community groups, while valuable, ran the risk of appearing esoteric, and those of them directed to actual language learning met resistance from children who saw them as extra schoolwork (Bhatnagar & Hamalian, 1981, 233–234).

Despite these efforts, there is a very strong tendency toward loss of the heritage languages; "by the third generation the question is not one of retention but of reacquisition and primary acquisition" (quoted by Cummins, 1984, 87). Swain points out that this is particularly true of dialect speakers, who may be ambivalent about or ashamed of their own manner of speaking and in consequence limit their verbal activities (discussion, reading aloud, games) with their children. Not only does this hasten the loss of the minority language (which, as a formal language, may never have been mastered in the first place) but it sends the children to school ill-prepared for a language-demanding environment (Swain, 1982, 95).

Denmark

Danish education policy, as formulated in 1976, supported home language instruction after school hours, so that "the students may maintain and develop their knowledge of their mother tongue and also their relation to their homeland." The education regulations provided that such instruction might be offered when there are twelve pupils using the same language, bringing them together from several communities if necessary. Local education authorities were required to provide three to five hours a week of "instruction in the minority pupil's mother-tongue or national language" if this was requested by the parents of at least twelve such pupils (Andersen, 1992, 31). It was to include the "mother tongue (national language)" and could deal with the homeland's history, geography and society, but should take as a starting point the pupil's situation in Denmark (Undervisningsministeriet, 1984a, 47–48).

The foreign pupils who participated voluntarily in this instruction had been in reception classes for a year or two and were then assigned to regular classes. Research suggested that

> the degree of participation in these national-language classes had little influence on the communication pattern or success rate of the student. Participation was also far from universal, even among the most "ethnic" students (Jørgensen, 1984).

The official position, as expressed by the Prime Minister in 1979, was that the immigrants came with a valuable "cultural ballast" that could offer much "to individuals who stretch out their hands and to Danish society as a whole. It is therefore important that the necessary integration be implemented with the greatest possible respect for the cultural identity of the immigrants."

A group of spokespersons for immigrant groups—Moroccan, Turkish, Yugoslavian, and Greek—issued, in 1980, a broad-ranging set of proposals for the improvement of their situation in Denmark. Among the recommendations was that instruction in home languages be obligatory for immigrant pupils as it is for Danish pupils in Danish. This instruction, they urged, should be included within the normal school hours. In grades 1 through 6 this should be through an extension of the timetable, while in grade 7 and above it should be in place of a second foreign language such as German (the need for English instruction starting in elementary school was not challenged). By "home language," the groups stressed, they meant the language spoken in the home and not the official language of the homeland. Home language instruction should take into account the new linguistic and cultural situation created for children and their parents by immigration (*Indvandrernes Forslag*, 1980, 20–21).

In 1990, however, the government decided home language support would be provided only through the 4th grade; after that, "if the children and their parents want to elaborate their mother-tongue, it should take place beyond the framework of the *folkeskole*." The Minister of the Interior added that "it is not the Government's task to strengthen immigrant culture, but a private matter" (quoted by Andersen, 1992, 56). Authorities in Ishøj, where there is an especially heavy concentration of immigrants, petitioned to give up mother-tongue teaching altogether.

France

It was in 1973 that courses in the language and culture of the homeland—originally, Portugal—penetrated officially into French public schools. Agreements were made with other nations subsequently: with Italy and Tunisia in 1974, with Spain and Morocco in 1975, with Yugoslavia in 1977, and with Turkey in 1978. Algerian Arabic classes had for some years been offered after school hours, and were introduced into a number of schools on an experimental basis starting in 1975; they were made official by an intergovernmental agreement (reached after long negotiations) in 1981 (Huart, 1988, 77–78). A government circular of 1975 specified that such instruction could be provided for three nonconsecutive hours a week during school time, by "foreign teachers recruited and paid by the governments of the countries" with which bilateral agreements had been made (Henry-Lorcerie, 1989, 37).

The 1973 circular authorizing home language and culture classes in Portuguese asserted that "the lack of mastery of the mother tongue leads to difficulties, for the newly-arrived, in learning French." Seksig comments that "this argument—really a postulate—would be systematically and literally repeated in the circulars that followed regulating the teaching of the languages of Yugoslavia, Tunisia, Algeria, etc." (Seksig, 1990, 24–25). That of 1981, announcing the agreement with Algeria, introduces in further justification the theme of self-esteem that was becoming so common in discussions of the education of minority pupils: maintaining the knowledge of the minority culture "constitutes an essential factor in the blossoming (*épanouissement*) of their personality" (Henry-Lorcerie, 1989, 43).

In 1983 the French government sought to regain control of this aspect of the instruction provided in its schools by issuing a directive specify-

TABLE 7.1. Participation in Home Language Instruction, 1986–87, in France

	School Hours	After School	% School Hours
Arabic (Algerian)	23,340	3,664	86.4
Arabic (Moroccan)	5,339	5,359	49.9
Arabic (Tunisian)	3,312	4,290	43.6
Italian	10,142	1,757	85.2
Portuguese	14,735	19,134	43.5
Spanish	411	3,133	11.6
Turkish	8,047	6,934	53.7
Yugoslav languages	108	1,428	7.0
	65,334	45,699	58.8

Source: Henry-Lorcerie, 1989, 77.

ing that the foreign governments would "make available" the teachers of their official languages but that school authorities would determine how they would be assigned and would direct their work (Henry-Lorcerie, 1989, 46–47). This measure seems to have been of limited utility, since the content of instruction in Arabic or Serbo-Croatian was necessarily opaque to French school inspectors.

By 1987, eight "homeland" countries assigned approximately 2,000 teachers to provide these language courses as a supplemental subject in schools, either during school hours (65,334 pupils) or after school hours but in school facilities (45,699 pupils). See Table 7.1. According to one study,

> [because] these teachers are trained, remunerated and supervised by the countries concerned . . . pedagogical integration has not proved to be very satisfactory . . . [participation has been] fewer than two per cent Yugoslavs and four per cent Spaniards, more than 25 per cent Turks and more than 20 per cent Portuguese. On the other hand, all Italians take these courses" (Costa-Lascoux, 1989, 74–75).

Most foreign pupils in French schools do not take part in such programs. During the school year 1989–90, in public elementary education, there were 60,926 pupils, or 17.26 percent of those potentially involved, taking part in home-language classes during school hours for a maximum of three hours a week; another 51,221 pupils took part in after-school classes, taught by 1,429 foreign teachers (Boulot & Boyzon-Fradet, 1991, 7). It has been noted, indeed, that the number of pupils participating is in a steady though not dramatic decline, having reached a high point of 20.24 percent of those eligible in 1984–85 (Boyzon-Fradet & Boulot, 1992, 249). Algerian Arabic classes, after growing from the mid-1970s to the mid-1980s, began to decline in enrollment in 1986–87, in part because the results achieved had been disappointing and in part because of a lack of consistent support from school authorities or from parents (Ali-Ammar, 1988, 18–20). The latter were not convinced that participation by their children contributed to their success in French schools, and they were encouraged in their skepticism by the regular teachers, who tended to resent the diversion of time and energy of their pupils (Huart, 1988).

Germany

The arrangements through which the various *Länder* chose to respond to the 1977 directive of the European Community differed widely, with some leaving the instruction up to the homeland governments to organize, support, and supervise, while others took on that responsibility in order to have greater control over content and pedagogy; in Hesse, the home language was made a normal part of the school program of foreign children, but in the other systems it was a voluntary extra subject (Nakipoğlu-Schimand, 1988, 89).

Home language instruction is provided through six organizational forms:

1.   Through arrangements made, paid for, and supervised by the consulates of the homelands, outside of school hours;

2.   Through arrangements made, paid for, and supervised by German education authorities, outside of school hours;

3.   Within ethnically homogeneous separate programs operated by German education authorities, either long-term "reception classes" with primary instruction in German or "mother-tongue classes" with primary instruction in the home language;

4.   Within the schedule of a German school, for pupils otherwise integrated into regular classes (generally this is only in pilot programs, according to Boos-Nünning, 1983a, 9);

5.   In privately-organized supplemental instruction, like the Koran schools maintained by the Turkish community independently of their government and its consulates; and

6.   In nonpublic bilingual schools, of which the most notable examples are the Greek schools in Bavaria (see Chapter 6).

When the decision was reached, in 1973, to halt recruitment of foreign workers, the German government stressed that efforts should be made to maintain the ties of those foreigners already in the country, and of their children, to the countries of origin. One way of doing so was through home language instruction. Thus a decision of the coordinating council of state education ministers called for a combined strategy:

> It is a question of enabling the foreign pupils to learn the German language and to obtain German school certificates while at the same time retaining and developing their knowledge of their home languages. At the same time the educational measures taken should contribute to the social integration of foreign pupils for the length of their stay in the Federal Republic of Germany. In addition they should serve the maintenance of their linguistic and cultural identity (quoted by Rixius & Thurmann, 1987, 25).

Altogether somewhat less than 40 percent of the foreign pupils in Germany take part in home language instruction, and the rate varies widely among the states. The differences reflect not only political decisions made in the states but also the differing goals of parents—and home governments— from various language groups (Mahler, 1983, 70). In addition, pupils or their parents may conclude (or be persuaded) that their efforts would be better spent on other aspects of the curriculum. For example, although Turkish pupils in Berlin may opt to substitute their language for English as the first "foreign" language studied, very few do so because English is required for secondary education and for much employment (Fase, 1987, 113).

According to one observer, it became increasingly clear in the late seventies that instruction in home languages could not fulfill its promise of developing and maintaining proficiency to a point that would allow children to re-enter the schools of their parents' homeland at grade level. As a result, "interest in home language instruction sank (at the end of the seventies the participation level in most states fell by 20–30%)" (Burk, 1988, 29).

Five *Länder* (Bavaria, Hesse, Lower Saxony, North Rhine/Westphalia, and Rhineland-Palatinate) make the funding and operation of such supplemental classes the responsibility of public education authorities. This instruction is in general limited to elementary and intermediate schools, with little at the preschool or the secondary level. North Rhine/Westphalia places first among the goals of supplemental home language instruction that it should "help the children to find their own identity"; there is no suggestion that it is an essential support to linguistic or cognitive development (Busges, 1988, 37). In 1987 new guidelines for such programs were issued, including the significant change that pupils of a single language group might be brought together full-time at specified schools (rather than assembled after school), so long as this did not lead to segregation; this was intended to facilitate real cooperation between home language and regular teachers. In addition, the home language teacher was to be consulted as decisions are made about the educational program of pupils of his or her group. The quite sensible intention of this provision was to take into account a student's achievement in the home language class when deciding on a further placement or a retention-in-grade (Accardo, 1987, 47).

In six other states the financing and operation of home language classes has been taken on by some of the foreign consulates, with limited German funding. Education authorities in Schleswig-Holstein decided that it would be contrary to their laws for public schools to provide such instruction and that it might therefore only be offered through private supplemental classes (Rixius & Thurmann, 1987, 53).

This issue of control reflects fundamental differences about the goals of home language instruction. This is in fact a three-sided tension, at least among the largest group of foreign residents. The Turkish Ministry of Education sent several hundred teachers to West Germany in the 1970s, where they provided supplementary instruction to more than ten thousand pupils outside of school hours. By contrast, Turkish teachers employed by German authorities were expected to work in cooperation with classroom teachers to promote the adjustment of Turkish pupils to the education system. One observer noted, in 1975, that "the co-existence of two types of teachers creates a number of conflict situations":

> There is a deep rift between former Turkish primary school teachers at present employed by German authorities, who are required to prepare Turkish pupils to adjust to the German curriculum, and Turkish teachers appointed by the Ministry of Education in Ankara. The latter's primary obligation is to maintain the pupils' allegiance to their home country (Abadan-Unat, 1975, 315, 318).

Despite concerns over the pedagogical effectiveness and the intellectual and political content of home language instruction, there are ample testimonies to the personal importance of the home language teacher to foreign students for whom he or she represents a primary source of support.

> For the children they are irreplaceable, because they alone, in the "majority school," represent for the children their ties to their own minority group; because they alone among the teachers have avail-

able a [to the foreign children] practical style of living; because they alone understand how the parents react in conflict situations; because they alone—if they have been in Germany long enough—have experience with the problems of migration; because they alone are not always judging the children by comparison with German children (Thurmann, 1988, 19).

In a *Gymnasium* in Oberhausen, a group of Turkish seventh graders were given the option of the formal study of Turkish in place of beginning a second "foreign language"—French or Latin—after English. Parents were told that this would not be an extra burden upon their children (as in the case of supplemental classes) but would rather provide an academic subject in which they could expect to be successful. It was reported that the pupils were enthusiastic to learn that there was a formal dimension—and thus a dignity equal to the German they had been taught at school—to a language which they had experienced only in conversational forms. On the other hand, and this is also typical, the course had to be improvised with no set goals, no curriculum, and inadequate materials, and the teacher conceded that there was little chance that the pupils would become fully proficient in Turkish, any more than they would have in French (Hofmann et al., 1993, 87–90).

In short, programs of supplemental home language instruction in Germany are often marginal to the educational process, but serve to humanize the school. They offer at least the possibility of a fruitful cooperation between foreign and German teachers. To the extent that they are brought into the curriculum and held to the same standards as other academic subjects, they could become a useful dimension of the education of the children of immigrants.

The Netherlands

Supplemental home language classes in the Netherlands were initially organized by the communities themselves—it is believed that the Spanish were first, in 1967—but the Dutch education authorities have taken responsibility since 1974, and a decade later the comprehensive Elementary Education Law provided for 2.5 hours a week of home language instruction within regular school time, and an equal amount, publicly funded, outside of regular school time, though the latter option is used only rarely. Of 1,350 home language programs surveyed in 1988, only southern European groups took relatively large advantage of the opportunity to organize after-school language classes (15.8 percent), while only 3.5 percent of the Moroccan supplemental classes were outside of school hours; a possible explanation is that such classes would be in competition with after-school Koran schools (Driessen et al., 1988). School authorities have in some cases sought to move home language instruction out of school hours to allow more time for regular instruction of language minority pupils, but this has met strong opposition from Turkish and Moroccan language activists, who insist upon the significance of the home language in connection with academic instruction (El Mouaden, 1990, 7), and presumably, fear that enrollment would drop if not sustained by a place in the school schedule. Spanish, Portuguese, and Italian home language instruction, by contrast, has more commonly been after school hours (though government subsidized) for several decades, because of the greater dispersal of those children and their greater integration into the regular program of schools.

The primary motivation for providing supplemental home language-and-culture (OETC) in Dutch schools, as expressed in both governmental documents and the views of minority language advocates, is psychological. The goals defined by the government were "developing a positive self-awareness, bridging the gap between school and home and contributing to the development of intercultural education" for Dutch as well as foreign children (Ministry of Education and Science, 1983). Advocates claim that immigrant youth are a "lost generation" and home language classes "give them their own identity and self-confidence" (Leunessen, 1994, 244).

The fundamentally "soft" character of these goals should be noted: They do not include developing a solid academic proficiency in the home language (Hajer & Meestringa, 1991, 73). Van Esch suggests that, if a language other than Dutch is to be studied in school, it should be approached in a way that stresses its equal seriousness with other subjects and the expectation of academically respectable accomplishment (Esch, 1982, 169). A recent government policy document pointed in this direction, stressing that "minority language teaching must not be allowed to become an isolated subject. It must be harmonized with other language teaching" (Ministry of Education and Science, 1991a, 148).

Schools differ in how they support the exercise of this right. In some cases the lessons are simply provided to all language minority pupils, unless parents refuse them. In others, the OETC teacher communicates with each language minority parent to determine their wishes in this respect. In yet other cases, a letter with a reply form is sent to parents, sometimes phrased to discourage participation by suggesting that it might deprive the child of important lessons in the regular class (Ersoy, 1993, 321).

It is estimated that about 75 percent of the language minority children in the Netherlands attend home language classes; participation of Turkish and Moroccan children, in particular, has been increasing (Aarssen et al., 1992, 9). This may result in part from the fact that 53 percent of the Turkish and 60 percent of the Moroccan home language teachers use their classes to provide Islamic religious instruction as well, even though this is not the intention of the government (Driessen, 1990, 23).

Many of the "Turkish" children in fact speak Kurdish at home, and an estimated 80 percent of the Moroccan children are speakers of one of the mutually unintelligible Berber languages or of one of the many dialectical forms of Moroccan Arabic. "There is no generally acceptable or standard way of writing Berber or Colloquial Moroccan Arabic . . . they are looked upon by Moroccan parents as *not fit to be taught in school*" (Khleif, 1991, 108; italics in original). This was confirmed by a study carried out in 1988 on behalf of the government by De Jong, Mol, and Oirbans, that found that "the vast majority of the parents involved favoured the official language rather than local languages or dialects" (Ministry of Education and Science, 1991a, 148). This raises the problem alluded to in Chapter 5, that Standard Arabic is taught to children for the fortunate of whom (the speakers of colloquial Arabic) it is as unfamiliar as "Latin for Italian speakers; or semi-Chaucerian, or rather Shakespearean, English for North Americans" (Khleif, 1991, 108), and for the others it is a completely new (and difficult) language. From the perspective of their access to an important world language, this is an excellent thing, but it is clearly more an additional burden to a child struggling to become proficient in Dutch, than it is support from a familiar "mother tongue."

Moroccan parents have a difficult time explaining *why* they want their children to learn formal written Arabic (which they themselves usually do not know), though it seems to be related to its closeness to the Classical Arabic used in the mosque and also symbolic of keeping open the possibility of returning, as a family, to Morocco even as that prospect grows more and more dim in actual reality. Tension arises in programs like that in Enschede (see below) where the home language—some variant of colloquial Arabic—is used as a means of promoting learning and adjustment to school (Pedagogisch Centrum Enschede, 1983b). An evaluator found that the Moroccan teacher himself experienced a serious conflict of expectations, since he had been trained to teach standard Arabic (as in Moroccan schools) and associated success with the ability of his pupils to use it correctly (Eldering, 1983b, 13); he was strongly supported in this by many of the Moroccan parents (Boos-Nünning et al., 1984, 37).

The fact that, according to an estimate by the secretary of the organization of home language teachers, 60 to 70 percent of the immigrant families in the Netherlands speak Berber or Kurdish at home removes two of the grounds often given for providing such instruction: that it allows the school to connect with the experience of the children in a way that enhances their self-esteem, and that it allows transfer into Dutch of skills developed through instruction in the home language (Driessen, 1990, 26). The function of home language classes, for parents as well as for school authorities, seems in such cases to be a largely symbolic acknowledgement of respect for diversity.

Sweden

Perhaps the most generous provisions are in Sweden, where bilingual pupils were entitled to two hours a week of supplemental home language instruction, though this commitment has been reduced under the fiscal austerity of recent years. In 1973, the National Board of Education adopted an ambitious goal for bilingual children of "a parallel command of both languages," and by 1978 55 percent of the 81,000 pupils with minority language backgrounds were participating in such programs. Another 40 percent did not wish home language instruction, and 5 percent wished it but did not receive it (McLaughlin, 1985, 30).

Swedish "compulsory" schools (grades 1 through 9) provided supplemental home language instruction in 105 different languages. Support for this program came from both sides of the political spectrum.

> The Social Democrats base the reform on the right of individuals to the free development of their personality and the claim to equal opportunity. The argument of the Conservatives is "the maintenance of linguistic and cultural diversity" (Belke, 1988, 40).

Paulston quotes Hanson (1980) as asserting that "Mothertongue classes do not aim 'directly' for bilingualism. They aim primarily to make children feel secure in their schoolwork. When children feel secure, they can do work in school" (Paulston, 1992e, 136). This assumes, of course, that devoting several hours each week to studying a language that is not used in schoolwork otherwise is more likely to create a feeling of security than would be the same amount of time spent on improving proficiency in the language of instruction.

Rather than rely upon teachers provided by homeland governments, Sweden decided to recruit and train teachers from immigrant communities in Sweden. A training program was established in 1974, and eventually came to include eleven languages (Linde & Löfgren, 1988). In this way they could ensure that the teachers understood the immigrant experience "from the inside out," and could serve as models to the pupils of living successfully in two cultures. Teachers recruited from other countries would have

> inadequate knowledge . . . concerning Sweden and concerning the difficulties and opportunities facing immigrants in this country. Home language teachers should be closely familiar both with the culture of their native country and with Swedish culture, so as to provide immigrant children with the cultural interpreters they need when they have to live in two cultures at once (*Investigation . . .*, 1979).

Home language classes in Sweden—in contrast to those in Denmark—are held during the regular school day, and school authorities have direct responsibility for appointing and supervising teachers. The necessity for many home language teachers to cover a number of schools may make it impossible to coordinate effectively with regular classroom teachers, as well as placing a tremendous burden on the traveling teacher; the Swedish Teachers' Association has identified this as a working-conditions issue (Sveriges Lärarforbund, 1989).

At the Rosengård School in Malmö, visited by the author, with more than forty languages represented among 300 pupils, grades 1–6, the solution was to schedule all part-time home language instruction for Wednesdays, so that at least those teachers were in the school together and teachers could plan their instruction for the other days without interruptions. The school also has full-time home language teachers of Spanish and Arabic—language groups represented in larger numbers in the school—who work cooperatively with the other teachers through the week.

Some immigrant organizations in Sweden have argued that home language instruction should be made a compulsory school subject for children of their groups.

> Among other things it is argued that home language must not be forced to compete with other subjects, and it is also argued that the free option concerning the immigrant children's native/home languages gives the latter an inferior and weaker position than the native language of Swedish children (*Immigrants and the Education System*, 1979, 28).

One of the more unusual arguments advanced for this position is that making the instruction mandatory would spare parents the burden of having to decide, since some "parents are unaware of the importance of the home language" (*Immigrants and the Education System*, 1979, 30). The government insisted upon keeping home language instruction voluntary, however, in part because of the difficulty of deciding which pupils should be required to participate, and in which language (and culture) they should be instructed.

> Home language lessons, like the teaching of Swedish to Swedish-speaking pupils, include elements relating to the culture, history, social structure, etc., of the country or the cultural region where the language is spoken. When some parents decline home language instruction for their children, this may be one of the reasons, particularly as regards certain political refugees and linguistic minorities from countries where only one language is officially recognized. In the latter case, children often have more than one home language, and sometimes they know the official language of their country of origin better than their parents' native language. Parents may therefore have powerful emotional reasons for objecting to their children being taught a particular language. . . . Parents and the individual pupil must have the last word as to whether the pupil is to be taught the home language (*Immigrants and the Education System*, 1979, 31).

Although it is not compulsory, there is a fundamental right to home language instruction in Sweden, and this right applies even when only one pupil with a particular language attends a school. The criteria for participating in such instruction are that (1) the pupil make daily use of the language in communication with one parent, for whom it is the mother tongue, (2) the pupil have a basic command of the language, and (3) participation be voluntary. A study of intermediate-level pupils found that

> one fifth of the students who take part in [home language] instruction say that they always speak Swedish at home. About half of these . . . also say that their parents usually speak Swedish. . . . A special analysis of these students shows that almost 90 percent of them were born in Sweden, that on average they have high grades in both English [a compulsory subject] and Swedish, and that most of them have parents with a secondary education (Balke-Aurell & Lindblad, 1983, 131).

There is thus no connotation that home language instruction is remedial; it is considered a form of educational enrichment to which pupils who already have some grasp of another language are entitled. By the same token, these programs are not justified as essential to achievement in the regular curriculum.

> Participation in home language instruction at 9-year compulsory comprehensive school can only predict participation in home language instruction at upper secondary level . . . we cannot prove any positive effects from the home language instruction in the form of a greater interest for further education. . . . On the other hand, there are no negative effects of the home language instruction with regard to future education (Löfgren, 1984, 22).

A nationwide study of all linguistic minority pupils who had been in the ninth grade in 1978–79 found that it was "impossible to draw any reliable conclusions . . . concerning the effect of home language instruction on the predisposition of pupils to start [noncompulsory] upper secondary school" (Liljegren & Ullman, 1981, 48).

There is in fact a correlation between lack of proficiency in Swedish and number of periods a week devoted to home language instruction. Of 2,138 linguistic minority pupils who received home language instruction in the ninth grade, 584 were not considered proficient in Swedish; 22 percent of these received five or more periods a week of home language instruction. Less than 3 percent of the 1,554 Swedish-proficient pupils received five or more periods a week of such instruction (Liljegren & Ullman, 1982, 25).

Among linguistic minority pupils with a limited proficiency in Swedish those who had received home language instruction were *less* likely to go on to upper secondary school than those who had not. By contrast, among linguistic minority pupils with a high proficiency in Swedish, those who had participated in home language instruction were *more* likely to go on with their education than those who had not (Liljegren & Ullman, 1981, 49). This suggests that home language instruction may have a positive effect on the self-concept and ambition of pupils who are doing well in school, while for those who are not, it may simply compete for instructional time with the regular program.

Ironically, in view of this pattern, the study found that pupils with a poor knowledge of Swedish were more likely to value home language instruction—and to have more periods a week of it—than those proficient in Swedish. For pupils from some language groups, the home language instruction was clearly enrichment for one or two periods a week, while for others it replaced major parts of the regular curriculum, causing problems with their achievement. A report prepared for the Council of Europe concluded that

Immigrant children in Swedish schools do not receive the consistent support they need to attain active bilingualism. Even in cases where provision is made for home language instruction or teaching of Swedish as a second language, the programmes to which children are subjected at one educational level are rarely consciously coordinated with the instructional programme at other levels. The immigrant child's educational career is marked more often than not by fragmented and inconsistent measures (Opper, 1985, 24).

The United Kingdom

To an increasing extent in the 1970s local authorities began to fund home language teachers to work in one or several schools, and to provide financial support to community-run programs (Tansley & Craft, 1984). This development was in part a response to the 1975 Bullock Report, which urged that

the school should adopt a positive attitude to its pupils bilingualism and wherever possible should help maintain and deepen their knowledge of their mother tongues (quoted in Linguistic Minorities Project, 1985, 60).

In a national survey conducted in 1983, twenty-three local education authorities reported providing home language instruction in primary schools, with 252 schools participating (Tansley & Craft, 1984).

Providing home language instruction in Britain, as elsewhere, is complicated by the fact that the home language, for many immigrant children, is not the official language of instruction of their homeland.

Asian children who speak Punjabi at home may well want to learn Urdu instead of Punjabi because this was the traditional language of learning for their parents. Those from the East Punjab may choose to study Hindi for religious reasons. A minority of Cantonese-speaking Chinese children may choose to learn Mandarin which is the national spoken language of the People's Republic of China and Taiwan (Tsow, 1983, 368).

British policymakers have not, by and large, accepted the contention of advocates of bilingual education, that use of the home language is essential, nor have they agreed that schools—rather then ethnic communities—have a responsibility to help to maintain heritage languages. Thus "it was not until the mid-eighties that the [government] formulated as its position that com-

433

munity languages could play a role in the first years of primary education in order to help ethnic minority children in acquiring proficiency in English" (Kroon, 1990, 48, 7). An experimental program in Bedfordshire formed two groups at each of four primary schools, serving Italian- and Punjabi-speaking children who were newly arrived in the country. These five- and six-year-old pupils received one lesson a day, after school hours, leaving the teachers free to develop curriculum; they seem not to have used this time to consult with the regular classroom teachers serving the same children.

> Visits by project teachers to mainstream classes and by the teachers of mainstream classes to mother tongue groups were organized only sporadically and only rarely led to mutual agreements on learning content, when the project teachers took up themes from the mainstream teaching (Boos-Nünning & others, 1986, 78–99).

This experimental project in home language instruction brought out again the difficulties which arise when the language of the home is not the standard form of the national language of the homeland. Italian parents in Bedford speak dialect and their

> inability to provide any model in the Standard [form of Italian] reduces considerably their control of and intervention in the child's language development. . . . despite the parents' determination to maintain their original idioms, they frequently cause the first gap in the vocabulary development of their children. This begins when they speak about the outside world in a language which is heavily affected by English borrowings (Tosi, 1984, 129).

For their children, these parents believed, learning standard Italian would increase future opportunities to relate to an evolving Italian society in which dialects have a decreasing role, though it would do little to maintain their communication with the parents themselves, for whom "the national [Italian] language has no place in the everyday speech" (Tosi, 1984, 130). The teachers were concerned to enable the pupils to pass language examinations in standard Italian as a regular school subject (Kroon, 1990, 39). Neither standard Italian nor dialect, indeed, compete successfully with English for children who

> excited by the access given by the common language to immediate membership of the English-speaking peer group, are also aware of the cohesion communicated by the local accent across the diversity of

surnames and skin colours. They will gradually associate with the English language sharply connotative and emotional values. . . . The young person is gradually learning to understand that [dialect and English], their speakers and the different values that they independently communicate, were not naturally created to co-exist in the same environment. These contrasts will reach them in the form of personal and emotional conflicts (Tosi, 1984, 111f).

There has been a tendency, as in other countries, for policies and school practices around the study of home languages to move in two directions. On the one hand, languages such as Bengali and Italian are increasingly offered as elective subjects within the curriculum for secondary pupils; on the other, home languages are sometimes used as part of the reception process rather than as supplemental programs. This tendency was already detectable fifteen years ago, and appears to be gaining in strength.

So the focus appears to be developing in favour of bilingual education as a transitional measure, to facilitate the move to English, rather than one that positively values the mother tongue and aims to maintain and develop it throughout the school system. This, it can be argued, is a more sophisticated assimilationist policy and does not involve, nor aim for, a truly multicultural, multilingual society where diversity is fostered (Saifullah Khan, 1980, 76).

The influence of American models of transitional bilingual education and of bilingual reception programs in the Netherlands (see below) may be partly responsible for this development, but it seems likely that there is also an element of disappointment with the results of supplemental classes, and an awareness of the growing unwillingness of language minority parents to support a form of education whose value was unclear. Criticism from "anti-racist" circles of the segregatory effect of "mother tongue teaching programmes that are isolated from the mainstream and restricted to only a particular section of pupils" (Houlton & King, 1985, 54) may have had an effect as well.

ASSIGNMENT TO A SPECIAL PROGRAM

Many immigrant children, as we have seen, are assigned to regular classes, either with or without part-time language development help and supplemental programs in the home language.

Others are placed in separate reception programs for a period of time, until they are judged ready to be assigned to regular, integrated classes. There are two primary types of reception programs, those that use only the language of the school and focus upon developing a "survival" proficiency in it, and those that also use the home language of the language minority children in some combination with the language of the school.

Each type of reception program may of course turn into a permanent segregated track within the educational system (see Chapter 6); here we are concerned with those that are, in practice as well as intention, essentially transitional.

Reception in the Language of the School

A variation on reception in the language of the school is structured immersion in a second language as implemented, most notably, for English-speaking pupils in Canada whose parents wish them to develop proficiency in French. By all accounts, these programs have achieved notable—though by no means complete—success (Lapkin & Cummins, 1984; Swain, 1984). To a limited extent, the model has been adapted to the schooling of majority children in the United States (Campbell, 1984) and elsewhere.

Canadian-style immersion programs may be considered reception classes in the sense that the pupils are taught entirely through a language that they do not speak at home. In several important respects, however, they differ from reception programs for the children of immigrants. One, frequently noted by advocates of the use of home languages for instruction, is that the pupils are in no risk of losing their first languages nor of coming to believe that it, and they, are somehow inferior (Siguán & Mackey, 1987, 87). Children from (usually middle-class) English-speaking families who have volunteered them for an immersion program as a form of enrichment presumably do not require that a stress be placed upon their home language either for the sake of their self-esteem or as a means of the political mobilization of their parents (see Chapter 5).

Rejection of Canadian-style second-language immersion for language minority children rests in most cases upon arguments that are more political than linguistic, as when one minority language advocate insists that

> the full and equal participation of language minorities in American society requires not that these groups try to become indistinguishable from the white majority, but rather than they strengthen themselves from within—culturally, socially, politically, and economically (Hernández-Chávez, 1984, 170).

For such opponents of assimilation, the primary lesson to be drawn from the Canadian immersion programs is not that Spanish-speaking children in the United States could learn English in the same way, but that they should receive instruction through Spanish for far longer than the three or four years typical of a bilingual reception program, indeed "throughout the school years" (Hernández-Chávez, 1984, 173; see the discussion of separate schooling in Chapter 6). The Canadian immersion programs also differ from reception programs in that they do not focus primarily on language as a preparation for mainstreaming, but are "fundamentally academic. That is to say, their primary objective is normal academic development" (Genesee, 1987, 17). The immersion programs are the schooling that the pupils receive, not a preparation for such schooling, and will therefore not be considered as examples of reception programs.

The United States

Creating special reception classes to teach the language skills considered essential for participation in an otherwise unmodified school program was considered an especially progressive measure in the period of heaviest immigration to the United States in the early twentieth century. So-called "steamer classes" were provided in many cities for children just off the boat from Europe. In Massachusetts alone, there were 26 cities and towns that reported providing such classes in 1914. A state-appointed commission applauded this practice, noting that

> where excellent methods are used and proper provision is made for the separate instruction of those who have had little schooling in Europe and of those who have had much, English is learned in an incredibly short time. Sometimes, however, newly arrived immigrant children are placed in a "special" class with the backward and subnormal children for whom quite different methods are needed, and a grave injustice is thus done to both groups (Commission on Immigration, 1914, 115–116).

The Boston school superintendent made the same case for reception programs in a book published in 1920,

> There is general agreement in the practice of progressive communities in grouping older immigrant children in special classes for intensive work in English, in order that they may acquire the common tongue as a tool for work through which they can be advanced rapidly to classes of children of their own age.

He contrasted this with

> the continuance in some communities of the bad practice originally
> in vogue in all cities—namely, the grouping of non-English-speaking
> children of all ages and degrees of maturity in the lowest grades of
> the schools. . . . This practice is demoralizing to the children who
> actually belong in the lower grades and discouraging to the immigrant
> child (Thompson, 1971, 118–119).

After World War II, Mexican-American veterans in the Southwest of the United States sought to overcome, for their children, the barriers that they themselves had experienced: "one typical result was the 'Little Schools of the 400,' community-supported preschool classes set up to help Chicano children learn the four hundred most common words of American English in preparation for entering the public school system" (Castellanos, 1983, 49). It is an indication of the shift in perspective away from integration and assimilation over recent decades that these reception programs, though community-sponsored, are characterized as "misguided" by Crawford in his study of efforts to insist upon the primacy of the English language in American life (Crawford, 1992b, 78).

Reception programs conducted exclusively in the majority language have become the exception in recent years in American schools, though many cities continue to provide them for pupils who belong to language groups whose numbers in local schools do not warrant a bilingual program. Typically, a reception program will mix Ukrainian-speakers and Hindi-speakers, but not Spanish-speakers, who will be assigned to a class conducted partly in Spanish. Most large cities with substantial language minority populations offer some form of bilingual program for each group represented in significant numbers.

Texas mandates what is called a "bilingual education program" for pupils of limited proficiency in English who are nonetheless stronger orally in English than in their home language: apart from 45 minutes a day of language arts in the home language, the balance of the classroom time is to be spent on language development and subject matter taught through English as a second language methodology (Texas Education Agency, no date, 16).

The most widely known nonbilingual reception program in the United States at present is that in Fairfax County, Virginia, a district with 4,200 language minority pupils from 75 language backgrounds among its total enrollment of 133,000. With pupils speaking fifty different languages, the district decided not to provide bilingual education in the usual sense but rather to provide an extensive program of English as a second language (ESL). This led to a challenge from the federal Office for Civil Rights, which had established bilingual instruction as the norm to meet the needs (and thus the rights) of language-minority pupils. After a five-year investigation, the government concluded that the program was in compliance with legal requirements since pupils were learning both English and the age-appropriate subject matter, and achieving at grade level after completing ESL (Porter, 1990, 146–147).

A low pupil-teacher ratio was provided, in Fairfax County, through substantial additional expenditure, and a tuition-free summer program in English was established.

> The district was using a well-coordinated, centralized registration procedure that enabled it to identify and assess potential LEP students within 48 hours. The district provided intensive instruction in understanding, speaking, reading, and writing English. Periods of instruction varied from a minimum of 45 minutes to a full day. One-on-one tutoring was also provided as necessary. Most importantly, there was close coordination between English instructors and regular classroom teachers to ensure their curricula meshed (Castellanos, 1983, 234–235)

Limited English-proficient pupils are clustered together for services in some areas when there are an insufficient number (less than forty) to provide services in each school; some school attendance district boundaries have been changed to ensure that the proportion of LEP pupils does not become so great in any school to impact upon the quality of instruction and expectations (Hadden, 1985, 66).

The success of this program was facilitated by the fact that a substantial proportion (though not the majority) of the language-minority pupils were the children of diplomats and others working in nearby Washington, D.C., rather than those of low-status immigrants.

"Newcomer" schools have been established recently in California—that in San Francisco has existed for decades—where most larger school districts have one. In Sacramento, for example, the Newcomer Center screens all immigrant language minority pupils as they enter the school system, and those at the appropriate age level for grades 1–8 are assigned to bilingual programs in the appropriate language if one exists in their section of the school district; otherwise, they are assigned to the Newcomer School where they receive instruction in English language and other subjects, supported by their home language if possible. After a maximum of one year they are assigned to a bilingual program or to a regular class (Hadden, 1985, 64).

Pupils at the Newcomer High School in San Francisco take six classes a day, three of them in different aspects of English as a second language, two "bilingual support classes" in mathematics and social studies, and a "sheltered English" class in physical education, art, biology, or physical science, in which they must use English with their classmates from diverse language backgrounds. The goal of the school, according to its principal, is not just fluency in English but "academic English, the kind of English that you need to do well in college, to evaluate, to criticize, to make judgments, to voice your opinion. That kind of English requires a lot of study and a certain amount of cultural literacy in the American context" (Cheng, in National Coalition of Advocates for Students, 1988, 88–89). Pupils stay one year, then are assigned to a regular high school where they continue to receive bilingual and English language support; no one graduates from Newcomer High School.

The newcomer school in Los Angeles serving grades 4 through 8 has as its objective to provide "English language training plus counseling designed to ease [the immigrant pupils'] eventual enrollment in a regular classroom." Other content, in science and mathematics, is provided only as a secondary aspect of the program (Stewart, 1993, 89–91). Such separate reception programs are expensive to operate because of their smaller class sizes, higher ratio of support staff, and need for varied materials corresponding to a highly diverse student population (McDonnell & Hill, 1993, 92–98).

La Guardia Community College in New York City operates an "international high school" that enrolls between four and five hundred pupils for forty or more nations at any time. The school provides a full educational program with intensive language support, and encourages pupils who have become bilingual to help newly arrived pupils through their first languages. This model, which goes beyond the emphasis of many reception programs upon language acquisition alone, has attracted considerable attention; the Dutch Ministry of Education has even distributed a videotape produced by the school, with an accompanying handbook in Dutch suggesting possible application to the Netherlands (Leeman, 1995, 228–230).

In a possibly unprecedented variation on such reception schools, the United States government established, in 1985, the PASS (Preparation for American Secondary Schools) program for Khmer and Vietnamese youth in refugee camps in Thailand and the Philippines; by June 1987, 5,533 pupils had graduated from these two sites. This program supplemented the English as a second language and cultural orientation classes already provided for adult refugees who had been accepted for resettlement in the United States. According to a contemporary evaluation, the PASS program attempts to simulate an American secondary school as much as possible by incorporating major features of junior and senior high schools in the U.S. The day is divided into six 40-minute class periods. Students move from class to class and follow customary American classroom procedures. The class periods include three periods of ESL, one period of basic math, and two periods of American studies. PASS also includes extracurricular activities such as poetry, math club and board games, and outdoor sports (Bureau for Refugee Programs, 1987, 2).

A follow-up study comparing the success in mainstream classes of American schools of these pupils with refugee pupils who did not take part in the PASS program found that 48 percent of the PASS pupils were rated by their teachers as "above average" compared with other refugees, compared with 23 percent of the non-PASS pupils.

The effect of the PASS program on student performance, while substantial for all . . . , was greatest for those with no or little previous education. For the students with 4+ years of previous education . . . , 55% more PASS students were rated Above Average. For students with 1–3 years previous education and with no previous education, the effect of the PASS program was roughly 3 to 10 times greater, respectively (the differentials are 143% and 575%) (Bureau for Refugee Programs, 1987, 25).

The strongest positive effect was in relation to English literacy, the weakest to "cultural orientation," suggesting that immigrant pupils need less help in making cultural adjustments than they do in acquiring a new language.

Khmer and Laotian pupils at Lowell (Massachusetts) High School were provided with a variety of support services by an outside agency funded by the state's Office of Educational Equity, then directed by the author. Project staff taught several brief orientation courses, including one on "being a teenager in America," and provided extensive counseling and crisis intervention services. It became apparent that learning English was only one of the challenging tasks facing these refugee pupils; many were struggling "to cope with past trauma and cultural transition as well as the normal developmental issues of adolescence" (Lockwood, 1987, 37). Contrary to the American stereotype of Asians as a "model minority," many of the refugee youth required mental health interventions for suicidal tendencies, family abuse and neglect, and social marginalization.

Australia

As Australia began, after the World War II, to admit an increasing number of Eastern European refugees and others for whom English was not the first language, educational policy was governed by the assumption that the acquisition of English was the short-term answer to all of their needs. A national policy study in 1960 concluded that

> migrant children have adjusted well, are above average in scholarship and present no problem of absorption (i.e. non-conformity); such problems as do arise with either parents or children result from lack of knowledge of English and evaporate when English has been mastered, which, for the children, happens "fairly quickly"; parents should therefore be encouraged to speak English in the home; "national groups" among school children, though not a "major problem," are undesirable because they hinder "the children's integration in the school community and their progress" (quoted by Bullivant, 1982, 132).

In addition to support for language acquisition within the regular curriculum, the national government also gives schools one-time grants for each newly arrived pupil who does not speak English, for a minimum of three months of intensive instruction in the language (*Commonwealth Programs for Schools*, 1986, 272–9).

In response to the flood of Vietnamese refugees in the seventies, residential hostels were provided in Melbourne for a transitional period, during which children were taught English in Reception Language Centres. Within six months they were transferred in groups of no more than twenty—"so as not to saturate any school or classroom with immigrants"—to local schools (Shafer, 1983, 423).

Belgium

Separate reception classes for immigrant pupils have not gained wide acceptance because of Belgium's emphasis upon assimilation (Fase, 1994, 94). Supporters argue that reception classes in Flanders are by no means an intermission in the educational process while children learn Dutch. The curriculum includes religion or ethics, French or English as a foreign language, mathematics, social studies (or history and economics), science, and art, while pupils study Dutch intensively (Bauwel & Verbeeck, 1993, 317–318).

The reception program in an intermediate school in Antwerp —regarded as a national pilot—has been described as a "language bath":

Many of these new pupils are newly-immigrated, even though in theory family reunification ended a few years ago, so that some teenagers enter the intermediate school speaking only an unwritten Berber dialect. . . . The usual approach of assignment of these pupils to a regular class with supplemental remedial instruction was not meeting their needs. Staff noted, for example, that pupils would be absent on those days when they would have lessons in which their inadequacies in Dutch would be obvious.

The answer seemed to be a special transitional program with a carefully-planned sequence of instruction stressing mastery of the ability to understand and communicate in spoken Dutch. Permission was received to launch this experiment in 1979. The transitional classes bring together a very heterogeneous group of pupils ranging in age from 12 to 17 or beyond, with a wide range of previous schooling.

Those who are not ready for a regular class are placed in one of the levels of the program; there is frequent movement among the groups. Students remain only one year in the program, unless they were illiterate when they entered it, since school authorities are concerned to avoid formation of an academic ghetto.

The heart of the program consists of eight hours a week of Dutch language instruction, provided by a language teacher and a Moroccan assistant teacher to a group of not more than fifteen pupils. The role of Moroccan assistant is regarded as a key to the success of the program, as a role model and a co-teacher in a flexible but intensive period of daily instruction.

The language teacher is responsible for coordinating with the other teachers working with these pupils (they have two hours of French, five of math, two of graphic arts, three of physical education, four of social studies, and four of industrial arts each week, as well as two each of religion (Islamic if appropriate) and native language each week. The purpose of this coordination is so they can all stress the same content and vocabulary in their different contexts; indeed the teachers of math and the other subjects should see themselves as first of all language teachers. Teacher schedules allow for time to discuss the progress of each pupil periodically (Glenn, 1987, 41–43).

A Newcomer Project in Ghent provides orientation and language support for immigrating teenagers, most of whom prefer to go directly to work rather than to continue their schooling (Maton, 1993, 221–222).

Denmark

Education regulations make provision for special reception classes for pupils arriving in Denmark at age 14 and above who are not capable of benefiting from a regular class; such classes may be offered by several communities jointly. Other pupils are to be placed in classes corresponding to their age, unless their parents agree to a lower grade, and may receive special instruction in Danish and, if necessary, in subject areas as well. "The principal will make the decision about this, after consultation with the pupils and parent and after discussion with the teachers' council" (Undervisningsministeriet, 1984a, 45).

For a time in the early 1980s, there was some interest in "national classes" like American bilingual classes, where literacy would be developed first in the home language of the pupils. This model was judged a failure because of the isolating of minority pupils and the lack of cooperation between bilingual and mainstream teachers—a familiar complaint! "Parallel classes" were then tried, in which Turkish pupils were in a separate class but integrated for music, physical education, and other activities, much as is required (though the requirement is commonly ignored) in bilingual programs in the United States; this model increased polarization between the foreign and Danish pupils. Finally, educators settled on a strategy of "integration on a bilingual/bicultural basis which implies that the teaching should take the bilingual child's linguistic and cultural background as a starting point." Immigrant pupils are placed in a reception class for special instruction in Danish for from three months to two years before assignment to a regular class; after such an assignment, they may receive continued remedial help but on the same basis as Danish pupils who are experiencing academic difficulties (Andersen, 1992, 44, 31).

France

The French government established, in response to a growing movement of family reunification, a system of *"classes d'initiation"* [CLIN] for elementary pupils requiring a period of intensive instruction in "written and spoken French particularly relevant to their daily lives" (Charlot, 1981, 103). As Charlot explains,

> There are three types of CLIN: those which extend over the whole school year, those lasting six months or a semester, and an integrated crash course (CRI = *Cours de rattrapage intégré*), in which the migrant children receive seven or eight special language lessons a week, but otherwise attend the same lessons as their French classmates (1981, 103).

For foreign pupils arriving in France age 12–14, the educational system provides a period of intensive instruction in French within an intermediate school: one year, in theory, if they have been "normally schooled" in their homeland, and two if they have not. If present in small numbers—as increasingly is the case with the shift from the reunification of guest-worker families to the more dispersed settlement of refugees—they may simply be put into a regular class. For example,

> Migrant children who enter the country after the age of twelve are placed in a *classe d'adaptation* (CLAD) in the type of secondary school that provides a general education or, if they are fourteen or over, in the type that offers vocational training or work preparation; attendance at these is compulsory for one or two years (Boos-Nünning & others, 1986, 102–103).

To ensure that responsibility for the newly arrived pupils would be felt by the whole school staff, the Ministry of Education directed in 1986 that they must be enrolled in a regular class from the start even though spending most of their time in the reception class, and thus "double-reported" for staffing purposes in the school rolls. Gradually over the course of a year they are to spend more time in the regular class, while the reception teacher uses the time thus freed up to provide individualized support to those experiencing difficulties or to start work with late-arriving pupils.

Germany

A common practice has been to place newly arrived immigrant children in reception classes within schools of the appropriate grade level for a period of language training before they are assigned to regular classrooms, usually on the basis of an informal assessment by the teacher that they are sufficiently prepared (McLaughlin, 1985, 42). The coordinating council of state education ministers issued an advisory bulletin on the education of foreign pupils in December 1971, calling for the establishment as necessary of public-school reception classes, with

> the assignment of facilitating and hastening the process of acclimatization to the German educational system. A reception class can be set up for approximately 15 children of the same or different language groups. The class may be divided for 24 children. . . . Pupils in reception classes may be taught together with German students in music, art, shop, sewing, home economics and physical education. In

445

these subjects and in reception classes foreign teachers may instruct along with German teachers. In such cases a close collaboration of foreign and German teachers is necessary. After sufficient advance in the German language the pupils in reception classes should be assigned to [regular] classes which correspond to their achievement level or their age. Participation in a reception class should last generally one year (quoted in Mahler, 1983, 201–202).

Striking differences are found among German states (as among nations in Europe) with respect to the proportion of all foreign students who are enrolled in reception classes and programs designed expressly for them. To some extent this reflects the characteristics of the different immigrant and refugee groups, including how recently they have arrived, but there are also clear policy differences which result in more or less integration. In Bavaria, for example, 47.8 percent of foreign students were in some form of separate program in a recent year, compared with 5.1 percent in Bremen, 3.7 percent in Lower Saxony, and 8.9 percent in Baden-Württemberg (Bottani, 1988, 10).

Providing special support has been complicated in Germany as elsewhere by the large number of pupils who arrive each year beyond the age at which language skills are usually taught in schools, the so-called *Seiteneinsteiger*. In 1980, for example, 55,000 foreigners between 15 and 20 were identified who had arrived in Germany within the previous year, and there were another 74,000 who had been there less than four years (Mahler, 1983, 74). Some had little or no previous formal education, yet were too old to be placed in a primary school. Others had completed compulsory schooling in their homeland but were still at the age of compulsory schooling in Western Europe (Brassé & De Vries, 1986, 147).

Experience with relying upon foreign teachers to instruct the pupils in German proved unsatisfactory and led to a requirement that only German teachers be used for the core subjects; this is by no means always the case, however, even two decades later. By the late 1970s, extended-time reception classes were common, keeping *Seiteneinsteiger* separate for several years during which they missed more and more of the instructional program provided to German pupils. The government of North Rhine/Westphalia, the largest German state, decided in 1982 that this was a mistake, and began to press for early integration with ongoing support (Hofman et al., 1993, 83–84).

In order to deal with the common problem of reception classes becoming a form of in-school segregation, a model was developed in Hamburg of assigning pupils to reception classes on a heterogeneous basis (that is, not by ethnic group), and at the same time assigning them to regular classes, with an increasing proportion of time during the reception year spent in the regular class (Institut für Zukunftsforschung, 1981, 136). In this way it was made clear from the start that these pupils had a place within the life of the school, and would be separate only to the extent required by their educational needs. Full integration, when it became appropriate, would be into a class with which relationships had already been formed through participating together in a variety of non-instructional activities.

The Netherlands

Language minority children arriving in the Netherlands have been either placed directly into regular classes with supplemental instruction in the Dutch language on a pull-out basis, or assigned to transitional reception programs with other language-minority pupils for a year or more, often in schools where such pupils are gathered from an entire town or section of a city (Appel, 1988, 60). In effect, the "steamer classes" that served European immigrants to the United States in 1910 have been reinvented for Third World immigrants to postwar Europe.

In most cases, such reception classes for language minority pupils who arrive during the years of mandatory schooling are intended to serve them for a limited period which ranges between half a year and two years; the appropriate duration is a matter of considerable disagreement, with some fearing the creation of "educational ghettos," while others call for an extended period of preparation to ensure the success of integration.

The stress of such classes is upon acquiring a "survival" proficiency in the host language and some basic orientation to the school system and society. Students in reception programs may be continuing their previous education in content areas at the same time, but this is a distinctly secondary concern (Coenen, 1982, 30). After the reception period they are placed in a regular class based upon an assessment of previous study, maturity, and ability to use the language of instruction.

In order to improve the effectiveness of reception classes, the government funded a number of three-year experimental programs starting in 1989. This has been especially necessary in the four largest cities; in Amsterdam, for example, there were in 1990 some 2,000 pupils of elementary school age who had come directly from their homelands into Dutch schools (Horst, 1990a). One approach tried there was to have newly arrived immigrant pupils spend half of their time in regular classes; this has required ensuring that all of the teachers in the school receive training in support for language development (Zandbergen, 1994, 281–283).

Reception centers were established in Utrecht in each of three neighborhoods with a large number of newly arrived immigrants. One described by Horst had about 60 pupils, divided into three groups by age but not (as in bilingual reception classes) by home language. Dutch was therefore the only language of instruction, though pupils were not forbidden to use other languages among themselves. Instruction was highly individualized because of the differences in age and previous schooling within each group; each pupil had a "log book" to keep track of daily progress. The goal was to place them in regular schools, with sufficient proficiency in Dutch for success, in no more than one year. Pupils aged less than 6 were assigned directly into regular classes, and those older than 12 were assigned to the "international linking classes" in secondary (middle/high) schools (Horst, 1990b, 36–38).

One notable characteristic of these Dutch reception classes is that they were "overstaffed" by American standards, to allow for intensive individual work with each pupil, and whole-class instruction—for example, to convey information important to life in the Netherlands—was supplemented with many individual assignments and one-on-one tutorials.

Initial reception into the Dutch system of schooling is not the only critical point for immigrant children; even those who have been in the system for some years often experience difficulty making the transition to the more demanding (and sorting) secondary schools. To ease this transition, the international linking classes were established in the mid 1970s. From 20 in 1975–76 the number grew by 1981–82 to 143 schools with such classes. While in theory these classes were to serve pupils for a single year of adjustment, in many cases the assignment lasted two and even three years because of the very uneven preparation with which pupils entered the program; for some, it became in effect the final schooling, a link not to further education but to the job market (Kloosterman, 1983, 89–101). In consequence, a too exclusive emphasis upon transition to secondary education would not have been appropriate; these adolescent pupils need the language and other skills to survive in Dutch society (Janssen-van Dieten, 1982, 43). Of 398 pupils followed in one study, only one had earned a diploma after three years, while 142 had left school with no school completion certificate (Eldering, 1986b, 193–195).

Social class plays an important part in the success of linking classes in the Netherlands. The author visited an ISK in the Hague which included mostly middle-class pupils, including two Americans; they were doing intellectually challenging work as they learned Dutch. A follow-up study of 50 pupils who had been in linking classes in Amsterdam found that of 45 who were the children of "guest workers," only three later earned secondary education diplomas. Four of the five who were *not* children of guest workers earned diplomas (Schumacher, 1981, 104–105). Three-quarters of the linking-class pupils in the early eighties were Turkish or Moroccan, with the remainder distributed among sixty nationalities. One study found that Moroccan pupils were most likely to go on to special education classes, Turkish pupils to the lower forms of vocational education, and pupils of other nationalities to the general forms of secondary education (Fase, 1985, 59).

After a period when the decline of family reunification seemed to reduce the need for international linking classes, they have experienced a certain revival since the mid-1980s with the increasing number of refugees in Western Europe (Fase, 1994, 112). Variations have been introduced in an effort to make these reception programs more effective. For example, a secondary school in Zeist places a heavy emphasis upon individual counseling of immigrant youth, with continual assessment and self-assessment of progress in adapting to Dutch life and schooling. A detailed "placement letter" is prepared for the teacher into whose class the pupil will be transitioned after a maximum of ten months in the reception program, having taken part in regular activities with that class from his first days in the school (Vliet, 1991, 89). Such a "combined reception" has also been implemented in the secondary schools of Emmen (Dongen, 1994). It is difficult to know whether to classify these models as reception programs with substantial amounts of integration or as assignment to regular classes with supplemental support.

Sweden

In addition to supportive Swedish instruction for immigrant pupils in regular classes, so-called preparatory classes with pupils from one or more language backgrounds can be set up as a temporary arrangement in schools with a large number of immigrant children. The aim of such classes is to introduce recent immigrants to the Swedish school and, in particular, to prepare the pupils for subject matter instruction in Swedish (Hyltenstam & Arnberg, 1988, 491).

Various efforts have been made to improve the transitional support provided to young immigrants who arrive at or shortly before the age for upper secondary school, which in Sweden is not compulsory but is essential to most decent jobs and to higher education. Such "introductory courses," some of them in the summer, teach Swedish intensively while also requiring civics, educational and vocational orientation, and physical education, with an emphasis upon flexibility and teamwork among staff. The fact that pupils in these courses have little contact with Swedish pupils, and that they are themselves very heterogeneous, have been identified as a significant drawback (*Introductory Course . . .* , 1977; *Local Experience . . .* , 1978, 11).

Switzerland

Swiss educational policy is largely set at the cantonal and local level, making it difficult to generalize. The delicate balancing-act among languages in Swiss national life has led—as in Belgium—to comparatively restricted provisions for home language instruction. Thus the emphasis of school systems is to prevent the formation of "foreign scholastic enclaves" in the form of alternative schools oriented toward the homelands of foreign pupils, or of long-term separate programs in the Swiss schools.

Reception classes for foreign pupils are provided in half of the cantons. For some schools these serve to prevent the creation of what is perceived as too high a proportion of foreign pupils in regular classes; thus, as in Berlin, creation of an all-foreign class is acceptable *if* that serves the perceived interests of native children. The *classes d'acceuil* in Geneva were set up in 1968 for pupils arriving in the canton without a knowledge of French; thus, they serve German-speaking or Italian-speaking Swiss children as well as foreigners. On the other hand, high-status foreign children (more than half of the Germans and English, for example) often enroll in private or international schools; the enrollment of the reception classes is disproportionately from southern Europe, and 72 percent (contrasted with 34 percent of the overall public school population) of the pupils entering in 1988–89 were from working-class families (Rastoldo & Rey, 1993, 9).

In theory, pupils remain in these classes for only one year, and of the 1988–89 sample, 72 percent enrolled in regular classes the following year. After four years, 32 percent of the group had continued their schooling without retention in grade, 38 percent had repeated one year, 8 percent two years, and 21 percent had dropped out of school. Follow-up evaluation concluded that much of the subsequent academic difficulty experienced by these children had to do with their "chaotic" schooling as a result of family movement (Rastoldo & Rey, 1993, 28).

The United Kingdom

As the work migrations of the postwar years changed the makeup of many British schools, it has not been the official norm—though it remains fairly common—for newly arrived foreign pupils to be placed directly in regular classes without special language support. This practice has generally come to be considered inappropriate; criticism was expressed when some Vietnamese refugee children in England were simply placed in classes for "slow learning" English-speaking pupils, and it was noted with approval that a residential program was created for others "offering a specially devised curricular diet of intensive English teaching" (*Education for All*, 1985, 724, 726).

In an effort to make more effective provision for immigrant pupils from the Indian subcontinent, many local education authorities set up "induction centres" providing short-term help in developing a survival proficiency in English (Reid, 1988, 186). Ministry of Education advice in 1963 was that these and other non-English-speaking children be brought together in one school or other facility for a "carefully planned, intensive course making full use of modern methods of language teaching" (quoted by V. Edwards, 1984, 51).

The practice of establishing physically separate facilities to teach the language of instruction to immigrant children was virtually unique to Britain among Western European educational systems, though it was explicitly emulated in Copenhagen starting in 1970 (Clausen & Horst, 1987, 98). Willke explains the differences among the various British centers:

> The [British] language centres might be built up of special classes designated: *reception class* (up to 12 children without any command of English, mostly for half day); *International English 1* (up to 26 children, any age or background, who have lived generally less than two years in England, where all subjects were taught, but concentration on the language skills was necessary for school subjects); *International English 2* (up to 10 children, who do not fit into either of the above classes, sometimes children who appear to be retarded in their own language as well). Children might be in these centres for two terms (two-year courses) in full-time special class learning English through the much-simplified subject-matter of the ordinary school curriculum (Willke, 1975, 317).

These reception centers discouraged use of the native languages (Linguistic Minorities Project, 1985, 284). Teachers had little preparation for this specialized work, and school authorities assumed that "once ethnic minority children had mastered English, their needs would have been fully met and they would then 'settle down' and cease to experience, or cause, educational problems" (*Education for All*, 1985, 223–224).

Although in the United States the practices of concentrating pupils of the same minority language background for bilingual programs and, at the point when they are judged ready for mainstreaming, to distribute them in the interest of desegregation have become largely routine and legally (if not politically) uncontested, this is not the case in some other legal contexts. While language minority pupils should be concentrated for services, it was stressed in the United Kingdom in 1965, they could be integrated more effectively if the number of immigrant pupils in a school was not allowed to rise too high. The Plowden Report in 1967, however, expressed reservations about deliberate efforts to disperse ethnic minority pupils for integration and urged that this should be done only if required to serve their language needs better (V. Edwards, 1984, 53). In fact, student assignments on the basis of language or ethnicity are rare in European educational systems (see Chapter 6).

The practice of assigning newly arrived immigrant children to language centers for a year or two became widespread, though it was criticized by the Bullock Committee report (*A Language for Life*) in 1975 and again, a decade later, by the Swann Committee report. The latter found that separate provision, though perhaps well-intended, was "discriminatory in *effect* in that it denies an individual child access to the full range of educational opportunities available" (*Education for All*, 1985, 389). The London outer borough of Haringey, mirroring this shift in policy, established an English Language Resource Centre in 1970, but by 1985 its strategy had changed and more than 30 peripatetic teachers were working alongside classroom teachers to provide support to linguistic minority pupils (Taylor, 1988, 44). It was not, however, until the decision by the Commission for Racial Equality, in 1986, that separate schooling in a language center violated both education and race relations laws that the practice was largely abandoned nationwide (Edwards & Redfern, 1992, 29).

Ironically, children who move from England to parts of Wales where schooling is provided through the Welsh language spend about 14 weeks in a Language Reception Centre where they acquire initial communicative competence in Welsh, but "this is in contrast to the situation in major cities of England where Reception Centres for non-English speaking in-migrants have been abandoned to maximize early integration" (Baker, 1993, 14).

Bilingual Reception Programs

In some cases in Europe, and in many or most cases in the United States (depending on state or local policy), reception programs for pupils arriving beyond the usual school-entry age make use of the home language of pupils to ease their adjustment and to speed their learning of language and other skills considered necessary before they are mainstreamed. Thus, for example, in the United Kingdom considerable attention has been devoted to producing materials that allow pupils to use their home languages and English in parallel while learning about important aspects of life in the immigration situation (Taylor, 1988, 203).

During the period of development of universal schooling, it was not uncommon for language minority groups to organize their own provision for their children, using a bilingual approach in an attempt to maintain the ancestral language while equipping their children to function in the host society. The "German-English Public School was established in 1837 in St. Louis a year before the first all-English public school opened in the city. . . . at least one million American children were educated in German and English during the period from 1880 to the end of the century" (Genesee, 1987, 2). Nor has this practice been abandoned, witness the hundreds of American, British, Japanese, French, and German schools in all parts of the globe where the number of foreign residents is sufficient to support them.

While such arrangements depend primarily upon the resources of middle-class expatriate parents and often of their home governments, and thus do not ordinarily raise policy issues, it often requires a major shift for public school systems to make provision for instruction through a minority language for the children of low-status immigrants. While bilingual programs as a means of transition into the mainstream are widely implemented in the United States, they tend, in Europe, to be local experiments involving only a small proportion of the children of immigrants.

The United States

The origins of bilingual education in postwar American education, in fact, were a form of reception program responding to demands of a relatively high-status refugee group, the Cubans who fled to Miami from the Castro regime in the early 1960s. Expecting to return to Cuba, this group was strongly motivated to maintain Spanish, and included many teachers. The American government provided nearly a billion dollars in resettlement assistance for Cuban refugees. The availability of supplemental funding, along with a Ford Foundation grant, enabled the Dade County school system to launch its first experiment in bilingual education at the Coral Way School. This was an unabashed Spanish-maintenance program for Cuban children and at the same time a Spanish "immersion" program for Anglo children. The goal was fluency in both languages for both groups (Crawford, 1992b, 93).

At Coral Way, a regular program of elementary school instruction through Spanish was provided to the children of Cuban refugees, supplemented by intensive English-as-a-second-language instruction leading quickly to instruction *through* English. In addition, Spanish for Spanish-speakers was offered as a subject. "In the mornings, students from the same first-language group received instruction in that language in language arts and other subjects. In the afternoons they switched over to their second language" and reviewed the same subject matter. The two groups [those dominant in Spanish and those dominant in English] mixed at lunch and in programs in arts, music, and physical education, but nor for the core instruction provided by the school (Hakuta, 1986, 195). The instructional model in this pioneering school changed subsequently into a "two-way bilingual" approach as the school population changed (Glenn & LaLyre, 1991, 47–48).

This is often seen as the first program in the United States since the nineteenth century to base the reception of immigrant language minority pupils partly upon their home language. Instruction through the language of the home is not ordinarily a matter of choosing a supplemental program in the United States, as it is in the other countries surveyed. Immigrant and language minority parents who might wish such instruction as an enrichment to the education of their children are not eligible for it, in most cases, unless the child has been assessed as "unable to perform ordinary classwork in English." Not only is this remedial or transitional function of instruction through the language of the home explicit in the federal and state laws permitting or mandating such instruction, but the courts have refused to order that a language-maintenance option for parents be included in remedies for previous discrimination against language minority pupils (Santiago, 1986, 158).

By contrast with part-time home-language programs in other countries, the use of home languages in the United States is almost exclusively within the context of full-time *transitional* bilingual programs; maintenance and development of the home language is usually not an explicit objective. The evidence that it may often be a tacit objective is discussed in Chapter 6, and will not be repeated here.

Transitional bilingual education programs are provided by hundreds of local school systems as a result of the requirements of state laws, of which the first was enacted in Massachusetts in 1971, or as a means of complying with the requirements of the *Lau v. Nichols* case decided by the United States Supreme Court in 1974. While federal law leaves it up to local education officials to determine how "to take appropriate action to overcome language barriers" (Equal Educational Opportunity Act)—which could include reception programs designed to teach English only—a strong encouragement is given to bilingual programs by federal funding that supports "educational programs using bilingual education practices, techniques and methods" (Bilingual Education Act). This provision of federal law was first enacted in

1968, and federal funding appropriated for bilingual education programs amounted to $245 million for FY 1995, up from $227 million the previous year (*Education Week*, October 19, 1994, 14). It should be noted that the amount spent for this purpose from state and local funds was undoubtedly much higher though impossible to separate out cleanly from well over $200 *billion* spent on schools by the state and local levels of government with the primary responsibility for education under the American polity.

Typically, pupils are assigned into transitional bilingual programs on the basis of an assessment that they are unable to perform ordinary classwork in English and require a period of adaptation; two to three years is the norm, though pupils often remain longer and advocates argue that five to seven years would be preferable. "Late-exit" bilingual programs, with an explicit intention of maintaining and developing the home language while English is learned, are less common.

Parents have the right to insist that their children be placed in regular classes rather than in separate bilingual classes, though they are often informed by school officials that their children will be ineligible for *any* supplemental support, including English as a second language, if they are not enrolled in the bilingual program. Typically, no choice is offered between the extremes of language and academic support in a segregated program and being placed in a regular class with no attention to needs arising in the course of second-language acquisition. Children in the second situation (including those in schools where no bilingual program is offered) not infrequently are subsequently diagnosed as having learning disabilities or other needs and end up segregated in special education programs; the failure of regular classes is indeed one of the strongest arguments used for separate bilingual programs.

A 1980 survey found that local school districts in thirty-eight of the fifty states provided bilingual education programs for Spanish-speaking youngsters; in twenty states they did so for Vietnamese children, in twelve for Korean youngsters, in ten for French-speaking children, and in nine for speakers of Greek. Half the states had laws which mandated or permitted bilingual instruction as needed—or were in the process of enacting such legislation—and the other half did not seem to have significant enrollments of LEP students (Castellanos, 1983, 210).

The Massachusetts Transitional Bilingual Education Act, adopted unanimously in 1971, requires that school districts enrolling altogether 20 pupils *at all grade levels* unable to perform ordinary classwork in English provide

> a full-time program of instruction (1) in all those courses or subjects which a child is required by law to receive and which are required

by the child's school committee which shall be given in the native language of the children of limited English-speaking ability who are enrolled in the program and also in English, (2) in the reading and writing of the native language of the children of limited English-speaking ability who are enrolled in the program and in the oral comprehension, speaking, reading and writing of English, and (3) in the history and culture of the country, territory [thus including Puerto Rico] or geographic area which is the native land of the parents of [the children] . . . and in the history and culture of the United States (Massachusetts General Laws, Chapter 71A, section 2).

California adopted a mandate of bilingual and "bicultural" education in 1976, requiring school districts with more than 50 pupils of limited proficiency in English to develop and implement district master plans. This law was not re-enacted in 1987, as part of the growing backlash against the presence of illegal and even legal immigrants, but most large school systems have continued to implement bilingual programs.

Texas has required bilingual education for districts with 20 or more pupils of limited English proficiency [LEP] at any grade level in the elementary grades; language minority pupils in grades 7 through 12 and in districts with fewer LEP pupils are entitled to English as a second language. Detailed state guidelines have been provided for language use in these programs. For example, kindergarten and first-grade bilingual programs for pupils initially stronger in another language than in English should devote 45 minutes daily to English and the balance of the time to teach language arts and other subjects through the home language (Texas Education Agency, no date, 6, 13).

Finding the right balance of time devoted to each language—and ensuring that each is used in an appropriate way—is a perennial problem of bilingual programs. Teachers have a natural tendency to fall into "concurrent translation," saying everything important twice in order to be sure that all children understand what has been said. The natural result is that children "tune out" the language with which they are less familiar, and fail to make the effort to communicate with their teacher in that language, knowing that she understands their stronger language. Well-designed programs often designate different teachers to use one language or the other exclusively, as is the practice of a particularly successful preschool program that has operated in Boston for more than 25 years.

There are three groups of 20 children in each center. Two groups utilize Spanish exclusively and the third group uses only English. Dur-

ing the morning academic program the groups of children rotate between the three sets of teachers, allowing for an "immersion" in each
of the two languages. Teachers repeat their activities with the three
different groups (Escuelita Agüeybana Inc, 1985, 5).

Belgium

One of the most interesting and well-documented bilingual reception programs is in Brussels. The Foyer program (described in Chapter 5) works with
kindergarten and primary school classes in Dutch-language schools to provide native-language support that is integral to the program rather than a
supplemental enrichment. In two of the project schools, the majority of
students (56 and 69 percent) are from immigrant families and a substantial
proportion (18 and 14 percent) from French-speaking Belgian families,
so that children from Dutch-speaking families are in a distinct minority
(Smeekens, 1985, 56).

An important element of the Foyer model is the intention that the
teachers who are members of the language minority groups represented in
the program serve as role models for the pupils and enable them to resist
what is seen as the pressure either to identify with the majority culture or
to accept a self-understanding as an inferior outsider. "The practices of the
Foyer Model are such that pupils are placed in situations in the early years
where they form significant relationships with these carriers of culture. It
is reasonable to suppose that the relationships will form a propitious environment in which their minority identity will be reinforced" (Byram
1990b, 135).

From this perspective, the personal competence of these language
minority teachers is a matter of crucial significance, since

> the foreign teachers share a special position. Their position in the staff,
> their permanent possibilities of interaction with the other teachers and
> their growing insight in the concrete interpretation of the project by
> the other teachers have given them a pivot function in the transfor-
> mation process. . . . One of the major objectives of the supervision
> will therefore be the expansion of the interpersonal skills of the for-
> eign teachers (Smeekens, 1990, 143).

A bilingual reception program in Waterschrei/Genk placed an emphasis upon teaching Dutch and orienting immigrant pupils to Flemish life as
quickly as possible, while maintaining the minority language and culture

(Esch, 1982, 103). Such bilingual approaches are the exception in Belgium as elsewhere in Western Europe, however. This is not to say that home languages are neglected, much less suppressed; in the Antwerp school described above,

> even in the reception class, with its intense focus on learning functional Dutch, pupils have two hours a week of their native culture and religion, and the Moroccan pupils have two hours of Arabic (not the Berber dialect spoken by many at home); others take two hours of English. Islamic religion is taught by teachers trained at the Islamic Center in Brussels. These classes are expected to keep open the possibility, for each pupil, of making an eventual choice of the elements of their native culture, which they may never have experienced in their "homeland," and the elements of Belgian culture that they will make their own (Glenn, 1987, 44).

Germany

Although some cities in North Rhine/Westphalia had since 1976 operated "reception classes in extended form"—similar to "transitional bilingual" programs in the United States—that might keep pupils separate for up to six years, the state education authorities decided in 1982 that foreign pupils must be integrated into regular classes no later than the fourth grade.

> Although these . . . classes distinguished themselves from other [German] bilingual models in that it was their explicit purpose to transition pupils to regular German classes, rather than to re-integrate them into the school systems of their homelands as in Baden-Württemberg and Bavaria, all of these models must be regarded primarily from the perspective that in practice they isolate foreign children and deny them "the opportunities for education available in the German school system" without offering them an education appropriate to the immigrant situation. One must assume that when they were established a more important motivation than the official goals was the "limited loading" [with foreigners] of German classes (Boos-Nünning & Henscheid, 1986, 68).

Exceptions are made, in some cases, when late-arriving adolescent pupils prove unable to profit from participation in regular classes, even after time in a reception program intended to teach them enough German to do academic work. A model in a *Hauptschule* in Oberhausen enrolled Turkish pupils up to age 18 who had performed poorly—even disruptively—in their previous classes. Although most of the teachers were dubious because of their previous experience with these pupils, the provision of a highly focused curriculum with instructional support in Turkish as needed produced very satisfactory results: "the pupils showed an enthusiastic readiness to learn, a high degree of diligence, and very good social behavior." Three out of four were able to earn a diploma (Hofmann et al., 1993, 93–95).

Home language support in reception classes depends, of course, upon enrolling mostly pupils of the same language background; it appears that this is becoming less easy to arrange with the change in immigration from labor migrants and their families from a few homelands to the worldwide refugee flow experienced in especially acute form by Germany in recent years (Hofmann et al., 1993, 164).

The Netherlands

In some programs of centralized reception in the Netherlands, in which pupils are brought together at a single site for a program not offered in each school, the home language of children may be used to some extent to facilitate their transition to the school. Thus some reception programs in Rotterdam use home languages to orient newly arrived pupils aged 12 to 16 to the Dutch educational system and to aspects of Dutch society that they need to learn about quickly. A Moroccan teacher may, for example, use both Arabic and a Berber language in the initial reception process (Horst, 1992, 305–306). The intention is that this transitional period will last one year, followed by enrollment in a secondary school, but those who arrive illiterate require two or three years (Horst, 1991, 262–263).

In contrast with this casually adaptive approach, an experimental reception program was implemented in Leiden in the late 1970s. The home language was used for the first year of schooling for newly arrived Turkish and Moroccan primary-school pupils brought together from all parts of the city, with a daily lesson in Dutch as a second language and some activity periods with Dutch pupils. During the second year there was an emphasis upon such integrated activities, some of them led by foreign teachers using Dutch (Appel, Everts, & Teunissen, 1986, 141–142). Half of the academic instruction in the second year for the immigrant children was provided by Dutch teachers, and half by foreign teachers following the same curriculum; for example, the Dutch teacher might give lessons 50 and 51 of the arithmetic program, and the Turkish teacher lessons 52 and 53 later in the week. After two years the children were mainstreamed into other schools. Compared with a control group of immigrant children assigned to regular classes with supplemental Dutch as a second language, those in the Leiden experimental bilingual reception program had a somewhat better proficiency in Dutch after two years and an equal proficiency after three (Everts, 1983, 85–87).

Subsequently, the municipal councils of The Hague and Amsterdam launched plans to use the mother tongue to instruct non-Dutch-speaking children in the basic skills during the first years of primary education (Eldering, 1989, 122). This became an element of the parental choice of schools which is guaranteed under the Dutch Constitution; for certain schools it was simply a matter of "school policy" that part of the instruction would be provided through, say, Turkish, and parents who didn't want that were encouraged to choose another school (Triesscheijn, 1990, 119–122).

Perhaps the best-known bilingual program in the Netherlands is that in Enschede, where careful attention was given to ensuring that the academic lessons provided through Dutch and through the home languages were closely coordinated, and that immigrant children benefited from many well-designed integrated experiences with Dutch children (Esch, 1982, 102). The program was established in two schools, once welcoming Moroccan and the other Turkish primary-level children, along with a majority of Dutch children. The home language was used to instruct the immigrant children approximately 56 percent of the time in the first year, decreasing to 44 percent in the second. There was no separate instruction in the Dutch language, but the immigrant children were exposed to it every day through activities with their Dutch-speaking classmates, including regular conversation times guided by their Dutch teachers (Pedagogisch Centrum Enschede, 1983a). Nor was there supplemental home language and culture instruction, as in other Dutch schools with many immigrant children—where it is often perceived as a useless "fifth wheel"—since Turkish or Arabic were simply languages of instruction (Pedagogisch Centrum Enschede, 1983c).

In the third year, children were assigned to mainstream classes, often in another school closer to their homes. Each child made a little book (corresponding to the portfolios much talked about now in American education) to give the new teacher an idea of his or her accomplishments and capabilities. Unfortunately, a study of the program after the first two-year cycle found that 9 out of 14 Moroccan pupils—but only 1 out of 17 Turkish pupils—were required to repeat the grade in making the transition to a regular class (Eldering, 1983b, (9).

The program was originally intended by those who planned it to help immigrant children to maintain and improve their home language and thus was not considered a reception model (Teunissen, 1986, 149–152), but the teachers actually involved with the children were keenly aware of the need to prepare them for a successful transition to regular Dutch schooling (Boos-Nünning & others, 1984, 36). Unlike many other experimental bilingual programs in Europe, that in Enschede has been incorporated into the regular functioning of the Europaschool (observed by the author in 1986), so that Turkish and Dutch children are taught separately part of the time and together part of the time, following the same curriculum, with the Turkish teacher considered a "regular" rather than a supplemental home-language teacher; he has his own classroom and essential role in teaching central aspects of the curriculum. "I think of myself as a Dutch teacher who speaks Turkish," he told a reporter recently (Barendse, 1995, 18–19).

The United Kingdom

While not recommending home language instruction in primary schools, the Swann Report urged that schools with many pupils of a particular non-English language group have staff, particularly at the early childhood level, capable of

> offering psychological and social support for the child, as well as being able to explain simple educational concepts in a child's mother tongue, if the need arises, but always working **within** the mainstream classroom situation and **alongside** the class teacher (*Education* for All, 1985, 407).

INTEGRATED BILINGUAL PROGRAMS

Chapter 8 will be devoted to discussing the pedagogical strategies employed in schools in which language minority and majority pupils learn together, with a carefully crafted emphasis upon both languages. There are unfortunately few examples of such an approach, whose structural dimension will be described briefly here.

Integrated bilingual programs seem to depend upon a continuously high level of commitment by both teachers and parents; those described here are not necessarily still in existence, or organized as described. At best, they describe what is *possible*.

A program in the Enghøj School near Copenhagen, visited by the author, set up Danish/Turkish classes which, on the Danish model, stayed together with the same teachers over a number of years. A Turkish and a Danish teacher worked together in the classroom, with shared responsibility for all the pupils, and supplemental home language instruction for the

Turkish pupils after their Danish classmates went home (Hvidovre Kommune, 1986).

The Spanish embassy in Brussels initiated an experimental project with two elementary Belgian schools in 1978–79, expanding it to five the following year and ten the year after. The purpose of the project was "that Spanish children in Belgium succeed in their academic life without having to renounce their distinctiveness" (Pino Romero, 1980, 234). The program was a response to the concern of the National Federation of Spanish Parent Associations that the usual supplemental classes failed to respond to the real situation and needs of the migrant child. Rather than experiencing two educational systems—a Belgian school for part of the day and an embassy-sponsored class representing a "simple prolongation of schooling in Spain" for the other—the parents asked for a close collaboration and interpenetration of the two that might take many different forms but should always be directly responsive to the migrant experience.

Unlike other embassy-sponsored programs, these were integrated fully into the life of the participating schools, without demanding after-school participation. The role of the Spanish teachers was to improve the adjustment of foreign children to Belgian schooling (thus it was essential that they speak adequate French) while "exercising and enriching" their proficiency in Spanish by using it as a language of instruction for part of the time. No more than ten Spanish students were assigned to each class, together with up to twenty Belgian and other students, and a Spanish and a Belgian teacher. While the Spanish lessons were conducted in that language, with homogeneous groups of students, there was an introduction and summary of each of the themes in French with the entire mixed group. The Spanish and Belgian teachers worked together to plan a common program and lessons, and these differed in each participating school. Only with a full commitment to such collaboration could the program be a success (Pino Romero, 1980, 240).

An evaluation of the first year's experience found strong support from students (91 wanted the new program continued, 11 wanted a resumption of the earlier model of supplemental classes, and 10 wanted the Spanish lessons dropped altogether). Parents preferred the new program as well (their comments generally stressed that supplemental classes after school were too tiring), and some reported that their children were doing better in their studies. Among teachers there was a sense that the collaboration was enriching to their teaching, and ensured that the Spanish students understood the subject matter, though improved coordination was needed.

In Sweden, some schools set up classes in which half of the pupils were of a single minority language and the other half were native speakers of the majority language, and assigned a teacher of the minority language full- or part-time to each class. During the 1987–88 school year, there were 558 such classes, enrolling 2,872 language-minority pupils (just under half of them Finnish-speaking) and an approximately equal number of Swedish pupils (*Hemspråks-* . . , 1988). This model, known as "consolidated" (*sammansatta*) classes, has reportedly produced excellent results. Löfgren describes in detail a program that he studied:

> The instructional model of the project included a two-year Finnish-speaking pre-school and a bilingual primary school lasting three years. The children spent three hours per day in the Finnish-speaking pre-school for two years. In the daily program half an hour was allocated for instruction in the Swedish language. In the elementary school the Finnish children were integrated with Swedish parallel classes, i.e. as a work team. The Swedish pupils in the project received essentially the same instruction as the Swedish pupils in other classes. The Finnish classes, on the other hand, were taught in both Finnish and Swedish, and their first reading and writing instruction was via Finnish instead of via Swedish. Since the project model was aimed at a transition to regular Swedish instruction at the intermediate level (grade 4), the number of Swedish-speaking periods was gradually increased. . . . The teaching group for a work team consisted of two Swedish class teachers, who were each responsible for a parallel class, a Finnish teacher, who was in charge of teaching Finnish, and a teacher to teach the immigrant children Swedish. In addition to these teachers, both Swedish and Finnish pupils with learning difficulties had access to remedial instruction in their native tongue. . . . From grade 4 to grade 6 the Finnish children followed regular instruction in all subjects via the Swedish language. However, the Finnish pupils were kept together and continued to have their Finnish teacher in home language training four lessons each week.

Results were highly satisfactory:

> the school achievement of the Finnish children taking part in the project were on a level with those of their Swedish classmates and . . . their grade 3 level of proficiency in the Swedish language was practically identical to that of comparable Swedish pupils. The Finnish project children had a command of their first language roughly one

standard deviation below that of the "Finnish children in Finland" reference group (Löfgren, 1986).

According to a leading researcher, "students in [integrated] composite classes reach the same mother tongue development as students in [separate] mother tongue classes, but reach a much higher proficiency in Swedish" (Ekstrand, 1985, 2407).

Another description of Swedish "composite" classes enrolling an equal number of Swedish and language-minority pupils notes that

> children from minority-language backgrounds receive about 60 percent of their instruction in the home language in grade 1, during which time they are separated from the Swedish students. In grade 2, the proportion of home language teaching is about 40 percent, in grade 3 it is about 30 percent, and in grades 4 to 6 there are about four or five hours of home language instruction in a week. In 1982 there were approximately 300 such programs in Sweden (McLaughlin, 1985, 30).

In the German city Krefeld, discussed as an example of desegregation in chapter 6, a pilot program was implemented in three schools, with a goal of creating classes in which the ratio would be one Greek or Turkish pupil to two German pupils, with an instructional program designed to promote interaction as well as academic achievement.

> Integrated homerooms were established, each with around 28 pupils. In the first grade pupils were together for arithmetic, music, art and physical education, together with part of *Sachunterricht* (a combination of science and social studies). The foreign pupils were instructed separately for home language, a part of *Sachunterricht* with a focus on their homelands, and religion, together with German as a second language. The German pupils, during this time, did language arts, a part of *Sachunterricht*, and religion. Thus the pupils were together for ten periods a week and apart for twelve, with the foreign pupils having one additional period of extra support. By the fourth grade pupils were together 22 periods a week, while the Greek or Turkish pupils had seven periods of separate home language, culture and religion instruction and one of extra support, and the German pupils seven periods of separate instruction including three of religion (Dickopp, 1982, 79–83).

Since home language, culture, and religious instruction were fully integrated into the curriculum, there was no reason for foreign pupils to be overburdened by supplemental classes outside of school hours. The decision was made to make home language instruction an integral part of the program for foreign pupils out of the conviction that language development and cognitive development are closely associated, and that everything should be done to stimulate both in the foreign pupils without waiting until their German was sufficiently advanced. Perhaps the most interesting aspect of the program was the handling of *Sachunterricht*, which provided an opportunity for the foreign and German teachers to plan together how they could supplement and enrich each other's work.

EVALUATING THE DIFFERENT MODELS

Little systematic research has been done on the effectiveness of these approaches to schooling language minority children, with the exception of a mountain of program evaluations of transitional bilingual education in the United States. "To rationalize its instructional base, bilingual education in the United States has had to look to related research in other fields, such as psychology and language acquisition, and to studies from other countries, principally Canada and Sweden" (Tikunoff & Vazquez-Faría, 1982, 241). Our brief discussion of the conclusions of Swedish researchers shows that they are by no means unanimously supportive of an emphasis upon the home language of language minority children; similarly, attempts to make use of the hundreds of program evaluation reports in the United States have not resulted in agreement among researchers on the benefits of employing the first language for instruction. In a much-cited paragraph in a book otherwise strongly supportive of bilingualism, Kenji Hakuta wrote that

> There is a sober truth that even the ardent advocates of bilingual education would not deny. Evaluation studies on the effectiveness of bilingual education in improving either English or math scores have not been overwhelmingly in favor of bilingual education. To be sure, there are programs that have been highly effective, but not very many. . . . An awkward tension blankets the lack of empirical demonstration of the success of bilingual education programs. Someone promised bacon, but it's not there (Hakuta, 1986, 219).

Similarly, a lawyer for the Mexican-American Legal Defense Fund (MALDEF), though engaged in litigation to require bilingual instruction, wrote that "no definitive conclusions can be drawn from the research about the relative merits of the different approaches for meeting the needs of" pupils with limited English-speaking ability (Roos, 1978, quoted by Rossell & Ross, 1985, 15).

The main source of evidence on the schooling received by language minority pupils is aggregate data on their academic success as measured by standardized tests and by persistence to the higher forms of secondary education. Such data, broken out for different ethnic groups or by citizenship status, does not tell us much about the approaches to instruction that have contributed to the results, since this is never consistent on a national level, and rarely consistent even locally. In Houston, Texas, for example,

> there was no more of an "immersion" program in the District than there was a "bilingual" program. What the District had was a hodge-podge of things happening to [language minority] students in each school—and should the students move about the District, as these students did very frequently, they could run the gamut of program types during their schooling (Stein, Gavito, & Veselka, 1988, 4).

Indeed, nationwide "an extreme diversity of instructional methodology exists *within* programs that are labeled 'bilingual.' Some classrooms in 'bilingual programs' looked very similar to some 'submersion' classrooms" (Hakuta & Gould, 1987, 40; Secada, 1987, 379); "great variation occurs on such variables as how the two languages are used as well as on the specific techniques adopted by teachers in promoting the development of English" (Gándara & Merino, 1993, 324).

The most ambitious study in any country of the effects of different modes of schooling language minority pupils is limited by this problem of the inaccuracy of program labels. Carried out by Ramirez and others under a contract with the U.S. Department of Education and costing $4.5 million over four years, the study gathered elaborate data on classroom practices and pupil outcomes in 46 schools in nine school districts. The intention was to compare the effects of "structured immersion" programs with bilingual teachers but all instruction through English, transitional bilingual programs seeking to mainstream children as early as possible, and programs seeking, over a longer period, to develop full bilingualism in the pupils (Ramirez et al., 1991).

It is disappointing that this massive effort did not produce clear and indisputable results. Rossell laments that, although "unlike most of the research in this field, there is an extraordinary amount of data on what went on in the classrooms," the authors "use *none* of these classroom characteristics to explain achievement" (Rossell, 1991, 14). The achievement data were simply allocated to the three program types, even though within each type there was—as revealed by the data—great variation in what actually occurred. Rossell continues,

> Teachers do appear on average to use very different amounts of English in the different programs and, not surprisingly, student usage of English follows teacher usage. These data indicate that the early-exit [bilingual] program is more like the immersion program in English language usage than it is like the late-exit [bilingual] program (Rossell, 1991, 15).

For example, in kindergarten social studies, teachers were observed to use Spanish none of the time in immersion classes, 9 percent of the time in early-exit (transitional) bilingual classes, and 93 percent of the time in late-exit (maintenance) bilingual classes. Corresponding use of Spanish in first-grade social studies was 2 percent, 18 percent, and 84 percent of the time (Rossell, 1991, 22).

Comparison of academic outcomes for pupils who were in immersion classes with those who were instructed largely through Spanish in "late-exit" classes would be highly instructive, but unfortunately this comparison was not made; instead, comparisons focused upon immersion and early-exit bilingual classes, though in fact the instruction did not differ greatly enough between the two models to permit a solid assessment of the effect of use of the home language. Rossell concludes that, although the report "presents a wealth of informative, carefully collected and constructed data, little of it was used in what most people would consider the raison d'être of this study—the analysis of program outcomes" (Rossell, 1991, 39).

In brief, policymakers are largely dependent upon aggregate data about the academic success or failure of groups of pupils defined by ethnicity and—at best—by program type, not by their actual experiences of schooling. The children of *certain* immigrant and language minority groups do badly in school compared with those of the majority; children of other immigrant groups, it is true, do better on average than national norms. Our focus in this study is primarily upon those minority groups that are educationally at risk, "schoolchildren who are marked both by the linguistic and cultural differences between their homes and schools, and by the low status of their parents and their ethnic identities in the host society" (Chapter 1).

In the Netherlands, on average, "ethnic minority children lagged behind educationally by two years at the end of the second year of secondary education;" Chinese children "were only six months behind their Dutch classmates, but Moroccan and Turkish children had an educational lag of 2.5 to three years" (Eldering, 1989, 126). The (since abolished) Inner London Education Authority reported that, in 1980, Greek Cypriot, West Indian, and Turkish Cypriot pupils had significantly lower reading scores (87.6, 85.9, and 84.9, respectively) than native English pupils (97.8) or pupils from Pakistan (94.9) or India (91.4).

Similarly, "the educational gap between Hispanics and non-Hispanics continues to widen . . . at each grade level a larger percentage of Hispanic children are enrolled below grade level than White or Black children" (De La Rosa & Maw, 1990, 1, 18). Secondary school completion rate for Hispanic pupils in the United States was, in 1992, 26 percentage points below that of white pupils (65 percent versus 91 percent), and 16 points below that of black pupils. Between 1990 and 1992 "the gap in mathematics performance actually widened . . . between Hispanic and White students in Grade 8 . . . as White students moved ahead, Black and Hispanic students fell further behind;" Hispanic 8th graders were 18 percentage points behind white pupils in mathematics in 1990, and 24 points behind in 1992. They were 21 percentage points behind in reading in 1992 (National Education Goals Panel, 1994, 30–36).

Such results suggest that schools are not effectively meeting the educational needs of certain groups of language minority pupils, but they do not permit conclusions about how much they have been helped by particular program models. When, for example, the Educational Testing Service conducted a special study of "the educational progress of language minority children," based upon data from the 1985–1986 National Assessment of Educational Progress, the author, as one of the reviewers, pointed out that

What we do not have is broad-based research reflecting the experience of the millions of language minority students who, over the past decade, either have or have not received an instructional program that builds their competence in their home language as a basis for English and general academic success. Nor do we have broad-based research that studies the relationship between developed proficiency in home language and in English. The NAEP study did not collect information on the extent to which home language had been used in the educational program of the individual students assessed. . . . it is lamentable that the study leaves us still clutching for indirect clues rather than having some solid information on how the instruction provided to language minority students (not in small-scale research projects but in a sample intended to be nationally representative) affects their performance on the assessment and also their sense of competence and 'locus of control'" (Glenn, 1988c, 1–5).

The variation of approaches to the schooling of language minority pupils reveals a fundamental disagreement about whether their needs can best be met in a setting in which they are integrated with language majority peers, or in a special program designed to serve only members of the minority. This has been described as the "difference dilemma":

> Are the stigma and unequal treatment encountered by minority groups better remedied by separation or by integration of such groups with others? Either remedy risks reinforcing the stigma associated with assigned differences by either ignoring it or focusing on it. This double-edged risk is the "difference dilemma" (Minow, 1985, 157).

The programs described in chapters 6 and 7 fall mostly along a continuum stretching between the extremes of segregated separate development and a refusal to recognize *any* needs deriving from language differences. At one extreme, language minority pupils are regarded as requiring a completely different form of schooling from the majority, while at the other they are regarded as being—as a group—indistinguishable from them. Between these extreme positions can be found a variety of attempts to make instruction relevant and effective for language minority pupils so that they will not be like the Hispanic pupils described to a Civil Rights Commission hearing as "spending most of their time doing art work in the back of their content subject classes. The [English as a second language] class had not equipped them with enough English to be able to understand what was going on in the class" (Stein, 1986, 14).

How to provide support targeted to the needs of language minority pupils without thereby making their education critically different from that of the majority, and reducing the quality of their interactions with majority pupils, is the theme of Chapter 8. Here we will review some of the criticisms leveled against the various program models described in the present chapter.

Evaluation of Assignment to a Regular Class with Supplemental Help

The reasoning behind assigning immigrant and other language minority pupils directly into a regular classroom is that in this way they will be exposed as quickly as possible to the same curriculum and learning experiences as majority pupils. Putting them together will provide more opportunities for interactions among peers and for using the second language, and will enhance social and cultural integration.

Advocates of this approach argue that a really well-designed program of immediate integration, with supplemental support for second language-learning and for social adjustment, can overcome the difficulties often observed in classes where the teachers have not been appropriately trained and assisted to adapt their class organization and instruction to the presence of second-language learners (Knijpstra, 1993b, 473–75).

Opponents charge that assigning pupils who are not proficient in the language of the school to regular classrooms with language support on a pull-out basis is not adequate to overcome their educational disadvantages. Premature integration, they say, leads to a prolonged period in which the language minority pupil understands and thus learns little and, in addition, creates a highly stressful situation which may discourage later attempts to be successful in school. Assignment to a reception program, they argue, provides a more effective because systematic exposure to the second language and is in the long run more conducive to successful integration (Meijerink & Appel, 1993, 292–295). They contend that

> it is in many cases plain impossible to offer late-arriving pupils adequate instruction in the regular class. You can professionalize teachers with respect to Dutch as a second language until they are stuffed full of it, but they still won't know what they should do with a late-arriving 11–year-old in—say—4th grade who understands hardly any Dutch, during social studies class. Teachers have classes with in general very large differences in level. To keep all the pupils up with the lesson is very hard, even without late arrivals, so how will the teacher provide special Dutch-as-a-second-language attention to the late arrival? (Appel 1993, 349).

Even when there is a consistent effort to provide supplemental support for language acquisition on a part-time basis, the effectiveness of this support may be limited. Immigrant pupils in Sweden were asked what they thought of Swedish as a second language classes; those who had attended such classes "were less satisfied with the amount of supportive Swedish language teaching received than those who received no such instruction at all. [This group], which received supportive Swedish lessons at all levels, knows less Swedish and receives less [advanced] education after compulsory school than other pupils who immigrated about the same time" (Liljegren &

Ullman, 1982, 3). Dissatisfaction with the supportive Swedish lessons was especially marked among those respondents who were employed or seeking work rather than continuing their schooling. In a later study, more than 70 percent of the immigrant pupils reported that Swedish as a second language classes had not really helped them (Löfgren, 1991).

Pupils who are in separate bilingual programs in the United States may also require but fail to receive supplemental help, especially if they have some form of physical or learning disability; this may not be diagnosed accurately because masked by their primary use of a language other than that used for screening by the school. In some states they are ineligible for services provided by federal Chapter 1 funding to pupils experiencing academic difficulty because that would entail "receiving assistance through more than one categorical program" and because regulations are designed to ensure that no federal funds supplant what should be provided through local efforts (Council of Chief State School Officers, 1990, 25).

Supplemental instruction in the host language may not be sufficient, if the teachers who provide the balance of instruction for language minority pupils in regular classes do not have the skills needed to support a second-language learner. In the Netherlands, Education Secretary Wallage stressed that every Dutch teacher should be trained in techniques for teaching Dutch as a second language. It is not enough, he said, to limit such efforts to reception classes for youth arriving from other countries after the age when schooling starts, since many language minority children born in The Netherlands arrive in school unprepared to take part successfully in the program (Wallage, 1993, 345–346). Unfortunately, materials for learning Dutch as a second language, especially in coordination with the regular school curriculum, have been inadequate or unavailable (Driessen, 1990, 12).

It is in fact only in recent years that Dutch as a second language has become an important pedagogical discipline; the Dutch have always learned the languages of other people! As a result, relatively few teachers have the skills to teach Dutch in connection with academic material, and it is sometimes assumed that once pupils have acquired a "survival" proficiency in the language, they need no further assistance (Egmond-van Helten, 1990, 111). Even the teachers assigned to work full-time with the children of immigrants on language acquisition may, as in Belgium, Sweden, and other countries, have no special training or competence in that specialization (Xhoffer, Codde, & Allery, 1984, 32; Boos-Nünning et al., 1986, 69; McLaughlin, 1985, 37).

Reportedly, some immigrant children in the Netherlands, and their parents, lack motivation to gain real proficiency in Dutch, which they consider to be of limited utility in the broader context of Europe. Their motivation is not increased if the Dutch teachers are unskilled in teaching their own language, and it has been suggested that all teachers should have such training since they are very likely to encounter pupils who need support in acquiring proficiency in Dutch (*Samenwijs*, November 1988). To date, however, a school like the one visited by one of the authors (De Jong) in Malmö, Sweden, which had required all of its staff to take a course in teaching Swedish as a second language, is still the exception.

Even schools with a well-organized program of supplemental support for language acquisition may find that language minority pupils are not making appropriate progress, if their regular classroom experiences do not include a sufficient amount of exposure to the spoken use of the target language and if language instruction is not integrated effectively with academic instruction. This requires close collaboration between the teachers. An English specialist calls for "bilingual children learning side by side with native English speakers, with the mainstream and language support teachers jointly doing developmental teaching." She points out that "bilingual children pick up things as they go along and learn from other pupils as well as directly from ESL teaching. If you withdraw them [for separate instruction] you are robbing them of interactions with others. They won't learn English as well and their language development will be delayed" (quoted by Klein, 1994, 14).

The effectiveness of programs of supplemental support is often undermined by a lack of connections with the balance of the instructional program. A study of an American high school, for example, found that a "vague state of affairs surrounding [English as a second language] programs . . . not only left [limited English-proficient] immigrant students feeling left out of the school—but it has contributed to their (and their teachers') lower status among mainstream teachers and students" (Grey, 1990, 419). The importance of ensuring that language minority pupils "study the same curriculum and acquire the same knowledge as their English-speaking counterparts" has frequently been emphasized, but supplemental support programs often are not designed to reinforce the material being covered in the regular classroom; this is particularly a problem at the secondary level, where pupils in an English as a second language group may be drawn from a number of different classes, and there is little communication, much less collaboration, among teachers (Crandall et al., 1987, 4). Pull-out programs need to be so designed that "language use is geared to the learners' special linguistic needs," as when it relates to the academic content with which they are dealing in their other classes (Garcia, 1987/1988, 3). Better yet, the supplemental staff could work in the regular classroom, helping pupils to learn how to respond to the demands of that situation and thus also to learn to function effectively in the language of the classroom.

> In contrast, students who are taken out of their regular classrooms to obtain (a) assistance with English acquisition, or (b) to complete class tasks with a person who speaks their [first language], are required to respond to very different task demands. Learning in a tutorial situation does not require the student to respond appropriately to the demands inherent in class tasks . . . when they return to the classroom (Tikunoff, 1985, 54).

It may be impossible to create such a positive language learning environment in some cases, however, because of the concentration of a high proportion of pupils who speak the target language in a limited way. Teachers may lament, as they did in one Amsterdam school, "what we need is more ordinary Dutch children . . . we now have less than 8 percent white pupils in the school; these children can't have an influence on language use. The teacher is the only one who speaks Dutch correctly" (Horst, 1990, 100).

Evaluation of Assignment to a Regular Class with Home-Language Maintenance
It has been difficult for researchers and policy-makers to determine how effective supplemental home language classes are because there is great uncertainty about their goals. Administrators typically have different perceptions of both the purpose and the effect of home language classes than do those who teach such classes, and both may have perceptions that differ significantly from those of language minority parents (Jungbluth & Driessen, 1989). Home language instruction may be mistrusted by public authorities who fear that it will retard the desired assimilation of the second and third generation of "foreigners." As a Moroccan educator describes the situation in Amsterdam, home language instruction "and Dutch education were considered two completely conflicting systems of education, with Dutch education promoting integration into Dutch society and [home language instruction] not doing so" (Amminh, 1986, 50).

As with bilingual reception programs, supplemental home language programs are commonly justified through two lines of argument. The first is that they enable language minority pupils to remain in touch with their distinctive cultures and communities, including their own families, while mastering the language of the majority and thus of academic success. Often the additional point is made, that academic proficiency in the home language will be useful in later study and employment. The second argument for supplemental home language programs is that they justify the presence in the school of adults drawn from the ethnic minority group, serving as role models of effective and equal participation in the host society and as advocates for the interests of pupils.

The first argument calls for reinforcing elements of the distinctiveness—understood as a strength rather than a deficiency—of ethnic minority pupils. *Anomie* and consequent low achievement, even delinquency, will be prevented by promoting the ethnic pride and self-esteem of minority pupils while developing a competence (the home language) in which they are ahead of their peers from the majority group. A positive adjustment will be promoted by making it unnecessary for pupils to choose between loyalty to their ethnic background and effective participation in the school. Advocates do not ordinarily ask whether these arrangements may not also give contradictory messages about whether the child is expected to become Dutch, for example, and at the same time to remain Turkish. West Indian sociologist Maureen Stone argues that

> it is the job of the [British] school to enable children to function with ease in the standard language. By the same token it is the job of the home, family and community to keep the dialect alive. The use of dialect in the classroom may obscure the basic role of the school, confuse issues, and create further contradictions (Stone, 1981, 111).

Lessons in the native language and culture of immigrant students, intended to maintain contact with the unknown homeland as well as communication between the generations, raise serious pedagogical questions, not least whether to use the language of schooling in the homeland or the language actually spoken by the family. For example, Haitian immigrants to the United States are sometimes puzzled that instruction is provided to their children in bilingual programs through Kreyol, though they themselves were schooled in Haiti through French, as do some Cape Verdean immigrants who wish that Portuguese rather than Kriolu were used for instruction and for school-home communication (Chapter 5). Cape Verdean parents in the Netherlands are reported to have the same preference for the use of Portuguese as a supplemental school language, and make little effort to ensure that their children learn to speak Kriolu (Rooy, 1986, 68).

In such cases immigrant parents want their children taught what was the high-status language in their homeland, even if they themselves do not speak it and the prospect of their children re-migrating is slight. This is especially the case with Arabic, the language of the Koran and of worship for many Muslims who do not otherwise speak or understand the language. But the Berber-speaking child learning Moroccan Arabic in a Belgian school, like the Kurdish-speaking child learning Turkish in a German school, or the dialect-speaking child learning standard Italian in a British school is not really maintaining linkages with her parents or receiving cognitive stimulation based upon her first language. This leads some to argue that the emphasis should be placed upon oral proficiency in the home language, not upon learning to write the official language (Driessen, 1990).

Those who see permanent bilingualism as a ticket to future opportunities, however, argue against bothering to teach children a low-status language, even if it is that of their parents. French, from this perspective, is far more useful for later life than is Kreyol. Whether a child will re-emigrate to his parents' homeland or will use his second language for employment or cultural purposes, it is well that this be a language of general currency, according to this argument.

A project of mother tongue teaching emphasizing to the second generation their ethnic minority traits derived from their parents' rural traditions, now incapsulated in the context of the indigenous urban mainstream school or contrasting the latter with urban patterns of life in the country of origin, would neither meet the community's expectations nor claim to be a true heritage program. On the other hand, if the social objective of a programme intends to equip socially underprivileged groups with bilingualism, including fluency and literacy in another modern language, there can be no regrets if it aims to provide competence in the Standard national language as opposed to the rural dialects (Tosi, 1984, 173).

In some cases public education authorities have begun to offer home language instruction as a means of luring children away from community-sponsored programs that were perceived as too nationalistic or ideological, too pedagogically backward or demanding upon the out-of-school time and energy of the linguistic minority pupil (Amersfoort, 1982, 203). An Australian advocate for home language programs warned that schools had *better* provide them or "the vacuum will be filled by ethnic separatist institutions. School multi-culturalism is required to avoid structural separation and division in society" (Smolicz, quoted by Bullivant, 1982, 141).

The fact that families themselves increasingly use the prevalent language of the host society, as does much of their environment, reduces the effectiveness of as well as the demand for home language classes. For Algerian children born in France

> Arabic, even in a dialect form, is essentially no longer a mother tongue, and can only be considered a "language of origin" in the sense that it permits youth who derive from the North African immigration to situate themselves in relation to their origins (Quijano, 1986, 89).

The effect of supplemental classes for some pupils, then, is not to maintain an inherited language and culture or to connect them effectively with their own families, much less to ease their integration into the host country's educational system, but rather to add an additional and difficult subject to their load. Whether or not this is educationally justifiable depends upon the circumstances of the individual pupil; if she is handling the regular curriculum with ease and success, it may well be a good idea to study the heritage language as an enrichment of that program, but not such a good idea if she is experiencing difficulties. Ironically, however, it is often the pupils for whom the regular program of the school is causing problems who are found in the supplemental home language classes, out of a misguided belief that this will somehow increase their self-esteem and thus lead to improved academic achievement.

The problem is that there is little clarity about how the time for home-language and -culture lessons should be used, or what the objectives are. Some see it as a means of easing the adjustment of language minority pupils to the school, while others insist that it must be seen as an academic subject in its own right (Driessen, 1990). A curriculum development process is needed to make such classes more effective and also to tie them more directly into the overall academic program of the school, serving as the basis for collaboration between the home-language teacher and the other members of the teaching team (Dekker, 1991, 55–56). A Dutch linguist who is a strong supporter of bilingual education notes that

> funds were provided for the appointment of teachers, but it stopped pretty much there. Little or nothing was done to develop curriculum materials in the minority language that were appropriate to the situation in the Netherlands, the training of teachers of other languages never really got off the ground, and integration with Dutch education was poorly supported (Appel, 1985, 76).

The second argument for supplemental home language programs, as noted, is that they justify the presence in the school of adults drawn from the ethnic minority group, serving as role models of effective and equal participation in the host society. Indeed, the most down-to-earth justification for supplemental home language and culture programs is that they can serve as an essential support system for a child experiencing the pressures of the immigrant situation. Such instruction should not seek to relate pupils to a homeland which they have left behind, but should rather deal with their present experience as members of an ethnic minority group.

In a Swedish bilingual kindergarten, Dutch researchers were told, the home language teacher was a cultural intermediary.

> Your behavior must show that it is very possible as an adult to be, in a balanced and secure way, both member of a small minority group and member of a dominant society. . . . Culture is always more than holidays, clothing and food. If you are not in close touch with the daily culture of the children, but stress unfamiliar aspects, that can precisely be alienating rather than reinforcing. . . . You must know:
>
> • What do parents want? Do they want to preserve their culture? What is their perspective? Is preserving the culture a possibility for them?
> • What elements of the culture do the parents themselves find important? What do they find indispensable?
> • What can they give the children themselves? What can immigrant organizations, social service institutions, and the like give? What aspects of the culture do parents want the school to help them to keep alive? (Hajer & Meestringa, 1986).

Thus the home language teacher is, more than anything, a "cultural interpreter," a person who is herself dealing successfully with an intercultural situation and can help to interpret, for pupils, not only the new situation and its demands but also their own parents as they react to the opportunities and disappointments of that situation. It is her task to help pupils to learn to handle two sets of norms and expectations in situation-appropriate ways, as much as to use two languages, just as many monolinguals use different "registers" of a single language. This capacity depends upon the development of a bicultural identity (Boos-Nünning, 1983, 5). It is not served by seeking either to assimilate completely to the pattern of the host society or to hold on tenaciously to that of the first generation.

This has been an area of considerable controversy, since the teachers of these supplemental classes are typically natives of the homelands of their pupils, trained in its institutions and often unfamiliar with the assumptions and practices which otherwise dominate schooling in the host society. It may in fact be the special role of these teachers to represent for the children an alternative to acculturation (Goetze, 1987, 91). In Belgium, where home language teachers have been recruited and paid by the homeland governments, it has been argued that this retards the adjustment of pupils to their actual circumstances. For example, in a "model" school visited by the author,

> in a Turkish language-and-culture class, the students were busy copying in their notebooks a great many words the teacher had written on the blackboard, all having to do with cereal products of Anatolia. The room was decorated with tourist posters of Turkey, mostly of Hellenistic ruins, and the inevitable photograph of Atatürk. The teacher's command of Dutch—when I spoke with him—was limited, and his rather old-fashioned suit and manner distinguished him clearly from his Belgian colleagues. . . . Memorizing irrelevant vocabulary, contemplating images of fallen Greek temples, under the supervision of a teacher himself poorly-adjusted to Belgian life, could, it seems to me, only heighten a sense of alienation in these young Belgians of Turkish ancestry. Their identification should presumably [rather] be with an emerging (and vital) culture-in-exile (Glenn, 1987, 76–77).

Dissatisfaction with such situations has led to a recent initiative by Flemish Community education authorities to recruit minority language teachers from the second and third generations of the language minority communities in Belgium, to be trained and paid by Belgian authorities (Verlot, 1994). The children of immigrants should be considered Belgian children, and their instruction, even in the minority languages, should reflect the immigrant experience in Flanders (Janssen, 1986, 13). Similarly, the Labor Party spokesperson for education in the Dutch Parliament has stressed the importance of recruiting home language teachers from among immigrants living in the Netherlands and fluent in Dutch (Vliet, 1991, 90).

For many immigrant parents, however, the participation of their children in home language instruction may represent a source of assurance that they continue to possess an identity distinct from the negative judgments offered by the society in which they are living. Thus some value home language instruction as an

> opportunity for reclaiming an original language and culture threatened by the host country's language and culture. . . . This rules out

any link between the course and normal day school; the whole atmosphere is one of drawing contrasts, warding off, making dialogue impracticable. The basis idea is that of returning home: life as it is being lived is only an unavoidable interlude in a time and place to which the child concerned refuses to belong (Campagnoni, 1987, 9).

Teachers who work on short-term contracts and look upon their appointment as a temporary interlude in a career in their homeland may have difficulty relating to the special circumstances of pupils who are growing up in an immigrant situation (even if in theory the children will eventually return to a "home" they may scarcely know).

Turkish children in The Netherlands are growing up in a migrant culture. . . . Sometimes teachers try to teach them about . . . things that were alive in Turkey fifty years ago but don't exist any more. Culture is not static . . . (Buvelot, 1986).

A related problem in several countries is the lack of coordination between home language instruction and the regular program of the school (Aarssen et al., 1992, 8, for the Netherlands; Hyltenstam, 1992, for Sweden). One study found that home language teachers typically meet "about once a month" or "never" with mainstream teachers (Driessen et al., 1989). The latter have reportedly little interest in what occurs in home language instruction and resent what they consider its diversion of energy from the "real" subjects that they themselves teach (Eldering, 1986b, 184). In Amsterdam, according to another study,

there is no consideration of any sort of integration or of coordinating with one another's reading and instructional materials; the Dutch teacher works with Dutch curriculum following a particular timetable and the foreign teacher works with a curriculum from the homeland following an entirely different timetable (Coenen, 1982).

The problem of coordination and setting common goals is frequently mentioned in Germany as well. Home language teachers sometimes complain that they have worked for a decade or more in German schools without a single teacher or principal taking the slightest interest in what they were doing with the children for several hours a week. The need, in many cases, to serve pupils at several different schools, and the frequent scheduling of home language instruction outside of normal school hours make it difficult to build collegial relationships. Working with groups drawn from different grades prevents co-ordination with what the children are doing in their regular classes.

Language minority pupils who are pulled out of their regular classes for supplemental home language instruction miss part of what's going on and have even more difficulty keeping up (Boos-Nünning, 1981a, 47), but problems also arise with the scheduling of home language instruction after school hours in order to avoid reduction in the regular instruction. It is not uncommon for the five periods a week of home language that many pupils receive to be scheduled one after another on the same afternoon, to reduce transportation and other costs, and this can mean a ten-hour day for the children (Rixius & Thurmann, 1987, 62). Regular teachers complain that their foreign pupils are overburdened with extra work and cannot complete their assignments. In addition, "afternoon home language instruction strengthens for many foreign children their 'Third World' situation [within German society], especially through external separation from German instruction" (Luchtenberg, 1984, 409).

Home language teachers often feel isolated and under stress, working with groups of very different proficiency levels and ages, in empty school buildings, without collegial support (Thurmann, 1988). A study by the Italian embassy found that Italian home language teachers worked with an average of more than six groups, and that 29 percent of them traveled more than 200 kilometers a week to cover these groups—5 percent of them more than 600 kilometers. Only 19 percent reported that they regularly exchanged information with their German colleagues (Rixius & Thurmann, 1987, 67). In many cases they are "skilled native speakers of their respective languages, but not necessarily skilled teachers of language"; they may have difficulty with pupils whose proficiency in their "native" language is much lower than they are used to through teaching in their homelands. Teachers of Asian community languages in the United Kingdom report, for example, that "the level of proficiency in these languages at the start of secondary education is diminishing" (Kroon, 1990, 59, 101).

Similar concerns are raised in Sweden, despite the government's extensive commitment to home language instruction. Some perceive it as having a relatively low status because supplemental and unrelated to the core curriculum. Others argue that immigrant pupils are already overburdened by the necessity of mastering all of the skills and subject-matter expected of Swedish pupils, including English starting in the fourth grade, and another language and its associated culture as well (Sveriges Lärarforbund, 1989).

Given this uncertainty about the purpose of supplemental home language classes, and the impediments to their effectiveness, it is not surprising to learn that many language minority pupils express negative attitudes toward these classes, some insisting that they already know their home language well enough, others that they don't want to know it (Löfgren, 1991). Some researchers suggest that home language "teaching underlines the 'failure' of their parents, their 'lack of culture,' and the gap between them and the society of origin" because "often impoverished and deformed, the languages spoken within families with little education, who emigrated several years previously, do not satisfy academic criteria" (Costa-Lascoux, 1989a, 77).

Other language minority pupils have more positive attitudes toward home language classes, though a study in Sweden found that the primary reason was not one of those often cited by advocates—remaining in contact with the culture of origin or with family members, self-esteem, or group solidarity—but the belief that bilingualism would be advantageous in the job market (Löfgren, 1991).

Christina Bratt-Paulston, in her review of Swedish research and practice, gently deflates the more grandiose claims made for home language programs:

> Mother tongue instruction [on a supplemental basis] is nice and makes possible a recognition of the values of the old country. As a linguist, I am very much in favour of it and recognize Swedish educational policy of mother tongue instruction as a very handsome gesture. . . . It is also a very expensive policy . . . and in the Swedish case, only indispensable for linguistic minority groups with a record of back migration (Paulston, 1982, 54–55).

Our conclusion supports this position. Home language maintenance and development is a good idea, provided that it can be achieved within a context of overall academic achievement and does not function as a diversion from the primary mission of the school, to enable the language minority pupil to develop real proficiency in the majority language and to be successful academically and (later) vocationally up to the limit of his or her ability and motivation.

To the extent that supplemental home language instruction is organized or taught badly, it may divert time and energy from the school's primary educational mission. An Australian study concluded that

> a curriculum that is unduly weighted with a selection of the expressive aspects from the ethnic group's cultural stock and stresses ethnic life styles may not provide students with sufficient instrumental

survival knowledge to compete for life chances when they leave school. Thus equipping children with a surfeit, say, of ethnic community languages, history and music in an attempt to improve their cultural awareness may be of far less survival value in the final analysis than mathematics, skills in using computers, and accountancy (Bullivant, 1989, 77).

Evaluation of the experimental program of home language instruction in Genk, Belgium, found that "the indigenous [Belgian] children, who remained all the time in the care of their mainstream class teacher and did not have to attend mother tongue classes, made better progress" (Boos-Nünning et al., 1986, 166). An interministerial committee in France that reviewed the effects of home language classes reached the conclusion that they "constitute, in the present state of things, a factor of discrimination and not of integration" (quoted by Boyzon-Fradet & Boulot, 1992, 249). Similarly, Henry Dors, a leading black researcher in the Netherlands, concluded that

> the extra psychic pressure placed on the foreign children through bi-cultural education is very clear: home-language instruction lays claim on part of the time and energy that as a child you desperately need to get a grasp on the instrumental cultural skills that work in this society. Meanwhile your white peers increase their educational headstart even more (quoted by Esch, 1982, 93).

Perhaps the most surprising research result is that participation in home language classes appeared to have little direct effect on achievement on tests of proficiency in the language and familiarity with the culture taught in those classes. For example, Turkish 6th graders who had not taken part in such classes outside of school outscored those who had done so, on both language and culture, including those who had taken three hours a week of home language and culture classes during school; for Turkish, Moroccan, and Spanish pupils, the number of hours of home language instruction in school appeared to have a largely random relationship with their proficiency. In addition, "it seems to make no difference to the children's attainments in regular education whether they attend OETC [home language and culture] or not . . . pupils attending OETC after school hours perform worse in the Dutch educational system and move on to lower levels of secondary education than pupils not attending" (Driessen, 1990, 122, 202).

The Dutch Labor Party's then Minister of Education, Sociologist Jos van Kemenade, argued in 1982 that extra attention to mastering the Dutch language, to academic coun-selling, to school choice and to a successful career in Dutch school-ing could be more important in the long run, not only for oppor-tunity in society, but also for the possibility of maintaining and de-veloping one's own identity than attention to native language and culture, especially when that in fact occurs only in isolation (Fase, 1987, 33).

And in 1983 he asked whether

the maintenance and strengthening of native cultural identity does not rather limit than assist equal participation in our society, and whether on the other hand a policy that is concerned with equal participation [of ethnic minority groups] in our society will not unavoidably lead to change and even to obscuring of cultural identity. . . . They result in a situation of social and economic dis-advantage which is decisive, not only for their chances to partici-pate on an equal basis in our society, but in the long run also for the possibility of giving shape to their own cultural identity (Kemenade, 1983, 76).

Strengthening the cultural identity and values of different groups, Van Kemenade argued, could also result in conflict with norms anchored in the Dutch Constitution and essential to Dutch society in its present form. Edu-cation and teachers should rather help immigrant children to change their identity and norms in order to participate fully in their new environment. Policy statements that stressed "full participation in Dutch society with maintenance of cultural identity" were more misleading than helpful. Home language and culture instruction could not make a positive contribution to the well-being of immigrant children when it

has an isolated position in education and does not form an integrated part of the whole schooling situation. Under such circumstances there is not the confrontation and exchange of cultural elements which in fact are precisely essential to the development of identity (Kemenade, 1983, 74).

Although Dutch policy pays tribute to the idea of the equal value of the vari-ous cultures represented among the immigrant population, this may be more of a high-minded principle than a realistic assessment of how the contact of cultures will play out in the Netherlands. Thus, as another critic points out,

> the government proceeds from the assumption that the cultures of the various ethnic groups are not only in principle but also in social actuality of equal value . . . [But] the policy aims at the participation of minority groups in common institutions that are based on Dutch values and norms. This makes the dominance of the majority culture and a one-sided acculturation virtually impossible to avoid (Eldering, 1986a, 189).

As we have pointed out in Chapter 5, efforts by the school to maintain active use of a minority language have little prospect of long-term success except in cases of unusually strong and isolated ethnic group life, which does not correspond to the "project" of most immigrant families. An extensive study of language minority parents in the United States, by the Educational Testing Service, found that 56 percent of Mexican-American but only 25 percent of Asian parents would want their children to be in a program that would maintain their home language while they learned English; 44 percent of each group responded positively to an immersion program in English. Asked who should teach children to read and write the non-English language, 10 percent of Asians but 48 percent of Mexican Americans assigned that responsibility to the school. Only 11 percent of the Asians and 12 percent of the Mexican Americans, however, wanted the school to provide such instruction if it meant less time for teaching English (Baratz-Snowden et al., 1988b, 54–61). The study of different program models by Ramirez and colleagues found that "an alarming 11 percent of late-exit [maintenance bilingual program] parents and 41 percent of early-exit [transitional bilingual program] parents want their child taught only in *English*. These children are obviously in the wrong program" (Rossell, 1991, 25).

That does *not* mean, of course, that the use of the minority language for academic instruction as part of a well-designed program will not have positive effects on pupil achievement; there is a fundamental difference between integrated bilingual education (see Chapter 8) and supplemental language programs.

The policy trend in several of the countries studied is toward continuing to provide language development instruction, but to do so within the context of an overall strategy for second-language acquisition by all pupils, treating the presence of language minority pupils in a school, and of teachers who speak their language, as a resource to improve foreign-language instruction in general.

Native-language content courses, with their enrollment of minority language students, can be incorporated into the foreign language—and content area—curriculum to provide English speakers with greater exposure to the foreign language and with real, purposeful communicative situations—factors which have been found to enhance language acquisition (Jaeger, 1985, 54).

Immigrant children might then study the official language of the homeland of their parents to meet school language requirements, and do so in a context of seriousness rather than as a poorly designed frill concerned more with self-esteem than with academic rigor. As an American education official put it, "lengthening the bilingual education schooling through high school, at least in selected languages, could help offset the need for initial specialist training in foreign language and area studies" (Thompson, 1983, 8). "Spanish for Spanish-speakers" in some American high schools, for example, aims to develop real competence in speaking and writing standard Latin-American Spanish so that it will be of actual vocational usefulness. According to one report, however, only 17 percent of pupils who have Spanish as their home language elect to take such courses (Benderson, 1986, 10). Arabic and Portuguese, as world languages, are taught in a growing number of French schools—though even pupils for whom these are "heritage languages" are likely to choose English as more useful for future employment.

Evaluation of Reception Classes in the Language of the School
In the United States a common criticism of nonbilingual reception programs has been that they seek to shift the language minority pupil too rapidly to a regular class on the basis of a superficial proficiency in spoken English, rather than taking the five to seven years that some researchers argue are needed in a language support program utilizing the home language for cognitive and expressive development. While this position is often advanced by specialists in the schooling of language minority pupils, the contrasting viewpoint is held by many educators, based upon what they consider a common-sense judgment that the only way to integrate pupils is to integrate them. A survey of school staff in metropolitan Toronto, for example, found that

> a strong assimilationist element was clearly evident. The solutions most frequently offered by Metro respondents included such statements as "have a holding center"; "culturize them"; "have a crash course in Canadian customs"; "give them one year to adjust to Ontario culture" (Samuda, 1980, quoted in Bhatnagar & Hamalian, 1981, 232).

In Europe, concerns have often been expressed that reception programs unduly prolong the segregation of language minority pupils. Thus the French government circular of January 1970 calling for the establishment of reception classes described their purpose as "a rapid integration into the normal school setting." Groups should if possible be set up on the basis of age, according to the circular, but one expert claims this has been the exception because of resistance to concentrating such students in any school.

The fear (sometimes justified) of local authorities that a ghetto will be created because of the presence, in significant numbers, of foreign children leads usually to a refusal to set up two reception classes in the same school. Research about "thresholds of tolerance" give [an apparent] scientific authority to these decisions. Thus the threshold of 12 percent foreigners in housing developments would be one danger signal, and that of 18 to 20 percent foreigners in elementary schools would be another. Although it is accurate that the grouping of pupils in difficulty in the same school can produce a defensive reaction on the part of French families leading as far as to the decision to change the school of their own children . . . the existence of two reception classes offers uncontestable advantages. In place of a heterogeneous mixture of children aged from 7 to 12 or 14, of differing linguistic backgrounds, of varied past schooling, it is possible to substitute an organization which is at the same time more supple and also more capable of responding to individual development (Clévy, 1978, 71–72).

A study carried out in 1973–74 found that nearly 90 percent of the reception programs in France were in full-time separate classes for an entire year. Short-term courses, relying upon language-teaching techniques often successful with middle-class foreign adults learning French, did not prove satisfactory as a means of preparing immigrant children to participate in French schooling. Teachers resented having to form relationships with two or three different groups of pupils the same year, and found relations with the families almost impossible. Full-year classes were more satisfactory, but it was important that

the class not remain closed to the school environment surrounding it, that it not become an isolated little island. Integration into the school takes place through the acquisition of the language but also through the relations that foreign and French children can establish.

Some call the reception class a "ghetto," but those who are in contact with daily realities describe it as a sheltered environment which permits a child to pass by controlled stages from one civilization to another. It is essential that activities shared by children of different nationalities permit all of them to become known and recognized. Physical education sessions—which are usually not just games—can be a first attempt from the start of the school year. In particular *activités d'éveil* [projects combining learning and doing, with a focus on direct experience of the world and on cooperation] carried out through the collaboration of two or three teachers should be especially favorable to this osmosis (Clévy, 1978, 73–74).

The goal of such classes, another French specialist argued, should be to give pupils as quickly as possible a basic proficiency in French and then to rely upon the regular class to extend that proficiency through interactions with the teacher and with other pupils. "One must be clear: even a school year constitutes too long a time to be schooled in a special class." Such a reception class "should not pretend to overcome all of the academic deficits that a pupil may have; that is the task of the regular class" (Porcher, 1978c, 125).

This concern was echoed a decade later in a report prepared for the French government by an expert on Islamic social history. Professor Jacques Berque reviewed the response of the education system to immigration and concluded that its goals needed to be rethought to ensure the full participation of immigrant pupils. Among other problems,

the "ghetto" or even "cocoon" CLIN [*classe d'initiation*] is generally too closed in on itself and in any case is too often marginalized in relation to the rest of the school. It demobilizes the other teachers . . ; because a "specialist" is concerned with these problems, the non-specialists feel relieved of them and have a tendency not to adapt their practices to the presence of these pupils and their specific [needs and strengths] (Berque, 1985, 11).

Placement of children who come from a French-speaking environment in a reception class, whether they have passed their early years in France or in a Francophone country abroad, was inappropriate; the CLIN should be limited to children who would be totally at a loss in a regular class, and the objective should be to integrate them as soon as possible. It was important that stress be placed on housing foreign pupils make progress not only in

French but also in other dimensions of the curriculum, and that they be

> permitted to participate together in activities corresponding to their age group (physical education and sports, art and music, etc.) where they will be able to learn to speak (acquire or practice) French in different situations, and to come to know the pupils of classes which they will be joining (Berque, 1985, 28).

On the occasion of publication of this report, Education Minister Jean-Pierre Chevènement charged that

> Reception classes in elementary and in secondary schools were originally intended to teach French to new arrivals and to integrate them as quickly and successfully as possible into regular classes. . . these classes have too often become ghettoes, contrary to the desire of those who created them, where sometimes even children born in France and speaking French are schooled. Thus too many young people from the immigrant community, desiring to succeed, find themselves excluded from the paths of success (Chevènement, 1985).

In a 1986 revision of French government requirements for reception classes, national education authorities responded to this concern by stressing that reception classes were intended only for

> non-French-speaking children newly arrived in France. For the much more numerous foreign students who were born or arrived very young in France, any difficulties encountered, whether they involve an insufficient mastery of the written language or insufficiencies in other basic skills, should be dealt with within the same framework as are analogous difficulties experienced by French pupils (*Apprentissage . . ,* 1986).

In the Netherlands there has been a debate about the practice of assigning language minority pupils to "centralized reception" while they learn a certain amount of Dutch and are otherwise prepared for a regular classroom. Opponents charge that this can lead to long-term segregation and is a less effective way of achieving integration and proficiency in Dutch than assignment to a predominantly Dutch class. Can immigrant youth afford to take several years to make the transition into schooling, and still complete an educational program that will be of some use in obtaining employment? The Dutch government is pressing intermediate schools to ensure that language minority pupils do not spend so much time on the transition process that their participation in formal schooling is unacceptably delayed (Zanderbergen, 1993a, 373). An even more fundamental question about the effectiveness of reception classes, however, may be whether the regular classes are ready to take in pupils who, in addition to limited proficiency in Dutch, may have had little formal schooling in their homelands (Fase, 1985, 53).

Questions have been raised in Germany about how effectively reception classes meet their goals—and whether they are really transitional or tend to become a permanent sidetrack for foreign pupils.

The instructional realities in preparation classes were identified early as one of the causes of the under-achievement and the problems of foreign children in the German educational system. Even in recent years there has been no decisive improvement, and even some worsening.

> Reception classes are often at a disadvantage even in external conditions. Often they are given the worst classrooms . . . often their enrollment is higher than that of regular classes, since the number of students is set at the start of the school year and then increases on an on-going basis. The heterogeneity of the pupils with respect to age, language proficiency and previous knowledge, and the heavy turnover make the instruction even more difficult, and it is generally not—contrary to the guidelines—aligned with the German curriculum. The teachers themselves don't especially like this instruction, which leads to a heavy turnover of teachers and to an assignment of the newest member of a faculty to this difficult task. Frustration and avoidance are increased by the lack of special teacher training in the education of foreign children. In addition the foreign children are generally instructed in isolation from the German children, since the integrated lessons are assigned little time in the schedule and suffer from a lack of pedagogical and methodological ideas. In many cases the instruction in reception classes is so arranged that foreign teachers proceed without supervision by German school authorities, using the curriculum and texts of their homelands. The language of instruction is as a result almost exclusively that of the homeland (Boos-Nünning, 1981b, 37).

Pupils in such classes do not continue any previous work in subject-matter; the reception period is a "timeout from learning." Nor is the German instruction—the primary reason for the programs—satisfactory. Often it is given by teachers who themselves have an inadequate command of the language.

When one considers the realities in the reception classes, it is not difficult to understand why they generally do not achieve their goal of preparing pupils for and transitioning them into regular classes. The result is that foreign pupils are transferred to regular classes after one or two years in a reception class, even though they don't have an adequate proficiency in German. They can't take part in the instruction and return to the reception class or repeat a year in the German class. Even when they have learned enough German in the reception class, they remain one, two, or more years behind in the content areas when they are transferred to a regular class at their age level (Boos-Nünning, 1981b, 38).

Integration into the mainstream of the school becomes more difficult, some believe, the longer an immigrant student has spent in a reception class. In addition, it is almost impossible for such a student to rejoin his age-mates who have in the meantime been mastering the age-appropriate content (Boulot & Boyzon-Fradet, 1986, 45).

The presence of a program specializing in serving immigrant pupils may have the result that

> the teachers of ordinary classes demobilize themselves with respect to welcoming foreign children and confide that responsibility to "specialists." . . . There is a great temptation to keep newly-arrived children in a closed CLIN (a serious deviation which is unfortunately common), reinforced by the attitude of other teachers who, using the pretext of the existence of the CLIN, often refuse to integrate the students during the course of the year, even if the CLIN teacher recommends that (Haeffele, 1988, 31).

The Swann Committee, in its study of the education of minority children in England, expressed strong reservations about arrangements for separate treatment, which they found to be "discriminatory in effect." "Nonspecialist teachers have been led to believe that they have little or no role to play in the language development of children from homes where English is not the first language." What, after all, the Committee had been asked, "is a teacher in the main school to do when a child appears for one lesson and not the next because that's his or her time to go to the language center? You do not have to be an ill-intentioned teacher to send a child to find a remedial teacher . . . an off-site withdrawal system takes the whole question out of their hands." One expert noted that "All too often the language teaching itself or the problems of the 're-inserted' child were seen to belong to those of the Remedial Department along with those of other backward children." The Committee was warned, in expert testimony, that

> separation of second language learners from the curriculum followed by all the other pupils cannot be theoretically justified since in practice it leads to both their curriculum and the social learning being impoverished, and thus both language and intellectual development is held up. It also means that the burden of joining in is always placed on the newcomers and never on those already established in the mainstream (*Education for All*, 1985, 388–390).

The fact that school staff tend to see responding to the concerns and educational needs of minority groups as something done by somebody else with a specialized assignment may have prevented an effective response to the overall educational needs of language minority pupils as an aspect of school improvement. Too often, a study in Birmingham found, they felt

> that lower standards and expectations were inevitable with a multiracial intake, and, although they tried to make schools a pleasant environment, did not expect high achievement. This, of course, was the antithesis of the expectations and understandings of minority parents as to what schools were all about (Tomlinson, 1984, 152).

A leading authority in France, where policy has placed a strong emphasis upon the integration of language minority pupils, insisted that

> we must have the courage to recognize that most of the "specialists" who have up to now concerned themselves with [the schooling of the children of immigrants] have fallen into this trap: considering that this population demands pedagogical responses which are *absolutely specific*, they have shut them, whether they wished to or not, whether they were aware of it or not, in the educational ghetto which in most cases they assert should be avoided (Porcher, 1978a, 11).

After all,

> Ghettoes are *always* dangerous. To socialize individuals separately is to run the risk of making them permanently unable to be anything but separate. The school ghetto has the essential characteristic of per-

petuating itself and of producing other ghettoes (or, if one prefers, of perpetuating the social ghettoes which already exist) . . . it's hard to understand how marginalization can help to fight against marginality (Porcher, 1978b, 122–123).

According to Costa-Lascoux, writing 20 years later, French teachers assigned to reception classes for immigrant pupils have a "low level of training and preparation," and these classes are still "isolated within the schools" (Costa-Lascoux, 1989a, 72).

Critics charge that reception programs tend to perpetuate themselves, marginalizing language minority pupils from the curriculum (in the broadest sense) of the school and thus of the host society, and also encourage on the part of nonspecialist teachers a belief that they do not have responsibility for language minority pupils and indeed are unable to help them.

Too much of the attention in reception classes may be given to poorly developed and stereotyped ideas of social adjustment rather than to creating the basis for success in the educational system. This has led over time to less emphasis on linking the instruction to further forms of schooling, which in turn have shown little inclination to make the adjustments necessary to serve foreign pupils with deficiencies in their previous schooling. Teachers in the mainstream classes upon which academic or vocational success depend expect the reception class to have corrected all such deficiencies so that a pupil can perform ordinary classwork without further support, a manifestly unrealistic objective. Too often, then, pupils in linking classes constitute an educational "lost generation" whose schooling will not continue beyond the reception stage (Fase, 1985, 53, 63).

Instructional isolation, even if in intention short-term and transitional, may have negative effects on pupils; it may also encourage nonspecialist teachers to see their responsibilities as not extending to language- and adjustment-related needs. Thus problems have arisen in the relationship between reception classes and the schools into which foreign students must be integrated. "Any specific treatment of a 'distinctive' question by a group of 'specialists' can be coherent and effective only if it is tied in well with the general context. Otherwise, they can only accentuate the effects of marginalization of the affected populations" (Seksig, 1990, 27).

Reception strategies run into the further difficulty that the concentration of language minority pupils to receive specialized services may bring with it consequences that work against their need sooner or later to be absorbed into regular classes.

In Germany, there are problems when having too few immigrant pupils makes it hard to provide support adapted to their needs, and problems when too many leads to isolation from German age-mates; either extreme can create difficulties in the development of proficiency in actually using the language. The results, so far as learning German is concerned, are uneven and often unsatisfactory:

1. There are a considerable number of migrant children in Germany who, during their schooling, have no contact at all with German children. They learn German as a foreign language . . . but they do not use it as a means of communication.

2. A significant number of migrant children live in areas where there are few migrants. These children are typically placed in regular classes with German children and get little or no additional help . . . these children rarely acquire written standard and academic German without additional help.

Thus most migrant children, including those with a functional conversational knowledge of German, cannot understand or use the academic language that constitutes the medium of instruction in higher education (Menk, 1986, 28–29).

An additional limitation of reception programs is that they tend to mix together pupils with a strong previous schooling in another language with pupils who have had very little school experience. One of the groups is likely to be short-changed: even the acquisition of the second language in a school setting is highly dependent upon literacy and study skills. A study of reception classes in Geneva found that refugee pupils with inadequate previous schooling remained longer in those classes and experienced considerable difficulty transferring into mainstream classes (Rastoldo & Rey, 1993). A teacher who is attempting to develop literacy and a functional understanding of grammar for such pupils will find it difficult to move quickly enough with other pupils who need only to apply academic skills that they have already acquired to a new language.

Evaluation of Bilingual Reception Programs

Criticisms of bilingual reception programs tend to focus less upon the theory behind them than upon their implementation. There are, of course, some critics who reject the very idea of using the home language during the reception period, as a distraction from a single-minded study of the language of the school; Christine Rossell and Michael Ross argue that transitional bilingual education is by its very nature likely to be ineffective, since

493

children who spend half their day being educated in their native tongue for three years and then all their time in the second language after that will not be very bilingual when they graduate many years later, and they will have lost one and one-half years of English language learning time (Rossell & Ross, 1986, 411).

Herbert Walberg, criticizing the "wretchedly planned and executed" research on bilingual education, insists upon "the superiority of large amounts of high-intensity exposure for learning a second language, which a gigantic amount of research on learning in general also supports" (General Accounting Office, 1987, 72).

Far more common, however, is the view that the idea of bilingual education is all very well, but is too often implemented ineptly and with an unnecessarily extended separation from majority pupils. In Germany, for example, the criticism has been leveled that

the foreign children are generally instructed in isolation from the German children, since the integrated lessons are assigned little time in the schedule and suffer from a lack of pedagogical and methodological ideas. In many cases the instruction in reception classes is so arranged that foreign teachers proceed without supervision by German school authorities, using the curriculum and texts of their homelands. The language of instruction is as a result almost exclusively that of the homeland (Boos-Nünning, 1981, 37).

Similar concerns have been expressed about transitional bilingual programs in the United States, where the argument has focused especially upon the lack of opportunity for second language learning. Research carried out for the federal government found that Spanish-speaking first graders in bilingual programs received 24 percent less time on oral development in English, 96 percent less time on reading in English, and 14 percent less time on mathematics than Spanish-speaking pupils in mainstream classrooms (Benderson, 1986, 11). It seems paradoxical, in addition, to establish separate programs and use the home language extensively for instruction in the name of fostering proficiency in the second language of the pupils, trying "to teach [language minority] children English by isolating them from the large numbers of native English speakers available in the mainstream classes of their schools" (Snow, 1990, 61). Separate programs tend to limit "the exposure of some Hispanic students to the native English discourse of peers" (Arias, 1986, 50).

On the other hand, there are many positive reports about the effectiveness of transitional bilingual programs, as measured, for example, by lower rates of retention-in-grade and subsequent dropping out of school and better academic achievement for pupils who had participated in such programs for more than a year compared with others who had not done so (Curiel, Rosenthal, & Richek, 1986).

The number of studies of bilingual programs in the United States is overwhelming, though this has not led to a consensus on the value of the programs. The evaluations generally consider primarily the extent to which language minority pupils become proficient in English, as measured by standardized tests. Most studies consider only the progress made in a few months of instruction, seldom with a control group since, as in Massachusetts, the law prohibits leaving a matched control group of limited English-proficient pupils in a "structured immersion" program of well-designed instruction in and through English. An exception is the multiyear follow-up study on the bilingual program in Redwood City, California, often cited as one of the examples of success, which found eventually that "reading taught bilingually may not facilitate reading in English; . . . children who learn to read first and exclusively in English appear to do better in English reading over time" (Cohen, Fathman, & Merino, 1976, quoted by Rossell & Ross, 1986, 404. This is consistent with Tikunoff's study of successful bilingual programs, which found that 80 percent of time was devoted to academic learning, and this academic content was taught in English, with the home language used primarily to clarify instructions (Tikunoff, 1985).

National studies of the results of many different program evaluations have produced generally inconclusive results, in large part because it proves impossible to control accurately for what actually occurs in the classroom; every teacher uses an idiosyncratic mix of languages and teaching methods, and evaluations do not—perhaps cannot—provide sufficient detail to identify the factors that may have contributed to the outcomes. "Poor study design and sloppy methodology abound" (Baker, no date, 38). A study by Okada and others of more than 1,000 evaluations of bilingual education projects found such inadequate information on the nature of what actually occurred in classrooms that no conclusions could be reached (Baker, 1987, 355).

The results of the summative studies, such as they are, seem to be that good bilingual programs are better than poor immersion (in English) programs, while good immersion programs are better than poor bilingual programs! A review of evaluations prepared for Congress found that the critical factors in successful programs for LEP students seem to be how teachers use language and instruct their LEP students, rather than how much English they use. It would appear that program characteristics such as direct instruction, highly structured curricular materials, maximum student time on task, high student participation, and well-trained bilingual teachers contribute more to improving LEP students' academic achievement than does the initial language of instruction (Holland, 1986, 37).

In short, how children are taught matters more than the language used. While of course this means—if true—that instruction can perfectly well be provided in the minority language without lasting ill effects, it also means that there is no *instructional* necessity to use the minority language, since the majority language will do just as well. The basis for insisting upon use of the minority language, then, must be psychological—security, identity, self-esteem—or political, arguments that we weighed in Chapter 5 and found wanting.

Other reviews of the program evaluations have yielded equally undefinitive results. For second language acquisition, Rossell and Ross's review found, 29 percent of the studies showed transitional bilingual education to (TBE) be superior to other methods of instruction, 21 percent found it to be inferior, and 50 percent found no systematic difference from placing the children in a regular class (Rossell & Ross, 1986, 399). Keith Baker and Adriana de Kanter's review found similarly mixed results ("most TBE programs produced insignificant effects . . . about 1 out of 3 times there were significant positive effects. But about 1 out of 4 times there were significant *negative* effects") (Baker, 1987, 352), as did that by Ann Willig. Her "meta-analysis of selected studies" found, for example, that "much of the variance in effect sizes stems from characteristics of the research rather than characteristics of the educational programs" (Willig, 1985, 296). Although Willig concluded that "bilingual education has been badly served by a predominance of research that is inadequate in design and that makes inappropriate comparisons of children in bilingual programs who are dissimilar in many crucial respects" (Willig, 1985, 312) and that "only when quality bilingual research becomes a norm will we be able to untangle the complex issues in bilingual education (Willig, 1987, 374), supporters of the use of the home language often cite her research as proving the superiority of this form of instruction.

This illustrates the difficulty in assessing evaluations of bilingual instruction caused by the fact that "bilingual educators and program advocates reach far more positive conclusions when reviewing the literature than do reviewers from outside the bilingual education field" (Baker, no date, 38).

"The evaluators and those who review and integrate the research are also passionate advocates of bilingual education for political or ideological reasons . . . [who] believe that any policy which ignores the mother tongue in favor of English is racist, and any policy which maintains the mother tongue, however inadequately, is equitable" (Rossell & Ross, 1986, 386). Christina Bratt Paulston, in her study of Swedish research on bilingual education, points out that

> in both the U.S. and Canada, virtually everyone involved in basic or evaluative research on bilingual education is also a firm supporter of the programs. . . . Many if not most proponents for mother tongue teaching have a vested interest in the maintained lack of assimilation of migrant children. This does not automatically invalidate the opinions of this group, but their lack of objectivity is marked, and their advice vis à vis educational language policy needs to be considered *cum grano salis*. They will strenuously object to this point and instead point out that no one is as familiar with the problems of migrant children as they are. This point is also true and needs to be considered (Paulston, 1982, 18, 54).

As Walberg put it more colorfully, "Getting information from such sources is like asking your barber if you need a haircut" (General Accounting Office, 1987, 71).

Many opponents of bilingual programs argue that they should not be provided if they do not produce better results than immersion programs; supporters argue that, if the outcomes in English are the same, the bilingual program is superior because the pupil becomes—allegedly—proficient in two languages (Zappert & Cruz, 1977). This seems an obvious point: if a bilingual reception produces an ability to participate successfully in the educational system which is comparable in every respect to that produced by a monolingual reception in the language of the school, the argument shifts to whether bilingualism is the goal of the educational system. A careful study of bilingual education in Sweden, following a group of pupils over eight years, reached the modest conclusion that

> teaching in the mother tongue does not seem to have the magical effect on the children's development, for good or ill, which it has sometimes been ascribed. Rather, we consider mother tongue teaching to be a human right. A child should not need to be cut off from his cultural inheritance, nor feel estranged from his cultural group or fam-

ily. Furthermore, bilingual teaching doesn't seem to have a negative effect on other skills. Therefore, why should children be monolingual when they obviously are capable of being bilingual? (Löfgren & Ouvinen-Birgerstam, quoted by Paulston, 1982, 49).

This is a policy question reminiscent of the debate, on the French Left, between "republicans" who seek to remove social inequalities through treating immigrants and citizens alike and "democrats" committed to respecting and making room for diversity within French society (see Chapter 1). But this policy question should be distinguished from claims for the *instrumental* role of the first language in learning the second language. In other words, the question of language policy can be allowed to cast the deciding vote about whether to use the home language for instruction if considerations of academic success in the mainstream program need not be taken into account.

Of course, the debate is rarely held on the ground of language policy, at least in the United States. Proponents of bilingual instruction, asserting that it is essential to academic success, pre-empt the policy debate by advancing a factual claim that seems to leave no room for legitimate disagreement. If bilingual instruction is the only educationally responsible way of educating language minority pupils, there are grounds for requiring that it be provided and, over time, for widening the definition of which pupils are entitled to it; the program—and associated employment—comes to have a life of its own, protected from the ups and downs of political support. The Baker and de Kanter review of research was conducted in order to inform a decision by the federal government on whether to issue such a mandate, reaching the conclusion that "the case for such a mandate [was] weak for two reasons: (a) there is an unacceptably high incidence of harmful results, and (b) the literature revealed examples of successful alternative methods" (Baker, 1987, 353). In addition, "An occasional, inexplicable success is not reason enough to make TBE the law of the land," they wrote, and the federal policy should be to support a variety of program models, encouraging "schools to develop instructional programs that suit the unique needs and circumstances of their students" (Baker & de Kanter, 1983, 51). Such programs, they stressed, could very well include bilingual education, since under some—undetermined—circumstances that appears to be highly effective.

Opponents of bilingual education go further, blaming it for the undeniable lack of academic success of a distressing number of language minority pupils, even though (as noted) the nature of the data on Hispanic underachievement does not enable us to determine how much is attributable to particular forms of instruction. In Hakuta's phrase, the opponents simply charge "Someone promised bacon, but it's not there" (Hakuta, 1986, 219).

Proponents reply that in most cases bilingual education has not been implemented properly, with sufficient additional resources, adequately trained teachers, appropriate materials, and supportive administrators; it has not had a fair trial. They are always able to point to model bilingual programs that have, by all accounts and measures, been a success for the pupils fortunate enough to be assigned to them (Krashen & Biber, 1988). The majority of experts consulted by the General Accounting Office of the American government concluded that the research evidence was "sufficient to support the law's requirement of some degree of use of the native language (to the extent necessary) in the classroom." On the other hand, most "rejected the idea that there was any support for connecting bilingual education, either positively or negatively, to later school outcomes." This led Chester Finn, then Assistant Secretary for Educational Research and Improvement, to protest against an "illogical and scientifically improper assertion that the inconclusive nature of the research argues against" the Department of Education's position that school districts should be permitted to decide whether or not to provide bilingual education rather than, for example, a structured immersion approach. "Especially where the research presents no conclusive evidence as to the superior effectiveness of one method," he wrote, "let us permit diversity, innovation, experimentation and local options to flourish" (General Accounting Office, 1987, 14, 21, 64).

Others believe that, as in the case of supplemental home language instruction, there has been a confusion of purpose about bilingual education that has undermined its effectiveness:

> while school boards favored the transitional approach, many staffs favored the maintenance approach, but without a concern for developing English. . . . At the national level, the people running the show were often those involved in minority politics, and they funded bilingual education projects designed to increase minority political involvement at the local level, all of which politicized the programs and increased local tensions (Charles Stansfield, quoted by Benderson, 1986, 12).

The pilot bilingual reception programs in the Netherlands, far from these political storms, appear to have been moderately successful, perhaps because of the modesty of their goals, though evaluation of their long-term effects tends to go no further than to conclude that "they have had no negative effects (Eldering, 1989); it is difficult to know to what extent a

"Hawthorne effect"—the tendency of all pilot programs to succeed—deserves part of the credit. In the Leiden and Enschede programs, according to early studies, the group receiving bilingual instruction outperformed control groups of immigrant children in oral and written Dutch language proficiency, and language minority participants expressed a more balanced sociocultural orientation and adapted better when transferred into regular classrooms. A crucial element in the success of these programs may have been the close collaboration among teachers—though this took a great deal of hard work, not least because of the language barriers among the teachers (Teunissen, 1986, 152)—and the systematic integration of pupils on a regular basis (Appel, 1988). More recently it has been reported that "children who take part in bilingual education achieve lower than do those in regular education" (Driessen, 1990, 28). As in the United States, it is difficult to judge among the claims of advocates and critics.

To a modest extent, it appears that bilingual schools—not only in Frisian and Dutch but also in immigrant languages and Dutch—are gaining in favor as supplemental home language classes fall further into disfavor, though the momentum of hundreds of foreign teachers not qualified to be employed in regular classrooms favors the continuation of the latter for some years more. An association of bilingual schools has been formed, with Frans Jacob of Enschede as its chairman and support from leading legislators and education officials (Zandbergen, 1993c, 448–449); three elementary schools in the Hague offer bilingual classes for parents who want their children to have a more intensive exposure to their heritage language than is provided through supplemental lessons (Triesscheijn & Geelen, 1993, 438). That was all very well for the primary grades, the city counselor responsible for education in Rotterdam said, but in the upper elementary grades pupils should concentrate on Dutch and take their home language as an elective if they wanted to, without cutting into time for instruction in and through Dutch (Hallensleben, 1992, 319).

SUMMARY

This has been an overview of programmatic responses to the presence of immigrant children in schools, and of the criticisms that have been leveled against them. A few conclusions are sufficiently clear to bear repeating at this point: coordination between special programs and regular classes is very important and generally very inadequate; home language maintenance programs have no clearly positive effects on academic achievement—and perhaps not even on maintenance of the target language; the question of *which* minority language to teach can be very difficult; the home language teacher is most effective if able to serve as a model of successful accommodation to the host society; and the minority language is most useful if taught as a regular academic subject.

Like any overview, this has been from the outside. In Chapter 8 we will look more closely from the inside of the classroom at the characteristics that make particular schooling arrangements successful or unsuccessful, and make suggestions about the elements that should be included in the classroom experience of children for whom the language of the school is not that of their homes.

8 INTEGRATED EDUCATION FOR LANGUAGE MINORITY CHILDREN*

Chapter 7 has provided an overview of the most common responses to linguistic and cultural diversity in schools. Although programs can differ largely in their actual practices, they share a common way of defining and conceptualizing language minority education. Schools have tended to add new programs to the existing program without considering the relationship between the two. Increasingly, however, the negative consequences of such an approach for language minority achievement have become clear and alternative ways to high quality language minority education are being implemented, though still on a small scale.

This chapter proposes a framework for looking at language minority education as an integral part of the school context instead of a separate entity. It presents integrated language minority education as an approach more consistent with what research says about bilingualism, second language learning, and the process of acculturation. Such an approach requires schools to take a whole school approach to language minority education, incorporating principles of effective learning, bilingual education, and bilingualism into all facets of schooling. This approach therefore stands in contrast to current approaches that often allow bilingual teachers, bilingual pupils, and language minority instruction to become marginal within the school.

This chapter consists of four main parts, starting with a description of some of the common characteristics of the approaches described in Chapter 7. This will be followed by a discussion of the framework for integrated language minority education and its theoretical premises regarding school organization, school curriculum, pupil integration, and the role of the first language. Since such a whole school approach to language education will require changes in many aspects of school life, the last section focuses on some of the conditions for successful integration.

---

* This chapter was written by Ester J. de Jong.

Regardless of their focus, current language minority education models have three aspects in common: they tend to concentrate on language issues, they represent a programmatic, "model"-based approach, and they expect a one-way change to occur. Each of these characteristics will be described and discussed below.

The first characteristic is that the approaches tend to focus on language issues, which assumes that language minority school failure can be best explained in linguistic terms. This is too simplistic an approach to the issues around language minority education for at least two reasons (see also Paulston, 1978a). First, it ignores other pupil characteristics, which range from socioeconomic to sociocultural, and learning-style differences that also impact a pupil's school success. The focus on language makes us forget that language minority pupils are not just learners of a second language but children with cognitive, social, affective, and linguistic needs.

> Bilingual learners are normal school students. They can engage, disengage, be committed to, and become alienated from school learning. They can acquire knowledge, reject it, take risks or refuse to do so. Each of them will acquire a use of the languages and language and language varieties around them to the degree it makes educational, political, social and psychological sense to do so (Levine, 1990, 11).

Moreover, the focus on language has often turned language minority programs into language classes, often at the cost of thinking about *education*. Even though bilingual programs in the United States are intended to be less limited in scope, one look at program evaluations makes clear that they too are ultimately evaluated in linguistic terms, more specifically in terms of second language proficiency. A meta-analysis of a number of well-designed evaluation studies by Willig (1985) illustrates the focus on linguistic issues. In her analysis, 73% of the effects considered are language-related. The remaining 27% refer to findings for math (16%), social studies (0.7%), general achievement (5.8%), and attitudes/self-concept (4.7%). This pattern seems representative of the great majority of the bilingual program evaluations. As Milk comments, "[w]hat is often lost sight of . . . is that the ultimate outcome of bilingual education must necessarily be school achievement, and that language development is only part of this desired outcome" (Milk, 1991, 35–36).

A second, and perhaps even more pervasive, characteristic of language minority education is that it has been perceived as a temporary, programmatic solution that is added on to the regular program. These solutions are preferably defined in terms of "models" that are implemented uniformly throughout a particular state or country. Besides the lack of flexibility that results from such an approach, another side effect is that language minority education has become the responsibility of specialists. School staff tend to see responding to the concerns and educational needs of minority groups as something done by somebody else with a specialized assignment. This fact may prevent an effective response to the overall educational needs of language minority pupils as an aspect of school improvement.

A final characteristic, which is closely related to the one above, is that each of these programs aims at fixing the language minority child's "problem" as quickly as possible so that she or he can then be inserted into the mainstream without difficulty (Ruiz, 1988). The *special* program is expected to change the language minority child in such a way that no changes have to be made in the *regular* program. This expectation implies first of all that the adaptation and change will occur in the special program, not in the regular program. Secondly, it is the regular program which sets the norm for the school, and the goals of the special program are considered subordinate to that. The relationship between the programs therefore becomes unidirectional in terms of responsibility for change and adaptation, and unequal in terms of status.

FROM SEPARATE PROGRAMS TO INTEGRATED EDUCATION

A concept that connects the three characteristics of language minority education is that together they marginalize language minority education. Marginalization refers in this case to a situation in which language minority programs operate separately in the periphery of the school and are not considered an integral part of the school context. Such marginalization affects not only the quality and organization of the language minority program but also its staff and the pupils. It narrowly defines the educational needs of language minority pupils in terms of linguistic needs. Moreover, it limits the responsibility of language minority education to specialists and excludes teachers and pupils from the overall school context.

The danger of marginalization is one of the central criticisms directed at the programs discussed in Chapter 7. Assigning pupils to special programs, critics point out, causes marginalization because of the academic, linguistic, and social isolation of language minority pupils. Marginalization can also occur, however, when pupils are assigned to "regular" classrooms and no further adaptations have been made regarding instructional strategies and curriculum content. In this case, marginalization occurs by not including the needs of language minority pupils, resulting in their exclusion from the learning process even through they are physically "integrated."

Marginalization can therefore be the result of overemphasizing or ignoring these differences. Minow has referred to this phenomenon as the "dilemma of difference," which she defines as the question whether "the stigma and unequal treatment encountered by minority groups [are] better remedied by separation or by integration of such groups with others" (Minow, 1985, 157). The choice for either side is not an easy one because "[e]ither remedy risks reinforcing the stigma associated with assigned differences by either ignoring it or focusing on it" (Minow, 1985, 157). Cardenas (1977, 62) pointed out that

> the placement of a child in a strange and alien cultural, linguistic, or economic instructional setting is no less an injustice or a barrier to learning than his placement in a segregated setting (cited by Gonzalez, 1979:26).

It is therefore not surprising that educators and policy makers have started to look for alternative approaches that recognize the specific needs of language minority pupils without making these needs a basis for segregation (Genesee, 1994; Levine, 1990; Natale, 1994). They try to find approaches that make language minority education an integral part of the school context instead of allowing it to become marginalized. These approaches define language minority education as a "whole school" responsibility, requiring a sense of ownership for all pupils, curriculum coordination, and pupil integration.

SCHOOL ORGANIZATION: OWNERSHIP

> Then I get all these other people in the system, administrators and teachers out of the bilingual program who are asking you "How come you're not teaching English?" I have to justify what I am doing. That's hard. . . . All the time you have to defend what you're doing. Some people who, no matter what you say, do not want to listen. This is typical of the majority of society. That's not only here, that's everywhere where there is bilingual. I get these questions all the time from teachers here about the English instruction [Bilingual teacher, USA] (De Jong, 1993a).

Making language minority education an integral part of the general educational context needs to start at the school level by developing a sense of ownership, a sense of shared responsibility for the education of all pupils. This factor has been found to be an important aspect of effective schools for language minority pupils, although few studies have been carried out in this area. These studies stress the fact that making language minority education an integral part of the general education context is a crucial factor for success.

For example, Lucas and others (1990; see also Lucas, 1993) looked at six high schools reported by education officials and principals to be effective with language minority pupils. They identified a schoolwide commitment to biliteracy and multiculturalism as one of the deciding factors for the schools' effectiveness. This commitment was expressed, among other things, by hiring of bilingual staff, by having high expectations for minority pupils, by offering advanced classes in the first language, and by providing counseling services which encouraged pupils to go to college. Positive attitudes towards the pupils' languages and culture were developed by allowing pupils to choose the language they felt most comfortable in for communication, by learning other languages and about other cultures and developing the pupils' first language. The authors conclude that

> this study strongly suggests that the diversity among students cannot simply be ignored. While the schools recognized the importance of integrating language-minority students with mainstream students and providing equally challenging instruction for all students, they did not try to minimize differences among mainstream and Latino students or among Latino students themselves. Approaches to schooling that value linguistic and cultural diversity and that promote cultural pluralism were welcomed and explored whenever possible. . . . Students' languages and cultures were incorporated into school programs as part of the efforts to create a context in which all students felt valuable and capable of academic success (Lucas & others, 1990, 338).

The interdependence between the bilingual program and the rest of the school is also supported by a study by Carter and Chatfield (1986). Carter and Chatfield collected various kinds of data on Lauderbach, an elementary school in California. They found that the effectiveness of the bilingual program was closely associated with the effectiveness of the entire school. Factors that contributed to the success of the school were a shared mission, community support, a safe and orderly environment, opportunities for learning, high expectations, and a good staff morale. Instructional leadership, continual instructional improvement, and the promotion of a positive climate promoted pupil outcomes. Carter and Chatfield point out that the relationship between the bilingual program and other aspects of the school organization is a complex and not a linear one. The projects implemented in the bilingual program affected the entire school and vice versa, the effectiveness of the entire school impacted the policies at the bilingual program level.

> Lauderbach is an effective school with an effective bilingual program. The bilingual program is not a separate part of the school but rather participates in, partakes of, *and contributes to* the positive student and educational climate outcomes (italics in the original; Carter & Chatfield, 1986, 226).

Woods and Grudgeon, looking at successful multiracial schools in Britain also identified an integrated approach to multiculturalism as a recurring theme. More specifically, they state that "a democratic regime emphasizing co-operation, collaboration, and participation is more suited to their advancement [of multicultural values] than an authoritarian one featuring dictatism [sic], hierarchy, competition, and individualism" (Woods & Grudgeon, 1990, 323).

In contrast, a lack of ownership tends to give nonspecialists the excuse not to deal with language minority pupils and reinforces the notion that language minority pupils have a temporary "problem" that a program can fix.

> If it's an Hispanic kid, many times, they show up at the office and they speak Spanish, so [they] send them to [our office]. It may have nothing to do with us. It's the attitude, we're responsible for the entire community. There's different degrees of ownership among mainstream staff in terms of owning the Hispanic community, feeling that they are responsible for them in the same way that they are responsible for the rest of the population [Bilingual Community Outreach Person, USA] (De Jong, 1993a).

> It demobilizes the other teachers . . . ; because a "specialist" is concerned with these problems, the non-specialists feel relieved of them and have a tendency not to adapt their practices to the presence of these pupils and their specific [needs and strengths] (Berque, 1985, 11).

> People deal with the kids because they're here. People deal with the program because it's the law. And they would rather not have the kids or the program to deal with [Bilingual Community Outreach Person, USA] (De Jong, 1993a).

In addition, adaptation to the needs of language minority pupils is expected to be made exclusively by the specialists. As a result, strategies that support the learning of language minority pupils are restricted to the second language classroom, or the bilingual program. Knowledge of instructional techniques to address the academic and linguistic needs and/or of pupils' cultural background are often not considered part of the regular education program. As one curriculum coordinator commented, the bilingual program is designed

> to include multicultural themes, particularly units around the Dominican Republic and Puerto Rico and that kind of thing. And I see that done more in [the bilingual program]. Right now we haven't really shared that with the mainstream [Bilingual curriculum coordinator, USA] (De Jong, 1993a).

Too often, expectations for language minority pupils are lowered in the regular program because teachers are unprepared to identify and meet the needs of language minority pupils. In a study in Birmingham, United Kingdom, it was found that

> lower standards and expectations were inevitable with a multiracial intake, and, although they tried to make schools a pleasant environment, [they] did not expect high achievement. This, of course, was the antithesis of the expectations and understandings of minority parents as to what schools were all about (Tomlinson, 1984, 152).

Similarly, Becker found in the United States that "teachers' attitudes and the resulting low expectations they had for Portuguese pupil achievement identified and separated the Portuguese as a distinct ethnic group within the high school" (Becker, 1990, 51). The recognition of these weaknesses often makes specialists reluctant to move their pupils out of the special program into the "regular" program.

A lack of shared mission may also result in teachers not communicating about each others' work, and participating in shared decision-making. This, in turn, reinforces the separate nature of language minority education in the school.

> We never had anybody who provided us with information, unfortunately, as to what we were supposed to be teaching. . . . Also, when I started there were so few materials that I couldn't even do what they

[i.e. the mainstream teachers] were doing even if I wanted to. A lot of stuff I had to find myself [Bilingual curriculum coordinator, USA] (De Jong, 1993a).

We don't really have enough representation. It is very hard for us too, to influence the curriculum because usually at each grade level there are five or six teachers and only one being a bilingual staff person. I felt for two years personally that a lot of what I said was not listened to. In fact, let's put it this way, there were five of them and one of me. . . . And I felt a lot of times that the conversation and the decision-making was dominated by the mainstream people that were on these committees. I was one-sixth of the committee. They all knew each other, they didn't know me [Bilingual curriculum coordinator, USA] (De Jong, 1993a).

The evidence above stresses the importance of a whole school approach to language minority education. A sense of ownership for all pupils by the staff (specialists and nonspecialists) is necessary to allow the sharing of experience and expertise and to increase the overall understanding of language minority pupils' needs. This, in turn, will allow for more open communication channels, for making language minority pupils visible within the school context in a positive way, and for maintaining high expectations for all pupils.

CURRICULUM COORDINATION

I: Do you have any idea what's going on in the other [monolingual] first grade?
T: Not about curriculum at all, none at all. I can't tell you what they're doing. Once, when we meet [in grade level meetings], we ask "is there anything you want to share with the others" . . . but nothing happened [Bilingual teacher, USA] (De Jong, 1993a).

I don't think that the teachers know from one grade to the other what skills are being taught and what is expected from the children from one grade to another [Bilingual teacher, USA] (De Jong, 1993a).

It is important to offer pupils a coherent curriculum in order to provide an opportunity for continuous cognitive and linguistic development. The existence of a special program does not preclude such continuous development but increases the need for collaboration and coordination of curriculum content as well as instruction. Only then will pupils be enabled to continue their academic development without significant developmental interruption when they move from one program to the other.

In reality, the existence of a "dual system" may significantly undermine such continuity. How this happens is best illustrated by looking at the process of "mainstreaming." Mainstreaming is the procedure which determines that a language minority pupil is ready to leave the special program and transfers him or her permanently into the regular program. It constitutes a part of all language minority programs, although it plays a more prominent role when pupils have been assigned to special programs for a longer period of time, such as a bilingual program, or a second language reception class. Given the segregated nature of such programs, mainstreaming often constitutes the only formal link between a language minority program and a mainstream program. A closer look at this process provides an important understanding of the educational discontinuities that language minority pupils are confronted with. This section will first look at the assumptions that mainstreaming makes about language minority pupils and their abilities. Then, the lack of *true* mainstreaming as a result of the lack of coordination among teachers and curriculum content will be discussed.

Mainstreaming makes certain assumptions about the language minority pupil. First, the pupil is expected to have second language skills sufficient to participate effectively in a regular classroom. Much of the debate about assessment and exit criteria has centered around what kinds of language skills would be necessary for such participation (Cummins, 1984a). However, meaningful and full participation requires more than just second language skills. Mainstreaming also assumes that bilingual pupils have had access to a similar knowledge base as pupils in the regular education context. This knowledge base includes academic knowledge in terms of subject matter (such as certain science concepts) as well as social and cultural knowledge (such as classroom expectations, being able to work independently, and knowing how to interact appropriately with others).

Given these assumptions, it is clear that lack of integration and curriculum coordination can undermine successful mainstreaming. First and foremost, language minority pupils are not necessarily exposed to the same materials and content matter as pupils in the "regular" program. In fact, given the different nature of the two programs, this exposure is very unlikely. Teachers comment frequently about language minority content differences:

> As far as the other subjects are concerned in the preparatory classes, the preparatory teacher told me that she will not start geography until they have come a long way in Swedish first. Then she will discuss

terms which can be found frequently in geography books, such as river, mountain, climate; and maps, the parts of the world. For biology, she might discuss things like the body parts, flowers, animals. Religion is discussed when it comes up, not as a subject. Then they will compare what different cultures do [Observation notes, Sweden] (De Jong, 1993b).

Everybody doesn't work with the same theme. That would be nice if we did it. [We all did an] apple unit in September. But then one wants to do dinosaurs, the other oceans. It would be nice to do the same theme. All the [bilingual] kids see the [other class's project] and say "O, I like dinosaurs. I would like to do dinosaurs" [Bilingual teacher, USA] (De Jong, 1993a).

These examples illustrate how pupils are confronted with gaps in the curriculum content as a result of the separateness and the linguistic focus of language minority programs. Imagine a fourth-grade pupil in the preparatory class in the first example who will be mainstreamed after one year of intensive Swedish as a Second Language instruction but little content instruction. How will she gain access to the concepts in science or geography which have been built up over the past five years in the regular classroom? Gaining access to the curriculum is not a matter of acquiring the second language alone.

The dinosaur example above shows another dimension of the lack of curriculum coordination. Here, differences among pupils are emphasized in such a way that it may result in language minority pupils feeling somehow inferior because they are not doing the same thing as the pupils in the regular classroom. Being aware of the norm set in the regular classroom and reinforced by the lower status of the language minority program, this may lead to a stigmatization of language minority pupils' work.

Moreover, the lack of coordination does not give the language minority pupil the opportunity to be exposed to the regular classroom and to gain familiarity with the teacher, classroom expectations, and the language majority pupils. This has two consequences. First, not knowing the "regular" classroom has been reported to result in a fear and reluctance to go into the regular classroom. Once mainstreamed, pupils will be uncomfortable in the regular classroom, which will naturally affect their interactions with peers and teachers.

Anne also mentioned that generally the students didn't want to leave the preparatory classes because they felt so comfortable. It's a luxury, she said, small groups [Director of home language classes, Sweden] (De Jong, 1993b).

... the preparatory classes as a small group is like a family and very good for the students as a first step. But then they need to broaden their horizons and move out. They are often afraid to do so . . . but they need to learn [Preparatory teacher, Sweden] (De Jong, 1993b).

Second, mainstreamed pupils are often required to make an important leap from their program to the regular program because of differences in instructional style. This is a direct result of the division of responsibility between regular and specialist teachers. The secure environment of the special program that has been adapted linguistically, and sometimes culturally, to the needs of the language minority child is rarely repeated in the mainstream class. In addition, in some programs pupils move from a small group to a large group setting. Pupils are therefore confronted with a significant change in the kind of classroom they are in. Often this means that they have to make adjustments in the regular classrooms which are difficult and may take time. Often, the regular teachers get frustrated, however, and lower their expectations.

The assumption is that they're only second language learners, they don't know the language, you can't demand much from them. . . . The attitude of the Swedish teachers is that if they don't speak Swedish, they're stupid [Preparatory teacher, Sweden] (De Jong, 1993b).

One can never bring them up to the same level, though, through the preparatory classes. Only the very smart ones can. There will always be a difference [Preparatory teacher, Sweden] (De Jong, 1993b).

Mainstreaming is not just a matter of matching curriculum content and instructional strategies. The actual process of mainstreaming involves the regular and the bilingual teacher and administrative decisions. The reality of mainstreaming reflects again the exclusion of language minority education, often at expense of the children. For example, at the organizational level, administrators often do not take mainstreaming into consideration and they forget to count bilingual pupils as part of both programs as they are putting classes together. As a result, regular classrooms may not have seats available for language minority pupils at the appropriate grade level once they are ready to be mainstreamed. This undermines the possibility for (part-time) mainstreaming and it may even lead to holding the bilingual pupil back in the program.

Asked whether they did any partial mainstreaming, the Hispanic bilingual teacher responded "We stopped because we break the rule of

28 students [maximum number of students allowed in the regular classroom]" [Bilingual teacher, USA] (De Jong, 1993a).

... we talked about locked-in-locked-out, about the opportunities the children have to go into a partial mainstream situation. I found those very lacking. I tried to set up a partial mainstream situation for a lot of the kids and was told I couldn't do it because there were no seats [Bilingual curriculum coordinator, USA] (De Jong, 1993a).

The mainstreaming process is often hard. Often the classes are full and then the students are stuck in the preparatory classes. With some teachers there are tensions around the mainstreaming process—especially the ones who aren't good teachers [Preparatory class teacher, Sweden] (De Jong, 1993b).

Even when bilingual pupils do have a physical space in the regular classroom, as was the case in some schools in Sweden, the situation may be far from ideal:

An issue is also . . . that although the teachers have students on their class list, they don't see them until later in the year, and therefore don't have them in their minds, they don't feel responsible [Preparatory class teacher, Sweden] (De Jong, 1993b).

This is also illustrated by the following situation in a regular classroom where a Jordanian is mainstreamed part-time for math.

9:00 The Jordanian girl and I leave the preparatory classroom and cross the school yard to go to the regular class for a math lesson. When we arrive, they are still doing language arts. The Jordanian girl and I sit down in the back of the classroom at a separate table. She is the only one at the set of four tables. She asks a student behind her something (about writing something down) but gets no response. She decides to continue working on her math, but stops several times to look around.

9:20 The other students get out their math books and work independently. . . . The math teacher looks at what she's doing; they exchange a few sentences. Towards the end of the class she calls the Swedish teacher and tells him she's ready with the page. He asks her something about copying it down. She first doesn't understand it, he repeats it. Then she understands and says yes. The teacher gets some paper for her to copy down her math.

9:40 We leave the classroom to go back to the preparatory class [Observation Sweden] (De Jong, 1993b).

In the example above, the Jordanian girl had minimal contact with the teacher, hardly any academic contact with peers, and in fact lost a lot of time-on-task because she had to move from one classroom to the other and because the teacher did not start the math lesson until 20 minutes later. The example illustrates some of the logistical and classroom issues which arise around mainstreaming, ranging from dealing with physical distance among classrooms to synchronizing instructional time and making the bilingual pupil part of the regular classroom. It shows that without coordination between the special program and the regular classroom, the quality of instruction of language minority pupils may be negatively impacted.

The analysis of the mainstreaming process shows how a language minority child is easily perceived as belonging either to the special program or the regular program but never to both. This reflects the lack of ownership discussed in the section above. The lack of shared responsibility and the subsequent lack of curriculum coordination significantly affect language minority pupils' learning environment. Curriculum coordination, in terms of academic and social expectations, is necessary to allow language minority pupils to develop cognitively and linguistically in a continuous way.

The Need for Pupil Integration

But there was very little integration. And you could see that too, the older ones especially. There was a lot of rivalry, a lot of bad blood between the fourth and the fifth graders. The older they got, the more I saw it at least at [school]. . . . they were identifying each other by their ethnic group and their language and there was very little integration. And it was tough even to get them together to go down to the specialist because there was the "Spanish" line and the "English" line. And they would fight on who would go first. I mean they would be together, but they would be separate [Bilingual curriculum coordinator, USA] (De Jong, 1993a).

Another aspect of an integrative approach to language minority education is the integration of pupils. It has been noted that language minority pupils who attend special programs tend to be and remain segregated from their peers (Meier & Stewart, 1991, 185). This, in turn, may negatively affect their academic achievement. Looking at educational attainment for Hispanic pupils, Meier & Stewart (1991, 144) find that "the segregation of Hispanic pupils in bilingual classes has an eventual negative effect on their future educational performance. If bilingual classes were integrated . . . we would not expect to find this relationship."

Pupil integration specifically focuses on the need to bring minority and majority pupils together in academic and social contexts. It has been primarily discussed in terms of its benefits for second language learning and acculturation. It is important to consider both factors in relationship to the role of the first language and culture of pupils. The next section will illustrate the importance of balancing the emphasis on the majority language and culture with the pupils' own language and culture. Grosjean (1989, 3) observes that "the bilingual is NOT the sum of two complete or incomplete monolinguals; rather, he or she has a unique and specific linguistic configuration." This recognition requires schools to incorporate both languages and cultures when trying to create a challenging learning environment for language minority pupils.

This section will first deal with the importance of integration for gaining access to the second language and then with the issue of becoming part of the majority culture.

Integration for Second Language Learning

> I think the only exposure the children have to English is when they go to their specialist classes, phys ed, art, music; and occasionally if they group the two classes [Bilingual teacher, USA] (De Jong, 1993a).

Exposure to the language is a necessary condition for learning the second language. The debate on second language acquisition has evolved around the quantity and the quality of the exposure needed and other factors that may influence becoming proficient in a second language. It is beyond the scope of this chapter to address in detail the process of second language acquisition and the factors that influence that process. The reader is referred to overviews of second language research and theories, such as Bialystok and Hakuta (1994), Baker (1993b), Larsen-Freeman & Long (1991), and Spolsky (1989).

The quantity of input is significantly related to the speed of second language acquisition. Exposure to the language is important because learners have to be able to hear the language being used in different contexts, learning to distinguish sounds and words, figuring out the meaning of utterances in certain social settings and having extensive opportunities to use the language (Snow, 1993; Wong Fillmore, 1989a). However, some researchers report no direct relationship between the amount of time spent in the second language and language proficiency (Swain, 1981). Wong Fillmore (1985a, 18) observes that despite extensive exposure to the second language, many limited English proficient pupils do not learn English very well. She suggests that the variability in language proficiency can be explained by considering the way the language is being presented to the language learner. This shifts the debate to the quality of the language that second language learners are exposed to.

Researchers have pointed out that exposure without comprehending some of what is being said will not be effective. The language input provided should instead build on the knowledge learners already have. This condition is known as the input hypothesis, which states that "[w]e acquire . . . only when we understand language that contains structure that is 'a little beyond' where we are now" (Krashen, 1982, 21). This knowledge will be comprised of strategies developed while learning the first language as well as knowledge about the second language itself.

There are several ways to provide second language learners with input that is comprehensible. For example, teachers can embed the language use in familiar contexts and clearly demonstrate ideas, using a variety of materials (Wong Fillmore, 1985a). Another way is to modify actual language use. Adults have been noted to adapt their language use to second language learners, similar to what parents do for small children (see R. Ellis, 1985, for an overview). Effective second language teachers, for example, use simpler structures, show a repeated use of same sentence patterns or routines, and use paraphrases for variation (Wong Fillmore, 1985a, 50).

Learners are not just passive recipients of modified input, however. The process of making modifications can be enhanced when it is the learner himself or herself who indicates that there is a breakdown in the communication due to a lack of understanding. Researchers such as Long (1983) and Pica (1992; 1994) claim that second language learners will gain more effective access to the second language as they try to actively engage in meaningful communication with native speakers. Within this context, second language learning is seen as the "outcome of learners' requests for clarification and indications of misunderstanding through a process which has come to be labelled 'negotiation'" (Pica, 1991, 191).

The negotiation for meaning can make the learning context more meaningful to the second language learner, if the purpose of the interaction is real communication. As with all learning, second language acquisition will be more effective when it is embedded within a context that is meaningful to the learner, that builds on what the learner already knows and that provides functional purposes for language use (Gersten & Woodward, 1994; Faltis, 1993) More important, though, is the fact that in interaction the impetus for modified input is with the learner. The learner indicates when she or he does not understand what is being said and the accommodations made as a result of this feedback are therefore more useful and can be targeted to the level of the learners' second language proficiency (Wong Fillmore, 1991a). These two factors (natural communication and learner-initiated modifications) contribute to the active engagement of the learner that "charges the input and allows it to penetrate deeply" in memory (Stevick 1971 quoted in Varonis and Gass, 1984, 82).

Swain (1985) has pointed out that negotiation for meaning should not only occur for comprehension. The same process can occur for language production, where learners learn to modify their output in order to communicate precisely what they want to say.

> The opportunity to engage in meaningful oral exchanges (in the classroom or in the community) is a necessary component in second language acquisition. In conveying meaning, a person learns about the structure and form of a language (Baker, 1993b, 88).

Within this framework, research has found that peer interactions can be more supportive of second language learning than adult-child interactions. Since adults tend to dominate interactions with children and direct the conversation, children often do not get the opportunity to interact and use the language themselves. Thus, although adult-child interactions may be good opportunities for modified input, they often do not provide the second language learner with opportunities to engage in meaningful negotiation.

To summarize, second language learning is enhanced when learning opportunities are created in contexts which have been adjusted to accommodate second language learner's needs.

> Those situations that promote frequent contacts are the best, especially if the contacts last long enough to give learners ample opportunity to observe people using the language for a variety of communicative purposes. Those which also permit learners to engage in the frequent use of the language with speakers are even better (Wong Fillmore, 1991a, 54).

Access to the second language can be enhanced when second language learners negotiate for meaning with others (especially peers), and when language use is contextualized within a natural communication context (Faltis, 1993). Based on the above, Wong Fillmore proposes that three ingredients are therefore necessary for successful second language learning, "the learners themselves, the speakers of the target language who provide the learners with the input they need, and the social setting in which learning takes place" (Wong Fillmore, 1989b, 316).

In her model, Wong Fillmore stresses the importance of interaction for language learning. This is a key issue for bilingual programs or other programs that separate language minority pupils from language majority pupils for the purpose of learning a second language. Zanger (1987; cited in Zanger, 1991) found that the social isolation of Vietnamese pupils negatively affected their English literacy skills. Their participation in a bilingual program was combined with avoiding English-speaking pupils, which hampered their learning of the second language. Snow points out that

> it seems paradoxical to try to teach children English by isolating them from the large numbers of native English speakers available in the mainstream classes of their schools (Snow, 1990, 61).

For the purposes of an integrated approach the question of interaction is important. What is the role of native speakers in acquiring the second language? Snow's comment suggest that separate programs are limited in the diversity of resources they can provide for second language learners as the teacher becomes the only target language model. Wong Fillmore (1992) warns therefore that this situation requires well-developed second language skills in bilingual teachers. The question is whether even this requirement will provide language minority pupils with adequate models and optimal resources for language learning. Garcia's conclusion of the literature seems to suggest the contrary:

> recent theoretical positions regarding second language acquisition propose that through natural conversations the learner receives the necessary input and structures which promote second language acquisition. This finding suggests that in schooling situations highly segregated Chicano classrooms may significantly limit L2 acquisition while L1–L2 integrated classrooms will promote L2 acquisition (Garcia, 1991, 104).

Bringing language minority speakers and native speakers of the target language together will create more and better opportunities for second language learning. If the classroom is organized well, pupils will engage in more negotiation and practice the language more. Two sources of evidence support this statement. On the one hand, it appears that language skills are developed only to a certain extent when there are only second language learners (referred to as "fossilization"). On the other hand, the presence of native speakers creates a natural context for second language use. Both arguments will be discussed below.

The first argument in favor of the presence of native speakers comes from immersion programs in Canada. In these programs, English-speaking pupils receive initial instruction in French only, with English being introduced later. There are no native speakers of the language in the classroom. The results of these programs have been impressive for promoting bilingualism (Genesee, 1987). However, it has also been noted that, first, the second language proficiency of pupils in these programs, although advanced, is characterized by a less complex grammar, less redundancy in speaking, and a lack of idiomatic expressions. In addition, research has found that pupils' second language proficiency in immersion programs tends to level off in the middle elementary grades, i.e., pupils seem to develop the second language only up to a certain level of proficiency and not beyond (Genesee, 1991; Swain, 1985).

The explanations for these findings can partially be attributed to the limitations of classroom instruction and the limited range of language functions that teachers use. Another explanation is that there are no interactions with native speakers in immersion classes (Genesee, 1991). Consequently, there are no opportunities to listen and interact with more natural models of language use that for example, would have more idiomatic expressions.

> Immersion students, and foreign language students in general, have difficulty in producing native-like speech in the second language. Part of this difficulty stems from an absence of the opportunity to talk with fluent speakers in the language they are learning (Lindholm, 1990, 98).

What is the difference between an integrated setting with majority speakers and a multilingual setting where all speakers are second language learners? Varonis and Gass (1984) found, for example, that more negotiation took place when pupils of different language backgrounds are placed together with varying abilities in language proficiency than when pupils had similar language backgrounds. The pupils in the multilingual setting had to use the second language to negotiate and interact since they had no other common language. This accounts for more negotiations. Creating a multilingual situation where all pupils are second language learners will not result in the same second language attainment as an integrated situation, however (Wong Fillmore, 1992). Although pupils who come from different linguistic backgrounds may use the second language more, this setting is still less optimal than an integrated setting. Within a setting with only second language learners, the likelihood is that pupils will develop their second language according to the not yet nativelike language model of their peers and not according to the native speaker's model. In other words, chances are that pupils will use this non-native second language model with each other without refining their own language skills. Wong Fillmore comments, "[s]econd language learners in such situations are indeed surrounded by people who speak English, but these are speakers of imperfect English" (Wong Fillmore, 1992,47). More research is needed to determine the ultimate consequences of such a setting.[1]

The second argument in favor of integrating language majority and language minority pupils for the purpose of second language learning is that it will stimulate language learners to practice and use the language in meaningful context. Brisk (1991) comments that

> Languages are learned and maintained because there is a real need to use them, rather than because they are a curricular requirement. Acquisition of English as a second language is not forced but a natural process driven by the presence of English speakers (Brisk, 1991, 122).

Strong (1983) suggests that "peer tutoring, when English learners have to explain in English something they know to an English speaker, may enhance language learning" (cited in August, 1987, 719; see also Hester, 1984). Hale & Burdar (1970) found that social contact with English speakers contributed more to second language learning in adolescents than formal English as a Second Language classes without such interaction. These findings support the importance of creating opportunities to interact with majority language peers.

From the discussion above it becomes clear that pupils need access to good language models. Integrated language minority education creates an optimal learning environment in which second language learners are exposed to modified input and in which language can be used in meaningful contexts with native speakers (McLaughlin, 1985, 162). A setting which segregates pupils, on the other hand, generally limits the available language models to the teacher.

Segregation denies them access to fluent English-speaking models other than their teacher and, therefore, fails to capitalize on an important source of help available (Handscombe, 1989, 10).

The advantage of an integrated setting is that it is able to provide both teacher and peer input. It creates a situation where second language learners are motivated to use the second language because "there is an authentic need on the part of the second language student to use the second language with such a partner" (Johnson, 1994, 197).

In its simplest form, the argument for such a solution is that since students need varied and multiple opportunities for both hearing and using language in meaningful situations, "many mouths (students' models) are better than one (the teacher's)" (Enright and Gomez, 1985, 6).

ACCULTURATION AND SOCIAL INTEGRATION

Well, they don't play together real well on the playground at the [school] because they don't get along that well. They don't have much chance to get to know each other [Bilingual teacher, USA] (De Jong, 1993a).

There is no integration between the Hispanic kids and American kids and I don't know whether that's because of the [bilingual] program, they're in different classrooms; there are a lot of issues [Bilingual teacher, USA] (De Jong, 1993a).

The Swedish children get angry at them because they can't understand what they're saying [Bilingual teacher, Sweden] (De Jong, 1993b).

These observations illustrate the social isolation of language minority and language majority pupils from each other. Partially, social isolation can be attributed to the segregated nature of some programs and/or the lack of classroom adaptation to a multicultural environment. On the other hand, friendship patterns seem to form themselves along ethnic lines from an early age onwards (Davey & Mullin, 1982). Tomlinson (1983, 129) concludes for the situation in Britain that

pupils in multiethnic schools do not appear to form inter-ethnic friendships to any great extent, being "racially aware" and preferring their own groups from an early age, becoming even more ethnocentric at the secondary level (cited in Woods & Grudgeon, 1990, 318).

Similar findings have been reported for the United States, although few studies have been carried out with language minority pupils. An exception is a study by Howes & Wu (1990) that looked at the patterns of peer interaction, social status, and reciprocated friendships. Their setting was unusual in that it was a demonstration school at a university with a socioeconomically and ethnically diverse pupil population. Within this context they found that the majority of the time children were engaged in positive social interaction with peers (72 percent of the observations) from different ethnic backgrounds. They also found that Euro-American children were less likely to attempt to enter cross-ethnic peer groups than Asian-American children and less likely to have cross-ethnic friends than the minority children (Howes & Wu, 1990, 539–540).

Jelinek & Brittan (1975) suggest that there are several possible barriers for inter-ethnic friendships, including pupil characteristics (language proficiency, length of stay in the country), home socialization patterns, and school characteristics (values and attitudes transmitted; opportunities to form friendships). Regarding the school environment, Davey and Mullin indicate that the proportion of majority and minority children may affect interaction patterns. Larger groups of minority students may encourage more within-group interactions and less intergroup interactions (Moldenhawer, 1992).

The immediate consequences of social isolation for second language learning opportunities have already been discussed in the previous section. The lack of interaction with speakers of the majority language may limit opportunities for natural and meaningful interactions in that language. In addition, it may affect the motivation to learn a second language. Motivation and attitudes have been found to significantly influence second language achievement (Gardner, 1985). Moreover, Schumann (1976) found that "Chicano children are more motivated to learn a second language if they do not perceive this learning process as alienation from their own culture" (cited in Garcia, 1991, 104).

The lack of interaction between minority and majority pupils also has consequences, however, for the opportunity for minority pupils to learn to function appropriately in two cultures, and to develop a sense of security within their own group as well as in the dominant group. As will be pointed out in this section, such lack of interaction also affects language majority children.

Interacting with members of the new culture can increase the opportunity to learn about the new culture and may avoid the development of negative attitudes and stereotypes. There is also a need for language majority pupils to learn how to interact with peers from diverse backgrounds. For them, integration is also an important condition to function successfully in a diverse society. As Parrenas & Parrenas point out, modern societies have developed in such a way that

> Students of today must learn to communicate and work well with others within the full range of social situations, especially within situations involving fluid social structures, human diversity, and interdependence (Parrenas & Parrenas, 1993, 186).

One way to achieve these goals is by integrating majority and minority pupils. Research with racial desegregation has found important long-terms gains for pupils, academically as well as socially (Braddock et al., 1984). One justification for the efforts to achieve desegregation is the "contact hypothesis," originally formulated by Allport (1954). This thesis states that in an integrated school, "everyday experiences with children of different ethnic backgrounds will increase the probability that cross-ethnic peers will be viewed as individuals rather than members of a stereotyped group" (Howes & Wu, 1990). Allport made clear that these results would be obtained only under very specific circumstances, which will be discussed in more detail in the next section. The lack of integration can therefore become a barrier to the process of learning about and functioning in the new culture.

Phinney (1991), in an overview of the relationship between ethnic identity and self-esteem, concludes that being acculturated is an important condition for psychological well-being and the ability to function in the mainstream. She finds that "[g]ood adjustment among minority group members is likely to be a factor of one's relationship to both the ethnic group and to the mainstream" (Phinney, 1991, 203). She compares different types of adaptation: marginalization, separation, assimilation, and biculturalism as defined by Berry and others (1987).

She concludes that marginalization is the least adaptive mode, as it results in minority pupils not identifying with either their own or the majority group. As an example she presents the situation of Native Americans, who as a result of lacking a clear identity, may suffer from feelings of hopelessness, alcoholism, and suicide (Berlin, 1987; cited in Phinney, 1991).

Efforts of the pupils to assimilate voluntarily may have the same result as marginalization, due to majority pupils' reactions towards language minority pupils who wish to become part of the majority group. Attempts at assimilation "may be met with prejudice and discrimination," leading to a rejection of the language minority pupil (Phinney, 1991, 204). Often, these students have also been rejected by their own group, reinforcing the marginalization process. Becker found such interaction patterns in the United States, where newly arrived Portuguese-speaking pupils were not accepted by either the established Portuguese-speaking pupils from Portugal or by the Anglo pupils. In this case the persistent labeling of teachers reinforced the differences among the groups.

> Total assimilation into the Anglo group was, however, prevented by the Anglo students' unwillingness to accept the Portuguese, and by the teachers' continued labelling of the early arrivals as Portuguese (Becker, 1990, 53).

Jelinek & Brittan (1975) found a significant discrepancy between desired friendships and actual friendships for the different ethnic groups involved in their study. In other words, actual friendship patterns did not reflect the friends the children wanted to have. This may have been because, even though the minority pupils wanted to assimilate, the majority pupils rejected them.

Separation from the majority and withdrawal within the own group may create more opportunities for ethnic identity development (for example, in the separate schools as discussed in Chapter 6). However, this may not adequately prepare pupils for a diverse society. Szapocznik & Kurtines (1980) suggest that "ethnic group members who remain monocultural may suffer adjustment problems due to their failure to learn to adapt to the mainstream" (cited in Phinney, 1991, 204).

Lastly, Phinney discusses an integrated identity which "involves a combined identification with one's own ethnic group and with mainstream culture" (Phinney, 1991, 204). There is some evidence that such an integrated, bicultural identity is most beneficial for language minority pupils. For example, Phinney (1991) discusses a study by Lang, Munoz, Bernal, & Sorenson (1982) who found that a bicultural orientation was related to a better psychological adjustment than either monoculturalism or assimilation. Similarly, Phinney and colleagues (1990) looked at high school and college pupils from different ethnic backgrounds and found "small but significant correlations between self-esteem[2] and endorsement of integration attitudes, whereas assimilation attitudes were negatively related to self-esteem, and separation attitudes were unrelated" (cited in Phinney, 1991, 205).

As with the process of second language learning, it can be argued that acculturation will best occur through contact and positive interactions with both the child's own ethnic group and with majority group members. Although separate programs may be able to develop the ethnic identity to a certain extent, it will be harder to introduce the pupils to the majority culture and values because the programs do not allow for interactions among pupils. Philips cautions against implementing programs that specifically adapt curriculum and instruction to the cultural background of the pupils because doing so may not adequately prepare language minority pupils for "the mainstream."

> The teachers who make these adjustments, and not all do, are sensitive to the inclinations of their students and want to teach them through means to which they most readily adapt. However, by doing so they are avoiding teaching the Indian children precisely in the contexts in which they are least able but most need to learn if they are "to do well in school" (Philips, 1972, 383).

This was one of the findings in a study by Brisk (1993) who interviewed successful bilingual adults about their experiences as children in bilingual programs. Subjects in the study felt that one of the drawbacks of the bilingual program was that it did not prepare them for dealing with the American culture.

> Students felt that although the bilingual program had been excellent in preparing them academically for college, they were not prepared to deal socially with their American peers. This problem is related to the school's structure as a whole. There was minimal integration between the bilingual and mainstream programs. . . . Both students and teachers did not feel accepted by the principal or their English-speaking peers (Brisk, 1993, 51).

Pupils in the study experienced difficulties in relating to their American peers and teachers. As one pupil recalls, "I had friends . . . that didn't dare walk into a monolingual class because they were scared and embarrassed. And if they had an accent it was worse" (Brisk, 1993, 52). It seems that such experiences are the result of an unfamiliarity of both groups with each other and a lack of time to adjust to each other's ways of interacting. Paulston argues,

> Beyond a superficial level, culture learning entails firsthand exposure to the members of the C2 [second culture], and it follows . . . that the

children must have access to Anglo teachers, if they are to learn the rules of mainstream culture. It will be the students' choice what aspects, if any, of mainstream culture they care to incorporate into their bicultural make-up, and no school or curriculum can dictate that choice. But to deny them the opportunity of choice I find reprehensible (Paulston, 1978b, 379).

An integrated setting, if properly implemented, can facilitate such positive contact among members of different cultures.

The findings above point to the importance of a dimension often left unaddressed in the literature. Successful acculturation depends on the attitudes and roles of the language majority students, not just on those of the minority students. Lindholm notes that

the achievement of language minority pupils is affected not only by the status perception of teachers but also by the status perceptions of majority peers. Allowing only unplanned or incidental contact between minority and majority students may only reinforce negative expectations (Lindholm, 1990, 101).

Findings regarding friendship patterns and attitude changes find that ethnic minority pupils are more likely to develop more positive attitudes and show more openness towards pupils from other groups. Anglo children, on the other hand, seem to have the tendency to be more ethnocentric and less willing to make friendships across ethnic lines, depending on the student body. Howes and Wu found that Euro-American children were less likely to attempt to enter cross-ethnic peer groups than Asian-American children, and were less likely to have cross-ethnic friends than the minority children (Howes & Wu, 1990, 539–540). Davey and Mullin found that "when white children are in the majority in a particular school there is a tendency for them to be less ethnocentric, but when either of the minority groups is highly represented in a school they tend to be more ethnocentric" (Davey & Mullin, 1982, 88).

If such attitudes and relationships among ethnic groups are maintained, this will negatively impact the linguistic minority pupils. Stereotypes and negative attitudes may decrease the willingness and ability of language majority students to be good role models, and to interact with their peers in ways that are effective for language learning and academic growth (Wong Fillmore, 1976; 1991a). The lack of majority pupils' exposure to different languages and cultures can create a lack of sensitivity and understanding, and an intolerance for hearing other languages. This will, in turn, negatively impact their relations with pupils from linguistically and culturally different backgrounds (Brisk, 1993).

The Role of the Home Language

Access to the second language and to the majority culture, as we have seen, will be promoted by exposing minority pupils to the language, through positive experiences, and to members of the culture itself. Where does this leave the pupils' first language and the role of the minority culture? Characteristically, the debate on this issue has been cast in either/or terms. Opponents of bilingual programs contend that these programs focus too much on the first language, decreasing opportunities for second language learning (Porter, 1990). Proponents of bilingual education argue that a singular emphasis on the second language diminishes the pupils' linguistic and cultural resources, returning to the decades of forced assimilation. Framing the debate in these terms excludes thinking about alternatives that are inclusive of different languages (and cultures) while stressing integration.

The second language learning process and the process of acculturation cannot be regarded in isolation from the first language and the pupil's own culture. At the same time, schools that allow for the development of the first language and create culturally sensitive learning environments have to consider the bridge with the second language and the majority culture. The previous section has critically examined the need for the latter. Rather than a disadvantage, the pupils' first language resources provide an important basis for second language learning, academic learning in general, and successful acculturation. Properly implemented,

> bilingual education is not just a quick route to English proficiency, but something much more profound: it is an educational alternative which provides the strongest route to academic achievement through L1 (a non-English language) as a means for attaining the paramount long-term goal of academic achievement in L2 (English) (Milk, 1993, 199).

Various arguments in favor of developing the first language have been put forward (Chapter 5). Often these arguments have included sociocultural aspects in addition to the role of language. Some of these arguments emphasize that using the first language in schools increases the school's ability to provide linguistic and cultural continuity for pupils when they move between the home and the school. This continuity is considered important for several reasons: to increase pupils' self-esteem, to allow pupils to maintain significant relations with their community, and to continue building on socialization patterns the pupil is familiar with and thus to increase the school's effectiveness in educating the pupils.

Other arguments in favor of the use of the first language are linguistic and cognitive in nature, stressing the advantages of bilingualism. Within this framework, the assumption is that using the first language will support learning the second language and facilitate academic learning. An unrelated argument is that bilingualism is a valuable skill for pupils in the global marketplace. Bilingualism as an enrichment is therefore advocated without necessary reference to any of the other factors. These arguments will be discussed separately in more detail below.

Home Language and Self-Esteem

The first argument regarding the use of the pupils' first language focuses on its importance for the way language minority pupils feel about themselves and school.

> Official recognition of the value of the home language and home culture, through native language instruction constitutes a major contribution to the maintenance of the self-esteem of language minority children (Snow, 1990, 64).

This argument has been discussed in detail in Chapter 5. In that chapter, it was pointed out that this psychological argument was not strongly supported by the literature for two reasons. First, language minority pupils often do not exhibit feelings of lower self-esteem as they enter schools. Secondly, pupils in bilingual programs have not been found to have a higher self-esteem than pupils in monolingual programs. Baral (1983b) adds that the effect of the first language on self-esteem may not be the same for all grade levels. He found that the most positive findings were found for pupils in grades one through three, whereas at the higher elementary and secondary level no differences were found. Overall, there does not seem to be a direct relationship between the use of the first language and self-esteem.

When the issue of language and self-esteem is considered within an integrated framework, a more complex picture emerges. Research on self-esteem and the use of the first language has been carried out without considering the educational context of the bilingual program, or the relationship between the bilingual program and the school setting.

For example, although bilingual programs are meant to use the first language as medium of instruction, observation in classrooms has shown that most programs tend to emphasize the second language (Wong Fillmore,

1989a). Moreover, bilingual programs are often marginalized within a school and have low status as a compensatory program. It is therefore not surprising that attending such bilingual programs in itself will not positively affect pupils' self-concept. Zanger (1989) (discussed in Zanger [1991]), documenting the experiences of Vietnamese and Hispanic adolescents who attended bilingual programs in a desegregated school setting, found that

> Students attributed their stigmatization by black and white native-born students to be the result of their language skills, their ethnicity, and *their membership in a low-status transitional bilingual program* (Zanger, 1991, 25; my emphasis).

The fact that home language classes in Europe are often taught after school hours and bear no relationship to the mainstream program contributes to the low status of these classes. When bilingual programs operate separately in the school, this does not reflect the official recognition Snow refers to. The pupils' language, and perhaps certain cultural aspects, may be recognized within the bilingual program but not within the institution. The pupils therefore still receive a negative message about their language and culture from the wider context in which they function.

Self-concept has to be developed within the entire school context. Language minority pupils have to be able to experience success in aspects of school life in which successful majority pupils are involved as well, especially if those activities have a higher status (Jungbluth & Driessen, 1989, 53).

Home Language and Socialization

It is also argued that the use of the first language in schools will provide linguistic and cultural continuity for language minority pupils. An assumption is made that there is a relationship between such continuity and academic achievement:

> native language instruction for language minority children promotes their educational success in English in a variety of ways, while at the same time preventing the alienation from the school culture that can undermine their educational achievement (Snow, 1990, 72).

Several programs have been established which take this assumption into consideration. In the Kamehameha Elementary Education Program (KEEP) for native Hawaiian children, extensive cultural analysis carried on in the pupils' home found characteristic patterns for learning style, helping skills, and sense of responsibility. Based on these characteristics, classroom adaptations were made, such as an open-door policy, teacher modeling behavior, and pupil-initiated leadership (Jordan, Tharp, & Baird-Vogt, 1992). In combination with other reform elements, this program succeeded in raising the pupils' reading achievement above the national norm. Au and Jordan state that the success in these programs is due to the fact that the instructional strategies "capitalize on the preexisting cognitive and linguistic abilities of the children" (Au & Jordan,1981, 140). Similarly, Moll speaks about the importance of incorporating the "funds of knowledge," which children acquire at home. Bringing these into the school allows teachers to make optimal use of "available resources, including the children's or the parents' language and knowledge, in creating new, advanced instructional circumstances for the pupils' academic development" (Moll, 1988, 23).

The home-school congruity argument merges issues of culture and learning with language issues. The implication for schools is that they should actively build on the linguistic and cultural resources that children bring to school to facilitate learning. Although the approach has been criticized for its lack of generalizability and explanatory power (Ogbu, 1987), its conclusion has been confirmed in effective school studies. For example, Tikunoff & Vasquez-Faria (1982) found that teachers in effective bilingual classrooms made pupils' experiences the basis of their curriculum.

The relationship between home and school has also been highlighted by two very different arguments in support of using the first language. The first argument points to the consequences of the breakdown of communication among children and their (grand)parents. The other argument refers to the effect of the use of the first language on parent involvement.

The danger of a breakdown of family ties and intergenerational communication was one of the conclusions that Wong Fillmore (1991b) drew after analyzing data on language maintenance and attrition patterns. Finding that pupils are quick to give up their own language, feeling the pressures of society, she questions the costs of not developing the first language for language minority children, their parents, and the community.

> What is lost is no less than the means by which parents socialize their children: When parents are unable to talk to their children, they cannot easily convey to them their values, beliefs, understandings, or wisdom about how to cope with their experiences. . . . Talk is a crucial link between parents and children: It is how parents impart their culture to their children and enable them to become the kind of men and women they want them to be. When parents lose the means for

socializing and influencing their children, rifts develop and families lose the intimacy that comes from shared beliefs and understanding (Wong Fillmore, 1991b, 343).

In his autobiography of growing up as a Mexican-American boy in California, Rodriguez describes how his relationship with his parents changed as he spoke more English and lost his command of Spanish.

> Matching the silence I started hearing in public was a new quiet at home. The family's quiet was partly due to the fact that, as we children learned more and more English, we shared fewer and fewer words with our parents. Sentences needed to be spoken slowly when a child addressed his mother or father. (Often the parents wouldn't understand.) The child would need to repeat himself. (Still the parent misunderstood.) The young voice, frustrated, would end up saying, "Never mind"—the subject was closed (Rodriguez, 1982, 23).

Little is known, however, about socialization patterns in bilingual households and the possible consequences for children. The situation is very complex, as Roossens (1989) indicates. He argues that immigrant children grow up in a home culture which is different from that in the home land, because "the social context that gives many elements of a culture meaning and significance has been lost" (Roossens, 1989, 88). The school confronts immigrant children with another culture, alien to that of their parents. Roossens concludes that immigrant children grow up in a fragmented culture, both at home and at school. Schools can assist immigrant children in the process of finding a way of functioning in both cultures.

> The home environment offers only a limited number of contact points with the cultural element that are transmitted to the children in the school context, whereas the home experiences are virtually ignored by the school programmes. Conflicts between norms, belief content, attitudes, and role patterns are not explained, and in most cases, no assistance in working through them is offered (Roossens, 1989, 90).

The use of the first language in school not only helps to maintain the pupil's ties with their family and community and to develop a sense of belonging but will also influence the relationship between parents and the school. The availability of bilingual staff and the fact that pupils' homework is in the native language may increase school participation opportunities for parents (Arvizu, 1992). The importance of parental involvement for pupil learning has been found as characteristics of many effective bilingual class-rooms (Pease-Alvarez and others, 1991; Garcia, 1987). In programs that continue to promote the first language the likelihood of parental involvement was greater (Cummins, 1994, 39). Such increased parent involvement may relate to the ability to assist in homework but probably more to the accessibility of teachers and the school for parents.

It's so wonderful to be able to talk to somebody in the language you are most comfortable in. I see that as such a difference for parents who have kids in the bilingual program. They really are able to make themselves understood, the [bilingual] teacher can ask "what do you want for your child?" "what do you see as the future for your child?" The parent has a chance to reflect and say something that really comes from the heart. Which is so hard to do, even when you do it through an interpreter. Let alone doing it through your broken English [Community outreach person, USA] (De Jong, 1993a).

Building on and expanding the resources language minority pupils bring to school is important. By including the pupils' language in the school and taking home socialization patterns into account, teachers are able to build on pupils' strengths. Such adaptations give pupils a supportive environment for learning, which makes learning about the majority culture and the language easier. It improves home-school relationships and allows pupils to maintain their ties with family and community.

Home Language and Cognitive Development

An often-cited argument in favor of the use of the first language is that it allows for continuous cognitive development. This was one of the main rationales for bilingual programs in the United States. The aim of these programs was to offer initial instruction in the first language, so that pupils would have access to a comprehensive curriculum and continue their cognitive and academic development, while learning the second language (Baez et al., 1985; Paulston, 1978a; S. Wong, 1988). There are two aspects of the cognitive argument. One aspect focuses on the continuation of knowledge and experiences the child has acquired at home in the formal school setting. The other aspect focuses on the fact that bilingualism can be cognitively advantageous.

When children come to school they have already developed concepts and have coded experiences in their native language. The use of the first language allows the teacher to tap into that potential as an important resource for learning. As Corder points out, "All that we know about learning insists that previous knowledge and skills are intimately involved in the acquisition of new knowledge and skills" (Corder, 1983, 95). In contrast, a one-sided focus on second language development does not seem to allow the same conceptual development to occur.

> If the mother tongue is not continuously practiced during the time when [the second language] has not yet reached a satisfactory level, there would be a period in which pupils would lack any adequate medium for knowledge attainment (Linde & Lofgren, 1988, 134).

It is important to reiterate the discussion above about differences in socialization and language use patterns in language minority families and the consequences for schooling (Trueba & Wright, 1992). Gaining access to the pupils' background and experiences and making them the basis for instruction is more successfully achieved through the first (or stronger) language.

The conclusion that it is harder to learn through the weaker language is supported by findings in immersion programs where pupils start in the second language, such as the Canadian programs. Pupils in these programs do very well on measures of first and second language proficiency (e.g., Genesee, 1987). However, a look at the achievement patterns for subject matter indicates that pupils may not do as well as those pupils who have been educated through their first language. Barik and Swain (1978; in Cummins & Swain, 1986) found that grade 6 pupils in partial immersion programs did not perform as well as their English-educated peers in science or mathematics. They conclude that "It may therefore be the case that their level of French was not adequate to deal with the more sophisticated level of mathematical and scientific concepts being presented to them in French" (in Cummins & Swain, 1986, 47). Pupils do not seem to learn as well through their weaker language. The key factor for conceptual development is that language skills have developed sufficiently in order to work in the curriculum in their second language (Baker, 1993b).

The use of the first language not only allows teachers to tap into the language minority pupil's resources but also provides a more efficient and effective learning environment. One of the implications is that first language development involves more than learning the technicalities of reading and writing. In addition to literacy development, it implies that pupils have to learn to manipulate the oral and written language within a cognitively demanding environment, such as the study of science or social studies.

In addition to the cognitive effects of developing the first language, bilingualism may also be associated with cognitive advantages. The idea that bilingualism itself is harmful to children has generally been refuted (Hakuta, 1986). Overviews of studies looking at the cognitive effects of bilingualism (Dolson, 1985a; Baker, 1993b) indicate that bilingualism may lead to higher metacognitive awareness and the ability to learn a third language more easily. Although these studies have been criticized for weak research designs because of the lack of control of background variables, it seems established that

> the development of the home language literacy skills by students entails no negative consequences for their overall academic or cognitive growth, and, in some situations, there may be significant educational benefits for students in addition to the obvious personal benefits of bilingualism (Cummins, 1994, 38).

Cognitive benefits only occur when subjects have developed both languages to a high extent. The implication for the goals that schools set for language minority pupils is clear: it takes time to develop abstract skills in a language; instead of implementing transitional programs in which the first language is phased out, schools should allow continuous development in the first (and the second) language to achieve high levels of proficiency in both language.

In conclusion, using the first language is important for a child's conceptual development. It allows teachers to gain access to what the child already knows and build on that conceptual framework. It also allows children to actively participate in what is going on in the class at a higher cognitively demanding level since they already have the language skills to express more complex thoughts. In addition, when both languages are developed well it seems that pupils have the ability to manipulate language and information in more creative ways than monolingual pupils.

Home Language and Second Language Development

One of the most prominent arguments for developing the first language is linguistic. Cummins (1981, 1984a, 1989) argued that proficiency in the first language can support and facilitate learning the second language. This section will describe Cummins's framework, empirical evidence in support of the framework, and some of its strengths and weaknesses.

The first central concept is that of *transfer*, which is used to explain why less time spent in the second language (but effectively spent on the first language) can result in high levels of second language proficiency. Despite the fact that bilingual programs spend less instructional time on the second language, it has been found that bilingual programs can do as well as submersion or second language programs in developing second language proficiency. This paradox can be explained if one assumes that skills developed in one language can transfer to the other language. This has been referred to as the interdependency hypothesis, which states that

> To the extent that instruction in L[anguage]$_x$ is effective in promoting proficiency in L[anguage]$_x$, transfer of this proficiency to L[anguage]$_y$ will occur provided there is adequate exposure to L[anguage]$_y$ (either in school or environment) and adequate motivation to learn L[anguage]$_y$ (Cummins, 1981, 29).

In the case of language minority pupils, the L$_x$ is generally the first language, and the L$_y$ is the second language. Within Cummins' framework, the assumption is that if the first language is developed to a certain level, transfer of those skills to the second language will occur. Much discussion occurred around what level and what kind of first language proficiency would be needed to reach the *threshold* for such transfer.

The answer to this question depends on the definition of language proficiency that one uses. Cummins (1981, 1982) makes a distinction between conversational and academic language skills (previously referred to as Basic Interpersonal Communication Skills or BICS, and Cognitive Academic Language Proficiency or CALP). Conversational skills are cognitively undemanding skills needed for daily interactions; much phrasing is automatic. Academic-language skills are required in context-reduced settings in cognitively demanding tasks, where the speaker does not have many contextual clues to figure out the meaning. It is the academic-language proficiency that transfers from one language to another since it refers to an underlying cognitive/academic proficiency common across languages (Cummins, 1982).

The distinction between conversational and academic language skills has been important because it appears that "very different time periods are required for pupils to attain peer-appropriate levels in conversational skills in English as compared to academic skills" (Cummins, 1994, 39). It is estimated that two years of exposure to the second language may be adequate for conversational proficiency, but that anywhere between four and nine years of school exposure may be necessary for full academic proficiency (Collier, 1987).

The interdependency hypothesis can then be summarized as follows:

in a Spanish-English program, Spanish instruction that develops L1 reading skills for Spanish-speaking students is not just developing Spanish skills, but is also developing a deeper conceptual and linguistic proficiency, which is strongly related to the development of English literacy and general academic skills. . . . This common underlying proficiency makes possible the transfer of cognitive/academic or literacy-related skills across languages (Cummins, 1985, 156).

The three elements together (transfer, academic vs. conversational skills, and time to learn a language) have important consequences for schools. Cummins' framework argues that in order for languages to support each other, both need to be developed beyond the threshold of literacy skills. Given the fact that it takes a long time to develop academic language skills, schools therefore have to allow for both languages to be developed throughout the school. It is important to note that Cummins indicates two additional conditions exposure and motivation—for successful second language learning both of which have been discussed in the section on pupil integration. Here, again, it is important to consider conditions of learning for both languages. Literacy skills in the first language will facilitate learning the second language, but this transfer will not succeed if the second language input is not sufficient. However, if the conditions of exposure and motivation have been met, literacy skills in the first language facilitate gaining access to the second language.

In addition to the higher level of language skills to interpret written text, it is also important to recognize that academic success requires such strategies as listening or reading for the main point, generalizing, making logical inferences from known information, and constructing more complex schemata—strategies which are not specific to a particular language. Again, once these strategies have been developed in the native language, they apparently transfer quite readily to academic tasks in a different language (Saville-Troike, 1991, 5).

Support for Cummins framework comes from several sources. The interdependency hypothesis has been supported by studies looking at the relationship between literacy skills in the first and the second language and studies comparing older and younger pupils' rate of second language acquisition.

The interdependent relationship between the first and the second language has been demonstrated in studies that correlate literacy and conversational skills in one language to those in the other language. The interdependency hypothesis predicts that such correlations will be significant across literacy skills for the two languages, and insignificant for conversational skills. This has been confirmed in several studies. A study that looked at pupils who had been schooled in another country than the United States showed that

> reading achievement in English as a second language is more dependent on reading achievement in their native language than it is on relative oral proficiency in English. This is true even when the language the students first learned to read is written in symbols which are quite different from our Roman alphabet, such as Japanese, Korean, and Arabic (cited in Saville-Troike, 1991, 5).

Cummins (1991) also found moderate to strong relationships between academic language skills in the first and the second language (predominantly as measured by reading scores). These studies suggest a common cross-linguistic proficiency in bilingual students for academic language skills, whereas conversational proficiency in one language seems unrelated to conversational proficiency in the other language.

A second source of evidence put forward in support of the interdependency hypothesis is that students who arrive in the host country at an older age, seem to be better second language learners. A widely cited study by Skutnabb-Kangas and Toukomaa with Finnish pupils found that

> those who attended school in Finland (prior to immigration) approached the level of achievement of normal Swedish pupils . . . in the written comprehension test considerably more than those who began school in Sweden. Those who attended school in Finland for at least three years did best (Skutnabb-Kangas and Toukomaa, 1976, 65–66; cited in Cummins, 1991, 73).

Skutnabb-Kangas and Toukomaa explain these findings in terms of the pupils' first language skills. They propose that since these pupils had already developed literacy skills in the first language, these skills transferred as they were acquiring the second language. A similar study found that "sixth graders who had immigrated to the U. S. after two years of education in Mexico consistently did better on the CTBS English reading comprehension test than students who had started school in this country" (Gonzales, 1986; cited in Saville-Troike, 1991, 6).

As critics have pointed out, the results of studies with older learners are hard to interpret because there are several confounding factors that may play a role. Swain, for example, presents the following explanations:

Their [i.e., older students'] ability to abstract, classify, and general-ize may aid the task of consciously formulating and applying second language rules. . . . Furthermore, older learners will already have mastered the skills of reading and writing and need only to learn the different surface realizations of these skills as demanded by the sec-ond language. Additionally, in such aspects of competence as vocabu-lary and grammatical knowledge, older learners come equipped to the task of second language learning with more knowledge than younger learners and presumably can transfer this knowledge to the second language context (Swain, 1981, 4).

Swain points to general knowledge and experiences, and general cog-nitive maturity as other explanations besides first language skills. Similarly, Saville-Troike (1991) points out that older pupils already have certain knowl-edge structures that, if they "match the experiences and expectations of school are going to transfer more readily" (Saville-Troike, 1991, 7). In other words, there is a general age factor that may really be the reason for better performance (Izzo, 1981; cited in Baker & Rossell, 1993).

Another explanation for the superiority of older learners emerges from research in second language acquisition. These studies find that older learners, at least initially, seem to learn the second language faster than younger pupils. For instance, Swain cites a study by Lapkin, Swain, Kamin, & Hann (1980) which found that "students who had accumulated 1400 hours of French [instruction] starting at age 12 would obtain French test scores equivalent to students who had accumulated over 4000 hours of French starting at age 5" (Swain, 1981, 3). Scarcella & Higa (1981) sug-gest that older pupils have easier access to more exposure in the second lan-guage. They point out that older learners are better able to sustain a con-versation and are therefore more likely to be exposed to and use the second language (see the section on Pupil Integration). Moreover, "adult native speakers seemed to expect more of older learners. Thus, the older learners were required to communicate even when they lacked the necessary linguistic competence to do so" (Scarcella & Higa, 1981, 425).

The Skutnabb-Kangas and Toukomaa study has been heavily criti-cized on methodological grounds (Hyltenstamm & Arnberg, 1988; Baker & Rossell, 1993) and it is surprising that it is still widely cited. Baker & Rossell (1993, 7), for example, point out that no statistical analysis is pre-sented (and reanalysis by Baker and de Kanter [1981] showed no statistical differences), and that Swedish was required for pupils in Finland from the third grade on. In other words, the older pupils had already been exposed to the second language before coming to Sweden, which facilitated their learning Swedish in Sweden.

Cummins's framework has also been criticized on theoretical grounds. For example, it is still unclear what academic language proficiency is, which language skills transfer, or what mental processes are involved in such transfer (Bialystok & Cummins, 1991; Cummins, 1991; Baker, 1993b). In addition, Cummins has been criticized for using a definition of language proficiency that is skill-oriented rather than wholistic in nature (Edelsky, 1991) as well as for proposing an untestable framework (Baker & Rossell, 1993).

Home Language and Enrichment

The last argument in favor of the use of the first language is that bilingualism is a valued ability to possess in a global market place. As the U.S. Congress declared in re-enacting the Bilingual Education Act,

> as the world becomes increasingly interdependent and as international communication becomes a daily occurrence in government . . . and family life, multilingual skills constitute an important national resource which deserves protection and development (Title VII. Part A; in Bilingual Education Commission, 1994, 13).

This position moves away from the compensatory nature of a bilingual education and emphasizes that being bilingual is an asset for everybody. This requires a school environment in which second language learning and bilingualism is valued and seen as an enrichment for pupils. The argument distinguishes itself clearly from the other arguments in this chapter. It moves away from politically and educationally motivated arguments to a more economic argument by stating that bilingualism will provide pupils with an advantage on the job market. There also is an integrative side to the argument. Bilingualism as enrichment is a reflection of a global reality which shows that countries are becoming more and more diverse. Being bilingual will allow individuals to avoid possible language barriers and breakdowns in communication. It needs to be pointed out that this economic argument is in reality often limited to languages being used beyond the school community. Whereas languages such as French and Spanish have an international status, regionally based languages such as Creole/Kreyol will give individuals limited opportunities to utilize their bilingual skills in a wide variety of jobs.

For language minority pupils the implication of this position is that the linguistic and cultural resources they bring to school will be recognized. If bilingualism is considered an enrichment, there is no reason to abandon the pupils' first language when they start school. Instead, capitalizing on the language resources these pupils already possess, a school would create an environment that favors bilingualism. A bilingual or multilingual labor force will play an important role in future economic success in the international labor market (Bilingual Education Commission, 1994, 13).

CHARACTERISTICS OF INTEGRATED LANGUAGE MINORITY EDUCATION

It is now possible to define more clearly some of the key elements of an integrated approach to language minority education. The need to make language minority education an integral part of the school is supported by insights into various aspects of the schooling process. As the previous discussion has illustrated, allowing language minority programs (and their pupils and teachers) to become marginalized in school will negatively influence academic and social integration and therefore academic achievement. Genesee provides a concise summary of the issues surrounding marginalization.

> Effective education of second language children calls for a more integrative approach than that which has characterized professional thinking and practice in the field to date. When I speak of an integrative approach, I am referring to more than integrating language and content, although this is important. All too often, teaching children who are learning a second language and learning through a second language has not been integrated with other important aspects of education. Educating second language children has been kept separate from issues concerning their social integration in mainstream classrooms and the school at large. It has been consigned to second language teaching specialists, thereby keeping grade level and second language teachers from integrating their professional competencies and resources and from cooperating extensively in planning whole educational programs for second language students (Genesee, 1994, 2).

An integrated approach aims at avoiding such marginalization while creating an environment that allows language minority pupils to actively build on the linguistic and cultural resources that they have. It therefore distinguishes itself from assimilation, when the latter is interpreted as requiring pupils to give up their language and cultural background in order to become part of the mainstream.

The previous sections have illustrated some of the key elements of integrated language minority education. The most important principle is that the education of language minority pupils becomes the responsibility of the entire school. At the teacher level, this implies that specialists (such as bilingual teachers, second language teachers) function as a crucial source of information and experience but are not perceived as the people solely responsible for meeting the needs of language minority pupils. Since language minority education is dealt with within the general education context, it is not restricted to language issues. Instead, a bilingual child is treated within an educational framework that considers cognitive and affective as well as linguistic factors. The "whole school approach" is a crucial prerequisite for the other characteristics of integrated language minority schooling, since it directs the efforts of teachers to a common mission.

The discussion of first language development, bilingualism, second language learning, and academic learning presented a complex picture. However, the common thread throughout this literature is that (1) the compensatory nature of current programs, and (2) the notion that language minority pupils' needs can be met through temporary solutions, will do more harm than good. The literature points to the importance of developing both languages to a high level of proficiency. This goal has implications for instruction and curriculum.

First of all, both languages need to be developed in cognitively demanding contexts of subject matter as well as of literacy skills. Language-rich classrooms are important for the acquisition of both languages. In addition, second language acquisition can be significantly supported by providing pupils with adult as well as peer language models.

The goal of high levels of proficiency in both languages also implies that the two languages need to be supported throughout a language minority pupil's school career. Language minority education can therefore no longer be defined as a temporary, compensatory program. A supportive environment allows pupils to use freely their two languages, build upon previous experiences, and not feel threatened in their own language as they are learning the second language. These factors will reduce anxieties around language learning and increase pupils' motivation to develop both languages.

It will be difficult to meet these goals for language minority pupils without a high quality curriculum that consistently builds on pupils' previous experiences. This background knowledge consists of knowledge learned in the home as well as in school (Moll, 1988). It also includes strategies and concepts learned in the first language. A high quality curriculum will require the coordination of curriculum content and instruction so that pupils are encouraged to transfer strategies and knowledge developed in one language to academic learning in the other language.

There are three general principles (see Handscombe, 1994; Cummins, 1994; Brisk & De Jong, 1993, for other listings) for such integrated education:

1. *A whole school approach*: integrated language minority education starts with the assumption that all staff members are responsible for all pupils in the school and have a strong sense of ownership for the education of all pupils.

2. *A cooperative approach*: integrated language minority education requires the coordination of curriculum content and instruction.

3. *An integrative approach*: integrated language minority education asks for the integration of pupils for academic purposes in an environment supportive of the pupils' languages and cultures.

These three characteristics are interdependent. A sense of ownership will direct much of the decisionmaking at the curriculum and instructional level. Without the acceptance of language minority education as an integral part of the general education system, it will be difficult to realize cooperation and successful integration of pupils. The next section will deal with some of the changes that have to be made at the classroom and school level and explain why these changes are necessary.

CONDITIONS FOR INTEGRATED LANGUAGE MINORITY EDUCATION

There is a need, then, for a whole school approach to language minority education: cooperation among teachers regarding curriculum and instruction, and integration of pupils. None of these goals will be met unless schools deliberately implement policies directed at collaboration and integration. Similar integration efforts for other target groups (African-Americans and special needs pupils) have emphasized the need for conscious efforts from teachers and administrators to achieve such integration.

Within the racial integration literature a distinction has been made between desegregation and integration after it was found that rsegregation frequently occurred within desegregated schools through tracking, grouping practices, special education referrals, or disciplinary action (Eyler, Cook, & Ward, 1983; Epstein, 1985; Meier & Stewart, 1991). "Desegregation" is therefore used to describe the situation in which minority and majority pupils are physically together in a school or classroom, whereas "integration" is reserved for "a social situation marked by mutual respect and equal dignity in an atmosphere of acceptance and encouragement of distinctive cultural patterns" (Weinberg, 1983, 172).

Similarly, the movement in favor of the inclusion of special needs pupils in regular classrooms has pointed out that such inclusion can be successful only if certain adaptations are made in instruction in the regular classroom. If such adaptations are lacking, the special needs pupil is excluded from the academic environment as well as from his and her peers.

The effectiveness of integrated language minority education will therefore highly depend on the way schools reform their school organization, curriculum, and instruction. Integration is not a process that will occur simply because pupils and teachers are put together. It can be successfully implemented only with deliberate planning and change. For this section, it will be assumed that schools will implement policies that aim at providing all pupils with access to a high-quality curriculum. Such policies will include current instructional techniques (e.g., a thematic approach to learning, hands-on learning, heterogeneous grouping), challenging curriculum content, and technology. These general characteristics of effective schools have also been identified in effective bilingual classrooms (Mace-Matluck, 1990; Garcia, 1988; Tikunoff & Vasquez-Faria, 1982).

Besides the need for general educational reform, integrated language minority education also addresses specific issues around collaboration and integration. This section will look at settings that integrate language minority and language majority pupils. To illustrate the importance of deliberate planning in such integrated settings, an example will be presented of the potential consequences when a classroom has not been adapted to the linguistic and cultural diversity within it. Then, two areas in which systematic change need to occur will be dealt with. The need for collaboration among bilingual and monolingual teachers will be described first. The section will conclude with curricular and instructional changes for language and academic learning in integrated settings.

The Need for Organizational Change

The issues of ownership, curriculum coordination, and pupil integration draw attention to the negative impact marginalization can have on learning. Based on such experiences, some have argued that pupils should be mainstreamed directly in the "regular" classroom. Handscombe (1989) uses the term "unplanned mainstreaming" for this strategy, where "students are placed in regular classes but receive no further special help in continuing to develop their English language proficiency" (p. 25). A nonadapted classroom will not achieve the academic, linguistic, nor social goals of integration. This section will explore the need for adaptation and changed attitudes towards languages and cultures.

A good way to gain insight into the need for changing curriculum and instruction is to look at classroom situations where no such adaptations have been made, as in a Danish school visited by the author. Five Turkish/Kurdish-speaking first-grade pupils are together with Danish-speaking peers most of the day. All five are pulled out for Danish as a Second Language class together with other Turkish/Kurdish first graders for five hours a week. The example is illustrative of a situation where modified instruction is seen as the responsibility of the second language teachers and where the regular teachers may not be aware of the specific educational needs of language minority pupils.

[Reading arts lesson in the Danish-only class]
There are two female Danish teachers. In the class there are five Turkish/Kurdish-speaking children (four girls and one boy) and 15 Danish-speaking children. Mehlike sits with two Danish girls in the front of the classroom; Nazen, who normally sits next to her, is absent today due to illness. Deniz and Nesrin sit next to each other in the back of the classroom with two Danish girls facing them. Mezaffa sits with three Danish boys at the table next to them.

One of the teachers starts with the lesson on the letter A. She starts by orally eliciting examples of words which start with the letter A from the pupils. Deniz is the only girl who volunteers an answer. The Danish teacher does not understand her response, however. The teacher draws a picture of the words the children come up with. The teacher then shows them how to write the letter A.

The children practice writing the letter A in the air, imitating the teacher. All instruction is large group. After that, the pupils have to work individually on work sheets on the letter A. When the pupils start working on their work sheets the two teachers go around the classroom helping individual pupils. At one point the Danish teacher comes by Deniz's and Nesrin's table and she asks them to label the objects on their work sheets in Danish.

During the lesson, Mehlike does not interact with the Danish pupils at her table. Several times she turns around and looks over at the other two Turkish girls with a questioning look on her face. Later, she gets up to show them her work. When the teacher is writing down the A-words, she is clearly working on something else. In the back of the classroom, Deniz and Nesrin discuss their class materials in Turkish with each other. They do not communicate with the other two girls at their table. Muzaffer is in constant physical contact with the neighbor on his left hand. They joke around, but do not seem to pay attention or talk about class work. [Observation notes, Denmark] (De Jong, 1993b).

This example raises a number of issues around the nature of integration and raises important questions to be addressed in integrated classrooms.

The first question is regarding the ways the teachers or peers provide access to the second language minority pupils during the lesson. In this particular lesson, the second language exposure the children receive is limited in several ways. First, the only way teachers contextualize their instruction is by providing drawings with the words that the pupils come up with. However, the vocabulary itself is unrelated to anything else and is not placed within a more meaningful context. If the teachers also had an additional goal of teaching vocabulary items, this strategy does not seem very effective. Secondly, the input the bilingual children receive is from the teacher and from the worksheet. Both are limited: the teachers' input focuses on instructional language (showing how to draw the letter A, telling pupils to do their worksheet), whereas the worksheets requires the pupils to trace the letter A and copy down three words with the letter A. Even when the teacher interacts briefly with the second language learners, she only asks them to label the pictures and does not provide extended comprehensible input nor requires the children to express themselves in more challenging ways. In other words, this way of organizing the classroom instruction does not provide pupils with a meaningful context for language learning.

If language input is not made comprehensible and meaningful, pupils may "tune out." Mehlike shows this when she works on something else during instruction. Similarly, Muzaffer acts out with his Danish peer during the lesson, talking about nonacademic matters. Saville-Troike (1984) has noted this "tendency of LEP [Limited English Proficient] children to disengage entirely either from group activity which is not focused on them or from individual activity that is given little direction" (cited by Flanigan, 1988, 30–31). This was also one of the findings of a study by Mendez who explored what happened to bilingual children after attending a transitional bilingual program in terms of their self-concept, attitudes, affective reactions, and academic achievement. Pupils indicated that they did not always understand the English spoken in the all-English classroom. However, since the regular classroom teacher did not respond to this, the pupils were allowed to "tune out." The pupils said,

> Sometimes I don't understand . . . they won't explain to you . . . if you get around you get around.

It is not bad to go to the Regular classroom without understanding English . . . one is just there and does not understand a thing and
one does not say a thing . . . one just looks (Mendez, 1982, 59).

Nonadapted instruction may therefore limit the access of language
minority pupils to the curriculum, which will in turn negatively impact academic learning for language minority pupils.

The instruction also has not been organized in such a way that access to the second language could be obtained through peers. Although the
language minority pupils sit together with Danish-speaking peers, there is
no interaction among the pupils. The isolation felt by the pupils becomes
especially evident when looking at Mehlike's behavior. Despite being in the
same classroom with the Danish children, she feels clearly isolated. She looks
for the other Turkish girls for support and encouragement but does not interact with their Danish peers, who are nearby. Neither do the Danish children reach out to her. Exposure to the second language is therefore limited
to the teachers' input, despite the fact that many native peer models are available. This situation illustrates the situation where pupils are often physically
integrated but little or no meaningful interaction takes place among minority and majority pupils (Faltis, 1993). Zanger (1987) found that, without
intervention, even "within the context of a desegregated school, the pupils
experienced significant isolation from native speakers of standard English"
(cited by Zanger, 1991, 24–25).

A last comment regarding the example above is the importance of the
opportunity to use the first language. Initially, the Turkish children had been
spread throughout the classroom (one at each table). At the suggestion of
the second language teacher it was decided to put two pupils together so that
they could use each other as a resource. For Deniz and Nesrin it was important that they shared a language because now they were able to figure
out together what was expected. It provided them with an additional resource to gain access to the curriculum.

This classroom example illustrates the importance of setting clear
goals for language learning. As it was a language arts lesson, issues of exposure to different models of the second language, using contextualized language use, and peer interactions were important things to think about and
plan. Similarly, teachers have to think about the nature of the task that they
present and its purpose and opportunities for meaningful language use
(Edelsky, 1991).

The importance of continuity between a special program and a regular
program in terms of the adaptive environment becomes very clear when com-

paring the behavior of a pupil attending an English as a Second Language class (adapted environment) and an all-English classroom (nonadapted environment). Flanigan (1988, 1991), for example, found a marked change in a pupil's behavior when going from the regular to the English as a Second Language classroom.

> The only time L. showed open and verbal pleasure, expressed opinions, asked for help, or claimed membership in a group was when she went to the ESL reading lab.
>
> . . . in the regular classroom she was allowed to "tune out" both verbally and physically more often than she was required to participate in activities.
>
> She tuned out only when she was unable to follow group activity. . . . However, this did not occur when she was engaged in group work in the ESL classroom; there, conscious teacher talk and a sense of equality with her peers seemed to encourage her acquisition of academic language proficiency (Flanigan, 1988, 30–32).

The phenomenon of tuning out when instruction is not modified and comprehensible has already been discussed above. Flanigan (1991) describes a Pakistani girl who functioned as a peer-tutor in the study and who showed a remarkable change when moving from the regular classroom to the English as a Second Language classroom.

> [O]ne of the most talkative of these tutors, a third-grade Palestinian girl (R), was reported by her classroom teacher to be very quiet and less than able to function in English with her academic peers; in the ESL classroom, however, she talked fluently and colloquially and frequently helped others even when not asked to (Flanigan, 1991, 149–150).

Such comparisons of behavior provide important insights into what environment creates the most optimal opportunities for learning for individual pupils. Communications among teachers becomes a very important factor in these situations: the ESL teacher will have a very different picture of the Pakistani girl than does the regular classroom teacher.

Besides the need to consider (second language) learning opportunities, peer interactions, and individual pupil behavior, it is also important to consider teacher-pupil relationships. Laosa (1979) looked at the treatment Mexican-American pupils received by teachers in comparison to Anglo pupils in desegregated classrooms. He found that Mexican-American pupils were reprimanded more and received less positive feedback. In addition, there were less interactions overall between the teacher and the Mexican-American pupils. He concludes that

> the Mexican American student is less likely to experience the quality of interaction and opportunity in the classroom that is experienced by students who are either Anglo or high-achieving, or of higher socioeconomic status, or who speak standard English (Laosa, 1979, 57).

Marginalization is most likely to occur when classrooms do not adapt to their pupils diverse linguistic and cultural backgrounds. The result is isolation within the classroom, limited access to the curriculum, lower expectations for language minority pupils, and little second language learning.

The Need for Collaboration

> If a bilingual teacher develops a relationship with a mainstream teacher, it does wonders what also happens. When there's no communication, it's like the kids. This is one camp and this is the other and it's not knowing what they're like. And they suspect. They think things about the person and make judgments while they don't really know the person. I have found that when the bilingual and the mainstream people get together, nine times out of ten everybody is really happy about it. And the whole operation just goes a lot more smoothly. . . .
>
> It was very important that we needed to collaborate. We need to find out what's going on in the mainstream and get involved with them and them with us. It's really proven to be a very positive thing because [before] the dialogue was initiated, there was so much misunderstanding between what was going on in the mainstream program, between the teachers and curriculum people [Bilingual curriculum coordinator, USA] (De Jong, 1993a).

The bilingual curriculum coordinator in the examples above addresses several important issues around teacher relationships. A lack of communication and collaboration between bilingual and monolingual teachers affects teachers' attitudes towards language minority education in general and towards their colleagues. A lack of interaction among teachers reinforces the separateness of a language minority program with regard to the regular program and does not allow for the sharing of the expertise of respective teachers. This in turn may undermine opportunities for curriculum coordination and the development of a sense of ownership.

The curriculum coordinator's statements are supported by literature that looks at the role of teacher collaboration in effective schools. Teacher collaboration and interaction have been identified as an important part of an effective school's climate or ethos, where staff share a mission and work toward common goals and objectives (Purkey & Smith, 1982). It is argued that the opportunity for sharing, reflective decisionmaking, and development on the job as part of teacher collaboration will improve the conditions for teaching and learning (Fullan, 1982; in Ellis, 1990). Ellis (1990) cites several studies which illustrate that teacher collaboration has been associated with a variety of positive school characteristics, such as collegiality, increased productivity and expertise, effective teaching practices, and teachers' perceptions of increased learning opportunities. Teacher isolation has been found to impede opportunities for improving the technical knowledge base in teaching and shared practical knowledge (Lortie, 1975; Sarason, 1982; both cited in Flinders, 1988)

Integrated language minority education requires a high level of teacher interaction and collaboration, given the issues of ownership, curriculum coordination, and mainstreaming. Carter and Chatfield found that teacher collaboration was an important characteristic of the effective school that they studied. Collaboration became an important mechanism to include the bilingual program in the larger school setting and to develop positive attitudes towards the program.

> Collaborative teaching has contributed to a total ownership of the bilingual program. The bilingual strand is not separated from the total school endeavor. Monolingual teachers and aides commented in interviews that the bilingual program was important and positive (Carter & Chatfield, 1986, 223).

Metz (1986) compared school practices in three magnet schools and found that interracial cooperation and interracial friendships were more common at the two schools where teacher collaboration was a key ingredient. In contrast, more racial tensions were found in the school where there was a teacher-centered approach to teaching and where there was little communication among teachers. It seems that teacher collaboration can also function as a model for pupil cooperation.

Despite the importance of teacher interaction, current practice still reflects a specialized, isolated approach to learning and teaching. This holds true for "regular" education as well as language minority programs. Goodlad (1984), in a study of teachers in 38 schools, concluded, "The classroom cells in which teachers spend much of their time appear . . . symbolic of their relative isolation from one another and from sources of ideas beyond their own background experience" (Quoted in Smith & Scott, 1990, 10).

Flinders (1988) distinguishes two ways of thinking about teacher isolation. Traditionally, teacher isolation has been defined as "a product of institutional characteristics firmly grounded in the historical development of public schools" (Flinders, 1988, 19). Issues of physical space, teacher turnover, and school organization are addressed as factors influencing the amount of collegial contact among teachers. For language minority education, such a definition of teacher isolation is reflected in studies that look at the amount of time teachers of language minority pupils spent with their colleagues. These studies indicate that such institutional isolation is part of the reality of language minority programs. For example, Driessen and others (1989) found that 60 percent of the home language teachers in their study in the Netherlands meet "once a month" to "never" with the mainstream teacher. Rixius & Thurmann (1987) report on a study by the Italian embassy which found that only 19 percent of the Italian home language teachers regularly exchanged information with their German colleagues. Coenen (1982) concludes that

> there is no consideration of any sort of integration or of coordinating with one another's reading and instructional materials; the Dutch teacher works with Dutch curriculum following a particular timetable and the foreign teacher works with a curriculum from the homeland following an entirely different timetable.

Another approach to teacher isolation reflects a psychological definition of teacher isolation in which "isolation depends more on how teachers perceive and experience collegial interaction than it does on the absolute amount of interaction in which they are involved" (Flinders, 1988, 20). More qualitative research on how teachers perceive their position in the school provide insights into this dimension of teacher isolation and its effects. Montero-Sieburth and Perez, for instance, documented a bilingual teacher's experiences in the United States. Although their study focused on classroom interactions between the teacher and the pupils, one important finding was that the teacher's ability to effectively address her pupils' needs was clearly influenced by the school's attitudes and the status of the bilingual program in the school.

> The fact that the special classes to which bilingual teachers are assigned are transitional — akin to a waiting room, where students are

to stay until they are admitted to the mainstream — induces a sense of marginality in the teacher. Thus the bilingual teacher comes to feel the very sense of isolation . . . that is also the fate of the migrant student (Montero-Sieburth & Perez, 1987, 187).

The bilingual teacher interviewed defined her position as "being a second-class member of an already devalued profession."

Lemberger (1992) interviewed four female, trained, experienced, bilingual primary school teachers about their experiences and perceptions about bilingual education in New York City. Besides curricular and instructional issues, the teachers commented on the lack of institutionalization of the bilingual program. All four teachers expressed "their pain over not having been accepted initially by their monolingual colleagues in their schools" (Lemberger, 1992, 9). As one of the teachers put it

> They really didn't want to have much . . . to do with us. They had these old faithfuls. There was really a schism. They would just go to their rooms for lunch and wouldn't have anything to do with you. They'd barely say hello (Lemberger, 1992, 9).

Grey, who looked at an ESL program in a high school, found that such lack of coordination can translate into a lack of clear goals for the program involved, which in turn may reinforce the isolation of both pupils and teachers.

> The vague state of affairs surrounding the ESL program . . . not only left LEP immigrant students feeling left out of the school—but it has contributed to their (and their teachers) lower status among mainstream teachers and students (Grey, 1990, 419).

Co-teaching situations between monolingual and bilingual teachers have not been documented systematically within the field of bilingual education. Some useful insights can be obtained, however, by looking at co-teaching situations between special education teachers and mainstream teachers. As special needs pupils are increasingly being served in regular classroom settings, this situation has become more common nowadays. As in integrated language minority education, interaction between a "special" program and a "regular" program is a necessary ingredient for such inclusion to be successful.

Redditt (1992) looked at teachers' perspective on their team-teaching. She found that the collaboration process was impeded when the relationship between the two teachers was negative due to philosophical and/or pedagogical disagreements. Modeling such behaviors would, according to the teachers involved in the study, also have negative consequences for pupils. Another obstacle was the lack of sufficient planning time. Redditt found that "talking through educational issues and making joint decisions in the classroom was time consuming" (Redditt, 1992, 111) In addition, she found that an important characteristic of her effective team was that the two teachers had addressed and solved the issue of power. Over time, the teachers had evened out their power in the classroom, reflecting an "evolution from a directive/accommodating style of interacting to a more collaborative one" (Redditt, 1992, 117). Redditt emphasizes that team-teaching is not an automatic process but "appears to be forged out of constant two-way communication, careful planning, compatible personalities, and an ongoing commitment to the concept of integration." (Redditt, 1992, 13).

Goessling (1994) characterizes the collaboration between special education teachers and regular teachers as a process of cultural adaptation, requiring the special needs educators to acquire the culture of the mainstream. Although Goessling does not address this issue, it is evident that the mainstream teacher also needs to adapt to the culture of inclusion and special education. As in Redditt's study, the integration specialists mentioned a lack of time as a barrier to effective collaboration and inclusion. In addition, Goessling's subjects also commented on the resistance of mainstream teachers against sharing the responsibility for special needs students within the context of the regular class.

In the schooling of language minority pupils similar issues arise. The conceptualization of language minority education can make it unlikely for teacher collaboration to occur. Unmatched schedules and the fact that only few hours a week exist for team-teaching are often enough to prohibit systematic planning and collaboration. If such collaboration does occur, however, issues of teacher status within the classroom and general teacher relationships play an important role in defining the relationship between the bilingual and the monolingual teacher.

The unequal status between monolingual and bilingual teachers appears most directly when monolingual and bilingual teachers are together within the classroom. For example, bilingual teachers in Sweden often function as support teachers in the "regular" Swedish classroom, besides teaching their home language classes. Although this situation theoretically allows for teacher collaboration, such collaboration seldom happens. Instead, the bilingual teacher fulfills the role of assistant either by helping pupils in the classroom or by pulling language minority pupils out for a particular lesson.

The [mainstream] teacher determines what the home language teacher is going to do with the pupil(s) and decides whether the home language teacher will pull the children out of the classroom or will work with them in the classroom [Preparatory class teacher, Sweden] (De Jong, 1993b).

Asked about the difference between teaching her home language classes and being in a co-teaching setting with Danish teachers, one of the bilingual teachers said the following:

When I'm alone, then I'm more independent. . . . There is no boundary. I am by myself. I decide what I'm going to teach; . . . It's my class and MY children. I have my own rules . . . I know them [the children] with their culture and their language. The other situation, with the Danish teacher. . . . I think it's the same for all bilingual teachers . . . the Danish teacher is the first person. I am a teacher or I am an assistant? What kind of picture does [the Danish teacher] have of a bilingual teacher? [Home language teacher, Denmark] (De Jong, 1993b).

Similarly, one of the Swedish preparatory class teachers commented that "playing the second fiddle in the classroom is much harder than being your own teacher outside the classroom" (De Jong, 1993b.) This role of the bilingual teachers is jokingly referred to as "radiator teacher"; the bilingual teacher sits on the radiator until the grade level teacher is done with the instruction and then gets up to help pupils do their work (Reid, 1989, 32 uses the term "whispering radiator teacher"). It is clear that such an arrangement for teacher collaboration only reinforces the subordinate role of language minority teachers. This will simultaneously affect the opportunities for pupils to be exposed to positive role models of a particular ethnic group.

Even when the intention is co-instruction rather than assistantship, the roles of the bilingual and monolingual teacher are difficult to keep equal. Hagman & Lahdenpera warn that

even when [the teachers] co-operated reasonably well, the children soon learned who was the "real" teacher. Two teachers from different cultures cannot reach equal status when one of them is the representative of the majority, unless something special is done about it (Hagman & Lahdenpera, 1988, 329).

Observations in co-taught classes confirm this pattern of inequality when no steps are taken to intervene.

The Turkish teacher also did some co-teaching with the Dutch as a Second Language teacher. At one session the Dutch as a Second Language teacher was standing up front going through a vocabulary listing related to bicycles in Dutch. The Turkish teacher sat on a bench behind the pupils. Later the Turkish teacher tells me that his main role in these classes is to translate. The Dutch teacher gives him the vocabulary list that they will deal with, so that he can translate the words and glue the work sheets in the children's notebooks. He feels that the Dutch teacher leaves all the handy work to him; sometimes he doesn't get the words to him in time to prepare. [Observation, the Netherlands] (De Jong, 1993b).

After a few more exchanges in Turkish between Tahsin [the bilingual teacher] and Nermin [pupil], Anne [the Danish teacher] asks whether they can continue [with the lesson]. She continues the lesson by asking where the bear book is that she had shown them the day before. She looks in her bag but cannot find it. She asks the children if they have it. They respond that they haven't. Anne questions Tahsin. It appears that Tahsin has the book in his bag. Tahsin takes the book out of his bag and wants to give it to Anne. She declines, saying that since it is in his bag, he has to read it. Tahsin then paraphrases the book in Turkish with Anne taking over at times. [Observation, Denmark] (De Jong, 1993b).

Note that in the last example Anne is the one getting the pupils' attention to continue the lesson and initiating the book reading sequence (searching for the book), and that Tahsin's first reaction is to give her the book to read as he considers her the lead teacher. Aware of their unequal interaction patterns, the Danish teacher insists, however, and passes on the leadership to the Turkish teacher.

Unfortunately, such role-switching between the teachers rarely occurs. An analysis of bilingual teachers co-teaching with three different Danish as a Second Language teachers confirmed this pattern. During seven co-taught lessons, it was the Danish teacher who started the class (either by some activity or by taking attendance), who initiated transitions to the next activity and who introduced anew activity. The bilingual teacher, in contrast, was the one to address home/school issues or quarrels among pupils, to clarify Danish instructions, and to explain vocabulary words. The roles between the teachers seem strictly divided, but they seldom switch roles, which may reinforce the inequality between the teachers.

Besides teacher equality within the classroom, the general relationship among bilingual and monolingual teachers may also affect teacher interactions. This relationship can be negatively influenced by external factors and by cultural differences regarding education and schools.

Bilingual teachers may be perceived as less professional or skilled as the result of contract differences (tenure vs. temporary contract) or educational background (mainly bilingual teachers are on waivers, or attend shorter teacher training programs). In addition, monolingual teachers may resent the fact that bilingual programs are entitled to a lower number of pupils, and to classroom assistants.

Besides these external factors, issues of cultural adaptation also seem to play a role.

The Turkish bilingual teacher explained how the Danish system is more democratic, that she has more freedom in what she teaches and what materials to use. She says that it took a long time to get to know the system and especially the way teachers interacted with each other [bilingual teacher, Denmark] (De Jong, 1993b).

The Danish teachers said that the Turkish teachers did not take initiative and refused to take responsibility. On the other hand, the Turkish teachers commented that the Danish teachers did not want to give them responsibility over the class [Notes, Denmark] De Jong, 1993b).

In the beginning there was no equal status because they [the Swedish teachers] didn't trust him [the bilingual teacher] that he could do the work. He didn't do the same amount of work. This has changed now and this has improved relations much. Of course he could do it but it's very hard to work together with the home language teacher. As one of the teachers said: "You have to give all the time, and you get nothing back. [He] never comes with his own initiative. Then you stop" [Notes, Sweden] (De Jong, 1993b).

Teunissen (1986) looked at a bilingual program in Enschede in the Netherlands and identifies three factors that influenced the success of the collaboration between the bilingual and the Dutch teacher. These factors are similar to the ones cited by the teachers above. One of the major barriers was the lack of real communication among the teachers. Teunissen indicates that miscommunications among teachers was only partially because of a lack Dutch proficiency of the bilingual teachers. Even more important perhaps was the absence of the teachers' skills in intercultural communication. Misinterpretations of verbal and nonverbal reactions and miscommunications were the result, inhibiting the collaboration process. Secondly, there was a lack of content-related preparation of teachers to ensure effective collaboration. Misunderstandings and misled expectations resulted from the lack of knowledge about each other's educational traditions and background. Lastly, the actual opportunities created by the schools to collaborate were often missing because the bilingual teachers worked at several schools. Informal contacts and chances to interact were therefore kept at a minimum.

One of the prerequisites for integrated language minority education is that teachers respect each other and collaborate to work toward common purposes. The need for such collaboration stems from a need for curriculum coordination and for ownership. However, there are several barriers that prevent successful collaboration among language minority and language majority teachers—the minority teachers' status in the school and cultural differences, for example. Collaboration requires a school culture that encourages communication among teachers, includes language minority teachers in the decisionmaking process, allows scheduled time for planning, and stimulates two-way communication among the teachers.

The Need for Instructional Change

As has been pointed out previously, the integration of pupils is expected to lead to academic and social integration. The previous section has clearly illustrated that the outcomes of integration are highly dependent on how the integrated setting is structured. For language minority pupils the situation is even more complex because the academic goals include second language development goals.

Teachers have to be aware of the needs of language minority student when the latter are integrated with language majority pupils to avoid a submersion situation. They have to make their curriculum content accessible for second language learning by using second language teaching techniques. Content matter can be an excellent way to develop second language skills. It provides a meaningful and natural context for language use, and teachers can adapt their content to the interests and level of their pupil, thus increasing pupil motivation (Met, 1994; Pierce, 1987). Teaching language through content has been associated especially with the Canadian immersion programs, where teachers continuously adapt their instruction because all pupils are second language learners (Krashen, 1991).

Wong Fillmore warns that, poorly implemented, this method can lead to "a classroom setting that is little more than submersion education—the teaching of subject matter in a language the students do not understand"

(Wong Fillmore, 1989a, 125). Based on studies in California and Toronto on effective instructional strategies, she identifies several characteristics for effective instruction of content through the second language. These strategies are, among others, heterogeneous grouping, appropriate content, attention to language, and corrective feedback. The role of the teacher is important in providing academic-language models, direction, and corrective feedback. Heterogeneous grouping allows students of different language abilities to interact and hear language at different levels of development. Appropriate content includes content matter that is designed to address different skills, draws from grade-level curriculum, and integrates different subject matter creatively. As language is a tool for communication but also the object of learning, lessons need to have both content and language goals. "The focus of this kind of instruction is the content rather than the language itself, but unless the language needed for talking about the content is considered an instructional objective, this approach will not succeed" (Wong Fillmore, 1989a, 141).

Another way teachers can effectively meet the needs of language minority pupils is through cooperative learning. Cooperative learning has been advocated as a way to increase academic achievement and improve pupil relationships (Slavin, 1985). Cooperative learning is particularly based on John Dewey's educational philosophy and Leon Vygotsky's ideas about the role of "better capable peers" for a child's cognitive development (Rich, 1993; De Villar & Faltis, 1991). Cooperative learning takes as its starting-point that peer-assisted learning is a more effective way of learning than a whole-class discussion by a teacher. It is an umbrella term for a variety of instructional strategies that have pupils work together in pairs or in small groups (see for descriptions, Slavin, 1985).

Cooperative learning has played an important role in the discussion on tracking and homogeneous grouping and there is a large body of research on its academic and social benefits (Rich, 1993, 61–84; Slavin, 1990; Sharan, 1990). The great majority of these studies have been carried out comparing African-American and Anglo pupil behavior, or low-achieving and high-achieving pupils. The conclusion from these studies is that cooperative learning leads to higher achievement and more positive interactions among all the pupils involved. It does appear that certain cooperative techniques may be better than others for developing particular skills (Slavin, 1985; Sharan, 1990) and their effect may depend on individual pupil characteristics (Rich, 1993).

The assumptions of cooperative learning also seem to hold true for language minority pupils, although fewer studies are available. For the effect of cooperative learning on academic achievement, Kagan (1986) cites a study by Aronson and others (1978), which found that African-American and Mexican-American pupils learned more in a cooperative setting than in traditional classes. Sharan (1990) reports on a study carried out in three junior high schools in Israel that served a mixed-ethnic population (42 percent of whom were Jewish families from Western countries, and 58 percent from the Middle East). Comparing the achievement of pupils in classes using cooperative methods of teaching with that of pupils taught in a frontal way, the researchers found that the former achieved higher scores in oral English proficiency. Sharan & Shachar (1988; in Sharan, 1990, 160–161) also found the cooperative method superior to whole-class instruction for a history and a geography unit.

Cooperative learning also improved social relations among language majority and language minority pupils. Kagan and colleagues (1985) (discussed in Kagan, 1986, 249–250) found strong interactions among technique (traditional classroom cooperative learning), age, and ethnicity. The researchers found strong segregation of pupils in the traditional classroom, whereas the cooperative classroom reduced such segregation, especially in the higher grades. Weiger, Wiser, & Cook (1975; in Sharan, 1990) conducted a study with 231 white, 54 black, and 39 Mexican-American seventh graders. They found that cross-ethnic and cross-racial friendships improved between the white and Mexican-American pupils, though not between the black pupils and either of the two other groups. In the cooperative classroom interpersonal conflict among ethnic groups was significantly less, and more helping behavior was observed. Similarly, the studies by Sharan & Shachar (1988), Sharan and others (1984) (both discussed in Sharan, 1990) found more helping behavior in the classrooms that employed cooperative methods than in classrooms that used whole-class teaching methods. In addition, they found more cross-ethnic interactions in the cooperative classrooms among the Middle-Eastern and Western pupils (in Sharan, 1990).

An additional goal of cooperative learning for language minority pupils is that it will improve their second language development. Interactions with peers are an important factor in second language learning. Cooperative learning is a good way to create a setting where "students have opportunities to use the second language for communicative purposes, and to do so under conditions which do not create high levels of anxiety" (De Villiers & Faltis, 1991, 24). Long and Porter (1985) argue that group work provides more opportunity for language practice, improves the quality of pupil talk, individualizes instruction, creates positive affective climate in the classroom, and increases pupil motivation. In addition, group work provides more comprehensible input through increased negotiation.

Studies by Doughty and Pica (1984; cited in Long & Porter, 1985) and by Pica and Doughty (1985) found indeed that small group discussions allowed for more opportunities to use the target language than whole-class instruction by the teacher. Organizing pupils in small groups seems to encourage second language learning more than does teacher-directed instruction. Kuhlman and others (1990; cited in Johnson, 1994) found that social interactions among Spanish-speaking and English-speaking pupils significantly influenced the pupils' reading and writing skills. Hawkins (1988; cited in De Villiers & Faltis, 1991) presents evidence that language minority pupils improved significantly towards nativelike proficiency in carefully structured small groups with native speakers, even though the instructional time was limited to one hour per day.

Cooperative learning is an instructional technique that seems to have much potential for integrated settings. For language minority pupils, it has been found to result in higher achievement, better social interactions, and increased second language skills. A closer look at the research indicates that teachers have to take several variables into account when organizing small group learning activities with ethnically diverse groups (Schofield & Sagar, 1983). Three factors are especially significant: the nature of the task, the pupils' status, and the need for pupil preparation.

The learning task itself will influence the extent and the quality of the interactions among pupils. From a second language learning perspective, individualized tasks will not easily create opportunities for meaningful interactions among peers. On the other hand, tasks that ask pupils to cooperate can initiate such interaction. Research indicates that tasks which require two-way communication between the participants are more supportive of second language acquisition than one-way tasks. Two-way tasks are tasks in which "the native speaker and the non-native speaker each start out a conversation with information the other needs in order for the pair to complete some task successfully" (Long & Porter, 1985, 214).

Once pupils work together in groups, the challenge is to ensure that all pupils have a chance to learn through interaction. Cohen (1975; described in Slavin, 1985) found that equal status among pupils is a crucial factor for successful cooperation. She points out that the societal unequal status of minority pupils will be sustained in the classroom if teachers do not intervene. As a result, interaction patterns among majority and minority pupils will be unequal, with the majority pupil dominating the interaction.

Cohen (1994) describes the negative impact of status inequality on learning because some pupils cannot gain access to the same opportunities to interaction and sharing ideas. Moreover, status inequalities may reinforce existing prejudice and stereotypes and undermine the process of group work. For example, in an integrated setting where there exists inequality, second language learners will be most likely to take the learners' role and majority pupils to take the leading role. If these roles are not changed, this will reinforce the lower status of the language minority pupil. The effect of these practices becomes clear when roles are changed. Edelsky describes how a monolingual Spanish teacher consciously violated the language norms in the class by refusing to take the learner's role and by teaching Spanish, the subordinate language in the classroom. The effect on the pupils was profound. It "gave the Spanish speaking peer partners a boost, evening up the usual asymmetry where they were always learners" (Edelsky, 1991, 27).

Varonis and Gass look at the issue of status inequality from a second language perspective. They express concern that the "inequality in the status of the participants (with regard to the language medium) actually discourages negotiation because it amplifies rather than masks the differences between them" (Varonis & Gass, 1984, 86). They contrast this assumption with a setting in which there are only second language learners. Since all pupils in this case know they are all still second language learners, the level of comfort for interaction can be higher.

Based on the above, Cohen (1994) suggests strategies to avoid status inequalities which may be detrimental for pupils. On the one hand, teachers have to learn how to be effective facilitators and models for their pupils (see also De Villers & Faltis, 1991). Pupils themselves also need to be trained to learn to listen to each other effectively, to work together, and to reach out for each other.

Tabors and Snow found in a preschool setting that "the English-speaking children chose to play with English-speaking playmates in the classroom until the second language learning children began to communicate in English" (Tabors & Snow, 1994, 119). The consequences for the bilingual children were immediate, as they had to wait for months before they were able to participate in more language-dependent and challenging activities. The only input they received until the moment they could engage in peer interaction was from the adult teacher. An intervention strategy implemented by Hirschler (1991; in Tabors and Snow, 1994) was successful in involving majority speakers in the learning process of second language learners. They taught children how to initiate and how to make certain modifications (rephrasing, asking for clarifications). These strategies were successful in increasing the interactions among pupils. Tabors and Snow conclude that although we know that children can modify their speech and are aware of the need to do so in certain circumstances, with younger children in particular, they are not as likely to understand this need when faced with same-age mates (Tabor & Snow, 1994, 121).

This holds true for cooperative learning as well. Pupils need to be exposed to a model of cooperation and to practice the different skills needed to complete certain tasks before they will be able to collaborate effectively (Johnson, 1983; Cochran, 1989).

Although cooperative learning has important potential for integrated settings under the conditions above, there are other considerations that teachers need to take into account. Research by Wong Fillmore (1982, 1985a, 1992) suggests that classroom composition and the pupils' cultural background may call for different approaches.

The first factor, classroom composition, has already been mentioned before with regard to second language learning. If there are few native speakers in a classroom, the teacher becomes the only nativelike model. Cooperative learning may be less effective for second language learning because the interaction partners do not provide target models based on the second language. Teacher-directed instruction may lead to more successful language acquisition in such cases (Wong-Fillmore, 1982). In contrast, when classes consist of a mixture of second language learners and native-speaking children, second language learners tend to do better with an open classroom organization. For these settings, cooperative learning can create a better second learning environment by providing opportunities for interaction with native peers and adult models. In other words, classroom teachers have to make opportunities for meaningful interactions with native models as optimal as possible given their classroom composition.

Cultural learning style may also play a role in whether pupils will do well in a cooperative setting. Wong Fillmore and co-workers (1985) looked at the influence of classroom practices on the development of oral English in Hispanic and Chinese background language minority pupils. One of the findings of this study was that

> Chinese students seemed to learn best in structured, fairly quiet classrooms, and profited most from interaction with their teachers. Hispanic students profited most from interaction with their peers, and were more sensitive to the quality of teaching and of instructional language than were Chinese students (cited in Chamot, 1988, 21).

These studies show the importance of adapting the classroom to the backgrounds of the pupils by allowing pupils to bring different knowledge, experiences, and learning styles to the academic environment.

A final remark regards the complexity of integrated settings and the goals teachers try to achieve for language minority pupils. As Rich points out,

> when certain educational practices are applied in the heterogeneous class, they often have positive effects on the advancement of one goal while negatively impacting another goal. In other words, means to achieve one goal may prove counterproductive in regards to the other goal (Rich, 1993, 43).

For example, conceptual development in a science class may be perhaps best achieved by allowing pupils to use their first language, even though they report in the second language. This allows pupils to build on their stronger language skills while being engaged in academically challenging second language contexts.

> [M]ost of the students who achieved best in content areas, as measured by tests in English, were those who had the most opportunity to discuss the concepts they were learning in their native language with peers or with adults, even when they were mainstreamed in English-medium classes (Saville-Troike,1984; in Saville-Troike, 1991, 6).

This finding supports the importance of allowing pupils to use their first language and access knowledge through their stronger language. However, at the same time, this practice can cause tensions with social goals that a teacher may have for a particular activity. Working in their native language may prevent language minority pupils from working together with language majority peers, which in turn may make the cooperating group process difficult. What this example illustrates is that meeting the cognitive, linguistic, and social goals will require careful planning and balancing of the positive impact of different tasks:

> we want to use methods that advance one goal without deleteriously affecting the other or, from a more ideal perspective, that positively influence both sets of goals simultaneously (Rich, 1993, 43–44).

Teachers need to be aware of the different factors that play a role in integrated settings. One the one hand, tasks and activities need to be designed to create meaningful and diverse contexts to allow for a varied used of the language. Cooperative learning strategies may enhance academic achievement and improve social relations among pupils, provided that issues of status, task, and preparation have been taken into account. Furthermore, classroom composition and cultural background encourage teachers to emphasize more teacher-directed instruction. Lastly, it is important to recognize the pupils' first language in integrated settings. Not only does this recognition validate the pupils' language, it also provides them with opportunities to further develop that language for academic use, and to access knowledge in their stronger language. In other words, teachers have to carefully balance the cognitive, linguistic, and social goals of integrated settings.

EXAMPLES OF INTEGRATED LANGUAGE MINORITY EDUCATION

The conceptualization of language minority education as a whole school effort is a relatively recent trend and few well developed examples exist as yet. Some schools have formulated integration goals, but have not been able to implement their policies as intended. Moreover, the great majority of efforts have been implemented at the program or classroom level, rather than at the school level. The implementation of integrated language minority programs is therefore still in its beginning stages. However, much can be learned from schools that have tried to address the issue of the academic and social integration of language minority students. Insights from these efforts will aid in formulating policies needed to support a whole school approach to language minority education.

So-called bi-cultural or consolidated classes (see Chapter 7) are the closest to an integrated model in the European context, especially in Denmark, Sweden, and Norway, although many are no longer in operation and no new programs are being implemented following this model, due to a lack of political support. The term is derived from the Swedish *sammansatta* classes, which are characterized by the fact that minority and majority students are put together in one classroom, instead of being assigned to separate classrooms. In the United States, there is a strong movement towards so-called two-way bilingual programs, in which language minority and language majority students are integrated for academics and in which bilingualism for all students is the goal. A model that characterizes a position between the bicultural and the two-way bilingual programs is an integration project developed by Brisk (1991), which involved the complete integration of a bilingual and a monolingual 5th grade. Experiences with these three models will be described below.

Consolidated Classes

Consolidated classes are comprised of 50 percent language minority students from the same language background and 50 percent language majority students. Language minority students learn to read in the minority language first before reading in the second language is introduced. The first language is also used to introduce the concepts of a new unit. For these activities, students are grouped by language group. Students are integrated for all other activities, which are conducted in the majority language, with the minority language teacher available for support. As language minority students acquire more second language skills, the role of the native language as a support language for subject matter is reduced. This role generally ends at the 4th-grade level. The minority language is continued to be taught in the home language classes, however (see Chapter 7). During the first three years, language minority students receive additional second language instruction during which material discussed in the home language is covered in the second language. After the third year, these second language classes become extra second language lessons, primarily focusing on language arts.

The Hvidovre community in Denmark started consolidated classes at the kindergarten and 1st-grade level for Turkish students at the Enghøjskole in 1984. Up until then, language minority students were held back in kindergarten for one year to increase their second language skills. Once they arrived in 1st-grade, it became clear, however, that they were academically still behind their peers and pull-out second language classes had to be organized. Moreover, the language minority students were not socially integrated with their peers. These issues caused teachers and parents to look for an alternative approach to language minority education, which they found in the consolidated classes.

At the Enghøjskole, teachers used a thematic approach and created "workstations" with hands-on activities. For example, when the students were working on the senses, there was a workstation for each of the senses. The workstation on "taste" asked students to taste several items and identify whether the items were sour, sweet, salty, or bitter. Teachers indicated that the process of integration confronted them with several issues they had not considered beforehand.

One issue was how to refer to the two classes. Students were separate for language arts and introductory lessons, but were otherwise together. The teachers noted the importance of treating the two groups as one class, instead of thinking about the integrated periods as "when 1.d [the Turkish group] goes to 1.c [the Danish group]." They felt that this usage would reinforce the unequal status between the two groups. Another issue was the physical environment. Things like different colors of work folders and cubby holes were felt to discourage a sense of belonging to the same class. An important aspect of the social integration was to teach students not to refer to each other as "the Turkish kid did it," or "the Danish kid did it," but to treat their peers "as somebody with a name and responsible for their own actions" (*To-Kulturel Skolestart*, 1985, 50–51). One important policy that the 1st-grade teachers implemented was to start the school year with two weeks of complete integration. During these first two weeks the children participated in nonverbal, hands-on activities, aimed at getting to know each other and establishing the sense of community.

An evaluation report of the 4th, 5th, and 6th grade consolidated classes describes the actual practices in the consolidated classes and explores some the barriers to successful implementation (Moldenhawer, 1992). Using observations and interviews and some standardized tests, the study looks at math skills, oral Danish skills, Danish reading skills, home language skills, social integration, ethnicity, parent involvement, teacher relationships. Although the data gathered was informal and limited in scope, it suggests some trends of student achievement and the social integration of students.

For oral Danish skills the study relied on teacher judgment for their measurement and found important differences between the Danish and the Turkish children in oral Danish, in favor of the Danish-speaking students. Whereas teachers indicated that 77.6 percent of the Danish children spoke Danish "well" or "very well," only 37.8 percent of the Turkish/Kurdish pupils were classified in these categories. In support of the framework presented before, the study also found that oral skills were better for those students who chose to work together with Danish and Turkish peers. Interestingly enough, this pattern held true for Danish students as well: working with students from both groups (v. working with members of own group) also positively affected their math and oral language skills. On the other hand, working predominantly within their own group only negatively affected the Turkish/Kurdish group.

This pattern of dominance almost disappears in mathematics. The data indicate that of all Danish children 67.7 percent were said to be "good" or "very good" in math, whereas 62.3 percent of the Turkish/Kurdish children fell into these categories. More Turkish/Kurdish students were classified as doing "badly" in math (10.1 percent v. 3.6 percent of the Danish children).

For academic integration, the study showed that about one-fifth of the boys and girls in either ethnic group chose to work with members of both groups. Compared to the other groups, Turkish/Kurdish boys preferred to work with members of their own group, whereas Turkish/Kurdish girls and Danish boys showed comparatively more preference for working alone. Since the study did not correct for proportion of Danish and Turkish/Kurdish students in the classroom, these results have to be interpreted with care. The patterns found may simply have been the result of the fact that there are more or fewer Danish or Turkish/Kurdish students to interact with. In 5th and 6th grade, the pupils tended to choose their friends first along gender and then along ethnic lines, but at the 4th-grade level, Turkish/Kurdish and Danish girls were friends. However, in neither grade did the pupils spend much time together outside of school.

It seems then that the social and academic integration poses a real challenge to the consolidated classes. Since the report does not address the issue of instructional strategies which are used to bring students together, it is difficult to determine whether these results reflect a shortcoming of the consolidated classes themselves or a lack of change in the classrooms towards more collaborative work.

Engelbrecht, Iversen, and Engel (1990, 1991, 1992) report on similar experiences with consolidated classes in Høje-Taastrup, Denmark. The teachers point out that they used different instructional strategies, such as a thematic curriculum and hands-on activities. They emphasize the need for intensive common planning to improve the coordination between the Turkish and the Danish component. The teachers felt that the consolidated classes improved students' self-esteem, allowed a more natural incorporation of the first language and culture in the curriculum, and significantly changed home-school relationships. The latter was, for example, reflected in how teachers succeeded in overcoming cultural barriers in getting permission of Turkish parents to allow their children (especially the girls) to go on field trips, and to participate in gym and swimming.

Interviews with teachers in Høje-Taastrup make clear that the role of bilingual teacher was different in the consolidated classes. As the school wrestled with fewer hours of home language support, the teachers became aware of the advantages they had had in previous years.

The bilingual teacher explains how she is unhappy in her current position. She used to be fulltime in the consolidated classes (first and second grade), but has now been assigned two hours for the fifth graders. Her schedule is filled up with teaching home language classes to second and fourth graders after school. She states that in the beginning the consolidated classes allowed her to be an equal to the Danish teacher, but that nowadays they don't plan anymore because of the two hours. The Danish teacher's response to the diminishing hours was also one of regret. She recalls how the two of them would plan every single detail every week for every lesson together. With the bilingual teacher coming in only two hours a week, this becomes almost superfluous: they continue what they have started earlier in the week [Notes, Denmark] (De Jong (1993b).

The bilingual teacher is also perceived as an important safeguard for quality by the Danish teachers.

The Danish teacher expressed how without the presence of the bilingual teacher in the consolidated class she is more nervous about whether the Turkish children really understand her. Similar experiences were reported by another Danish teacher in the same situation, who added that she started to go over the same materials again and again to ensure understanding, thus feeling that she is losing much time. She comments that the bilingual teacher was always able to tell when the students did not understand something and jump in to explain the concepts in Turkish, or ask comprehension questions [Notes, Denmark] (De Jong, 1993b).

These examples show the importance of collaboration and the importance of the bilingual teacher. The bilingual teacher played an important part in maintaining high expectations for language minority students, and the Danish teachers trusted their professional judgment.

A formal and long-term evaluation of a consolidated program was carried out by Löfgren & Ouvinen-Birgerstam (1982) with Finnish-speaking children in Lund, Sweden. They looked at student achievement from preschool and up until 3rd-grade at the elementary school level in a program, where there was "composite [sammansatta] instruction in mathematics and general subjects, the children being mainly taught Swedish together with the rest of the class, but with some terms being explained in Finnish by the teacher" (Löfgren & Ouvinen-Birgerstam, 1982, 325). The first language was used for instruction or added explanation for the entire period of the study. Students were expected to be ready for full instruction in Swedish by grade 4, which gives the program a transitional goal although Finnish home language classes would continue after grade 4.

They had language arts in Swedish with Swedish children (they had studied Swedish as a foreign language (Sfs) in a two year K program), parallel classes separated in Finnish and Swedish and some other subjects, combined classes in mathematics and other subjects in Swedish (Paulston, 1982, 49).

The study found that Finnish children had an increased opportunity to develop a functional bilingualism. Their skills in Finnish were better than those of other comparable Finnish pupils. Furthermore, "school achievement of the Finnish children taking part in the project are on level with their Swedish classmates . . . their grade 3 level of proficiency in the Swedish language is practically the same as that of comparable Swedish pupils" (Löfgren & Ouvinen-Birgerstam, 1982, 329).

Although the consolidated classes are transitional in nature, they are different in several ways from transitional bilingual reception programs. First, whereas transitional bilingual programs often employ a curriculum separate and independent from the regular curriculum, consolidated classes integrate the curriculum conducted in the first and the second language. Secondly, although the role of the first language diminishes for instruction in consolidated classes, students are able to continue developing their first language through the mother tongue classes. In transitional bilingual education programs, such option for maintenance does not exist. Moreover, since these home language classes have started as part of the consolidated classes, they often attempt to maintain the relationship with the second language curriculum. Lastly, whereas transitional bilingual programs segregate students, consolidated programs offer students the opportunity to share experiences and work together for academic and social purposes.

The lack of formal, long-term evaluations makes it hard to draw conclusions about the consolidated classes. The study by Löfgren & Ouvinen-Birgerstam (1982) indicates that the positive academic effects for language minority students with an emphasis in the early years is on the first language and integration with majority speakers. Experiences with the Danish consolidated classes illustrate that the consolidated classes have been successful at the social and academic integration of language minority students and teachers. The studies also stress the need for school reform, including the use of the first language as medium of instruction, instructional innovation (such as a thematic approach, hands-on experiences), close curriculum coordination, adequate materials, and teacher collaboration.

Multilingual and Multicultural Mainstream Education

Brisk (1991) documents experiences with a model that integrated a monolingual and a transitional bilingual education class. Two 5th-grade classes, one transitional bilingual classroom, and one monolingual classroom were clustered together. The project involved two monolingual English teachers and one bilingual Spanish/English teacher. Students were grouped by their own homeroom (i.e., monolingual or bilingual classroom) for morning activities, social studies, and English as a Second Language. They were integrated for reading and language arts, math and science. Flexible grouping practices were important to the success of the program: bilingual students were grouped by homeroom, with English-speaking peers or with mainstreamed bilingual students. The language of instruction changed accordingly: Spanish-only, English-only, or both languages (with the bilingual teacher). Adjustments in the groups were made for individual students throughout the year. As an example, Brisk gives the schedule for Carlos:

> Carlos, a recent arrival from El Salvador, has a math class taught bilingually; reading, language arts, and social studies class taught in Spanish; a science class with some units done bilingually and others in English (depending on the teacher); and special subjects such as art, music and gym in English. In addition, he does 30 minutes of ESL daily with the bilingual teachers. Therefore, Carlos receives most of the instruction in the language he understands, while receiving a considerable and varied amount of instruction in English (Brisk, 1991, 118–119).

The grouping exposed the English-speakers to Spanish, although no attempt was made to formally teach the language to them. However, it sensitized the students to hearing other languages around them, and multilingualism rather than monolingualism was considered the norm in classes.

The integrated cluster appeared to be a positive experience for all involved. Brisk reports that majority and minority students developed positive attitudes towards their own language and towards the language of the other students. Although the learning of Spanish was not a goal of the program, several English-speaking students picked up the language and the Spanish-speaking students did not feel threatened in their efforts to learn English. The supportive environment for the first language allowed students to continue learning, an important factor especially for those students who took longer to adjust to a new country due to personal traumas or homesickness. The study also found a positive effect on bilingual students who had been previously mainstreamed. The model allowed them to continue to use their native language, instead of having to drop or hide their first language after being mainstreamed.

The model also impacted the teachers who "learned to trust each other's ability to educate all students" (Brisk, 1991,125). Monolingual teachers improved their strategies to teach a class with second language learners, and bilingual teachers "have benefitted because their status has changed not only among their colleagues but among mainstreamed students. Bilingual teachers bring a new image of the bilingual adult to English-speaking students" (Brisk, 1991, 126).

Overall, then, this model had positive results for everyone involved. Important factors contributing to the success of the model were the fact that both languages were used for academic learning and communication, and that individual student's needs constituted the basis for the teachers' decisionmaking regarding how they could best learn. Moreover, the three teachers considered all students as students of one class, thus sharing ownership and including students' needs in their teaching.

Two-Way Bilingual Programs

Two-way bilingual programs come perhaps closest to the goal of integrated education in the United States (other labels for these programs are dual immersion, developmental bilingual, bilingual immersion; Christian & Mahrer, 1992).

The first two-way bilingual school was the Coral Way school in Dade County (Miami), Florida. It was established for the children of Cuban refugees in the late 1960s who wanted to maintain their Spanish. The success of the school influenced the establishment of several other bi-language programs before the passing of the Bilingual Education Act (BEA) in 1974. After the BEA was passed the focus of bilingual education shifted to transitional programs and it was not until the late 1980s that two-way bilingual programs reappeared as an alternative model of language minority education in the United States.

Two-way bilingual programs integrate language minority and language majority students, and use both languages for instruction. There is a wide range of ways that two-way programs have been organized to meet the needs of their local circumstances. The two languages can be employed in a variety of ways: by content area (for example, math in Spanish; science in English), by time (for example, mornings in Spanish, afternoons in English), or by person (for example, one teacher uses only Spanish, and another teacher uses only English for instruction). Students are likely to be grouped by language for language arts instruction, while heterogeneous grouping occurs for other subjects. The distribution of the two languages also differs largely. Some schools have a 50-50 percent distribution from the beginning, other schools emphasize the minority language more in the lower grades.

Two-way programs have the potential of avoiding the negative effects associated with a loss of cultural bearings and of preventing segregation, while creating a supportive learning environment as discussed in this chapter. Lindholm (1992) summarizes the principles which guide two-way bilingual programs and their relationship to the literature on first and second language learning. Students in two-way programs are taught together, the native language of language minority students is used for academic learning and is maintained throughout the program. Minority teachers can serve as positive models. Two-way bilingual programs also allow for natural and extensive exposure to the dominant language, while at the same time giving the minority language a high status in the school. The integrated activities can enhance cross-cultural attitudes, and improve teacher relationships (Glenn & LaLyre, 1991).

> The only school that has made great strides in eliminating that is [the two-way program]. I really do think that. Because the integration is a very big part of that program. Alice [a two-way teacher] also said it yesterday that they don't consider that this is my group, these are Alice's kids, these are Donna's kids. They're our kids. And I really get that sense of it's a real team, the teachers really team together and the kids feel that also too. They look at themselves as program, an overall program, where they all connect some way [Bilingual curriculum coordinator, USA] (De Jong, 1993a).

The directory of two-way bilingual programs compiled by the Center for Applied Linguistics (Christian & Mahrer, 1992, 1993, 1994) indicates that there are 174 two-way bilingual programs nationwide. The great majority uses Spanish and English (160 schools) and have been implemented at the K–6 level (144 schools) (Christian & Mahrer, 1992). Two-way bilingual programs have generally been implemented at the program level, i.e., they are a program within a school. Few schools exist that have established a whole school two-way approach.

Little is known about the effects of the different two-way models that have been implemented, or the actual contexts of two-way bilingual programs. An exception is a report issued by the Massachusetts Department of Education that presents profiles of two-way bilingual programs in Massachusetts, including classroom observations. There have been some formal evaluations, however, and they support the success of two-way bilingual education. Most of these evaluations have focused on language skills and math.

For example, Lindholm & Alclan (1991) and Lindholm (1991) looked at an English/Spanish bilingual/immersion program that aimed at developing high levels of proficiency in the two languages, at demonstrating normal to superior proficiency in the two languages, and at showing high levels of psychosocial competence and positive cross-cultural attitudes. Both studies only reported on academic achievement as measured by standard-ized test scores for English, Spanish, and math. They found advanced math skills and reading and language skills in both languages for all learners com-pared to students in other programs. It is important to point out that these two-way programs were part of a general educational innovation that in-cluded training teachers to interact equitably with language minority and language majority students, and to promote equal status in the classroom. Students were integrated for all content instruction in a high-quality curricu-lum equivalent to the curriculum taught in mainstream classes. Moreover, instructional strategies included whole language, discovery math, integrated thematic subject matter, and cooperative learning.

One formally evaluated program is the AMIGOS-program in Cam-bridge, Massachusetts. Cazabon, Lambert, & Hall (1992) compared student achievement on Spanish and English between the students in the AMIGOS program and matched control groups. Except for Spanish-reading skills, the study found that the students in the AMIGOS program outscored their con-trol group peers on English, Spanish, and math. In a later study, Lambert & Cazabon (1994) looked at students' self-perceptions as developing bilinguals. The small number of participating students makes the interpre-tation of the results difficult but certain trends can be indicated. Whereas the Spanish-speaking students feel comfortable and proficient in both lan-guages (including the ability to translate), the English-speaking students feel more proficient in English and feel their Spanish reading skills are stronger than writing or oral skills in that language. The two groups do not show an ethnic or linguistic preference for their choice of close friends and prefer the bilingual classes over monolingual classes. Finally, students favor speak-ing English over Spanish in any given social situation, especially the older students.

The strengths of the two-way programs is also illustrated in studies by Collier and colleagues (reported in Olsen & Leone, 1994; Thomas & Collier, 1995), who found more long-term educational gains in five urban school districts for students who attended two-way programs than for stu-dents in other bilingual or English as a Second Language programs. She also indicates the following school characteristics that support the academic out-comes: integrated schooling with English speakers, high expectations, equal status of the two languages, parent involvement, and staff development. Continuous support for the first language results in higher long-term achieve-ment levels after the 6th-grade level.

Two-way bilingual programs represent a successful way to language minority education. It is clear that the overall school reform that has accompanied two-way programs is a crucial contributor to the success of these programs. The studies by Collier and Lindholm emphasize that changes in instructional strategies, parent involvement, and expectations play an important role in the implementation of two-way bilingual programs. This fact reinforces the notion that language minority education has to be concerned with education, not just with language learning.

Although two-way bilingual programs aim at bilingualism for all students, many are wrestling with the development of Spanish language skills. Among students, English is the preferred language. Observations in two-way bilingual classes often indicate that students will use English, even when instruction is in Spanish (Edelsky, 1991). As stated earlier, Lambert & Cazabon (1994) found that pupils preferred speaking English for all social situations. This is not surprising. In classroom situations, the Spanish-speakers speak better English than the English-speakers speak Spanish. Moreover, in language-contact situations it is the higher status language that tends to dominate, unless there is a clear case of diglossia, in which case each language has been assigned a particular domain. Not only does this mean that English-speaking students have less opportunities to develop their second language, it also results in language loss for the language minority students. Snow goes as far as to say that two-way programs are subtractive environments, because "if the Spanish speakers in those two-way programs learn English, they are very likely to lose Spanish" (Snow, 1993, 408).

Two-way bilingual programs do not constitute a feasible alternative for all situations, however. Their applicability is limited as they require, among other things, a stable pupil population, a second language which is valued by majority parents, and a student body which represents the two languages in the school. The reality is that school districts are often dealing with low-incidence groups, with students from various language background in the same school, and with a transient language minority population. For these groups, the principles that are underlying integrated language minority education need to be implemented in accordance with the local needs.

Conclusions

Consolidated classes, the multilingual and multicultural mainstream education model, and two-way bilingual programs represent ways in which schools have tried to implement an integrated approach to language minority education. Although rarely schoolwide approaches, these programs take a first step into the direction of making the education of language minority pupils a more integral part of the general education context. They show that language minority education must deal with educational issues, not just linguistic issues. They illustrate the importance of allowing students to use their own language freely, and of trying to give that language equal status within the school. Experiences with the programs also stress the need for change. The success of these programs depended largely on changing curriculum and instruction, on teacher collaboration, and on having the flexibility to adapt to local circumstances without compromising the principles of integrated education for language minority pupils.

NOTES

1. In fact, Wong Fillmore uses the term "semilingualism" (not knowing either language) as a potential outcome of these situations if the teacher is not a fluent second language speaker.

> Given the conditions under which they were learning English, we might ask: What are the chances that they are going to learn a fully realized version of their second language? What happens when children do not learn a second language completely after deciding to give up their first language? One hesitates to suggest that the result may be what some people have described as "semilingualism" (Wong Fillmore, 1992, 55).

The concept of "semilingualism" was introduced in Sweden in the 1960s by Hansegård (1968) to refer to the imperfect learning of two languages. It has generally been dismissed as no a valid theoretical construct due to lack of research evidence, however (Paulston, 1982).

2. "Self-esteem" is used here as an index of psychological well-being.

9 CONCLUSIONS AND RECOMMENDATIONS

The Policy Context

The presence of immigrants from developing nations has become a major policy issue in most industrialized countries (Chapter 1). Some charge that this presence places an unacceptable cost burden upon the native population, others that educational underachievement by the children of immigrants threatens them with permanently subordinate status. Concern with *class* is paralleled by a concern with *culture*: Does the presence of a large number of immigrants who are culturally very distinct from the majority threaten to distort or corrupt the host society? Or will immigrants form an inassimilable minority within that society and threaten its security or ability to act in a coherent way? Ironically, all of these concerns were raised in the 1840s in the United States, when many opinion-shapers were deeply worried about the Irish and German Catholic immigrants who were believed to threaten the loss of the American character and democratic political system (Glenn, 1988b).

In response to these fears, anti-immigrant sentiment has risen in each of the countries surveyed, expressing itself both in violent incidents directed against immigrants and refugees and also in political pressure for the exclusion of new immigrants and the repatriation or rapid assimilation of those already present. Schools are asked to bear a major share of the responsibility for ensuring that the children of immigrants become neither a permanent underclass nor an unassimilated minority.

They must be enabled to play an 'American role.' That is, they must learn to lend themselves to a cultural situation that requires a new extension of their identity . . . it is our moral obligation to teach people English—otherwise we are engaging in an insidious kind of veiled discrimination that discourages the young national origin minority students from investing in education (Alatis, 1983, 30).

Ensuring the success of the children of immigrants has led education authorities, in many cases, to create programs for them intended to meet their needs more effectively than by simply putting them into classes with majority children. In order to prevent the perpetuation of separate and noncooperating ethnic minority groups, and to provide full access to educational opportunities, however, there are compelling arguments for integrating the children of immigrants as quickly as possible, "to treat them just like everyone else." For many parents of majority children and for cultural conservatives, the adjustments to school programs made to promote integration and mutual understanding seem to confirm the fear of *Überfremdung*, of a loss of familiar and essential cultural goods. Recently, growing sensitivity about the costs of the presence of immigrants makes it difficult to develop new programs targeted to their children, or even to maintain those already in place. Some of the programs described in Chapter 7, indeed, have been scaled back or abandoned since they were visited by the authors.

Chapter 2 discusses the origins and character of postwar immigration to the industrialized nations of the West. Of particular significance for this study is the shift from the European immigration of the fifties and sixties to the Third World immigration of recent decades, creating far greater cultural tensions and ensuring that immigrants and their children are highly visible. Also significant is the family reunification that began in the 1970s and led to a rapid change in the profile of the immigrant population of Western Europe, from a group made up disproportionately of workers to a group made up disproportionately of children. This pattern was reinforced by the changing economies of the host societies, which had less and less place for unskilled workers; while foreign workers were invited, explicitly or implicitly, in earlier decades, the refugees and asylum-seekers of recent years are defined more by their plight than by their potential.

Countries differ in their policies toward the naturalization of foreigners— and the groups of resident foreigners differ in their eagerness to *be* naturalized, particularly when this requires renunciation of their previous nationality. On the other hand, for many immigrants the choice is stark: either "make it" in the host society through extensive participation (and loss of much distinctiveness) or become trapped in a marginal position; "families no longer have three generations in which to enter the mainstream" (González, 1981, 31).

Government interventions to address the social needs created by immigration have changed in response to this evolution. The tendency in recent years has been away from programs targeted to particular minority groups and toward broader social reconstruction, usually as an aspect of policies to address poverty and marginalization among the native population as well; some experts insist, however, that the problems facing members of minority groups require distinctive approaches. The contrast with the optimistic reception programs for postwar immigrants to Canada or Australia, assuming that with a little assistance they would fit right in, is evident.

Minority Groups and Their Languages

In Chapter 3, the situation of "indigenous" language minority groups is used to explore how societies manage to accommodate the active use of more than one language. Minority languages have survived in such situations only when associated with territories where they are in active and daily use and serve as a symbol and instrument of demands for regional autonomy; the "territorial principle," under which the right to use a language for official purposes is associated with a geographical area rather than with individual preference, is thus guarded jealously in Belgium, Switzerland, Quebec, and Catalonia. Bilingualism, under such circumstances, may be perceived as a threat to the continued use of the minority language. "The more bilingual our children become," a French-Canadian lamented, "the more they use English; the more they use English, the less they find French useful; the less they find French useful, the more they use English. The paradox of French-Canadian life is the following: the more we become bilingual, the less it is necessary to be bilingual" (quoted by McLaughlin, 1985, 76). Any acknowledgment of the languages of immigrant groups might threaten the status of the officially protected minority language under such circumstances.

The case of Ireland suggests that, when the political significance of a minority language fades, it is maintained in active use only half-heartedly despite government sponsorship. The situation of Spanish in Puerto Rico, though similarly protected at present by its symbolic function, is more secure than that of the Irish language a century ago, largely because it is spoken daily by the local majority and because of contacts with the wider Latin-American language and culture sphere; it is unlikely that simply using it for governmental functions, as with the Irish language, would preserve its use absent these other factors. Among Puerto Ricans in the continental United States, continual contact with the island and the importance of Spanish for ethnic awareness and solidarity have maintained the symbolic significance of the language, though in most cases not in the form of extensive and accurate proficiency among the younger generation.

"Native peoples," the aboriginal inhabitants of areas later settled by colonists from northwestern Europe—Maori in New Zealand, Aboriginal and Torres Straits groups in Australia, Lapps or Sami of Scandinavia, Indians and Inuit of North America—have in most cases not been able to continue the use of their ancestral languages apart from a few religious and other traditional spheres. Participation in modern economies, even in a rather marginal position, requires use of the majority language, and maintenance of another language in the home seems not to persist over more than two or three generations of extensive contact with the majority society, particularly if that contact is successful. "Rhetoric about cultural pluralism," as Paulston points out, "accounts for little if the objectives [of effective participation] are not implemented; the community-run Navajo school, as measured by the achievement test . . . , was markedly inferior academically to the government run school" (Paulston, 1992a, 24).

That the attitudes of indigenous language minority groups toward official use of their home languages is highly varied should warn us against overgeneralization about the significance of language in relation to culture and identity. Bernard Spolsky describes two Indian "pueblos with the same language: in one, where there is high language maintenance, there is strong opposition to bilingual education because it might bring the school into areas best left to the home and the community; in another, where few of the children speak the language, bilingual education is encouraged because it will teach the native language and thus help to preserve the native religion" (Spolsky, 1978a, 277).

Chapter 4 turns to the situation of immigrants, considered in relation to the varying welcome extended to them by the host societies, and in relation to their homelands, to immigrant "communities" (some more deserving than others of that name), to religious traditions and beliefs, and to ethnic leadership. Ties to the homeland are quickly broken in most cases in North America and Australia and—though sometimes promoted vigorously by homeland governments hoping to maintain influence, and by host governments hoping to encourage reverse migration—scarcely more enduring in most cases in Europe. Ethnic communities are far more significant for most (though by no means all) immigrants, either as a support during the adjustment process or, for some, as an alternative to completing that adjustment.

Religion seems to be the most enduring aspect of a previous existence in the homeland, persevering both as belief and as practice over a number of generations (though of course not in the case of every individual) and adapting to new languages and new cultural forms with relative ease. Many immigrants indeed become more rather than less strict in their religious observance, though others simply abandon all practice in the secularized host societies. Few immigrants make a change of religion—from, say, Islam to Catholicism—though they may switch from lukewarm participation in the established religion of their homelands to more fervent sectarian forms of the same. The apparent exception, the high rate of Protestant church participation among Korean immigrants to the United States, was in fact already well-established through missionary activity in Korea before the emigration. For Koreans and other immigrant groups, participation in a religiously-based ethnic organization may serve an important transitional function into the host society, since such organizations have a greater capacity to acculturate without losing their reason for existence than do groups whose only basis is shared ethnicity.

Chapter 4 also considers the situation of the second generation, and several patterns of response are described. Some are marginalized from both the culture and communal solidarities of their immigrant parents and also from those of the host society. Other move easily in both, while yet others cleave to the one and reject the other. Thus, "it would be too simple to understand the choices faced by immigrants and their children as lying along a single continuum running between maintenance of the original identity, language, and mores intact, and their complete abandonment for those of the host society." Policy prescriptions that attempt to make the decision for the children of immigrants, or that make it more difficult for them to participate fully in the host society, are a recipe for maintaining social and economic inequalities. Unfortunately, "there has been a loss of nerve among elites, in recent decades, about the possibility that immigrants or their children can—or should—become fully-assimilated members of the host society. This has been more the result of currents of intellectual fashion than of any actual loss, on the part of Western countries, of their capacity to absorb and transform new populations. The *process* of assimilation has been continuing, by and large, even as the concept has been challenged."

It's not always clear, in policy discussions, what is meant by the terms "assimilation," "acculturation," and "integration" (Just, 1985c, 23–24). This lack of clarity may be intentional, with the chosen words intended to signal different intentions to different audiences; "in France the term 'insertion' is used sometimes because it has no precise meaning" (Lapeyronnie, 1993, 22).

The Dutch government tried for years to pursue an ambiguous "two-track" policy of "integration with maintenance of a distinctive identity"—

given official expression in 1974—while failing to recognize that cultural elements that may be entirely functional in the homeland may be highly dysfunctional in the immigration situation (Entzinger, 1986, 52).

> Integration without assimilation, integration of minorities which remain culturally distant from the majority, these notions we would propose to call "ideological" because from a sociological point of view they obviously neglect the determinants and regularities which operate in social reality. . . . Ideologists who would like to exploit the migrant's situation for power reasons or for the sake of their "true belief" might perhaps not be interested in "solving" the minority problem by integration or assimilation. A *Realpolitiker*, however, acting in the interest of the immigrants, would opt in the first instance for the removal of barriers against integration and assimilation; recognizing that their lifespans are limited and they would like to enjoy a higher status (which was the motivation to emigrate) during their lifetime, he would not want the immigrants to wait for the realization of a Utopia. . . . There would be very little tolerance if immigrants were to claim, for example, the right to a deviating work culture (Hoffmann-Nowotny, 1986, 204–205).

On the other hand, in a free society people presumably have the right to be "backward" or unadapted, like the Amish in the United States, and not have their efforts to maintain a way of life that is important to them continually undermined by well-meaning government policies and helping professionals, like teachers and social workers, who have very different beliefs and values. Professional interventions not uncommonly have the effect of weakening the problem-solving strategies of the immigrants themselves and replacing them with a dependence upon government.

Some have suggested that a wiser policy would seek to strengthen the capacity of ethnic organizations and institutions to meet the needs of their members; on the other hand, we have seen in Chapter 4 the tendency of those who come to depend for status and livelihood upon being "professional ethnics" to maintain the marginal position of the rank and file whose marginality provides the justification for their services and advocacy. In Manchester (England) in 1989–1990, for example, there were 272 full-time government jobs tied directly to serving ethnic minority groups (Lapeyronnie, 1993, 285), and, according to critics, there are ethnic spokesmen "for whom no prospect is more frightful than the emergence of a Black and Asian bourgeoisie in Britain" (Levy, 1986, 122). In France, by contrast, there are very few special units or positions designated for minority concerns, resulting in "a feeble institutionalization of the representation of immigrant minorities and a feeble professionalization of action on their behalf" (Lapeyronnie, 1993, 340). Ethnic leadership plays a double role in relation to immigrants, both representing their interests in relation to the host society and seeking to maintain group loyalty at some cost to full participation in that society. For those ethnic groups that come to occupy a favorable niche in the host economy—Hasidim in the diamond trade, or Koreans in the grocery business—ethnic group solidarity may be advantageous, but for others it may reinforce a marginal and disadvantaged position.

Cultural distinctiveness can only be maintained through distinct parallel institutions that make it unnecessary for members of an ethnic group to subject themselves to the assimilating effects of the majority institutions—schools, most kinds of employment, the legal system, political structures. As Lotty Eldering has pointed out, for most immigrants and their children, "multi-culturalism" will be largely confined to the private spheres of life, including the religious institutions in which their distinctiveness and alternative values have the best chance of finding semipublic expression and validation (Eldering, 1986b, 266–268). Hawkins adds,

> The most important fact about immigrants . . . is their primary motive for migrating. It is fair to say that the majority of immigrants . . . do not uproot themselves and leave their native land in order to lead the same kind of life in a foreign country . . . a great many immigrants look forward to becoming Canadians or Australians. The preservation of cultural heritage is a lesser concern and for them the whole concept of multiculturalism can be confusing (Hawkins, 1989, 217).

Immigrant groups, Chapter 5 points out, rarely maintain the active use of their original languages beyond the second generation. Apart from the "territorial" language groups described in Chapter 3, and individuals for whom it is occupationally advantageous, stable bilingualism—as contrasted with transitional bilingualism within an individual or a family over the course of several generations—is a fairly rare phenomenon in the industrialized nations of the West (though reportedly much more common in parts of India and of Africa). Well-educated Canadians or Belgians or Swiss, especially those working in government, are likely to be reasonably bilingual, as are merchants or professionals serving language minority communities, and political and cultural leaders in those communities who must deal extensively with the majority society, but they are the exceptions.

Chapter 5 presents data on intergenerational language maintenance and reviews the factors that in most cases lead to eventual monolingualism in the language of the host society, whatever schools may seek to do. Proficiency in the majority language is continually rewarding: "whether or not one comes from a home where a second language is frequently spoken is not an important issue in itself, but whether or not one is competent in English is" (Baratz-Snowden et al., 1988a, 173). Under such circumstances, there is no need for the host society to seek to suppress the use of immigrant languages, and in fact it is exceedingly rare that it does so, or needs to do so. Generally, as proficiency in carrying out academic, work, and other tasks in the second language increases, that in doing so in the first declines; "research suggests that language balance—in the sense of native-like proficiency in two languages—is impossible to obtain in practice" (McLaughlin, 1985, 33). After all,

> if over the course of time a language loses exclusivity within a domain, and one (other) language comes to serve across all, then an unstable bilingualism results which does not bode well for the continued survival within the group of both languages (Edwards, 1988, 203).

Schools are often called upon to help in the maintenance of minority languages, and Chapter 5 reviews the arguments advanced for and against programs to teach these languages to the children and grandchildren of immigrants, on the assumption that they will not attain a sufficient mastery through practice and example in the home. The principle of "minority language rights" has been enshrined in some international covenants, in studiously unspecific language that leaves it up to each government to determine what this will mean in practice.

A case has also been made that the academic underachievement of many minority children results from a lack of emphasis upon their home language and culture, leading to low self-esteem and to alienation from the school. The research evidence for this theory is notably weak. For example, the French government's circular, in 1973, authorizing the first home language classes (in Portuguese) asserted that "a lack of mastery of the mother tongue leads to difficulties for the newly-arrived in learning French," and subsequent official statements repeated this postulate again and again without ever offering objective evidence based upon "serious observations, statistical studies or evaluations" (Seksig, 1992, 91). Questioning along the same lines, an American expert on sociolinguistics has written that she knows of no research which investigates whether equal educational opportunity as manifest through bilingual education programs really leads to raised socioeconomic status. It is the major assumption of bilingual education, but among structural-functional research it remains not only untested but also unquestioned—it is a question outside the paradigm (Paulston, 1992b, 73–74).

Programs to maintain home languages come into existence under differing forms of sponsorship: homeland governments seeking to maintain loyalty, ethnic organizations (often religious) seeking to reinforce community cohesion, and the education authorities of the host country, convinced by appeals to one or more of the arguments discussed. These modalities and their implications are discussed in Chapter 5, and Chapter 7 returns in greater depth to the actual experiences and to evaluations of them.

The conclusion of Chapter 5 is that two of the lines of argument for language maintenance—the asserted right of ethnic groups to maintain an identity inseparably linked to their ancestral language, and the alleged importance of the home language to the self-esteem of minority pupils—provide an unconvincing basis for making language maintenance a goal of public policy. "The only ones who can legitimately—and effectively—decide whether language-minority children and youth will maintain and develop the language and the culture of their ancestors are those children and youth and parents acting on their behalf, and they will have to do so in their daily lives. School programs supporting that resolution are a generous and possibly a wise accommodation, so long as participation is truly voluntary and not based upon an automatic assignment of minority children in ways which make their schooling differ from that of their majority peers." There is however no reason to believe that such efforts will be successful, absent strong community support for language maintenance.

> I will not be surprised to find that successful transitional [bilingual] programs will encourage more rapid acquisition of English and consequent loss of use of the native language by groups which have no strong internal desire for language maintenance. In other words, I do not think that bilingual education is a causal factor by itself in language loss or maintenance, but plays its part among other factors, depending upon the situation and attitude of the rest of the community (Spolsky, 1978a, 281).

On the other hand, Chapter 5 shows, the arguments commonly used *against* the use of minority languages in schooling—"that immigrant groups will not fit within society and that social order will be threatened if immigrants and their children are not required to use the majority language" and "that it may divert attention and time away from giving the children of immigrants the skills and habits, the attitudes and expectations that they will need to participate successfully in the host society, in its political system, and in its economy"—are equally groundless, at least when minority language instruction is well-integrated into the program of an effective school. The chapter concludes by looking ahead to Chapter 8, which "will consider a third, and potentially the strongest, argument for the use of minority languages in schooling, based upon how language is learned rather than upon ethnic group interests or dubious psychological theories."

Program Models

Chapter 6 turns to consider the educational segregation experienced by many language minority children. The children and even grandchildren of immigrants may be segregated through administrative practices or the avoidance, by majority parents, of the schools that they attend; Chapter 6 reviews briefly the (very scarce outside of the United States) efforts to reduce such isolation. Separate schooling may also be sought and indeed created by ethnic minority communities, with the most notable examples being the Islamic schools in the Netherlands and the United Kingdom, and "Afro-centric" community schools in the United States. Public education authorities may also in some cases adopt a policy of separate development of minority children out of the conviction that this is necessary to their academic success or social adjustment, as in Bavaria and Sweden and some "transitional" bilingual programs in the United States.

Where separate education enjoys strong support from minority parents, the motivation appears to be religious more than a desire to provide instruction through the home language; it is based on "a concern to transmit a religious heritage with its associated behavioral norms, especially when the latter are threatened by a host society that seems anomic and corrupting. It seems, indeed, that the demand for schooling based on religious dimensions of the immigrant heritage is growing even as (and perhaps because) the linguistic minority community becomes better established and more comfortable with the language of the host society. After all, as children become proficient in the language of the host society, it becomes more difficult for parents to protect them from its corrupting influences—especially those which the parents themselves do not understand."

Chapter 7 reviews the most common arrangements for the schooling of the children of immigrants, and the meager evidence—mostly anecdotal—

that exists for the effectiveness of each; the exception is bilingual education, for which there is an enormous quantity of inconclusive evidence. A distinction is made between policies that integrate language minority children from the start, often providing supplemental support as they adjust to and encounter difficulties in "regular" classrooms, and policies that provide a year or two (or longer) of transitional instruction in a reception class or program. A further distinction is made between policies that rely exclusively upon the language of the host society and its schools, whether in providing supplemental support or in separate reception programs, and policies that use the home language of minority children for part of their schooling.

Supplemental home language programs are provided in a number of countries (though rarely in the United States), as are separate reception programs, employing either the language of the school exclusively or the home language of the pupils. Serious concerns have been expressed about each. Supplemental home language programs are often out of touch with the experience, interests, and language capability of children in whose homes the language may (or may not) be spoken, and seldom rise to the level of academic respectability (Timmers, 1995). Reception programs teaching *through* the majority language by a structured immersion method using "comprehensible input" to present academic material can produce good results, by some accounts. "Immersion can and does work with low-income Hispanic and Asian children and . . . the effects seem to endure even after students enter the mainstream" (Gersten & Woodward, 1985, 78). The focus in immersion programs is not on the language itself, but on what is learned through the language; this is, after all, the way in which children acquire their first language. "For the students in immersion, second language learning is incidental to learning about their school subjects, their community, the world, and one another" (Genesee, 1985, 542).

Even in these cases, the absence of classmates who are native speakers of the majority language, and the tendency of reception programs to become low-level instructional tracks, with minority pupils remaining in them far longer than intended, suggest that structured immersion methods might better be used as one aspect of integrated schooling rather than as a separate program.

A combination of the two, reception or transitional programs that employ the home language of pupils for instruction for a period of several years, is the norm in the United States (in the form of "transitional bilingual education"), and is less frequently implemented—though often advocated—in other countries. Bilingual education has been strongly supported on the basis of linguistic theory (Chapter 8), and just as strongly opposed on that of common sense, as when critics insist that the need for "time on task" in learning the majority language makes time devoted to the home language wasteful. They point to "a logical paradox in the model: if students do not begin to read in English until the 2nd or 3rd grade, how will they ever catch up with their English-speaking peers?" (Gersten & Woodward, 1985, 76), and insist that "we fail to see any empirical evidence of bilingual students taught in Spanish ever catching up after a seven-year period" (Gersten & Woodward, 1985b, 84). A compromise position suggests that use of the home language for part of the time can contribute to motivation and reduce stress, but that there is no reason to believe that it has a *direct* effect upon acquisition of the second language and that overreliance upon it may retard second-language learning.

> It is possible that bilingual education programs, because they provide a needed rest from constant exposure to the new language, can produce better learning at the early stages of learning a second language. Later on, however, instruction entirely in the second language probably works better than bilingual education when English is comprehensible enough so that new words are a minority (Rossell & Baker, 1995, 43).

Equally if not more common than separate programs for language minority pupils are less visible arrangements under which students are placed directly in regular classrooms with extra support provided as needed through programs designed for any pupils in academic difficulty, whatever their origin. Some educators and policymakers consider this approach preferable to special programs for minority pupils, because less stigmatizing and isolating. Others contend that government policies developed to "bring along" the lagging elements of the indigenous population, those who for whatever reason have not shared in the growing prosperity of the post-war years, should not be applied willy-nilly to immigrant groups. Though the latter may have many of the same objectively measurable characteristics as low-achieving natives, the causes may be entirely different and compensatory interventions quite inappropriate.

While education authorities often formulate the goal for immigrant children as "integration with maintenance of cultural identity," in the overwhelming majority of cases either the first or the second goal is given priority and "as before, foreign children are either put in regular classes or taught in [separate] bilingual classes" (Uhl, 1992, 7).

Reports of educational outcomes show in almost all cases "that schools are not effectively meeting the educational needs of certain groups of language minority pupils, but they do not permit conclusions about how much they have been helped by particular program models." There *is* abundant evidence of the encouraging results produced by experimental programs of every description, but also unfortunately of the inadequacy of these models as they are "put into production" on a large scale.

Assessing the research and evaluation evidence on alternative strategies to serve language minority pupils is complicated by the fact that much of it is by no means unaffected by the agendas of those who report it, either because they support or oppose the use of minority languages for ideological reasons, or because their career interests are closely tied to the continuing use of those languages. Van den Berghe wrote that "in the race relations field, more than in many others, social science theory is little more than a weathercock shifting with ideological winds" (quoted by Doorn, 1985, 74); the same might be said of the schooling of minority children. Although there is anecdotal and some research evidence that individual bilingual programs have produced good results, requiring bilingual instruction has not been a highly successful government intervention in the United States.

> Reviews of research findings comparing the effects of alternative instructional approaches on student achievement have shown that bilingual programs are neither better nor worse than other instructional methods . . . federal attempts to require specific instructional approaches do not result in positive programmatic changes but simply increase the complexity of running an educational system . . . In general, there is little evidence that program regulations have had a significant impact on the quality of instruction at the local level (Rotberg, 1982, 165).

The challenge is to devise approaches to instruction that can be adapted flexibly at the school level to combine the best features of the different models while avoiding their problems. In Chapter 8, Ester de Jong describes the elements of an effective schooling for language minority children, in which "the education of language minority pupils becomes the responsibility of the entire school" and the emphasis is academic achievement rather than upon language acquisition alone. "The compensatory nature of current programs and the notion that language minority pupils' needs can be met through temporary solutions" do more harm than good. She draws upon the research evidence and describes classroom practices that promote integration of language minority and majority pupils while stimulating the use of both languages.

Integrated education is recommended not only for what could be called sociological reasons—because it can contribute to a reduction in intergroup tensions and stereotyping and to the later ability to live successfully in a pluralistic society—but also for the pedagogical reason that a second language is best acquired through interaction with native speakers of that language. "Second language learning is facilitated in programmes which allocate a significant part of the school day to English language development, which provide for interaction between LEP and English proficient students, and which provide native language support" (Chamot, 1988, 23).

What Kind of Society?

Before turning to specific policy conclusions and recommendations, it is important to place the schooling of language minority children within the larger discussion of the significance of *differences* within contemporary societies. The phrase clutched in the beak of the eagle on the back of American one-dollar bills, "*e pluribus unum*," has always been more a prayer and a statement of intention than a boast of accomplishment. Its original application was to the formation of a single nation out of thirteen "Free and Independent States," as the Declaration of Independence has it, a project only completed by the Civil War or, according to some accounts, by the economic flourishing of the Sun Belt in recent decades. Another resonance of the phrase was its expression of the concern to "control the violence of faction" through a "well-constructed Union," as Madison put it in *Federalist No. 10*; this also is perpetually unfinished business for American society as for others where the people elect their leaders.

A third application of *e pluribus unum*, and perhaps the most potent of all, has been to the challenge of reconciling diverse peoples—deriving largely from immigration—in a workable society. John Jay could express his pleasure, in *Federalist No. 2*, that "Providence has been pleased to give this country to one united people—a people descended from the same ancestors, speaking the same language, professing the same religion, attached to the same principles of government, very similar in their manners and customs" . . . but this did not long remain even approximately true. Ethnic diversity—initially with respect to religion and then to language—has long aroused fears and political controversy in the United States, reaching an early climax with the Nativist movement of the decades before the Civil War. Following the election of 1854, in which the membership of the Massachusetts Legislature was almost completely replaced and 99 percent of the legislators elected were members of the anti-immigrant American Party, the new governor called for a vigorous use of schooling to shape the children of immigrants to the American pattern.

> It is a great problem of statesmanship wisely to control the mingling
> of races into one nationality. The dominant race must regulate the
> incoming class. . . . It is the only salvation of both. . . . To dispel
> from popular use every foreign language, so great a preserver of
> unassimilating elements of character . . . to ordain that all schools
> aided by the State shall use the same language . . . to Americanize
> America . . . to nationalize before we naturalize, and to educate be-
> fore either (quoted by Glenn, 1988b, 72–73).

The creation and development of systems of public schooling in the
United States were profoundly shaped, between the 1830s and the 1920s,
by a concern to "Americanize" the children of immigrants. Americans were
reassured that "to be great a nation need not be of one blood, it must be of
one mind" (John Commons, 1907, quoted by Pole, 1978, 227). Progressive
thinkers and leaders were especially concerned that America not become "a
replica of the racial, religious, and social complexities of the rest of the
world" (Pole, 1978, 236).

"Fashion into one united people," American Episcopalians pray, "the
multitudes brought hither out of many kindreds and tongues." It is not clear,
however, that all Americans or citizens of the other countries whose policies and practices we have been considering would add their "amen" to this
prayer. The belief that diversity should somehow be forged into unity is much
disparaged as the "ideology of the melting-pot," and alternate metaphors
have been suggested: the salad-bowl, the mosaic. Nor is this advocacy of
pluralism only a recent fashion. Israel Zangwill's influential play *The Melting Pot* (1909) was criticized by his contemporary Horace Kallen, who "held
that the special duty of government in a free society . . . was to permit free
development of the ethnic group, for the individual's happiness was 'implied
in ancestral endowment'" (Pole, 1978, 245). Kallen, a philosopher and early
Zionist, "has been acknowledged as the originator and leading philosophical exponent of the cultural pluralism idea." While he favored "participation for the individual in a wide variety of types of associational groups, he
attaches to ethnic group membership and participation special significance
for personality satisfaction and development" (Gordon, 1964, 144–145).

Even the salad bowl metaphor is rejected by those who insist, in the
name of minority groups, upon separate tables, contending that their real
interests demand a distinctly separate space, expressed in their own institutions and without a common ground of shared culture or even of language.

Much of the emotional energy behind bilingual schooling has derived from this fear of loss; thus at the 1967 hearings that led to adoption of the federal law providing funding for bilingual education, a Puerto Rican activist argued that "the psychic cost of the melting pot" was responsible for much of the "mental and emotional illness" in the United States, since learning a new language gives children "a negative self-image" (quoted by Ravitch, 1983, 272). Similarly, in the 1970 hearings, a witness, significantly an "intergroup specialist" with the Philadelphia public school system, insisted that "the old concept of the melting pot is another arm of destruction for the Puerto Rican in the schools" (Franco, 1970, 3810). Reacting to this undercurrent in arguments for publicly funded bilingual education programs, one of the early critics argued, in 1977, that "the idea that the federal government should finance and promote pupil attachments to their ethnic languages and histories while the students also go through the normal process of learning the common English language and the common national history . . . might be called *affirmative ethnicity*" (N. Epstein, 1992, 337).

The ultimate extension of the logic of separate development is the insistence upon separate "gerrymandered" electoral districts, municipalities (as in the effort to form the largely black section of Boston into a separate city called "Mandela"), college dormitories, academic departments, and public schools. To a surprising degree, progressive intellectuals look benevolently upon such developments, as when Claude Lévi-Strauss "insists that the disappearance of differences would be fatal for all cultures. . . . Beyond a certain threshold, communication is therefore harmful, for it leads to homogenization, which in turn is tantamount to a death sentence for humanity. . . . Auguste Comte's utopian dream [of a single humanity] is for Lévi-Strauss a nightmare" (Todorov, 1993, 71).

Surprising because, before the last quarter-century, the progressive position was to deplore all expressions of ethnic or racial distinctiveness. Today, however, "the 'progressive' position in one country" or situation "can well be the 'reactionary' position in another" (Lapeyronnie, 1993, 23). Language activist Tove Skutnabb-Kangas supports separate programs in Sweden identical to those that she condemns in Germany (Chapter 6). Within Germany, as we have seen, it is in conservative-dominated Bavaria that separate schooling has been provided for immigrant groups, while in the *Länder* controlled by social democrats there has been an insistence upon integrated schooling as the means to full participation in German society (Röhr-Sendlmeier, 1986). Muslim girls in France who choose to wear the *hijab* to school are defended by elements of the Right, insisting that cultures cannot be mixed or compromised, as well as by elements of the Left, insisting upon equal rights of cultural expression.

Subjects of the policy debates in Western Europe, Canada, and Australia are parallel to those in the United States: *the meaning of equal opportunities and outcomes, the role of native language and culture in schooling, the extent to which integration can and should be promoted.* Decisions at the policy level are based upon judgments about the goals of each nation with respect to ethnic minorities, the extent to which cultural unity and social justice are seen as appropriate objects of government intervention.

In a recent study, Willem Fase found a wide variety of practices in the schooling of language minority pupils, based sometimes more upon implicit than upon explicit policies.

> The two poles that I see are Germany and England. The English are extremely cautious about considering special measures for minorities, and if they do so it is purely and simply for egalitarian reasons. In Germany there is more or less a "do your own thing policy." Special measures are contrived for minorities for all sorts of reasons and on the initiative of divergent groups. These can be egalitarian in nature but there can also be all sorts of other reasons lying behind them. The Netherlands waver between the two extremes (quoted by Triesscheijn, 1994, 201).

A stress on differences, some argue, leads inevitably to the reinforcement of hierarchies and thus inequality. This was pointed out, in the United States, by the first Commission on Civil Rights, in 1947, and given canonical form by the Supreme Court in its 1954 ruling that "separate educational facilities are inherently unequal" (*Brown v. Board of Education*, 347 U.S. 483). After all, "success in institutions—schools, workplaces, and so on—is predicated upon acquisition of the culture of those who are in power . . . children from other kinds of families operate within perfectly wonderful and viable cultures but not cultures that carry the codes or rules of power" (Delpit, 1995, 25). Insisting that they continue to function in the terms of their minority culture may satisfy an ideological insistence upon its equal value, but does nothing for their chances in life.

Conversely, strong egalitarianism inevitably dissolves differences, subordinating them to individualism and dealing a fatal blow to ethnically-based communities (Lapeyronnie, 1993, 103). "How can a discourse [dominated by the concept of] minority groups be reconciled with the extension of personal rights, of persons unbound from imposed memberships and prescribed roles, mobile and autonomous persons who will change their status on the basis of free choice?" (Costa-Lascoux, 1992b, 107). There is thus a growing "distance between participative demands for equality and affirmations of identity," leading to a tendency for ethnic groups to close in upon themselves and to "the appearance of authoritarian and racist ideologies that seek to establish a new [form of] socio-political integration" (Lapeyronnie, 1993, 344).

By confirming members of minority groups in a sense that ethnic status is the most important thing about them and carries with it a package of attitudes and orientations that cannot be changed without a deep betrayal of their identity, the culturalist perspective can be a source of unequal achievement and of conflict within a society. Diane Ravitch points out that

> instead of promoting reconciliation and a sense of shared community, particularism rekindles ancient hatreds in the present; its precepts set group against group. Instead of learning from history the dangers of prejudging individuals by their color or religion, students learn that it is appropriate to think of others primarily in terms of their group identity (Ravitch, 1990c, 20).

Didier Lapeyronnie warns of "the dangers of an institutionalization of racial categories and a 'racialization' of social life under cover of the struggle against racism" (Lapeyronnie, 1993, 200), while Jacqueline Costa-Lascoux notes that "from the early eighties, some [guess who?] warned that affirmations of identity would lead to an ethnicization of social relations; they were not heeded" (Costa-Lascoux, 1992b, 106).

A strongly culturalist perspective can also threaten individual freedom. After all, "When one responds to demands based upon identity or when one surrenders to the pressure of collective membership, that implies imposing silence on marginal individuals, those outside of the norms, ostracized by their communities, or simply those who wish to exercise their free choice over against prescribed identities" (Costa-Lascoux, 1992b, 131). As Milton Gordon summed up the problem, "while cultural pluralism may be democratic for groups, how democratic is it for individuals?" (Gordon, 1964, 152).

On the other hand, respect for cultural differences, appreciation for diversity of cultural expressions, understanding that how individuals perceive and react to the world around them can be influenced by their cultural backgrounds, are appropriate and even essential in a pluralistic society. Of course, the same could be said of differences in individual psychology, in family traditions, in physical appearance and condition, and in religious convictions, *inter alia*. If a "free society" means anything, it is surely that such differences, to the extent that they rest upon free choice, are left undisturbed provided that they do not themselves disturb public order. Cultural background is only one of the ways in which individuals differ, and they have considerable freedom to choose to what extent it will have a continuing significance for them; culture should not be absolutized.

In a pluralistic society, cultural identity and orientation are always to some extent chosen. That is the source of the discontent but also the enormous attractiveness of modernity (Berger, Berger, & Kellner, 1974). This reality is denied by those who insist upon cultural determinism, reaching an extreme form in the insistence, among postmodern multiculturalists, that "race, gender, class, and similar factors do not function merely as biases influencing cognition but rather serve as *determinants* of cognition, consciousness and experience, and integral parts of one's personal identity; they are no more capable of being transcended than it is possible to step outside of one's own skin" (Yates, 1992). This contention has been most influential where one would expect it to have been most quickly dismissed, in the universities, and has led to accommodations of presumed differences, under the cover of the most benevolent rhetoric, that subvert the functioning of what should be equal opportunity to participate in a common education and what follows from it.

Placing emphasis upon culture (though ignoring its most central expression, religion) in attempts to make schools responsive to immigrants and their families may have something to do with the fact that anthropologists discovered they could do their field research near their universities by focusing upon immigrant and other marginal groups in their own societies. "The very strong position of anthropologists in research on the question of minorities in the Netherlands may have contributed to accentuation of its 'cultural' aspect" (Doorn, 1988, 103). A more important reason, however, was undoubtedly that cultural differences provide a reason for the underachievement of many minority children in schools that places the blame neither upon the schools nor upon the children: it is not that schools teach ineffectively, by this account, nor that minority children are genetically unable or lacking in motivation to succeed. Culture is a cause that leaves no one at fault, and multicultural education the presumed solution.

Showing respect for minority cultures is in fact nothing but rhetoric if no significant social space exists within which they can serve as the basis for group life; a culture is above all a way of structuring relationships, and cannot meaningfully be considered "alive" apart from the social conditions which it requires (Bastenier & Dassetto, 1993, 227). Worse, a stress on cultural distinctions can serve to confirm the stratification of society on an ethnic basis. The plain fact is that the only alternative to participation in the majority culture—except for "ethnic specialists" such as certain entrepreneurs and the clergy of ethnic religious organizations—is an economically and socially marginal position.

Pierre-André Taguieff explored the intellectual confusion over equality and valued differences with particular lucidity in *La force du préjugé*, distinguishing between inegalitarian racism, based upon biological scientism, and differentialist racism, based upon concepts of culture (Taguieff, 1987, 14). The latter, masking as antiracism in the name of "the right to be different," seeks just as firmly as the former to keep the subordinate or excluded group in its place. "If inegalitarian racism is haunted by the loss of status, the abasement of superiors," he writes, "then differentialist racism is haunted by the loss of distinctiveness, the eradication of the distinctive identity of the group" (Taguieff, 1993/1994, 105, 122).

"Differentialist racism" is not altogether new, in France or elsewhere. In the nineteenth century, Renan and Le Bon "simply transpose[d] onto culture the prejudices that are commonly attached to race. And the determinism they profess[ed] is no less inflexible for being cultural rather than physical." By the end of the century, however, the concept of race was often used broadly to include cultural elements that were considered to be inflexibly determined by inheritance, "in the genes" as we might now say. As a southern senator declared at the time of the debate over whether the United States should take over the Philippines,

> There is one thing that neither time nor education can change. You may change the leopard's spots, but you will never change the different qualities of the races which God has created in order that they may fulfill separate and distinct missions in the cultivation and civilization of the world (John W. Daniel, quoted by Hofstadter, 1955, 192).

This form of biological racism has been thoroughly discredited through its espousal by the Nazis in the 1930s and the consequences, but it has re-emerged in a "culturalist" form that can be equally deterministic. "In our day, racist behaviors have clearly not disappeared, or even changed; but the discourse that legitimizes them is no longer the same; rather than appealing to racialism, it appeals to nationalist or culturalist doctrine, or to 'the right to difference'" (Todorov, 1993, 145, 157).

The heart of the confusion that Taguieff has sought to elucidate is that differentialist racism employs many of the categories of thought and offers many of the prescriptions associated with a strong tradition of *anti*-racism. The German-American anthropologist Franz Boas insisted on the primacy of culture, in 1911, in the face of the prevailing biological determinism; the traits of black Americans could be explained by their history and social status, and there was no essential difference in the ways that primitive and civilized peoples thought. The observed differences could be explained by the influence of culture. As the exploration of the role of culture developed, it stressed three principles: that cultural phenomena are autonomous from material conditions, that culture dominates in a deterministic way mental structures and forms of life, and that all cultures are equal in value (Taguieff, 1992b, 23). From this culturalist perspective, associated more recently with Claude Lévi-Strauss and others, the universalization of particular values and norms, with its concomitant relegation of others to a lower status, is a form of racism. This is of course the central article of faith of the multicultural education movement (if something so inchoate yet already overripe can be called a movement) in the United States and other Western countries. France, it is true, is relatively free from it, though Adler exaggerates when he writes of "the universally pejorative sense with which the French today use the term multi-culturalism (most often dismissed as *connerie* [imbecility, in an especially rude sense] *américaine*)" (Adler, 1993/1994, 29).

Of course, there is a self-contradiction at the heart of assertions of the equal value of all cultures, a universalistic position that emerged through such "dead white male" thinkers as Montesquieu and would be rejected by almost all of the non-Western cultures that are so greatly prized by the multiculturalists! Cultures that absolutely reject the validity of alternative perspectives cannot readily be domesticated into part of an optimistic rainbow of "values" (see Friesenhahn, 1993).

It is a mistake, Taguieff argues, to "see racism only in the rejection of difference (*heterophobia*)" and thus to be blinded "to the appearance of softer, new and euphemistic forms of racism praising difference (*heterophilia*) and substituting 'culture' for 'race'." Under this guise, "the praise of difference translates as respectably as possible into the will to hold others at a distance" (Taguieff, 1993/1994, 123–125). Fundamentally, racism has several distinguishing characteristics that are shared by its inegalitarian (biological) and differentialist (cultural) forms, including: "(1) rejection of universals, (2) fixed categorization of individuals, (3) absolutization of collective differences." In rejecting universals, racism rejects also the concept of the individual in (at least theoretical) freedom from biological or cultural determinisms (Taguieff, 1987, 314–315). Thus it would disagree profoundly with the understanding of modernity expressed by the philosopher Emmanuel Lévinas, describing his arrival in France as an adolescent from Lithuania. In his teachers, he wrote later, he encountered "a dazzling vision of a people equivalent to humanity itself (*qui égale l'humanité*) and of a nation to which one could be attached as firmly by mind and heart as by roots" (quoted by Taguieff, 1987, 472).

According to Taguieff, the problem faced by "republicanism" is to find the philosophical tools "to clear the horizon of the opaque vapors given forth by the fetishism of differences, either in the form of tribal particularism which claims" that there is no escape from it, or in that of "the humanitarian idolatry of the individual" detached from the social world.

Just as there are two forms of racism (though the culturalist form is seldom labeled as such and in fact masquerades as antiracism), so Taguieff identifies two forms of antiracism prevalent in contemporary Western societies, and illustrates them with the famous debate, in book form, between Margaret Mead and James Baldwin. Mead's form of antiracism stresses the unity of humanity in all its forms, and looks upon the past of ethnic and religious divisions as a sad burden to be forgotten as soon as possible; its opponent is the common human tendency to cling to one's own group and to exclude or subordinate others. Baldwin's form of antiracism is more concerned with the alienation of mass society than it is with segregation, more with loss of identity ("roots") than with isolation as a result of that identity; its opponent is "ethnocentric universalism," which desires to assimilate all differences to itself (Taguieff, 1987).

This second form of antiracism, respectful of cultural and other differences, may produce the unintended consequence of reinforcing unequal participation in societal institutions, in particular formal schooling, and thus in economic and other opportunities. Indeed, the cultural determinism that insists upon attributing to different groups "no conceptual or experiential points in common" can be employed just as well by those who would prevent societal change as by those who would accelerate its pace. "A relativist, after all, need not advocate social change . . . [but] can just as easily be an ultraconservative" (Yates, 1992). Thus Alain de Benoist, a leading figure in the French New Right, wrote in 1986,

> Already on the international level, the major contradiction is no longer between Right and Left, liberalism and socialism, fascism and communism, "totalitarianism" and "democracy." It is between those who want the world to be one-dimensional and those who support a plural world grounded in the diversity of cultures (quoted by Taguieff, 1993/1994, 108).

A decade earlier he told an interviewer that "every egalitarian or univer-salist ideology is *necessarily* totalitarian because it tries to *reduce* all so-cial and spiritual reality to a single model" (quoted by Taguieff, 1994/1995, 109).

Very much the same determination to define as being in the inter-est of minority groups resisting inclusion in the majority culture and soci-ety is frequently expressed by some elements of the Left, with what some critics consider "a consistent political purpose: to create and foster disaf-fection, social tension and inter-group conflict" as a way of exacerbating the "crisis of Capitalism" (Cox, 1986, 80). In England, "'integration' has indeed become something of a dirty word in 'anti-racist' literature, sug-gesting, as it does, that adjustments are required from the ethnic minori-ties as well as from the white population, and that, once these occur, race relations can be improved *within* the established social order" (Levy, 1986, 122). In this spirit, an article in Boston University's *Journal of Education*, in 1987, argued that

> civic inclusion came from the minds (and, some would argue, hearts) of the white dominant class, those in power. It was a bourgeois aber-ration, an attempt at assimilation that in no way represented the ef-forts of the subordinate class. . . . for many Latino students . . . the use of culturally based discourse and other cultural practices provides for a *community inclusion* which supplants the civic inclusion pro-moted by social institutions like schools (Walsh, 1987, 127).

Similarly, an article the next year in the *Harvard Educational Review* con-tended that the efforts of American schools, including bilingual education, to serve immigrant and other minority children had no other purpose than to miseducate them in the interest of an exploitative system.

> In the United States, a long history of racism and the existence of a stratified opportunity structure combine to work against assimilation into the host society's higher status, dominant White group. What could be the rationale for assimilating immigrant children away from their own culture? . . .
>
> In order to prepare students for caste-minority status in the host society, whether in the United States or Europe, several things must be accomplished. . . . they must internalize the caste ideology of the host society. That is, they must not have a value system and a way of life independent of that of the society at large (Spener, 1988, 146–147).

If U.S. society needs to recruit and prepare new candidates for a growing number of low-status, poorly compensated slots in the opportunity structure, transitional bilingual education programs . . . may be construed by the majority as part of a "reasonable" set of educational policies for the nation. If political and social considerations dictate that Black and other non-White and/or foreign-born people bear a greater share of the hardships, poverty, and unemployment in the U.S. economy, it is "reasonable" to expect the educational system to reflect such considerations . . . by providing, more or less intentionally, non-White people with an inferior education (Spener, 1988, 149–150).

Clearly, the goal of such a program in this scheme . . . is the acquisition of English as a badge of American identity. The insights gained from sociological and linguistic investigation seem to show that this goal serves the interest of society at the expense of the needs of language-minority students (Spener, 1988, 151).

According to this line of argument—derived ultimately from the French radical sociology of Bourdieu and Passeron (*Les héritiers*, 1964; *La reproduction*, 1970) and from Bowles and Gintis (*Schooling in Capitalist America*, 1976)—it is not that schools inadvertently fail to educate poor and minority children effectively but that they do so deliberately. Schools succeed very well, this conspiracy theory contends, in confirming children of poor and working-class families, including immigrants, in their exploitable status, to the benefit of an unjust social and economic order. The ahistorical and superficial nature of such an analysis has been pointed out frequently, though (as with psychoanalysis) the convictions of true believers are only the more confirmed by criticism; they remain convinced against all the evidence that a highly evolved economy has a use for poorly educated workers.

The association of what we might call "alienating multiculturalism" with the political Left made its appearance in Western Europe in the 1980s as an aspect of the post-modern critique of Western society. Disappointed in their ambition of controlling social processes through government action as the bankruptcy of Socialism in Eastern Europe apparent, the Left embraced multiculturalism as a way of relativizing what seemed to be the triumph of liberalism. Radtke suggests that it served to give the aesthetic critique of modernity associated with post-modernism the moral dimension demanded by the Left: rejection of the authority of the dominant order could be linked with insistence upon the equal validity of non-Western worldviews. But this strategy was self-contradictory: allowing space for the expression of diversity within society and its schools requires that all groups accept common groundrules which themselves derive from Western liberalism. In the last analysis these groundrules are more concerned to protect the rights of individuals than the interests of groups, and indeed of individuals against groups when they are in conflict. Assertion of the equal validity of other ways of understanding the common life of society, Radke suggests, is regressive in the psychoanalytical sense of a return to an earlier stage of development, giving a status which is no longer appropriate in a pluralistic social order to "the basic triad of *child* of the soil, *father* land, and *mother* tongue [*Landeskind, Vaterland und Muttersprache*]." When ethnic categories are introduced into the competition for economic and social advantages, he argues, it tends to absolutize them and thus to remove the possibility of compromise on the basis of less absolute categories of material interests (1992, 28).

In the final analysis, stressing how they differ from the majority tends to work against the interests of members of minority groups. In order to prevent the development of a form of caste-based society with the increasing marginalization of the second generation of foreigners, policy-makers must choose between two strategies: "the stabilization of the minority group as a minority" with the goal of achieving "ethnic/cultural pluralism," or the promotion of assimilation, in order "so far as possible to eliminate all characteristics that can serve as the basis for discrimination" (Nieke, Budde & Henscheid, 1983, 95). From the perspective of social justice, there can be little doubt which course is preferable.

But integration can take different forms, and government policies encouraging members of immigrant minority groups to participate fully in the host society through becoming proficient in its language and responsive to its expectations need not discourage their preservation of forms of distinctiveness that are not in conflict with the goal of full participation. Nor—though care must be exercised here to avoid new forms of inequality—need public policy be concerned to eliminate the "ethnic specialization" in particular occupations or residential areas that has characterized some immigrant groups in the United States to the third generation and beyond. As Jacqueline Costa-Lascoux has pointed out,

> integration is a fluid concept which can mean coordinating policies that favor a process of acquiring individual rights, the free construction of a chosen identity. A contrasting meaning which would consist of making [integration] the sum of institutional, economic or cultural indicators—a sort of values scale to apply to immigrants, the poor, or the excluded—would tend to frustrate European policies cen-

tered on the concept of citizenship. The danger of bureaucratic imperialism is real . . . (1992a, 292–293).

On the other hand, governments do—though usually inadvertently—
often implement policies or support practices that have the effect of perpetuating (even creating) ethnic divisions. Indeed, in none of the countries under review have programs been widely implemented in recent years that were
as unapologetically intended to "naturalize" immigrants as were those in the
United States early in this century, or in Australia after World War II.

Individuals can be—immigrants usually become—bilingual, though
their children, as we have seen, often revert to monolingualism in the language of the adopted society. Can individuals be *bicultural* in the same way?
If so, does maintenance of a distinctive culture alongside that of the host
society serve as the basis for maintenance of an ethnic community over several generations, even as a language switch occurs?

Some would deny the possibility, insisting that culture is inseparably
tied to the language in which it finds expression. Ethnic activists argue that
culture and language are inextricably connected, and that the preservation
of both is essential to an ethnic group's ability to continue to serve important functions in the lives and self-understanding of its members. Some assert that

> language is not merely a medium of communication, however impor-
> tant that medium is—but the unifying factor of a particular culture
> and often a prerequisite for its survival. No other factor is as power-
> ful as language in maintaining *by itself* the genuine and lasting dis-
> tinctiveness of an ethnic group (Giles & Saint-Jacques, 1979, quoted
> by Smolicz, 1986, 50).

A Puerto Rican social worker and cultural activist testified at the 1970 Senate hearings on equal educational opportunity that the language and culture
of Puerto Rico "are not only the treasures we as a poor people possess, which
enrich our lives, but they are also the life savers which will succor us in this
our hour of crisis. . . . The difference between the situation of the Puerto
Rican and the situation of the previous . . . newcomers is that the ties [with
their culture] seem to strengthen with time rather than lessen" (Pantoja,
1970, 3696).

On the other hand, experience of many immigrants suggests that when
we stop using the language of our ethnic group, only the language

use aspect of our ethnic identity changes; the primordial sense of who
we are and what group we think we belong to . . . remains intact. . . .
[Thus] language shift or change can only affect one aspect of our ethnic identity—the language use aspect, which is a very low level manifestation of our cultural belief system (Eastman, 1984, 261, 275).

To the extent that cultural identity is a framework for understanding and
relating to the world, "a way of structuring experience and the perception
of it, a cognitive system of knowledge and belief which determines the way
in which norms and values are taken up, attitudes and behaviours exercised" (Brock & Tulasiewicz, 3), it can presumably survive translation into
another language with some unimportant amount of distortion. One can
be bilingual without that requiring two distinct ways of understanding the
world.

Paulston contends, on the basis of her own experience as a Swedish American as well as of research, that there is no such thing as being
"bicultural," switching between cultures in the sense that one can switch
between languages to express a single culture. Since a cultural system is a
way of understanding the world, she argues, it can evolve through contact with another culture without abandoning a basic continuity, and its
elements can be reassembled in another pattern, but this is inevitably an
idiosyncratic process of picking and choosing what the individual will retain from the first culture and what she will adopt from the second, with
some apparently contradictory elements perhaps remaining in a certain
tension. "When you speak Swedish or English," she writes, "it is perfectly
obvious which set of rules you are drawing on. But with behavior it is
not necessarily clear just which cultural system your performance rules
belong to" (Paulston, 1992d, 125). It would be more accurate to describe
certain individuals as *trans*cultural, in the process of switching from one
system of meaning and behavior to another and using elements of each
as appropriate.

Sociolinguist Joshua Fishman criticizes the use of the term "bicultural" in connection with transitional bilingual education programs in the
United States, pointing out that "most of modern life is inhospitable—
whether ideologically or pragmatically—to compartmentalization between
a people's behaviours and values. . . . Neither the institutional stability nor
the functional compartmentalization of this phenomenon, if it is to pursued seriously and societally, is recognized [by bilingual educators]. Indeed,
unknowingly, the arrangements entered into usually foster biculturalism
in the most dislocative sense, i.e. they are . . . commonly condescending,

trivializing and peripheralizing" toward the minority culture (Fishman, 1980, 13).

The concept of biculturalism, as more than a temporary transitional phase, has been extensively criticized in Germany, as well, as a form of what Taguieff calls "differentialist racism," distancing "the Other" as retaining an essence that is totally foreign beneath a misleading surface of conformity to "us" (Hamburger, 1991, 39).

On the other hand, sociologists note how commonly individuals manage to inhabit "plural life-worlds," for example, believing in healing by prayer and by modern medicine, inhabiting roles that are not only functionally different but rest upon different perceptions of reality as we pass from the home to the office to the political rally to the mosque or nightclub. "My consciousness," Berger notes, "is capable of moving through different spheres of reality" (Berger, 1967, 21). It seems perfectly reasonable that an immigrant could behave according to bureaucratic rationality in the workplace and according to traditional customs in the bosom of his family. Although there would be evident tensions between the two modes of behavior and of perceiving reality, it is possible that the undisturbed traditionalism of his home might sustain him in dealing with the unsettling modernity of his workplace, that being a patriarch in the family might help him to endure being ordered around in the factory or jostled on the street.

Ethnic identity *is* invoked by most Americans of European ancestry, but generally in marginal aspects of their lives, as Alba's research found (see Table 9.1). "For most white Americans," Alba concludes, "ethnic experiences do not appear to constitute a rich tapestry of everyday life. But most do have some experiences which they think of in ethnic terms" (Alba, 1990, 80). On the other hand, this is not a society where "ethnicity represents a fundamental social cleavage," in contrast with some societies where trust "may be largely limited to one's fellow ethnics, and interactions across ethnic boundaries may be marked by some degree of suspicion or wariness" (Alba, 1990, 125).

That ethnicity is a way of thinking about oneself positively, and of claiming special qualities in contrast with other members of a pluralistic and confusing society, is clear from Waters's interviews with American Catholics from a variety of ethnic backgrounds. *Whatever* their ethnic group,

> Individuals claimed that their ethnic group was different from all the rest because of three important characteristics: (1) the high value put on the family, (2) the high value put on education, which is clear

TABLE 9.1. Reported Frequency of "Ethnic Experiences"

Percent of native-born white Americans reporting the following
"ethnic experiences" in the preceding five years

Teaching your children about your ethnic background	15.0
Using words or phrases from an ancestral language	29.8
Being discriminated against because of your ethnic background	4.3
Feeling a special sense of relationship with someone else because that person has your ethnic background	21.3
Getting special help in your business or profession from someone with your ethnic background	2.2
Eating special foods of your ethnic background	47.0

Source: Alba, 1990, 79.

from the sacrifices of parents for their children's education, and (3) less often, but still quite common, greater loyalty to God and country (Waters, 1990, 134).

This does not resolve the question whether cultural maintenance efforts can sustain the cohesion of ethnic *groups* as functioning communities, as distinguished from the sense of individual identification with a particular ethnicity. "Their culture starts to go first, followed by the community, as the newcomers . . . or their descendants no longer need or want to depend on the people with whom they or their parents grew up, or on the institutions they brought with them" (Gans, 1991, 13). After all, ethnicity is only one of many forms of identity which people draw upon in a complex modern society, and most invoke it only occasionally (Doorn, 1985, 88). Culture, by the same token, has many variations, and it is

very well possible for cultural differences between one subgroup and another within the same ethnic group to be greater than that between it and Dutch people in the same circumstances in life. It is quite conceivable that there would on some points be no "cultural conflict" between the Dutch school and parents, but rather between the ethnically-mixed peer group on the one side and the school and parents on the other (Vermeulen, 1992, 15).

Fragments of a heritage culture make up a marginal aspect of ordinary life for most of those who choose to practice them, as among immigrant ethnic groups in Australia, where "the traditional and the colourful can most easily find their expression at the weekend rather than during the week, in leisure rather than work, in the domestic rather than the public arena." Thus

> [t]here can be flurries of colour but, by and large, only within spaces made for them by industrialism (commodities, the weekend, the realm of the private and so on), or within limits defined by industrialism. . . . We should stick to being multicultural about the culture that it is possible to be "multi" about (Kalantzis, Cope, & Slade, 1989, 14, 21).

Australian policy has not swung back to the position articulated by an earlier government official in the late 1960s, that "[w]e must have a single culture. . . . I am quite determined we should have a monoculture, with everyone living in the same way, understanding each other, and sharing the same aspirations. We don't want pluralism" (Bill Snedden, quoted by Bullivant, 1981, 173), but the rhetoric about a multicultural society has faded considerably in recent years. The more successful immigrants have quietly acculturated and the problems of the others are more clearly seen as social and educational rather than cultural. Those who have managed (and chosen) to fit in have presumably done so, in most cases, without a crisis of identity in which they rejected their previous lives and loyalties; "taking to oneself of new elements of identity, and abandonment of others, should be referred to as 'identity change.' By that is not meant giving up one's own identity, but the achievement of a new identity" (Abali, 1983, 176).

As we have seen, the position taken toward the maintenance of immigrant minority languages and associated cultures can be affected by the situation of indigenous language diversity in a society. "It's not entirely clear," a Flemish scholar wrote, "how the distinct culture of foreigners can be maintained in a situation of total integration." The experience of Dutch-speakers in Belgium was one of many years in which their culture was suppressed or disadvantaged, leaving them with "little experience in sharing our culture" with others; "we have as a people more experience in relation to a culture dominating us than in relation to minorities" (Dumon, 1982, 137).

There are those, like Diane Ravitch and John Edwards, who insist that the process of assimilation is largely undertaken by members of immigrant groups on their own initiative. "To assume that they have been indoctrinated by some mass conspiracy is to credit them with little intelligence or self-interest; here, the words and actions of cultural pluralists often have a very condescending and paternalistic tone" (Edwards, 1984, 282).

The effort to maintain or somehow to create a sense of an oppositional culture on the basis of ethnicity—in contrast with economic interest or religious convictions—is in most cases destined to be futile. Edwards concludes that "retention of public, visible markers of ethnicity is unlikely, with or without government support, except in cases where segregation is involved and maintained. It is clear that such segregation is not an attractive long-term option for most groups" (Edwards, 1984, 282–283). Even Lévi-Strauss acknowledges that many indigenous peoples, though more sheltered than immigrants from the acculturating force of modernity, "desire nothing more than to share in the benefits of industrialization; peoples who prefer to look at themselves as temporarily backward rather than permanently different" (quoted by Todorov, 1993, 88).

The exception to this generalization is the "culture of victimization" that has emerged in the United States since William Ryan's influential book *Blaming the Victim* (1971). If a group experiences extensive and persistent discrimination—especially based upon unchangeable characteristics like race—or, as John Ogbu has noted, develops a "folk theory" that explains their difficulties as beyond their power to confront by their own efforts, the result may be that such efforts seem futile (Ogbu, 1991). This may lead to an "*oppositional cultural system or cultural frame of reference* that contains mechanisms for maintaining and protecting the group's social identity" (Ogbu & Matute-Bianchi, 1986, 94). Such essential measures of acculturation as use of the majority language and academic success may under these circumstances come to be seen as a betrayal of the minority group (see Chapter 4).

In theory, this pattern of rejection of the majority culture and of success by its rules should not be found among immigrant groups; indeed, Ogbu's concern is precisely to explain why immigrants ("voluntary minorities") usually do better than nonimmigrant minority groups. In recent years, however, there have been troubling indications among second-generation immigrants and especially ethnic activists of a tendency to understand their situation by analogy with that of "involuntary minority" groups, and thus to place responsibility for improving their socioeconomic situation upon societal changes rather than upon their own efforts (see Chapters 3 and 4).

Perhaps the strongest resistance to public support for—or open tolerance of—ethnic-group maintenance has been in France, where there is a strong tradition of assimilation and acceptance of members of racial and ethnic minority groups provided that they embrace wholeheartedly all aspects of French culture, including proficiency in the language and its associated cultural patterns.

The proposals of some on the Left, in the early 1980s, to stress a "right to be different" and evolution toward a multicultural society, ran deeply counter to this theme of assimilation; "it is difficult to think of anything further removed from the French tradition than bilingual education" (Kaplan, 1992, 42). There was a tendency on the Right, by contrast, to insist that immigrants "should break completely and definitively with their original culture" (Khellil, 1991, 39). Both Left and Right were concerned about signs that France might develop what is thought of as the "Anglo-Saxon pattern" of ethnocultural pluralism. This would be deeply harmful for the society, many argued, as well as for the future of members of the minority groups.

> The appeal to identity threatens to exhaust itself quickly in a group self-isolation (*clôture communautaire*) and, thereby, in a new exclusion unless the content which is given to it does not become less and less cultural and more and more political. . . . Wouldn't the reproduction of mechanisms of domination accommodate itself very well today to giving consideration to the cultural singularity of immigrants, to the extent that this would serve basically to mark them socially, with a stigmatization perpetuating their subordinate position in the social hierarchy? (Bastenier, 1986, 89).

French political thinking, influenced by the bitter struggles between Catholics and "anticlericals" during much of the nineteenth century, has little tolerance for the expression of religious or ethnic solidarities in the political arena. "We are not in the USA and this mode of structuring [of society] by communities flies in the face of the 'French model' of integrating communities of foreign origin. The foreigners assimilated over more than a century have frequently had to experience this integration on an individual level and not through communities" (Roux, 1990, 96). There is thus no place in French politics for the familiar (though now fading) American tradition of seeking the "ethnic vote" in local, state, and national elections.

> Will we from now on think of each foreigner living in France, of each child of a foreigner, as first of all a member of a community? Will we discuss integration with the representatives (usually self-proclaimed) of these "communities"? Will entrance into the national society be made through the mediation of a community? But in that case, how will the relationship between "communities" and democracy be articulated on the national stage? (Gaspard, 1992, 23).

The emphasis upon "the right to be different" has increasingly been replaced, on the Left as well as the Right, with a concern to revive what was seen as the prewar capability of France to absorb immigrants and make them into Frenchmen (Gaspard, 1992, 18–21). It is not altogether clear whether this will be possible. With the economic difficulties of the 1990s, it became increasingly evident that problems of "insertion" into the job and housing markets were not limited to immigrants and their children; the concept came to be applied to youth in general. The weakening of the socializing power of elementary schools, the army, labor unions, political parties, youth clubs, and the social class structure in its varied associational forms was evident in a growing population of disconnected youth of French ancestry, and left the children of immigrants even more marginal. It may be, some pointed out, that the emphasis upon the cultural dimensions of integration was a diversion from the failure to achieve effective "insertion" of the second generation of North Africans who are in fact already highly assimilated culturally, but socially and economically marginalized (Dubet & Lapeyronnie, 1992, 141).

The growing anti-immigrant sentiment in the country at large began to call into question the wisdom of stressing cultural and social differences. Socialist Education Minister Jean-Pierre Chevènement issued an official circular in October 1984 calling for more effective efforts, by schools, to achieve the *integration* of the children of immigrants. "It is necessary for national unity," he wrote, "to continue to develop the policy of insertion and integration of immigrants in French society."

> [T]hese children, most of them born in France, will remain in France. They have no other country. They will grow up in France. They will work in France, and marry here. They must therefore be integrated into the French community. That means sharing with other Frenchmen a language, references, a culture, perspectives about work, rights and duties, a civic conscience. . . . to teach a little Algerian to speak and write French correctly is not to show disrespect for his culture but [rather] to respect his right to be educated equally with his schoolmates, to give him every chance of success in the society where he will live. This does not excuse the school from helping the child, if he desires, to come to know the culture and the language of the country of his fathers. But the priorities are clear: the French language and culture are at the base of educational integration, as of social and professional success (Chevènement, 1985).

Such plain speaking causes discomfort, and not only among nativist groups. It may

> provoke the anger and resistance of those French people infected with xenophobia; cause discontent in the homelands for whom the immigrants are a transplanted piece of the nation over whom they wish to retain some rights; finally shock, by plain speaking, those most directly concerned, the migrants who would at last have to make a choice [of nationality], if not for themselves, then at least for their children (Gaspard & Servan-Schreiber, 1985, 17).

It is significant that the school principal in Creil who barred Muslim girls wearing their headscarves (see Chapter 1) was himself an immigrant "of color" from the French colonies, and that the Socialists' top government official charged with integration of France's ethnic minorities was a black man from Togo who, like many immigrants, was "far more interested in being included in French society than in being 'different' outside. . . . In a sense Kofi Yamgname is symbolic of a kind of 'republican reaction' on the left, one that rejects any sort of concession to the ideology of 'the right to be different'" (Kaplan, 1992, 46, 43), including programs to maintain minority cultures.

For many analysts, the problem faced by France and other countries is no longer that of the integration of foreigners as such—with increased mobility as a result of the European Union they are becoming a familiar presence—but "that of the formation of a social group which is excluded and racialized, no longer having access to citizenship and to individuality. In postnational societies, social exclusion and cultural marginality are separated" (Lapeyronnie, 1993, 347). It is not the foreigner who is the problem, but the minority person whose parents or even grandparents immigrated from a Third World country.

> Under these circumstances, while respect for diversity is a fundamental civic virtue, the right to difference is only a *secondary implication* of a well-grounded antiracism—to accord it a primary place would be to succumb to the premises of racism. The respect for persons includes respect for their "cultural" choices. It is because universalism is not sufficiently universalist that it admits a racism which is at once reductive and homogenizing and which does not respect the diversity of forms of life and thought (Taguieff, 1993/1994, 123).

A decision to place integration ahead of ethnic pluralism as a guide to public policy would require the courage not to practice a sort of colonial-style "indirect rule" through relying excessively upon those who offer themselves as spokesmen for minority-group interests. There is in fact a fundamental tension between the very concept of "minority-group interests" and the real interest of most of the rank and file in becoming part of the majority, with all of the social and economic advantages that go with successful integration. Insisting upon that point has its price, however. In France, the conversion of leading voices in the Socialist Party to a policy of integration was challenged by others on the Left who accused them of wishing to continue to colonize an "internal Algeria," and charged that, in using the term integration, these Socialists were really preaching assimilation (Bonnafous, 1992a, 26). Support for assimilation, of course, was tantamount to racism in the twisted logic of what Taguieff calls the second form of anti-racism.

SHOULD SCHOOLS EMPHASIZE CULTURAL DIFFERENCES?
Making a virtue of and even promoting cultural differences is a comparatively recent fashion in the public schools of the Western nations. It is often presented in the context of an agenda of social and cultural change based upon the belief that, for example, "education has worked with the long-term objective of weakening Indian nations through causing the children to lose sight of their identities, history and spiritual knowledge" (Diane Longboat, quoted by Jordan, 190). Such charges echo the contention of Bourdieu and others that "capitalist" schools deliberately miseducate. Didier Lapeyronnie suggests that

> Multiculturalism is the ideology of an elite integrated into institutions and the State, an elite cut off from the underclass and slum areas [*quartiers marginaux*]. With no ability to solve the problems and to deal with social demands, and above all without being representative, the elite becomes moralizing and authoritarian through concentrating on symbols, denouncing racism in all its forms and, today, appealing for "political correctness" (Lapeyronnie, 1993, 346).

Promotion of cultural differences emerged in France in the 1960s, for example, in opposition to what was considered an oppressive emphasis upon uniformity, "formalistic, aseptic, a masked and deceiving expression of the interests of the dominant class." Many on the Left supported

> a right to cultural expression which was different and outside of the norms, the diversity and equal dignity of symbolic forms produced over the course of history by different communities, by the cultural

practices of the people. Against the "symbolic violence of the bourgeois and capitalist school," we called for a culture of resistance by the immigrant proletariat and its children (Charlot, 1990, 47).

The contemporary fashion in intellectual circles of "bashing" Western culture was mediated into actual practice in schools through the belief that the underachievement of minority pupils was the result of a cultural discontinuity between the school and the home, often associated in the United States with the theory of incompatibilities advanced by José Cardenas (Chapter 5). In a typical prescription based upon this theory, Margaret Gibson calls for what she terms a "policy of *additive acculturation*" parallel to the "additive bilingualism" advocated by those who want schools to maintain minority languages. This would, she argues, help minority students "to view the acquisition of academic learning and proficiency in the dominant language and culture as additional sets of skills that would lead not to a replacement of their minority cultures but to successful participation in both mainstream and minority worlds" (Gibson, 1991b, 375). This has led in some cases, as John Rex notes of English schools, to programs "encouraging West Indian children to organise steel bands or giving Asian children special lessons on rice-growing" (Rex, 1985b, 240). It has also provided important support to the demand for bilingual education, increasingly referred to as "bilingual/bicultural," with the original stress on "transitional" quietly dropped out of sight.

> Most writers [supporting] bilingual education are also proponents of a continuing cultural pluralism and ethnic diversity . . . bilingual education is considered a potentially powerful servant to the cause. It can only operate as such, however, in a "maintenance" mode. . . . Much of the current effort, therefore, is based upon the hope and desire that bilingual education will undergo a metamorphosis into something better (Edwards, 1981, 31).

We have seen (Chapter 5) that the alleged relationship between use of the home language for instruction and the self-esteem and psychological well-being of language minority pupils is, at best, unproven. It may indeed be that the belief that minority children are alienated from school because of cultural incompatibility is simply mistaken. Driessen found that Turkish, Moluccan, Chinese, and Spanish children in the Netherlands expressed more enjoyment of school than did Dutch pupils, and Moroccan children as much (Driessen, 1990, 109); this argues against the thesis that a fundamental alienation from the "culture of the school" explains the underachievement of most immigrant minority children. The first major study of bilingual program effects in the United States

> found no difference in attitudes toward school and school-related activities between students in Title VII [bilingual] and non-Title VII classes. Similarly, a study of a comprehensive bilingual-bicultural program for Mexican-American students in Texas, specifically designed to increase students' psychological as well as cognitive development, found no difference between experimental and comparison students on a range of measures including attitudes, self-concept, motivation, social values, absenteeism, grade retention, and dropout rates (Rotberg, 1982, 161).

The causes of the underachievement of many language minority pupils must be sought elsewhere, in their inability to perform tasks that the academic program of the school requires at the level of proficiency expected of majority pupils.

Second thoughts have occurred as it has become increasingly clear that the emphasis upon multiculturalism in schools was not overcoming but, if anything, reinforcing the unequal academic results of the children of immigrants.

> Making people feel good about their cultures and languages, by officially viewing them as nice pieces of the national mosaic, does nothing about the structural inequalities written through this same plurality. Besides, there is a rash presumption in thinking that people unproblematically want to maintain the diversity they have, when immigrants almost invariably aspire to the all but universal goals (within industrialism) of a good job, a good education, a good house, and so on (Kalantzis, Cope, & Slade, 1989, 13).

This is particularly true of the more extreme forms of particularistic multiculturalism, which seek to convince minority children "that something in their blood or their race memory or their cultural DNA determines who they are and what they may achieve" (Ravitch, 1990c, 46). What is most mischievous about these efforts is that

> cultural diversity is not a diversity of equals. . . . How will diversification of curriculum . . . avoid reproducing social stratification at the same time? . . . Simplistic pluralist assessment procedures and pedagogy with limited objectives of esteem and cultural maintenance do

not necessarily help students acquire those educational skills necessary for social access (Kalantzis, Cope & Slade, 1989, 102–103).

Martine Abdallah-Pretceille has warned against the risk of attributing a stable character to the phenomenon of culture, "one of whose characteristics is movement." Educators should avoid presenting cultures as though they were new forms of determinism, thus forcing individual pupils to conform themselves and indeed submit to a cultural identity, which "would come down to denying the individual any role in the very elaboration of his culture" (Abdallah-Pretceille, 1984, 39).

West Indian sociologist Maureen Stone has described the resistance of minority parents to "multiracial" programs in English schools serving Afro-Caribbean pupils. Concern for their underachievement led, through a fundamental misunderstanding of its causes, to an emphasis upon "social, as opposed to educational goals" and thus upon activities designed to raise the self-esteem of black pupils rather than to develop their academic skills.

> In spite of contradictory research evidence, the belief in black low self-esteem persists, and along with it goes the parallel belief that schools can and should compensate black children for the negative social stereotypes which exist in the wider society (Stone 1981, 25–26).

Too often, in American programs for minority children as in French *classes d'initiation*, questions of identity and culture have over the years come to be stressed more than improving the content and methods of instruction (Seksig, 1992, 90). Lisa Delpit describes the "negative outcry in the black community when well-intentioned white liberals introduced 'dialect readers.' These were seen as a plot to prevent the schools from teaching the linguistic aspects of the culture of power" (Delpit, 1995, 29).

There is an unfortunate tendency toward stereotyping in attempts to adapt school programs to the supposed demands of cultural diversity. It is conventional wisdom, for example, that Latino pupils recoil from the competitive atmosphere that allegedly rules in American classrooms, and would do better if instruction were organized on a cooperative basis. Actual research on preferred styles, however, has in at least one case found that Anglo pupils were more cooperative than Latino pupils! (Concha, Garcia, & Perez, 1975, 273–274). Research has also failed to confirm the belief that Mexican-American teachers, parents, and children differ from their Anglo counterparts in how they perceive classroom interactions (Stewart, 1975, 21–23). Common sense and the research on styles of cognition suggest that there is far more difference *within* ethnic groups in how individuals learn or relate to school than there is between groups.

Even when there are culturally-based differences in learning style, it is not clear what implications for instruction are appropriate. A study of American Indian children in school found that their participation styles were very different from those of non-Indian American children; however, Philips concluded, placing the Indian children in a separate class, while it would reduce that conflict, would prepare them poorly for participation in the wider society. "The point is not that one set of values or behaviors replaces the other, but that the children have access to both sets so that they can form from both their unique bicultural identity" (quoted by McKay, 1988, 350). Another study did not "find support for the common conclusion that adapting instruction to Native Americans' learning style will increase achievement" (Kleinfeld & Nelson, 1988, quoted by Pitman, 1995, 25). Earlier research found that "culturally relativistic" teachers, influenced by anthropological literature on culture and teaching for altruistic reasons, were ineffective with Indian children and reinforced their differences from majority children (Kleinfeld, 1975, 269–274).

Attempts to make schools more supportive of minority pupils by incorporating elements of minority cultures run the risk of becoming patronizing; it is "an easier goal to state than to realize in practice, especially when Swedes are asked to appreciate the 'beneficial influence' of customs and habits of poor, rural Mediterranean cultures that are quite at variance with those of affluent, urban Swedish society" (McLaughlin, 1985, 38). Too much "sensitivity" can mislead children about the real costs of making it in the dominant culture, a cost that cannot be wished away.

> Intercultural teaching should not seek to spare individuals and groups from predictable conflicts . . . which cannot be removed by compromises which seek to embrace both positions . . . the notion of cultural openness must be distinguished from "cultural neutrality" (Boos-Nünning et al., 1986, 206).

There can also be unanticipated consequences of school programs that stress cultural differences, including reinforcement of the belief, among children, that race and ethnicity are defining characteristics of fundamental importance. Thus one of the disconcerting results of even reportedly successful schooling based upon minority languages, as in the Leiden experiment described in Chapter 7, is that primary-level children "developed more and more into an ethnic group. . . . the children became more and more aware of their ethnic identity as a minority group" (Appel, Everts, & Teunissen, 1986, 143). The same phenomenon has frequently been noted in criticisms of multicultural and antiracism programs in American schools.

Of course, some educators believe that it is a central function of schooling to raise the consciousness of pupils about social injustice and their own victimization through a "critical pedagogy" that aims at heightening the contradictions of an oppressive society. There is thus a critique of multicultural education from the Left:

> the anti-racists argue that such changes as "permeating" the history or geography syllabus, adding Indian languages to the list of taught languages or doing comparative religion are largely tokenistic. Unless the school adopts an anti-racism, anti-prejudice policy as part of the hidden curriculum, and unless the existing power structures and injustices, both nationally and internationally, are critically examined, then schools are failing (Watson, 1988, 547).

Although substantial efforts are made, in each nation included in this study, to address the unequal outcomes of foreign pupils in the educational system, the efforts are based upon differing assumptions about the real nature of the issue. Underlying patterns of societal oppression are, quite naturally, less popular among educators than theories of cultural incongruity.

> During the late 1960s and early 1970s, educational authorities began to recognise the disadvantages immigrant school children have suffered. The catch-cry has become multi-cultural education providing for the diversity and integrity of different cultural patterns and languages (Sherington, 1980, 157).

Policies assuming that these pupils differ in fundamental ways from native children of the same social class (and level of academic achievement) may lead to part- or full-time instruction with other pupils of the same background, focusing upon those differences, rather than to adaptations within the standard curriculum and school program. Instruction that stresses the language and culture of foreign pupils' homes is often intended to contribute to a positive identity and thus to the self-confidence required for a successful school career, but it may also have the effect of perpetuating the "foreignness" of the children and thus preventing their full participation in the host society.

The definition of a method of instruction based upon a cultural profile runs the risk of racializing the idea of culture and thus of instruction. Labeled on the basis of his cultural identity (by whom? with what right? with what degree of appropriateness?), the child runs the risk of seeing his personality dissolved into a collective identity which will act as a stigma. In short, he will have an identity in the sense of a caricature, but not be recognized as a complete individual (Abdallah-Pretceille, 1984, 35).

The Commonwealth Immigrants Advisory Council in the United Kingdom concluded more than 30 years ago that "If their parents were brought up in another culture and another tradition, children should be encouraged to respect it, but a national system cannot be expected to perpetuate the different values of immigrant groups" (quoted by Fernández Bragado, 1992, 114).

Policy development in this area has been strongly affected by the differing ways in which the issues have been defined. "Culture" is frequently employed as an umbrella concept to conceal a refusal (usually well-meaning) to disentangle the ways in which typical language minority pupils differ from the native middle-class pupils whom schools tend to be best prepared to educate. The positive connotations of the term, in such combinations as "cultural diversity" and "multicultural education," can lead to a failure to address the real disabilities which the former may bring with them to school, disabilities related more to the educational and social class position of their parents than to cultural distinctiveness.

An idealized "minority culture" presented in little doses in the school may have little reality for the child of immigrants who is exposed much more intensively through the media and the peer culture of the street to an overwhelmingly seductive majority culture. We may deplore this seduction, we may insist upon the unique virtues of the minority culture that is being lost, but "the native culture is not in the first place a jewel box of the beauties of the country of origin, but rather the here-and-now lived everyday culture of the families" (Reich, 1991, 165). That "lived everyday culture" is something that is created out of the materials of daily life and the mainstream media available to youth for whom the homeland is often no more than a story that might as well be a fairy tale. Multicultural programs often present culture as something static which has little in common with the way that living cultures unfold dynamically over time and through encounters with other cultures, leading to adaptations and mutual borrowing (Perret-Clermont, 1984, 23).

Concerns have been raised about the possibly negative effects upon equal opportunity of stressing the culture of a society that has been left behind for good. The frustrations and powerlessness of many immigrant families, indeed, may lead them to hold stubbornly to patterns of behavior and expectations that are dysfuntional in the host society—patterns that may be disappearing in their homelands. Such uncritical idealization of the past is their absolute right in a free society, but it should not be reinforced by the common public school (Boos-Nünning 1981a, 15).

EFFECTIVE EDUCATION FOR LANGUAGE MINORITY CHILDREN

Since these children live in American society and must find their place in this society, the particularist message may actually damage the self-esteem of minority children by implying that they are not part of the mainstream culture and that their ancestors had little or no part in shaping the common culture. If children are taught that their real identity must be found on another continent or in a vanished civilization, they may suffer an intense sense of marginalization in relation to the culture they now live in (Ravitch, 1990c, 47).

To the extent that minority cultures are taught about in separate classes, as in the home-language-and-culture classes for the children of immigrants in many European schools, this may disadvantage them academically in comparison with their peers who are spending the same time continuing work central to the curriculum. The same concern has been expressed about proposals to teach "African science" or "Mayan mathematics" in American schools: "If, as seems likely, ancient mathematics is taught mainly to minority children, the gap between their achievement levels and those of middle-class white children seems likely to grow" (Ravitch, 1990c, 47). The enthusiasm over multicultural education in France had similar unintended consequences:

Sometimes, in the name of the right to be different, teaching practices functioned which were paternalistic, folkloristic, artificial. Even more, social and academic practices of segregation, of marginalization, of ghettoization were justified in the name of the right to be different. Some of us began then to demand a right to be the same [*un droit à la ressemblance*] (Charlot, 1990, 47).

It cannot be emphasised too strongly, for American readers, that stress upon access to the "dominant" culture is not the position exclusively of social and cultural conservatives, especially in Europe. It is if anything progressives, like Antonio Gramsci, founder of the Italian Communist Party, whose concern for the economic and political participation of minority groups leads to a demand for their cultural participation as well.

> I reached the conclusion that the desire to promote or to restore the cultural identity of their pupils, which then passed for the pedagogical panacea, was a total mistake, at once an interference in much too delicate a domain and at the same time an alibi in the face of difficulties in meeting academic objectives (Pierrot 1990, 29).

After all, "by the time [minority] children come to school they have already internalized a great deal of the home culture and what they very much need, if they are to succeed in school, is to learn the cultural ways of mainstream America" (Paulston, 1992c, 127). The futility of attempts to teach minority cultures (except, of course, in the freely-chosen "minority schools" described in Chapter 6) is exacerbated by the problem of what culture to teach:

> Educational intervention programs and policies aimed at improving academic achievement among Mexican-descent students assume a cultural homogeneity that does not exist and typically focus on single-cause assessments and solutions to perceived problems (Matute-Bianchi, 1991, 242).

The remedy is to "stop creating special programs to fit stereotypic perceptions of students and their perceived problems and to begin changing the school climate, structure and practices to ones that are more broadly sensitive, responsive and challenging to this diverse student clientele" (Matute-Bianchi, 1991, 243).

In particular, it is essential that language minority pupils be given abundant opportunities to become proficient in *and to use* the majority language. The process is a "virtuous circle": foreign pupils who speak the language of the school well are more likely to participate in formal and informal activities in the school and on the playground and to form friendships with majority pupils that give them constant opportunities to use the majority language and to be exposed (in a nonthreatening way) to its correct or at least colloquial use (Jong & Battenburg, 1985b, 126).

The Swann Commission in the United Kingdom was told by John Rex that "the question of underachievement by an ethnic group or class is a real one in our schools, but its practical solution must lie in better educational practice rather than in emphasizing the cultural and environmental differences between children outside the school" (Rex, 1985b, 231). Nor is such a strategy "insensitive" to the concerns of minority families. A study in four urban areas of England found that immigrant parents were quite clear about what they wanted from the educational system. They wanted "as good as possible an education," they wanted some form of home language instruction, they (especially Muslims) wanted a recognition of their customs in school practices, and they wanted schools to "play a supportive role in the moral education of children, supportive, that is, of the kind of morality which parents see themselves as trying to inculcate in their homes." What immigrant parents did *not* call for was some sort of multicultural education.

> There may be in the minority communities a commitment to cultural pluralism, it is true, but this does not usually lead to general demands on teachers and the school as distinct from the specific demands mentioned above. Minority parents expect that their language, culture and religion should be treated with respect and that it [*sic*] should not become the object of denigration and abuse, but there is widespread recognition of the schools as agencies which can promote or restrict equality of opportunity, and a fear that the provision of special education designed for minorities might hold children back from academic achievement (Rex, 1985b, 238).

The study found also that "when minority-specific policies were developed they were often based upon incoherent and conflicting assumptions about the problems of a multicultural society" (Rex, 1985b, 239).

Maureen Stone studied the phenomenon of "Saturday schools" established and supported by West Indian parents to provide supplemental instruction, not in Caribbean culture, but in the academic subjects to which the parents believed schools were devoting insufficient attention in their concern to be "relevant" to the cultural distinctiveness of their pupils. After observing school classes in which white teachers led discussions on the value of speaking West Indian dialects of English, Stone concluded:

> I would argue that it is the job of the school to enable children to function with ease in the standard language. By the same token it is the job of the home, family and community to keep the dialect alive. The use of dialect in the classroom may obscure the basic role of the school, confuse the issues and create further contradictions (Stone 1981, 111).

The implication of Stone's recommendation is that it would be desirable for children from ethnic minority families to be capable of moving comfortably between two cultural and linguistic domains, but that it is not the mission of the school to see to the development of both capabilities. This is consistent with the affirmation of the American Anthropological Association, in 1975, that pluriculturalism is the normal human condition. Culture is understood by anthropologists as a dynamic reality, in evolution, never fixed, generated and regenerated by the relationships which the different cultural groups maintain among themselves, parallel to the relationships which social groups maintain among themselves (Rebaudière Paty, 116). It calls into question the assumption that schools can treat minority cultures as curriculum packages to be defined and applied.

> Intercultural education must seek to unveil what is for the migrants and their teachers often the idealized folkloristic characteristics of their culture of origin (often a myth of the national culture) and interpret freshly their real situation in the host society; . . . children must be given . . . the possibility of using their own family histories to construct their own identities (Hofmann & others, 1993, 44).

Intercultural education should be "not primarily concerned with what we are used to calling the 'cultures of origin', but with the actual cultures of the new minority groups in their new settings" (Wittek, 1992, 11). This means showing respect for what parents and children themselves most value about their cultural heritage—"to teach 'against' the parents is inconceivable in a democratic, participatory society" (Hofmann & others, 1993, 99)—and also showing respect for the desire of most of them to be accepted as full participants in the host society.

> Although "first generation" migrants sometimes see the culture of their country of origin as a "refuge" or a means of asserting their cultural identity, young people often refuse to be confined to "specific," "separate" areas and types of cultural expression, which they see as likely to relegate them to a fringe existence, if not isolate them from the society and culture of the receiving country. . . . This is hardly surprising, given that, in our Western societies . . . the development of a "cultural identity" by an individual or community does not stop with the acceptance of established cultural practices. Culture is a constantly changing process (Perotti, 1987, 5–6).

Robert Merton has pointed out, of course, that "anticipatory social-ization" can be dysfunctional if in fact the real opportunities for participa-tion in the society to which the outsider is adapting are very limited or blocked entirely. Rhetoric to the contrary, that is not generally true for im-migrant minority children in the Western democracies.

Becoming well integrated into the host society does not have to imply abandoning convictions and private behaviors that have continu-ing meaning in the new situation; "dutchifying [*vernederlandsing*] does not have to mean that the grandchildren of Muslim and Hindu foreigners immediately become Protestants or Catholics" (Jong, 1987, 19).

> Whenever someone leaves a cultural society in order to emigrate, there can be no question of "keeping" his own culture. Like it or not, the immigrant will acculturate, adjust to the foreign culture through taking over cultural elements from the new society and through dropping, conforming, modifying elements of the [original] culture. . . . That's why I find the formula "right to maintain one's own cultural values and norms" incorrect. Each individual and each group has a right to its own identity, which is based in, develops from, and builds upon the culture—with its values and norms—from which they have come, but in the case of migration not without ac-commodation, reshaping, new developments (Kloosterman, 1983, 100).

As the Swann Commission concluded, "the fundamental change that is necessary is the recognition that the problem facing the education system is not how to educate children of ethnic minorities, but how to educate *all* children" (*Education for All*, 1985, 769). This requires, obvious as it may seem, that minority children attend effective schools.

> Of the seven projects that existed in Brussels in 1988–1989, one was in a highly prestigious school, two were in really good schools, three in less prestigious middle quality schools, and one is a lower middle quality school. None was in any of the really poor schools that exist in some parts of Brussels (Leman, 1991, 133).

It seems reasonable to assume, indeed, that in general good programs for immigrant children are those found in good schools, which support the edu-cation of all children with high expectations and effective teaching (Carter & Chatfield, 1986). The German federal official with responsibility for immigrant policy wrote in 1988 that what was needed was "a common education from the earliest years [*von klein auf*] that keeps an eye on both the distinctiveness of *all* children—especially in elementary school—and also the shared characteristics of childhood [*gemeinsame Daseinsformen des Kindseins*]" (Funcke, 1988, 7). There are those who argue, indeed, that efforts to modify instruction to make schools more effective for minority pupils can result in improved education for majority pupils as well (Paelman, 1995), though more commonly majority parents fear that instruction will simply be "dumbed down" at a cost to their children.

This is a concern that cannot simply be dismissed; it is unfortunately true that expectations are often lowered and instruction made more mechanical because of the presence of low-achieving children, though the essential issue, once again, is social class rather than national origin. Schools that employ such methods tend to be ineffective for all of the children who attend them. On the other hand, schools that are effective for minority children tend also to be effective for those of the majority. A recent study in Rotterdam found that minority children in the most effective elementary schools scored as high as Dutch children in the least effective schools. The gap between minority and Dutch children remained in the effective schools, but the quality of the school clearly made a difference in absolute if not in relative achievement (Geelen, 1995, 347).

The desire of many educators of language minority children to shelter them from the difficulties and occasional discouragement associated with becoming proficient in a new language, to make it all fun and self-affirming, is profoundly misguided. Children will face a day of reckoning—indeed many such—eventually, and "the important thing is to equip children to meet this selection as fairly as possible."

> It is absurd to say that only the school is selective, or that its main function is to select. General social selection is much more rigorous, more segregative, than academic selection. It is therefore not through the former that we can hope to fight against the latter. To the contrary, it is the school alone which is in a position to contribute to minimizing the handicaps (Porcher, 1978b, 122).

EFFECTIVE TEACHING OF LANGUAGE MINORITY PUPILS
How can the school go about minimizing the handicaps faced by low-status language minority children and ensuring that more of them achieve high academic performance?

Integrated schooling is an important aspect of preparation for integration into the society, both because of the attitudes formed thereby and because of the language skills that develop through interaction with peers; "students will profit from being exposed to a large variety of styles and levels of language" (Valdés, 1988, 133). A careful study of second-language learning by foreigners in the Netherlands, for example, found that the most important factor was the extent to which they were surrounded by Dutch-speakers (Hoefnagel-Höhle, 1982, 97). Tikunoff's studies of classrooms that are reputedly effective for language minority children in the United States have found a high level of active use of English and a close integration with the rest of the school; "in the daily learning experience for a language minority student, it was not clear where an exemplary program ended, and where 'regular' school began" (quoted by Gersten, Keating, & Brengelman, 1995, 66; see Tikunoff, 1985). Labov's research has shown that "underlying grammatical patterns of standard English are learned through 'meaningful' and intensive interaction with those who already use standard English grammar, not 'simply by exposure in the mass media or in schools'" (quoted by Farr & Daniels, 1986, 35). Similarly, Lily Wong Fillmore points out that

> in order to learn a language, learners must be exposed to it as it is used by people who know it well. It is in the process of trying to understand what the speakers are saying and in trying to communicate with them that the learners acquire the new language. . . . Getting them to interact together in ways that promote language learning . . . requires that attention be given to the social climate within the setting. Learners need opportunities to hear and practice the language in order to learn it, but they have to be motivated to take advantage of these opportunities. . . . The ideal situation is one in which there is, in addition to teachers, a balance between language learners and classmates who know the target language well enough to help in its learning, and there are many reasons for them to talk with one another. Fathman (1976) found . . . that LEP students generally did not achieve well in English when they were greatly outnumbered by English speakers, or when they outnumbered English speakers (Wong Fillmore & Valadez, 1986, 668).

Unfortunately, the instructional specifics of schooling of ethnic minority and majority children *together* have received very little attention (Reich, 1982, 13). Human relations are important, and "by reorganizing the social structure of the classroom, radical improvements in race relations can be obtained consistently" (Kagan, 1986, 235), but far too little attention has been given to what children will actually be learning, and how, and to what extent they will be learning from one another. Physical integration creates the possibility, but only through the way that teaching and learning are organized will real integration be possible (Dickopp, 1982, 164).

Integration from the start does not have to mean that the home language is excluded from instruction, but it does imply that language minority pupils will be learning through the majority language throughout their early years of schooling. Virginia Collier's research has found that "students between the ages of 8 and 12 seem to be the fastest acquirers of second language for academic purposes" (Collier & Thomas, 1988, 20); this contradicts earlier claims by Cummins and others that adolescence is the best time for learning a second language and therefore instruction should stress the first language until then.

In chapter 8, Ester de Jong explains why classroom integration is important:

> The lack of interaction with speakers of the majority language may limit opportunities for natural and meaningful interactions in that language. In addition, it may affect the motivation to learn a second language. Motivation and attitudes have been found to significantly influence second language achievement elements of effective instruction in linguistically-integrated classrooms. . . . If there are few native speakers in a classroom, the teacher becomes the only native-like model. Cooperative learning may be less effective for second language learning because the interaction partners do not provide target models based on the second language. . . . In contrast, when classes consist of a mixture of second language learners and native-speaking children, second language learners tend to do better with an open classroom organization. For these settings, cooperative learning can create a better second learning environment by providing opportunities for interaction with native peers and adult models.

This educational considerations constitute a strong case against separate programs for language minority children. Gary Orfield warned a congressional hearing, in 1977, about

> expensive, highly segregated programs of no proven educational value to children. Worse, I believe there is sometimes a tendency to train children who do not need the program and may be hurt by it. Some

programs pursue not successful integration in American society but deeper cultural and linguistic identity and separation. . . . There is nothing in the research to suggest that children can effectively learn English without continuous interaction with other children who are native English speakers (quoted by Ravitch, 1983, 277).

Despite such warnings, separate development has become the norm in the schooling of language minority pupils in the United States, to such an extent that advocates periodically complain that many are *not* in separate programs, referring to them as "not receiving services." Bilingual education policy has evolved in the United States in a climate of intense suspicion, on the part of advocates and government officials, about the intentions of teachers and principals toward language minority children, and their capability of making wise decisions about the best educational interests of the children. The then Commissioner of Education, Harold Howe, urged that bilingual education legislation should allow "flexible and experimental attacks upon the problem in the future," since "the program which best meets the needs of Puerto Rican children in New York is not necessarily appropriate for the needs of Mexican-American children in the Southwest or Cuban children in Florida" (quoted by Spolsky, 1978a, 277). Despite this caution, the Bilingual Education Act of 1974 "represented the first time since the enactment of federal aid that the Congress had dictated a specific pedagogical approach to local educational agencies" (Ravitch, 1983, 276). The government guidelines ("*Lau Remedies*") stipulated that school districts could not rely exclusively upon English in teaching language minority pupils below 9th grade since that did not "consider the affective nor cognitive development of the students in this category and the time and maturation variables are different" than those of newly arrived high school students (quoted by Rotberg, 1982, 153).

The whole thrust of the legislation and of its implementation was away from the integrated education of language minority and majority children, and toward creating so far as possible an alternative educational system within bilingual programs. Thus

the federal government funded the preparation of teaching materials in sixty-eight languages, including not only those with sizable numbers of speakers . . . but also in seven Eskimo languages . . . and a score of American Indian languages (some of which had no written form) (Ravitch, 1983, 276).

The more a curriculum was elaborated in other languages, of course, the less language majority had common ground with their language minority peers in the same school buildings.

This reliance upon separate schooling for language minority pupils should be replaced with a concerted effort to ensure their effective integration. Not *programs*, then, but *schools* should be the focal point of policies for the education of language minority pupils, and that education should be the responsibility of all of the staff of the school to which such students are assigned. This responsibility implies assigning these pupils only to schools that are prepared to serve them effectively and in an integrated way. The creation or maintenance of separate programs, inevitably coming to have a life of their own and sustained by bureaucratic vested interests as well as by a conviction of their unique virtue, should be abandoned as contrary to effective schooling.

The languages that children speak at home should, so far as possible, be part of the repertory of at least some of the educators who teach and counsel them. Pupils of different language minority groups present in sufficient numbers locally should be assigned to different schools to allow for a measure of specialization in language provision. This is already the practice in the United States, where language minority pupils often receive school assignments based upon the location of bilingual programs in the appropriate language, and it has been adopted to some extent in Germany as well (Piroth, 1982). Better than either would be to assign the pupils to particular schools where they can be served most effectively, but not to separate programs within those schools.

A stress upon integration of language minority pupils does not imply that they should simply be scattered into regular classes. As Ursula Boos-Nünning has pointed out, teachers and fellow-pupils are more likely to relate with positive interest and appropriate adaptations to groups of language minority pupils within a well-structured program of collaboration that includes teachers of the same background than they are to isolated individuals (Boos-Nünning, 1981b, 54).

The isolation of bilingual teachers from other teachers in the same school (Chapter 8) must be decisively overcome; their collaboration must be *structurally* guaranteed rather than resting on good will and good intentions. Not only should teachers work together, but their pupils should know that they work together and respect one another (Papi-Rovini, 1984, 86). It is unlikely, with the best of intentions, that such a collaboration will work, and will be seen to work, in a large school. One reason that the increasing interest in breaking up large schools into several smaller schools sharing the same building may be especially valuable for language minority pupils is that in a smaller school they are more likely to have sustained relationships and unstructured communication with nonminority pupils, and their teachers are more likely to work together closely (Valdivieso, 1986, 43).

Keith Baker, author of several reviews of the literature on bilingual education in the United States, makes the further suggestion

> to put LEP [limited-English proficient] students in *very* small classes, classes of 8–12 students. It would be nice if the teacher knew some of the students' native language, but at this class size I do not think it is critical. The principal should give the teacher the following instructions at the start of the school year: "Make sure these students master the required curriculum for this grade." The principal, consultants, special teachers, lawyers, and policymakers should then get the hell out of the teacher's way and let her have at it. With classes this small, the teacher can individualize a program that fits the needs of each student. . . . The research shows that communicating in a second language is the key to learning it (Krashen, 1982). But . . . *such exchanges cannot occur often enough in large classes for effective language learning to take place* (Baker, no date, 55) (emphasis in original).

We would modify Baker's prescription to the extent that it continues to assume separate schooling, if only for a limited number of months or years. The evidence presented in Chapter 8 suggests that it is preferable to assign a language minority child to an integrated class from the start, and to provide first-language support and "comprehensible input" in the majority language within the context of and as a variation upon or adaptation of the common schooling of minority and majority pupils.

Baker's comment about the desirability of teacher knowledge of "some of the students' native language" is supported by a recent review of the research that he conducted with Christine Rossell, in which they concluded that the best situation for second-language learning and academic achievement is when the teacher can speak the first language somewhat but is not sufficiently fluent in it to be tempted to use it much of the time. "The psychological and perhaps initial pedagogical advantage one may gain from having a fluent bilingual, same ethnic group teacher may be offset by the tendency of such teachers to teach too much and too long in the native tongue" (Rossell & Baker, 1995, 36).

Active language use is essential, and even the most favorable pupil/

teacher ratio is unlikely to prove effective if language minority pupils are not encouraged to produce free responses in the second language. Simply giving expected formulaic responses to teacher questions, which Ramirez and Merino found to be typical of all programs in their study, is unlikely to lead to real proficiency. Curiously, they found an especially high rate of "expected responses" in 1st-grade classes conducted primarily in Spanish—twice as high as in those conducted in English—and an especially low rate of "free responses," suggesting that the use of the home language does not necessarily lead to the rich language environment that is often claimed for it (Ramirez & Merino, 1988, 38). As the author wrote in a 1988 state government report,

> It is important, in educating these students, to provide a period of intense stimulation of conceptual and communicative proficiency, which for many students may best be done to a substantial extent in the language spoken in the home. There is no reason to fear that development of the home language will prevent learning English nor, conversely, should the use of English be delayed to avoid "linguistic confusion." With appropriate instructional methods, such as avoiding a mixture of languages at any one time, children are fully capable of learning through two languages and thus of acquiring proficiency in both (Glenn, 1988d, 7).

Because language minority pupils face the double task of learning the language of the school and also learning the same academic material that their nonminority peers are studying, it seems appropriate to consider how their school day or school year can be lengthened to allow additional time (Harant, 1987, 260). It is astonishing that the common practice of pulling children out of their regular classes for supplemental language or remedial instruction has persisted for 30 years in spite of frequent testimony to its ill effects. Presumably it is the force of the bureaucratic rationality by which most publicly funded schools operate that dictates that all teachers and all children be in the school for precisely the same period of time; it would be far more sensible to adopt a flexible school day or year allowing for more instructional time.

There is a danger that this would widen the existing gulf between "regular" and specialist teachers, as demonstrated by the experience of supplemental home language classes in Europe (Chapter 7), but this is not the inevitable consequence if (1) two or more teachers are assigned shared responsibility for all aspects of the schooling of the same group of pupils, (2) their schedules are set so as to provide several hours of overlap each day, and (3) they are given the discretion to work out the apportioning of instructional tasks among themselves in the hours available for that purpose.

Where does attention to the *culture* of language minority pupils fit into such a whole-school model? If schools take culture seriously, as they must if they are to educate effectively, they will not address either the majority culture nor those cultures of minority pupils lightly, as a way to add a little flavor and variety to the curriculum. Culture has to do with the rules by which we live, and the assumptions and ways of understanding the world that underlie those rules; both a culture's outward and its inner expressions are the result of our loyalties to and participation in groups that matter to us. Schools that function well work at creating a sense of shared culture, which usually borrows heavily from that dominant in the surrounding environment; alternatively, schools may set themselves explicitly in opposition to aspects of their environment, as is often the case with religiously based schools. We would thus expect an Islamic school in the Netherlands to be culturally different from a Catholic school in the same country, though it fact it would be likely to be culturally closer to the Catholic school than to an Islamic school in Pakistan. Culture is, as we have noted several times, always in the process of renegotiation and reinvention.

Whether congruent or at odds with the dominant culture, schools need to be culturally coherent *within themselves*, or they will educate badly. An effective school, a school of character, is very likely to rest upon a shared ethos among the teachers and other staff, one that is at least vaguely understood and supported by the parents and in any case is not in opposition to their own beliefs about education for their children.

If the culture of the family is odds with that of the school, the only intellectually honest course is to make what the school stands for explicit and give parents the choice of enrolling their children in different schools or allowing them to be exposed in a consistent way to the school's culture. The school's job, in such a situation, "is to teach about the second culture, and how to operate within it effectively—without requiring changes in students' cultural identity and loyalty," since "a major hazard in teaching a second culture is that students may reject parts of their native culture without knowing or accepting comparable parts of the second" (Saville-Troike, 1978, 12–13). Of course, this rejection is likely to occur in the immigrant situation with or without encouragement by the school (see Chapter 4); the urgent task for teachers is to ensure that the majority culture, its rules, and underlying assumptions, are presented clearly enough that they can be mastered by minority pupils. On the other hand, teachers should avoid stressing areas in which pupils are likely to experience conflict between home and school values.

The practice of beginning social studies with topics closest to the experience of the child ('the family') does not seem appropriate . . . as it is these topics which probably include the most culturally sensitive content. . . . Older students may be taught *about* aspects of the second culture which conflict with native religious or moral teaching, for purposes of *receptive* knowledge, but these should never be required as part of the students' *productive* cultural competence (Saville-Troike, 1978, 49).

This recommendation has particular force with respect to teaching about sexuality.

A common public school (as contrasted with a school organized on the basis of religious convictions and freely chosen by parents who share those convictions) should exemplify respect for cultural—especially religious—diversity, but without making assumptions about what aspects of traditional cultures have meaning for individual pupils nor imprisoning them in an identity with which they may not at that point in their lives wish to identify. This is why phrases like "dialogue between cultures" or "contact of cultures" are meaningless; it is people who enter into dialogue and have meaningful contacts. Nor, as we have seen, is it useful to assume that there is such a thing as a single "Latino culture" or "Native American culture" that can be presented by the school.

Of course, as we are constantly told, the diversity of cultural backgrounds among the pupils in a school can be an occasion for enrichment of instruction, so long as teachers do not assume that children have any detailed knowledge of the countries and the cultures that were familiar to their parents or grandparents, or of the language used by older family members (Burk, 1988, 38). The author described a particularly insensitive "multicultural" lesson that he observed in a much praised school in a coal-mining region of Belgium:

the Belgian teacher was displaying three models of houses: a large model of a Belgian single-family house of the sort that a professional class family might live in, and two models to a smaller scale of a more traditional type of house in Turkey and in Morocco. The Turkish model had an outdoor toilet. The teacher called upon a Moroccan boy to describe how "his people" lived: "You sleep on the floor on rugs, right?" "No, no, we sleep in beds!" "Oh, then, but you eat sitting on the floor, right?" "No, no, we eat at table, sitting on chair, like you!" Her intentions were entirely benign, to teach that traditional cultures may have other ways of doing familiar things that are interesting and to be respected, and to do so in a way that allowed the student to be an "expert." For the student, though, the lesson was clearly threatening; it suggested, in front of his giggling classmates, that his people were primitive and poor. His own family in Limburg presumably lives very much like working-class Belgians. Multi-cultural education too often assumes that children relish having pointed out how they are different! (Glenn, 1988a, 34).

It is easy to stress differences, Martine Abdallah-Pretceille warns, and even the most insignificant can become an occasion for rejection of the one who is different; children do not require a sophisticated theory of racialism to give each other a hard time. Emphasis on what those who seem different have in common, and the development of a sense of mutual respect based upon that, require a higher level of conceptualization. The process of coming to such an awareness of commonality is itself an important intellectual exercise, a way to develop a scientific spirit and a measure of detachment and objectivity. *Inter*cultural education is thus entirely different from and more demanding than multicultural education as it is ordinarily practiced (Abdallah-Pretceille, 1984, 34). Intercultural education seeks to build bridges rather than to define differences, and it depends above all upon cooperation by teachers who represent in their own persons and relationships the possibility of successful adaptation of minorities to the majority without loss of valued aspects of distinctiveness (Gondolf et al., 1983, 23). In the Massachusetts state report, the author wrote that

The culture that Cambodian students in Lowell live and can share with their classmates is one that they and their families and their community are developing today, made up of elements of their heritage (while other elements are abandoned or rejected) and a creative response to their present situation, including selective adoption of elements from the mainstream American culture. It is thus a matter for extreme tact and sympathy to presume to interpret the cultures of our students to them and to others.

It is essential that our schools be sensitive to and celebrate cultural differences, while taking care not to reinforce stereotypes.

The multi-cultural dimension of a school's program should be developed in close consultation with parents. The institutions of the ethnic community, its churches or temples, its performance groups, its associations and media, can play an important role in this process. It is, however, important to recognize their tendency to stress distinctiveness and group cohesion rather than integration. No student should be forced to identify with someone else's interpretation of the heritage "culture," and every student will have to decide, over time, which elements of that culture will be retained and built upon.

The very best "multi-cultural education" is provided by the daily example of a teacher or principal who is herself living the heritage culture in the context of contemporary American life, and who unselfconsciously shares what that means in every dimension of school life. This is an additional benefit of integrated bilingual education: both linguistic minority and majority children see teachers of their respective groups working together in mutual respect.

In Great Britain and elsewhere multi-cultural education has been criticized as a way of seeking to pacify ethnic minorities so that they will not focus on the realities of discrimination and the requirements of personal and group struggle for achievement. It must not be allowed to become a substitute for high expectations and demanding instruction.

There are some aspects of the cultural heritage of the majority— prejudices, stereotypes, forms of injustice—that we are laboring to change, and there are similarly aspects of the cultural heritage of some linguistic minority students—for example, attitudes toward equal opportunities for women—that do not deserve to be maintained. Rhetoric about the "equal value of all cultures" reflects a lack of reflection on the uneven value of the disparate elements making up each cultural system, including one's own (Glenn, 1988d, 21).

ORGANIZING SCHOOLS TO SERVE LANGUAGE MINORITY PUPILS
Detailed recommendations for school policies that would support an effective education for language minority pupils were prepared by the author for the final report of the Massachusetts Governor's Commission on Bilingual Education, on which he served, and were included with some modifications in that report (Bilingual Education Commission, 1994). The original version, stressing a "whole-school" emphasis, follows:

> The [Massachusetts Transitional Bilingual Education] Law places an obligation upon school committees in whose districts are "twenty or more children of limited English-speaking ability" [defined by the statute as "(1) children who were not born in the United States whose

native tongue is a language other than English and who are incapable of performing ordinary classwork in English; and (2) children who were born in the United States of non-English speaking parents and who are incapable of performing ordinary classwork in English" (M.G.L. c.71A, s.1)] to provide a full-time program of instruction (1) in all those courses or subjects which a child is required by law to receive and which are required by the child's school committee which shall be given in the native language of the children of limited English-speaking ability, (2) in the reading and writing of the native language of the children of limited English-speaking ability who are enrolled in the program and in the oral comprehension, speaking, reading, and writing of English, and (3) in the history and culture of the country, territory, or geographic area which is the native land of the parents of children of limited English-speaking ability who are enrolled in the program and in the history and culture of the United States (M.G.L. c.71A, s.1).

There are now 51 school systems which provide such bilingual education programs, twice as many as provided reception classes for immigrant children 80 years ago, and these programs serve pupils with 18 different home languages who are unable to participate effectively in English-only classes.

Beneath the technical statutory language lie several important educational principles that have been this Commonwealth's policy for more than two decades, and continue to be valid.

(a) the initial reception in school of children who are not yet proficient in English should be in the language which they have already acquired, to make their first school experiences here successful ones and to facilitate communication with their families

The Commission finds that the record of transitional bilingual education (TBE) programs in Massachusetts over the past 23 years has provided very significant support in this respect. By and large, schools have been secure and welcoming places for language minority children, not least because of hundreds of bilingual teachers and directors who have bridged the gap between home and what could otherwise have been an alienating school environment.

Communication with families in their primary language, though explicitly mandated by law and regulations, has been less consistent; the Commission finds that the purpose and procedures of programs and the rights and responsibilities of pupils and parents have not always been made clear in language and in terms that are readily grasped by parents unfamiliar with our educational system. The Commission's recommendations suggest how families can become a more integral and supportive part of what happens in school.

(b) pupils should be able to do the schoolwork appropriate to their age and grade level in their first language while developing proficiency in English

The Commission finds that the record of TBE programs in Massachusetts over the past 23 years has been generally successful in this respect in the lower grades of schooling. State monitoring and other reports suggest that most pupils in TBE programs make progress in reading, writing, and the other subjects taught in elementary schools while studying through the medium of their first languages as well as through English.

State monitoring over the years has found that language minority pupils who begin their schooling in Massachusetts schools in the middle and high school grades may not find the range of academic and vocational courses available to them in their first languages that are available in English, and may therefore encounter severely limited educational opportunities while they acquire proficiency in English.

The Massachusetts Common Core of Learning, adopted in June 1994, gives strong support to proficiency in other languages as well as in English as a goal of academically demanding education: "all students should learn or maintain a second language, beginning in elementary school, and should be expected to master the language." The best way to develop mastery of a language is to use it, and the Commission recommends that secondary schools provide instruction in academic subjects through languages other than English for both native speakers of those languages and native speakers of English who are learning the languages, as is the practice already in a number of "two-way bilingual" schools.

*(c) the goal is participation **on equal terms** in the mainstream of American education, and thus eventually of American society*

The Commission finds that there is insufficient hard evidence in the form of follow-up studies of former TBE pupils to reach a conclusion about the success of TBE programs in this respect. Some anecdotal evidence is encouraging, but the high drop-out rate of Hispanic youth in particular causes the Commission deep concern about how adequately our education system is serving these pupils.

The 1971 statute itself is unfortunately silent on how *schools* should adapt to the presence of language minority pupils; its concern is with a discrete program, and with entry and exit, but not with the overall schooling experience.

The Massachusetts Education Reform Act of 1993 is whole-school oriented, and bilingual education will have to become an integral part of the mission of each school which enrolls pupils who require and desire it. The Commission's recommendations, in a significant shift from the emphasis of the 1971 TBE statute, address explicitly what should be expected of *schools*.

(d) accountability for educational results is built into the statute

The Commission finds that the administration of TBE programs in Massachusetts over the past 23 years, with honorable exceptions, has been severely deficient in this respect. We are disturbed by the paucity of hard data on educational outcomes, both in the subjects that make up the curriculum and also in the acquisition of English.

The Massachusetts Education Reform Act of 1993 is strongly oriented toward accountability for educational results. A process—now well advanced—is established for setting educational standards, and consequences are laid out for schools that fail to educate their pupils effectively. Explicit reporting requirements are placed upon school systems with respect to bilingual education, and a pupil identifier system will make it possible, for the first time, to track the progress of pupils and to do follow-up studies. A series of assessments will permit much closer state-wide monitoring of pupil achievement than in the past. The Commission's recommendations spell out explicitly how schools, school committees, and language-minority pupils themselves should be held accountable for the quality and scope of learning which occurs.

(e) the statute recognizes the need for additional resources to meet the needs of classes in which pupils are at widely varying stages in the acquisition of English as a second language and in the adequacy of their previous schooling

The various school finance arrangements over the past 23 years have reflected the need for smaller class sizes, supplemental staff, and other extraordinary expenses of TBE such as teaching materials in languages other than English, as well as the expenses to school systems of keeping space available in regular classrooms for partial and full mainstreaming of language minority pupils. The new funding formula in the Education Reform Act, similarly, recognizes the additional costs of serving these pupils.

The Commission finds that the Department of Education has not required a method of accounting for expenditures on TBE programs which would ensure that additional resources (or even equal resources) were available to support the education of language minority pupils. Such evidence as is available (and it must be used with great caution) suggests that many school districts have failed to meet their obligation to provide the additional support contemplated by the statute and by the various local aid arrangements.

The Commission's recommendations address the need for an adequate system of accountability for the expenditures required for the education of language minority pupils, consistent with the emphasis of the Education Reform Act upon the whole school (rather than discrete programs) as the primary locus of responsibility for decision-making about the organization of instruction.

(f) teachers and other staff who work with language minority pupils require a variety of skills and insights that go beyond what was expected of teachers in the past

The Commission finds that the Commonwealth faces a severe shortage of certified bilingual teachers who have received a preparation of sufficient breadth and depth and possess the necessary language skills, and that this will grow more critical as the number of language minority pupils continues to increase.

The Commission also finds that few teachers of mainstream or special education classes, and few teachers in Chapter 1 (compensatory education) and talented-and-gifted programs, have received training in language acquisition and cross-cultural communication, and reports from bilingual program directors across the Commonwealth suggest a need for more understanding of and sensitivity to these issues on the part of administrators and mainstream teachers. With pupils whose first language is not English now representing 12 percent (and increasing) of the total public school enrollment, it is essential that these competencies become widely distributed. The Education Reform Act's strong emphasis upon whole-school responsibility makes it clear that the need for them will no longer be limited to teachers who work within bilingual programs.

The Commission's recommendations suggest how these competencies can become part of what is expected of every teacher, principal, and educational specialist, since every educator in the Commonwealth is increasingly likely to be called upon to serve language minority pupils.

The Whole-School Emphasis

Providing transitional bilingual classes—even very effective ones—but no adaptation of the regular classes into which pupils will be mainstreamed is educationally irresponsible. Becoming proficient in a second language is not a process that is complete after several years; it is rather an on-going task even for pupils whose first language is English. For pupils who are becoming bilingual, the whole-school program should provide support for language development. It is not enough to prepare language minority pupils to take advantage of the whole-school program; the whole-school program must be prepared to support and challenge them as well.

On the other hand, failure to integrate language minority pupils on the basis that the mainstream is not prepared to serve them well is an abdication of the responsibility to offer them access to the full range of opportunities available. Separate schooling beyond what is essential tells these pupils that they are not considered capable of full participation in our educational system, and denies them the opportunity to develop full proficiency in English through using it with classmates for whom English is the first language, in settings where it is a means of communication and not just a subject to be studied. Responsibility for educating language minority pupils effectively cannot be placed upon bilingual programs and their staff alone; that responsibility belongs to all of the educators in schools which those children attend. The whole staff of the school must be trained in techniques for supporting second language development and be committed to well-understood strategies to ensure that language minority pupils can take part in their classes with profit.

Integration of language minority pupils involves more than physical proximity to other pupils: it requires that they be enabled to participate fully in classroom and other activities, while receiving on-going support for their distinctive learning needs. This calls for a different way of thinking about how their schooling is organized. For the past two decades, great stress has been placed upon "mainstreaming" as an event through which a pupil leaves a bilingual program and subsequently is in a sense lost from view as a "regular" student receiving no services related to language background. There has often been little communication between bilingual and other teachers about what pupils are learning at each stage, and few opportunities for the pupils to establish relationships with the peers with whom they will suddenly be mainstreamed. It is no wonder that some teachers and parents hesitate to take this definitive step, while pupils who are mainstreamed often experience considerable difficulty participating in the regular classroom.

A whole-school strategy, by contrast, would begin the integration of language minority with other pupils in regular classrooms from the start of their schooling, while continuing to provide support in the first language and in English as a second language for as long as school staff and parents believe it is appropriate. Instruction through the first language should not be seen as a temporary, remedial measure, but as a means of developing a high level of bilingualism when instruction is provided through English as well.

Staff of an integrated bilingual school plan together for the education of all; they do not think in terms of "my kids" and "those kids." This requires *time*, it requires willingness and an open attitude on the part of all staff, and it requires that all staff be knowledgeable about how first languages and second languages are learned. Principals of integrated bilingual schools must themselves be skilled bilingual educators, and they must be able to select staff compatible with the mission of the school, staff who are willing to and capable of working effectively with all the pupils in the school.

Bilingual staff should be seen as a valuable resource who share in responsibility for every pupil, and they must have the English-language skills and the professional training to do so. A whole-school strategy considers languages central to the mission of the school, and the learning of languages as an important dimension of its academic rigor.

Pupils whose first language is English may be offered the opportunity to study the first language of other pupils in the school; in some cases, when enrollment is on the basis of parental choice, this may be a fundamental dimension of the school's program. But the "two-way" approach is not essential to integration; what *is* essential is clear respect for second-language learners as expressed in organizational and instructional arrangements that promote their full participation in the educational mission of the school.

Such an approach can only work when class sizes of the regular classes into which language minority pupils are integrated are kept low enough to permit their participation. This should not be considered a problem (though often it is presented as an insurmountable barrier); the extra funding provided for pupils requiring bilingual education should be seen as providing them with "seats" in two classrooms and with two teachers, just as most pupils with special needs are assigned to a regular classroom as well as to a resource room, and are taught by two different teachers who (at least in principle) collaborate closely.

The number of state-approved charter schools and the number allowed in a particular community should be expanded to include bilingual charter schools in each community where a program of transitional bilingual education now exists and where such a school is proposed by local initiative and otherwise meeting state requirements for charter schools. A bilingual charter school should (a) enroll pupils whose first language is not English of a single language background as between 25 percent and 45 percent of its total enrollment, (b) be headed by a principal eligible for certification in bilingual education or English as a second language as well as in school administration, (c) be staffed with teachers knowledgeable of and skilled in second language teaching, including several proficient in the language other than English spoken by a substantial proportion of the pupils of the school, and (d) be organized to provide high-quality integrated instruction that employs two languages as media of instruction.

SPECIFIC RECOMMENDATIONS

1. Bilingual education programs in grades k–6 (k–5 or k–8 in school districts with those forms of organization of the first level of schooling) should be established only in school facilities that are large enough to allow at least two and preferably three classes at each grade level for which bilingual education is provided.

2. The principal assigned to each school housing a bilingual education program should be thoroughly familiar with strategies for language acquisition and bilingual education.

3. Each k–6 (k–5, k–8) bilingual education teacher should be paired with at least one and preferably two regular program teachers of the same grade level, and their schedules should in every case allow for at least bi-weekly joint planning time.

4. Each pupil in grades k–6 (k–5, k–8) requiring bilingual instruction should from the start and each subsequent year receive a double assignment, to a bilingual class and to a partner regular program class; both teachers should be considered responsible for the pupil's academic progress.

5. A pupil in grades k–6 (k–5, k–8) requiring bilingual instruction

should for the first three years (including kindergarten) be counted as 1.5 pupils for the purpose of establishing pupil/teacher ratios: as a full-time pupil for the bilingual program teacher and as a half-time pupil for the regular program teacher.

6. A pupil in grades k–6 (k–5, k–8) who has completed three years of bilingual instruction may continue to receive such instruction after the third year, if by judgment of the principal in consultation with the parents and the pupil's bilingual and regular program teachers this would enhance the academic success of the pupil. In this case the pupil should be counted as a half-time pupil for the bilingual program teacher and as a full-time pupil for the regular program teacher.

7. Bilingual program teachers may be assigned responsibility for half-time pupils at several different grade levels if, in the judgment of the principal, this is consistent with sound education.

8. A pupil in grades 7–12 (6–12, 9–12) requiring bilingual instruction will in most cases be a recent immigrant or refugee. He or she should in every case be evaluated for previous academic progress as well as language proficiency, and should be individually scheduled to ensure an appropriate mix of language instruction in English and academic instruction through English and the home language to support academic progress. In every case, the instruction should be so scheduled and designed that the student in question will be able to participate to the greatest extent possible in the regular school program as soon as possible. At no time can a program be selected to place the student in a situation where the method of instruction will result in a substantial delay in providing the student with necessary English language skills needed by or required of other students at the time of graduation. The guiding principle for the secondary education program of pupils unable to perform ordinary classwork in English shall be those articulated by the Office for Civil Rights and reaffirmed by the Supreme Court in 1974: "Any ability grouping or tracking system employed by the school system to deal with the special language skill needs of national origin-minority group children must be designed to meet such language skill needs as soon as possible and must not operate as an educational deadend or permanent track" (*Lau v. Nichols*).

9. Groups of bilingual and non-bilingual teachers should work together to ensure effective instruction of bilingual pupils in academic areas.

The findings of the Massachusetts Commission on which the author served are strikingly consistent with those of a legislatively mandated study of the schooling of language minority children in California: state officials responsible for bilingual education had never, in more than twenty years, required the collection of data on the academic achievement and the English language proficiency of pupils in their programs; school districts had retained pupils in programs for year after year without assessment of their readiness for mainstreaming; bilingual program pupils in secondary school did not have available the full range of courses required for graduation, much less college admission; and there was no accountability for the significant amount of additional funding provided to school districts to meet the needs of language minority pupils (Rossier, 1995).

Despite the obvious shortcomings of these state-mandated programs, and abundant evidence of the dismal school achievement of many Hispanic pupils in particular, Hispanic activists continue to make protection of the semimonopoly position of separate bilingual programs a high priority. They have little patience with suggestions that

> school districts should be allowed to experiment in a responsible and informed manner. Similarly, parents and community members, once provided with accurate and reliable background information, should be given more opportunity to select program options which they feel are best suited for their individual children and communities (Dolson, 1985b, 24).

A bill filed by Massachusetts Governor William Weld in the spring of 1995, for example, sought to increase the presumption that language minority pupils should be integrated with other pupils to the greatest extent possible, while continuing to require providing instruction also through home languages; it was soundly defeated after hundreds of parents and schoolchildren packed the hearing room to denounce the amendment as an effort to abolish bilingual education.

Similar criticism of separate home language programs in the Netherlands has been met with similar indignation. When Dutch Education Secretary Tineke Netelenbos proposed that supplemental home language classes be made the responsibility of local government, with flexibility to determine how best to organize them, this was denounced as "a stab in the back" at a stormy meeting of home language advocates. Learning minority languages actually furthers the integration process, the Labor Party education spokesman (former

Education Secretary Wallage) told an approving audience, "because integration requires that you know who you are" (Withagen, 1995, 340).

The response reflects a shift of emphasis away from arguments based upon academic and cognitive considerations toward arguments based upon social-psychological and political considerations; indeed Wallage insisted that the debate over home language instruction had for more than twenty years been about politics and not about education. This shift in the argument for home language instruction can be traced in a single sentence by Jim Cummins:

> data from both Sweden and the United States suggest that minority students who immigrate relatively late (about ten years of age) often appear to have better academic prospects than students of similar socioeconomic status born in the host country (Cummins, 1984a; Skutnabb-Kangas, 1984c). *Is this because their L1 cognitive/academic skills on arrival provide a better foundation for L2 cognitive/academic skills acquisition* [the only explanation given earlier by Cummins], *or alternatively, because they have not experienced devaluation of their identity in the societal institutions, namely schools of the host country . . . ?* (Cummins, 1986, 23; emphasis added).

This new line of argument leads to downplaying linguistic considerations and stressing cultural ones instead. The important thing now is that teachers convey to their pupils—whether in the home language or in that of the school—that they can add the second language and culture without abandoning their heritage. "It should be noted," according to Cummins,

> that an additive orientation does not require the actual teaching of the minority language. . . . Even within a monolingual school context, powerful messages can be communicated to students regarding the validity and advantages of language development (Cummins, 1986, 25–26).

Well-structured programs based exclusively upon the second language of children may be quite effective linguistically, Cummins concludes, but they do not deal with the other causes of the underachievement of minority pupils, including their "ambivalence" about both languages and their need to have their "cultural identity" reinforced (Cummins, 1984a, 156–157).

Conversely, it is not enough—according to this line of argument—to provide instruction through the home language, without more fundamental changes designed to give a message of empowerment.

[I]t is not sufficient to merely use the students' home language in bi-lingual programs, nor is it sufficient to employ members of the minority group in the school only as teachers and support personnel. What is called for is the use of the students' home language and the employment of minority language group members in ways that upgrade their status and power relative to that of English and English-speaking people. This might mean "over-using" the minority language or "over-representing" the minority group in the administrative hierarchy of the school, relative to their predominance in the community at large, in order to offset the inferior social status otherwise associated with the group (Genesee, 1984, 168).

The pursuit of status-equality in the school in order to affect how language minority pupils feel about themselves has no obvious limit. For example, many opponents of tracking practices based upon academic achievement that disproportionately place minority children in lower groups and thus give them low expectations for themselves, call for the use of "cooperative learning" in place of tracking. Even this may not be enough if *within* heterogeneous cooperative-learning groups the differing ability of pupils to carry out the assigned tasks will "entail differential status effects" (Genesee, 1984, 169).

Beneath the prescriptions for separate and distinctive forms of schooling for minority children lies the fundamental mistrust of the intentions and capabilities of "majority" educators and the educational system in general toward language minority children that has characterized bilingual education advocates for decades.

Fase suggests a helpful way of categorizing policy approaches to schooling according to whether they seek the same or distinctive outcomes for particular groups of pupils by identical or differentiated means. In the case of ethnic minority pupils, seeking the same outcome as for majority pupils is the egalitarian and assimilative goal of postwar educational policy; it can be sought by making no distinction among groups of pupils (model 1) or precisely by treating minority pupils as different and providing them with a distinctive program or instructional approach, such as a reception class or a transitional bilingual program (model 2) (see Table 9.2). Even in the last-mentioned case, the use of the minority language is not primarily intended to maintain that language but rather to support transition to instruction in the majority language (Fase, 1994, 133).

Seeking distinctive outcomes for ethnic minority pupils may (as in South Africa under *apartheid*) be intended to maintain a castelike hierarchy of groups in the society, but more commonly it is an expression of the goal

TABLE 9.2. Policy Models Based on Treatment/Desired Outcomes		
Desired Outcomes	Same	Distinctive
Treatment		
Identical	model 1	model 2
Differentiated	model 3	model 4

Source: Fase, 1994, 133 (adapted).

of societal pluralism advocated from various quarters of late, though not commonly made an explicit public policy (see Chapter 4). Different outcomes are accepted on the basis of the assumption "that several groups of pupils, or their parents and communities, do have a different set of orientations and perceptions [about] what constitutes a valuable education outcome" (Fase, 1994, 133). This may lead, at least within some aspects of the school program, to different goals for different groups of pupils, not just, as in model 3, different means of seeking to reach the same goals. In some cases, this may involve simply rationalizing the expectation that minority pupils will not benefit in the same way or to the same extent from participating in the regular program (model 2), while in other cases it may involve such differentiated practices as maintenance programs in the minority language that entail largely separate schooling for a number of years (model 4). Multicultural programs that are based upon an understanding of cultural differences as being of fundamental significance may, in an inadvertent and fuzzy-thinking way, fit in model 2 as well: Children of different ethnic backgrounds may be in the same classroom, but receiving the message from the curriculum that they are expected to end up quite different.

If the only goal were full participation of language minority children on an equal basis in the educational system and the later rewards offered by the host society, one would expect advocates for their interests to support a variety of responsible experimental approaches that might do a better job than the present arrangements. Another agenda, political rather than educational, seems to lie behind the strong opposition to such alternatives as structured immersion. Bilingual education advocates argue that immersion works for middle-class Canadian pupils but would not work for language minority children in the United States because of their subordinated status. They base this contention upon generalizations from linguistic and social theory, not from examination of actual programs that seem to demonstrate that a well-constructed immersion program can work effectively.

Canadian immersion programs were successfully replicated for low-ability children and for children from working-class families. Similarly, in Redwood City, California study, low-income Mexican-American children, taught exclusively in English, performed better in English-language skills than children in bilingual programs. Neither finding would have been predicted from the generalizations drawn above (Rotberg, 1982, 160).

Structured immersion has also been used successfully in the United States to teach foreign languages to English-speaking children.

Students in the Cincinnati immersion program demonstrated the same levels of achievement in English and mathematics as their peers in English-medium schools. Of particular significance, this was equally true for working class and black students as well as for middle class and white students. . . . There were clear performance differences . . . that favoured the white and middle class students but these differences were independent of the programs they were in . . . the disadvantaged students were not disadvantaged when it came to second language learning (Holobow, Genesee, & Lambert, 1990, 24).

The success of such instructional strategies undermines the contention that minority children are somehow fundamentally different and must be educated differently from majority children. Fase offers another helpful analytical distinction, based upon the extent to which program interventions are based upon singling out the minority group on the basis of its ethnic or language characteristics or, by contrast, offering particular services to all pupils with similar educational needs (see Table 9.3). Here the question is, to what extent ethnicity is considered a relevant category for policy formulation.

From our perspective, *none* of the options shown in Table 9.3 is fully desirable; only two have the intellectual coherence that should be required of acceptable policy choices. Seeking to support societal pluralism through separate educational provisions is rational and, in the case of differing religious convictions, must be allowed as necessary in a free society. Muslim or Catholic parents have a right to arrange that their children be schooled apart from the mainstream, and each of the countries in our study except the United States provides public funding for Catholic schooling, though the Netherlands are the exception at present in providing it for Islamic schooling as well. Choice on the basis of ethnicity does not deserve the same level

TABLE 9.3. Practices According to Orientation and Categorization

	Categorization Is High	Categorization Is Low
Pluralistic	separate mother tongue classes	expansion of modern language offerings
	minority religious instruction	language awareness
	"nationality schools"	multicultural education
	Islamic and Hindu schools	"anti-racism education"
Egalitarian	reception classes	compensatory education
	transitional bilingual education	

Source: Fase, 1994, 134 (adapted).

of public support, and in fact is unlikely to be attractive to parents unless supported by religious considerations.

Seeking to achieve egalitarian goals through what Fase calls compensatory education is also rational. That is, to the extent that language minority pupils have difficulty with schooling, they can be served through arrangements that are provided also to majority pupils who are experiencing similar difficulties. This is fair on the face of it (if effective, of course), and does not result in stigmatization or marginalization. As noted above, the confusion of national origin with social-class origin has led to a misleading attribution to ethnic and language factors of academic difficulties that some language minority pupils share with other children of the same social-class background.

It cannot be stressed too often that the fact that a pupil entering an educational system does not speak the language used for instruction in that system is, in itself, usually only a temporary problem; hundreds of thousands of children have risen to that challenge successfully over the past decade. Difficulty arises from the fact that language is often a surrogate for other ways in which a particular pupil is disadvantaged in pursuing a formal education. If the parents are themselves poorly educated (in any language), if the child belongs to an ethnic group of which little is expected by the school, if she comes to school with physical or emotional or what could be called social disabilities, there is a good chance that she will not do well academically. This conditions require different remedies, and it is not helpful to lump them under the heading of language or cultural differences. Unfortunately, "the isolation of the language variable [as the cause of difficulties], which researchers and bilingual advocates have embraced somewhat uncritically, has particularized and fragmented the learning problems faced by Hispanics and other national-origin students" (Baez et al., 1985, 206). As the author wrote in a Massachusetts government report,

> We in education have erred by thinking of what is really an issue of language development as being one of transition between two languages. As a result, bilingual programs have been seen by non-specialists as mysterious "black boxes" into which Khmer-speaking or Spanish-speaking students are fed, to emerge three years later as English-speaking students. If the results are less than satisfactory—and we should admit candidly that this is often the case—bilingual education itself is incorrectly seen as the problem. It would be more useful to say that the whole educational system fails these children when it defines their home language as a problem and does not from the start set clear objectives for their overall education. It fails them if it does not provide opportunities to be actively engaged in learning from the first day in school, through use of the language in which the student is most secure.
>
> Language development is a much more complex and long-term process than simply the acquisition of a surface fluency in a second language, and it should not be isolated from the other aspects of learning that go on in the school. It is one of the tasks that must be undertaken by *every* student, and seems to pose particular difficulties for those from poor families.
>
> It is inappropriate to provide special support only to those students who exhibit the "problem" of preferring to use another language than English. Some of these students may in fact need language development help *less* than schoolmates who are not eligible for a bilingual program. Urban schools should assess individual needs and provide a flexible program of challenge and support to every student (Glenn, 1988d, 10–11).

Educational policy has seldom taken into account the ways in which language and social class interact to influence pupil achievement. Bilingualism seems to confer educational advantages on high-status pupils. That is, high-status, English-dominant Hispanic pupils who also speak Spanish do better in school than do Hispanic pupils of similar social status who are monolingual in English. On the other hand, "frequent use of a non-English language was negatively associated with achievement," and this was increasingly true the longer a pupil had lived in the United States. This suggests not only that bilingualism is a sort of cultural luxury item which produces benefits if it is not indulged in too extensively, but also that remaining within a language ghetto has a negative effect on school achievement, at least for Hispanics in the United States (Baratz-Snowden et al., 1988a, 5).

It would not do to end this study on a note that could appear critical of bilingual education. *We are strongly favorable toward bilingual education, for all children.* What we oppose is *separate* education for language minority children, especially when it is based upon separatist ideologies involving absolutization of culture as destiny. We also oppose simply assuming that physical integration in schools or classrooms will by itself lead to equal participation and outcomes. Language minority children will benefit most from schools in which they are integrated from the start and continually with majority children for instruction that is adapted as to language use but not as to intellectual expectations, while also having opportunities to continue to use and to develop their first languages.

We would, with Löfgren and Ouvinen, "disassociate ourselves from those arguments for teaching in the mother tongue which attempt to frighten parents into choosing mother tongue-teaching by threatening emotional and intellectual under-development in those children who do not receive" it (quoted by Löfgren, 1984, 19). The best reason for providing instruction through more than a single language is that—if it is done in a way appropriate to the comprehension level of the pupils—this is the best way of becoming proficient in several languages, and much more effective than simply "teaching" languages. The best reason for so organizing instruction that pupils become proficient in several languages is that this is intellectually and (later) professionally advantageous. The schooling of children of elite groups in most societies has always stressed several languages; as Sy Fliegel is fond of saying, "in [New York's] District No. 4 we hold the general belief that what is good for the children of the rich is good enough for the children of East Harlem"!

The only rationale for bilingual education that is likely to be effective in the long run is that learning several languages is preferable to learning only one. "It cannot survive long as an adjunct program which bears close resemblance to makeshift measures intended to meet only transient needs," Diego Castellanos has pointed out. "Neither can it survive as a 'special' program for a minority group. It desperately needs the support of the wider community as part and parcel of the total educational system" (Castellanos, 1983, 266). Language minority pupils—like majority pupils—should receive instruction through the minority language only if that instruction is serious and disciplined, not dilettantish or concerned more with promoting good feelings than with training minds. As the author wrote in the 1988 Massachusetts report,

> Instruction in the home language of linguistic minority students has been promoted largely as a means of assisting the transition to English. There is a better reason: that it has the potential of providing a higher-quality all-around education. Students are more likely to grapple with challenging material, to take intellectual risks, to apply themselves fully to learning if they feel secure in the language they are using. We can teach industrial arts in simplified English, but not philosophy, and the civics discussion that has to limit itself to a 700 word vocabulary will not train much of a citizen.
>
> But instruction in the home language is justified only if it is purposeful, demanding, and accountable for results; it must not be a backwater. It is most likely to have these characteristics if it looks toward secondary-school courses, including the option of advanced placement in the home language. Study in the home language must be considered intellectually demanding and not simply remedial. . . .
>
> To define the education of linguistic minority students primarily in terms of their acquisition of English is too narrow. The [State] Board has adopted nine goals for education in Massachusetts, and each of these may be sought in the language with which children come to school as well as in English. It should never be the intention of teachers to suppress or devalue the language used in the home.
>
> Our expectation should be that every linguistic minority students will acquire a solid proficiency in English and a well-rounded education. Maintenance of the first language and of the heritage culture are matters for individual choice, but public schools should assure that there is a real opportunity to make that choice (Glenn, 1988d, 14–15).

As David Baral put it rather wistfully, "I feel that we must be cautious about adopting a theory of bilingual education that is primarily linguistic in character. . . . It would be highly desirable to examine an alternative rationale for bilingual education which is based on the broader social perspectives of a national language policy" (Baral, 1983a, 18–19). Most governments have not been quick, however, to make the maintenance of immigrant minority languages a specific policy objective; Australia and Canada are exceptions, and their enthusiasm has waned in recent years. In these cases, significantly, the stress upon immigrant languages was within the context of policies intended to promote a measure of bilingualism on the part of the entire population, for reasons of national rather than ethnic-group interest. This is consistent with Kenji Hakuta's comment that bilingual education would best be promoted through "diluting its association with ethnicity and making functional bilingualism the goal for all students" (Hakuta, 1986, 233).

Bilingual education, yes, definitely; segregated minority schooling, no!

REFERENCES *

Aarssen, J., De Ruiter, J.J., and Verhoeven, L. (1992). *Toetsing Turks en Arabisch aan het einde van het basisonderwijs*. Tilburg (The Netherlands): Tilburg University Press.

Abadan-Unat, Nermin (1975). Educational Problems of Turkish Migrants' Children, *International Review of Education, 21*, 3.

Abali, Marie-Luise (1983). Entwicklungsprobleme bei Türkischen Kindern und Jugendlichen in Berlin: Psychologische Aspekte der Identitätsbildung. In Christoph Elsas (Ed.), *Identität: Veränderungen kultureller Eigenarten im Zusammenleben von Turken und Deutschen*. Hamburg: Rissen.

Abbott, Edith (1926). *Historical Aspects of the Immigration Problem: Select Documents*. Chicago: University of Chicago Press.

Abdallah-Pretceille, Martine (1984). Pédagogie interculturelle: de la pratique à la théorie, réflexions à partir de la situation française. In Micheline Rey (Ed.), *Une pédagogie interculturelle*. Berne (Switzerland): Commission nationale suisse pour l'UNESCO.

Abdallah-Pretceille, Martine (1987). Prologèmes à une pédagogie interculturelle. In *L'Immigration en France: Le choc des cultures*. L'Arbresle (France): Centre Thomas More.

Abou-Sada, Georges and Milet, Hélène (1986). Introduction. In Georges Abou-Sada and Hélène Milet (Eds.), *Générations issues de l'immigration*. Paris: Arcantère Éditions.

Accardo, Armando (1987). Die Neuregelung des muttersprachlichen Unterrichts an den Schulen in NRW am Beispiel des Faches Italienisch. *Gemeinsam, 7*, December.

Adler, Frank (1993–1994). Left Vigilance in France. *Telos 98–99*, Winter-Spring.

Afdeling Onderwijs, Gemeente Amsterdam (1988). *Discussienota: Gemeentelijk Minderhedenbeleid Onderwijs*, Part 2, January.

Ahmad, Asad (1987a). De to-kulturelle klasser stryker ikke modersmålet. *Samspil* (Denmark), 1.

Ahmad, Asad (1987b). Fri os fra de frelste folkeskolelærere. *Samspil*, 2.

Aikio, Marjut (1991). The Sámi Language: Pressure of Change and Reification. In Kjell Herberts and Christer Laurén (Eds.), *Papers from the Sixth Nordic Conference on Bilingualism*. Clevedon (United Kingdom): Multilingual Matters.

Alaluf, Mateo (1982). *Migrant Culture and Culture of Origin*. Strasbourg (France): Council of Europe.

---

*Articles from periodicals for which no author was given are referenced directly in the text and are not included below. These include *Berlingske* (Denmark), *The Boston Globe* (United States), *The Economist* (United Kingdom), *Le Figaro* (France), *Gemeinsam* (Germany), *Le Monde* (France), *Het Parool* (The Netherlands), *Samenwijs* (The Netherlands), *Der Spiegel* (Germany), *The Times Educational Supplement* (United Kingdom).

Alatis, James E. (1983). The Role of Language Study in Bilingual Education. *Exploring Strategies for Developing a Cohesive National Direction toward Language Education in the United States*, Rosslyn (VA): National Clearinghouse for Bilingual Education.

Alba, Richard D. (1990). *Ethnic Identity: The Transformation of White America*. New Haven: Yale University.

Alba, Richard D. (1995). Assimilation's Quiet Tide. *The Public Interest*, 119, Spring.

Alexander, Susan and Baker, Keith. (n.d.). A Case Study of Educational Reform and the Adequacy of the Research Base: Bilingual Education and Self-esteem. Unpublished manuscript.

Alfatli, Jacqueline and Alfatli, Nazim (1980). Ensemble de pressions contradictoires exercees sur les enfants à travers la scolarité. In *Codes et pratiques des populations immigrées: identité culturelle et modeles de socialisation*. Brussels: Ministère de l'Education Nationale et de la Culture Française.

Ali-Ammar,–(1988). Allocution. In *Les algériens et l'enseignement de l'arabe en France*, Paris: Centre culturel algérien.

Allegro, Annalisa (1985). Approaches for the Mainstream Classroom: LEP and English-Proficient Students Learning Together. In Stefan Jaeger (Ed.), *Educating the Minority Language Student: Classroom and Administrative Issues I*. Rosslyn (VA): The National Clearinghouse for Bilingual Education.

Allport, G.W. (1954). *The Nature of Prejudice*. Cambridge (MA): Addison-Wesley.

Allsup, Carl (1977). Education Is Our Freedom: The American G.I. Forum and the Mexican American. School Segregation in Texas, 1948–1957. *Aztlan 8*, Spring-Fall, 27–50.

Amersfoort, Hans van (1982). *Immigration and the Formation of Minority Groups* (Robert Lyng, Transl.). Cambridge: Cambridge University Press.

Amersfoort, Hans van (1986). Nederland als immigratieland. In Lotty van den Berg-Eldering (Ed.), *Van gastarbeider tot immigrant: Marokkanen en Turken in Nederland, 1965–1985*. Alphen aan den Rijn (The Netherlands): Samson.

Amminh, Hassan. (1986). OETC voor Marokkaanse kinderen. *Onderwijs in eigen taal en cultuur, MOER* (The Netherlands) 1–2.

A Nation Prepared: Teachers for the 21st Century (1986, May). New York: Carnegie Forum on Education and the Economy.

Ancart, R., Tommissen, R. and Xhoffer, J. (1982). De concentratie van migrantenleerlingen in het Rijksonderwijs. *Informatieblad, xvii*, 1 (January), 2 (February), Brussels: Ministerie van Onderwijs.

An Coiste Comhairleach Pleanála [The Advisory Planning Committee] (1988). *The Irish Language in a Changing Society*. Dublin: Bord na Gaeilge.

An Coiste Comhairleach Pleanála [The Advisory Planning Committee] (n.d.). *The Irish Language in a Changing Society*. Dublin: Bord na Gaeilge.

Anderiesen, Gerard and Reijndorp, Arnold (1991). Op zoek naar de onderklasse: heterogeniteit en sociaal isolement in stadsvernieuwingswijken. *Migrantenstudies*, 7, 3.

Andersen, Ole Stig and Nielsen, René Mark (1987). *Noget fremmed—en bog om integration*. Copenhagen: Dunya.

Andersen, Suzanne (1992). *Ethnic Minority Children and Education in Denmark*. Copenhagen: Danmarks Lærerhøjskole.

Andersson, Theodore and Boyer, Mildred. (1970). *Bilingual Schooling in the United States I and II*. Austin, Texas: Southwest Educational Development Laboratory.

André, Bernard (1988). Une expérience d'autonomisation des apprenants d'une classe d'accueil. *Migrants formation no. 73*, June. Special theme issue: L'accueil scolaire des nouveaux arrivants.

André, Robert (1983). *La population de la Wallonie dans la dualité démographique de la Belgique*. Brussels: Fondation Charles Plisnier.

Andress, Karen (1988, March 17). Letter to the Editor: Deaf Culture Threatened by Research in Hearing. *The Boston Globe*.

Angel, Frank. (1972). Social Class or Culture? In B. Spolsky (Ed.), *A Fundamental*

Issue in the Education of Culturally Different Students. The Language Education of Minority Children. Rowley (MA): Newbury House.

Anglejan, Alison d' (1981). The Education of Minorities in Canada: An Examination of Policies. In *World Yearbook of Education 1981: Education of Minorities.* New York: Kogan Page.

Anglejan, Alison d' (1984). Language Planning in Quebec: An Historical Overview and Future Trends. In Richard Y. Bourhis (Ed.), *Conflict and Language Planning in Quebec.* Clevedon (United Kingdom): Multilingual Matters.

Appel, René (1980). De voertaal op school en tweedetaalverwerving van anderstalige kinderen. In René Appel, Cees Cruson, Pieter Muysken and J.W. de Vries (Eds.), *Taalproblemen van buitenlandse arbeiders en hun kinderen.* Muiderberg (Netherlands): Coutinho.

Appel, René (1985). Pleidooien voor Arabisch en Turks op school. *Samenwijs, 6* (3).

Appel, René (1988). The Language Education of Immigrant Workers' Children in The Netherlands. In Tove Skutnabb-Kangas and Jim Cummins (Eds.), *Minority Education: From Shame to Struggle.* Clevedon (United Kingdom): Multilingual Matters.

Appel, René (1993). Het enge gezichtsveld van Harm Kijpstra. *Samenwijs, 13,* 8.

Appel, René, Everts, Henk, & Teunissen, Joop (1986). Het Leidse onderwijsexperiment. In *Onderwijs in eigen taal en cultuur,* MOER (The Netherlands) 1–2.

Appel, René and Nalbantoglu, Papatya. (1990). Onderwijs in eigen taal en cultuur. *Samenwijs, 11* (1).

Apprentissage du français pour les enfants étrangers nouvellement arrivés en France, Circulaire no. 86–119, Paris: Ministère de l'Education nationale, March 13, 1986.

Arfert, Gerd and Hegele, Irmintraut (1985). *Sprachstandserhebung und Sprachforderung unter besonderer Berucksichtigung ausländischer Kinder, part 2,* Hildesheim (Germany): Niedersachsisches Landesinstitut fur Lehrerfortbildung, Lehrerweiterbildung und Unterrichtsforschung.

Arias, M. Beatriz (1982). When Hispanics Become the Majority: The Multiracial Challenge to Educational Equity. *Metas, 2* (3), 24–43.

Arias, M. Beatriz (1986). The Context of Education for Hispanic Students: An Overview. *American Journal of Education, 95* (1).

Arnau, Joaquim and Boada, Humbert (1986). Languages and School in Catalonia. *Multilingual and Multicultural Development, 7* (2 & 3).

Aronowitz, Michael (1984). The Social and Emotional Adjustment of Immigrant Children: A Review of the Literature. *International Migration Review, 18* (2).

Arons, Stephen (1986). *Compelling Belief: The Culture of American Schooling.* Amherst: University of Massachusetts Press.

Artigal, Josep Maria (1991a). *The Catalan Immersion Program: A European Point of View.* (Jacqueline Hall, Transl.). Norwood (MA): Ablex.

Artigal, Josep Maria (1991b). The Catalan Immersion Program: The Joint Creation of Shared Indexical Territory. In Kjell Herberts and Christer Laurén (Eds.), *Papers from the Sixth Nordic Conference on Bilingualism.* Clevedon (United Kingdom): Multilingual Matters.

Artigal, Josep Maria (1993). Catalan and Basque Immersion Programmes (Jacqueline Hall, Transl.). In Hugo Baetens Beardsmore (Ed.), *European Models of Bilingual Education.* Clevedon (United Kingdom): Multilingual Matters.

Arvizu, S.F. (1992). Home-school linkages: A Cross-cultural Approach to Parent Participation. In M. Saravia-Shore and S. Arvizu (Eds.), *Cross-cultural Literacy: Ethnographies of Communication in Multiethnic Classrooms.* (Pp. 37–56). New York: Garland.

Asante, Molefi Kete and Ravitch, Diane (1991). Multiculturalism: An Exchange Between Molefi Kete Asante and Diane Ravitch. *American Scholar, 60* (2), Spring.

Ascher, Carol (1989). Southeast Asian Adolescents: Identity and Adjustment. *ERIC Digest 51.*

Ashruf, George (1986). OETC Hindi, Urdu en Sarnami voor Surinamers. *Onderwijs in eigen taal en cultuur, MOER (The Netherlands)* 1–2.

Askolovitch, Claude (1994). Le voile de discorde. *Esprit Libre*. December.

Atkins, J.D.C. (1887). Barbarous Dialects Should Be Blotted Out. In James Crawford (Ed.), *Language Loyalties*. Chicago: University of Chicago Press, 1992.

Au, K.H. and Jordan, C. (1981). Teaching Reading to Hawaiian Children: Finding a Culturally Appropriate Solution. In H. Trueba, G. Guthrie, K.H. Au (Eds.), *Culture and the Bilingual Classroom: Studies in Classroom Ethnography* (pp. 139–152). Rowley (MA): Newbury House.

August, D.L. (1987). Effects of Peer Tutoring on the Second Language Acquisition of Mexican American Children in Elementary School. *TESOL Quarterly, 21* (4), 717–736.

August, D. and Garcia, E.E. (1988). *Language Minority Education in the United States: Research, Policy, and Practice*. Springfield (IL): Charles Thomas.

Baerdsmore, Hugo Baetens and Swain, Merrill (1985). Designing Bilingual Education: Aspects of Immersion and "European School" Models. *Multilingual and Multicultural Development, 6* (1).

Baert, G. (1984). Schoolorganisatie en externe controle en inspectie in Belgie, *3 HSO* (Belgium), November.

Baez, T., Fernandez, R.R., Navarro, R.A., and Rice, R.L. (1985). Litigation Strategies for Educational Equity: Bilingual Education and Research. *Issues in Education, 3* (3), 198–214.

Bagley, Christopher. (1989). Education for All: A Canadian Dimension. In Gajendra K. Verma (Ed.), *Education for All: A Landmark in Pluralism*. London: Falmer Press.

Baker, Colin (1993a). Bilingual Education in Wales, European Models of Bilingual Education. In Hugo Baetens Beardsmore (Ed.), *European Models of Bilingual Education*. Clevedon (United Kingdom): Multilingual Matters.

Baker, C. (1993b). *Foundations of Bilingual Education and Bilingualism*. Clevedon (United Kingdom): Multilingual Matters.

Baker, Keith A. (n.d.). *Bilingual Education's 20 Year Failure to Provide Civil Rights Protection for Language Minority Students*. (Typescript.)

Baker, Keith A. (1987). Comment on Willig's "A Meta-Analysis of Selected Studies in the Effectiveness on Bilingual Education." *Review of Educational Research, 57* (3).

Baker, Keith A. and de Kanter, Adriana A. (1983). Federal Policy and the Effectiveness of Bilingual Education. In Keith A. Baker and Adriana A. de Kanter (Eds.), *Bilingual Education: A Reappraisal of Federal Policy*. Lexington (MA): D.C. Heath.

Baker, Keith A. and Rossell, Christine H. (1987). An Implementation Problem: Specifying the Target Group for Bilingual Education. *Educational Policy, 1* (2).

Baker, Keith and Rossel, Christine H. (1993). Blinded by Theory in the Search for Effective Programs for LEP Students: A Call for Testing New research Hypotheses. Paper presented at Annual Meeting of the American Educational Research Association, April 12–16, Atlanta, GA.

Balinge, Gré van (1988). In nieuwe schooljaar gaan islamitische en hindoeïstische scholen open, *Samenwijs, 8* (9).

Balke-Aurell, Gudrun and Lindblad, Torsten (1983). *Immigrant Children and Their Languages*. Gothenburg (Sweden): University of Gothenburg.

Banks, James A. (1981). *The Nature of Multiethnic Education, Education in the 80's: Multiethnic Education*. Washington, DC: National Education Association.

Banks, James A. (1986). Multicultural Education and Its Critics: Britain and the United States. In Sohan Mogdil, Gajendra Verma, Kanka Mallick, and Celie Mogdil (Eds.), *Multicultural Education: The Interminable Debate*. London: Falmer Press.

Banks, James A. (1988).The Influence of Ethnicity and Class on Cognitive Styles: Implications for Research and Education. In W. J. Lonner and Vernon O. Tyler, Jr. (Eds.), *Cultural and Ethnic Factors in Learning and Motivation: Implications for Education*. Bellingham (WA)Western Washington University, 1988.

Baral, David P. (1983a). Second-Language Acquisition Theories Relevant to Bilingual Education. In Raymond V. Padilla (Ed.), *Theory, Technology, and Public Policy on Bilingual Education*. Rosslyn (VA): The National Clearinghouse for Bilingual Education.

Baral, David P. (1983b). Self-concept Studies in Bilingual Education: A Review and Critique. Paper presented at Annual International Bilingual Bicultural Education Conference, Washington, DC.

Baratz-Snowden, J., Rock, D., Pollack, J., and Gita Wilder, G. (1988a). *The Educational Progress of Language Minority Students: Findings from the NAEP 1985–86 Special Study*. Princeton: Educational Testing Services.

Baratz-Snowden, J., Rock, D., Pollack, J., and Gita Wilder, G. (1988b). *Parent Preference Study*. Princeton: Educational Testing Service.

Barendse, Jan (1995). "Ik voel mij een Nederlandse leerkracht die Turks spreekt." *Inzicht* (Netherlands), 129, 1 (February).

Barman, J., Hébert, Y., and McCaskill, D. (1986). The Legacy of the Past: An Overview. In J. Barman, Y. Hébert, and D. McCaskill (Eds.), *Indian Education in Canada: vol. 1: The Legacy*. Vancouver: University of British Columbia Press.

Barou, Jacques (1989). Les immigrations africaines á la croisée des chemins. *Migrants-Formation*, 76 (March).

Barrera, Mario (1979). *Race and Class in the Southwest: A Theory of Racial Inequality*. Notre Dame (IN): University of Notre Dame Press.

Barrington, John M. (1991). The New Zealand Experience: Maoris. In Margaret A. Gibson and John U. Ogbu (Eds.), *Minority Status and Schooling*. New York: Garland.

Barrows-Chesterfield, K., Chesterfield, R.A., and Chavez, R. (1982). Peer Interaction, Language Proficiency, and Language Preferences in Bilingual Preschool Classrooms. *Hispanic Journal of Behavioral Sciences*, 4 (4), 467–486.

Barton, Josef J. (1978). Eastern and Southern Europeans. In John Higham (Ed.), *Ethnic Leadership in America*. Baltimore: Johns Hopkins University Press.

Bassa, Ramon (1989). *El Catalá a l'escola (1936/39–1985)*. Barcelona: La Llar del Llibre.

Bastenier, Albert (1986). La question de l'identité: genèse des représentations et révision des paradigmes. In Georges Abou-Sada and Hélène Milet (Eds.), *Générations issues de l'immigration*. Paris: Arcantère Éditions.

Bastenier, Albert (1988). Islam in Belgium: Contradictions and Perspectives. In Tomas Gerholm and Yngve Georg Lithman (Eds.), *The New Islamic Presence in Western Europe*. London: Mansell.

Bastenier, Albert and Dassetto, Felice (1993). *Immigration et espace public: La controverse de l'intégration*. Paris: Éditions l'Harmattan.

Batenburg, Th. A. van (1985). Taalachterstand bij allochtone leerlingen. In Mart-Jan de Jong (Ed.), *Allochtone kinderen op Nederlandse scholen: Prestaties, problemen en houdingen*. Lisse (The Netherlands): Swets & Zeitlinger.

Batenburg, Th. A. van and M. J. de Jong (1985). Problemen met en houding tegenover het Nederlandse onderwijs. In Mart-Jan de Jong (Ed.), *Allochtone kinderen op Nederlandse scholen: Prestaties, problemen en houdingen*. Lisse (The Netherlands): Swets & Zeitlinger.

Battiste, Marie (1986). Micmac Literacy and Cognitive Assimilation. In J. Barman, Y. Hébert, and D. McCaskill (Eds.). *Indian Education in Canada: vol. 1: The Legacy*. Vancouver: University of British Columbia Press.

Baudelaire, Charles (1954). *Oeuvres complètes*. Paris: Gallimard.

Bauer, Evelyn (1971). A History of Bilingual Education in BIA Schools. In *Bilingual*

Education for American Indians. Washington (DC): Bureau of Indian Affairs.

Bauwel, Griet van and Verbeeck, Kris (1993). NT2 neveninstromers. *Samenwijs, 13* (7).

Bayard, Mary Prieto (1978). Ethnic Identity and Stress: The Significance of Sociocultural Context. In J. Manuel Cases and Susan E. Keefe (Eds.), *Family and Mental Health in the Mexican American Community.* Los Angeles: Spanish Speaking Mental Health Research Center.

Bayaz, Ahmet and Weber, Florian (1984). Die Rechnung ohne den Gast. In Ahmet Bayaz, Mario Damolin, and Heiko Ernst (Eds.), *Integration: Anpassung an die Deutschen?* Weinheim and Basel: Beltz Verlag.

Baylon, Leah (1994). Analysis of California referendum on illegal immigrants (typescript).

Bean, Frank D., Chapa, Jorge, Berg, Ruth R., and Sowards, Kathryn, A. (1994). Educational and Sociodemographic Incorporation among Hispanic Immigrants to the United States. In Barry Edmonston and Jeffrey S. Passel (Eds.), *Immigration and Ethnicity.* Washington, DC: The Urban Institute.

Béaud, Stéphane & Noiriel, G. (1992). Penser l' "intégration" des immigrées. In Pierre-André Taguieff (Ed.). *Face au racisme, 2: Analyses, hypothèses, perspectives.* Paris: Éditions La Découverte.

Beauftragten der Bundesregierung fur die Integration der auslændischen Arbeitnehmer und ihrer Familienangehuerigen, Daten und Fakten zur Auslændersituation. (1987) Bonn.

Beck, Jan Mansfelt (1993). Spanje, van emigratie-naar immigratieland. *Migrantenstudies, 9* (4).

Becker, A. (1990). The role of the school in the maintenance and change of ethnic group affiliation. *Human Organization, 49* (1), 48–55.

Beckett, Francis (1993, April 2). Listening Out for the Bandwagon. *The Times Educational Supplement.*

Beebe, L.M. (1985). Input: Choosing the Right Stuff. S.M Gass, and C.G. Madden (Eds.), *Input in Second Language Acquisition.* Rowley (MA): Newbury House

Begay, Sally, Dick, Galena Sells, Estell, Dan W., Estell, Juanita, McCarty, Teresa L., and Sells, Afton (1995). Change from the Inside Out: A Story of Transformation in a Navajo Community School. *Bilingual Research Journal, 19* (1).

Beleidsplan culturele minderheden in het onderwijs, The Hague: Ministerie van Onderwijs en Wetenschappen, 1981.

Bel Ghazi, Hazzan (1982). *Over twee culturen, uitbuiting en opportunisme.* Rotterdam: Futile.

Belke, Gerlind, (1988). Zweisprachige Kinder—ein ungenutzter Reichtum!. *Gemeinsam, 9,* June.

Bell, Daniel (1975). Ethnicity and Social Change. In Nathan Glazer and Daniel P. Moynihan (Eds.), *Ethnicity: Theory and Experience.* Cambridge (MA): Harvard University Press.

Bell, Derrick (1983). Time for the Teachers: Putting Educators Back into the Brown Remedy. *Journal of Negro Education, 52* (3).

Benderson, Albert (1986). Educating the New Americans. *Focus* (Princeton, NJ: Educational Testing Service), *17.*

Benoist, Alain de (1993–1994). Three Interviews. *Telos 98–99,* Winter 1993-Spring 1994.

Benson, P. L., Yeager, R.J., Wood, P.K., Guerra, M.J., and Manno B. (1986). *Catholic High Schools: Their Impact on Low-income Students.* Washington, DC: National Catholic Education Association.

Berg, G. van den and Fase, W.(1985). Over beleid en praktijk van intercultureel onderwijs. In Mart-Jan de Jong (Ed.), *Allochtone kinderen op Nederlandse scholen: Prestaties, problemen en houdingen.* Lisse (The Netherlands): Swets & Zeitlinger.

Bergen, John J. (1978a). The Holdeman Mennonites (Church of God in Christ, Mennonite) and Schools. Unpublished manuscript.

Bergen, John J. (1978b). The Alberta Mennonite Holdeman Private School Controversy (A Case Study in Minority Group Maintenance). Unpublished manuscript.

Bergen, John J. (1978c). A Decision That Shook Education in Alberta. *Challenge, 18* (1).

Bergen, John J. (1982). The Private School Movement in Alberta. *Alberta Journal of Educational Research, 28* (4), December.

Berger, Peter (1977). *Facing Up to Modernity*. New York: Basic Books.

Berger, Peter, Berger, Brigitte, and Kellner, Hansfried (1974). *The Homeless Mind: Modernization and Consciousness*. New York: Random House Vintage Books.

Berger, Peter and Luckmann, Thomas (1967). *The Social Construction of Reality*. Garden City (NY): Doubleday Anchor.

Berger, Peter and Neuhaus, Richard John (1977). *To Empower People: The Role of Mediating Structures in Public Policy*. Washington, DC: American Enterprise Institute.

Berque, J. (1985). *L'Immigration à l'école de la République*. Paris: Centre National de Documentation Pédagogique.

Bhagwati, Jagdish (1990, May 14). Behind the Green Card. *The New Republic*.

Bhatnagar, Joti and Hamalian, Arpi (1981). Educational Opportunity for Minority Group Children in Canada. In *World Yearbook of Education 1981: Education of Minorities*. New York: Kogan Page.

Bialystok, E. (Ed.) (1991). *Language Processing in Bilingual Children*. Cambridge: Cambridge University Press.

Bialystok, E. and Cummins, J. (1991). Language, Cognition, and Education of bilingual children. In E. Bialystok, (Ed.), *Language Processing in Bilingual Children*. Cambridge: Cambridge University Press.

Bialystok, E. and Hakuta, K. (1994). *In Other Words: The Science and Psychology of Second-Language Acquisition*. New York: Basic Books.

Bikker, Frans (1986). Samenwerken. *Onderwijs in eigen taal en cultuur, MOER* , 1–2.

Bilingual Education Commission (1994). *Striving for Success: The Education of Bilingual Pupils*. Boston: Commonwealth of Massachusetts.

Billiet, J. (1977). *Secularisering en verzuiling in het onderwijs: Een sociologisch onderzoek naar de vrije schoolkeuze als legitimatieschema en als sociaal proces*. Louvain (Belgium): Louvain University Press.

Bloemberg, Lucie and Nijhuis, Dorrit (1993). Hindoebasisscholen in Nederland. *Migrantenstudies, 9* (3).

Bloom, David E. and Grenier, Gilles (1992). Economic Perspectives on Language: The Relative Value of Bilingualism in Canada and the United States. In James Crawford (Ed.), *Language Loyalties*. Chicago: University of Chicago Press.

Blot, B.(1978a). Bilinguisme. In Louis Porcher (Ed.), *La scolarisation des enfants étrangers en France*. Paris: CREDIF.

Blot, B.(1978b). L'immigration en France. In Louis Porcher (Ed.), *La scolarisation des enfants étrangers en France*. Paris: CREDIF.

Boef, Suus van der, Bronneman, R., and Konings, M. (1983). *Schoolkeuzemotieven en meningen over onderwijs*. Rijswijk (The Netherlands): Sociaal Cultureel Planbureau.

Bolhuis, Maryse (1994). Is de angst voor concentratiewijken gerechtvaardigd? *Samenwijs, 14* (4), December.

Bonnafous, Simone (1992a). Le terme 'intégration' dans le journal *Le Monde*: Sens et non-sens. *Hommes & Migrations*, 1154 (May).

Bonnafous, Simone (1992b). "Immigrés," "immigration." De quoi parler? In Pierre-André Taguieff (Ed.), *Face au racisme, 2: Analyses, hypothèses, perspectives*. Paris: Éditions La Découverte.

Boos-Nünning, Ursula (1981a). *Schulmodelle für ethnische Minderheiten, Drei Bundesländer im vergleich.* Essen/Landau (Germany): ALFA.

Boos-Nünning, Ursula (1981b). Muttersprachliche Klassen fur ausländische Kinder: Eine kritische Diskussion des bayerischen "Offenen Modells.". *Deutsch Lernen,* 2.

Boos-Nünning, Ursula (1983a). Kulturelle Identität und die Organisation des Muttersprachlichen Unterrichts für Kinder ausländischer Arbeitnehmer. *Deutsch Lernen,* 4.

Boos-Nünning, Ursula (1983b). Fordern die muttersprachlichen Klassen in Bayern die Zweisprachigkeit ausländischer Schuler? Ausländerkinder. *Forum für Schule und Sozialpädagogik,* 13.

Boos-Nünning, Ursula, Gogolin, Ingrid, Hohmann, Manfred, Reich, Hans H., and Wittek, Fritz (1984). *Der Modellversuch in der Niederlanden: Enschede.* Essen/Landau: Forschungsgruppe ALFA.

Boos-Nünning, Ursula and Henscheid, Renate (1986). Ausländische Kinder an deutschen Schulen. *Politische Bildung,* 1 (19).

Boos-Nünning, Ursula and Hohmann, Manfred (1989). The Educational Situation of Migrant Workers' Children in the Federal Republic of Germany. In Lotty Eldering and Jo Kloprogge (Eds.), *Different Cultures—Same School: Ethnic Minority Children in Europe.* Amsterdam: Swets & Zeitlinger.

Boos-Nünning, Ursula, Hohmann, Manfred, Reich, Hans H., and Wittek, Fritz (1986). *Towards Intercultural Education: A Comparative Study of the Education of Migrant Children in Belgium, England, France and the Netherlands.* London: Center for Information on Language Teaching and Research, 1986 [first published as *Aufnahmeunterricht, Muttersprachlicher Unterricht, Interkultureller Unterricht,* Munich: Olderbourg, 1983].

Boos-Nünning, Ursula, Driessen, G., and Jungbluth, P. (1991). An Evaluation of Migrant Language Teaching in The Netherlands. In Koen Jaspaert and Sjaak Kroon (Eds.), *Ethnic Minority Languages and Education.* Amsterdam/Lisse: Swets & Zeitlinger.

Bott, Peter, Merkens, Hans, and Schmidt, Folker (Eds.) (1991). *Türkische Jugendliche und Aussiedlerkinder in Familie und Schule,* Hohengehren (Germany): Schneider Verlag.

Bottani, Norberto (1988). Les structures scolaires pour les enfants de migrants dans les pays de l'OCDE. *Migrants formation: L'accueil scolaire des nouveaux arrivants,* 73 (June).

Boulot, Serge and Boyzon-Fradet, Danielle (1986). Diversité de références des publics scolaires et réponses institutionnelles. In Georges Abou-Sada and Hélène Milet (Eds.), Générations issues de l'immigration. Paris: Arcantère Éditions.

Boulot, Serge and Boyzon-Fradet, Danielle (1988). L'accueil des enfants étrangers non francophones. *Migrants formation: L'accueil scolaire des nouveaux arrivants* 73 (June).

Boulot, Serge and Boyzon-Fradet, Danielle (1990). Touche pas à mon école! *Hommes & Migrations,* 1129–1130 (February-March).

Boulot, Serge and Boyzon-Fradet, Danielle (1991a). De qui parle-t-on? *Hommes & Migrations,* 1146 (September).

Boulot, Serge and Boyzon-Fradet, Danielle (1991b). Élèves étrangers: obligation scolaire et classes d'accueil. *Cahiers pédagogiques,* 296 (September), 16–18.

Boumaza, Nadir and Neves, Gwendoline (1994). Jeunes d'origine portugaise: du bon usage de la communauté. *Hommes & Migrations,* 1180 (October).

Bourdieu, P. and Passeron, J. C. (1964). *Les heritiers. Les étudiants et la culture,* Paris: Minuit.

Bourgarel, Alain (1992). Immigration et ZEP. *Cahiers pédagogiques,* 309 (December).

Bourhis, Richard Y. (1984a). Introduction: Language Policies in Multilingual Settings. In Richard Y. Bourhis (Ed.), *Conflict and Language Planning in Quebec.*

Clevedon (United Kingdom): Multilingual Matters.

Bourhis, Richard Y. (1984b). The Charter of the French Language and Cross-Cultural Communication in Montreal. In Richard Y. Bourhis (Ed.), *Conflict and Language Planning in Quebec*. Clevedon (United Kingdom): Multilingual Matters.

Bovenkerk, F, Bruin, K., Brunten, L., and Wouters, H (1985). *Vreemd volk, gemengde gevoelens: Etnische verhoudingen in een grote stad*. Amsterdam: Boom Meppel.

Boyzon-Fradet, Danielle with Serge Boulot (1992). Le système scolaire français: aide ou obstacle à l'intégration? In Pierre-André Taguieff (Ed.), *Face au racisme, 2: Analyses, hypothèses, perspectives*. Paris: Éditions La Découverte.

Brabant, Stephane (1983). *Preface, La Population de la Wallonie dans la dualité démographique de la Belgique*. Brussels: Fondation Charles Plisnier.

Braddock, J.H. II, Crain, R.I., and McPartland, J.M. (1984). A long-term view of school desegregation: Some recent studies of graduates as adults. *Phi Delta Kappan*, December, 259–264.

Brassé, Paul (1988). Heeft minderheid toekomst? In F. Lindo (Ed.), *Balans van het minderhedenbeleid: Vier jaar na de Nota*. Utrecht: Nederlands Centrum Buitenlanders.

Brassé, Paul and De Vries, Marlene (1986). Jonge Turken en Marokkanen: hun positie in het onderwijs en op de arbeidsmarkt. In Lotty van den Berg-Eldering (Ed.), *Van gastarbeider tot immigrant: Marokkanen en Turken in Nederland, 1965–1985*. Alphen aan den Rijn (The Netherlands): Samson.

Brecht, Bertold (1959). *Hundert Gedichte 1918–1950*. Berlin: Aufbau-Verlag.

Brimelow, Peter (1987). A Cautionary Case of Bilingualism. *Commentary*, November.

Brimelow, Peter (1995). *Alien Nation: Common Sense About America's Immigration Disaster*, New York: Random House.

Brisk, M.E. (1991). Towards Multilingual and Multicultural Mainstream Education. *Journal of Education*, 173 (2), 114–129.

Brisk, M.E. (1993). Reflections on bilingual education. A report card from elementary and secondary graduates. Paper presented at the Massachusetts Association for Bilingual Education conference, March.

Brisk, M.E. and De Jong, E.J. (1994). Conditions for quality bilingual education. Paper presented at the National Association for Bilingual Education Conference, February, Los Angeles.

Brock, Colin and Tulasiewicz, Witold (1985). The Concept of Identity. In C. Brock and W. Tulasiewicz (Eds.), *Cultural Identity and Educational Policy*. London: Croom Helm.

Broek, Bart ten (1991). Een week op een christelijk-islamitische school. *Samenwijs*, 12 (4).

Bromley, Mary Ann (1987). New Beginnings for Cambodian Refugees—or Further Disruptions? *Social Work*, May-June.

Brubaker, Rogers (1993). Political Dimensions of Migration From and Among Soviet Successor States. In Myron Weiner (Ed.), *International Migration and Security*. Boulder (CO): Westview Press.

Brumlik, Micha (1984). Was heißt Integration? Zur Semantik eines sozialen Problems. In Ahmet Bayaz, Mario Damolin, and Heiko Ernst (Eds.), *Integration: Anpassung an die Deutschen?* Weinheim and Basel: Beltz Verlag.

Brussell, Charles B. (1968). *Disadvantaged Mexican American Children and Early Educational Experience*. Austin (TX): Southwest Educational Development Corporation.

Buiks, Peter (1986). Maatschappelijke dienstverlening aan buitenlanders. In Lotty van den Berg-Eldering (Ed.), *Van gastarbeider tot immigrant: Marokkanen en Turken in Nederland, 1965–1985*. Alphen aan den Rijn (The Netherlands): Samson.

Bullivant, Brian (1981). *The Pluralist Dilemma in Education*. Sydney (Australia): George Allen & Unwin.

Bullivant, Brian (1982). Pluralist Debate and Educational Policy—Australian Style. *Multilingual and Multicultural Development, 3* (2).

Bullivant, Brian (1986). Towards Radical Multiculturalism: Resolving Tensions in Curriculum and Educational Planning. In Sohan Mogdil, Gajendra Verma, Kanka Mallick, and Celie Mogdil (Eds.), *Multicultural Education: The Interminable Debate*. London: Falmer Press.

Bullivant, Brian (1989). The Pluralist Dilemma Revisited. In Gajendra K. Verma (Ed.), *Education for All: A Landmark in Pluralism*. London: Falmer Press.

Bunge, Robert (1992). Language: The Psyche of a People. In James Crawford (Ed.), *Language Loyalties*. Chicago: University of Chicago Press.

Bureau for Refugee Programs (1987). *The PASS Tracking Study: Final Report*. Washington, DC: U.S. Department of State (July).

Burk, Karlheinz (1988). *Rahmenbedingungen und Rahmenvorgaben des interkulturellen Lernens in der Schule, Und im Ausland sind die Deutschen auch Fremde! Interkulturelles Lernen in der Grundschule*. Frankfurt am Main: Arbeitkreis Grundschule.

Burleson, Helen (1986). Lessen in het Sranan voor Surinaamse kinderen. *Onderwijs in eigen taal en cultuur, MOER*, 1–2.

Busges, Heinz (1988). Die Beschäftigung ausländischer Lehrer im muttersprachlichen Ergænzungsunterricht an allgemeinbildenden Schulen im Lande Nordrhein-Westfalen, *Gemeinsam, 8*, March.

Bustamante, Hugo, Van Overbeke, Maurits, and Verdoodt, Albert (1978). Bilingual Education in Belgium. In Bernard Spolsky and Robert L. Cooper (Eds.), *Case Studies in Bilingual Education*. Rowley (MA): Newbury House.

Buvelot, B. (1986). Tweetaligheid is gewenst van het begin tot het einde van de school, *Samenwijs, 7* (4).

Byram, Michael (1981). Minority Schools in the Former Duchy of Schleswig. *Multilingual and Multicultural Development, 2* (3).

Byram, Michael (1988). Bilingualism and Education in Two German Minorities. *Multilingual and Multicultural Development, 9* (5).

Byram, Michael (1990a). Return to the Home Country: The "Necessary Dream" in Ethnic Identity. In Michel Byram and Johan Leman (Eds.), *Bicultural and Trilingual Education*. Clevedon (United Kingdom): Multilingual Matters.

Byram, Michael (1990b). Teachers and Pupils: The Significance of Cultural Identity. In Michel Byram and Johan Leman (Eds.), *Bicultural and Trilingual Education*. Clevedon (United Kingdom): Multilingual Matters.

Byram, Michael (1991). Bilingualism in Minority Education: The Conflict of Interest Between Minorities and Their Members. In Koen Jaspaert and Sjaak Kroon (Eds.), *Ethnic Minority Languages and Education*. Amsterdam/Lisse: Swets & Zeitlinger.

Byram, Michael (1993). Bilingual or Bicultural Education and the Case of the German Minority in Denmark. In Hugo Baetens Beardsmore (Ed.), *European Models of Bilingual Education*. Clevedon (United Kingdom): Multilingual Matters.

Cahill, Desmond (1986). An Evaluation of Australia's Multicultural Education Program. *Multilingual and Multicultural Development, 7* (1).

Cakir, Sedat (1992). Warum in der monokulturellen Schule monokulturelldenkende Lehrer keine interkulturelle Pædagogik umsetzen können. *Gemeinsam, 25* (December).

Caldwell, Gary (1984). Anglo-Quebec: Demographic Realities and Options for the Future. In Richard Y. Bourhis (Ed.), *Conflict and Language Planning in Quebec*. Clevedon (United Kingdom): Multilingual Matters.

California State Department of Education (1983). *Basic Principles for the Education of Language-Minority Students: An Overview*. Sacramento: California State Department of Education.

Camilleri, Carmel (1990). Différences culturelles et laicité. *Hommes & Migrations*, 1129–1130 (February-March).

Campagnoni, Ezio (1987). Methods of Teaching the Mother Tongue in the Migration Situation. In *Teaching Children of Migrant Workers Their Mother Tongue*, Strasbourg: Council of Europe.

Campbell, Russell N. (1984). The Immersion Approach to Foreign Language Teaching. In *Studies on Immersion Education*. Sacramento: California State Department of Education.

Canada's Charter of Rights and Freedoms. In James Crawford (Ed.), *Language Loyalties*. Chicago: University of Chicago Press.

Cardoso, Luis (1990). Au coeur de "l'Affaire": Un professeur de Creil témoigne. *Hommes & Migrations*, 1129–1130 (February-March).

Carter, T. and Chatfield, M. (1986). Effective schools for language minority students. *American Journal of Education*, 97, 200–233.

Casanova, Jean-Claude (1989, December 29). L'état des droites. *L'Express*.

Castaneda, Alfredo (1971). Persisting Ideological Issues of Assimilation in America: Implications for Assessment Practices. In Edgar G. Epps (Ed.), *Psychology and Education, Cultural Pluralism*. Berkeley: McCutcheon.

Castellanos, Diego, with Pamela Leggio (1983). *The Best of Two Worlds: Bilingual/Bicultural Education in the U.S.* Trenton: New Jersey State Department of Education.

Castles, Stephen (1985). The Guests Who Stayed—The Debate on "Foreigners Policy" in the German Federal Republic. *International Migration Review, 19* (3), Fall.

Castles, Stephen (1986). The Guest-Worker in Western Europe—An Obituary. *International Migration Review, 20* (4) Winter.

Castles, Stephen, with Booth, Heather, and Wallace, Tina (1984). *Here for Good: Western Europe's New Ethnic Minorities*. London: Pluto Press.

Cate-Dhont, R.M. ten (1988). Minderhedenbeleid op gemeentelijk niveau. In F. Lindo (Ed.), *Balans van het minderhedenbeleid: Vier jaar na de Nota*. Utrecht: Nederlands Centrum Buitenlanders.

Cazabon, M., Lambert, W.E., and Hall, G. (1993). *Two-way Bilingual Education: A Progress Report on the Amigos Program*. Santa Cruz (CA): The National Center for Research on Cultural Diversity and Second Language Learning.

Cebollero, Pedro (1970). A Second Language Policy for Puerto Rico. In Erwin H. Epstein (Ed.), *Politics and Education in Puerto Rico: A Documentary Survey of the Language Issue*. Metuchen (NJ): Scarecrow Press, 1970.

Centre for Educational Research and Innovation (1987). *Immigrants' Children at School*. Paris: Organisation for Economic Cooperation and Development.

Chamot, Anna Uhl (1983). Application of Second Language Acquisition Research to the Bilingual Classroom. *NCBE Focus*, 12 (October).

Chamot, Anna Uhl (1988). Bilingualism in Education and Bilingual Education: The State of the Art in the United States. *Papers from the 5th Nordic Conference on Bilingualism*. Copenhagen: Royal Danish School of Educational Studies. [Also in *Multilingual and Multicultural Development, 9*, 1 & 2, 1988]

Chamot, Anna Uhl and O'Malley, J. Michael (1984). Using Learning Strategies to Develop Skills in English as a Second Language. *NCBE Focus, 8* (September).

Chamouni, Rachid (1988). *Evaluation de l'enseignement de la langue nationale, Les Algériens et l'enseignement de l'Arabe en France*. Paris: Centre Culturel Algérien.

Charlot, Bernard (1990). Droit à la différence, droit à l'universel, droit au sens. *Hommes & Migrations*, 1129–1130 (February-March).

Charlot, M. (1981). The Education of Immigrant Children in France. In B.K. Bhatnagar (Ed.), *Educating immigrants*. New York: St. Martin's Press.

Chavez, Linda (1990, July 18). The Real Aim of the Promoters of Cultural Diversity Is to Exclude Certain People and to Foreclose Debate. *Chronicle of Higher Education*.

Chavez, Linda (1991). *Out of the Barrio.* New York: Basic Books.

Chawaf, Adel (1980). L'intégration des populations arabo-musulmanes: le rôle des intermédiaires sociaux. In *Codes et pratiques des populations immigrées: identité culturelle et modèles de socialisation.* Brussels: Ministère de l'Education Nationale et de la Culture Française.

Chesnais, Jean-Claude (1990). The Africanization of Europe? *The American Enterprise,* May/June.

Chesterfield, R., Barrows-Chesterfield, K., Hayes-Latimer, K., and Chavez, R. (1983). The Influence of Teachers and Peers on Second Language Acquisition in Bilingual Preschool Programs. *TESOL Quarterly, 17* (3), 401–419.

Chevènement, Jean-Pierre (1985). *Conférence de Presse,* December 19, 1985.

Chobeaux, François (1994). L'identité collective de jeunes en difficulté d'insertion sociale. *Hommes & Migrations,* 1180 (October).

Choron-Baix, Catherine (1989). L'insertion linguistique de la communauté lao; une stratégie d'accommodement. *Migrants-Formation, 76* (March).

Christelijk Pedagogisch Studiecentrum (1987). *GAMMA: bronnenboek intercultureel onderwijs,* Hoevelaken (The Netherlands): CPS.

Christian, D. & Mahrer, C. (1992). *Two-way Bilingual Programs in the United States, 1991–1992.* Santa Cruz, CA and Washington, DC: National Center for Research on Cultural Diversity and Second Language Learning.

Chung, Chuong Hoang (1988). The Language Situation of Vietnamese Americans. In Sandra Lee McKay and Sau-ling Cynthia Wong (Eds), *Language Diversity: Problem or Resource?* Cambridge (MA): Newbury House.

Churchill, Stacy (1986). *The Education of Linguistic and Cultural Minorities in the OECD Countries.* Clevedon (United Kingdom): Multilingual Matters.

Cibulka, James G., O'Brien, Timothy J., and Zewe, Donald (1982). *Inner-City Private Elementary Schools: A Study.* Milwaukee: Marquette University Press.

Cintrat, Iva (1987). *Recognition of Cultural Diversity in the Teaching of School Subjects.* Strasburg: Council of Europe.

Citrin, Jack (1990). Language Politics and American Identity. *The Public Interest, 99,* Spring.

Claes, Beda (1962). *De sociale integratie van de Italiaanse en Poolse immigranten in Belgisch-Limburg.* Hasselt: Heideland.

Claessens, A.M. (1980). *Compte rendu des travaux de groupe, Code et practiques des populations immigrées: identité culturelle et modèles de socialisation.* Brussels: Ministere de l'Education nationale et de Culture Française.

Clausen, Inger M. and Horst, Christian (1987). Udvikling frem mod en interkulturel pædagogik, *Dansk Pædagogisk Tidsskrift, 35* (3).

Clerck, K. de (1974). *Momenten uit de geschiedenis van het Belgisch onderwijs.* Antwerp: De Sikkel.

Clévy, J. (1978). L'institution scolaire devant l'immigration. In Louis Porcher (Ed.), *La scolarisation des enfants étrangers en France.* Paris: CREDIF.

Coates, Ken (1986). A Very Imperfect Means of Education: Indian Day Schools in the Yukon Territory, 1890–1955. In Barman, J., Hébert, Y., and McCaskill, D. (Eds.), *Indian Education in Canada: Volume I: The Legacy.* Vancouver: University of British Columbia Press.

Cochran, C. (1989). *Strategies for involving LEP Students in the all-English Medium Classroom: A Cooperative Learning Approach.* Washington, DC: National Clearinghouse for Bilingual Education.

Codding, George Arthur, Jr. (1961). *The Federal Government of Switzerland.* Boston: Houghton Mifflin.

Coenen, Josée (1982). Opvang en taalonderwijs voor buitenlandse kinderen op de basisschool. In René Appel, Cees Cruson, Pieter Muysken and J. W. de Vries (Eds.), *Taalproblemen van buitenlandse arbeiders en hun kinderen.* Muiderberg: Coutinho.

Cohen, Andrew D. (1976). The Case for Partial or Total Immersion Education. In Antonio Simões, Jr. (Ed.), *The Bilingual Child: Research and Analysis of Existing Educational Themes.* New York: Academic Press.

Cohen, Andrew D. (1982). Bilingual Schooling and Spanish Language Maintenance: An Experimental Analysis. In Joshua A. Fishman and Gary D. Keller (Eds.), *Bilingual Education for Hispanic Students in the United States.* New York: Teachers College Press.

Cohen, David K. (1970). Immigrants and the Schools. *Review of Educational Research, 40.*

Cohen, E.G. (1994). *Designing Groupwork. Strategies for the Heterogeneous Classroom.* 2d ed. New York: Teachers College Press.

Coleman, James S. and Hoffer, Thomas (1987). *Public and Private High Schools: The Impact of Communities.* New York: Basic Books, 1987.

Collet, Beate (1992). La construction politique de l'Ausländer: le modèle allemand en question. In Jaqueline Costa-Lascoux and Patrick Weil (Eds.), *Logiques d'états et immigrations.* Paris: Éditions Kimé.

Collier, Virginia P. (1987). Age and Rate of Acquisition of Second Language for Academic Purposes. *TESOL Quarterly, 21,* 617–641.

Collier, Virginia P. and Thomas, Wayne P. (1988). Acquisition of Cognitive-Academic Second Language Profiency: A Six-Year Study.

Comerford, Richard Vincent (1991). The British State and the Education of Irish Catholics, 1850–1921. Janusz Tomiak (Ed.), *Schooling, Educational Policy, and Ethnic Identity.* New York: New York University Press.

Commissie Allochtone Leerlingen in het Onderwijs (1992). *Ceders in de tuin,* The Hague.

Commission on Immigration (1914). *The Problem of Immigration in Massachusetts.* Boston: Massachusetts House of Representatives.

Commonwealth Programs for Schools. Canberra: Commonwealth Schools Commission, 1986.

Concha, P., Garcia, L., and Perez, A. (1975). Cooperation versus Competition: A Comparison of Anglo-American and Cuban-American Youngsters in Miami. *Social Psychology, 95.*

Connor, Walker (1985a). Who Are the Mexican-Americans? A Note on Comparability. In Walker Connor (Ed.), *Mexican-Americans in Comparative Perspective.* Washington, DC: The Urban Institute.

Connor, Walker (1985b). Conclusions: Through a Comparative Prism Darkly. In Walker Connor (Ed.), *Mexican-Americans in Comparative Perspective.* Washington, DC: The Urban Institute.

Coombs, L. Madison (1971). A Summary of Pertinent Research in Bilingual Education. In *Bilingual Education for American Indians.* Washington, DC: Bureau of Indian Affairs.

Coppens, Martine (1985). Observation sur l'expression française chez les enfants italiens et espagnols. In *Four Years Bicultural Education in Brussels: An Evaluation.* Brussels: The Foyer Committee of Bicultural Education.

Cordasco, Francesco and Bernstein, George (1981). Puerto Rican Children in American Mainland Schools. In *World Yearbook of Education 1981: Education of Minorities.* New York: Kogan Page.

Cordeiro, Albano (1989). La communauté portugaise de France à l'heure de l'Europe de 93. *Migrants-Formation, 76* (March).

Cordeiro, Albano (1990). La méthode Coué appliquée à l'immigration. *Hommes & Migrations, 1129–1130* (February-March).

Corder, S.P. (1978). Language-learner Language. In Richards, J.C. (Ed.), *Understanding Second and Foreign Language Learning. Issues and Approaches.* Rowley (MA): Newbury House.

Corder, S.P. (1983). A Role for the Mother Tongue. In S.M. Gass and L. Selinker (Eds.),

Language Transfer in Language Learning. (Pp. 85–97). Rowley (MA): Newbury House.

Corredera Garcia, Maria, Paz & Santiago Diez Cano, L. (1992). L'Espagne, nouveau pays d'immigration. In Jaqueline Costa-Lascoux & Patrick Weil (Eds.), *Logiques d'états et immigrations.* Paris: Éditions Kimé.

Cortés, Carlos E. (1986). The Education of Language Minority Students: A Contextual Interaction Model. In *Beyond Language: Social and Cultural Factors in Schooling Language Minority Students* Los Angeles: Evaluation, Dissemination and Assessment Center, California State University, Los Angeles.

Costa-Lascoux, Jacqueline (1986). Les politiques migratoires dans les états européens. In Georges Abou-Sada and Hélène Milet (Eds.), *Générations issues de l'immigration.* Paris: Arcantère Éditions.

Costa-Lascoux, Jacqueline (1989a). Immigrant Children in French Schools: Equality or Discrimination. In Lotty Eldering and Jo Kloprogge (Eds.), *Different Cultures—Same School: Ethnic Minority Children in Europe.* Amsterdam: Swets & Zeitlinger.

Costa-Lascoux, Jacqueline (1989b). *De l'immigrée au citoyen.* Paris: La Documentation française.

Costa-Lascoux, Jacqueline (1991). Intégration et civisme. *Hommes & Migrations, 1146* (September).

Costa-Lascoux, Jacqueline (1992a). Vers une Europe des citoyens? In Jaqueline Costa-Lascoux and Patrick Weil (Eds.), *Logiques d'états et immigrations.* Paris: Éditions Kimé.

Costa-Lascoux, Jacqueline (1992b). Des lois contre le racisme. In Pierre-André Taguieff (Ed.). *Face au racisme, 2: Analyses, hypothèses, perspectives.* Paris: Éditions La Découverte.

Council of Chief State School Officers (1990). *School Success for Limited English Proficient Students: The Challenge and State Response.* Washington, DC.

Council of Ministers of Education (1983). *The State of Minority-Language Education in the Provinces and Territories of Canada.* Toronto.

Council of Ministers of Education (1985). *Report on French- and English-Language Education in Minority Settings and Teaching of English and French as Second Languages.*

Cox, Caroline (1986). From "Auschwitz—Yesterday's Racism" to GCHQ. In Frank Palmer (Ed.), *Anti-Racism—An Assault on Education and Value.* London: The Sherwood Press.

Craft, Maurice (Ed.) (1984). Education for Diversity. *Education and Cultural Pluralism.* London: The Falmer Press.

Craft, Maurice (1989). Teacher Education in a Multicultural Society. In Gajendra K. Verma (Ed.), *Education for All: A Landmark in Pluralism.* London: Falmer Press.

Crandall, JoAnn, Spanos, George, Christian, Donna, Simich-Dudgeon, Carmen, and Willetts, Karen (1987). *Integrating Language and Content Instruction for Language Minority Students.* Teachers Resource Guide Series, 4, Washington, DC: National Clearinghouse for Bilingual Education.

Crawford, James (1988, May 18). Study Charts Hispanics' Acquisition of English. *Education Week.*

Crawford, James (1989). *Bilingual Education: History, Politics, Theory, and Practice.* Trenton: Crane\.

Crawford, James (1992a). *Language Loyalties: A Source Book on the Official English Controversy.* Chicago: University of Chicago Press.

Crawford, James (1992b). *Hold Your Tongue: Bilingualism and the Politics of English Only.* Reading (MA): Addison-Wesley.

Crawford, James (1995). Endangered Native American Languages: What Is To Be Done, and Why? *Bilingual Research Journal, 19* (1).

Croall, Jonathan (1993a, January 15). Principal Role. *The Times Educational Supplement.*

Croall, Jonathan (1993b, January 15). The Call of the Valleys. *The Times Educational Supplement.*

Croall, Jonathan (1993c, February 19). More than a Hint of Gaelic. *The Times Educational Supplement.*

Croall, Jonathan (1993d, May 28). The Fall and Rapid Rise of Manx Gaelic. *The Times Educational Supplement.*

Croall, Jonathan (1993e, October 1). The Language of Land's End. *The Times Educational Supplement.*

Crowley, John (1992). Consensus et conflits dans la politique de l'immigration et des relations raciales du Royaume-Uni. In Jaqueline Costa-Lascoux and Patrick Weil (Eds.), *Logiques d'états et immigrations.* Paris: Éditions Kimé.

Cummins, Jim (1978). Immersion Programs: The Irish Experience. *International Review of Education, 24.*

Cummins, Jim (1979). Linguistic Interdependence and the Educational Development of Bilingual Children. *Review of Educational Research, 49 (2).*

Cummins, Jim (1980a). The Entry and Exit Fallacy in Bilingual Education. *NABE Journal, 4 (3).*

Cummins, Jim (1980b). Four Misconceptions about Language Proficiency in Bilingual Education. *NABE Journal, 5 (3).*

Cummins, J. (1981). Empirical and Theoretical Underpinnings of Bilingual Education. *Journal of Education, 63 (1), 16 - 29.*

Cummins, Jim (1982). The Role of Primary Language Development in Promoting Educational Success for Language Minority Students. *Schooling and Language Minority Students,* Sacramento (CA): Office of Bilingual Education, California State Department of Education.

Cummins, Jim (1984a). *Bilingualism and Special Education: Issues in Assessment and Pedagogy.* Clevedon (United Kingdom): Multilingual Matters.

Cummins, Jim (1984b). Linguistic Minorities and Multicultural Policy in Canada. In John Edwards (Ed.), *Linguistic Minorities, Policies and Pluralism.* London: Academic Press.

Cummins, Jim (1985). The Construct of Language Proficiency in Bilingual Education. In James E. Alatis and John J. Staczek (Eds.), *Perspectives on Bilingualism and Bilingual Education.* Washington: Georgetown University Press.

Cummins, Jim (1986). Empowering Minority Students: A Framework for Intervention. *Harvard Educational Review, 56 (1).*

Cummins, Jim (1988a). From Multicultural to Anti-racist Education: An Analysis of Programmes and Policies in Ontario. In Tove Skutnabb-Kangas and Jim Cummins (Eds.), *Minority Education: From Shame to Struggle.* Clevedon (United Kingdom): Multilingual Matters.

Cummins, Jim and Skutnabb-Kangas, Tove (1988b). Introduction. In Tove Skutnabb-Kangas and Jim Cummins (Eds.), *Minority Education: From Shame to Struggle.* Clevedon (United Kingdom): Multilingual Matters.

Cummins, J. (1989). *Empowering Minority Students.* Sacramento (CA): California Association for Bilingual Education.

Cummins, J. (1991). Interdependence of First- and Second-Language Proficiency in Bilingual Children. In E. Bialystok (Ed.), *Language Processing in Bilingual Children.* Cambridge: Cambridge University Press.

Cummins, J. (1994). Knowledge, Power, and Identity in Teaching English as a Second Language. In F. Genesee (Ed.), *Educating Second Language Children. The Whole School, the Whole Curriculum, the Whole Community* (Pp. 33–58). Cambridge: Cambridge University Press.

Cummins, J. and M. Swain (1986). *Bilingualism in Education: Aspects of Theory, Research and Practice.* New York: Longman.

Cunha, Fernando (1986a). Het is wenselijk dat allochtonen verantwoordelijkheid dragen voor het O.E.T.C. *Samenwijs, 6* (6).

Cunha, Fernando (1986b). De vorming van de Zuid Europese gemeenschappen in Amsterdam. *Samenwijs, 6* (7).

Cunha, Maria (1989). Les parents portugais et l'école française. *Migrants-Formation, 76* (March).

Curiel, H., Rosenthal, J.A., and Richek, H.G. (1986). Impacts of Bilingual Education on Secondary School Grades, Attendance, Retention and Drop Out. *Hispanic Journal of Behavioral Sciences, 8* (4), 357–367.

Curriculum Branch (1985). *The Implementation of Bilingual and Community Language Programs in Primary Schools.* Melbourne: Ministry of Education (Schools Division), Victoria.

Curriculum Branch (1986). *Education in, and for, a Multicultural Victoria.* Melbourne: Ministry of Education (Schools Division), Victoria.

Curriculum Branch (1987). *First Language and Second Language Development.* Melbourne: Ministry of Education (Schools Division), Victoria.

Curriculum Branch (1988). *The LOTE Framework P–10.* Melbourne: Ministry of Education (Schools Division), Victoria.

Dahl, Robert A. (1982). *Dilemmas of Pluralist Democracy: Autonomy vs. Control.* New Haven: Yale University Press.

Damanakis, Michael (1982a). Empfehlungen der Kultusministerkoferenz. In Michael Damanakis and Hans H. Reich (Eds.), *Ausländerunterricht: Schulrechtliche, bildungspolitische und unterrichtsorganisatorische Beiträge.* Essen/Landau: ALFA.

Damanakis, Michael (1982b). Beschulungsmodelle fur Ausländerkinder in Bayern und Berlin. In Michael Damanakis and Hans H. Reich (Eds.), *Ausländerunterricht: Schulrechtliche, bildungspolitische und unterrichtsorganisatorische Beiträge.* Essen/Landau: ALFA.

Davey, A.G. and Mullin, P.N. (1982). Inter-ethnic Friendship in British Primary Schools. *Educational Research, 24* (2), 83–92.

Day, Elaine M. and Shapson Stan M. (1988). *Provincial Assessment of Early and Late French Immersion Programs in British Columbia, Canada.* New Orleans: AERA.

Dean, Clare (1990, August 24). Muslim Voters Divided over Separate Schools. *The Times Educational Supplement.*

Dean, Clare (1993, September 1993). Christians Blaze a GM trail. *The Times Educational Supplement.*

De Avila, Edward (1985). *Motivation, Intelligence, and Access: A Theoretical Framework for the Education of Minority Language Students, Issues in English Language Development.* Rosslyn (VA): The National Clearinghouse for Bilingual Education.

De Bot, Kees, Buster, Alex, and Janssen-van Dieten, Anne-Mieke (1985). Educational Settings, Teaching Methods and Second Language Proficiency of Turkish and Moroccan Children. In Guus Extra and Ton Vallen (Eds.), *Ethnic Minorities and Dutch as a Second Language.* Dordrecht (The Netherlands): Foris.

De Jong, E.J. (1993a). [Evaluation of a Spanish-English transitional bilingual program] Unpublished raw data.

De Jong, E.J. (1993b). [Observation data and interview transcripts from Dutch, Swedish, and Danish language minority programs] Unpublished raw data.

Dekker, Ellen (1991). OETC structuren. *Samenwijs, 12* (2), October.

Dekker, Paul and Ester, Peter (1993). *Social and Political Attitudes in Dutch Society.* Rijswijk (The Netherlands): Social and Cultural Planning Office.

Dekker, Paul and Van Praag, C.S. (1990). Xenofobie in West-Europa. *Migrantenstudies, 6* (4).

De la Garza, Rodolfo O. (1985). As American as Tamale Pie: Mexican-American Political Mobilization and the Loyalty Question. In Walker Connor (Ed.), *Mexican-Americans in Comparative Perspective.* Washington: The Urban Institute.

De la Garza, Rodolfo O., Falcon, A., Garcia, F.C., and Garcia, J. (1994). Mexican Immigrants, Mexican Americans, and American Political Culture. In Barry Edmonston and Jeffrey S. Passel (Eds.), *Immigration and Ethnicity*. Washington, DC: The Urban Institute.

De La Rosa, Denise and Maw, Carlyle E. (1990). *Hispanic Education: A Statistical Portrait 1990,.* Washington, DC: National Council of La Raza.

DeLey, Margo (1983). French Immigration Policy since May 1981. *International Migration Review*, 17 (2), Summer.

Delpit, Lisa (1995). *Other People's Children: Cultural Conflict in the Classroom.* New York: The New Press.

Department of Employment, Education and Training (1991a). *Australia's Language: The Australian Language and Literacy Policy.* Canberra: Australian Government Publishing Service.

Department of Employment, Education and Training (1991b). *Companion Volume to Australia's Language: The Australian Language and Literacy Policy.* Camberra: Australian Government Publishing Service.

Dericioglu, Mujgan and Orfali, Nuri (1982). Memorandum der tünkischen Regierung zur Unterrichtung türkischer Kinder in der Bundesrepublik Deutschland. In Michael Damanakis and Hans H. Reich (Eds.), *Ausländerunterricht: Schulrechtliche, bildungspolitische und unterrichtsorganisatorische Beiträge.* Essen/Landau: ALFA.

Derouet, Jean-Louis (1992). *École et Justice.* Paris: Métailié.

Desbarats, Jacqueline (1986). Ethnic Differences in Adaptation: Sino-Vietnamese Refugees in the United States. *International Migration Review*, 20 (2), Summer.

Devereux, George (1982). Ethnic Identity: Its Logical Foundations and Its Dysfunctions. In George De Vos and& Lola Romanucci-Ross (Eds.), *Ethnic Identity: Cultural Continuities and Change.* Chicago: University of Chicago Press.

De Villar, R.A. and Faltis, C.J. (1991). *Computers and Cultural Diversity. Restructuring for School Success.* New York: SUNY Press.

De Vos, George (1982). Ethnic Pluralism: Conflict and Accommodation. In George De Vos & Lola Romanucci-Ross (Eds.), *Ethnic Identity: Cultural Continuities and Change.* Chicago: University of Chicago Press.

De Vos, George and Romanucci-Ross, Lola (1982a). Introduction. In George De Vos and Lola Romanucci-Ross (Eds.), *Ethnic Identity: Cultural Continuities and Change.* Chicago: University of Chicago Press.

De Vos, George and Romanucci-Ross, Lola (1982b). Ethnicity: Vessel of Meaning and Emblem of Contrast. In George De Vos and Lola Romanucci-Ross (Eds.), *Ethnic Identity: Cultural Continuities and Change.* Chicago: University of Chicago Press.

Dezell, Maureen (1995, Janauary 12). Koreans Keep the Faith. *The Boston Globe*, pp. 20, 32.

Dickopp, Karl-Heinz (1982). *Erziehung ausländischer Kinder als pädagogische Herausforderung: Das Krefelder Modell.* Dusseldorf: Schwann.

Diouf-Kamara, Sylviane (1994). La montée du sentiment anti-immigrés aux États-Unis, *Hommes & Migrations*, 1180 (October).

Dodson, C.J. (1985). Second Language Acquisition and Bilingual Development: A Theoretical Framework. *Multilingual and Multicultural Matters*, 6 (5).

Dodson, C.J. and Thomas, Sara E. (1988). The Effect of Total L2 Immersion Education on Concept Development. *Multilingual and Multicultural Development*, 9, 6.

Dolson, David P. (1984). Introduction. *Studies on Immersion Education.* Sacramento: California State Department of Education.

Dolson, David P. (1985a). Bilingualism and Scholastic Performance: The Literature Revisited, *NABE Journal*, Fall.

Dolson, David P. (1985b). *The Application of Immersion Education in the United States*, Rosslyn (VA): National Clearinghouse for Bilingual Education.

Donato, R., Menchaca, M., and Valencia, R.R. (1991). Segregation, Desegregation, and Integration of Chicano Students: Problems and Prospects. In R.R. Valencia (Ed.). *Chicano School Failure and Success*. London: Falmer Press.

Dongen, Joseé van (1993). Aparte meisjeklas. *Samenwijs, 13* (5), January.

Dongen, Joseé van (1994). Internationale taalklas. *Samenwijs, 14* (7), March.

Donselaar, Jaap van (1982). Racistische partijen in drie Europese landen. In J.M.M. van Amersfoort and H.B. Entzinger (Eds.), *Immigrant en Samenleving*. Deventer (The Netherlands): Van Loghum Slaterus.

Donselaar, Jaap van (1993). Racistisch geweld en entreem-rechts. *Migrantenstudies, 9* (2).

Doolittle, J.R. (1974). A Report on Boarding Schools for Indians in Oregon (1867). In Sol Cohen (Ed.), *Education in the United States: A Documentary History*. (pp. 1734–1735). New York: Random House.

Doorn, J.A.A. van (1985). Het miskende pluralisme: een herformulering van het minderhedenvraagstuk. In J.S. Weiland and J.H.P. Paelinck (Eds.), *Etnische minderheden: Wetenschap en Beleid*. Amsterdam: Boom Meppel.

Doorn, J.A.A. van (1988). Minderhedenbeleid: tussen sociale emancipatie en culturele bevestiging. In F. Lindo (Ed.), *Balans van het minderhedenbeleid: Vier jaar na de Nota*. Utrecht: Nederlands Centrum Buitenlanders.

Dore, Antony (1993, May 28). Unwanted English Imports. *The Times Educational Supplement*.

Dors, Henry (1983). Intercultureel onderwijs als pedagogisch perspectief. In Nitha Neuwahl and Aletta de Raad (Eds.). *Kinderen van medelanders: Buitenlandse kinderen in de Nederlandse samenleving*. Deventer (The Netherlands): Van Loghum Slaterus.

Dors, Henry (1987). "Zwarte" en "Witte" scholen anti-racistisch bezien, Amsterdam: Stichting advies- en begeleidingscentrum.

Dors, Henry (1989). Apartheid in het Nederlandse onderwijssysteem? *Samenwijs, 9* (6), February.

Dors, H., Karsten, S., Ledoux, G., Steen, A.H.M., and Meijer, P.G. (1991). *Etnische segregatie in het onderwijs: Beleidsaspecten*. Amsterdam: Universiteit van Amsterdam.

Downing, John (1978). Strategies of Bilingual Teaching. *International Review of Education, 24* (3).

Drake, Glendon F. (1984). Problems of Language Planning in the United States. In John Edwards (Ed.), *Linguistic Minorities, Policies and Pluralism*. London: Academic Press.

Draper, Jamie B. and Jiménez, Martha (1992). A Chronology of the Official English Movement. In James Crawford (Ed.), *Language Loyalties*. Chicago: University of Chicago Press.

Driessen, Geert (1990). *De onderwijspositie van allochtone leerlingen*, Nijmegen (The Netherlands): ITS.

Driessen, G., De Bot, K., and Jungbluth, P. (1989). *De effectiviteit van het onderwijs in eigen taal en cultuur*. Nijmegen (The Netherlands): ITS/ITT.

Driessen, G., Jungbluth, P. and Louvenburg, J. (1988). *Onderwijs in eigen taal en cultuur. Doelopvattingen, leerkrachten, leermiddelen en omvang*. The Hague: Instituut voor Onderzoek van het onderwijs.

Dubet, François and Lapeyronnie, Didier. (1992). *Les quartiers d'éxil*. Paris: Éditions du Seuil.

Dubreuil, Jean (1989). École et ethnopsychiatrie. *Migrants-Formation, 78* (September).

Duhamel, Alain (1993). *Les peurs françaises*. Paris: Flammarion.

Duhamel, Olivier (1989, November 3). Tolérer le foulard. *L'Express*.

Dumon, Wilfried (1982). *Het profiel van de vreemdelingen in Belgie*. Leuven: Davidsfonds.

Dunning, Anneke (1995). "De Nederlandse multi-culturele samenleving zal nog jarenlang een utopie blijven," *Samenwijs*, 15, 7 (March).

Dupont, Pascal (1994, November 3). L'Algérie décervelée. *L'Express*, pp. 122–123.

Duquesne, A. (1987). *Accord culturel belgo-marocain: Cours intégré de culture marocaine et de langue arabe*. Brussels: Ministère de l'Education nationale.

Duraffour, Annick and Guittonneau Claudine, (1992). Des mythes aux problèmes: L'argumentation xénophobe prise au mot. In Pierre-André Taguieff (Ed.), *Face au racisme, 2: Analyses, hypothèses, perspectives*. Paris: Éditions La Découverte.

ECCE (1992). A Summary Guide to the Fifteen "ECCE" Projects. In Euan Reid and Hans Reich (Eds.), *Breaking the Boundaries: Migrant Workers' Children in the EC*. Clevedon (United Kingdom): Multilingual Matters.

Edelsky, C. (1991). *With Literacy and Justice for All. Rethinking the Social in Language and Education*. Bristol (PA): Falmer Press.

Edmonston, Barry and Passel, Jeffrey, S. (1994a). Ethnic Demography: U.S. Immigration and Ethnic Variations. In Barry Edmonston and Jeffrey S. Passel (Eds.), *Immigration and Ethnicity*. Washington, DC: The Urban Institute.

Edmonston, Barry and Passel, Jeffrey, S. (1994b).The Future Immigrant Population of the United States. In Barry Edmonston and Jeffrey S. Passel (Eds.), *Immigration and Ethnicity*. Washington, DC: The Urban Institute.

Education for All: The Report of the Committee of Inquiry into the Education of Children from Ethnic Minority Groups (the "Swann Report"), London: HMSO, 1985.

Edwards, John (1984). Language, Diversity and Identity. In John Edwards (Ed.), *Linguistic Minorities, Policies and Pluralism*. London: Academic Press.

Edwards, John (1981). The Context of Bilingual Education. *Journal of Multilingual and Multicultural Development 2*, 25–44.

Edwards, John (1988). Bilingualism, Education and Identity. *Multilingual and Multicultural Development, 9*, (1 & 2).

Edwards, Viv (1984). Language Policy in Multicultural Britain. In John Edwards (Ed.), *Linguistic Minorities, Policies and Pluralism*. London: Academic Press.

Edwards, Viv and Redfern, Algela (1992). *The World in a Classroom: Language in Education in Britain and Canada*. Clevedon (United Kingdom): Multilingual Matters.

Egmond-van Helten, H.M. van (1990). Dringend aan kwaliteitsverbetering toe. *Samenwijs, 11* (3), November.

Ekstrand, Lars H. (1978). Migrant Adaptation: A Cross-Cultural Problem. In R. Freudenstein (Ed.), *Teaching the Children of Immigrants*. Brussels: Didier.

Ekstrand, Lars H. (1979). *Early Bilingualism: Theories and Facts*. Malmö (Sweden): Malmö School of Education, University of Lund.

Ekstrand, Lars H. (1980a). *Questioning Some Popular Beliefs about Immigrant Children: Contemporary Problems and Practices in Sweden*. Malmö (Sweden): Malmö School of Education, Lund University.

Ekstrand, Lars H. (1980b). *Att Utveckla Tvåspråkighet och Bikulturell Identitet*. Malmö (Sweden): Malmö School of Education, Lund University.

Ekstrand, Lars H. (1981a). Unpopular Views on Popular Beliefs about Immigrant Children: Contemporary Practices and Problems in Sweden. In J. Bhatnagar (Ed.), *Educating Immigrants*. London: Croom Helm.

Ekstrand, Lars H. (1981b). Theories and Facts about Early Bilingualism in Native and Immigrant Children. *Grazer Linguistische Studien, 14*, Spring.

Ekstrand, Lars H. (1985a). Immigrant Children: Policies for Educating. *The International Encyclopedia of Education*.Oxford; Pergamon Press.

Ekstrand, Lars H. (1985v). Bilingual Learning: Problems, Results and Theoretical Advances. typescript, 1988; quoted with permission of the author.

Elam, Sophie L. (1967). Acculturation and Learning Problems of Puerto Rican Children. In Joan I. Roberts (Ed.), *School Children in the Urban Slum*. New York: Free Press.

Eldering, Lotty van den Berg (1983a). Marokkaanse en Turkse kinderen en hun ouders. In Nitha Neuwahl and Aletta de Raad (Eds.), *Kinderen van medelanders: Buitenlandse kinderen in de Nederlandse samenleving*. Deventer (The Netherlands): Van Loghum Slaterus.

Eldering, Lotty van den Berg (1983b). *Bikultureel onderwijs aan Turkse en Morokkaanse kinderen in Enschede*. Amsterdam: University of Amsterdam.

Eldering, Lotty van den Berg (1986a). Onderwijs en etnische ongelijkheid. In J.A. Van Kemenade, J.M.G. Leune, & J.M.M. Ritzen (Eds.), *Onderwijs en samenleving*. Groningen: Wolters-Noordhoof.

Eldering, Lotty van den Berg (1986b). Onderwijs: beleid en praktijk. In Lotty van den Berg-Eldering (Ed.), *Van gastarbeider tot immigrant: Marokkanen en Turken in Nederland, 1965-1985*. Alphen aan den Rijn (The Netherlands): Samson.

Eldering, Lotty van den Berg (1989). Ethnic Minority Children in Dutch Schools: Underachievement and Its Explanations. In Lotty Eldering and Jo Kloprogge (Eds.), *Different Cultures—Same School: Ethnic Minority Children in Europe*. Amsterdam: Swets & Zeitlinger.

Ellis, N.E. (1990). Collaborative interaction for improvement of teaching. *Teaching and Teacher Education*, 6 (3), 267-277.

Ellis, R. (1985). *Understanding Second Language Acquisition*. Oxford University Press.

El Mouaden, El Amin. (1990). Arabisch OETC op weg naar buiten schooltijd. *Samenwijs, 11* (1), September.

El Mouaden, El Amin (1990). Arabisch OETC op weg naar buiten schooltijd. *Samenwijs, 11, 1* (September).

Elsas, Christoph (1983). Religiöse Faktoren für Identität: Politische Implikationen Christlich-Islamischer Gespräche in Berlin. In Elsas, C. (Ed.), *Identität: Veränderungen kultureller Eigenarten im Zusammenleben von Türken und Deutschen*. Hamburg: Rissen.

Elwert, Georg (1984). Die Angst vor dem Ghetto. Binnenintegration als erste Schritt zur Integration. In Ahmet Bayaz, Mario Damolin, and Heiko Ernst (Eds.), *Integration: Anpassung an die Deutschen?* Weinheim and Basel: Beltz Verlag.

El Yazami, Driss (1988). Présence Musulmane et immigration. In *L'Immigration dans l'histoire nationale*. Paris: CEFISEM.

Enderwitz, Susanne (1983). Der Schleier im Islam—Ausdruck von Identität? In Elsas, C. (Ed.), *Identität: Veränderungen kultureller Eigenarten im Zusammenleben von Türken und Deutschen*. Hamburg: Rissen.

Engelbrecht, M., Iversen, K.A., and Engel, M. (1990). *Danskundervisningen i de to-kulturelle klasser in Høje-Taastrup*. Høje-Taastrup Kommune (Denmark).

Engelbrecht, M., Iversen, K.A., and Engel, M. (1991). *Arbejdet i de to-kulturelle klasser i Høje-Taastrup*. Høje-Taastrup Kommune.

Engelbrecht, M., Iversen, K.A., and Engel, M. (1992). *Status ved afslutningen af forsøget med tokulturelle klasser i Høje-Taastrup*. Høje-Taastrup Kommune.

Enright, D.S. and Gomez, B. (1985). Pro-act: Six Strategies for Organizing Peer Interaction in Elementary Classrooms. *NABE Journal*, 9 (3), 5-24.

Entzinger, Han B. (1982). Migratie- en minderhedenbeleid in Europees perspectief. In J.M.M. van Amersfoort and H.B. Entzinger (Eds.), *Immigrant en Samenleving*. Deventer (The Netherlands): Van Loghum Slaterus.

Entzinger, Han B. (1984). *Het Minderhedenbeleid*. Meppel: Boom.

Entzinger, Han B. (1985). The Netherlands. In Tomas Hammar (Ed.), *European Immigration Policy: A Comparative Study*. Cambridge: Cambridge University Press.

Entzinger, Han (1986). Overheidsbeleid voor immigranten. In Lotty van den Berg Eldering (Ed.), *Van gastarbeider tot immigrant: Marokkanen en Turken in Nederland, 1965-1985*. Alphen aan den Rijn (The Netherlands): Samson.

Entzinger, Han B. (1987). Een kleine wereld. *Migrantenstudies*, 3 (4).

Entzinger, Han B. (1988). Voorwaarden voor een multiculturele samenleving. In F. Lindo (Ed.), *Balans van het minderhedenbeleid: Vier jaar na de Nota*. Utrecht:

Nederlands Centrum Buitenlanders.

Ephimenco, Sylvain (1986, October 1). Belgique et Islam. *Actualité de l'émigration, 57.*

Epstein, Erwin H. (1970a). General Introduction. In Erwin H. Epstein (Ed.), *Politics and Education in Puerto Rico: A Documentary Survey of the Language Issue.* Metuchen (NJ): Scarecrow Press, 1970.

Epstein, Erwin H. (1970b). La Enseñanza del Idioma y el Status Politico. In Erwin H. Epstein (Ed.), *Politics and Education in Puerto Rico: A Documentary Survey of the Language Issue.* Metuchen (NJ): Scarecrow Press, 1970.

Epstein, Erwin H. (1970c). National Identity and the Language Issue. In Erwin H. Epstein (Ed.). *Politics and Education in Puerto Rico: A Documentary Survey of the Language Issue.* Metuchen (NJ): Scarecrow Press, 1970.

Epstein, Erwin H. (1970d). English and Politics in the Schools. In Erwin H. Epstein (Ed.). *Politics and Education in Puerto Rico: A Documentary Survey of the Language Issue.* Metuchen (NJ): Scarecrow Press, 1970.

Epstein, J. (1985). After the Bus Arrives: Resegregation in Desegregated Schools. *Journal of Social Issues, 41* (3), 23–43.

Epstein, Noel (1992). Affirmative Ethnicity. In James Crawford (Ed.), *Language Loyalties.* Chicago: University of Chicago Press.

Eriksen, Knut (1991). Norwegian and Swedish Educational Policies vis-á-vis Nondominant Ethnic Groups, 1850–1940. In Janusz Tomiak (Ed.), *Schooling, Educational Policy, and Ethnic Identity.* New York: New York University Press.

Eriksen, K., Kazamias, A., Okey, R., and Tomiak, J. (1991). Governments and the Education of Non-Dominant Ethnic Groups in Comparative Perspective. In Janusz Tomiak (Ed.), *Schooling, Educational Policy, and Ethnic Identity.* New York: New York University Press.

Ersoy, Durgut (1993). Ontmoediging OETC. *Samenwijs, 13* (7), March.

Esch, W. van (1982). *Etnische groepen en het onderwijs: Een verkennende studie.* The Hague (The Netherlands): Stichting voor Onderzoek van het Onderwijs.

Escuelita Agueeybana Inc. (1985). *Parent Manual,* Boston.

Espinosa, Ruben and Ochoa, Alberto (1986). Concentration of California Hispanic Students in Schools with Low Achievement: A Research Note. *American Journal of Education, 95* (1), November.

Esser, Hartmut and Korte, Hermann (1985). Federal Republic of Germany. In Tomas Hammar (Ed.), *European Immigration Policy: A Comparative Study.* Cambridge University Press.

European Communities (1985). Guidelines for a Community Policy on Migration. *Bulletin of the European Communities,* September.

Everts, Henk (1983). Onderwijsorganisatievormen, toegespitst op het zgn. Leidse opvangmodel. In Nitha Neuwahl and Aletta de Raad (Eds.), *Kinderen van medelanders: Buitenlandse kinderen in de Nederlandse samenleving.* Deventer (The Netherlands): Van Loghum Slaterus.

Everts, Henk, Golhof, A., Stassen, P., and Teunissen, J. (1987). *De kultureel-etnische situatie op OVB-scholen.* 2d ed., Utrecht: Vakgroep Onderwijskunde.

Eyler, J., Cook, V.J. and Ward, L.E. (1983). Resegregation: Segregation within Desegregated Schools. In C.H. Rossell and H.D. Hawley (Eds.), *The Consequences of School Desegregation.* Philadelphia: Temple University Press.

Fallows, James (1988). Immigration: How It's Affecting Us. *The Atlantic Monthly,* November.

Faltis, C.J. (1993). *Joinfostering: Adapting Teaching Strategies for the Multilingual Classroom.* New York: Merrill.

Farr, Marcia and Daniels, Harvey (1986). *Language Diversity and Writing Instruction.* New York: ERIC Clearinghouse on Urban Education.

Fase, Willem (1985). Schoolloopbanen van leerlingen uit internationale schakelklassen. In Mart-Jan de Jong (Ed.), *Allochtone kinderen op Nederlandse scholen: Prestaties, problemen en houdingen.* Lisse (The Netherlands): Swets & Zeitlinger.

Fase, Willem (1986a). Over de betekenis van onderwijs in eigen taal en cultuur in Frankrijk. *Samenwijs*, 6, 10 (June).

Fase, Willem (1986b). In Berlijn hooguit sprake van keuzevak Turks. *Samenwijs*, 6, 6 (February).

Fase, Willem (1987). *Voorbij de grenzen van onderwijs in eigen taal en cultuur: Meertaligheid op school in zes landen verkend*. The Hague: Instituut voor Onderzoek van het Onderwijs.

Fase, Willem (1990). Maatschappelijke actergronden van de verdeling van etnische groepen in her scholenveld. *Migrantenstudies*, 6 (2).

Fase, Willem (1994). *Ethnic Divisions in Western European Education*. Muenster (Germany): Waxmann.

Federal Government Initiatives Relating to Multiculturalism in Education, Toronto (Canada), May, 1987.

Federal-Provincial Cooperation in Language Programs. *Dialogue*, 3 (2), October.

Fernandez, R.M. and F. Nielsen, F. (1986). Bilingualism and Hispanic Scholastic Achievement: Some Baseline Research. *Social Science Research*, 377.

Fernandez, R.R., Guskin, J.T. (1981). Hispanic students and school desegregation. In W.D. Hawley (Ed.), *Effective School Desegregation. Equity, Quality and Feasibility*. (Pp. 107–140). London: Sage.

Fernández Bragado, José (1992). Anti-racist Education: An Approach to the Schooling of Children from Ethnic Minority Communities. In Euan Reid and Hans Reich (Eds.), *Breaking the Boundaries: Migrant Workers' Children in the EC*. Clevedon (United Kingdom): Multilingual Matters.

Ferré, Luis A. (1970). Une Amenaza Contra Escuelas Privadas. In Erwin H. Epstein (Ed.), *Politics and Education in Puerto Rico: A Documentary Survey of the Language Issue*. Metuchen (NJ): Scarecrow Press.

Ferrier, Joan M. (1985). *De Surinamers*. Muiderberg (The Netherlands): Coutinho.

Fichte, Johann Gottlieb (1922). *Addresses to the German Nation* (R.F. Jones and G.H. Turnbull, transl.). Chicago: Open Court.

Fishman, Joshua A. (1967). Childhood Indoctrination for Minority-Group Membership. In Milton L. Barron (Ed.), *Minorities in a Changing World*. New York: Alfred A. Knopf.

Fishman, Joshua (1970). Some Facts about Bilingualism in the United States: A Sociohistorical Overview. In Theodore Andersson and Mildred Boyer (Eds.), *Bilingual Schooling in the United States* II. Austin, Texas: Southwest Educational Development Laboratory.

Fishman, Joshua (1980). Bilingualism and Biculturalism as Individual and as Societal Phenomena. *Multilingual and Multicultural Development*, 1 (1).

Fishman, Joshua A. (1985). The Ethnic Revival in the United States: Implications for the Mexican-American Community. In Walker Connor (Ed.), *Mexican-Americans in Comparative Perspective*. Washington: The Urban Institute.

Fishman, Joshua A. (1989). *Language and Ethnicity in Minority Sociolinguistic Perspective*. Clevedon (United Kingdom): Multilingual Matters.

Fishman, Joshua A. (1992). The Displaced Anxieties of Anglo-Americans. In James Crawford (Ed.), *Language Loyalties*. Chicago: University of Chicago Press.

Fitzpatrick, Joseph P. (1967). The Adjustment of Puerto Ricans to New York City. In Milton L. Barron (Ed.), *Minorities in a Changing World*. New York: Alfred A. Knopf.

Fix, Michael and Passel, Jeffrey S. (1994). *Immigration and Immigrants: Setting the Record Straight*, Washington, DC: The Urban Institute.

Fix, Michael and Zimmermann, Wendy (1994). After Arrival: An Overview of Federal Immigrant Policy in the United States. In Barry Edmonston and Jeffrey S. Passel (Eds.), *Immigration and Ethnicity*. Washington, DC: The Urban Institute.

Flanigan, B.O. (1988). Second Language Acquisition in the Elementary Schools: The

Negotiation of Meaning by Native-speaking and Nonnative-speaking Peers. *Bilingual Review, 14* (3), 25–40.

Flanigan, B.O. (1991). Peer Tutoring and Second Language Acquisition in the Elementary School. *Applied Linguistics, 12* (2), 141–158.

Fletcher, Peri L. and Taylor, J. Edward (1990). A Village Apart. *California Tomorrow, 5* (1), Winter/Spring.

Flew, Antony (1986a). Education Against Racism. In Dennis O'Keefe (Ed.), *The Wayward Curriculum*. London: The Social Affairs Unit.

Flew, Antony (1986b). Clarifying the Concepts. In Frank Palmer (Ed.), *Anti-Racism— An Assault on Education and Value*. London: Sherwood Press.

Fligstein, N. and Fernandez, R.M. (1985). Hispanics and Education. In P. Cafferty and W. McCready (Eds.), *Hispanics in the United States: A New Social Agenda*. New Brunswick (NJ): Transaction.

Flinders, D.J. (1988). Teacher Isolation and the New Reform. *Journal of Curriculum and Supervision, 4* (1), 17–29.

Flores, Estevan T. (1984). Research on Undocumented Immigrants and Public Policy: A Study of the Texas School Case. *International Migration Review, 18* (3), Fall.

Fluegel, Christoph (1987). *Modele suisse. in La Suisse—un défi: Une approche de l'enseignement des langages nationales en Suisse*. Berne: CDIP.

Follain, Mary (1989, November 17). Ex-minister Backs Head against Muslim Scarves. *The Times Educational Supplement*.

Fonteyn, Guido (1985). The specific characteristics of the Brussels situation. In *Four Years Bicultural Education in Brussels: An Evaluation*. Brussels: The Foyer Committee of Bicultural Education.

Foster, Lois and Stockley, David (1988). *Australian Multiculturalism: A Documentary History and Critique*. Clevedon (United Kingdom): Multilingual Matters, 1988.

Förster, P., Friedrich, W., Müller, H., and Schubarth, W. (1992). Jugendliche in Ostdeutschland, *Gemeinsam*, 25, December.

Franco, Juan N. (1983). Developmental Analysis of Self-concept in Mexican-American and Anglo School Children. *Hispanic Journal of Behavioral Sciences, 5* (2), June.

Franco, Ralph A. (1970). Statement. In *Hearings before the Select Committee on Equal Educational Opportunity of the United States Senate: Part 8—Equal Educational Opportunity for Puerto Rican Children*. Washington, DC, November.

Frederking, Monika (1985). Zweisprachigkeit bei türkischen Kindern in der Bundesrepublik Deutschland. *Zielsprache Deutsch, 3*.

Freeman, Gary P. (1979). *Immigrant Labor and Racial Conflict in Industrial Societies: The French and British Experience 1945–1975*. Princeton (NJ): Princeton University Press.

Freeman, Gary P. (1993). From "Populate or Perish" to "Diversify or Decline": Immigration and Australian National Security. In Myron Weiner (Ed.), *International Migration and Security*. Boulder (CO): Westview Press.

Freeman, Kate, Stairs, Arlene, Corbière, Evelyn, and Lazore, Dorothy (1995). Ojibway, Mohawk, and Inuktitut Alive and Well? Issues of Identity, Ownership, and Change. *Bilingual Research Journal, 19* (1).

Friedberg, Maurice (1988). Varieties of Yiddish Verse—In English. *Commentary*, April.

Friedrich, Carl J. (1970). Federalism, Nationalism and Language. In Erwin H. Epstein (Ed.), *Politics and Education in Puerto Rico: A Documentary Survey of the Language Issue*. Metuchen (NJ): Scarecrow Press.

Friesenhahn, Günter J. (1993). Multikulturelle Gesellschaft als pädagogische Aufgabe? *Unsere Jugend 45* (2 & 3).

Frisch, Max (1967). *Öffentlichkeit als Partner*. Frankfurt am Main: Suhrkamp.

Fristad i sigtuna: *En rapport om flyktingbarn i grundskolan* (1988). Stockholm: Skolöverstyrelsen.

Frost, Joan (1970). Ukrainian Schools and Organizations. In Theodore Andersson and Mildred Boyer (Eds.), *Bilingual Schooling in the United States, II*. Austin (TX): Southwest Educational Development Laboratory.

Frost, Joan (1970). The Norwegian Language in America. In Theodore Andersson and Mildred Boyer (Eds.), *Bilingual Schooling in the United States, II*. Austin (TX): Southwest Educational Development Laboratory.

Frost, Joan (1970). Polish Speakers in the United States. In Theodore Andersson and Mildred Boyer (Eds.), *Bilingual Schooling in the United States, II*. Austin (TX): Southwest Educational Development Laboratory.

Funcke, Liselotte (1988). Vorwort. In *"Und im Ausland sind die Deutschen auch Fremde!" Interkulturelles Lernen in der Grundschule*. Frankfurt am Main: Arbeitkreis Grundschule.

Gaarder, A. Bruce (1977). *Bilingual Schooling and the Survival of Spanish in the United States*. Rowley (MA): Newbury House.

Gabaccia, Donna (1988). *Immigrant Women and Acculturation. Einwandererland USA/Gastarbeiterland BRD*. Berlin: ARGUMENT-Sonderband AS 163.

Galang, Rosita (1988). The Language Situation of Filipino Americans. In Sandra Lee McKay and Sau-ling Cynthia Wong (Eds), *Language Diversity: Problem or Resource?* Cambridge (MA): Newbury House.

Gandara, Patricia and Merino, Barbara (1993). Measuring the Outcomes of LEP Programs: Test Scores, Exit Rates, and Other Mythological Data. *Educational Evaluation and Policy Analysis, 15* (3), Fall.

Gans, Herbert J. (1991). *Middle American Individualism*. New York: Oxford University Press.

Garcia, Ofelia and Otheguy, Ricardo (1988). The Language Situation of Cuban Americans. In Sandra Lee McKay and Sau-ling Cynthia Wong (Eds), *Language Diversity: Problem or Resource?* Cambridge (MA): Newbury House.

Garcia, Eugene E. (1987). Effective Schooling for Language Minority Students. *Focus*, Washington, DC: National Clearinghouse for Bilingual Education, Winter.

Garcia, E.E. (1988). Attributes of Effective Schools for Language Minority Students. *Education and Urban Society, 20* (4), 387–398.

Garcia, Eugene E. (1991). Bilingualism, Second Language Acquisition, and the Education of Chicano Language Minority Students. In R.R. Valencia (Ed.), *Chicano School Failure and Success*. London: Falmer Press.

Garcia Garrido, José Luis (1991). Spanish Education Policy Towards Non-Dominant Linguistic Groups, 1850–1940. In Janusz Tomiak (Ed.), *Schooling, Educational Policy, and Ethnic Identity*. New York: New York University Press.

Garcia Hoz, Victor. (1980). *La Educacion en la España del Siglo XX*. Madrid: Rialp.

Gardner, R.C. (1985). *Social Psychology and Second Language Learning. The Role of Attitudes and Motivation*. London: Edward Arnold.

Gaspard, Françoise (1992). Assimilation, Insertion, Intégration: Les mots pour devenir français. *Hommes & Migrations, 1164*, May.

Gaspard, Françoise and Servan-Schreiber, Claude (1985). *La fin des immigrés*. 2d ed. Paris: Éditions du Seuil.

Gaustad, Edwin S. (1983). *A Documentary History of Religion in America since 1865*. Grand Rapids (MI): Eerdmans.

Gedmin, Jeffrey (1992). Germany's Growing Pains. *The American Enterprise*, March/April.

Geelen, Eva (1995). Effectieve school zorgt voor kleinere achterstand. *Samenwijs, 15* (8), April.

Geiss, Bernd, Hartmut Reichow, Bernhard Schmidt and Beate Winkler-Poehler (1985). *Ausländer in europäischen Staaten*. Bonn: Mitteilungen der Beauftragten der Bundesregierung für die Integration der ausländischen Arbeitnehmer und ihrer Familienangehörigen.

Gelder, Paul van (1990). Het Surinaamse begrip "hosselen." *Migrantenstudies, 6* (3).

Gellner, Ernest (1987). *Culture, Identity, and Politics*. Cambridge: Cambridge University Press.

General Accounting Office (1987). *Bilingual Education: A New Look at the Research Evidence*. Washington, DC.

Genesee, Fred (1984). Historical and Theoretical Foundations of Immersion Education. In *Studies on Immersion Education*. Sacramento: California State Department of Education.

Genesee, Fred (1985). Second Language Learning through Immersion: A Review of U.S. Programs. *Review of Educational Research, 55* (4), Winter.

Genesee, Fred (1987). *Learning Through Two Languages*. Cambridge (MA): Newbury House.

Genesee, F. (1991). Second Language Learning in School Settings: Lessons from Immersion. In A.G. Reynolds (Ed.), *Bilingualism, Multiculturalism, and Second Language Learning* (Pp. 183–201). Hillsdale (NJ): Laurence Erlbaum Association.

Genesee, F. (1994). Introduction. In F. Genesee (Ed.), *Educating Second Language Children. The Whole Child, the Whole Curriculum, the Whole Community*. (Pp. 1–12). New York: Cambridge University Press.

George, Jacques (1992). Les ZEP et le reste. *Cahiers pédagogiques, 309,* December.

Georgel, Jacques and Thorel, Anne-Marie (1995). *L'enseignement privé en France du VIIIe au XXe siècle*. Paris: Dalloz.

Gerritsen, J. H. (1986). Christelijke ontmoetingsschool in wording. *INKOM.*

Gerritsen, J. H. (1989). *In samenklank en tegenspraak*, Kampen: Kok.

Gersten, Russell (1985). Structured Immersion for Language Minority Students: Results of a Longitudinal Evaluation. *Educational Evaluation and Policy Analysis, 7* (3), Fall.

Gersten, Russell, Keating, Thomas J., and Brengelman, Susan Unok (1995). Toward an Understanding of Effective Instructional Practices for Language Minority Students: Findings From a Naturalistic Research Study. *READ Perspectives, II* (1), Spring.

Gersten, Russell and Woodward, John (1985). A Case for Structured Immersion. *Educational Leadership*, September.

Gersten, Russell and Woodward, John (1994). The Language-Minority Student and Special Education: Issues, Trends, and Paradoxes. *Exceptional Children, 60* (4), 310–322.

Gerth, Klaus-Erich (1988). Latest Developments in Early Bilingual Education in France and Southern Europe. *Multilingual and Multicultural Development, 9* (1 & 2).

Gianturco, Adriana and Aronin, Norman (1971). *Boston's Spanish Speaking Community: Findings of a Field Survey*. Boston: Action for Boston Community Development.

Gibson, Margaret A. (1991a). Ethnicity, Gender and Social Class: The School Adaptation Patterns of West Indian Youths. In Margaret A. Gibson and John U. Ogbu (Eds.), *Minority Status and Schooling*. New York: Garland.

Gibson, Margaret A. (1991b). Minorities and Schooling: Some Implications. In Margaret A. Gibson and John U. Ogbu (Eds.), *Minority Status and Schooling*, New York: Garland.

Gibson, Margaret A. and Parminder K. Bhachu (1991). The Dynamics of Educational Decision Making: A Comparative Study of Sikhs in Britain and the United States. In Margaret A. Gibson and John U. Ogbu (Eds.), *Minority Status and Schooling*. New York: Garland.

Gilbert, M. Jean (1978). Extended Family Integration Among Second-Generation Mexican Americans. In J. Manuel Casas and Susan E. Keefe (Eds.), Family and Mental Health in the Mexican American Community. Los Angeles: Spanish Speaking Mental Health Research Center.

Gilhotra, Manjit S. (1985). Maintenance of Community Languages in Multicultural Australia. *Multilingual and Multicultural Development, 6* (1).

Gimbel, Jorgen (n.d.). *Immigrant Danish—A Multitude of Languages.* Copenhagen: Royal Danish School of Educational Studies.

Gimbel, Jorgen (1988). Modersmålet og barnets sociokulturelle forudsøtninger: Om at tage udgangspunkt i barnets forudsøtninger. In Christian Horst (Ed.), *Den Flerkulturelle Udfordring: Socialisation og bærn fra etniske mindretal.* Copenhagen: Kultursociologiske Skrifter.

Giotitsas, Napoleon (1988). "Scholiko": Das bedeutet fur uns alles—Integrierter muttersprachlicher Unterricht. In *"Und im Ausland sind die Deutschen auch Fremde!" Interkulturelles Lernen in der Grundschule.* Frankfurt am Main: Arbeitkreis Grundschule.

Girardon, Jacques, Vincent Hugeux and Sylviane Stein. (1993, May 6). Les Islamistes en Europe. *L'Express.*

Glazer, Nathan (1967). The Peoples of America. In Milton L. Barron (Ed.), *Minorities in a Changing World.* New York: Alfred A. Knopf.

Glazer, Nathan (1977). Public Education and American Pluralism. In James S. Coleman and others (Eds.), *Parents, Teachers, and Children: Prospects for Choice in American Education.* San Francisco: Institute for Contemporary Studies.

Glazer, Nathan (1983). *Ethnic Dilemmas 1964–1982.* Cambridge: Harvard University Press.

Glazer, Nathan (1985). The Political Distinctiveness of the Mexican-Americans. In Walker Connor (Ed.), *Mexican-Americans in Comparative Perspective.* Washington, DC: The Urban Institute.

Glazer, Nathan (1991). The Lessons of New York City. *The Public Interest, 104,* Summer.

Glazer, Nathan and Moynihan, Daniel P. (1963). *Beyond the Melting Pot.* Cambridge (MA): MIT Press.

Glazer, Nathan and Moynihan, Danile P. (1975). Introduction. In Nathan Glazer and Daniel P. Moynihan (Eds.), *Ethnicity: Theory and Experience.* Cambridge: Harvard University Press.

Glazer, Sarah (1988). Bilingual Education: Does It Work? *Educational Research Reports 1* (10), March. Washington DC: Congressional Quarterly.

Glenn, Charles L. (1985a). Two Schools in Rotterdam. *The Reformed Journal,* November.

Glenn, Charles L. (1985b). Bilingual Assignments in Boston. In *Report No. 5 to the Federal District Court on Boston School Desegregation,* II. Quincy (MA): Commonwealth of Massachusetts Board of Education, July.

Glenn, Charles L. (1986a). How We Are Failing "Linguistic Minority" Students. *Equity and Choice, 2* (3), Spring.

Glenn, Charles L. (1986b). *Seeking Educational Equity for Linguistic Minority Students.* Quincy (MA): Massachusetts Department of Education.

Glenn, Charles L. (1987a). *Creating the New Common School.* Quincy (MA): Massachusetts Department of Education.

Glenn, Charles L. (1987b). Religion, Textbooks and the Common School. *The Public Interest,* July.

Glenn, Charles L. (1988a). *Immigrant Students in Belgian Schools.* Quincy (MA): Massachusetts Department of Education.

Glenn, Charles L. (1988b). *The Myth of the Common School.* Amherst (MA): University of Massachusetts Press.

Glenn, Charles L. (1988c). *NAEP Language Minority Study: Review for the Center for Education Statistics.* Quincy (MA): Massachusetts Department of Education.

Glenn, Charles L. (1988d). *Educating Linguistic Minority Students.* Quincy (MA): Office of Educational Equity.

Glenn, Charles L. (1989a). Just Schools for Minority Students: Remarks to Educators in Denmark and West Germany. *Phi Delta Kappan*, June.

Glenn, Charles, L. (1989b). *Choice of Schools in Six Nations*. Washington, DC: U.S. Department of Education.

Glenn, Charles L. (1989c). Variations on the Education of Immigrant Students. Joseph J. Foley and Lisanio R. Orlandi (Eds.), *Proceedings of the Annual MABE Conference*. Massachusetts Association for Bilingual Education.

Glenn, Charles L. (1990). Gebruik de keuzevrijheid voor een rechtvaardiger en beter onderwijssysteem. *Inkom, 14* (2), February.

Glenn, Charles L. (1995). Minority Schools on Purpose. In Erwin Flaxman and A. Harry Passow (Eds.), *Changing Populations, Changing Schools: 94th Yearbook of the National Society for the Study of Education*, Part II. Chicago: National Society for the Study of Education.

Glenn, Charles L. and Joshua Glenn (1991). Making Room for Religious Conviction in Democracy's Schools. In Stanley Hauerwas and John H. Westerhoff (Eds.), *Schooling Christians*. Grand Rapids (Michigan): Eerdmans Publishing Company.

Glenn, Charles L. and LaLyre, Ivonne (1991). Integrated Bilingual Education in the USA. In Koen Jaspaert and Sjaak Kroon (Eds.), *Ethnic Minority Languages and Education*. Amsterdam/Lisse: Swets & Zeitlinger.

Glenn, Charles L., McLaughlin, Kahris and Salganik, Laura (1993). *Parent Information for School Choice: The Case of Massachusetts*. Boston: Center on Families, Communities, Schools and Children's Learning, May.

Goessling, D.P. (1994). *We can't go back! The Journey from Special Education Teacher to Integration Facilitator*. Dissertation. Boston University Press.

Goetze, Dieter (1987). Probleme der Akkulturation und Assimilation. In Helga Reimann and Horst Reimann (Eds.), *Gastarbeiter: Analyse und Perspektiven eines sozialen Problems*. Opladen (Germany): Westdeutscher Verlag.

Gondolf, Ursula, Hegele, I., Pommerin, G., Rober-Siekmeyer, R., Schellong, I., and Steffen, G. (1983). *Gemeinsames Lernen mit ausländischen und deutschen Schülern*. Tübingen: Deutsches Institut für Fernstudien.

González, Josué M. (1979). *Bilingual Education in the Integrated School: Some Social and Pedagogical Factors*. Rosslyn (VA): National Clearinghouse for Bilingual Education.

González, Josué M. (1981). Short Answers to Common Questions About Bilingual Education." *Agenda* (National Council of La Raza), *11* (4).

González-Quijano, Yves (1986). "Comme si on etait des étrangers": Enquête sur l'image de la langue arabe chez les jeunes d'origine maghrébine. *Migrants Formation*, December.

Gordon, Milton M. (1964). *Assimilation in American Life*. New York: Oxford University Press.

Gordon, Milton M. (1975). Toward a General Theory of Racial and Ethnic Group Relations. In Nathan Glazer and Daniel P. Moynihan (Eds.), *Ethnicity: Theory and Experience*. Cambridge: Harvard University Press.

Gorter, Durk (1991). Lesser Used Languages in Primary Education in the European Community. In Koen Jaspaert and Sjaak Kroon (Eds.), *Ethnic Minority Languages and Education*. Amsterdam/Lisse: Swets & Zeitlinger.

Grant, Nigel. (1988). The Education of Minority and Peripheral Cultures: Introduction. *Comparative Education, 24* (2).

Greeley, Andrew M. and McCready, William C. (1975). The Transmission of Cultural Heritages: The Case of the Irish and the Italians. In Nathan Glazer and Daniel P. Moynihan (Eds.), *Ethnicity: Theory and Experience*. Cambridge (MA): Harvard University Press.

Greenbaum, William (1974). America in Search of a New Ideal: An Essay on the Rise of Pluralism. *Harvard Educational Review, 44* (3), August.

Gresko, Jacqueline (1986). Creating Little Dominions Within the Dominion: Early Catholic Indian Schools in Saskatchewan and British Columbia. In J. Barman, Y. Hébert, and McCaskill, D. (Eds.), *Indian Education in Canada: vol. 1: The Legacy*. Vancouver: University of British Columbia Press.

Grey, M.A. (1990). Immigrant Students in the Heartland: Ethnic Relations in Garden City, Kansas, High School. *Urban Anthropology, 19* (4).

Griffiths, Sian (1989, July 21). Rousing Speech. *The Times Educational Supplement*.

Griffiths, Sian (1990a, September 14). Pressure Points. *The Times Educational Supplement*.

Griffiths, Sian (1990b, November 30). Voices of the People. *The Times Educational Supplement*.

Griffiths, Sian (1991, April 19). A Language Is Put at the Very Core. *The Times Educational Supplement*.

Groenendijk, C.A. (1989). Migratiecontrole in Europa: Angsten, Instrumenten en Effecten. In *Migranten in her Europa van de Burger*. Utrecht: Mederlands Centrum Buitenlanders.

Groenendijk, Kees (1992). Europese migratiepolitiek: Fort Europa of het in stand houden van denkbeeldige grenzen. *Migrantenstudies, 8* (4).

Groenendijk, Petra (1992). Voorportaal is nuttig. *Samenwijs, 13* (2), September.

Grosjean, F. (1989). Neurolinguists, Beware! The Bilingual Is Not Two Monolinguals In One Person. *Brain and Language, 36*, 3–15.

Groth, Annette (1985). Bürgerliche und politische Rechte der Wanderarbeitnehmer in der EG. In Wolf-Dieter Just and Annette Groth (Eds.), *Wanderarbeiter in der EG*. vol. 1. Munich: Kaiser.

Gueler, Ome and Van der Heijden, Jos (1990). Van Kemenade: Ik ben niet bang voor opbloeiend fundamentalisme. *Samenwijs, 11* (2), October.

Guenter, A., Janssen, T., Petit, G., Uytterhoeven, A., Van Echelpoel, H., and Willems, R. (1987). 74 nationaliteiten in onze scholen! Immigrantenleerlingen in het katholiek secondair onderwijs. *Pedagogische Bijdragen voor Technisch en Beroepsonderwijs*, 86, June.

Guenter, A. and Guttentag, Marcia. (1970). Group Cohesiveness, Ethnic Organization, and Poverty. *The Journal of Social Issues, 26* (2), Spring.

Gutfleisch, Ingeborg and Rieck, Bert-Olaf (1981). Immigrant Workers (Gastarbeiter) in West Germany: Teaching Programmes for Adults and Children. In *World Yearbook of Education*. London: Kogan Page.

Haan, Dorian de and Nalbantoglu, Papatya (1986). Onderwijs in eigen taal en cultuur op de basisschool: ontwikkeling en perspectieven. *Onderwijs in eigen taal en cultuur, MOER*, 1–2.

Hackett, Geraldine (1992, August 7). The Scramble for State Funding. *The Times Educational Supplement*.

Hadden, Betsy (1985). Scattered, Diverse, and Fluctuating Minority Language Populations: School District Responses. In Stefan Jaeger (Ed.), *Educating the Minority Language Student: Classroom and Administrative Issues*. Vol. 2. Rosslyn (VA): National Clearinghouse for Bilingual Education.

Hadden, Betsy (1988). *Educating Language Minority Children in the United States: Classroom and Administrative Issues. Einwandererland USA/Gastarbeiterland BRD*. Berlin: ARGUMENT-Sonderband AS 163.

Haeffele, Henri (1988). L'accueil des primo-arrivants: Pour . . . quoi? Comment? *Migrants formation, 73*, June. Special issue *L'accueil scolaire des nouveaux arrivants*.

Haest, Guus (1989). *De Ouwe Garde, het Andere Slag, en de Buitenlanders*. Assen/Maastricht: Van Gorcum.

Hagman, T. and Lahdenpera, J. (1988). Nine Years of Finnish-medium Education in Sweden. In Tove Skutnabb-Kangas and Jim Cummins (Eds.), *Minority Education: From Shame to Struggle*. Clevedon (United Kingdom): Multilingual Matters.

Hajer, Maaike and Meestringa, Teun (1986). Tien jaar OETC aan kleuters in Zweden: Wat kan de rol van de etc-leerkracht zijn? *Samenwijs, 7,* (1), September.

Hajer, Maaike and Meestringa, Teun (1991). Curriculum Development in Migrant Languages and Cultures at the Primary School Level. In Koen Jaspaert and Sjaak Kroon (Eds.), *Ethnic Minority Languages and Education.* Amsterdam/Lisse: Swets & Zeitlinger.

Hakuta, Kenji (1986). *Mirror of Language: The Debate on Bilingualism.* New York: Basic Books.

Hakuta, Kenji and Gould, Laurie J. (1987). Synthesis of Research on Bilingual Education. *Educational Leadership, 44* (6), March.

Hale, T. and Burdar, E. (1970). Are TESOL Classes the Only Answer? *Modern Languages Journal, 59,* 15–18.

Hamburger, Franz (1984). Erziehung in der Einwanderungsgesellschaft. In Hartmut M. Griese (Ed.), *Der gläserne Fremde: Bilanz und Kritik der Gastarbeiterforschung und der Ausländerpädagogik.* Leske & Budrich.

Hamburger, Franz (1989). Auf dem Weg zur Wanderungsgesellschaft—Migratieprozesos und politische Reaktion in der Bundesrepublik Deutschland. *Deutsch lernen, 14* (1).

Hamburger, Franz (1991). Die fremden Kinder. In Heiner Ullrich (Ed.), *Kinder am Ende ihres Jahrhunderts.* Langenau-Ulm (Germany): Vaas Verlag.

Hammar, Tomas (1985a). Sweden. In *European Immigration Policy: A Comparative Study.* Cambridge: Cambridge University Press.

Hammar, Tomas (1985b). Comparative Analysis. In *European Immigration Policy: A Comparative Study.* Cambridge: Cambridge University Press.

Hamilton, Leslie (1985). Zu den Ursachen der Migration in Europa. In *Wanderarbeiter in der EG.* Vol. 1. Munich: Kaiser.

Handboek voor de ontmoeting in het protestants-christelijk voortgezet onderwijs, Hoevelaken: Christelijk Pedagogisch Studiecentrum, 1987.

Handlin, Oscar (1951). *The Uprooted,* New York: Grosset & Dunlap.

Handscombe, J. (1989). Mainstreaming: Who Needs It? In Esling, J.H. (Ed.), *Multicultural Education and Policy: ESL in 1990.* Toronto: Institute for Studies in Education.

Handscombe, J. (1994). Putting It All Together. In F. Genesee (Ed.), *Educating Second Language Children. The Whole Child, the Whole Curriculum, the Whole Community.* (Pp. 331–356). New York: Cambridge University Press.

Hannoun, Hubert (1987). *Les ghettos de l'école: Pour une éducation interculturelle.* Paris: Editions ESF.

Hansen, Georg (1986). *Diskriminiert: Uber den Umgang der Schule mit Minderheiten.* Basel: Beltz.

Hansen, Iren (1987). En 2–kulturel klasse fra det virkelige liv. *Samspil, 3.*

Hansen, Marcus Lee (1938). *The Problem of the Third Generation Immigrant.* Rock Island (IL): Augustana Historical Society.

Hansen, Marcus Lee (1961). *The Atlantic Migration 1607–1860,* ed. by Arthur M. Schlesinger, New York: Harper Torchbook, 1961.

Hansen, Sven-Erik (1987). Mother-Tongue Teaching and Identity: The Case of Finland-Swedes. *Multilingual and Multicultural Development, 8* (1–2).

Harant, Stefan (1987). Schulprobleme von Gastarbeiterkindern. In Helga Reimann and Horst Reimann (Eds.), *Gastarbeiter: Analyse und Perspektiven eines sozialen Problems.* Opladen (Germany): Westdeutscher Verlag.

Harris, John (1991). The Contribution of Primary Schools to the Maintenance of Irish. In Koen Jaspaert and Sjaak Kroon (Eds.), *Ethnic Minority Languages and Education.* Amsterdam/Lisse: Swets & Zeitlinger.

Harzig, Christiane (1988). *Ethnische Nachbarschaften: Hemmnis oder Basis für Akkulturation. Einwandererland USA/Gastarbeiterland BRD.* Berlin: ARGUMENT-Sonderband AS 163.

Haugen, Einar (1992). The Curse of Babel. In James Crawford (Ed.), *Language Loyalties*. Chicago: University of Chicago Press.

Hawkins, Freda (1989). *Critical Years in Immigration: Canada and Australia Compared*. Kingston and Montreal: McGill-Queen's University Press, 1989.

Heath, Shirley Brice (1985). Language Policies: Patterns of Retention and Maintenance. In Walker Connor (Ed.), *Mexican-Americans in Comparative Perspective*. Washington: The Urban Institute.

Heath, Shirley Brice (1986). Sociocultural Contexts of Language Development. In *Beyond Language: Social and Cultural Factors in Schooling Language Minority Students*. Los Angeles: Evaluation, Dissemination and Assessment Center, California State University, Los Angeles.

Heath, Tony (1993, October 22). Welsh Language Patchy in Life after School. *The Times Educational Supplement*.

Heiliger, Christian and Kürten, Karen (1992). Jugend '92: Ergebnisse der IBM-Jugendstudie. *Gemeinsam, 25*, December.

Hemmingsen, Signe (1988). Børn fra etniske mindretal i danske daginstitutioner. Det social-pådagogiske grundlag. In Christian Horst (Ed.), *Den Flerkulturelle Udfordring: Socialisation og bærn fra etniske mindretal*. Copenhagen: Kultursociologiske Skrifter nr. 24.

Hemspråk och hemspråksundervisning: Grundskolan och gymnasieskolan 1987/88 (1988). Stockholm: Statistiska centralbyran.

Henderson, David (1994, October 21). Mosque Has to Fill the Shortfall. *The Times Educational Supplement*, 12.

Henry-Lorcerie, Françoise (1989). Bilan d'une réglementation. In Claude Liauzu, Françoise Henry-Lorcerie, and Josette Liauzu (Eds.), *Immigration et école: la pluralité culturelle: État des questions, Dossiers documentaires*. Aix-en-Provence: Travaux et Documents de l'I.R.E.M.A.M.

Héraud, Guy (1982). The Status of Languages in Europe. In Beverly Hartford, Albert Valdman and Charles R. Foster (Eds.), *Issues in International Bilingual Education: The Role of the Vernacular*. New York: Plenum.

Herberg, Will (1955). *Protestant, Catholic, Jew: An Essay in American Religious Sociology*. Garden City (NY): Doubleday.

Hernández-Chávez, Eduardo (1978). Language Maintenance, Bilingual Education, and Philosophies of Bilingualism in the United States. In Alatis, James E. (Ed.), *International Dimensions of Bilingual Education*. Washington: Georgetown University Press.

Hernández-Chávez, Eduardo (1984). The Inadequacy of English Immersion Education as an Educational Approach for Language Minority Students in the United States. In *Studies on Immersion Education*. Sacramento: California State Department of Education.

Hernández-Chávez, Eduardo (1988). Language policy and language rights in the United States. In Tove Skutnabb-Kangas and Jim Cummins (Eds.), *Minority Education: From Shame to Struggle*. Clevedon (United Kingdom): Multilingual Matters.

Hester, H. (1984). Peer Interaction in Learning English as a Second Language. *Theory into Practice, 23* (3), 208–217.

Hewitt, Suzanne (1988, December 16). Primary Purposes: Children Need to Develop and Express Their Own Beliefs. *The Times Educational Supplement*.

Higham, John (1975). *Send These to Me: Jews and Other Immigrants in Urban America*. New York: Atheneum.

Hily, Marie-Antoinette and Poinard, Michel (1986). Les jeunes et la dynamique associative portugaise. In Georges Abou-Sada and Hélène Milet (Eds.), *Générations issues de l'immigration*. Paris: Arcantère Éditions.

Hirsch-Ballin, E.M.H. (1992). Morele vorming. *Samenwijs, 13* (2), October.

Hoefnagel-Höhle, Marian (1982). Tweede-taal verwerving. In René Appel, Cees Cruson, Pieter Muysken, and J.W. de Vries (Eds.), *Taalproblemen van buitenlandse arbeiders en hun kinderen*. Muiderberg (The Netherlands): Coutinho.

Hoerder, Dirk (1988). *Zur Akkulturation von Arbeitsmigranten. Einwandererland USA/Gastarbeiterland BRD*. Berlin: ARGUMENT-Sonderband AS 163.

Hof, Louise van't and Dronkers, Jaap (1993). Onderwijsachterstanden van allochtonen: klasse, gezin of etnische cultuur? *Migrantenstudies, 9* (1).

Hoffmann-Nowotny, Hans-Joachim (1985). Switzerland. In Tomas Hammar (Ed.), *European Immigration Policy: A Comparative Study*. Cambridge: Cambridge University Press.

Hoffmann-Nowotny, Hans-Joachim (1986). Assimilation and Integration of Minorities and Cultural Pluralism: Sociocultural Mechanisms and Political Dilemmas. In Dietmar Rothermund and John Simon (Eds.), *Education and the Integration of Ethnic Minorities*. New York: St. Martin's Press.

Hoffmann-Nowotny, Hans-Joachim (1987). Gastarbeiterwanderungen und soziale Spannungen. In Helga Reimann and Horst Reimann (Eds.), *Gastarbeiter: Analyse und Perspektiven eines sozialen Problems*. Opladen: Westdeutscher Verlag.

Hofmann, Klaus, Petry, Christian, Raschert, Jürgen, and Schlotmann, Barbara (1993). *Schulöffnung und Interkulturelle Erziehung*. Weinheim (Germany) and Basel (Switzerland): Beltz Verlag.

Hofstadter, Richard (1955). *Social Darwinism in American Thought*. Boston: Beacon Press.

Hohmann, Manfred, with Wittek, F., Chmielorz, A., and Gogolin, I. (1983). *Intercultural Education in Primary Schools. Compendium of Information on Intercultural Education Schemes in Europe*. Strasbourg: Council of Europe.

Holland, Rick (1986). *Bilingual Education: Recent Evaluations of Local School District Programs and Related Research on Second-language Learning*. Washington DC: Congressional Research Service.

Holm, Agnes and Holm, Wayne (1990). Rock Point, a Navajo Way to Go to School: A Valediction. *The Annals of the American Academy of Political and Social Science, 508*, March.

Holm, Agnes and Holm, Wayne (1995). Navajo Language Education: Retrospect and Prospects. *Bilingual Research Journal, 19*, 1.

Holobow, Naomi, Genesee, Fred, and Lambert, Wallace E. (1990). The Effectiveness of a Foreign Language Immersion Program for Children from Different Ethnic and Social Class Backgrounds: Report 2. Typescript, April.

Homan, Roger (1986). The Supplementary School: Development and Implications. In Sohan Mogdil, Gajendra Verma, Kanka Mallick, and Celie Mogdil (Eds.), *Multicultural Education: The Interminable Debate*. London: Falmer Press.

Honeyford, Ray (1986). Anti-Racist Rhetoric. In Dennis O'Keefe (Ed.), *The Wayward Curriculum*. London: The Social Affairs Unit.

Honkala, T., Leporanto-Morley, P., Liukka, L., and Rougle, E. (1988). Finnish Children in Sweden Strike for Better Education. In Tove Skutnabb-Kangas and Jim Cummins (Eds.), *Minority Education: From Shame to Struggle*. Clevedon (United Kingdom): Multilingual Matters.

Hornberger, Nancy H. (1990). Bilingual Education and English-only: A Language-planning Framework. *The Annals of the American Academy of Political and Social Science, 508*, March.

Horowitz, Donald L. (1985). Conflict and Accommodation: Mexican-Americans in the Cosmopolis. In Walker Connor (Ed.), *Mexican-Americans in Comparative Perspective*. Washington, DC: The Urban Institute.

Horst, Christian (1980). *Arbejdskraft: Vare eller menneske?* Copenhagen: Akademisk Forlag.

Horst, Christian (1988). Integration og assimilation. In *Den Flerkulturelle Udfordring: Socialisation og børn fra etniske mindretal*, Copenhagen: Kultursociologiske Skrifter nr. 24.

Horst, Jacqueline van der (1990a). De schoolnabije aanpak van Amsterdam: naar werkbare oplossingen in een meertalige klas. *Samenwijs, 10* (6), March.

Horst, Jacqueline van der (1990b). Een ochtend in een opvangklas voor neveninstromers. *Samenwijs, 11* (1), September.

Horst, Jacqueline van der (1990c). Schoolnabije aanpak neveninstromers in Amsterdamse Bijlmermeer. *Samenwijs, 11* (3), November.

Horst, Jacqueline van der (1991). Neveninstromers in het v.o. *Samenwijs, 11* (7), March.

Horst, Jacqueline van der (1992). Neveninstromers. *Samenwijs, 12* (7), March.

Houlton, David and King, Edith W. (1985). Mother-Tongue Teaching in Britain and the United States: Some Current Developments. *Multilingual and Multicultural Development, 6* (1).

Howes, C. and Wu, F. (1990). Peer Interactions and Friendships in an Ethnically Diverse School Setting. *Child Development, 61,* 537–541.

Huart, Michelle (1988). L'Intégration des enseignements de langue et culture des pays d'origine. In *Les Algériens et l'enseignement de l'Arabe en France.* Paris: Centre Culturel Algérien.

Hughes, Everett C. (1963). *French Canada in Transition.* Phoenix Edition. Chicago: University of Chicago Press.

Hussenet, André (1991). Une politique scolaire de l'intégration (extracts). *Hommes & Migrations, 1129–1146,* September.

Hutmacher, Walo (1987). Passport or Social Position? In *Immigrants' Children at School.* Paris: Organization for Economic Cooperation and Development.

Hvidovre Kommune (1985). (Denmark). *To-Kulturel Skolestart: Enghøjskolen 1984/85.*

Hvidovre Kommune (1986). *To-Kulturel Skolestart: Enghøjskolen 1985/86.*

Hyltenstam, Kenneth and Arnberg, Lenore (1988). *Bilingualism and Education of Immigrant Children and Adults in Sweden.* Stockholm: National Swedish Board of Education.

Hyltenstam, Kenneth and Stroud, Christopher (1985). Bilingualism and Its Educational Effects, Especially with Regard to Handicapped Children. Typescript.

Ickes, Harold (1970). In Erwin H. Epstein (Ed.), *Politics and Education in Puerto Rico: A Documentary Survey of the Language Issue.* Metuchen (NJ): Scarecrow Press.

Iglesias, César Andreu (1970). Argumentos Politicos. In Erwin H. Epstein (Ed.), *Politics and Education in Puerto Rico: A Documentary Survey of the Language Issue.* Metuchen (NJ): Scarecrow Press.

Imhof, Edith (1988). *La scolarisation des enfants de travailleurs migrants en Suisse.* Geneva: Centre suisse de documentation en matière d'enseignement et d'éducation.

Imhoff, Gary (1990). The Position of U.S. English on Bilingual Education. *The Annals of the American Academy of Political and Social Science, 508,* March.

Immigrants and Immigrant Teaching in Sweden (1983). Stockholm: Statistics Sweden.

Immigrants and the Education System: An Action Programme for the Work of the National Board of Education in Connection with Immigrant Affairs (1979). Stockholm: National Swedish Board of Education.

Indvandrernes Forslag til Læsning af deres Problemer i Danmark (1980). Copenhagen: Forbundet af Arbejdere fra Tyrkiet.

Inglehart, Ronald F. and Woodward, Margaret (1992). Language Conflicts and Political Community. In James Crawford (Ed.), *Language Loyalties.* Chicago: University of Chicago Press.

Inglis, Christine and Manderson, Lenore (1991). Turkish Immigrants in Australia. In Margaret A. Gibson and John U. Ogbu (Eds.), *Minority Status and Schooling.* New York: Garland.

Institut für Zukunftsforschung (1981). *Ausländer oder Deutsche: Integrationsprobleme griechischer, jugoslawischer und türkischer Bevolkerungsgruppen.* Cologne: Bund-Verlag.

Introductory Course for Young Immigrants (1977). Stockholm: National Swedish Board of Education.

Invandrar- och minoritetspolitiken: Slutbetankande av Invandrarpolitiska Kommitten (1984). Stockholm: Statens offentliga utredningar.

Investigation of the Necessity and Feasibility of Temporary Recruitment of Home Language Teachers from Certain Emigration Countries (1979). Stockholm: National Swedish Board of Education.

Iram, Yaacov (1985). Education Policy and Cultural Identity in Israel. In C. Brock and W. Tulasiewicz (Eds.), *Cultural Identity and Educational Policy*. London: Croom Helm.

Irvine, Jacqueline Jordan (1990). Cultural Mismatch in Schools a Barrier to Learning. *Catalyst: Voices of Chicago School Reform*, 2 (4), December.

Isaacs, Harold R. (1975). Basic Group Identity: The Idols of the Tribe. In Nathan Glazer and Daniel P. Moynihan (Eds.), *Ethnicity: Theory and Experience*. Cambridge: Harvard University Press.

Isaacs, Harold R. (1992). Language as a Factor in Inter-Group Conflict. In James Crawford (Ed.), *Language Loyalties*. Chicago: University of Chicago Press.

Jackson, Henry M. and Javits, Jacob K. (1970). Language in Puerto Rico as Viewed by the United States Senators Serving on STACOM. In Erwin H. Epstein (Ed.), *Politics and Education in Puerto Rico: A Documentary Survey of the Language Issue*. Metuchen (NJ): Scarecrow Press.

Jaeger, Stefan (1985). Foreign Language and Bilingual Education: A Possible Link. In *Educating the Minority Language Student: Classroom and Administrative Issues* II. Rosslyn (VA): The National Clearinghouse for Bilingual Education.

Jaenen, Cornelius J. (1986). Education for Francization: The Case of New France in the Sevententh Century. In J. Barman, Y. Hébert, & D. McCaskill (Eds.), *Indian Education in Canada. vol. 1: The Legacy*. Vancouver: University of British Columbia Press.

Jansen, Dirk (1992). Reorganisatie OETC. *Samenwijs, 13* (1), September.

Jansen, Dirk and Terkessidis, Koula (1992). Nieuw beleid werkt. *Samenwijs, 13* (2), October.

Janssen, Piet (1986). OETC in Vlaanderen. De Antwerpse situatie. *Onderwijs in eigen taal en cultuur, MOER* 1–2.

Janssen-van Dieten, Anne-Mieke (1982). Buitenlandse jongeren in het voortgezet onderwijs. In Rene Appel, Cees Cruson, Pieter Muysken, and J.W. de Vries (Eds.), *Taalproblemen van buitenlandse arbeiders en hun kinderen*. Muiderberg (The Netherlands): Coutinho.

Jaspaert, Koen and Lemmens, Getrud (1990). Linguistic Evaluation of Dutch as a Third Language. In Michel Byram and Johan Leman (Eds.), *Bicultural and Trilingual Education*. Clevedon (United Kingdom): Multilingual Matters.

Javier Leunda (1980). *Quelques réflexions sur la situation biculturelle des enfants espagnols en Belgique. Code et pratiques des populations immigrées: Identité culturelle et modèles de socialisation*. Brussels: Ministère de l'Education nationale et de Culture Française.

Jeffcoate, Robert (1984). Ideologies and Multicultural Education. In Maurice Craft (Ed.), *Education for Diversity, Education and Cultural Pluralism*. London: Falmer.

Jelinek, M.M. and Brittan, E.M. (1975). Multiracial Education. 1. Inter-ethnic friendship patterns. *Educational Research*, 18 (1), 44–53.

Johannesson, Ingvar (1975). Bilingual-Bicultural Education of Immigrant Children in Sweden. *International Review of Education, 21* (3).

Johnson, D.M. (1983). Natural Language Learning by Design: A Classroom Experiment in Social Interaction and Second Language Acquisition. *TESOL Quarterly, 17* (1), 55–68.

Johnson, D.M. (1994). Grouping Strategies for Second Language Learners. In F. Genesee (Ed.), *Educating Second Language Children. The Whole Child, the Whole Curriculum, the Whole Community.* (Pp. 183–211). New York: Cambridge University Press.

Johnstone, Diana (1990, January 24–30). In "Great Kerchief Quarrel" French Unite Against "Anglo-Saxon Ghettos." *In These Times.*

Joly, Daniele (1988). Making a Place for Islam in British Society: Muslims in Birmingham. In Tomas Gerholm and Yngve Georg Lithman (Eds.), *The New Islamic Presence in Western Europe.* London: Mansell.

Jones, Maldwyn Allen (1960). *American Immigration.* Chicago: University of Chicago Press.

Jones-Wilson, Faustine C., Arnez, Nancy L., and Asbury, Charles A. (1992). Why Not Public Schools? *The Journal of Negro Education, 61* (2).

Jong, Cheryl de (1995, May 7). Only Place for Kriolu Is Here. *The Boston Globe.*

Jong, Mart-Jan de (n.d). Allochtone leerlingen en het onderwijsbeleid: een pleidooi voor integratie. Typescript.

Jong, Mart-Jan de (1985a). Ethnic Minorities in Dutch Education: Practice and Policies. Paper presented in Dubrovnik, 1985a.

Jong, Mart-Jan de (1985b). Integratie en gelijke kansen. Unpublished manuscript. Rotterdam: Vakgroep Onderwijssociologie, 1985b.

Jong, Mart-Jan de (1987). *Herkomst, kennis en kansen: Allochtone en autochtone leerlingen tijdens de overgang van basis- naar voortgezet onderwijs.* Lisse (The Netherlands): Swets & Zeitlinger.

Jong, Mart-Jan de and Batenburg, Th.A. Van (1984). Etnische herkomst, intelligentie en schoolkeuzeadvies. *Pedagogische Studien,* 61.

Jong, Mart-Jan de and Batenburg, Th.A. Van (1985a). Over de zin voor realiteit. *Pedagogische Studien, 62.*

Jong, Mart-Jan de and Batenburg, Th.A. Van (1985b). Integratie van allochtone leerlingen. In Mart-Jan de Jong (Ed.), *Allochtone kinderen op Nederlandse scholen: Prestaties, problemen en houdingen.* Lisse (The Netherlands): Swets & Zeitlinger.

Jonkman, Reitze J. (1991). Triangulation and Trilingualism. In Kjell Herberts and Christer Laurén (Eds.), *Papers from the Sixth Nordic Conference on Bilingualism.* Clevedon (United Kingdom): Multilingual Matters.

Jordan, C., Tharp, R.G., and Baird-Vogt, L. (1992). "Just open the door": Cultural Compatibility and Classroom Rapport. In M. Saravia-Shore and S. Arvizu (Eds.), *Cross-cultural Literacy: Ethnographies of Communication in Multiethnic Classrooms.* (Pp. 3–18). New York: Garland.

Jordan, Deirdre F. (1988). Rights and Claims of Indigenous People: Education and the Reclaiming of Identity. In Tove Skutnabb-Kangas and Jim Cummins (Eds.), *Minority Education: From Shame to Struggle.* Clevedon (United Kingdom): Multilingual Matters.

Jorgensen, Jens Normann (1979). *Linguistics and Politics in Bilingual Education.* Texas Linguistic Forum 15, Austin, Texas: University of Texas at Austin, Department of Linguistics.

Jorgensen, Jens Normann (1984). *Sociolinguistic Papers.* Copenhagen: Royal Danish School of Educational Studies.

Jorgensen, Jens Normann (1984). Communication Strategies as Phenomena Related to Boundaries of Ethnicity. *Multilingual and Multicultural Development, 5,* (3–4).

Jorgensen, Jens Normann (1987). Minority Language Speaking Students' First and Second Language Vocabulary. *Multilingual and Multicultural Development, 8* (1–2).

Jorgensen, Jens Normann (1988). Turkish Children's Communication Strategies in Danish. In Anne Holmen and others (Eds.), *Bilingualism and the Individual.* Clevedon (United Kingdom): Multilingual Matters.

Julliard, Jacques (1987, October 9, October 15). La France aux mille mosquées. *Le nouvel observateur.*

Jungbluth, P. and Driessen, G. (1989). Onderwijs in eigen taal en cultuur. Pretenties aanzienlijk, verwachtingen gering. *Pedagogische Studien, 66,* 52–60.

Just, Wolf-Dieter (1985a). Einwanderungsgeschichte und Ausländerpolitik in den Hauptaufnahmeländern der EG—ein Überblick. In *Wanderarbeiter in der EG.* vol. 1. Munich: Kaiser.

Just, Wolf-Dieter (1985b). Die Situation der (Im-)Migrantenkinder—Vergleichende Analyse. In *Wanderarbeiter in der EG.* vol. 1. Munich: Kaiser.

Just, Wolf-Dieter (1985c). Selbstorganisation der Wanderarbeitnehmer in der EG. In *Wanderarbeiter in der EG.* vol. 1. Munich: Kaiser.

Kagan, Spencer (1986). Cooperative Learning and Sociocultural Factors in Schooling. In *Beyond Language: Social and Cultural Factors in Schooling Language Minority Students.* Los Angeles: Evaluation, Dissemination and Assessment Center, California State University.

Kagitçibasi, Çigdem (1989). Child Rearing in Turkey: Implications for Immigration and Intervention. In Lotty Eldering and Jo Kloprogge (Eds.), *Different Cultures—Same School: Ethnic Minority Children in Europe.* Amsterdam: Swets & Zeitlinger.

Kalantzis, Mary, Cope, Bill, and Slade, Diana (1989). *Minority Languages and Dominant Culture.* London: Falmer Press.

Kanavakis, Michael (1982). Die Einstellung griechischer Eltern zum bayerischen Beschulungsmodell. In Michael Damanakis and Hans H. Reich (Eds.), *Ausländerunterricht: Schulrechtliche, bildungspolitische und unterrichtsorganisatorische Beiträge.* Essen/Landau: ALFA.

Kaplan, Roger (1992). Through Kofi's Eyes. *The Atlantic,* April.

Karajannidis, Dimitrios (1982). Leitlinien der griechischen Botschaft. In Michael Damanakis and Hans H. Reich (Eds.), *Ausländerunterricht: Schulrechtliche, bildungspolitische und unterrichtsorganisatorische Beiträge.* Essen/Landau: ALFA.

Karaman, Muharrem (1980). *Problèmes scolaires des enfants Turcs. Code et pratiques des populations immigrées: identité culturelle et modèles de socialisation.* Brussels: Ministère de l'Education nationale et de Culture Française.

Kastoryano, Riva (1989). L'identité turque immigrée. *Migrants-Formation, 76,* March.

Kastoryano, Riva (1992). Relations interethniques et formes d'intégration. In Pierre-André Taguieff (Ed.), *Face au racisme, 2: Analyses, hypothèses, perspectives.* Paris: Éditions La Découverte.

Kemenade, Joos van (1983). Onderwijs en culturele identiteit. In Nitha Neuwahl and Aletta de Raad (Eds.), *Kinderen van medelanders: Buitenlandse kinderen in de Nederlandse samenleving.* Deventer (The Netherlands): Van Loghum Slaterus.

Kepel, Gilles (1987). *Les banlieues de l'Islam.* Paris: Éditions du Seuil.

Kepel, Gilles (1991). *La revanche de Dieu.* Paris: Éditions du Seuil.

Kepel, Gilles (1993, May 6). Interview by Sylviane Stein: L'exploitation du malaise beur. *L'Express.*

Kepel, Gilles (1994). *A l'ouest d'Allah.* Paris: Éditions du Seuil.

Kerr, A. N. (1984). Language and Education of Immigrants' Children in Sweden. In Chris Kennedy (Ed.), *Language Planning and Language Education.* London: George Allen & Unwin.

Khellil, Mohand (1991). *L'intégration des Maghrébins en France.* Paris: Presses universitaires de France.

Khleif, Bud B. (1991).The Place of Arabic in Identity Maintenance of Moroccans in The Netherlands: An Exploratory Study of Some School Textbooks. In Koen Jaspaert and Sjaak Kroon (Eds.), *Ethnic Minority Languages and Education.* Amsterdam/Lisse: Swets & Zeitlinger.

Kibbe, Pauline R. (1946). *Latin Americans in Texas*. Albuquerque (NM): University of New Mexico Press.

Kim, Bok-Lim (1988). The Language Situation of Korean Americans. In Sandra Lee McKay and Sau-ling Wong (Eds.), *Language Diversity: Problem or Resource?* Cambridge (MA): Newbury House, 1988.

Kirp, David L. (1991). Textbooks and Tribalism in California. *The Public Interest, 104*, Summer.

Klein, Reva (1992a, March 15). Saturday Is the Only Alternative. *The Times Educational Supplement.*

Klein, Reva (1992b, October 23). Issues of Islam. *The Times Educational Supplement*,

Klein, Reva (1993, Hune 25). Islam in West London. *The Times Educational Supplement.*

Klein, Reva (1994, September 9). Lost for Words in an Unequal World. *The Times Educational Supplement.*

Kleinfeld, J. (1975). Positive Stereotyping: The Cultural Relativist in the Classroom. *Human Organization, 34*.

Klooss, Wolfgang (1988). *Vom Bikulturalismus zum kanadischen Multikulturalismus. Historische Grundlagen und gesellschaftliche Implikationen eines politischen Programms. Einwandererland USA/Gastarbeiterland BRD*. Berlin: ARGU-MENT-Sonderband AS 163.

Kloosterman, Alphons (1983). Internationale schakelklassen (ISK). In Nitha Neuwahl and Aletta de Raad (Eds.), *Kinderen van nedelanders: Buitenlandse kinderen in de Nederlandse samenleving*. Deventer (The Netherlands): Van Loghum Slaterus.

Kloosterman, Alphons (1986). OETC in het voortgezet onderwijs. *Onderwijs in eigen taal en cultuur, MOER* 1–2.

Kloprogge, Jo. (1989). Etnische minderheden in het onderwijs: wat gebeurt er in her onderzoek? *Samenwijs, 9* (6), February.

Kloss, Heinz (1977). *The American Bilingual Tradition*. Rowley (MA): Newbury House.

Kluckhohn, Clyde and Leighton, Dorothea (1946). *The Navajo*. Cambridge (MA): Harvard University Press

Knijpstra, Harm (1991). NT2 leerplan meertalige klas. *Samenwijs, 11* (6), February.

Knijpstra, Harm (1993a). Te eng gezichtsveld. *Samenwijs, 13* (7), March.

Knijpstra, Harm (1993b). Blij met onderzoek. *Samenwijs, 13* (10), June.

Köbben, A.J.F. (1985). Oordeel en discriminatie. In J.S. Weiland and J.H.P. Paelinck (Eds.), *Etnische minderheden: Wetenschap en Beleid*. Amsterdam: Boom Meppel.

Köbben, A.J.F (1988). Tussen optimisme en pessimisme. In F. Lindo (Ed.), *Balans van het minderhedenbeleid: Vier jaar na de Nota*. Utrecht: Nederlands Centrum Buitenlanders.

Koch-Arzberger, Claudia (1985). *Die schwierige Integration*. Opladen (Germany): Westdeutscher Verlag.

Koekebakker, Olof (1990). *Immigrant in Europa*. Utrecht: Mederlands Centrum Buitenlanders.

Koeslag, Mieke and Dronkers, Jaap (1993). *Overadvisering en de schoolloopbanen van migrantenleerlingen en autochtone leerlingen in het voortgezet onderwijs*. Amsterdam: SCO-Kohnstamm Instituut, Universiteit van Amsterdam.

Kohler, Janine (1990). Les perplexités d'une enseignante. *Hommes & Migrations* 1129–1130 (February-March).

Kohn, Hans (1967). *The Idea of Nationalism*. New York: Collier Books.

Koot, Willem, Tjon-a-Ten, Varina and Uniken Venema, Petrien (1985). *Surinaamse kinderen op school*. Muiderberg (The Netherlands): Dick Coutinho.

Kossmann, E.H., (1978). *The Low Countries 1780–1940*. Oxford: Clarendon Press.

Kotkin, Joel (1992). *Tribes*. New York: Random House.

Kramer, Betty Jo (1991). Education and American Indians: The Experience of the Ute Indian Tribe. In Margaret A. Gibson and John U. Ogbu (Eds.), *Minority Status and Schooling*. New York: Garland.

Krashen, Stephen D. (1981). Bilingual Education and Second Language Acquisition Theory. In *Schooling and Language Minority Students: A Theoretical Framework*. Los Angeles: California State Department of Education.

Krashen, Stephen D. (1982). *Principles and Practice in Second Language Acquisition*. Oxford: Pergamon.

Krashen, Stephen D. (1983). Second Language Acquisition Theory and the Preparation of Teachers: Toward a Rationale. In James E. Alatis and others (Eds.), *Applied Linguistics and the Preparation of Second Language Teachers*. Washington, DC: Georgetown University Press.

Krashen, Stephen D. (1991). Sheltered subject matter teaching. *Cross Currents, 18*, Winter, 183–188.

Krashen, Stephen D. and Biber, Douglas (1988). *On Course: Bilingual Education's Success in California*. Sacramento: California Association for Bilingual Education.

Krieger-Krynicki, Annie (1988). The Second Generation: The Children of Muslim Immigrants in France. In Tomas Gerholm and Yngve Georg Lithman (Eds.), *The New Islamic Presence in Western Europe*. London: Mansell.

Kroon, Sjaak (1990). *Opportunities and Constraints of Community Language Teaching*. New York: Waxmann Muenster.

Kühl, Joergen (1987). Zur Bedeutung der Ausländerbeschäftigung für die Bundesrepublik Deutschland. In Helga Reimann and Horst Reimann (Eds.). *Gastarbeiter: Analyse und Perspektiven eines sozialen Problems*. Opladen (Germany): Westdeutscher Verlag.

Kugelmann, Cilly and Löw-Beer, Peter (1984). Bürger, Mitbürger und das ewige Durcheinander vom Miteinander. Ein Puzzle. In Ahmet Bayaz, Mario Damolin, and Heiko Ernst (Eds.), *Integration: Anpassung an die Deutschen?* Weinheim and Basel: Beltz Verlag.

Lahdenpera, Juoko (988). Barn från etniske minoriteter i svenskan skolan. Mågnåriga erfarenheter med modersmålklasser. In Christian Horst (Ed.), *Den Flerkulturelle Udfordring: Socialisation og børn fra etniske mindretal*, Copenhagen: Kultursociologiske Skrifter nr. 24.

Lambert, Wallace E. (1984). An Overview of Issues in Immersion Education. In *Studies on Immersion Education*. Sacramento: California State Department of Education.

Lambert, Wallace, E. and Cazabon, Mary (1994). *Students' Views of the Amigos Program*. Santa Cruz (CA): The National Center for Research on Cultural Diversity and Second Language Learning.

Lambert, Wallace E. and Taylor, Donald M. (1988). Assimilation versus Multiculturalism: The Views of Urban Americans. *Sociological Forum, 3* (1).

Lambert, Wallace E. and Taylor, Donald M. (1990). *Coping with Cultural and Racial Diversity in Urban America*. New York: Praeger.

Lambert, Wallace E. and Tucker, G. Richard (1972). *Bilingual Education of Children: The St. Lambert Experiment*. Cambridge (MA): Newbury House.

Landry, Walter J. (1983). Future Lau Regulations: Conflict Between Language Rights and Racial Nondiscrimination. In Raymond V. Padilla, (Ed.), *Theory, Technology, and Public Policy on Bilingual Education*. Washington, DC: The National Clearinghouse for Bilingual Education.

Language Policy Task Force (1992). English and Colonialism in Puerto Rico. In James Crawford (Ed.), *Language Loyalties*. Chicago: University of Chicago Press.

Laosa, Luis M. (1979). Inequality in the Classroom: Observational Research on Teacher-Student Interactions. *Aztlan, 8* (283), 51–67.

Laosa, Luis M. and Henderson, Ronald W. (1991). Cognitive Socialization and Competence: The Academic Development of Chicanos. In R.R. Valencia (Ed.), *Chicano School Failure and Success*. London: Falmer Press.

Lapeyronnie, Didier (1993). *L'individu et les minorités*. Paris: Presses universitaires de France.

Lapkin, Sharon and Cummins, Jim (1984). Canadian French Immersion Education: Current Administrative and Instructional Practices. In *Studies on Immersion Education*. Sacramento: California State Department of Education, 1984.

Laporte, Pierre E. (1984). Status Language Planning in Quebec: An Evaluation. In Richard Y. Bourhis (Ed.), *Conflict and Language Planning in Quebec*. Clevedon (United Kingdom): Multilingual Matters.

Laquière, Marc (1992). Welkom op school? *Samenwijs, 13* (2), October.

Laquière, Marc (1993). Einde discriminatie? *Samenwijs, 14* (1), September.

Laquière, Marc (1994). Het loopt (nog) niet van een leien dakje. *Samenwijs, 15* (1–2), September-October.

Lara, Julia and Hoffman, Ellen (1990). *School Success for Limited English Proficient Students: The Challenge and State Response*. Washington: Council of Chief State School Officers.

Larsen-Freeman, Diane (1985). *Overview of Theories of Language Learning and Acquisition. Issues in English Language Development*. Rosslyn (VA): The National Clearinghouse for Bilingual Education.

Larsen-Freeman, D. and Long, M.H. (1991). *An Introduction to Second Language Acquisition Research*. New York: Longman.

Lau v. Nichols. In Keith A. Baker and de Kanter, Adriana A. (Eds.). (1983). *Bilingual Education: A Reappraisal of Federal Policy*. Lexington: D.C. Heath.

Layton-Henry, Zig (1985). Great Britain. In Tomas Hammar (Ed.), *European Immigration Policy: A Comparative Study*. Cambridge: Cambridge University Press.

Leake, Donald (1990, November 28). Averting "A Lifetime of Segregation," *Education Week*.

Leake, Donald and Leake, Brenda (1992). African-American Immersion Schools in Milwaukee: A View From the Inside. *Phi Delta Kappan*, June.

Le Bras, Hervé (1988). La France, pays d'immigration. In *L'Immigration dans l'histoire nationale*. Paris: CEFISEM.

Leca, Jean (1992). Nationalité et citoyenneté dans l'Europe des immigrations. In Jaqueline Costa-Lascoux and Patrick Weil (Eds.), *Logiques d'états et immigrations*. Paris: Éditions Kimé.

Leclerc, Gerard (1985). *La bataille de l'école: 15 siècles d'histoire, 3 ans de combat*. Paris: Denoel.

L'Ecole québécoise et les communautés culturelles. Montreal: Ministère de l'Education, 1985.

Lee, Carol D. (1992). Profile of an Independent Black Institution: African-Centered Education at Work. *Journal of Negro Education, 61* (2), Spring.

Lee, Everett S. and Rong, Xue-lan (1988). The Educational and Economic Achievement of Asian-Americans. *The Elementary School Journal, 88* (5).

Lee, Yongsook (1991). Koreans in Japan and the United States. In Margaret A. Gibson and John U. Ogbu (Eds.), *Minority Status and Schooling*. New York: Garland.

Leeman, Yvonne (1995). Over koude en warme scholen. *Samenwijs 15* (5), January.

Leemans, R., Verhulst, J. and J. Xhoffer, J. (1983). *Vademecum migrantenonderwijs*. Lier (Belgium): J. Van In.

Legrand, Louis (1981). *L'école unique: à quelles conditions?* Paris: Scarabée.

Leibowicz, Joseph (1992). Official English: Another Americanization Campaign? In James Crawford (Ed.), *Language Loyalties*. Chicago: University of Chicago Press.

Leibowitz, Arnold H. (1971). A History of Language Instruction in American Indian Schools: The Imposition of English by Government Policy. In *Bilingual Education for American Indians*, Washington: Bureau of Indian Affairs.

Leman, Johan (1985a). The Foyer-Project: How a Confusing Trilingual Situation Can Be Converted into an Advantage for Immigrant Children in Brussels. In *Four Years Bicultural Education in Brussels: An Evaluation*. Brussels: The Foyer Committee of Bicultural Education.

Leman, Johan (1985b). The Foyer Project: A Brussels Model of Bicultural Education in a Trilingual Situation. *Studi Emigrazione/Etudes Migrations, 23* (78), June.

Leman, Johan (1990). Multilingualism as Norm, Monolingualism as Exception: The Foyer Model in Brussels. In Michel Byram and Johan Leman (Eds.), *Bicultural and Trilingual Education*. Clevedon (United Kingdom): Multilingual Matters.

Leman, Johan (1991). Between Bi- and Intercultural Education: Projects in Dutch™ Language Kindergartens and Primary Schools in Brussels. In Koen Jaspaert and Sjaak Kroon (Eds.), *Ethnic Minority Languages and Education*. Amsterdam/Lisse: Swets & Zeitlinger.

Leman, Johan (1993). The Bicultural Programmes in the Dutch-Language School System in Brussels. In Hugo Baetens Beardsmore (Ed.), *European Models of Bilingual Education*. Clevedon (United Kingdom): Multilingual Matters.

Lemann, Nicholas (1991). The Other Underclass. *The Atlantic Monthly,* December.

Lemberger, N. (1992). *Bilingual Teachers' Voices.* Paper presented at AERA, San Francisco, CA.

Lemco, Jonathan (1992). Quebec's "Distinctive Character" and the Question of Minority Rights. In James Crawford (Ed.), *Language Loyalties*. Chicago: University of Chicago Press.

Les principaux passages de l'avis du Conseil d'Etat. *Hommes & Migrations* 1129–1130 (February-March) 1990.

Lessow-Hurley, Judith (1990). *The Foundations of Dual Language Instruction.* New York: Longman.

Leunessen, Janine (1994). Beter les in eigen taal. *Samenwijs, 14* (6), February.

Leurin, Marcel (1985). *Querying the Intercultural Approach.* Strasbourg: Council of Europe.

Leveau, Rémy (1988), The Islamic Presence in France. In Tomas Gerholm and Yngve Georg Lithman (Eds.). *The New Islamic Presence in Western Europe.* London: Mansell.

Levine, J. (1990). Responding to Linguistic and Cultural Diversity in the Teaching of English as a Second Language. In J. Levine (Ed.), *Bilingual Learners and the Mainstream Curriculum* (pp. 11–28). New York: Falmer Press.

Levy, David J. (1986). Here Be Witches! "Anti-Racism" and the Making of a New Inquisition. In Frank Palmer (Ed.), *Anti-Racism—An Assault on Education and Value*. London: Sherwood Press.

Lewis, E. Glyn (1978). The Morality of Bilingual Education. In Alatis, James, E. (Ed.). *International Dimensions of Bilingual Education*. Washington: Georgetown University.

Lewis, Gordon K.(1968). *Puerto Rico: Freedom and Power in the Caribbean.* New York: Harper Torchbooks.

Lewis, Oscar (1966). The Culture of Poverty. *Scientific American, 215*, October.

Lewis, Ramon, Rado, Marta, and Foster, Lois (1982). Secondary School Students' Attitudes towards Bilingual Learning in Schools. *Australian Journal of Education, 26* (3).

Liauzu, Claude, Henry-Lorcerie, Françoise, and Liauzu, Josette (1989). *Immigration et école: la pluralité culturelle: État des questions.* Dossiers documentaires. Aix-en-Provence: Travaux et Documents de l'I.R.E.M.A.M.

Liensol, Bruno (1992). Photographie et typologie des ZEP de la période 1990–1993; Évolutions dans les établissements situés en ZEP depuis 1982. In *L'Évaluation des zones d'éducation prioritaires*. Paris: Ministère de l'Éducation nationale.

Lijphart, Arend (1968). *The Politics of Accommodation: Pluralism and Democracy in the Netherlands.* Berkeley: University of California Press.

Liljegren, Thomas and Ullman, Lilian (1981). *Interim Report 1. Compulsory School Leavers in 1979 with Home Languages Other Than Swedish.* (Roger G. Tanner, Transl.) Stockholm: National Swedish Board of Education.

Liljegren, Thomas and Ullman, Lilian (1982). *Interim Report 4. Compulsory School Leavers in 1979 with Home Languages Other Than Swedish.* (Roger G. Tanner, Transl.) Stockholm: National Swedish Board of Education.

Linde, Sylvia G. and Lofgren, H. (1988). The Relationship between Medium of Instruction and School Achievement for Finnish-speaking Students in Sweden. *Language, Culture and Curriculum, 1* (2).

Lindholm, K.J. (1990). Bilingual Immersion Educaton: Criteria for Program Development. In Padilla, A.M., Fairchild, H.H., Valadez, C.M. (Eds.), *Bilingual Education: Issues and Strategies*. (Pp. 91–105). Newbury Park (CA): SAGE.

Lindholm, K. J. (1991). Theoretical Assumptions and Empirical Evidence for Academic Achievement in Two Languages. *Hispanic Journal of Behavioral Sciences, 13* (1), 3–17.

Lindholm, K.J. and Alclan, Z.A. (1991). Bilingual Proficiency as a Bridge to Academic Achievement. Results from Bilingual/Immersion Programs. *Journal of Education, 173* (2), 99–113.

Lines, Patricia M. (1993). Parents and Their Informational Resources: A Reassessment of Findings From Alum Rock. Presentation at the American Education Research Association Annual Meeting in Atlanta, April.

Linguistic Minorities Project (1985). *The Other Languages of England*. London: Routledge and Kegan Paul.

Lithman, Yngve Georg (1988). Social Relations and Cultural Continuities: Muslim Immigrants and their Social Networks. In Tomas Gerholm and Yngve Georg Lithman (Eds.), *The New Islamic Presence in Western Europe*. London: Mansell.

Local Experience of Experimental Introductory Courses and Supplementary Summer Courses for Young Immigrants Attending Upper Secondary School. Stockholm: National Swedish Board of Education, 1978.

Lockwood, Holly, (1987). *Support Services for Limited-English Proficient Khmer and Laotian at Lowell High School*. Chelsea (MA): Metropolitan Indochinese Children and Adolescent Services, September.

Lodge, Bert and Sanders, Claire (1990, August 17). CRE Accused of Putting Down Christians. *The Times Educational Supplement*.

Löfgren, Horst (1984). Immigrant Adolescents in Sweden. *Pedagogical Bulletin*, University of Lund.

Löfgren, Horst (1986). *Bilingual Instruction of Immigrant Children: A Theoretical Overview and Results from Empirical Research*. Malmö (Sweden): Malmö School of Education, University of Lund.

Löfgren, Horst (1991). *Elever med annat hemspråk än Svenska*. Malmö: Institutionen for pedagogik och specialmetodik.

Löfgren, Horst and Ouvinen-Birgerstam, Pirjo (1982). A Bilingual Model for the Teaching of Immigrant Children. *Multilingual and Multicultural Development, 3* (4).

Lomotey, Kofi (1992). Independent Black Institutions: African-Centered Education Models. *Journal of Negro Education 61* (4), Fall.

Long, M.H. (1983). Native Speaker/Non-native Speaker Conversation and the Negotiation of Comprehensible Input. *Applied Linguistics, 4* (2), 126–141.

Long, M.H. and Porter, P.A. (1985). Group Work, Interlanguage Talk, and Second Language Acquisition. *TESOL Quarterly, 19* (2), 207–228.

Loos, Rinus de and Calbo, Sjoerd (1989). Samenwerking Nederlandse en Buitenlandse leerkrachten in basisschool. *Samenwijs*, January.

Lopez, Julian T. (1980). *Self-concept and Academic Achievement of Mexican-American Children in Bilingual Bicultural Programs*. Dissertation. United States International University.

Lorcerie, Françoise (1990). L'école pourrait être un laboratoire de civilité. *Hommes & Migrations*, 1129–1130 (February-March).

Lorimer, R. (1984). *The Nation in the Schools*. Toronto: Ontario Institute for Studies in Education.

Lorwin, Val R. (1966). Belgium: Religion, Class, and Language in National Politics. In Robert A. Dahl (Ed.), *Political Oppositions in Western Democracies*. New Haven: Yale University Press.

Lubbers, Ruud (1989). Het Europa van de Burger. In *Migranten in her Europa van de Burger*. Utrecht: Mederlands Centrum Buitenlanders.

Lucas, T. (1993). Secondary Schooling for Students Becoming Bilingual. In M.B. Arias and U. Casanova (Eds.), *Bilingual Education: Politics, Practice, Research*. (Pp. 113–143). Ninety-second yearbook of the National Society for the Study of Education, Part II. Chicago: University of Chicago Press.

Lucas, T., Henze, R., and Donato, R. (1990). Promoting the Success of Latino Language-minority Students: An Exploratory Study of Six High Schools. *Harvard Educational Review, 60* (3), 315–340.

Luchtenberg, Sigrid (1984). Diskriminierung ausländischer Kinder im Unterricht? Darstellung und Wege zu ihrem Abbau. *International Review of Education, 30* (4).

Luebke, Frederick (1978). The Germans. In John Higham (Ed.), *Ethnic Leadership in America*. Baltimore: Johns Hopkins University Press.

Lum, Philip A. (1978). The Creation and Demise of San Francisco Chinatown Freedom Schools: One Response to Desegregation. *Amerasia Journal 5* (1), 57–73.

Lynch, James (1989). International Interdependence: Swann's Contribution. In Gajendra K. Verma (Ed.), *Education for All: A Landmark in Pluralism*. London: Falmer.

Lyons, James J. (1990). The Past and Future Directions of Federal Bilingual-education Policy. *The Annals of the American Academy of Political and Social Science, 508*, March.

MacDonald, Barry, Adelman, C., Kushner, S., and Walker, R. (1982). *Bread and Dreams—A Case Study of Bilingual Schooling in the USA*. Norwich (England): Center for Applied Research in Education.

Mace-Matluck, B.J. (1990). The Effective Schools Movement: Implications for Title VII and Bilingual Education Projects. *Annual Conference Journal NABE '88–89*. (Pp. 83–95). Washington, DC: NABE.

Macias, Reynaldo F. (1979). Language Choice and Human Rights in the United States. In James E. Alatis and G. Richard Tucker (Eds.), *Language in Public Life*. Washington, DC: Georgetown University.

Macias, Reynaldo F. (1985). National Language Profile of the Mexican-origin Population in the United States. In Walker Connor (Ed.), *Mexican-Americans in Comparative Perspective*. Washington, DC: The Urban Institute.

Macias, Ysidro Ramon (1974). Description of the Chicano Movement (1970). In Sol Cohen (Ed.), *Education in the United States: A Documentary History*. (Pp. 2944–2948). New York: Random House.

Mackey, William F. (1984). Bilingual Education and Its Social Implications. In John Edwards (Ed.), *Linguistic Minorities, Policies and Pluralism*. London: Academic Press.

Made-Yuen, Mary van der (1986). Chinees OETC in Nederland. *Onderwijs in eigen taal en cultuur, MOER 1–2.*

Madrid, Arturo (1990). Official English: A False Policy Issue. *The Annals of the American Academy of Political and Social Science, 508*, March.

Madsen, William (1964). *Mexican-Americans of South Texas*. New York: Holt, Rinehart and Winston.

Mahler, Gerhart (1983). Bildungspolitische Schwerpunkte. In Gerhart Mahler and Michael Steindl (Eds.), *Zweitsprache Deutsch fur Ausländerkinder*. Donauworth: Auer.

Mahnig, Hans (1992). Immigration et émancipation des minorités aux Pays-Bas. In Jaqueline Costa-Lascoux and Patrick Weil (Eds.), *Logiques d'états et immigrations*. Paris: Éditions Kimé.

Malaurie, Guillaume (1990, February 16). Islam: le débat escamoté. *L'Express.*

Malherbe, Jacques (1994, September 21). Tchador à l'école: la réponse de Bayrou. *Le Figaro.*

Mallea, John (1984). Minority Language Education in Quebec and Anglophone Canada. In Richard Y. Bourhis (Ed.), *Conflict and Language Planning in Quebec*. Clevedon (United Kingdom): Multilingual Matters.

Marchi, Loredana (1985). Un processo di integrazione: Momenti di un cammino nel progretto italiano—fiammingo a Laken. In *Four Years Bicultural Education in Brussels: An Evaluation*. Brussels: The Foyer Committee of Bicultural Education, 1985.

Marschalck, Peter (1984). *Bevölkerungsgeschichte Deutschlands im 19. und 20. Jahrhundert*. Frankfurt am Main: Suhrkamp.

Marschalck, Peter (1990). Language in Immigration: Creativity and Linguistic Mobility. In Michel Byram and Johan Leman (Eds.), *Bicultural and Trilingual Education*. Clevedon (United Kingdom): Multilingual Matters.

Marshall, Jane (1994, September 23). Compromise Sought over Muslim Veils. *The Times Educational Supplement*.

Martinson, Jane (1993, February 25). Racial Attacks Drive Pupils Out. *The Times Educational Supplement*.

Masemann, V. (1978). Ethnography of the Bilingual Classroom. *International Review of Education, 24* (3).

Massenet, Michel (1994). *Sauvage Immigration*. Paris: Éditions du Rocher.

Masson, C.N. and De Jong, W. (1985). Leerprestaties op scholen met hoge concentraties allochtone leerlingen. In Mart-Jan de Jong (Ed.). *Allochtone kinderen op Nederlandse scholen: Prestaties, problemen en houdingen*. Lisse (The Netherlands): Swets & Zeitlinger.

Maton, Els (1993). Nieuwkomersprojekt. *Samenwijs, 13* (5), January.

Matute-Bianchi, Maria Eugenia (1986). Ethnic Identities and Patterns of School Success and Failure among Mexican-Descent and Japanese-American Students in a California High School: An Ethnographic Analysis. *American Journal of Education 95* (1), November.

Matute-Bianchi, Maria Eugenia (1991). Situational Ethnicity and Patterns of School Performance among Immigrant and Nonimmigrant Mexican-Descent Students. In Margaret A. Gibson and John U. Ogbu (Eds.), *Minority Status and Schooling*. New York: Garland.

Maurais, Jacques (1991). A Sociolinguistic Comparison Between Québec's Charter of the French Language and the 1989 Language Laws of Five Soviet Republics. In Kjell Herberts and Christer Laurén (Eds.), *Papers from the Sixth Nordic Conference on Bilingualism*. Clevedon (United Kingdom): Multilingual Matters.

Mauri, R. (1980). L'enseignement de la langue et de la culture italiennes. In *Codes et pratiques des populations immigrées: identité culturelle et modèles de socialisation*. Brussels: Ministère de l'Education Nationale et de la Culture Française.

Mayer, Nonna (1992). Racisme et antisémitisme dans l'opinion publique française. In Pierre-André Taguieff (Ed.), *Face au racisme, 2: Analyses, hypothèses, perspectives*. Paris: Éditions La Découverte.

McArthur, Edith K.(1993). *Language Characteristics and Schooling in the United States, a Changing Picture: 1979 and 1989*. Washington, DC: National Center for Education Statistics.

McConnell, Beverly B. (1983). Individualized Bilingual Instruction: A Validated Program Model Effective with Both Spanish and Asian Language Students. In Raymond V. Padilla (Ed.), *Theory, Technology, and Public Policy on Bilingual Education*. Rosslyn (VA): The National Clearinghouse for Bilingual Education.

McDonnell, L.M. and Hill, P.T. (1993). *Newcomers in American Schools. Meeting the Educational Needs of Immigrant Youth*. Santa Monica, CA: RAND.

McGavin, Harvey (1993, October 15). Catalans' future perfect creates present tense. *The Times Educational Supplement*.

McGroarty, Mary (1988). Second Language Acquisition Theory Relevant to Language Minorities: Cummins, Krashen, and Schumann. In Sandra Lee McKay and Sau-ling Cynthia Wong (Eds), *Language Diversity: Problem or Resource?* Cambridge (MA): Newbury House.

McInerney, Dennis M. (1987). Teacher Attitudes to Multicultural Curriculum Development. *Australian Journal of Education 31*, 2, 129–144.

McKay, Sandra Lee (1988). Weighing Educational Alternatives. In S.L. McKay and Sau-ling Cynthia Wong (Eds.), *Language Diversity: Problem or Resource?* Cambridge (MA): Newbury House.

McLaughlin, Barry (1985). *Second-Language Acquisition in Childhood: Volume 2. School-Age Children.* 2d ed. Hillsdale (NJ): Lawrence Erlbaum.

McLean, Martin (1985). Private Supplementary Schools and the Ethnic Challenge to State Education in Britain. In C. Brock and W. Tulasiewicz (Eds.), *Cultural Identity and Educational Policy.* London: Croom Helm.

Mead, Margaret (1982). Ethnicity and Anthropology in America. In George De Vos and Lola Romanucci-Ross (Eds.), *Ethnic Identity: Cultural Continuities and Change.* Chicago: University of Chicago.

Medina, Marcello (1988). Hispanic Apartheid in American Public Education. *Educational Administration Quarterly, 24* (3), August, 336–349.

Medina, Marcello and Sacken, D.M. (1988). Passing Arizona's Bilingual Education Legislation: A Case Study in the Management of Policy Symbols. *Educational Policy, 2* (3), September. Mehrlander, Ursula (1986). The Second Generation of Migrant Workers in Germany: The Transition from School to Work. In Dietmar Rothermund and John Simon (Eds.), *Education and the Integration of Ethnic Minorities.* New York: St. Martin's Press.

Meier, Kenneth J. and Stewart, Joseph, Jr. (1991). *The Politics of Hispanic Education.* Albany (NY): SUNY Press.

Meijerink, Joke and Appe, R. (1993). Voor spek en bonen. *Samenwijs, 13* (3), March.

Meijnen, G. Wim (1991). Cultural Capital and Learning Process. *International Journal of Educational Research, 15.*

Menk, Antje-Katrin (1986). Language Training and Social Integration of Migrants in the Federal Republic of Germany. In Dietmar Rothermund and John Simon (Eds.), *Education and the Integration of Ethnic Minorities.* New York: St. Martin's Press.

Merino, Barbara J. (1991). Promoting School Success for Chicanos: The View from Inside the Bilingual Classroom. In R.R. Valencia (Ed.), *Chicano School Failure and Success.* London: Falmer Press.

Met, M. (1994). Teaching content through a second language. In F. Genesee (Ed.), *Educating Second Language Children. The Whole School, the Whole Curriculum, the Whole Community.* (Pp. 159–182). Cambridge: Cambridge University Press.

Meyer-Ingwerson, Johannes (1988). Auch sie haben eine Muttersprache. *Gemeinsam,* June.

Miedema, Wietske (1988). Alle aandacht geven aan organisatorische, professionele, didactische en inhoudelijke verbetering van zwarte school. *Samenwijs,* April.

Miles, Jack (1985). The Coming Immigration Debate. *The Atlantic Monthly,* April.

Miles, Jack (1994). A Bold Proposal on Immigration. *The Atlantic Monthly,* June.

Milk, R.D. (1990). Integrating Language and Content: Implications for Language Distribution in Bilingual Classrooms. In R. Jacobson and C. Faltis (Eds.), *Language Distribution Issues in Bilingual Schooling.* Clevedon (United Kingdom): Multilingual Matters.

Milk, R.D. (1993). Bilingual Education and English as a Second Language: The Elementary school. In M.B. Arias and U. Casanova (Eds.), *Bilingual Education: Politics, Practice, and Research.* (Pp.88–112). Ninety-second Yearbook of the National Society for the Study of Education, Part 2, Chicago: The University of Chicago Press.

Miller, Kate (1990, September 14). Welsh Training Sparks a Monmouth Rebellion. *The Times Educational Supplement.*

Miller, Mark J. (1992). La politique américaine: la fin d'une époque? In Jaqueline Costa-Lascoux and Patrick Weil (Eds.), *Logiques d'états et immigrations.* Paris: Éditions Kimé.

Minces, Juliette (1988). Les ambiguités de l'immigration. In *L'Immigration dans l'histoire nationale.* Paris: CEFISEM.

Minderhout, Rob (1993). Allochtone leerling krijgt te weinig kansen. *Inzicht, 127* (2), April.

Ministère de l'Education (1984). *Services éducatifs aux communautés culturelles. Les classes d'accueil, les classes de françisation, l'enseignement des langues d'origine 1973–1984.* Montreal.

Ministère de l'Education nationale (1986). *Educational Developments in Belgium.* Brussels.

Ministerial Advisory Committee on Multicultural and Migrant Education (1986). *Education in, and for, a Multicultural Victoria.* Melbourne, Victoria: Ministry of Education.

Ministry of Education and Science [The Netherlands] (1983). *Beleidsnotitie Onderwijs in Eigen Taal en Cultuur.* The Hague (The Netherlands).

Ministry of Education and Science (1991a). Ethnic Minority Language Teaching in the Dutch Educational System in the Nineties. In Koen Jaspaert and Sjaak Kroon (Eds.), *Ethnic Minority Languages and Education.* Amsterdam/Lisse: Swets & Zeitlinger.

Ministry of Education and Science (1991b). *Nederlands als tweede taal op lerarenopleidingen.* Zoetermeer (The Netherlands).

Ministerie van Onderwijs [Flanders, Belgium] (1985). *Informatiebrochure voor buitenlandse leerkrachten van het Nederlandstalig basis- of secondair onderwijs in Belgie.* Brussels.

Minow, M. (1985). Learning to Live with the Dilemma of Difference: Bilingual and Special Education. *Law and Contemporary Problems, 48* (2).

Mizrahi, Maurice (1970). The Italian Americans. In Theodore Andersson and Mildred Boyer (Eds.), *Bilingual Schooling in the United States* II. Austin (TX): Southwest Educational Development Laboratory.

"Mit der Nadel einen Brunnen graben." *Der Spiegel,* February 27, 1989.

Mogdil, S., Verma, G., Mallick, K. and Mogdil, C. (Eds.) (1989). *Multicultural Education: The Interminable Debate.* London: Falmer Press.

Mol, Paulien (1995). Onderwijsprestaties van alloctone leerlingen verbeteren. *Samenwijs, 15* (7), March.

Moldenhawer, B. (1992). *Dig og mig og vi to. Evaluaering af tokulturelle klasser.* Copenhagen: Institut for Filosofi, Pædagogik & Retorik.

Molesky, J. (1988). Understanding the American Linguistic Mosaic: A Historical Overview of Language Maintenance and Language Shift. In Sandra Lee McKay & Sau-ling Cynthia Wong (Eds). *Language Diversity: Problem or Resource?* Cambridge; Newbury House.

Moll, L.C. (1988). Some Key Issues in Teaching Latino Students. *Language Arts, 65*(5), 465–472.

Montero-Sieburth, Martha (1988). Conceptualizing Multicultural Education: From Theoretical Approaches to Classroom Practice. *Equity and Choice, 4* (3) Spring.

Montero-Sieburth, Martha and Perez, Marla (1987). Echar Pa'lante, Moving Onward: The Dilemmas and Strategies of a Bilingual Teacher. *Anthropology and Education Quarterly, 18.*

Montvalon, Dominique de and Léotard, Marie-Laure de (1989, November 1989). Les consignes du Sphinx. *L'Express.*

Morales, Luis Muñoz (1970). El Idioma y el Status. In Erwin H. Epstein (Ed.), *Politics and Education in Puerto Rico: A Documentary Survey of the Language Issue.* Metuchen (NJ): Scarecrow Press.

Morokvasic, Mirjana (1986). Doubles orientations des jeunes yougoslaves. In Georges Abou-Sada and Hélène Milet (Eds.), *Générations issues de l'immigration*. Paris: Arcantère Éditions.

Mousavizadeh, Nader (1995, January 30). Sanctuary. *The New Republic*.

Moynihan, Daniel Patrick (1993). *Pandaemonium: Ethnicity in International Politics*. Oxford University Press.

Mullis, I.V.S. (et al.) (1994). *NAEP 1992 Trends in Academic Progress*. Washington, DC:National Center for Educational Statistics.

Muñoz, Marie-Clair (1987). Le rôle de la langue dans l'affirmation de l'appartenance nationale. In *L'Immigration en France: Le choc des cultures*. L'Arbresle: Centre Thomas More.

Muñoz Hernandez, Shirley and Santiago Santiago, Isaura (1983). Toward a Qualitative Analysis of Teacher Disapproval Behavior. In Raymond V. Padilla (Ed.), *Theory, Technology, and Public Policy on Bilingual Education*. Rosslyn (VA): The National Clearinghouse for Bilingual Education.

Murphy, Brian (1993). *The Other Australia*. Cambridge University Press.

Muus, Philip (1992). Internationale migratie en de Europese Gemeenschap met bijzondere aandacht voor Nederland. *Migrantenstudies, 8* (4).

Muysken, Pieter and Vries, J.W. de (1982). Een sociolinguïstische kijk op het taalgebruik van buitenlandse arbeiders. In René Appel, Cees Cruson, Muysken and De Vries (Eds.), *Taalproblemen van buitenlandse arbeiders en hun kinderen*, Muiderberg (The Netherlands): Coutinho.

Naess, Ragnar (1988). Being an Alevi Muslim in South-western Anatolia and in Norway: The Impact of Migration on a Heterodox Turkish Community. In Tomas Gerholm and Yngve Georg Lithman (Eds.), *The New Islamic Presence in Western Europe*. London: Mansell.

Nair, Sami. (1990). A propos de l'intégration. *Hommes & Migration*s 1129–1130, February-March.

Nakipoglu-Schimand, Berrin (1988). Zur alphabetisierung turkischer Kinder. In *"Und im Ausland sind die Deutschen auch Fremde!" Interkulturelles Lernen in der Grundschule*. Frankfurt am Main: Arbeitkreis Grundschule.

Natale, J. (1994). Homeroom to the world. *The Executive Educator, 16* (1), 14–18.

National Center for Education Statistics (1992). *Digest of Education Statistics 1992*. Washington, DC: U.S. Department of Education

National Coalition of Advocates for Students (1988). *New Voices: Immigrant Students in U. S. Public Schools*. Boston.

National Commission on Secondary Education for Hispanics (1984). *"Make Something Happen"—Hispanics and Urban High School Reform*. Washington, DC: Hispanic Policy Development Project.

National Council for Mother Tongue Teaching (1985). The Swann Report: Education for All? *Multilingual and Multicultural Development, 6* (6).

National Education Goals Panel, (1994). *The National Education Goals Report: Building a Nation of Learners: 1994*. Washington, DC.

National Swedish Board of Education (1980). *The 1980 Compulsory School Curriculum*, Stockholm.

Native American Language Act (1992). In James Crawford (Ed.), *Language Loyalties*. Chicago: University of Chicago Press.

Naylor, Fred (1989). *Dewsbury: The School Above the Pub*. London: Claridge Press.

Navarre, François-Régis (1990, February 23). Clichy: du rouge au noir. *L'Express*.

Nebioglu, Ersan (1989). Quelques aspects de l'organisation de la vie religieuse des turcs en France. *Migrants-Formation 76*, March.

Neuhaus, Richard John (1984). *The Naked Public Square: Religion and Democracy in America*. Grand Rapids (Michigan): Eerdmans.

New Mexico Legislature (1992). English Plus Resolution. In James Crawford (Ed.). *Language Loyalties*. Chicago: University of Chicago Press.

New South Wales Department of Education (1983). *Multicultural Education Policy Statement.* Sydney (Australia): Multicultural Education Centre.

Nieke, Wolfgang, Budde, H., and Henscheid, R. (1983). *Struktuelle Benachteiligung auslaendischer Jugendlicher: Die Marginalisierung der zweiten Generation.* Essen/Landau: ALFA.

Noboa, Abdin (1980). Hispanics and Desegregation: Summary of Aspira's Study on Hispanic Segregation Trends in U.S. School Districts. *Metas, 1* (3), 1–24.

Norbelie, Bertil (1983). Mother Tongue Teaching in Classes Comprising Two Nationalities. In *Compendium of Information on Intercultural Education Schemes in Europe.* Strasbourg: Council of Europe.

Novak, Michael (1973). *The Rise of the Unmeltable Ethnics.* New York: Macmillan Paperback.

Nyhan, David (1994, September 4). So, Is It to Be Cpl. or Cmdr. Clinton? *The Boston Globe.*

Office of Pastoral Research (1982). *Hispanics in New York: Religious, Cultural and Social Experiences.* New York: Archdiocese of New York.

Ogbu, John U. (1986). The Consequences of the American Caste System. In Ulric Neisser (Ed.), *The School Achievement of Minority Children: New Perspectives.* Hillsdale (NJ): Lawrence Erlbaum Associates.

Ogbu, J. (1987). Variability in Minority School Performance: A Problem in Search of an Explanation. *Anthropology and Education Quarterly, 18* (4), 312–357.

Ogbu, John U. (1991a). Immigrant and Involuntary Minorities in Comparative Perspective. In Margaret A. Gibson and John U. Ogbu (Eds.), *Minority Status and Schooling.* New York: Garland.

Ogbu, John U. (1991b). Low School Performance as an Adaptation: The Case of Blacks in Stockton, California. In Margaret A. Gibson and John U. Ogbu (Eds.), *Minority Status and Schooling.* New York: Garland.

Ogbu, John, U. and Matute-Bianchi, Maria Eugenia (1986). Understanding Sociocultural Factors: Knowledge, Identity, and School Adjustment. In *Beyond Language: Social and Cultural Factors in Schooling Language Minority Students.* Los Angeles: Evaluation, Dissemination and Assessment Center, California State University, Los Angeles.

Ohannessian, Sirarpi (1971). Planning Conference for a Bilingual Kindergarten Program for Navajo Children. In *Bilingual Education for American Indians.* Washington: Bureau of Indian Affairs.

OIDEL (Organisation internationale pour le développement de la liberté d'enseignement) (n.d.). *Liberté d'enseignement. Les textes.* Geneva.

Oirbans, Peter (1986). Impressies over onderwijs in eigen taal en cultuur in Belgie. *Samenwijs, 6* (9), May.

Okey, Robin (1991). Education and Nationhood in Wales, 1850–1940. In Janusz Tomiak (Ed.), *Schooling, Educational Policy, and Ethnic Identity.* New York: New York University Press.

Oliveras, Candido (1970). Acerca de la Enseñanza en los Idiomas Español e Ingles: Entrevista. In Erwin H. Epstein (Ed.), *Politics and Education in Puerto Rico: A Documentary Survey of the Language Issue.* Metuchen (NJ): Scarecrow Press.

Olneck, Michael R. (1990). The Recurring Dream: Symbolism and Ideology in Intercultural and Multicultural Education. *American Journal of Education, 98* (2), February.

Olneck, Michael R. (1993). Terms of Inclusion: Has Multiculturalism Redefined Equality in American Education? *American Journal of Education 101,* (3), May.

Olsen, Laurie (1988). *Crossing the Schoolhouse Border: Immigrant Students and the California Public Schools.* San Francisco: California Tomorrow.

Olsen, Roger E. and Leone, B. (1994). Sociocultural Processes in Academic, Cognitive, and Language Development. *TESOL Matters, 4* (3), June/July.

Olson, Shelly L.(1990). *Language Shift and Bilingual Education: A Long-Term Analysis of a National Sample of Mexican-American Sophomores.* Paper presented at the AERA, Boston.

O'Malley, J. Michael (1981). *Language Minority Children with Limited English Proficiency in the United States.* Rosslyn (VA): National Clearinghouse for Bilingual Education.

Ontmoetingsonderwijs: Een onderwijskundige invulling van de ontmoeting tussen moslims en christenen op een p. c. basisschool. Hoevelaken: Christelijk Pedagogisch Centrum, 1985.

Ontwerp-Minderhedennota. The Hague: Ministerie van Binnenlandse Zaken, 1981.

Opper, Susan (1985). *The Function of Home and Parents in an Intercultural Society.* Strasbourg: Council of Europe, March.

Orfield, Gary (1978). *Must We Bus? Segregated Schools and National Policy.* Washington, DC: The Brookings Institution.

Orfield, Gary (1986). Hispanic Education: Challenges, Research, and Policies. *American Journal of Education,* 95 (1), November.

Organisation for Economic Cooperation and Development (1987). *Immigrants' Children at School.* Paris.

Organisation for Economic Cooperation and Development, SOPEMI: Continuous Reporting System on Migration, 1988. Paris, 1989 [and subsequent reports].

Organisation for Economic Cooperation and Development (1994). *Trends in International Migration: Annual Report 1993.* Paris.

Ornan, Olga (1986). Onderwijs in het Papiamento. *Onderwijs in eigen taal en cultuur, MOER 1–2.*

Ørzerk, Kamil Zihni. (1988). Språklige minoriteter i Norge og erfaringer fra tospråklig undervisningen av en del språklige minoriteter i tokulturelle klasser i Oslo. In Christian Horst (Ed.), *Den Flerkulturelle Udfordring: Socialisation og børn fra etniske mindretal,* Copenhagen: Kultursociologiske Skrifter.

Otheguy, Ricardo (1982). Thinking About Bilingual Education: A Critical Appraisal. *Harvard Educational Review,* 52 (3), August.

Ovando, Carlos J. and Collier, Virginia P. (1985). *Culture. Bilingual and ESL Classrooms: Teaching in Multicultural Contexts.* New York: McGraw-Hill.

Overbeek, Henk (1994). Mondialisering en regionalisering. *Migrantenstudies, 10* (2).

Oxford-Carpenter, R., Pol, L., Lopez, D., Stupp, P., Gendel, M., and Peng, S. (1984). *Demographic Projections of Non-English-Language-Background and Limited-English-Proficient Persons in the United States to the Year 2000 By State, Age, and Language Group.* Rosslyn (VA): The National Clearinghouse for Bilingual Education.

Padilla, Amado M. (1982). Bilingual Schools: Gateways to Integration or Roads to Separation. In Joshua A. Fishman and Gary D. Keller (Eds.), *Bilingual Education for Hispanic Students in the United States.* New York: Teachers College Press.

Padilla, Amado, M. and Liebman, Ellen (1982). Language Acquisition in the Bilingual Child. In Joshua A. Fishman and Gary D. Keller (Eds.), *Bilingual Education for Hispanic Students in the United States.* New York: Teachers College Press.

Padilla, Elena (1958). *Up From Puerto Rico.* New York: Columbia University Press.

Padilla, Raymond D. (1983). Articulating a Positive Orientation Toward Bilingual Education. In Raymond V. Padilla (Ed.), *Theory, Technology, and Public Policy on Bilingual Education.* Rosslyn (VA):The National Clearinghouse for Bilingual Education.

Padrun, Ruth (1983). The Saint-Quentin-en-Yvelines Intercultural Project. In *Compendium of Information on Intercultural Education Schemes in Europe.* Strasbourg: Council of Europe.

Paelman, Filip (1995). Migranten een zegen voor het onderwijs of andersom? *Samenwijs, 15* (7), March.

Palmer, Frank (1986a). English: Reducing Learning to Short-cut Skills. In Dennis O'Keefe (Ed.), *The Wayward Curriculum*. London: The Social Affairs Unit.

Palmer, Frank (1986b). *Moral Understanding and the Ethics of Indignation. in Anti-Racism—An Assault on Education and Value*. London: The Sherwood Press.

Pantoja, Antonia (1970). Prepared Statement. In *Hearings before the Select Committee on Equal Educational Opportunity of the United States Senate: Part 8—Equal Educational Opportunity for Puerto Rican Children*. Washington, DC, November.

Papendorp, B.J.L. and Teunissen, J.M.F. (1983). Projekt Thuisland. In *Compendium of Information on Intercultural Education Schemes in Europe*. Strasbourg: Council of Europe.

Papi-Rovini, Franca (1984). Pointe de vue de la responsable des cours de langue et culture italienne. In Micheline Rey (Ed.). *Une pédagogie interculturelle*. Berne (Switzerland): Commission nationale suisse pour l'UNESCO.

Parrenas, C.S. and Parrenas, F.Y. (1993). Cooperative Learning, Multicultural Functioning, and Student Achievement. In L. Malave (Ed.), *NABE '90–'91 Annual Conference Journal*. vol. 4, Washington, DC: National Association for Bilingual Education.

Parekh, Bhikhu (1986). The Concept of Multi-Cultural Education. In Sohan Mogdil, Gajendra Verma, Kanka Mallick, and Celie Mogdil (Eds.), *Multicultural Education: The Interminable Debate*. London: Falmer Press.

Parekh, Bhikhu (1989). The Hermeneutics of The Swann Report. In Gajendra K. Verma (Ed.), *Education for All: A Landmark in Pluralism*. London: Falmer Press.

Parker-Jenkins, Marie (1994, October 21). Islam Shows Its Diverse Identities. *The Times Educational Supplement, 13*.

Parsons, Talcott (1975). Some Theoretical Considerations on the Nature and Trends of Change of Ethnicity. In Nathan Glazer and Daniel P. Moynihan (Eds.), *Ethnicity: Theory and Experience*. Cambridge: Harvard University Press.

Passel, Jeffrey S. and Barry Edmonston, Barry (1994). Immigration and Race: Recent Trends in Immigration to the United States. In Barry Edmonston and Jeffrey S. Passel (Eds.), *Immigration and Ethnicity*. Washington, DC: The Urban Institute.

Passmore, Biddy (1993, September 30). Section 11 Cuts "appall" Shephard. *The Times Educational Supplement*.

Paulston, C.P. (1978a). Rationales for Bilingual Educational Reforms: A Comparative Assessment. *Comparative Education Review, 22* (3), 402–419.

Paulston, C.P. (1978b). Biculturalism: Some Reflections and Speculations. *TESOL Quarterly, 12* (4), 369–380.

Paulston, Christina Bratt (1980b). *Bilingual Education: Theories and Issues*. Rowley (MA): Newbury House.

Paulston, Christina Bratt (1982). *Swedish Research and Debate about Bilingualism*. Stockholm: National Swedish Board of Education.

Paulston, Christina Bratt (1980a). Bilingual/Bicultural Education. *Review of Research in Education, 6*.

Paulston, Christina Bratt (1992a). Ethnic Relations and Bilingual Education: Accounting for Contradictory Data. In *Sociolinguistic Perspectives on Bilingual Education*. Clevedon (United Kingdom): Multilingual Matters. [Originally published in 1975]

Paulston, Christina Bratt (1992b). Theoretical Perspectives on Bilingual Education Programs. In *Sociolinguistic Perspectives on Bilingual Education*. Clevedon (United Kingdom): Multilingual Matters. [Originally published in 1977]

Paulston, Christina Bratt (1992c). Biculturalism: Some Reflections and Speculations. In *Sociolinguistic Perspectives on Bilingual Education*. Clevedon (United Kingdom): Multilingual Matters. [Originally published in 1978]

Paulston, Christina Bratt (1992d). Quantitative and Qualitative Research on Bilingual Education in the United States. In *Sociolinguistic Perspectives on Bilingual Education*. Clevedon (United Kingdom): Multilingual Matters. [Originally published in 1981]

Paulston, Christina Bratt (1992e). Language Planning. In *Sociolinguistic Perspectives on Bilingual Education*. Clevedon (United Kingdom): Multilingual Matters. [Originally published in 1984]

Paulston, Christina Bratt, with R.G. Paulston (1992). Language and Ethnic Boundaries. In *Sociolinguistic Perspectives on Bilingual Education*. Clevedon (United Kingdom): Multilingual Matters. [Originally published in 1977]

Pautard, André (1986, October 31)). Immigrés: qui deviendra français. *L'Express*.

Pearce, Simon (1986). Swann and the Spirit of the Age. In Dennis O'Keefe (Ed.). *The Wayward Curriculum*. London: The Social Affairs Unit.

Pease-Alvarez, L., Garcia, E.E., and Espinosa, K. (1991). Effective Instruction for Language Minority Students: An Early Childhood Case Study. *Early Childhood Research Quarterly, 6* (3), 347–363.

Pedagogisch Centrum Enschede, Project Moedertaal Klassen (1983a). *Enschedese Project Cahiers, Deel I, Doel en Organisatie van het Project.*

Pedagogisch Centrum Enschede, Project Moedertaal Klassen (1983b). *Enschedese Project Cahiers, Deel II, Het onderwijs in het arabisch.*

Pedagogisch Centrum Enschede, Project Moedertaal Klassen (1983c). *Enschedese Project Cahiers, Deel III, Het onderwijs in her turks.*

Peeters, Kris (1992). De kiezerssnede. *Samenwijs, 12* (7), March.

Penninx, Rinus (1986). International Migration in Western Europe Since 1973: Developments, Mechanisms and Controls. *International Migration Review, 20* (4), Winter.

Penninx, Rinus and Selier, Frits (1992). Theorievorming over internationale migratie: een historisch overzicht en een stand van zaken. *Migrantenstudies, 8* (4).

Perotti, Antonio (1986). Les Italiens en France: Un archipel à découvrir. *Migrants-Formation, 67*, December.

Perotti, Antonio (1987). Presentation of the Theme and the Objectives of the Meeting. In *The Culture of Immigrant Populations and Cultural Policies: Socio-cultural Innovations in the Member States of the CDCC*. Strasbourg: Council of Europe.

Perret-Clermont, Anne-Nelly (1984). Risques et chances des rencontres intergroupes. In Micheline Rey (Ed.), *Une pédagogie interculturelle*. Berne (Switzerland): Commission nationale suisse pour l'UNESCO.

Perrineau, Pascal (1992). Le Front national: du désert à l'enracinement. In Pierre-André Taguieff (Ed.), *Face au racisme, 2: Analyses, hypothèses, perspectives*. Paris: Éditions La Découverte.

Persson, Diane (1986). The Changing Experience of Indian Residential Schooling: Blue Quills, 1931–1970. In Barman, J., Hébert, Y., and McCaskill, D. (Eds.), *Indian Education in Canada. vol. 1: The Legacy*. Vancouver: University of British Columbia Press.

Peters, Alice Perez (1979). *Self-Esteem as it Relates to Reading Facility and Bilingual Schooling of Puerto Rican Students*. Dissertation. Loyola University of Chicago.

Petersen, William (1975). On the Subnations of Western Europe. In Nathan Glazer and Daniel P. Moynihan (Eds.), *Ethnicity: Theory and Experience*. Cambridge: Harvard University Press.

Philips, S. (1972). Participant Structures and Communicative Competence: Warm Springs Children in Community and Classrooms. In C.B. Cazden, V.P. John, and D. Hymes (Eds.), *Functions of language in the classroom*. (Pp. 370–394). New York: Teachers College Press.

Phillipson, Robert (1988). Linguicism: Structures and Ideologies in Linguistic Imperialism. In Tove Skutnabb-Kangas and Jim Cummins (Eds.), *Minority Education: From Shame to Struggle*. Clevedon (United Kingdom): Multilingual Matters.

Phinney, J.S. (1991). Ethnic Identity and Self-esteem: A Review and Integration. *Hispanic Journal of Behavioral Sciences, 13* (2), 193–208.

Pica, T. (1991). Input as a Theoretical and Research Construct: From Corder's Original Definition to Current Views. *IRAL, 29,* (3), 185–196.

Pica, T. (1992). The Textual Outcomes of Native Speaker–Non-native Speaker Negotiation: What Do They Reveal About Second Language Learning? In C. Kramsch and S. McConnell-Ginet (Eds.), *Text and Context. Cross-disciplinary Perspectives on Language Study.* (Pp. 198–237). Lexington (MA): D.C. Heath.

Pica, T. (1994). Research on Negotiation: What Does it Reveal about Second-language Learning Conditions, Processes, and Outcomes? *Language Learning, 44* (3).

Pica, T. and Doughty, G. (1985). Input and Interaction in the Communicative Language Classroom: A Comparison of Teacher-fronted and Group Activities. S.M. Gass and C.G. Madden (Eds.), *Input in Second Language Acquisition.* Rowley (MA): Newbury House.

Piccone, Paul (1993–1994). Confronting the French New Right: Old Prejudices or a New Political Paradigm. *Telos 98–99,* Winter-Spring.

Pierce, L. V. (1987). *Cooperative Learning: Integrating Language and Content-area Instruction.* Washington, DC: National Clearinghouse for Bilingual Education.

Pierre-Brossolette, Sylvie (1989, November 10). Laïcité: enfin un débat d'idées. *L'Express.*

Pierrot, Alain (1988). L'école et l'immigration. In *L'Immigration dans l'histoire nationale.* Paris: CEFISEM.

Pierrot, Alain (1990). La règle du jeu. *Hommes & Migrations* 1129–1130 (February-March).

Pierrot, Alain (1991). Le nous est-il haïssable? *Hommes & Migrations* 1146 (September).

Pino Romero, A.(1980). L'expérience d'intégration de cours d'espagnol en Belgique. In *Codes et pratiques des populations immigrées: identité culturelle et modèles de socialisation.* Brussels: Ministère de l'Education Nationale et de la Culture Française.

Piroth, Gunter (1982). Das Mainzer Modell zur schrittweisen Integration auslaendischen Schuler. In Michael Damanakis and Hans H. Reich (Eds.), *Ausländerunterricht: Schulrechtliche, bildungspolitische und unterrichtsorganisatorische Beiträge.* Essen/Landau: ALFA.

Pitman, A. Lynette (1995). The Debacle of Native American Education. Typescript [paper for seminar with the author].

Platiel, Suzy (1989). Les langues d'Afrique noire en France: Des langues de culture face a une langue de communication. *Migrants-Formation, 76,* March.

Plummer, Robert (1988, May 6). When Variety Can Add Too Much Spice to School Life. *The Times Educational Supplement.*

Poblete, Renato (1986). Anomie and the "Quest for Community"; The Formation of Sects Among the Puerto Ricans of New York. In Francesco Cordasco and Eugene Bucchioni (Eds.), *Puerto Rican Children in Mainland Schools.* Metuchen (NJ): Scarecrow Press, 1986.

Pole, J.R. (1978). *The Pursuit of Equality in American History.* Berkeley: University of California Press.

Pommerin, Gabrielle (1988a). Gemeinsame Grundschule fur alle Kinder—Hirngespinst oder konkrete Utopie? In *"Und im Ausland sind die Deutschen auch Fremde!" Interkulturelles Lernen in der Grundschule.* Frankfurt am Main: Arbeitkreis Grundschule.

Pommerin, Gabrielle (1988b). Clustern macht Spass—Kreatives Schreiben im interkulturellen Kontext. In *"Und im Ausland sind die Deutschen auch Fremde!" Interkulturelles Lernen in der Grundschule.* Frankfurt am Main: Arbeitkreis Grundschule.

Ponty, Janine (1986). Quand être Polonais se conjugue en français. *Migrants Formation*, December.

Ponty, Janine (1988). L'immigration polonaise. In *L'Immigration dans l'histoire nationale*. Paris: CEFISEM.

Poole, Millicent E. and Sachs Judith, M. (1989). Education for All: Social Reconstruction or Status Quo? In Gajendra K. Verma (Ed.), *Education for All: A Landmark in Pluralism*. London: Falmer Press.

Porcher, Louis (1978a). Introduction. In Louis Porcher (Ed.), *La scolarisation des enfants étrangers en France*. Paris: CREDIF.

Porcher, Louis (1978b). Pour et contre les classes d'initiation. In Louis Porcher (Ed.), *La scolarisation des enfants étrangers en France*. Paris: CREDIF.

Porcher, Louis (1978c). Unilingisme et multilinguisme. In Louis Porcher (Ed.), *La scolarisation des enfants étrangers en France*. Paris: CREDIF.

Porter, John (1975). Ethnic Pluralism in Canadian Perspective. In Nathan Glazer and Daniel P. Moynihan (Eds.), *Ethnicity: Theory and Experience*. Cambridge: Harvard University Press.

Porter, Rosalie Pedalino (1990). *Forked Tongue: The Politics of Bilingual Education*. New York: Basic Books.

Porter, Rosalie Pedalino (1995). A Review of the U.S. GAO Study on Limited-English Speaking Students. *READ Perspectives*, *II* (1), Spring.

Porter, J.R. and Washington, R.E. (1979). Black Identity and Self-Esteem: A Review of Studies of Black Self-Concept, 1968–1978. *Annual Review of Sociology, 5*.

Portes, Alejandro and Rumbaut, R.G. (1990). *Immigrant America*. Berkeley: University of California Press.

Portes, Alejandro and Zhou, Min (1994). Should Immigrants Assimilate? *The Public Interest, 116*, Summer.

Portmann, Rosemarei (1988). An der Zweisprachigkeit allein kann es nicht liegen. In *"Und im Ausland sind die Deutschen auch Fremde!" Interkulturelles Lernen in der Grundschule*. Frankfurt am Main: Arbeitkreis Grundschule.

Postel-Vinay, Karoline (1992). L'immigration au Japon: le tournant des années quartrevingt. In Jaqueline Costa-Lascoux and Patrick Weil (Eds.), *Logiques d'états et immigrations*. Paris: Éditions Kimé.

Predaris, Theodora G. (1984). American Indian/Alaskan Native Program Study. In *Educating the Minority Language Student: Classroom and Administrative Issues*. Rosslyn (VA): National Clearinghouse for Bilingual Education.

Prestage, Michael (1991, November 22). Parents Challenge "Enforced" Welsh. *The Times Educational Supplement*.

Prestage, Michael (1992, August 14). Opt-out Vote Sparks Welsh Language Row. *The Times Educational Supplement*.

Prestage, Michael (1993, March 12). First Welsh Primary Opts Out. *The Times Educational Supplement*.

Prewitt-Diaz, Joseph O. (1983). The Role of Bilingual Education in the Cultural Adjustment of Puerto Rican Students. In Raymond V. Padilla, (Ed.), *Theory, Technology, and Public Policy on Bilingual Education*. Rosslyn (VA): The National Clearinghouse for Bilingual Education.

Provinciale Dienst voor Onthaal van Gastarbeiders (1980). *Onderwijsnota. Migrantenkinderen in onze scholen: aandachtspunten en suggesties*. Hasselt (Belgium): Provincie Limburg.

Purkey, S.C. and Smith, M.P. (1983). Effective Schools: A Review. *The Elementary School Journal, 83*(4), 427–452.

Pyke, Nicholas (1991, September 13). Bengalis Shy Away from Separatism. *The Times Educational Supplement*.

Pyke, Nicholas (1994, October 21). Discontentment in Search of a Voice. *The Times Educational Supplement*.

Pyke, Nicholas (1995, February 24). Muslims Vow to Try Again. *The Times Educational Supplement*.

Quatremer, Jean (1989, November 18). L'expression religieuse tolérée mais cadrée. *Libération*.

Rado, Marta (1978). The Language of Instruction of Immigrant Children: An Australian Solution. *International Review of Education 24* (3).

Radtke, Frank-Olaf (1992). Multikulturalismus: Ein postmoderner Nachfahre des Nationalismus? In *Vorgänge* (Germany), *3* (31).

Ramakers, J. (1993). Onpraktische pragmatiek. *Samenwijs, 13* (7), March.

Ramirez, M., III, Casteneda, A. (1974). *Cultural Democracy, Bicognitive Development and Education*. New York: Academic Press.

Ramirez, J. David and Merino, Barbara J. (1988). Classroom Talk in English Immersion, Early-exit and Late-exit Transitional Bilingual Education Programs. Typescript.

Ramirez, J. David, Yuen, S.D., Ramey, D.R., and Pasta, D. (1991). *Final Report: Longitudinal Study of Structured English Immersion Strategy, Early-Exit and Late-Exit Transitional Bilingual Education Programs for Language-Minority Children*. San Mateo (CA): Aguirre International.

Rashid, Hakim M. and Muhammad, Z. (1992). The Sister Clara Muhammad Schools: Pioneers in the Development of Islamic Education in America. *Journal of Negro Education 61* (2), Spring.

Rasmussen, Henrik Egede (1987). Det dur ikke at drukne indvandrerbørnene i sprog. *Samspil, 2*.

Rastoldo, F. and Rey, F. (1993). *Les filières après la classe d'accueil*. Geneva: Centre de Recherches Psychopédagogiques.

Rath, Jan (1991). *Minorisering: de sociale constructie van etnische minderheden*, Amsterdam: SUA.

Rath, J, Groenendijk, K., and Penninx, R. (1992). Nederland en de islam. Een programma van onderzoek. *Migrantenstudies, 8* (1).

Rath, J. and Meyer, A. (1994). Ruimte voor islamitisch godsdienstonderwijs op openbare basisscholen. *Migrantenstudies, 10* (1).

Ratteray, Joan Davis (1992). Independent Neighborhood Schools: A Framework for the Education of African Americans. *Journal of Negro Education, 61* (2), Spring.

Raufer, Xavier (1993, May 6). France: les sous-marins du FIS. *L'Express*.

Raun, Toivo U. (1987). *Estonia and the Estonians*. Stanford (CA): Hoover Institution Press.

Ravitch, Diane (1983). *The Troubled Crusade: American Education 1945–1980*. New York: Basic Books.

Ravitch, Diane (1990a). Multiculturalism. E Pluribus Plures. *The American Scholar*, Summer.

Ravitch, Diane (1990b). *What's At Stake With Multicultural Education?* New York: Center for Educational Innovation, Manhattan Institute for Policy Research.

Ravitch, Diane (1990c). Diversity and Democracy: Multicultural Education in Democracy. *Executive Educator*. Spring.

Ravitch, Diane (1990d, October 24). Multiculturalism Yes, Particularism No. *Chronicle of Higher Education*.

Ravitch, Diane (1990e). Diversity and Democracy: Multicultural Education in America. *American Educator*, Spring.

Raymond, Chris (1990, September 12). Global Migration Will Have Widespread Impact on Society, Scholars Say. *Chronicle of Higher Education*.

Rebaudière Paty, Madeleine (1986). Examen de la question de l'identité culturelle telle qu'elle surgit dans le champ des sciences sociales des vingt dernières années: Révision des paradigmes et question du sujet. In Georges Abou-Sada and Hélène Milet (Eds.), *Générations issues de l'immigration*. Paris: Arcantère Éditions.

Rebell, Michael A. and Block, Arthur R. (1982). *Educational Policy Making and the Courts*. Chicago: University of Chicago Press.

Recommandations de la Conférence suisse des directeurs cantonaux de l'instruction publique. In *La Suisse—un défi: Une approche de l'enseignement des langues nationales en Suisse*, Berne: CDIP 1987.

Redditt, S.A. (1992). *Working Together as One*. Dissertation. Boston: Boston University.

Regeringsnota over het Minderhedenbeleid. (1983). The Hague: Tweede Kamer. Zitting 1982–83.

Reich, Hans H. (1982). Die Rechtlinien der EG - Ansätze zu einer zweisprachigen Erziehung der Gastarbeiterkinder. In Michael Damanakis and Hans H. Reich (Eds.), *Ausländerunterricht: Schulrechtliche, bildungspolitische und unterrichtsorganisatorische Beiträge*. Essen/Landau: ALFA.

Reich, Hans H. (1991). Developments in Ethnic Minority Language Teaching within the European Community. In Koen Jaspaert and Sjaak Kroon (Eds.), *Ethnic Minority Languages and Education*. Amsterdam/Lisse: Swets & Zeitlinger.

Reich, Hans H. and Reid, Euan (1992). Education for Bilingualism. In Euan Reid and Hans Reich (Eds.), *Breaking the Boundaries: Migrant Workers' Children in the EC*. Clevedon (United Kingdom): Multilingual Matters.

Reid, Euan (1988). Linguistic Minorities and Language Education—The English Experience. *Multilingual and Multicultural Development, 9*, 1, and 2.

Reid, Euan (1989). English as a Second Language in England. In G. Tingbjorn (Ed.), *Svenska som Andrasprȧk*, Goteborg: Skriptor Forlag.

Rellini, Giampiero (1992). Les étrangers en Italie: une politique à l'épreuve des faits. In Jaqueline Costa-Lascoux and Patrick Weil (Eds.), *Logiques d'états et immigrations*. Paris: Éditions Kimé.

Rex, John (1985a). Integratie, multiculturalisme, of etnische en rassentegenstelling. In J.S. Weiland and J.H.P. Paelinck (Eds.), *Etnische minderheden: Wetenschap en Beleid*. Amsterdam: Boom Meppel.

Rex, John (1985b). Extract from . . . Introduction to the Report on the Development of Multicultural Education Policy in Four Local Education Authority Areas. In *Education for All: The Report of the Committee of Inquiry into the Education of Children from Ethnic Minority Groups* (the "Swann Report"). London: HMSO.

Rex, John (1986). Equality of Opportunity and the Ethnic Minority Child in British Schools. In Sohan Mogdil, Gajendra Verma, Kanka Mallick, and Celie Mogdil (Eds.), *Multicultural Education: The Interminable Debate*. London: Falmer.

Rex, John (1988). The Urban Sociology of Religion and Islam in Birmingham. In Tomas Gerholm and Yngve Georg Lithman (Eds.), *The New Islamic Presence in Western Europe*. London: Mansell.

Rex, John (1989). Equality of Opportunity, Multiculturalism, Anti-racism and "Education for All." In Gajendra K. Verma (Ed.), *Education for All: A Landmark in Pluralism*. London: Falmer.

Rey-von Allmen, Micheline (1979a). *L'éducation des enfants (de) migrants dans le canton de Genève: Vers une éducation interculturelle. Annuaire de l'instruction publique en Suisse*. Lausanne: Editions Payot.

Rey-von Allmen, Micheline (1979b). *Identité et intégration. Schule und Fremdarbeiterkinder*. Geneva: Schweizerische Konferenz der kantonalen Erziehungsdirektoren.

Rey-von Allmen, Micheline (1981). De la classe d'acceuil à une classe interculturelle. In *Etre migrant*, Berne: Peter Lang.

Rey-von Allmen, Micheline (1983). Conclusions: Main Lines of Intercultural Education. In *Compendium of Information on Intercultural Education Schemes in Europe*. Strasbourg: Council of Europe.

Rey-von Allmen, Micheline (1984). Pièges et défi de l'interculturalisme. *Éducation permanente, 75.*

Rey-von Allmen, Micheline (1986). *Former les enseignants à l'éducation interculturelle?* Strasbourg: Council of Europe.

Reyhner, Jon (1992). Policies toward American Indian Languages: A Historical Sketch. In James Crawford (Ed.), *Language Loyalties.* Chicago: University of Chicago Press.

Rich, Y. (1993). *Education and Instruction in the Heterogeneous Class.* Springfield (IL): Thomas Books.

Riehl, Carolyn (1985). Bilingual Education: An Introduction to the Issues. *Equity and Choice II, 1,* Fall. New York: ERIC Clearinghouse on Urban Education.

Rigaux, F. (1980). La Condition Juridique des travailleurs migrants en Belgique. In *Aspects socio-culturels et juridiques de l'immigration.* Brussels: Ministère de l'Éducation Nationale et de la Culture Française.

Ritsch, Wolfgang (1987). *Die Rolle des Islams fuer die Koranschulerziehung in der Bundesrepublik Deutschland.* Cologne: Pahl-Rugenstein.

Rixius, Norbert and Thurmann, Eike (1987). *Muttersprachlicher Unterricht fur ausländische Schuler.* Berlin: EXpress Ed.

Rodriguez, Ramon (1970). El Idioma Español con la Estatidad Entraña en Periodo de Disolucion: Comentarios de Rubén Del Rosario. In Erwin H. Epstein (Ed.), *Politics and Education in Puerto Rico: A Documentary Survey of the Language Issue.* Metuchen (NJ): Scarecrow Press.

Rodriguez, Richard (1983). *Hunger of Memory: The Education of Richard Rodriguez.* New York: Bantam Books.

Rodriguez, Richard (1992). The Romantic Trap of Bilingual Education. In James Crawford (Ed.), *Language Loyalties.* Chicago: University of Chicago Press.

Roegiers, J. (1983). Socicultureel leven in de Zuidelijke Nederlanden 1794–1814. In *Algemene Geschiedenis der Nederlanden 11,* Weesp: Fibula-Van Dishoeck.

Rogers, Rosemarie (1985). Migration Theory and Practice. In Walker Connor (Ed.), *Mexican-Americans in Comparative Perspective.* Washington, DC: The Urban Institute.

Rogers, Rosemarie (1993). Western European Responses to Migration. In Myron Weiner (Ed.), *International Migration and Security.* Boulder (CO): Westview Press.

Röhr-Sendlmeier, Una M. (1986). Die Bildungspolitik zum Unterricht für ausländische Kinder in der Bundesrepublik Deutschland—Eine kritische Betrachtung der vergangenen 30 Jahre. *Deutsch lernen, 11* (1).

Roossens, Eugeen (1989). Cultural Ecology and Achievement Motivation: Ethnic Minority Children in the Belgian System. In Lotty Eldering and Jo Kloprogge (Eds.), *Different Cultures—Same School: Ethnic Minority Children in Europe.* Amsterdam: Swets & Zeitlinger.

Rooy, Willemieke van (1986). OETC voor Spaanse, Kaapverdiaanse en Portugese kinderen. *Onderwijs in eigen taal en cultuur, MOER 1–2.*

Rosario, Rubén del (1977). *La lengua de Puerto Rico.* Rio Piedras: Editorial Cultural.

Rosen, Jeffrey (1995, January 30). The War on Immigrants. *The New Republic.*

Rossell, Christine H. (1989). The Effectiveness of Educational Alternatives for Limited English Proficient Children. Unpublished manuscript. Boston: Boston University.

Rossell, Christine H. (1991). Nothing Matters? A Critique of the Ramirez, et al. Longitudinal Study of Instructional Programs for Language Minority Children. Unpublished manuscript. Boston: Boston University.

Rossell, Christine H. and Baker, Keith (1995). The Educational Effectiveness of Bilingual Education: A Report to Pioneer Institute. Boston. Draft, quoted by permission.

Rossell, Christine H. and Ross, J. Michael (1985). The Social Science Evidence on Bilingual Education. Boston: Center for Applied Social Science, Boston University, Working Paper 85–6, May.

Rossell, Christine H. and Ross, J. Michael (1986). The Social Science Evidence on Bilingual Education. *Journal of Law and Education*, 15 (4), Fall.

Rossier, Robert E. (1985). A Critique of California's Evaluation of Programs for Students of Limited-English Proficiency. *READ Perspectives*, II (1), Spring.

Rotberg, Iris C. (1982). Some Legal and Research Considerations in Establishing Federal Policy in Bilingual Education. *Harvard Educational Review*, 52 (2), May.

Rout, Leslie B., Jr. (1976). *The African Experience in Spanish America*. Cambridge University Press.

Roux, Michel (1990). Vers un Islam français. *Hommes & Migrations* 1129–1130, February-March.

Rueda, Robert (1991). An Analysis of Special Education as a Response to the Diminished Academic Achievement of Chicano Students. In R.R. Valencia (Ed.), *Chicano School Failure and Success*. London: Falmer Press.

Ruiter, Jan Jaap de (1990). De taalsituatie van jonge Marokkanen in Nederland. *Migrantenstudies*, 6 (1).

Ruíz, Richard (1988). Orientations in Language Planning. In Sandra Lee McKay and Sau-ling Cynthia Wong (Eds), *Language Diversity: Problem or Resource?* Cambridge (MA): Newbury House.

Ruíz, Richard (1995). Language Planning Considerations in Indigenous Communities. *Bilingual Research Journal*, 19 (1).

Sacken, Donal M. and Medina, Marcello, Jr. (1990). Investigating the Context of State-Level Policy Formation: A Case Study of Arizona's Bilingual Education Legislation. *Educational Evaluation and Policy Analysis*, 12 (4).

Sahin, Numan Kema and Heyden, Manfred (1982). "Seiteneinsteiger": Zum besseren Verstaendnis einer Schulergruppe. In Helmut Birkenfeld (Ed.), *Gastarbeiterkinder aus der Turkei*. Munich: C.H. Beck.

Sahl, Freddy and Carl Skjelmose, Carl (1986). *Fremmed i skolen?* Tåstrup: Paedagogisk-Psykologisk Rådgivning.

Sahl, Freddy (1987). Er en to-kulturel identitet mulig? *Dansk Pædagogisk Tidsskrift*, 35 (3).

Saifullah Khan, Verity (1980). The "Mother-tongue" of Linguistic Minorities in Multicultural England. *Multilingual and Multicultural Development*, 1 (1).

Salameh, Eva-Kristina (1988). Svenska som andraspråk i førskolan. In Christian Horst (Ed.), *Den Flerkulturelle Udfordring: Socialisation og børn fra etniske mindretal*, Copenhagen: Kultursociologiske Skrifter.

Salinas, Guadalupe (1971). Mexican Americans and the Desegregation of Schools in the Southwest. *El Grito* 4, (4), 36–69.

Salom, Gaye (1989). Propos sur l'éxil turc: Comment defaire les valises? *Migrants-Formation*, 76 (March).

Samuda, Ronald (1986). The Canadian Brand of Multiculturalism: Social and Educational Implications. In Sohan Mogdil, Gajendra Verma, Kanka Mallick, and Celie Mogdil (Eds.), *Multicultural Education: The Interminable Debate*. London: Falmer.

San Miguel, Guadalupe, Jr. (1987a). The Status of Historical Research on Chicano Education. *Review of Educational Research*, 57 (4), Winter.

San Miguel, Guadalupe, Jr. (1987b). *"Let All Of Them Take Heed": Mexican Americans and the Campaign for Educational Equality in Texas, 1910–1981*. Austin (TX): University of Texas Press.

Sansone, Livio (1992). *Schitteren in de schaduw*. Amsterdam: Het Spinhuis.

Santiago, Isaura Santiago (1986). *Aspira v. Board of Education* Revisited. *American Journal of Education*, 95 (1), November.

Sarup, Madan (1986). *The Politics of Multiracial Education*. London: Routledge & Kegan Paul.

707

Savary, Alain, with Catherine Arditti (1985). *En toute liberté*. Paris: Hachette.

Saville-Troike, Muriel (1978). *Culture in the Classroom*. Rosslyn (VA): National Clearinghouse for Bilingual Education.

Saville-Troike, Muriel (1991). *Teaching and Testing for Academic Achievement: The Role of Language Development*. Occasional Papers in Bilingual Education. Washington, DC: National Clearinghouse for Bilingual Education.

Sayad, Abdelmalek (1987). L'Islam "immigré." In *L'Immigration en France: Le choc des cultures*. L'Arbresle: Centre Thomas More.

Scarcella, R.C. and Higa, C. (1981). Input, Negotiation, and Age Differences in Second Language Acquisition. *Language Learning, 31* (2), 409 -437.

Schalburg, Kirsten (1987). Den flerkulturelle skole. *Dansk Pådagogisk Tidsskrift, 35* (3), April.

Schalburg, Kirsten (1988). Børn fra etniske minoriteter i folkeskolen: Er kulturel integration mulig? In Christian Horst (Ed.), *Den Flerkulturelle Udfordring: Socialisation og børn fra etniske mindretal*, Copenhagen: Kultursociologiske Skrifter nr. 24.

Schemla, Elisabeth (1994, December 8–14). Taslima face aux filles voilées. *Le nouvel Observateur*.

Schierup, Carl-Ulrik (1987). *Integration? Invandrere, kultur og samfund*. Copenhagen: Billesø & Baltzer, 1987.

Schindler, Dominique (1982). *Etre migrant ou les données d'une vie*. Bern: Federal Office of Education and Science.

Schlesinger, Arthur M., Jr. (1992). *The Disuniting of America: Reflections on a Multicultural Society*. New York: W.W. Norton.

Schlossman, Steven (1983). Self-Evident Remedy? George I. Sanchez, Segregation, and Enduring Dilemmas in Bilingual Education. *Teachers College Record, 84* (4), 871–907.

Schmidt, Peter (1993, August 4). Study Finds Immigrants' Children Face Some Risks in Assimilating. *Education Week*.

Schmidt, Peter (1994, January 12). Desegregation Study Spurs Debate Over Equity Remedies. *Education Week*.

Schoeneberg, Ulrike (1985). Participation in Ethnic Associations: The Case of Immigrants in West Germany. *International Migration Review, 19* (3), Fall.

Schofield, J.W. and Sagar, H.A. (1983). Desegregation, School Practice, and Student Race Relations. In Rossell, C.H. and Hawley, W.D. (Eds.), *The Consequences of School Desegregation*. (Pp.58–102). Philadelphia: Temple University Press.

Schoten, Fons van and Wansink, Hans (1984). *De Nieuwe Schoolstrijd: Knelpunten en Conflicten in de hedendaagse onderwijspolitiek*. Utrecht: Bohn, Scheltema & Holkema.

Schumacher, Peter (1981). *De Minderheden*. Amsterdam: Van Gennep.

Schuricht, Klaus. (1982) Sinn und Aufgabe eines Faches Türkisch im Fächerkanon der deutschen Schule. In Helmut Birkenfeld (Ed.), *Gastarbeiterkinder aus der Türkei*. Munich: C.H. Beck.

Schwartz, Bernard (Ed.) (1970). *Statutory History of the United States: Civil Rights, Part I*. New York: Chelsea House.

Schwencke, H.J. (1994). Schoolstrijd in Den Haag. Veranderingen in de religiuze cultuur van Surinaamse Hindoes in Nederland. *Migrantenstudies, 10* (2).

Scruton, Roger (1986). The Myth of Cultural Relativism. In Frank Palmer (Ed.), *Anti-Racism—An Assault on Education and Value*. London: Sherwood Press.

Secada, Walter G. (1987). This Is 1987, Not 1980: A Comment on a Comment. *Review of Educational Research, 57* (3), Fall).

Secada, Walter G. (1990). Research, Politics and Bilingual Education. *The Annals of the American Academy of Political and Social Science, 508*, March.

Second Thoughts in Wales. *The Times Educational Supplement*, August 6, 1993.

Seidner, Stanley S. and Medina Seidner, Maria (1983). In the Wake of Conservative Reaction: An Analysis. In Raymond V. Padilla (Ed.), *Theory, Technology, and Public Policy on Bilingual Education*. Rosslyn (VA): The National Clearinghouse for Bilingual Education.

Seksig, Alain (1990). A l'école, l'intégration: rassembler ou différencier? *Hommes & Migrations* 1129–1130 (February-March).

Seksig, Alain (1992). Que peut l'école contre le racisme? In Pierre-André Taguieff (Ed.), *Face au racisme, 1: Les moyens d'agir*. Paris: Éditions La Découverte, 1992.

Seligson, Anne G. (1979). *Study of the Self-concept of Mexican-American Children in a Bilingual Program*. Dissertation. United States International University.

Seminario Internacional Sobre Educacion Bilingue (1986). Premisas. Unpublished manuscript. Oaxtepec, Mexico, November 2–6.

Sen, Faruk (1987). *Turks in the Federal Republic of Germany: Achievements, Problems, Expectations*. Bonn: Zentrum fur Türkeistudien.

Senior, Clarence (1965). *The Puerto Ricans: Strangers—Then Neighbors*. Chicago: Quadrangle Books.

Sexton, Patricia Cayo (1965). *Spanish Harlem: Anatomy of Poverty*. New York: Harper & Row.

Shadid, W. and Van Koningsveld, P.S. (1990). Islamitische basisscholen in Nederland. *Samenwijs, 1* (1), September.

Shafer, Susanne M. (1983). Australian Approaches to Multicultural Education. *Multilingual and Multicultural Development, 4* (6).

Shain, Yossi (1993). Democrats and Secessionists: US Diasporas as Regime Destabilizers. In Myron Weiner (Ed.), *International Migration and Security*. Boulder (CO): Westview Press.

Sharan, S. (1990). Cooperative Learning and Helping Behavior in the Multi-ethnic Classroom. In H.C. Foot, M.J. Morgan, and R.H. Shute (Eds.), *Children Helping Children*. (Pp. 151–176). New York: John Wiley & Sons.

Sheffer, Gabriel (1993). Ethnic Diasporas: A Threat to Their Hosts? In Myron Weiner (Ed.). *International Migration and Security*. Boulder (CO): Westview Press.

Sherington, Geoffrey (1980). *Australia's Immigrants 1788–1978*. Sydney: George Allen & Unwin.

Shimahara, Nobuo K. (1991). Social Mobility and Education: Burakumin in Japan. In Margaret A. Gibson and John U. Ogbu (Eds.), *Minority Status and Schooling*. New York: Garland.

Shujaa, Mwalimu J. (1992). Afrocentric Transformation and Parental Choice in African American Independent Schools. *Journal of Negro Education 61* (2), Spring.

Siguén, Miguel and Mackey, William F. (1987). *Education and Bilingualism*. London: Kogan Page.

Simon, John (1986). Models versus Reality, or, Let's Call Racism by Its Name. In Dietmar Rothermund and John Simon (Eds.), *Education and the Integration of Ethnic Minorities*. New York: St. Martin's Press.

Simons, H.J. (1985). Synthese van onderzoek en beleid ten aanzien van minderheden. In J.S. Weiland and J.H.P. Paelinck (Eds.), *Etnische minderheden: Wetenschap en Beleid*. Amsterdam: Boom Meppel.

Sitbon, Guy (1994, December 8, December 14). Quand les voiles tombent. *Le nouvel Observateur*.

Skerry, Peter (1989). Borders and Quotas: Immigration and the Affirmative-Action State. *The Public Interest, 96*, Summer.

Skerry, Peter (1993). *Mexican Americans: The Ambivalent Minority*, New York: Free Press.

Skerry, Peter (1995, January 30). The Black Alienation. *The New Republic*.

Skutnabb-Kangas, Tove. (1979). *Language in the Process of Cultural Assimilation and Structural Incorporation of Linguistic Minorities*. Rosslyn (VA): National Clearinghouse for Bilingual Education.

Skutnabb-Kangas, Tove (1981). Guest Worker or Immigrant—Different Ways of Reproducing an Underclass. *Multilingual and Multicultural Development, 2* (2).

Skutnabb-Kangas, Tove (1984a). Children of Guest Workers and Immigrants: Linguistic and Educational Issues. In John Edwards (Ed.), *Linguistic Minorities, Policies and Pluralism*. London: Academic Press.

Skutnabb-Kangas, Tove (1984b). Why Aren't All Children in the Nordic Countries Bilingual? *Multilingual and Multicultural Development, 5* (3–4).

Skutnabb-Kangas, Tove (1984c). *Bilingualism or Not: The Education of Minorities.* Clevedon (United Kingdom).

Skutnabb-Kangas, Tove (1988a). Multilingualism and the Education of Minority Children. In Tove Skutnabb-Kangas and Jim Cummins (Eds.), *Minority Education: From Shame to Struggle*. Clevedon (United Kingdom): Multilingual Matters.

Skutnabb-Kangas, Tove (1988b). Resource Power and Autonomy Through Ciscourse in Conflict—a Finnish Migrant School Strike in Sweden. In Tove Skutnabb-Kangas and Jim Cummins (Eds.), *Minority Education: From Shame to Struggle*. Clevedon (United Kingdom): Multilingual Matters.

Skutnabb-Kangas, Tove and Cummins, Jim (1988). Concluding Remarks: Language for Empowerment. In Tove Skutnabb-Kangas & Jim Cummins (Eds.) *Minority Education: From Shame to Struggle*. Clevedon (United Kingdom): Multilingual Matters.

Slavin, R.E. (1985). Cooperative Learning: Applying Contact Theory in Desegregated Schools. *Journal of Social Issues, 41* (3), 45–62.

Slavin, R.E. (1990). Cooperative Learning and Language Minority Students. Paper presented at the Annual Convention of the American Educational Research Association, Boston, April.

Smail, Messaoud (1988). Pour une nouvelle approche de l'enseignement de la langage et de la culture d'origine. In *Les algériens et l'enseignement de l'arabe en France*. Paris: Centre culturel algérien.

Smedt, Hilde de (1985a). Language Activation Within the Dutch-speaking Educational System for Infants Who Do Not Speak Dutch. In *Four Years Bicultural Education in Brussels: An Evaluation*. Brussels: The Foyer Committee of Bicultural Education.

Smedt, Hilde de (1985b). Didactical Realisation of Mother Tongue Education in the Bicultural Foyer Project. In *Four Years Bicultural Education in Brussels: An Evaluation*. Brussels: The Foyer Committee of Bicultural Education.

Smedt, Hilde de (1985c). The Turkish Project After One Year. In *Four Years Bicultural Education in Brussels: An Evaluation*, Brussels: The Foyer Committee of Bicultural Education, 1985.

Smedt, Hilde de (1985d). The Turkish Project After One Year. In *Four Years Bicultural Education in Brussels: An Evaluation*. Brussels: The Foyer Committee of Bicultural Education.

Smedt, Hilde de (1986). De didactische realisatie van het moedertaal-onderwijs binnen het bi-cultureel Foyer-project: de ervaringen van Italiaanse en Spaanse leerkrachten. *Onderwijs in eigen taal en cultuur, MOER, 1–2.*

Smeekens, Ludo (1985). The Foyer Bicultural Project: A Few Aspects of the Guidance in Educational Projects. In *Four Years Bicultural Education in Brussels: An Evaluation*. Brussels: The Foyer Committee of Bicultural Education.

Smeekens, Ludo (1990). Structural Change: From Monocultural to Bicultural Schools. In Michel Byram and Johan Leman (Eds.), *Bicultural and Trilingual Education*. Clevedon (United Kingdom): Multilingual Matters.

Smith, Iola (1987, May 8). A Passionate Campaigner Who Minds His Language. *The Times Educational Supplement.*

Smith, Iola (1988a, February 26). Tongue Sandwich. *The Times Educational Supplement.*

Smith, Iola (1988b, November 18). Exemption Sought for Native Speakers. *The Times Educational Supplement.*

Smith, Iola (1991, June 21). Black Pupils Will Study in Welsh. *The Times Educational Supplement.*

Smith, S.C. and Scott, J.J. (1990). *The Collaborative School: A Work Environment for Effective Instruction.* Eugene (OR): ERIC Clearinghouse on Educational Management.

Smolicz, J. J. (1983). Modification and Maintenance: Language Among School-children of Italian Background in South Australia. *Multilingual and Multicultural Development, 4* (5).

Smolicz, J. J. (1984). Minority Languages and the Core Values of Culture: Changing Policies and Ethnic Response in Australia. *Multilingual and Multicultural Development, 5* (1).

Smolicz, J. J. (1985). Greek-Australians: A Question of Survival in Multicultural Australia. *Multilingual and Multicultural Development, 6* (1).

Smolicz, J. J. (1986). National Policy on Languages: A Community Language Perspective. *Australian Journal of Education, 30* (1).

Snow, Catherine E. (1990). Rationales for Native Language Instruction: Evidence from Research. In A. M. Padilla, H.H. Fairchild, and C.M. Valadez (Eds.), *Bilingual Education: Issues and Strategies.* Newbury Park (CA): Sage.

Snow, C.E. (1992). Perspectives on Second-language Development: Implications for Bilingual Education. *Educational Researcher, 21* (2), 16–20.

Snow, C.E. (1993). Bilingualism and Language Acquisition. In J. Berko Gleason and N. Bernstein Ratner (Eds.), *Psycholinguistics.* (Pp. 391–416). New York: Harcourt Brace Javonovich.

Snow, Catherine E. and Kenji Hakuta (1992). The Costs of Monolingualism. In James Crawford (Ed.), *Language Loyalties.* Chicago: University of Chicago Press.

Social and Cultural Planning Office (1993). *Social and Cultural Report 1992.* Rijswijk (The Netherlands).

Sociaal en Cultureel Planbureau (1993). *Rapportage minderheden 1993.* Rijswijk (The Netherlands).

Søndergaard, Bent (1993). The Problem of Pedagogy versus Ideology: The Case of a Danish-German Bilingual School-Type. In Hugo Baetens Beardsmore (Ed.), *European Models of Bilingual Education.* Clevedon (United Kingdom): Multilingual Matters.

Sorensen, Elaine and Enchautegui, Maria E. (1994). Immigrant Male Earnings in the 1980s: Divergent Patterns by Race and Ethnicity. In Barry Edmonston and Jeffrey S. Passel (Eds.), *Immigration and Ethnicity.* Washington, DC: The Urban Institute.

Sowell, Thomas (1978). *Essays and Data on American Ethnic Groups.* Washington, DC: The Urban Institute.

Sowell, Thomas (1993). Middleman Minorities. *The American Enterprise,* May/June.

Spencer, Diane (1989, December 15). Countries Seek Unity in Diversity. *The Times Educational Supplement.*

Spener, David (1988). Transitional Bilingual Education and the Socialization of Immigrants. *Harvard Educational Review, 58* (2), May.

Spolsky, Bernard (1978a). Bilingual Education in the United States. In Alatis, James, E. (Ed.). *International Dimensions of Bilingual Education.* Washington, DC: Georgetown University Press.

Spolsky, Bernard (1978b). A Model for the Evaluation of Bilingual Education. *International Review of Education, 24* (3).

Spolsky, Bernard and Holm, Wayne (1971). Literacy in the Vennacular: The Case of Navajo. In *Bilingual Education for American Indians.* Washington, DC: Bureau of Indian Affairs.

Spolsky, B. (1989). *Conditions for Second Language Learning.* Oxford University Press.

Spörl, Gerhard (1989, February 24). Wir bleiben gern liberal, aber . . . *Die Zeit.*

Språk-och kulturstod for invandrar-och minoritetsbarn i forskolealdern (1982). Stockholm: Statens offentliga utredningar.

Stacy, Palmer and Lutton, Wayne (1985). *The Immigration Time Bomb*. Alexandria (VA): The American Immigration Control Foundation.

"Statehood as a Status Alternative: The STACOM Report." (1970). In Erwin H. Epstein (Ed.), *Politics and Education in Puerto Rico: A Documentary Survey of the Language Issue*. Metuchen (NJ): Scarecrow Press.

Stein, C.B., Jr. (1986). *Sink or Swim: The Politics of Bilingual Education*. New York: Praeger.

Stein, Terri, Gavito, Alfredo A., and Veselka, Ron E. (1988). *A Longitudinal Study of the Programs Designed for Students Whose First Language Is Not English*. Houston (TX) Independent School District.

Steinberg, L., Blinde, P.L., and Chan, K.S. (1984). Dropping Out Among Language Minority Youth. *Review of Educational Research, 54* (1).

Steinberg, Stephen (1982). *The Ethnic Myth: Race, Ethnicity, and Class in America*. Boston: Beacon Press.

Steindl, Michael (1983). Didaktische Grundlagen. In Gerhart Mahler and Michael Steindl (Eds.), *Zweitsprache Deutsch fur Ausländerkinder*. Donauworth: Auer.

Steiner, Stan (1970). *La Raza: The Mexican Americans*. New York: Harper Colophon.

Steiner, Stan (1975). *The Islands: The Worlds of the Puerto Ricans*. New York: Harper Colophon.

Stewart, D.W. (1993). *Immigration and Education. The Crisis and the Opportunities*. New York: Lexington Books.

Stewart, I. S. (1975). Cultural Differences Between Anglos and Chicanos. *Integrated Education, 13* (6).

Stone, John (1985). Ethnicity and Stratification: Mexican-Americans and European Gastarbeiter. In Walker Connor (Ed.), *Mexican-Americans in Comparative Perspective*. Washington, DC: The Urban Institute.

Stone, Maureen (1981). *The Education of the Black Child: The Myth of Multiracial Education*. London: Fontana.

Stora, Benjamin (1992). L'intégrisme islamique en France: entre fantasmes et réalités. In Pierre-André Taguieff (Ed.), *Face au racisme, 2: Analyses, hypothèses, perspectives*. Paris: Éditions La Découverte.

Storimans, Theo (1993). *Het recht op anders-zijn*. Nijmegen: Ars Aequi Libri.

Stowe, Calvin (1974). The Americanization of the Immigrant (1836). In Sol Cohen (Ed.), *Education in the United States: A Documentary History*. (Pp. 993–994). New York: Random House.

Strijbosch, Fons (1992). Hoe heilloos is nu eigenlijk minorisering? *Migrantenstudies, 8* (3).

Strijp, Ruud (1990). Witte vlekken op de landkaart. Recente publikaties over islam en moslims in Nederland. *Migrantenstudies, 6* (4).

Stuurgroep PC-onderwijs en culturele minderheden (n.d.). *Nota Toelatingsbeleid*. Hoevelaken.

Suarez-Orozco, Marcelo M. (1991). Immigrant Adaptation to Schooling: A Hispanic Case. In Margaret A. Gibson and John U. Ogbu (Eds.), *Minority Status and Schooling*. New York: Garland.

Sung, B.L. (1971). *The Story of the Chinese in America*. New York: Macmillan.

Sunier, Thijl. (1994). Islam en etniciteit onder jonge leden van Turkse islamistische organisaties in Nederland. *Migrantenstudies 10*, 1.

Suny, Ronald Grigor (1988). *The Making of the Georgian Nation*. Stanford (CA): Hoover Institution Press.

Susam, Huseyin (1986). Het Turkse OETC. in *Onderwijs in eigen taal en cultuur, MOER* 1–2.

Sveriges Lärarforbund (1989). SLs policy angaende invandrarundervisning, hemspråksundervisning och hemspråkslärarnas arbetsvillkor.

Swain, Merrill (1981). Time and timing in bilingual education. *Language learning, 31* (1), 1–15.

Swain, Merrill (1982). Immersion Education: Applicability for Nonvernacular Teaching to Vernacular Speakers. In Beverly Hartford, Albert Valdman, and Charles R. Foster (Eds.), *Issues in International Bilingual Education: The Role of the Venacular.* New York: Plenum.

Swain, Merrill (1984). Research and Evaluation Studies. In *Studies on Immersion Education*, Sacramento: California State Department of Education.

Swain, M. (1985). Communicative Competence: Some Roles of Comprehensible Input and Comprehensible Output in Its Development. In S.M. Gass and C.G. Madden (Eds.), *Input in Second Language Acquisition*. Rowley (MA): Newbury House.

Swain, Merrill and Barik, H. (1978). Bilingual Education in Canada: French and English. In Bernard Spolsky and Robert L. Cooper (Eds.), *Case Studies in Bilingual Education*. Rowley (MA): Newbury House.

Swing, Elizabeth Sherman (1982). Education for Separatism: The Belgian Experience. In Beverly Hartford, Albert Valdman, and Charles R. Foster (Eds.). *Issues in International Bilingual Education: The Role of the Vennacular.* New York: Plenum.

Swing, Elizabeth Sherman (1985). Colonials Subordinates, or Superordinates: Puerto Ricans and Educational Policy on the United States Mainland. In C. Brock and W. Tulasiewicz (Eds.), *Cultural Identity and Educational Policy.* London: Croom Helm.

Szasz, Margaret (1974). *Education and the American Indian.* Albuquerque: University of New Mexico Press.

Taboada-Leonetti, Isabelle (1986). L'immigration espagnole et la langue de Cervantes. *Migrants Formation*, December.

Taboada-Leonetti, Isabelle (1987). Stratégies culturelles des immigrés: complexité des enjeux et ambiguité des politiques culturelles (Le cas des femmes immigrées). In *L'Immigration en France: Le choc des cultures.* L'Arbresle (France): Centre Thomas More.

Tabors, P.O. and Snow, C.E. (1994). English as a Second Language in Preschool Programs. In F. Genesee (Ed.), *Educating Second Language Children. The Whole School, the Whole Curriculum, the Whole Community.* Cambridge: Cambridge University Press.

Taguieff, Pierre-André (1987). *La force du préjugé: essai sur le racisme et ses doubles.* Paris: Éditions La Découverte.

Taguieff, Pierre-André (1988). Les métamorphoses du racisme. In *L'Immigration dans l'histoire nationale*, Paris: CEFISEM.

Taguieff, Pierre-André (1992a). La lutte contre le racisme, par-delà illusions et désillusions. In Pierre-André Taguieff (Ed.). *Face au racisme, 2: Analyses, hypothèses, perspectives.* Paris: Éditions La Découverte.

Taguieff, Pierre-André (1992b). Les métamorphoses idéologiques du racisme et la crise de l'antiracisme. In Pierre-André Taguieff (Ed.), *Face au racisme, 2: Analyses, hypothèses, perspectives.* Paris: Éditions La Découverte.

Taguieff, Pierre-André (1993–1994). From Race to Culture: The New Right's View of European Identity. *Telos*, 98–99, Winter-Spring.

Tansley, Paul and Craft, Alma (1984). Mother Tongue Teaching and Support: A Schools Council Enquiry. *Multilingual and Multicultural Development*, 5 (5).

Tappeiner, Imelda (1990). Italiaanse jongeren: een portret. *Migrantenstudies*, 6 (1).

Tarrow, Norma Bernstein (1985). The Autonomous Basque Community of Spain: Language, Culture and Education. In C. Brock, W. Tulasiewicz (Eds.),*Cultural Identity and Educational Policy.* London: Croom Helm.

Tauvel, Jean-Paul (1988). Editorial. *Migrants-Formation 73.* Special theme issue: L'accueil scolaire des nouveaux arrivants.

Taylor, Monica J. (1988). *Worlds Apart? A Review of Research into the Education of Pupils of Cypriot, Italian, Ukrainian and Vietnamese Origin, Liverpool Blacks and Gypsies.* Windsor (United Kingdom): NFER-Nelson.

Teitelbaum, Herber and Hiller, Richard J. (1977). Bilingual Education: The Legal Mandate. *Harvard Educational Review,* 47 (2), May.

Tennant, Edward A. (1971). The Bilingual Education Act and the American Indian. In *Bilingual Education for American Indians.* Washington: Bureau of Indian Affairs.

Tennekes, J. (1991). Een antropologische visie op de islam in Nederland. *Migrantenstudies,* 7, 4.

Tesser, Paul T.M. (1993). *Rapportage minderheden 1993.* Rijswijk (The Netherlands: Sociaal en Cultureel Planbureau, 1993.

Tesser, Paul and Mulder, Lia (1990). Concentratie en prestatie van allochtone leerlingen in het basisonderwijs. *Migrantenstudies,* 6 (2).

Teunissen, Frans (1986). Project Moedertaalklassen: tweetalig en bicultureel onderwijs voor de tweede generatie. *Onderwijs in eigen taal en cultuur, MOER 1–2.*

Teunissen, Frans (1992). Equality of Educational Opportunity for Children from Ethnic Minority Communities. In Euan Reid and Hans Reich (Eds.), *Breaking the Boundaries: Migrant Workers' Children in the EC.* Clevedon (United Kingdom): Multilingual Matters.

Teunissen, Joop (1982). Immigratie en onderwijspolitiek: een overzicht van het onderwijsbeleid in Frankrijk, Engeland en West-Duitsland. In J.M.M. van Amersfoort and H.B. Entzinger (Eds.), *Immigrant en Samenleving.* Deventer: Van Loghum Slaterus.

Teunissen, Joop (1990). Basisscholen op islamitische en hindoeistische grondslag. *Migrantenstudies,* 6 (2).

Texas Education Agency (n.d.). *Guidelines for Language Usage in Bilingual Education and English as a Second Language Programs.* Austin (TX).

The European Schools (n.d.). Brussels: Central Office of the Representative of The Board of Governors of The European Schools.

The Evolution of Equal Educational Opportunity for Negroes, Indians, and Chinese in California (1860–90). (1974). In Sol Cohen (Ed.), *Education in the United States: A Documentary History.* (Pp. 1761–1776). New York: Random House.

Thibaud, Paul (1991, April 26). La grandeur de la France. *L'Express.*

Thiessen, Elmer J. (1982). Religious Freedom and Educational Pluralism. In Michael E. Manley-Casimir (Ed.), *Family Choice in Schooling: Issues and Dilemmas.* Lexington (MA): D.C. Heath.

Thiessen, Elmer J. (1986). How Religious Freedom Postulates Educational Pluralism in Alberta Province, Canada. *Educational Freedom,* 19 (2), Spring/Summer.

Thomas, Wayne P. and Collier, V.P. (1995). Research summary of study in progress: Language minority student achievement and program effectiveness. Paper presented at NABE conference, Phoenix, Arizona.

Thoma-Venske, Hanns (1988). The Religious Life of Muslims in Berlin. In Tomas Gerholm and Yngve Georg Lithman (Eds.), *The New Islamic Presence in Western Europe.* London: Mansell.

Thomas, Peter Wynn (1991). Children in Welsh-medium Education: Semilinguals or Innovators? In Kjell Herberts and Christer Laurén (Eds.), *Papers from the Sixth Nordic Conference on Bilingualism.* Clevedon (United Kingdom): Multilingual Matters.

Thompson, Frank V. (1971). *Schooling of the Immigrant.* Montclair (NJ): Patterson Smith. [originally published Harper Brothers 1920]

Thompson, Richard E. (1983). Matching Appropriate Actions to Specific Linguistic Inadequacies. In *Exploring Strategies for Developing a Cohesive National Direction toward Language Education in the United States.* Rosslyn (VA): The National Clearinghouse for Bilingual Education.

Thorning, Inge (1988). Oplæg om en to-kulturel model i børnehaven Svalen i Århus. In Christian Horst (Ed.), *Den Flerkulturelle Udfordring: Socialisation og børn fra etniske mindretal.* Copenhagen: Kultursociologiske Skrifter.

Thurmann, Eike (1988). Ausländische Lehrer, Gastarbeiter im deutschen Bildungssystem? *Gemeinsam, 8,* March.

Tikunoff, William J. (1985). *Applying Significant Bilingual Instructional Features in the Classroom.* Rosslyn (VA): National Clearinghouse for Bilingual Education.

Tikunoff, William J. and Vasquez-Faria, J.A. (1982). Successful instruction for bilingual schooling. *Peabody Journal of Education, 59* (4), 234–271.

Timberlake, Elizabeth M. and Cook, Kim Oanh (1984). Social Work and the Vietnamese Refugee. *Social Work, 29* (2), March-April.

Timera, Mohamet (1989). Identité communautaire et project éducatif chez les immigrés Sonikés en France. *Migrants Formation, 7* (6), March.

Timmers, Andrea (1995). Leermiddelen OET sluiten slecht aan bij belevingswereld leerlingen. *Samenwijs, 15* (7), March.

Tincq, Henri (1987, March 6). Sur la voie de l'intégration. *Le Monde.*

Tingbjørn, Gunnar (1988a). Tvåspråkig utbildning i Sverige. In Christian Horst (Ed.), *Den Flerkulturelle Udfordring: Socialisation og børn fra etniske mindretal,* Copenhagen: Kultursociologiske Skrifter.

Tingbjørn, Gunnar (1988b). Active Bilingualism—the Swedish Goal for Immigrant Children's Language Instruction. In Tove Skutnabb-Kangas and Jim Cummins (Eds.), *Minority Education: From Shame to Struggle.* Clevedon (United Kingdom): Multilingual Matters.

Todd, Emmanuel (1994). *Le destin des immigrés: Assimilation et ségrégation dans les démocracies occidentales.* Paris: Éditions du Seuil, 1994.

Todorov, Tzvetan (1993). *On Human Diversity.* Cambridge: Harvard University Press.

Tomlinson, Sally (1984). Home, School and Community. In Maurice Craft (Ed.), *Education for Diversity, Education and Cultural Pluralism.* London: Falmer Press.

Tomlinson, Sally (1989a). Ethnicity and Educational Achievement in Britain. In Lotty Eldering and Jo Kloprogge (Eds.), *Different Cultures—Same School: Ethnic Minority Children in Europe.* Amsterdam: Swets & Zeitlinger.

Tomlinson, Sally (1989b). The Origins of the Ethnocentric Curriculum. In Gajendra K. Verma (Ed.), *Education for All: A Landmark in Pluralism.* London: Falmer Press.

Toro, Arturo Ortiz (1970). Language and Statehood. In Erwin H. Epstein (Ed.), *Politics and Education in Puerto Rico: A Documentary Survey of the Language Issue.* Metuchen (NJ): Scarecrow Press.

Tosi, Arturo (1984). *Immigration and Bilingual Education.* Oxford: Pergamon Press.

Tosi, Arturo (1988). The Jewel in the Crown of the Modern Prince: The New Approach to Bilingualism in Multicultural Education in England. In Tove Skutnabb-Kangas and Jim Cummins (Eds.), *Minority Education: From Shame to Struggle.* Clevedon (United Kingdom): Multilingual Matters.

Toukomaa, Pertti and Skutnabb-Kangas, Tove (1977). *The Intensive Teaching of Mother Language to Migrant Children at Pre-school Age.* University of Tampere: UNESCO Tutkimusia Research Reports.

Triesscheijn, Ton M. (1985). O.E.T.C. heeft een brugfunctie naar de integratie. *Samenwijs, 6* (3), November.

Triesscheijn, Ton M. (1987a). Het openen van Turkse scholen in Nederland moet voorkomen worden. *Samenwijs, 7* (5), January.

Triesscheijn, Ton M. (1987b). Gelijke kansen geven aan alloctone kinderen vraagt heel wat meer dan alleen Nederlands leren. *Samnwijs, 7* (5), January.

Triesscheijn, Ton M. (1990). Tweetaligheid is schoolbeleid op Tweezaamschool in Den Haag. *Samenwijs, 11* (3), November.

Triesscheijn, Ton M. (1992). Leraren ongerust. *Samenwijs, 12* (10), June.

Triesscheijn, Ton M. (1994). Onderwijs minderheden in West-Europa. *Samenwijs, 14* (5), January.

Triesscheijn, Ton M. and Geelen, Eva (1991a). Nuttig voor onderwijs. *Samenwijs, 12* (4), December.

Triesscheijn, Ton M. and Geelen, Eva (1991b). Rotterdam wil daden. *Samenwijs, 12* (4), December.

Triesscheijn, Ton M. and Geelen, Eva (1992). In algemeen beleid. *Samenwijs, 12* (10), June.

Troike, Rudolph (1978). Bilingual Education in the United States: The First Decade. *International Review of Education, 24* (3).

Trotter, Rhonda (1988). Immigrant Students and the Black Community: Strangers in an Already Underserved Land. *California Tomorrow, 3* (1–2), Spring.

Trueba, Henry T. (1989). *Raising Silent Voices: Educating the Linguistic Minorities for the 21st Century*. Cambridge: Newbury House.

Trueba, Henry T. (1991). From Failure to Success: The Roles of Culture and Cultural Conflict in the Academic Achievement of Chicano Students. In R.R. Valencia (Ed.), *Chicano School Failure and Success*. London: Falmer Press.

Trueba, H.T. and Wright, P.G. (1992). On Ethnographic Studies and Multicultural Education. In M. Saravia-Shore and S. Arvizu (1992). *Cross-cultural Literacy: Ethnographies of Communication in Multiethnic Classrooms*. New York: Garland.

Truetas, Miguel Strubell (1978). *¿Bilinguismo en Madrid? In Bilinguismo y Biculturalismo*. Barcelona: Ediciones CEAC.

Tsow, Ming (1983). Ethnic Minority Community Languages: A Statement. *Multilingual and Multicultural Development, 4* (5).

Tucker, G. Richard (1977). The Linguistic Perspective. In *Bilingual Education: Current Perspectives—Linguistics*. Arlington (VA): Center for Applied Linguistics.

Tucker, G. Richard (1980). Implications for U. S. Bilingual Education: Evidence from Canadian Research. *NCBE Focus*, 2, February.

Uhl, Siegfried (1992). Schulerziehung in der "Multikulturellen Gesellschaft." *Mitteilungsblatt des Institutes für Bildung und Wissenschaft*, January.

Ulvhammar, Birgitta and Jakobsson, Bertil (1984). *Intercultural Education*. Stockholm: Allmaenna Foerlaget.

Undervisningsministeriet (1984a). *Regler: Bekendtgorelse om folkeskolens undervisning af fremmedsprogede elever*, Copenhagen.

Undervisningsministeriet (1984b). *Undervisning af fremmedsprogede elever i folkeskolen: En håndbog*. Copenhagen.

Ungar, Sanford J. (1995). *Fresh Blood: The New American Immigrants*. New York: Simon & Schuster.

Unterricht für Kinder ausländischer Arbeitnehmer (1984, August 29). Munich: Bayrischen Staatsministeriums fur Unterricht und Kultus.

United States Bureau of the Census (1975). *Historical Statistics of the United States*. Washington, DC.

United States Commission on Civil Rights (1976). *Puerto Ricans in the Continental United States: An Uncertain Future*. Washington, DC.

United States Commission on Civil Rights (1992). Language Rights and New Mexico Statehood. In James Crawford (Ed.), *Language Loyalties*. Chicago: University of Chicago Press.

U.S. English (1992). In Defense of Our Common Language. In James Crawford (Ed.), *Language Loyalties*. Chicago: University of Chicago Press.

Valdés, Guadalupe (1988). The Language Situation of the Mexican Americans. In Sandra Lee McKay and Sau-ling Cynthia Wong (Eds), *Language Diversity: Problem or Resource?* Cambridge (MA): Newbury House.

Valdivieso, Rafael (1986). *Must They Wait Another Generation? Hispanics and Secondary School Reform*. New York: ERIC Clearinghouse on Urban Education.

Valencia, Richard R. (1991). The Plight of Chicano Students: An Overview of Schooling Conditions and Outcomes. In R.R. Valencia (Ed.), *Chicano School Failure and Success*. London: Falmer Press.

Valencia, Richard R. and Aburto, Sofia (1991). The Uses and Abuses of Educational Testing: Chicanos as a Case in Point. In R.R. Valencia (Ed.), *Chicano School Failure and Success*. London: Falmer Press.

Valentine, Charles (1968). *Culture and Poverty.* Chicago: University of Chicago Press.

Vandermeulen, H. (1987). *Migranten in Limburg: Enkele kanttekingen bij het integratieproces.* Provincieraad van Limburg (Belgium).

Vanhoren, Ingrid (1991). Registratie herkomst. *Samenwijs, 12,* (2), October.

Varonis, E.M.' and Gass, S. (1984). Non-native/native Conversations: A Model for Negotiation of Meaning. *Applied Linguistics,* 6 (1), 71–90.

Veltman, Calvin (1988). *The Future of the Spanish Language in the United States.* New York and Washington: Hispanic Policy Development Project.

Verbunt, Gilles (1985). France. In Tomas Hammar (Ed.), *European Immigration Policy: A Comparative Study.* Cambridge: Cambridge University Press.

Verbunt, Gilles (1986). Jusqu'à va le rôle de l'Education nationale? *Migrations santé, 49.*

Verbunt, Gilles (1987). Le cloisonnement des communautés. In *L'Immigration en France: Le choc des cultures.* L'Arbresle (France): Centre Thomas More.

Verbunt, Gilles (1994). Culture, identité, intégration, communauté: des concepts à revoir. *Hommes & Migrations,* 1180, October.

Vereniging voor Openbaar Onderwijs (1983). *Openbaar onderwijs en culturele minderheden.* Amsterdam: VOO.

Verkuyten, M. (1985). Etnische identiteit en sociaal-emotionele problemen: een theoretische en empirische exploratie. In Mart-Jan de Jong (Ed.), *Allochtone kinderen op Nederlandse scholen: Prestaties, problemen en houdingen.* Lisse (The Netherlands): Swets & Zeitlinger.

Verkuyten, M. (1987). Etnische identiteit en identificatie bij allochtone adolescenten. *Kind en adolescent, 8* (2).

Verkuyten, M. (1988). *Zelfbeleving en identiteit van jongeren uit etnische minderheden.* Arnhem (The Netherlands): Gouda Quint.

Verlot, Marc (1994). Interview with Charles Glenn. Brussels: Ministry of Education.

Verma, Gajendra K. (1989). Postscript—Cultural Pluralism: Strategies for Change. In Gajendra K. Verma (Ed.), *Education for All: A Landmark in Pluralism.* London: Falmer Press.

Vermeulen, Hans (1984). *Etnische groepen en grenzen: Surinamers, Chinezen en Turken.* Weesp: Het Wereldvenster.

Vermeulen, Hans (1992). De cultura. Een verhandeling over het cultuurbegrip in de studie van allochtone etnische groepen. *Migrantenstudies, 8* (2).

Villanova, Roselyne de (1986). La langue du "retour" ou le retour de la langue: les pratiques d'alternance linguistique dans la famille portugaise emigrée en France. In Georges Abou-Sada and Hélène Milet (Eds.). *Générations issues de l'immigration.* Paris: Arcantère Éditions.

Vliet, Mario van (1991). Beleidsmatige aanpak. *Samenwijs,* 12 (2), October.

Voisard, Jacques and Ducastelle, Christiane (1986). *La question immigrèe en France.* Fondation Saint-Simon.

Voorstel eindtermen secundair onderwijs—eerste graad, Brussels: Ministerie van de Vlaamse Gemeenschap, Departement Onderwijs, December 1993.

Vries, Marlene de (1983). De gevolgen van de huidige ontwikkelingen voor onderwijs en arbbeidsmarkt. In Nitha Neuwahl and Aletta de Raad (Eds.), *Kinderen van medelanders: Buitenlandse kinderen in de Nederlandse samenleving.* Deventer (The Netherlands): Van Loghum Slaterus.

Vroede, M. de (1983). Onderwijs en opvoeding in de Zuidelijke Nederlanden 1815–circa 1840. In *Algemene Geschiedenis der Nederlanden 11.* Weesp (The Netherlands): Fibula-Van Dishoeck.

Vroede, M. de (1991). Language in Education in Belgium up to 1940. In Janusz Tomiak (Ed.), *Schooling, Educational Policy, and Ethnic Identity.* New York: New York University Press.

Waardenburg, Jacques (1988). The Institutionalization of Islam in the Netherlands, 1961–86. In Tomas Gerholm and Yngve Georg Lithman (Eds.), *The New Islamic Presence in Western Europe.* London: Mansell.

717

Wade, Barrie and Souter, Pam (1992). *Continuing to Think: The British Asian Girl.* Clevedon (United Kingdom): Multilingual Matters.

Wagenaar, Erin (1993). *Tweetaligheid in het aanvangsonderwijs.* Amsterdam: Het Spinhuis.

Waggoner, Dorothy (1988). Language Minorities in the United States in the 1980s: The Evidence from the 1980 Census. In Sandra Lee McKay and Sau-ling Cynthia Wong (Eds), *Language Diversity: Problem or Resource?* Cambridge (MA): Newbury House.

Waggoner, Dorothy (1994, September 15). Language-Minority School-Age Population Now Totals 9.9 Million. *NABE News 18* (1).

Wallage, Jacques (1993). Iedere leerkracht moet basiskennis verwerven voor het geven van NT2. *Samenwijs, 13* (8), April.

Wallraff, Guenter (1985). *Ganz unten.* Cologne: Kiepenheuer & Witsch.

Walsh, Catherine E. (1987). Schooling and the Civic Exclusion of Latinos: Towards a Discourse of Dissonance. *Journal of Education* (Boston University), *169* (2).

Walshe, John (1989, December 22). EC Throws Out Language Bias Claim. *The Times Educational Supplement.*

Wammen, Lotte Halby, and others (1985). *Børnehaveklasse for indvandrerbørn en multietnisk børnehaveklasse på Brobjergskolen.* Århus: Kommunale Skolevasen.

Wande, Erling (1984). Two Finnish Minorities in Sweden. *Multilingual and Multicultural Development, 5* (3–4).

Waters, Mary C. (1990). *Ethnic Options: Choosing Identities in America.* Berkeley: University of California Press.

Watson, J.K.P. (1988). From Assimilation to Anti-Racism: Changing Educational Policies in England and Wales. *Journal of Multilingual and Multicultural Development, 2, 6,* 531–552.

Wattenberg, Ben J. (1990). Why Not? *The American Enterprise,* March/April.

Weber, Eugen (1976). *Peasants into Frenchmen.* Stanford: Stanford University Press.

Weber, Max (1964). *The Theory of Social and Economic Organization.* Talcott Parsons (Ed.). New York: Free Press Paperback.

Webster, Noah (1992). Declaration of Linguistic Independence. In James Crawford (Ed.), *Language Loyalties.* Chicago: University of Chicago Press.

Wehrung, Melodye (1992). *Evaluation Report: Boston Public Schools Parent Information Centers, School Year 1991–1992.* Boston: Office of Research & Development, Boston Public Schools.

Weil, Patrick (1992). Convergences et divergences des politiques de flux. In Jaqueline Costa-Lascoux and Patrick Weil (Eds.), *Logiques d'états et immigrations.* Paris: Éditions Kimé.

Weinberg, Meyer (1983). *The Search for Quality Integrated Education.* Westport (CT): Greenwood Press.

Weiner, Myron (1993). Security, Stability and International Migration. In Myron Weiner (Ed.), *International Migration and Security.* Boulder (CO): Westview Press.

Westerman, W.E. (1990). *Integration versus Remigration: A Pedagogical Dilemma?* Hoevelaken (The Netherlands): Christelijk Pedagogisch Studiecentrum.

Wheatcroft, Geoffrey. (1993) The Disenchantment of Ireland. *The Atlantic Monthly* July.

Wheelock, Anne E. (1990). *The Status of Latino Students in Massachusetts Public Schools: Directions for Policy Research in the 1990's.* Boston: Mauricio Gaston Institute for Latino Community Development and Public Policy.

Whitaker, D.P. (et al.) (1974). *Area Handbook for Australia.* Washington, DC: U.S. Government Printin Office.

Willems, Wim and Cottaar, Annemarie (1990). Ethnocentrisme en het beeld van minderheden over Nederland. *Migrantenstudies, 6* (3).

Williams, Colin H. (1984). More than Tongue Can Tell: Linguistic Factors in Ethnic Separation. In John Edwards (Ed.), *Linguistic Minorities, Policies and Pluralism*. London: Academic Press.

Willig, Ann C. (1985). A Meta-Analysis of Selected Studies on the Effectiveness of Bilingual Education. *Review of Educational Research, 55* (3), Fall.

Willig, Ann C. (1987). Examining Bilingual Education Research Through Meta-Analysis and Narrative Review: A Response to Baker. *Review of Educational Research, 57* (3), Fall.

Willke, Ingeborg (1975). Schooling of Immigrant Children in West Germany—Sweden—England: The Educationally Disadvantaged. *International Review of Education, 21* (3).

Wilpert, Czarina (1987). Zukunftsorientierungen von Migrantenfamilien: Türkische Familien in Berlin. In Helga Reimann and Horst Reimann (Eds.), *Gastarbeiter: Analyse und Perspektiven eines sozialen Problems*. Opladen (Germany): Westdeutscher Verlag.

Wilpert, Czarina (1988). Religion and Ethnicity: Orientations, Perceptions and Strategies among Turkish Alevi and Sunni Migrants in Berlin. In Tomas Gerholm and Yngve Georg Lithman (Eds.), *The New Islamic Presence in Western Europe*. London: Mansell.

Wilson, J. Donald (1986). "No Blanket to Be Worn in School": The Education of Indians in Nineteenth-Century Ontario. In J. Barman, Y. Hébert, and D. McCaskill (Eds.), *Indian Education in Canada: vol. 1: The Legacy*. Vancouver: University of British Columbia Press.

Wilson, J. Donald and Lazerson, Marvin (1982). Historical and Constitutional Perspectives on Family Choice in Schooling: The Canadian Case. In Michael E. Manley-Casimir (Ed.), *Family Choice in Schooling: Issues and Dilemmas*. Lexington (MA): D.C. Heath.

Winkler, Karen, J. (1990, October 10). Evidence of "Cultural Vitality." Researcher's Examination of California's Poor Latino Population Prompts Debate Over the Traditional Definitions of the Underclass. *The Chronicle of Higher Education*.

Wirth, Louis (1956). *The Ghetto*. Chicago: University of Chicago Press.

Wit, Walter de (1990). De etnische samenstelling van basisscholen. *Migrantenstudies* 6 (2).

Withagen, Walter (1995). OETC-plannen Netelenbos zijn een 'dolksteek in de rug'. *Samenwijs, 15* (8), April.

Witte, E.M. and Meynen, A. (1982). Het maatschappelijk-politieke leven in Belgie 1945–1980. In *Algemene Geschiedenis der Nederlanden, 15*, Haarlem (The Netherlands): Fibula-Van Dishoeck.

Wittek, Fritz (1990). *Intercultural Education in a Multi-lingual Europe. Migrants' Children: Report of the 1990 EPA-Seminar on Education Policy and Migration*. Rotterdam: European Parents' Association, 1990.

Wittek, Fritz (1992). The Historical and International Context for Current Action on Intercultural Education. In Euan Reid and Hans Reich (Eds.), *Breaking the Boundaries: Migrant Workers' Children in the EC*. Clevedon (United Kingdom): Multilingual Matters.

Wolfe, Alan (1990, December 31). The Return of the Melting Pot. *The New Republic*.

Wollenberg, Charles (1974). *Mendez v. Westminster*: Race, Nationality and Segregation in California Schools. *California Historical Quarterly, 53* (4), 317–322.

Wong, Sau-ling Cynthia (1988). The Language Situation of Chinese Americans. In Sandra Lee McKay and Sau-ling Wong (Eds.), *Language Diversity: Problem or Resource?* Cambridge (MA): Newbury House.

Wong Fillmore, L. (1976). *The Second Time Around: Cognitive and Social Strategies in Second Language Acquisition*. Dissertation. Stanford University.

Wong-Fillmore, L. (1982). Instructional Language as Linguistic Input: Second Language Learning in Classrooms. In L.C. Wilkinson (Ed.), *Communicating in the classroom*. New York: Academic Press.

Wong Fillmore, L. (1985a). When Does Teacher-Talk Work as Input? In S.M. Gass, and C.G. Madden (Eds.), *Input in Second Language Acquisition*. Rowley (MA): Newbury House.

Wong Fillmore, L. (1985b). *Second Language Learning in Children: A Proposed Model. Issues in English Language Development*. Rosslyn (VA): The National Clearinghouse for Bilingual Education.

Wong Fillmore, L. (1989a). Teaching English Through Content: Instructional Reform in Programs for Language Minority Students. In J.H. Esling (Ed.), *Multicultural Education and Policy: ESL in 1990*. Toronto: Institute for Studies in Education

Wong Fillmore, L. (1989b). Teachability and Second Language Acquisition. In M.L. Rice and R.L. Schiefelbusch (Eds.), *The Teachability of Language*. (Pp. 311–332). Baltimore (MD): Paul H. Brookes.

Wong Fillmore, L. (1991a). Second-language Learning in Children: A Model of Language Learning in Social Context. In E. Bialystok (Ed.), *Language Processing in Bilingual Children*. (Pp. 49–69). Cambridge: Cambridge University Press

Wong Fillmore, L. (1991b). When Learning a Second Language Means Losing the First. *Early Childhood Research Quarterly, 6*, 323–346.

Wong Fillmore, L. (1992). Learning a Language from Learners. In C. Kramsch and S. McConnell-Ginet (Eds.), *Text and context. Cross-disciplinary perspectives on language study*. (Pp. 46–66). Lexington (MA): D.C. Heath.

Wong Fillmore, L., Ammon, P., McLaughlin, B., and Ammon, M.S. (1985). *Final Report for Learning English Through Bilingual Instruction*. NIE report. Washington, DC.

Wong Fillmore, Lily, with Concepción Valadez (1986). Teaching Bilingual Learners. In M.C. Wittrock (Ed.), *Handbook of Research on Teaching*. 3d ed. New York: Macmillan.

Woods, P. and Grugeon, E. (1990). Pupils and "Race": Integration and Disintegration in Primary Schools. *British Journal of the Sociology of Education, 11* (3), 309–326

Wulf, Kristel de (1993). Magneetproject Gent. *Samenwijs, 13* (5), January.

Wulf, Kristel de and Janssen, Dirk (1992). Sociale mobiliteit. *Samenwijs, 12* (10), June.

Xhoffer, J. (1983). Pedagogische opvangvormen voor leerlingen uit migrantgezinnen in het L.S.O. *Informatieblad, Brussels, 18* (3), March.

Xhoffer, J., Codde, A., and Allery P. (1984). Drievoudige stageweek over culturele minderheden in Belgie, Duitsland en Nederland. *Informatieblad, Brussels, 19* (6), June.

Yankelovich, Skelly, and White, Inc. (1984). *Spanish USA, 1984: A Study of the Hispanic Market*. New York: SIN Television Network.

Yates, Steven (1992). Multiculturalism and Epistemology. *Public Affairs Quarterly*, October.

Yinger, J. Milton (1985). Assimilation in the United States: The Mexican-Americans. In Walker Connor (Ed.), *Mexican-Americans in Comparative Perspective*. Washington, DC: The Urban Institute.

Yuan, D. Y. (1967). Voluntary Segregation: A Study of New York Chinatown. In Milton L. Barron (Ed.), *Minorities in a Changing World*. New York: Alfred A. Knopf.

Zakhartchouk, Jean-Michel (1992). Couleur gris-rose. *Cahiers pédagogiques, 309*, December.

Zaki, Yaqub (1982). The Teaching of Islam in Schools: A Muslim Viewpoint. *British Journal of Religious Education*, Autumn.

Zandbergen, Ellen (1993a). Naar basisvorming. *Samenwijs, 13* (8), April.

Zandbergen, Ellen (1993b). Ouders positief. *Samenwijs, 13* (8), April.
Zandbergen, Ellen (1993c). Nut van tweetaligheid. *Samenwijs, 13* (10), June.
Zandbergen, Ellen (1994). Eerste opvang in BO. *Samenwijs, 14* (6), February.
Zanger, Virginia Vogel (1985). *Face to Face: The Cross-Cultural Workbook.* Cambridge (MA): Newbury House.
Zanger, V. (1991). Social and Cultural Dimensions of the Education of Language Minority Students. In A.N. Ambert (Ed.), *Bilingual Education and English as a Second Language. A Research Handbook, 1988–1990.* New York: Garland.
Zappert, L. and Cruz, B. (1977). *Bilingual Education: An Appraisal of Empirical Research.* Berkeley (CA): Berkeley Unified School District.
Zentella, Ana Celia (1988). The Language Situation of Puerto Ricans. In Sandra Lee McKay and Sau-ling Cynthia Wong (Eds), *Language Diversity: Problem or Resource?* Cambridge (MA): Newbury House.
Zolberg, Aristide R. (1992). Reforming the back door: perspectives historiques sur la réforme de la politique américaine d'immigration. In Jaqueline Costa-Lascoux and Patrick Weil (Eds.), *Logiques d'états et immigrations.* Paris: Éditions Kimé.

Index

REFERENCE BOOKS IN INTERNATIONAL EDUCATION
EDWARD R. BEAUCHAMP, *Series Editor*